250 Best-Paying Jobs

Part of JIST's Best Jobs™ Series

Michael Farr and Laurence Shatkin, Ph.D.

Foreword by Cheryl Buhl, Director, Oregon Career Information System, University of Oregon

Also in JIST's Best Jobs Series

- Best Jobs for the 21st Century
- 200 Best Jobs for College Graduates
- 300 Best Jobs Without a Four-Year Degree
- 250 Best Jobs Through Apprenticeships
- 50 Best Jobs for Your Personality
- 40 Best Fields for Your Career
- 225 Best Jobs for Baby Boomers
- 150 Best Jobs for Your Skills

JIST Works
America's Career Publisher

250 Best-Paying Jobs

© 2007 by JIST Publishing, Inc.

Published by JIST Works, an imprint of JIST Publishing, Inc.
8902 Otis Avenue
Indianapolis, IN 46216-1033

Phone: 1-800-648-JIST   Fax: 1-800-JIST-FAX
E-mail: info@jist.com Web site: www.jist.com

Some Other Books by the Authors

Michael Farr

Seven-Step Job Search

The Quick Resume & Cover Letter Book

100 Fastest-Growing Careers

Overnight Career Choice

Laurence Shatkin

90-Minute College Major Matcher

Quantity discounts are available for JIST products. Have future editions of JIST books automatically delivered to you on publication through our convenient standing order program. Please call 1-800-648-JIST or visit www.jist.com for a free catalog and more information.

Visit www.jist.com for information on JIST, free job search information, book excerpts, and ordering information on our many products. For free information on 14,000 job titles, visit www.careeroink.com.

Acquisitions Editor: Susan Pines
Development Editor: Stephanie Koutek
Cover and Interior Designer: Aleata Howard
Interior Layout: Toi Davis
Proofreader: Linda Seifert
Indexer: Cheryl Lenser

Printed in the United States of America

11 10 09 08 07 06   9 8 7 6 5 4 3 2 1

Library of Congress Cataloging-in-Publication Data

Farr, J. Michael.
    250 best-paying jobs / Michael Farr and Laurence Shatkin.
       p. cm. -- (Best jobs series)
    Includes index.
    ISBN-13: 978-1-59357-355-3 (alk. paper)
    ISBN-10: 1-59357-355-3 (alk. paper)
    1. Vocational guidance--United States. 2. Occupations--United States. I. Shatkin, Laurence. II. Title.
    HF5382.5.U5F366 2007
    331.7020973--dc22

                              2006026310

We have been careful to provide accurate information throughout this book, but it is possible that errors and omissions have been introduced. Please consider this in making any career plans or other important decisions. Trust your own judgment above all else and in all things.

Trademarks: All brand names and product names used in this book are trade names, service marks, trademarks, or registered trademarks of their respective owners.

ISBN-13: 978-1-59357-355-3
ISBN-10: 1-59357-355-3

This Is a Big Book, But It Is Very Easy to Use

An old Russian proverb says, "It's not money that brings happiness; it's *lots* of money." Most people consider income one of the main reasons they go to work. If a high income is especially important to you, this book can help you identify high-paying career goals, including many that you may have never considered before.

The lists in the first part of this book identify not only the best-paying jobs, but also high-paying jobs that are growing fast and promising lots of openings, plus industries and locations where workers are paid especially well.

But let's be honest about job satisfaction: Money is not the *only* important factor. That's why this book also provides lists of high-paying jobs based on interests, education or training level, personality type, and many other criteria that affect your perception of work on the days between paychecks. Are you looking for high-paying jobs in the arts? Jobs in which women are not greatly underpaid? Jobs with a lot of self-employed workers? You'll find them all here, and more.

The lists are fun and easy to use, and they tell basic facts about a job. But this book also lets you dig deeper. When you find a job that interests you in one of the lists, turn to the second part of the book and read a description of the job—the work tasks, major skills, educational programs, industries and locations that pay best, and many other informative facts.

Using this book, you'll be surprised how quickly you get new ideas for career goals that can provide both a good income and the satisfactions that money can't buy.

Some Things You Can Do with This Book

- Identify better-paying jobs that don't require you to get additional training or education.
- Develop long-term career plans that may require additional training, education, or experience.
- Explore and select a training or educational program that relates to a high-paying career objective.
- Find reliable earnings information to negotiate pay.
- Prepare for interviews.

(continued)

(continued)

These are a few of the many ways you can use this book. We hope you find it as interesting to browse as we did to put together. We have tried to make it easy to use and as interesting as occupational information can be.

When you are done with this book, pass it along or tell someone else about it. We wish you well in your career and in your life.

Credits and Acknowledgments: While the authors created this book, it is based on the work of many others. The occupational information is based on data obtained from the U.S. Department of Labor and the U.S. Census Bureau. These sources provide the most authoritative occupational information available. The job titles and their related descriptions are from the O*NET database, which was developed by researchers and developers under the direction of the U.S. Department of Labor. They, in turn, were assisted by thousands of employers who provided details on the nature of work in the many thousands of job samplings used in the database's development. We used the most recent version of the O*NET database, release 9.0. We appreciate and thank the staff of the U.S. Department of Labor for their efforts and expertise in providing such a rich source of data.

Table of Contents

Summary of Major Sections

Introduction. An overview to help you better understand and use the book. *Starts on page 1.*

Part I: The Best-Paying Jobs Lists. Very useful for exploring career options! Lists are arranged into easy-to-use groups. The first group of lists presents the 250 best-paying jobs, ranking them first by earnings and then showing the 100 fastest-growing jobs and the 100 with the largest projected number of job openings. Another series of lists gives insights into jobs that offer unique ways to command a particularly high income—for example, by becoming a "star" earner or moving into a hot industry. More-specialized lists follow, presenting the best jobs by age, gender, level of education or training, personality type, and interest. The column starting at right presents all the list titles. *Starts on page 17.*

Part II: Descriptions of the Best-Paying Jobs. Provides complete descriptions of the jobs that met our criteria for high pay. Each description contains information on earnings, projected growth, job duties, skills, related job titles, education and training required, related knowledge and courses, and many other details, plus tables showing industries and metropolitan areas where income is highest. *Starts on page 117.*

Appendix: Skills Referenced in This Book. Defines all the skills listed in the descriptions in Part II. It also identifies the skills most closely associated with high earnings and lists the jobs in Part II that demand a high level of each of these skills. *Starts on page 443.*

Detailed Table of Contents

Table of Contents

Foreword

If you are taking the time to look through the pages of this book, you must be thinking about your career. Whether you are a student engaged in career planning or an adult in a career transition, take a moment to think about what is important to you. What do want from your work? Is it a sense of achievement, the support of your supervisors and co-workers, recognition for your accomplishments, an opportunity to work with people you like, the chance to use your skills? Do you want to earn enough to support your chosen lifestyle? There are numerous aspects of work that you may value. Make a list of those that are most significant for you.

Chances are good that one of the work values you listed involves wages. Most of us want a reasonable-to-excellent salary—a paycheck that enables us to do the things we enjoy. If we are continuing our education, we hope that our investment pays off in the earnings we eventually bring home. *250 Best-Paying Jobs* addresses this fairly universal value–to have a high-paying job–and allows you to examine the world of work through this filter. Using the most current U.S. aggregate data available, it lists more than 250 occupations with the best pay.

But it doesn't stop there. Most of us also look for a career in which opportunities will be numerous enough that we can find employment over time through economic swings and in a variety of work settings. *250 Best-Paying Jobs* helps you examine high-wage jobs by their projected growth and by the projected number of openings. It also combines other work aspects, such as age and education level and interests, with pay and growth factors. Best-paying jobs lists are organized by these additional characteristics, thus making your exploration more personalized and targeted to your needs.

Taking advantage of our societal obsession with lists (how many lists of Top 10s or Top 100s have you seen in the last month?), the authors make it fun to explore the possibilities in a meaningful way. Do you want to work for yourself? Go to the list of high-paying jobs for self-employed workers. Did some of the 250 best-paying jobs require education that you don't want to pursue? Go to the lists of high-paying jobs requiring short-, moderate-, or long-term on-the-job training.

Career decision making is a lifelong process that requires an open mind about opportunities and a positive attitude toward change. Self-awareness, knowledge about the world of work, and sound planning and decision making are essential steps in the process. *250 Best-Paying Jobs* will help you think about what you value (one facet of knowing yourself) and learn how one of those values, good pay, matches the realities of the labor market. From there, you can learn more about the occupations listed and pursue additional information to help you make decisions and formulate an action plan.

So what are you waiting for? Explore!

Cheryl Buhl
Director, Oregon Career Information System
University of Oregon

Introduction

We kept this introduction short to encourage you to actually read it. For this reason, we don't provide many details on the technical issues involved in creating the job lists or descriptions. Instead, we give you short explanations to help you understand and use the information the book provides for career exploration or planning. We think this brief and user-oriented approach makes sense for most people who will use this book.

Who This Book Is For and What It Covers

We created this book to help students and adults learn about high-paying careers and the educational and training pathways that lead to them. Employers, educators, program planners, career counselors, and others will also find this book to be of value.

If you are a young career planner and high income is important to you, this book can be especially useful. Are you impatient with the idea of starting at the bottom and working your way up the corporate ladder toward a better-paying job? The research of labor economists shows that you are right to set your sights high for your first job. Economists compared the earnings of people who started out in lower- and higher-paying jobs and found that those who began at a lower level generally had not caught up to the others even 10 or 20 years later. So you are wise to use this book to identify a high-paying job as your initial career goal.

People who are considering a career change later in life will also find this book useful. Do you feel stuck in a low-paying job? This book can point you toward high-paying jobs that are a good fit with your interests and, perhaps best of all, do not require a great amount of additional education or training. You will be particularly interested in the lists of high-paying jobs organized by level of required education or training.

To create this book, we started with approximately 900 major jobs at all levels of training and education. From these, we selected those with earnings of at least $46,300 per year. That figure represents an income level higher than what three-quarters of Americans earn as wages. The national median wage for all jobs is $29,430. Part I contains lists that rank these high-paying jobs according to many criteria, including earnings, growth, openings, education level, and interest area. Part II contains job descriptions for all of the jobs.

We think you will find many of the job lists in Part I interesting and useful for identifying high-paying career options to consider, even if they require you to get more education or training. The job descriptions are also packed with useful information.

Cautions About Choosing a Career Based on the Earnings

One of the most important reasons people work is to earn money, and many people aspire toward the best-paying job they can obtain. On the other hand, it is often said that money cannot buy happiness. This book is not the appropriate place for a philosophical discussion of the comparative merits of wealth versus poverty, but some cautionary statements are warranted nevertheless if you are basing your career choice largely on the criterion of earnings.

Working at a job means a lot more than just collecting the pay. It means putting in the required hours, doing the required tasks, being exposed to a particular work setting and to co-workers, and experiencing all the many other aspects of work. Therefore, when you choose a career goal, you need to consider *all* its potential rewards, as well as its possible drawbacks. Will you find the work interesting? Is the work setting an environment where you will feel comfortable? Will you work with people who don't get on your nerves? Does the work impose stress, travel, long hours, or physical demands that you would not be able to tolerate? This book can help answer some of these questions. For example, one set of lists in Part I breaks down the high-paying jobs by interest fields and another set breaks them down by personality types so you can identify jobs that are more likely to suit you. The job descriptions in Part II can also help you get some insights into the work. Finally, the appendix shows which skills are most closely associated with high-paying jobs. Nevertheless, any job choice you make using this book should be tentative, and before you make a commitment you should investigate the work in greater depth, ideally from seeing and talking to people on the job.

To qualify for entry to a high-paying job, you'll probably need to get some additional education or training. If you turn to the lists in Part I that group jobs by the amount of required education or training, you'll see that most of the high-paying jobs require a commitment of several years of preparation. You can learn the name of the specific educational or training program that you'll need to complete by looking at the job description in Part II. But the name of the program by itself does not tell you all you need to know about it. Can you can meet the program's demands for time, money, and motivation, which may be considerable? Is it offered in a location near you or where you are willing to relocate? What sorts of academic skills does it require? Do you feel comfortable in the setting where the learning will take place (e.g., library, classroom, lab, or clinic)? To answer these questions, you need to look at brochures and catalogs from providers of education and training and speak to people who are currently in the program, as well as people who have completed it and are now in the workforce.

After you talk to people in the career or preparatory program, you may start to question the assumption that more income is always better. You may find that earning a very high income will reduce some other satisfactions. For example, qualifying for a high-paying career may require you to complete years of study or an arduous training program. It may mean working under the stress of making decisions with high financial risks or with life-or-death consequences. And it may demand long work hours and travel that interfere with family life and leisure-time activities.

To gain more insights into the nature of high-paying jobs, we investigated whether certain aspects of *work context* are more closely associated with high income than others. Using data from the U.S. Department of Labor and a statistical procedure called correlation (which shows how well one variable can predict another), we found that various aspects of work context are better than others for predicting high income. Here are the factors that are most closely associated with high income:

- Freedom to Make Decisions
- Electronic Mail
- Letters and Memos
- Structured versus Unstructured Work
- Coordinate or Lead Others
- Impact of Decisions on Co-workers or Company Results
- Responsibility for Outcomes and Results
- Telephone
- Importance of Being Exact or Accurate
- Face-to-Face Discussions
- Consequence of Error
- Spend Time Sitting
- Level of Competition
- Indoors, Environmentally Controlled
- Frequency of Conflict Situations
- Public Speaking
- Contact with Others
- Exposed to Radiation

Some of these factors may sound pretty good to you—for example, "Freedom to Make Decisions." But consider the responsibilities that accompany this freedom: "Impact of Decisions on Co-workers or Company Results," Responsibility for Outcomes and Results," "Importance of Being Exact or Accurate," and "Consequence of Error."

Are some of the factors listed here unappealing or even distasteful to you? Be aware that not every high-paying job has all of these characteristics. For example, people who find indoor work confining may find satisfaction as Park Naturalists or Insurance Appraisers, Auto Damage. People with an aversion to public speaking may work as Credit Analysts, Electronics Engineering Technicians, or Dental Hygienists. But the highest-paying jobs are likely to have the largest number of these characteristics, so you need to decide how you feel about each of these factors (among others) and determine how much they characterize the kind of work you are considering. If a job on a list in Part I appeals to you because of its income, read its description in Part II thoroughly and don't stop there—explore it in depth using some of the resources listed at the end of this introduction under the heading "Sources of Additional Information."

Note that "Level of Competition" is one of the factors listed above. A lot of other people may be pursuing the same high-paying career goal that appeals to you, so you need to get a realistic sense of your chances of entering and succeeding in the job. One clue may be found in this book's information about how fast the job is growing and how many job openings are expected—figures you can find both in the lists in Part I and in the job descriptions in Part II. But this tells you only the demand for the occupation, not the supply of job-seekers, so you need to do more research to find out the amount of competition you may expect. The *Occupational Outlook Handbook* is a good place to start, and people who do the hiring or have recently been employed can also supply useful insights. If you talk to someone who works for an educational or training institution, especially a for-profit venture, remember that what they tell you may be partly a sales pitch, and be sure to ask about their recent job-placement track record.

After reading all these cautions and learning more about the highest-paying jobs, you may decide to lower your salary expectations and aim for a job that falls somewhere in the middle or lower range of the high-paying jobs in this book. This does not mean choosing a life of poverty! Remember that every job in this book pays, on average, better than what three-quarters of Americans earn from their work. Furthermore, the jobs in this book are ranked by their *average* earnings. Why not aspire to be an above-average earner in your occupation? One of the lists in Part I identifies 20 jobs with a few "star" earners, but every occupation has at least a few workers whose pay greatly exceeds the average. Here are some factors that can increase your chances of becoming one of those high-end earners:

- You have outstanding natural abilities.
- You become highly skilled.
- You move into a specialization, geographic location, or industry where demand is high but you have little competition.

- You have a flair for self-promotion.
- You take on managerial duties.
- You work out a business arrangement to direct your work output to a very large market.

For example, you won't find Chefs and Head Cooks included in this book because the average earnings are $32,330. But those employed by the government earn an average of $50,950, and the head pastry chef at the White House, who was paid $120,000 per year, recently left that job for a position at a casino hotel where he could earn *almost double* that salary. Chefs who author best-selling cookbooks and who get television shows earn even more. So it is possible to be a high earner even in an occupation that, on average, does not offer outstanding pay. But to achieve that exceptional income, you will have to beat the odds. You may have to expend exceptional effort, such as working long hours, to establish yourself in the occupation, perfect your skills, and demonstrate your abilities. Reaching peak earning power in your occupation also can take many years and put strains on your home life.

So as you explore the jobs in this book, keep in mind that every career choice involves trade-offs; you will have to give up some things to get other things. But if you follow up on the research that you are beginning by using this book, you can identify the job that will require you to give up the least in order to get a comfortable income and other satisfactions.

Where the Information Comes From

The information we used in creating this book comes from three major government sources:

- **The U.S. Department of Labor:** We used a variety of data sources to construct the information we used in this book. We started with the jobs included in the U.S. Department of Labor's O*NET database. The O*NET includes information on more than 1,000 occupations and is now the primary source of detailed information on occupations. The Labor Department updates the O*NET on a regular basis, and we used the most recent version available, release 9.

- **The U.S. Census Bureau:** Because we wanted to include earnings, growth, number of openings, and other data not included in the O*NET, we used information on earnings from the U.S. Department of Labor's Bureau of Labor Statistics (BLS). Some of this data came from the Current Population Survey (CPS), conducted by the U.S. Census Bureau, and other data came from the BLS's own Occupational Employment Statistics (OES) survey. The information on earnings is the most reliable information we could obtain. The OES and CPS use a slightly different system of job titles than the O*NET does, but we were able to link most of the OES and CPS data to the O*NET job titles we used to develop this book. The CPS also provided information about the proportion of workers in each job who are self-employed, work part time, or are in various age brackets. The 2000 Census provided information about the relative earnings of men and women.

⊚ **The U.S. Department of Education:** We used the Classification of Instructional Programs, a system developed by the U.S. Department of Education, to cross-reference the education or training programs related to each job.

Data Complexities

For those of you who like details, we present some of the complexities inherent in our sources of information and what we did to make sense of them here. You don't need to know this to use the book, so jump to the next section of the introduction if you are bored with details.

Earnings, Growth, and Number of Openings

We include information on earnings, projected growth, and number of job openings for each job throughout this book. We think this information is important to most people, but getting it for each job is not a simple task.

Earnings

Since so much of the emphasis of this book is on earnings, we want you to understand exactly what our earnings statements represent and where the information comes from.

The employment security agency of each state gathers information on earnings for various jobs and forwards it to the U.S. Bureau of Labor Statistics. This information is organized in standardized ways by a BLS program called the Occupational Employment Statistics, or OES. To keep the earnings for the various jobs and regions comparable, the OES screens out certain types of earnings and includes others, so the OES earnings we use in this book represent straight-time gross pay, exclusive of premium pay. More specifically, the OES earnings include the job's base rate; cost-of-living allowances; guaranteed pay; hazardous-duty pay; incentive pay, including commissions and production bonuses; on-call pay; and tips, but they do not include back pay, jury duty pay, overtime pay, severance pay, shift differentials, non-production bonuses, tuition reimbursements, or stock options. Also, self-employed workers are not included in the earnings estimates, and they can be a significant segment in certain occupations. The most recent earnings figures available apply to May 2005, so if the mild rate of inflation continues until you read this book, you can expect current earnings to have risen slightly above the figures reported here.

The OES earnings data is reported under a system of job titles called the Standard Occupational Classification system, or SOC. Most of these jobs can be cross-referenced to the O*NET job titles we use in this book, so we can attach earnings information to most job titles and descriptions. But a small number of the O*NET jobs simply do not have earnings data available for them from the sources we used and therefore were not included. In some other cases, an SOC title cross-references to more than one O*NET job title. For example, the O*NET has separate information for Accountants and for Auditors, but the OES reports earnings for a single SOC occupation called Accountants and Auditors. Therefore you may notice that the salary we report for Accountants ($52,210) is identical to the salary we report for Auditors. In reality there probably is a difference, but this is the best information that is available.

OES does not collect data on the comparative earnings of men and women, but we wanted to create a list of the best-paying jobs in which women's earnings are not greatly lower than men's. For this information we relied on the 2000 Census, which was the most recent source that reported statistics at the level of detail we needed for this book. Although the figures are a few years old and differ from the OES figures somewhat (they are based on the *total weekly* earnings), they are useful for computing the *comparative* earnings of the two sexes, a ratio that is likely to remain accurate for several years. Nevertheless, we decided it was advisable to report these percentage figures without any decimal places so the figures would not look more precise than they really are.

Projected Growth and Number of Job Openings

This information comes from the Office of Occupational Statistics and Employment Projections, a program within the Bureau of Labor Statistics that develops information about projected trends in the nation's labor market for the next ten years. The most recent projections available cover the years from 2004 to 2014. The projections are based on information about people moving into and out of occupations. The BLS uses data from various sources in projecting the growth and number of openings for each job title—some data comes from the Census Bureau's Current Population Survey and some comes from an OES survey. The projections assume that there will be no major war, depression, or other economic upheaval.

Like the earnings figures, the figures on projected growth and job openings are reported according to the SOC classification, so again some of the SOC jobs crosswalk to more than one O*NET job. To continue the example we used earlier, SOC reports growth (19.5%) and openings (119,000) for one occupation called Accountants and Auditors, but in this book we report these figures separately for the occupation Accountants and for the occupation Auditors. When you see that Accountants has a 19.5 percent project-ed growth rate and 119,000 projected job openings and Auditors has the same two numbers, you should realize that the 19.5 percent rate of projected growth represents the *average* of these two occupations—one may actually experience higher growth than the other—and that these two occupations will *share* the 119,000 projected openings.

It's especially important that you understand that (in this example) the figure of 119,000 job openings represents the *total number of job openings for the two jobs*. They share this figure—each job is projected to have *some fraction* of 119,000 job openings, but we don't know exactly how many. On the list of the "100 Best-Paying Jobs with the Most Openings" in Part I, jobs that share a figure for job openings are listed together because their position on this list depends on this shared figure. To remind you about how to read these figures, we print footnotes below lists in Part I to identify all the jobs that share data. In the job descriptions in Part II, we identify any occupations that share the job-openings figure listed for an occupation.

While salary figures are fairly straightforward, you may not know what to make of job-growth figures. For example, is projected growth of 15 percent good or bad? The average (mean) growth projected for all occupations by the Bureau of Labor Statistics is 14.8 percent. One-quarter of the occupations have a growth projection of 4.7 percent or lower. Growth of 12.4 percent is the median, meaning that half of the occupations have more, half less. Only one-quarter of the occupations have growth projected at more than 19.4 percent.

Fortunately the 250 best-paying jobs are also comparatively fast-growing. The weighted average of their growth is a lofty 19.6 percent, meaning that they exceed 75 percent of occupations in projected growth just as they exceed 75 percent of wage-earners in pay. Among these 250 high-powered jobs, one-quarter have projected job growth of 7.7 percent or lower, the median is 14.2 percent, and three-quarters have projected job growth of 19.8 percent or better.

Perhaps you're wondering why we present figures on both job growth *and* number of openings. Aren't these two ways of saying the same thing? Actually, you need to know both. Consider the occupation Geographers, which is projected to grow at the impressive rate of 19.5 percent. There should be lots of opportunities in such a fast-growing job, right? Not exactly. This is a tiny occupation, with only about 1,000 people currently employed, so even though it is growing rapidly it will not create many new jobs (fewer than 500 per year, in fact). Now consider Postal Service Mail Carriers. This occupation is actually *shrinking* slightly rather than growing (its growth rate is –0.5 percent), partly because automation does much of the mail-sorting for these workers and allows them to spend more of their time actually delivering mail and thus covering longer routes. Nevertheless, this is a huge occupation, employing one-third of a million workers, so even as it shrinks it is expected to take on 20,000 new workers each year to replace those who are retiring or moving into other careers. That's why we report both of these economic indicators and why you should pay attention to both when you scan our lists of best jobs.

Finally, don't forget that the job market consists of both job openings and job-*seekers*. The figures on job growth and openings don't tell you how many people will be competing with you to be hired. The Department of Labor does not publish figures on the supply of job candidates, so we are unable to tell you about the level of competition you can expect. Competition is an important issue that you should research for any tentative career goal. In some cases the *Occupational Outlook Handbook* provides informative statements. You should speak to people who educate or train tomorrow's workers; they probably have a good idea of how many graduates find rewarding employment and how quickly. People in the workforce also can provide insights into this issue. Use your critical thinking skills to evaluate what people tell you. For example, educators or trainers may be trying to recruit you, whereas people in the workforce may be trying to discourage you from competing. Get a variety of opinions to balance out possible biases.

Information in the Job Descriptions

We used a variety of government and other sources to compile the job descriptions we provide in Part II. Details on these various sources are mentioned later in this introduction in the section "Part II: The Job Descriptions."

How the 250 Best-Paying Jobs Were Selected

If you have read up to this point, you know that the jobs in this book were selected because they pay at least $46,300 per year. Here are a few more details about how we created the list of 250 jobs:

1. We began by creating our own database of information from the O*NET, the Census Bureau, and other sources to include the information we wanted. This database covers 1,167 job titles at all levels of education and training.

2. We eliminated 219 O*NET jobs for which we lacked useful information, such as work tasks or earnings, plus 13 jobs that are expected to employ fewer than 500 workers per year and to shrink rather than grow in workforce size. We also combined 36 very similar college teaching jobs into one job.

3. From the remaining 900 jobs, we removed all the jobs except those that pay what is earned by the highest-paid 25 percent of Americans—that is, those with average earnings of $46,300 or higher. Note that this figure is based on people's occupational earnings, not earnings from investments and other sources. (The exact figure is $46,180, but for this book we rounded it upward slightly.) This left a list of 250 high-paying jobs.

Why This Book Has More Than 250 Jobs

We didn't think you would mind that this book actually provides information on more than 250 jobs. Among the jobs it includes are 36 specialized postsecondary education jobs that we combined into one job called Teachers, Postsecondary. We use this one job title throughout the *lists* but provide *descriptions* for all 36 specialized postsecondary teaching jobs in Part II. You can find the titles of all of these jobs in the "Some Details on the Lists" section at the beginning of Part I.

This means that although we used 250 job titles to construct the basic list of high-paying jobs, we have a total of 285 job descriptions in Part II.

The Data in This Book Can Be Misleading

We use the most reliable data we can obtain for the earnings, projected growth, number of openings, and other information to create this book, but keep in mind that this information may or may not be accurate for your situation. This is because the information is true on the average. But just as there is no precisely average person, there is no such thing as a statistically average example of a particular job. We say this because data, while helpful, can also be misleading.

Take, for example, the yearly earnings information in this book. This is highly reliable data obtained from a very large U.S. working population sample by the Bureau of Labor Statistics. It tells us the median annual pay received by people in various job titles. This sounds very useful until you consider that half of all people in that occupation earn less than that amount and half earn more. (We often use "average" instead of "median" elsewhere in this book for ease of explanation.)

For example, people just entering the occupation or people with few years of work experience will often earn much less than the average. People who live in rural areas or who work for smaller employers typically earn less than those who do similar work in cities, where the cost of living is higher, for larger employers, or in high-growth industries. To help you focus on the most lucrative opportunities, for every occupation described in Part II we list the five industries in which income is highest and the five metropolitan areas where income is highest. But remember that just as these instances exceed the average, other industries and geographical locations offer earnings that are considerably below the average.

So, in reviewing the information in this book, please understand the limitations of the data it presents. You need to use common sense in career decision-making as in most other things in life. Even so, we hope that you find the information helpful and interesting.

Part I: The Best-Paying Jobs Lists

There are 59 separate lists in Part I of this book—look in the table of contents for a complete list of them. The lists are not difficult to understand because they have clear titles and are organized into groupings of related lists.

Depending on your situation, some of the jobs lists in Part I will interest you more than others. For example, if you are young, you may be interested to learn the best-paying jobs that employ high percentages of workers age 16–24. Other lists show best-paying jobs within interest groupings, by personality type, by level of education, and in other ways that you might find helpful in exploring your career options.

Whatever your situation, we suggest that you use the lists that make sense for you in beginning your exploration of best-paying career options. Following are the names of each group of lists along with short comments on each group. You will find additional information in a brief introduction provided at the beginning of each group of lists in Part I.

The Best-Paying Jobs

The first three lists in this group are the ones that most people want to see first. The first list presents all 250 job titles in order of their average earnings. The second list are subsets of the first list: the 100 jobs projected to grow most rapidly and the 100 jobs with the most openings.

Two lists highlight jobs where the earnings are particularly high: 20 jobs with a few "star" earners and 43 jobs in which almost everyone is well-paid. The next two lists get even more specific, identifying situations in which average earnings are over $100,000 per year: one in terms of jobs and industries, the other in terms of jobs and metropolitan areas. Finally, there is a list of jobs in which women's average earnings are not greatly lower than men's.

Best-Paying Jobs with High Percentages of Workers Age 16–24, Workers Age 55 and Over, Part-Time Workers, Self-Employed Workers, Women, and Men

This group of lists presents interesting information for a variety of types of people based on data from the U.S. Census Bureau. The lists are arranged into groups for workers age 16–24, workers age 55 and older, part-time workers, self-employed workers, women, and men. Each group of lists includes jobs in which the concentration of the specific type of people is significantly above the average for all jobs. We created three lists for each group, basing the last two on the information in the first list:

- The jobs with the highest earnings (the number of jobs varies)
- The 25 jobs with the highest growth rates
- The 25 jobs with the largest number of openings

Best-Paying Jobs Lists Based on Levels of Education, Training, and Experience

We created separate lists for each level of education and training as defined by the U.S. Department of Labor and put each of the 250 best-paying jobs into the list that indicates the education and training required for entry. Jobs within these lists are presented in order of their earnings. The lists include jobs in these groupings:

- Short-term on-the-job training
- Moderate-term on-the-job training
- Long-term on-the-job training
- Work experience in a related job
- Postsecondary vocational training

- Associate degree
- Bachelor's degree
- Work experience plus degree
- Master's degree
- Doctoral degree
- First professional degree

Best-Paying Jobs Lists Based on Interests

These lists organize the 250 best-paying jobs into groups based on interests. Within each list, jobs are presented in order of their earnings. Here are the 16 interest areas used in these lists: Agriculture and Natural Resources; Architecture and Construction; Arts and Communication; Business and Administration; Education and Training; Finance and Insurance; Government and Public Administration; Health Science; Hospitality, Tourism, and Recreation; Human Service; Information Technology; Law and Public Safety; Manufacturing; Retail and Wholesale Sales and Service; Scientific Research, Engineering, and Mathematics; Transportation, Distribution, and Logistics.

Best-Paying Jobs Lists Based on Personality Types

These lists organize the 250 best-paying jobs into six personality types, which are described in the introduction to the lists: Realistic, Investigative, Artistic, Social, Enterprising, and Conventional. The jobs within each list are presented in order of their earnings.

Part II: Descriptions of the Best-Paying Jobs

This part of the book provides a brief but information-packed description for each of the 285 best-paying jobs that appear on lists in this book. The descriptions in Part II are presented in alphabetical order. This makes it easy to look up any job you identify in a list from Part I that you want to learn more about.

We used the most current information from a variety of government sources to create the descriptions. We designed the descriptions to be easy to understand, and the sample that follows—with an explanation of each of its component parts—will help you better understand and use the descriptions.

Job Title

Data Elements

Industries in Which Income Is Highest

Metropolitan Areas Where Income Is Highest

Summary Description and Tasks

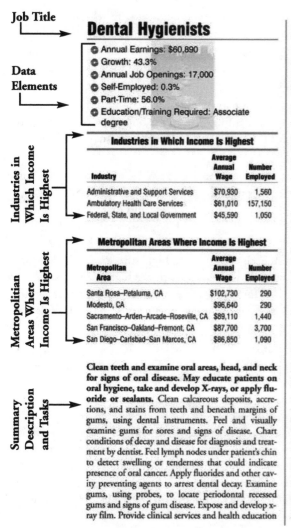

Dental Hygienists

- Annual Earnings: $60,890
- Growth: 43.3%
- Annual Job Openings: 17,000
- Self-Employed: 0.3%
- Part-Time: 56.0%
- Education/Training Required: Associate degree

Industries in Which Income Is Highest

Industry	Average Annual Wage	Number Employed
Administrative and Support Services	$70,930	1,560
Ambulatory Health Care Services	$61,010	157,150
Federal, State, and Local Government	$45,590	1,050

Metropolitan Areas Where Income Is Highest

Metropolitan Area	Average Annual Wage	Number Employed
Santa Rosa–Petaluma, CA	$102,730	290
Modesto, CA	$96,640	290
Sacramento–Arden-Arcade–Roseville, CA	$89,110	1,440
San Francisco–Oakland–Fremont, CA	$87,700	3,700
San Diego–Carlsbad–San Marcos, CA	$86,850	1,090

Clean teeth and examine oral areas, head, and neck for signs of oral disease. May educate patients on oral hygiene, take and develop X-rays, or apply fluoride or sealants. Clean calcareous deposits, accretions, and stains from teeth and beneath margins of gums, using dental instruments. Feel and visually examine gums for sores and signs of disease. Chart conditions of decay and disease for diagnosis and treatment by dentist. Feel lymph nodes under patient's chin to detect swelling or tenderness that could indicate presence of oral cancer. Apply fluorides and other cavity preventing agents to arrest dental decay. Examine gums, using probes, to locate periodontal recessed gums and signs of gum disease. Expose and develop x-ray film. Provide clinical services and health education

to improve and maintain oral health of school children. Remove excess cement from coronal surfaces of teeth. Make impressions for study casts. Place, carve, and finish amalgam restorations. Administer local anesthetic agents. Conduct dental health clinics for community groups to augment services of dentist. **SKILLS**—Active Learning; Time Management; Persuasion; Social Perceptiveness; Instructing; Learning Strategies; Reading Comprehension; Service Orientation.

GOE—Interest Area: 08. Health Science. **Work Group:** 08.03. Dentistry. **PERSONALITY TYPE:** Social. Social occupations frequently involve working with, communicating with, and teaching people. These occupations often involve helping or providing service to others.

EDUCATION/TRAINING PROGRAM—Dental Hygiene/Hygienist. **RELATED KNOWLEDGE/ COURSES**—**Biology:** Knowledge of plant and animal organisms and their tissues, cells, functions, interdependencies, and interactions with each other and the environment. **Medicine and Dentistry:** Knowledge of the information and techniques needed to diagnose and treat human injuries, diseases, and deformities. This includes symptoms, treatment alternatives, drug properties and interactions, and preventive health-care measures. **Chemistry:** Knowledge of the chemical composition, structure, and properties of substances and of the chemical processes and transformations that they undergo. This includes uses of chemicals, their danger signs, production techniques, and disposal methods. **Psychology:** Knowledge of human behavior and performance; individual differences in ability, personality, and interests; learning and motivation; psychological research methods; and the assessment and treatment of behavioral and affective disorders. **Customer and Personal Service:** Knowledge of principles and processes for providing customer and personal services. This includes customer needs assessment, meeting quality standards for services, and evaluation of customer satisfaction. **Sales and Marketing:** Knowledge of principles and methods for showing, promoting, and selling products or services. This includes marketing strategy and tactics, product demonstration, sales techniques, and sales control systems.

Skills

GOE Information

Personality Type

Education/ Training Programs

Related Knowledge/ Courses

- **Job Title:** This is the job title for the job as defined by the U.S. Department of Labor and used in its O*NET database.

- **Data Elements:** The information on earnings, education, growth, annual openings, percentage of self-employed workers, and percentage of part-time workers comes from various government databases, as we explain earlier in this introduction.

- **Industries in Which Income Is Highest:** When you are applying for jobs, or even while you are planning your education or training, you can use this information to aim for industries where workers are paid best. This list includes only industries where 50 or more workers in the occupation are employed, unless total U.S. employment in the occupation is less than 10,000. This information, as well as that in the next topic, is derived from the Occupational Employment Survey of the Department of Labor.

- **Metropolitan Areas Where Income Is Highest:** If you are willing to relocate, this information may help you find where the pay is best. Of course, high-paying localities often have high living costs, but not always. This list includes only metropolitan areas where 50 or more workers in the occupation are employed, unless total U.S. employment in the occupation is less than 10,000.

- **Summary Description and Tasks:** The first part of each job description provides a summary of the occupation in bold type. It is followed by a listing of tasks that are generally performed by people who work in the job. This information comes from the O*NET database.

- **Skills:** The O*NET database provides data on 35 skills, so we decided to list only those that are most important for each job rather than list pages of unhelpful details. For each job, we identify any skill that is rated at a level that is not low and that is significantly higher than the average level for this skill for all jobs and that also is rated as of significant importance in the occupation. We order these skills by the amount by which their ratings exceed the average rating for all occupations, from highest to lowest. If there are more than eight such skills, we include only those eight with the highest ratings. We include up to 10 skills if scores were tied for eighth place. If no skill has a rating significantly higher than the average for all jobs, we say "None met the criteria." All skills are defined in the appendix.

- **GOE Information:** This information cross-references the Guide for Occupational Exploration (or the GOE), a system developed by the U.S. Department of Labor that organizes jobs based on interests. We use the groups from the fourth edition of the *New Guide for Occupational Exploration*, as published by JIST. This edition uses a set of interest fields based on the 16 career clusters developed by the U.S. Department of Education and used in a variety of career information systems. The description includes the major Interest Area the job fits into, its more-specific Work Group, and a list of related O*NET job titles that are in this same GOE Work Group. This information will help you identify other job titles that have similar interests or require similar skills. You can find more information on the GOE and its Interest Areas in the introduction to the lists of jobs based on interests in Part I.

- **Personality Type:** The O*NET database assigns each job to its most closely related personality type. Our job descriptions include the name of the related personality type as well as a brief definition of this personality type. You can find more information on the personality types in the introduction to the lists of jobs based on personality types in Part I.

- **Education/Training Program(s):** This part of the job description provides the name of the educational or training program or programs for the job. It will help you identify sources of formal or informal training for a job that interests you. To get this information, we used a crosswalk created by the National Crosswalk Service Center to connect information in the Classification of Instructional Programs (CIP) to the O*NET job titles we use in this book. We made various changes to connect the O*NET job titles to the education or training programs related to them and also modified the names of some education and training programs so they would be more easily understood.

- ⊚ **Related Knowledge/Courses:** This entry in the job description will help you understand the most important knowledge areas that are required for the job and the types of courses or programs you will likely need to take to prepare for it. We used information in the Department of Labor's O*NET database for this entry. We went through a process similar to the one described for the skills (noted earlier) to end up with entries that are most important for each job.

Getting all the information we used in the job descriptions was not a simple process, and it is not always perfect. Even so, we used the best and most recent sources of data we could find, and we think that our efforts will be helpful to many people.

Sources of Additional Information

Hundreds of sources of career information exist, so here are a few we consider most helpful in getting additional information on the jobs listed in this book.

Print References

- ⊚ *O*NET Dictionary of Occupational Titles:* Revised on a regular basis, this book provides good descriptions for all jobs listed in the U.S. Department of Labor's O*NET database. There are 950 job descriptions at all levels of education and training, plus lists of related job titles in other major career information sources, educational programs, and other information. Published by JIST.

- ⊚ *New Guide for Occupational Exploration,* **Fourth Edition:** The new edition of the GOE is cross-referenced in the descriptions in Part II. The GOE provides helpful information to consider about each of the Interest Areas and Work Groups, descriptions of all O*NET jobs within each GOE group, and many other features useful for exploring career options. This most recent edition is published by JIST.

- ⊚ *Enhanced Occupational Outlook Handbook:* Updated regularly, this book provides thorough descriptions for almost 270 major jobs in the current *Occupational Outlook Handbook,* brief descriptions for the O*NET jobs that are related to each, brief definitions of thousands of more-specialized jobs from the *Dictionary of Occupational Titles,* and other information. Published by JIST.

Internet Resources

- ⊚ **The U.S. Department of Labor Bureau of Labor Statistics Web site:** The Department of Labor Bureau of Labor Statistics Web site (http://www.bls.gov) provides a lot of career information, including links to other Web pages that provide information on the jobs covered in this book. This Web site is a bit formal and, well, confusing, but it will take you to the major sources of government career information if you explore its options.

- **O*NET site:** Go to http://www.onetcenter.org for a variety of information on the O*NET database, including links to sites that provide detailed information on the O*NET job titles presented in Part II of this book.

- **CareerOINK.com:** This site (http://www.careeroink.com) is operated by JIST and includes free information on thousands of jobs (including all O*NET jobs included in *250 Best-Paying Jobs*), easy-to-use crosswalks between major career information systems, links from military to civilian jobs, sample resumes, and many other features. A link at http://www.jist.com will also take you to the CareerOINK Web site.

Thanks

Thanks for reading this introduction. You are surely a more thorough person than those who jumped into the book without reading it, and you will probably get more out of the book as a result.

We wish you a satisfying career and, more importantly, a good life.

PART I

The Best-Paying Jobs Lists

This part contains a lot of interesting lists, and it's a good place for you to start using the book. Here are some suggestions for using the lists to explore career options:

◎ The table of contents at the beginning of this book presents a complete listing of the list titles in this section. You can browse the lists or use the table of contents to find those that interest you most.

◎ We gave the lists clear titles, so most require little explanation. We provide comments for each group of lists.

◎ As you review the lists, one or more of the jobs may appeal to you enough that you want to seek additional information. As this happens, mark that job (or, if someone else will be using this book, write it on a separate sheet of paper) so that you can look up the description of the job in Part II.

◎ All data used to create these lists comes from the U.S. Department of Labor and the Census Bureau. The earnings figures are based on the average annual pay received by full-time workers. Some occupations have high percentages of part-time workers, and those workers would receive, of course, proportionately less pay on a weekly or annual basis. Because the earnings represent the national averages, actual pay rates can vary greatly by location, amount of previous work experience, and other factors.

Some Details on the Lists

The sources of the information we used in constructing these lists are presented in this book's introduction. Here are some additional details on how we created the lists:

◎ **We excluded some jobs for which very little information is available.** In the full list of 1,167 jobs that are described in release 9 of the U.S. Department of Labor's O*NET database, 212 have no information beyond a definition and, in some cases, a list of tasks. These are either catch-all titles (such as "Financial Specialists, All Other") that make the O*NET as comprehensive as possible or dummy occupations that help the O*NET match up better with occupational information from other government agencies. Census

Bureau data is available for some of them, but no O*NET data is available for them, so we dropped them from consideration. We also reluctantly excluded seven jobs because no wage information is available for them: Actors; Biologists; Dancers; Human Resources Managers; Hunters and Trappers; Musicians, Instrumental; and Singers.

- **We excluded some jobs that are shrinking or that offer very few opportunities.** Among the 948 jobs for which we have both O*NET and wage information, 13 are expected to employ fewer than 500 workers per year and to shrink rather than grow in workforce size: Camera and Photographic Equipment Repairers; Fabric Menders, Except Garment; Fire Inspectors; Fire Investigators; Forest Fire Inspectors and Prevention Specialists; Loading Machine Operators, Underground Mining; Mathematicians; Mine Cutting and Channeling Machine Operators; Mining and Geological Engineers, Including Mining Safety Engineers; Radio Operators; Refractory Materials Repairers, Except Brickmasons; Shoe Machine Operators and Tenders; and Shuttle Car Operators. These jobs can't be considered "best jobs," so we excluded them from consideration for this book.

- **We collapsed a number of specialized postsecondary education jobs into one title.** The government database we used for the job titles and descriptions included 36 job titles for postsecondary educators, yet the data source we used for growth and number of openings provided data only for the more general job of Teachers, Postsecondary. To make our lists more useful, we included only one listing—Teachers, Postsecondary—rather than separate listings for each specialized postsecondary education job. We did, however, include descriptions for all the specific postsecondary teaching jobs in Part II (except two for which no detailed information is available). Should you wonder, here are the more-specialized titles: Agricultural Sciences Teachers, Postsecondary; Anthropology and Archeology Teachers, Postsecondary; Architecture Teachers, Postsecondary; Area, Ethnic, and Cultural Studies Teachers, Postsecondary; Art, Drama, and Music Teachers, Postsecondary; Atmospheric, Earth, Marine, and Space Sciences Teachers, Postsecondary; Biological Science Teachers, Postsecondary; Business Teachers, Postsecondary; Chemistry Teachers, Postsecondary; Communications Teachers, Postsecondary; Computer Science Teachers, Postsecondary; Criminal Justice and Law Enforcement Teachers, Postsecondary; Economics Teachers, Postsecondary; Education Teachers, Postsecondary; Engineering Teachers, Postsecondary; English Language and Literature Teachers, Postsecondary; Environmental Science Teachers, Postsecondary; Foreign Language and Literature Teachers, Postsecondary; Forestry and Conservation Science Teachers, Postsecondary; Geography Teachers, Postsecondary; Graduate Teaching Assistants; Health Specialties Teachers, Postsecondary; History Teachers, Postsecondary; Home Economics Teachers, Postsecondary; Law Teachers, Postsecondary; Library Science Teachers, Postsecondary; Mathematical Science Teachers, Postsecondary; Nursing Instructors and Teachers, Postsecondary; Philosophy and Religion Teachers, Postsecondary; Physics Teachers, Postsecondary; Political Science Teachers, Postsecondary; Psychology Teachers, Postsecondary; Recreation and Fitness Studies Teachers, Postsecondary; Social Work Teachers, Postsecondary; Sociology Teachers, Postsecondary; Vocational Education Teachers, Postsecondary.

- **Some jobs have the same scores for one or more data elements.** For example, in the list of occupations ordered by rate of job growth, two occupations (Astronomers and Construction Managers) are growing at the same rate, 10.4%. Therefore we ordered these two jobs alphabetically, and their order has no other significance. There was no way to avoid these ties, so simply understand that the difference of several positions on a list may not mean as much as it seems.

⊙ **Some jobs share certain data elements.** In some cases, our data sources do not provide separate information for several separate jobs but instead provide it for an umbrella occupation. In these cases we have to print the same information for two, three, or more jobs. That can be misleading if you don't understand that these jobs *share* data. The section on "Data Complexities" in the introduction explains the full implications of this data-sharing. For here, we'll say simply that when occupations share data, the figures for earnings and job growth represent the *averages* for the occupations, and the figure for job openings represents the *total number* of job openings for the occupations. To remind you about how to read these figures, we print footnotes below lists to identify all the jobs that share job-openings data.

We hope you find these lists both interesting and helpful. They can help you explore your career options in a variety of interesting ways. We suggest you find the ones that are most helpful to you and focus your attention on them. Enjoy!

The Best-Paying Jobs

The first three lists in this section are the most important of all. First is the list of the 250 best-paying jobs, listed in order of their annual earnings. These jobs are the basis for most of the other lists in this book. For each job you'll find figures for the average earnings, the projected growth through 2014, and the expected annual job openings during that time period.

Of course, a high-paying job does you no good if you can't get hired for it. Some of the occupations on the list of 250 are growing much faster than others and producing many more job openings than others, so the next two lists present the 100 jobs with the best figures for projected percentage growth and number of annual openings.

This section also includes two lists of best-paying jobs in which the pay is distributed in certain desirable patterns (for example, jobs in which almost everyone is well-paid); a list of the jobs and industries where pay is highest; a list of the jobs and metropolitan areas where pay is highest; and a list of jobs where women's average earnings are not greatly lower than men's.

Descriptions for all of the jobs in these lists are included in Part II.

The 250 Best-Paying Jobs

This is the list that most people want to see first. It includes the 250 jobs that pay on average better than what 75 percent of American wage-earners make. (The section in the introduction called "How the 250 Best-Paying Jobs Were Selected" explains in detail how we selected the jobs on this list.)

Although health-care jobs dominate the top 20, you'll also find jobs in management, transportation, science, and the law. Not far behind you'll see jobs in engineering, finance, and technology. If you're interested in seeing the 250 jobs broken down by interest areas, turn to some of the lists later in Part I. If you're wondering how much education, training, or experience you'll need to qualify for these jobs, we also have lists that break down the 250 jobs by these requirements.

Consider this first list a starting place, not the final word. Your career decision should not be based solely on expected income, so look at the other lists, read the job descriptions in Part II for any job that interests you, and do a lot of additional career exploration before committing to a career goal.

The 250 Best-Paying Jobs

Job	Annual Earnings	Percent Growth	Annual Openings
1. Anesthesiologists	more than $145,600	24.0%	41,000
2. Internists, General	more than $145,600	24.0%	41,000
3. Obstetricians and Gynecologists	more than $145,600	24.0%	41,000
4. Oral and Maxillofacial Surgeons	more than $145,600	16.2%	fewer than 500
5. Orthodontists	more than $145,600	12.8%	1,000
6. Prosthodontists	more than $145,600	13.6%	fewer than 500
7. Psychiatrists	more than $145,600	24.0%	41,000
8. Surgeons	more than $145,600	24.0%	41,000
9. Chief Executives	$142,440	14.9%	38,000
10. Government Service Executives	$142,440	14.9%	38,000
11. Private Sector Executives	$142,440	14.9%	38,000
12. Family and General Practitioners	$140,400	24.0%	41,000
13. Airline Pilots, Copilots, and Flight Engineers	$138,170	17.2%	7,000
14. Pediatricians, General	$136,600	24.0%	41,000
15. Dentists, General	$125,300	13.5%	7,000
16. Air Traffic Controllers	$107,590	14.3%	2,000
17. Astronomers	$104,670	10.4%	fewer than 500
18. Engineering Managers	$100,760	13.0%	15,000
19. Podiatrists	$100,550	16.2%	1,000
20. Lawyers	$98,930	15.0%	40,000
21. Judges, Magistrate Judges, and Magistrates	$97,570	6.9%	1,000
22. Computer and Information Systems Managers	$96,520	25.9%	25,000
23. Natural Sciences Managers	$93,090	13.6%	5,000
24. Petroleum Engineers	$93,000	−0.1%	1,000
25. Marketing Managers	$92,680	20.8%	23,000
26. Pharmacists	$89,820	24.6%	16,000
27. Physicists	$89,810	7.0%	1,000
28. Nuclear Engineers	$88,290	7.3%	1,000
29. Optometrists	$88,040	19.7%	2,000

The 250 Best-Paying Jobs

Job	Annual Earnings	Percent Growth	Annual Openings
30. Sales Managers	$87,580	19.7%	40,000
31. Financial Managers, Branch or Department	$86,280	14.8%	63,000
32. Treasurers, Controllers, and Chief Financial Officers	$86,280	14.8%	63,000
33. Industrial-Organizational Psychologists	$84,690	20.4%	fewer than 500
34. Computer Hardware Engineers	$84,420	10.1%	5,000
35. Political Scientists	$84,100	7.3%	fewer than 500
36. Aerospace Engineers	$84,090	8.3%	6,000
37. Computer Software Engineers, Systems Software	$82,120	43.0%	37,000
38. Actuaries	$81,640	23.2%	3,000
39. General and Operations Managers	$81,480	17.0%	208,000
40. Electronics Engineers, Except Computer	$78,030	9.7%	11,000
41. Chemical Engineers	$77,140	10.6%	3,000
42. Computer Software Engineers, Applications	$77,090	48.4%	54,000
43. Public Relations Managers	$76,450	21.7%	5,000
44. Purchasing Managers	$76,270	7.0%	8,000
45. Industrial Production Managers	$75,580	0.8%	13,000
46. Education Administrators, Elementary and Secondary School	$75,400	10.4%	27,000
47. Sales Engineers	$74,200	14.0%	8,000
48. Training and Development Managers	$74,180	25.9%	3,000
49. Atmospheric and Space Scientists	$73,940	16.5%	1,000
50. Economists	$73,690	5.6%	1,000
51. Electrical Engineers	$73,510	11.8%	12,000
52. Marine Architects	$72,920	8.5%	fewer than 500
53. Marine Engineers	$72,920	8.5%	fewer than 500
54. Construction Managers	$72,260	10.4%	28,000
55. Physician Assistants	$72,030	49.6%	10,000
56. Biomedical Engineers	$71,840	30.7%	1,000
57. Geologists	$71,640	8.3%	2,000
58. Materials Scientists	$71,450	8.0%	fewer than 500
59. Biochemists	$71,000	21.0%	1,000
60. Biophysicists	$71,000	21.0%	1,000
61. Administrative Law Judges, Adjudicators, and Hearing Officers	$70,680	10.1%	1,000
62. Education Administrators, Postsecondary	$70,350	21.3%	18,000
63. Medical and Health Services Managers	$69,700	22.8%	33,000
64. Materials Engineers	$69,660	12.2%	2,000
65. Compensation and Benefits Managers	$69,130	21.5%	4,000

(continued)

(continued)

The 250 Best-Paying Jobs

Job	Annual Earnings	Percent Growth	Annual Openings
66. Storage and Distribution Managers	$69,120	12.7%	15,000
67. Transportation Managers	$69,120	12.7%	15,000
68. Veterinarians	$68,910	17.4%	8,000
69. Advertising and Promotions Managers	$68,860	20.3%	9,000
70. Computer Systems Analysts	$68,300	31.4%	56,000
71. Environmental Engineers	$68,090	30.0%	5,000
72. Mechanical Engineers	$67,590	11.1%	11,000
73. Chiropractors	$67,200	22.4%	4,000
74. Sales Agents, Financial Services	$67,130	11.5%	37,000
75. Sales Agents, Securities and Commodities	$67,130	11.5%	37,000
76. Industrial Engineers	$66,670	16.0%	13,000
77. Management Analysts	$66,380	20.1%	82,000
78. Nuclear Power Reactor Operators	$66,230	–0.5%	1,000
79. Civil Engineers	$66,190	16.5%	19,000
80. First-Line Supervisors/Managers of Police and Detectives	$65,570	15.5%	9,000
81. Fire-Prevention and Protection Engineers	$65,210	13.4%	2,000
82. Industrial Safety and Health Engineers	$65,210	13.4%	2,000
83. Product Safety Engineers	$65,210	13.4%	2,000
84. Agricultural Engineers	$64,890	12.0%	fewer than 500
85. Administrative Services Managers	$64,020	16.9%	25,000
86. Art Directors	$63,950	11.5%	10,000
87. Financial Analysts	$63,860	17.3%	28,000
88. Hydrologists	$63,820	31.6%	1,000
89. Geographers	$63,550	6.8%	fewer than 500
90. Personal Financial Advisors	$63,500	25.9%	17,000
91. Computer Programmers	$63,420	2.0%	28,000
92. Database Administrators	$63,250	38.2%	9,000
93. Financial Examiners	$63,090	9.5%	3,000
94. Physical Therapists	$63,080	36.7%	13,000
95. Architects, Except Landscape and Naval	$62,850	17.3%	7,000
96. Statisticians	$62,450	4.6%	2,000
97. Radiation Therapists	$62,340	26.3%	1,000
98. Operations Research Analysts	$62,180	8.4%	7,000
99. First-Line Supervisors/Managers of Non-Retail Sales Workers	$61,970	1.9%	38,000
100. Network Systems and Data Communications Analysts	$61,750	54.6%	43,000
101. Medical Scientists, Except Epidemiologists	$61,730	34.1%	15,000

The 250 Best-Paying Jobs

Job	Annual Earnings	Percent Growth	Annual Openings
102. Nuclear Equipment Operation Technicians	$61,120	13.7%	1,000
103. Nuclear Monitoring Technicians	$61,120	13.7%	1,000
104. Dental Hygienists	$60,890	43.3%	17,000
105. Fashion Designers	$60,860	8.4%	2,000
106. Forest Fire Fighting and Prevention Supervisors	$60,840	21.1%	4,000
107. Municipal Fire Fighting and Prevention Supervisors	$60,840	21.1%	4,000
108. Sales Representatives, Agricultural	$60,760	14.4%	47,000
109. Sales Representatives, Chemical and Pharmaceutical	$60,760	14.4%	47,000
110. Sales Representatives, Electrical/Electronic	$60,760	14.4%	47,000
111. Sales Representatives, Instruments	$60,760	14.4%	47,000
112. Sales Representatives, Mechanical Equipment and Supplies	$60,760	14.4%	47,000
113. Sales Representatives, Medical	$60,760	14.4%	47,000
114. Logisticians	$60,110	13.2%	7,000
115. Gaming Managers	$59,940	22.6%	1,000
116. Computer Security Specialists	$59,930	38.4%	34,000
117. Network and Computer Systems Administrators	$59,930	38.4%	34,000
118. Nuclear Medicine Technologists	$59,670	21.5%	2,000
119. Elevator Installers and Repairers	$59,190	14.8%	3,000
120. Power Distributors and Dispatchers	$59,160	0.0%	1,000
121. Budget Analysts	$58,910	13.5%	6,000
122. Chemists	$57,890	7.3%	5,000
123. Market Research Analysts	$57,300	19.6%	20,000
124. Real Estate Brokers	$57,190	7.8%	12,000
125. Clinical Psychologists	$57,170	19.1%	10,000
126. Counseling Psychologists	$57,170	19.1%	10,000
127. School Psychologists	$57,170	19.1%	10,000
128. Microbiologists	$56,870	17.2%	1,000
129. Occupational Therapists	$56,860	33.6%	7,000
130. Commercial Pilots	$55,810	16.8%	2,000
131. Child Support, Missing Persons, and Unemployment Insurance Fraud Investigators	$55,790	16.3%	9,000
132. Criminal Investigators and Special Agents	$55,790	16.3%	9,000
133. Immigration and Customs Inspectors	$55,790	16.3%	9,000
134. Police Detectives	$55,790	16.3%	9,000
135. Police Identification and Records Officers	$55,790	16.3%	9,000
136. Locomotive Engineers	$55,520	–2.5%	2,000

(continued)

(continued)

The 250 Best-Paying Jobs

Job	Annual Earnings	Percent Growth	Annual Openings
137. Urban and Regional Planners	$55,170	15.2%	3,000
138. Technical Writers	$55,160	23.2%	5,000
139. Teachers, Postsecondary	$55,100	32.2%	329,000
140. Electrical and Electronics Repairers, Powerhouse, Substation, and Relay	$54,970	–0.4%	2,000
141. Speech-Language Pathologists	$54,880	14.6%	5,000
142. Registered Nurses	$54,670	29.4%	229,000
143. Plant Scientists	$54,530	13.9%	1,000
144. Soil Scientists	$54,530	13.9%	1,000
145. Diagnostic Medical Sonographers	$54,370	34.8%	5,000
146. Arbitrators, Mediators, and Conciliators	$54,360	15.5%	fewer than 500
147. Landscape Architects	$54,220	19.4%	1,000
148. Railroad Conductors and Yardmasters	$54,040	20.3%	3,000
149. Directors—Stage, Motion Pictures, Television, and Radio	$53,860	16.6%	11,000
150. Producers	$53,860	16.6%	11,000
151. Program Directors	$53,860	16.6%	11,000
152. Talent Directors	$53,860	16.6%	11,000
153. Technical Directors/Managers	$53,860	16.6%	11,000
154. Agents and Business Managers of Artists, Performers, and Athletes	$53,800	11.8%	2,000
155. Orthotists and Prosthetists	$53,760	18.0%	fewer than 500
156. Occupational Health and Safety Specialists	$53,710	12.4%	3,000
157. Audiologists	$53,490	9.1%	fewer than 500
158. Park Naturalists	$53,350	6.3%	2,000
159. Range Managers	$53,350	6.3%	2,000
160. Soil Conservationists	$53,350	6.3%	2,000
161. Auxiliary Equipment Operators, Power	$53,170	–0.4%	5,000
162. Power Generating Plant Operators, Except Auxiliary Equipment Operators	$53,170	–0.4%	5,000
163. Ship Engineers	$52,780	12.7%	1,000
164. Sociologists	$52,760	4.7%	fewer than 500
165. Postmasters and Mail Superintendents	$52,710	0.0%	2,000
166. Environmental Scientists and Specialists, Including Health	$52,630	17.1%	8,000
167. Aerospace Engineering and Operations Technicians	$52,450	8.5%	1,000
168. Accountants	$52,210	22.4%	157,000
169. Auditors	$52,210	22.4%	157,000

The 250 Best-Paying Jobs

Job	Annual Earnings	Percent Growth	Annual Openings
170. Commercial and Industrial Designers	$52,200	10.8%	7,000
171. Epidemiologists	$52,170	26.2%	1,000
172. Zoologists and Wildlife Biologists	$52,050	13.0%	1,000
173. Cost Estimators	$52,020	18.2%	15,000
174. First-Line Supervisors/Managers of Mechanics, Installers, and Repairers	$51,980	12.4%	33,000
175. First-Line Supervisors and Manager/Supervisors—Construction Trades Workers	$51,970	10.9%	57,000
176. First-Line Supervisors and Manager/Supervisors—Extractive Workers	$51,970	10.9%	57,000
177. Gas Distribution Plant Operators	$51,920	7.7%	2,000
178. Gas Processing Plant Operators	$51,920	7.7%	2,000
179. Food Scientists and Technologists	$51,440	10.9%	1,000
180. Insurance Underwriters	$51,270	8.0%	13,000
181. Agricultural Crop Farm Managers	$51,160	4.0%	20,000
182. Fish Hatchery Managers	$51,160	4.0%	20,000
183. Nursery and Greenhouse Managers	$51,160	4.0%	20,000
184. Gaugers	$51,060	–8.6%	6,000
185. Petroleum Pump System Operators	$51,060	–8.6%	6,000
186. Petroleum Refinery and Control Panel Operators	$51,060	–8.6%	6,000
187. Mates—Ship, Boat, and Barge	$50,940	4.8%	2,000
188. Pilots, Ship	$50,940	4.8%	2,000
189. Ship and Boat Captains	$50,940	4.8%	2,000
190. Central Office and PBX Installers and Repairers	$50,620	–4.9%	21,000
191. Communication Equipment Mechanics, Installers, and Repairers	$50,620	–4.9%	21,000
192. Frame Wirers, Central Office	$50,620	–4.9%	21,000
193. Station Installers and Repairers, Telephone	$50,620	–4.9%	21,000
194. Telecommunications Facility Examiners	$50,620	–4.9%	21,000
195. Instructional Coordinators	$50,430	27.5%	15,000
196. Credit Analysts	$50,370	3.6%	3,000
197. Multi-Media Artists and Animators	$50,290	14.1%	14,000
198. Electrical Power-Line Installers and Repairers	$50,150	2.5%	11,000
199. Railroad Yard Workers	$49,700	–38.5%	1,000
200. Train Crew Members	$49,700	–38.5%	1,000
201. Social and Community Service Managers	$49,500	25.5%	17,000
202. Aviation Inspectors	$49,490	11.4%	2,000

(continued)

(continued)

The 250 Best-Paying Jobs

Job	Annual Earnings	Percent Growth	Annual Openings
203. Freight Inspectors	$49,490	11.4%	2,000
204. Marine Cargo Inspectors	$49,490	11.4%	2,000
205. Motor Vehicle Inspectors	$49,490	11.4%	2,000
206. Public Transportation Inspectors	$49,490	11.4%	2,000
207. Railroad Inspectors	$49,490	11.4%	2,000
208. Loan Officers	$49,440	8.3%	38,000
209. Coroners	$49,360	11.6%	17,000
210. Environmental Compliance Inspectors	$49,360	11.6%	17,000
211. Equal Opportunity Representatives and Officers	$49,360	11.6%	17,000
212. Government Property Inspectors and Investigators	$49,360	11.6%	17,000
213. Licensing Examiners and Inspectors	$49,360	11.6%	17,000
214. Pressure Vessel Inspectors	$49,360	11.6%	17,000
215. Signal and Track Switch Repairers	$49,200	2.3%	1,000
216. Purchasing Agents, Except Wholesale, Retail, and Farm Products	$49,030	8.1%	19,000
217. Pile-Driver Operators	$48,900	11.9%	fewer than 500
218. Compensation, Benefits, and Job Analysis Specialists	$48,870	20.4%	15,000
219. Transit and Railroad Police	$48,850	9.2%	fewer than 500
220. Foresters	$48,670	6.7%	1,000
221. First-Line Supervisors/Managers of Correctional Officers	$48,570	9.4%	2,000
222. Postal Service Clerks	$48,310	0.0%	4,000
223. Cartographers and Photogrammetrists	$48,250	15.3%	1,000
224. Insurance Appraisers, Auto Damage	$48,090	16.6%	2,000
225. Boilermakers	$48,050	8.7%	2,000
226. Calibration and Instrumentation Technicians	$48,040	9.8%	18,000
227. Electrical Engineering Technicians	$48,040	9.8%	18,000
228. Electronics Engineering Technicians	$48,040	9.8%	18,000
229. Medical and Clinical Laboratory Technologists	$47,710	20.5%	14,000
230. Funeral Directors	$47,630	6.7%	3,000
231. First-Line Supervisors/Managers of Transportation and Material-Moving Machine and Vehicle Operators	$47,530	15.3%	22,000
232. Subway and Streetcar Operators	$47,500	13.7%	1,000
233. Librarians	$47,400	4.9%	8,000
234. Sales Representatives, Wholesale and Manufacturing, Except Technical and Scientific Products	$47,380	12.9%	169,000
235. Aircraft Body and Bonded Structure Repairers	$47,310	13.4%	11,000
236. Aircraft Engine Specialists	$47,310	13.4%	11,000

The 250 Best-Paying Jobs

Job	Annual Earnings	Percent Growth	Annual Openings
237. Airframe-and-Power-Plant Mechanics	$47,310	13.4%	11,000
238. Vocational Education Teachers, Secondary School	$47,090	9.1%	10,000
239. Film and Video Editors	$46,930	18.6%	3,000
240. Special Education Teachers, Secondary School	$46,820	17.9%	11,000
241. Chemical Plant and System Operators	$46,710	-17.7%	8,000
242. Purchasing Agents and Buyers, Farm Products	$46,680	7.0%	2,000
243. Flight Attendants	$46,680	16.3%	7,000
244. Avionics Technicians	$46,630	9.1%	2,000
245. Educational, Vocational, and School Counselors	$46,440	14.8%	32,000
246. Caption Writers	$46,420	17.7%	14,000
247. Copy Writers	$46,420	17.7%	14,000
248. Creative Writers	$46,420	17.7%	14,000
249. Poets and Lyricists	$46,420	17.7%	14,000
250. Postal Service Mail Carriers	$46,330	0.0%	19,000

Jobs 1, 2, 6, 7, 8, 12, and 14 share 41,000 job openings. Jobs 9, 10, and 11 share 38,000 job openings. Jobs 52 and 53 share fewer than 500 job openings. Jobs 59 and 60 share 1,000 job openings. Jobs 66 and 67 share 15,000 job openings. Jobs 74 and 75 share 37,000 job openings. Jobs 81, 82, and 83 share 2,000 job openings. Jobs 102 and 103 share 1,000 job openings. Jobs 106 and 107 share 4,000 job openings. Jobs 108, 109, 110, 111, 112, and 113 share 47,000 job openings. Jobs 116 and 117 share 34,000 job openings. Jobs 125, 126, and 127 share 10,000 job openings. Jobs 131, 132, 133, 134, and 135 share 9,000 job openings. Job 136 shares 2,000 job openings with two other jobs not included in this list. Jobs 143 and 144 share 1,000 job openings. Jobs 149, 150, 151, 152, and 153 share 11,000 job openings. Jobs 158, 159, and 160 share 2,000 job openings. Jobs 161 and 162 share 5,000 job openings. Jobs 168 and 169 share 157,000 job openings. Jobs 175 and 176 share 57,000 job openings. Jobs 177 and 178 share 2,000 job openings. Jobs 181, 182, and 183 share 20,000 job openings. Jobs 184, 185, and 186 share 6,000 job openings. Jobs 187, 188, and 189 share 2,000 job openings. Jobs 190, 191, 192, 193, and 194 share 21,000 job openings. Jobs 199 and 200 share 1,000 job openings. Jobs 202, 203, 204, 205, 206, and 207 share 2,000 job openings. Jobs 209, 210, 211, 212, 213, and 214 share 17,000 job openings. Jobs 226, 227, and 228 share 18,000 job openings. Jobs 235, 236, and 237 share 11,000 job openings. Jobs 246, 247, 248, and 249 share 14,000 job openings.

The 100 Best-Paying Jobs with the Fastest Growth

Of the 250 jobs that met our criteria for this book, this list shows the 100 that are projected to have the highest percentage increase in the number of people employed through 2014. (The average growth rate for *all* occupations in the workforce is 14.8 percent.)

Jobs in the computer and health-care fields dominate the 20 fastest-growing jobs. Network Systems and Data Communications Analysts is the job with the highest growth rate—the number employed is projected to increase by better than half during this time. You can find a wide range of rapidly growing jobs in a variety of fields and at different levels of training and education among the jobs in this list.

The 100 Best-Paying Jobs with the Fastest Growth

Job	Annual Earnings	Percent Growth	Annual Openings
1. Network Systems and Data Communications Analysts	$61,750	54.6%	43,000
2. Physician Assistants	$72,030	49.6%	10,000
3. Computer Software Engineers, Applications	$77,090	48.4%	54,000
4. Dental Hygienists	$60,890	43.3%	17,000
5. Computer Software Engineers, Systems Software	$82,120	43.0%	37,000
6. Computer Security Specialists	$59,930	38.4%	34,000
7. Network and Computer Systems Administrators	$59,930	38.4%	34,000
8. Database Administrators	$63,250	38.2%	9,000
9. Physical Therapists	$63,080	36.7%	13,000
10. Diagnostic Medical Sonographers	$54,370	34.8%	5,000
11. Medical Scientists, Except Epidemiologists	$61,730	34.1%	15,000
12. Occupational Therapists	$56,860	33.6%	7,000
13. Teachers, Postsecondary	$55,100	32.2%	329,000
14. Hydrologists	$63,820	31.6%	1,000
15. Computer Systems Analysts	$68,300	31.4%	56,000
16. Biomedical Engineers	$71,840	30.7%	1,000
17. Environmental Engineers	$68,090	30.0%	5,000
18. Registered Nurses	$54,670	29.4%	229,000
19. Instructional Coordinators	$50,430	27.5%	15,000
20. Radiation Therapists	$62,340	26.3%	1,000
21. Epidemiologists	$52,170	26.2%	1,000
22. Computer and Information Systems Managers	$96,520	25.9%	25,000
23. Personal Financial Advisors	$63,500	25.9%	17,000
24. Training and Development Managers	$74,180	25.9%	3,000
25. Social and Community Service Managers	$49,500	25.5%	17,000
26. Pharmacists	$89,820	24.6%	16,000
27. Anesthesiologists	more than $145,600	24.0%	41,000
28. Family and General Practitioners	$140,400	24.0%	41,000
29. Internists, General	more than $145,600	24.0%	41,000
30. Obstetricians and Gynecologists	more than $145,600	24.0%	41,000
31. Pediatricians, General	$136,600	24.0%	41,000
32. Psychiatrists	more than $145,600	24.0%	41,000
33. Surgeons	more than $145,600	24.0%	41,000
34. Actuaries	$81,640	23.2%	3,000
35. Technical Writers	$55,160	23.2%	5,000
36. Medical and Health Services Managers	$69,700	22.8%	33,000
37. Gaming Managers	$59,940	22.6%	1,000

The 100 Best-Paying Jobs with the Fastest Growth

Job	Annual Earnings	Percent Growth	Annual Openings
38. Accountants	$52,210	22.4%	157,000
39. Auditors	$52,210	22.4%	157,000
40. Chiropractors	$67,200	22.4%	4,000
41. Public Relations Managers	$76,450	21.7%	5,000
42. Compensation and Benefits Managers	$69,130	21.5%	4,000
43. Nuclear Medicine Technologists	$59,670	21.5%	2,000
44. Education Administrators, Postsecondary	$70,350	21.3%	18,000
45. Forest Fire Fighting and Prevention Supervisors	$60,840	21.1%	4,000
46. Municipal Fire Fighting and Prevention Supervisors	$60,840	21.1%	4,000
47. Biochemists	$71,000	21.0%	1,000
48. Biophysicists	$71,000	21.0%	1,000
49. Marketing Managers	$92,680	20.8%	23,000
50. Medical and Clinical Laboratory Technologists	$47,710	20.5%	14,000
51. Compensation, Benefits, and Job Analysis Specialists	$48,870	20.4%	15,000
52. Industrial-Organizational Psychologists	$84,690	20.4%	fewer than 500
53. Advertising and Promotions Managers	$68,860	20.3%	9,000
54. Railroad Conductors and Yardmasters	$54,040	20.3%	3,000
55. Management Analysts	$66,380	20.1%	82,000
56. Sales Managers	$87,580	19.7%	40,000
57. Optometrists	$88,040	19.7%	2,000
58. Market Research Analysts	$57,300	19.6%	20,000
59. Landscape Architects	$54,220	19.4%	1,000
60. Clinical Psychologists	$57,170	19.1%	10,000
61. Counseling Psychologists	$57,170	19.1%	10,000
62. School Psychologists	$57,170	19.1%	10,000
63. Film and Video Editors	$46,930	18.6%	3,000
64. Cost Estimators	$52,020	18.2%	15,000
65. Orthotists and Prosthetists	$53,760	18.0%	fewer than 500
66. Special Education Teachers, Secondary School	$46,820	17.9%	11,000
67. Caption Writers	$46,420	17.7%	14,000
68. Copy Writers	$46,420	17.7%	14,000
69. Creative Writers	$46,420	17.7%	14,000
70. Poets and Lyricists	$46,420	17.7%	14,000
71. Veterinarians	$68,910	17.4%	8,000
72. Architects, Except Landscape and Naval	$62,850	17.3%	7,000
73. Financial Analysts	$63,860	17.3%	28,000

(continued)

(continued)

The 100 Best-Paying Jobs with the Fastest Growth

Job	Annual Earnings	Percent Growth	Annual Openings
74. Airline Pilots, Copilots, and Flight Engineers	$138,170	17.2%	7,000
75. Microbiologists	$56,870	17.2%	1,000
76. Environmental Scientists and Specialists, Including Health	$52,630	17.1%	8,000
77. General and Operations Managers	$81,480	17.0%	208,000
78. Administrative Services Managers	$64,020	16.9%	25,000
79. Commercial Pilots	$55,810	16.8%	2,000
80. Directors—Stage, Motion Pictures, Television, and Radio	$53,860	16.6%	11,000
81. Insurance Appraisers, Auto Damage	$48,090	16.6%	2,000
82. Producers	$53,860	16.6%	11,000
83. Program Directors	$53,860	16.6%	11,000
84. Talent Directors	$53,860	16.6%	11,000
85. Technical Directors/Managers	$53,860	16.6%	11,000
86. Atmospheric and Space Scientists	$73,940	16.5%	1,000
87. Civil Engineers	$66,190	16.5%	19,000
88. Child Support, Missing Persons, and Unemployment Insurance Fraud Investigators	$55,790	16.3%	9,000
89. Criminal Investigators and Special Agents	$55,790	16.3%	9,000
90. Flight Attendants	$46,680	16.3%	7,000
91. Immigration and Customs Inspectors	$55,790	16.3%	9,000
92. Police Detectives	$55,790	16.3%	9,000
93. Police Identification and Records Officers	$55,790	16.3%	9,000
94. Oral and Maxillofacial Surgeons	more than $145,600	16.2%	fewer than 500
95. Podiatrists	$100,550	16.2%	1,000
96. Industrial Engineers	$66,670	16.0%	13,000
97. First-Line Supervisors/Managers of Police and Detectives	$65,570	15.5%	9,000
98. Arbitrators, Mediators, and Conciliators	$54,360	15.5%	fewer than 500
99. Cartographers and Photogrammetrists	$48,250	15.3%	1,000
100. First-Line Supervisors/Managers of Transportation and Material-Moving Machine and Vehicle Operators	$47,530	15.3%	22,000

Jobs 6 and 7 share 34,000 job openings. Jobs 27, 28, 29, 30, 31, 32, and 33 share 41,000 job openings. Jobs 38 and 39 share 157,000 job openings. Jobs 45 and 46 share 4,000 job openings. Jobs 47 and 48 share 1,000 job openings. Jobs 60, 61, and 62 share 10,000 job openings. Jobs 67, 68, 69, and 70 share 14,000 job openings. Jobs 80, 82, 83, 84, and 85 share 11,000 job openings. Jobs 88, 89, 91, 92, and 93 share 9,000 job openings.

The 100 Best-Paying Jobs with the Most Openings

Of the 250 jobs that met our criteria for this book, this list shows the 100 jobs that are projected to have the largest number of job openings per year. They are ordered by the number of openings, so look to the top of the list for the occupations that will have the most job openings. Occupations that have equal figures for job openings are ordered alphabetically, but note that in some cases the figures are equal because two closely related occupations share the figure. We indicate all such occupations here in a footnote and list them one atop the other. If you are interested in job 99 or 100, you may also want to consider three related jobs—Program Directors, Talent Directors, and Technical Directors/Managers—that share economic data with 99 and 100 but had to be kept off this list to keep the number to 100.

Jobs with many openings present several advantages. Because there are many openings, these jobs can be easier to obtain. If part-time work is your goal, the odds of achieving that work arrangement are better when there are more openings. Although some occupations with many openings have low pay, all the jobs listed below met the criteria for this book and therefore have average earnings of at least $46,300.

It is interesting to note that high technology does not play a large role among most of the top 20 jobs on this list. Therefore it is not really true that nowadays you must master high-tech skills to be employable. In fact, most of these jobs have so many openings precisely because they require hands-on work and workers cannot be replaced by technology. Most of these jobs also require on-site work, sometimes in-person work, and therefore cannot be outsourced to overseas workers.

The 100 Best-Paying Jobs with the Most Openings

Job	Annual Earnings	Percent Growth	Annual Openings
1. Teachers, Postsecondary	$55,100	32.2%	329,000
2. Registered Nurses	$54,670	29.4%	229,000
3. General and Operations Managers	$81,480	17.0%	208,000
4. Sales Representatives, Wholesale and Manufacturing, Except Technical and Scientific Products	$47,380	12.9%	169,000
5. Accountants	$52,210	22.4%	157,000
6. Auditors	$52,210	22.4%	157,000
7. Management Analysts	$66,380	20.1%	82,000
8. Financial Managers, Branch or Department	$86,280	14.8%	63,000
9. Treasurers, Controllers, and Chief Financial Officers	$86,280	14.8%	63,000
10. First-Line Supervisors and Manager/Supervisors—Construction Trades Workers	$51,970	10.9%	57,000

(continued)

(continued)

The 100 Best-Paying Jobs with the Most Openings

Job	Annual Earnings	Percent Growth	Annual Openings
11. First-Line Supervisors and Manager/Supervisors—Extractive Workers	$51,970	10.9%	57,000
12. Computer Systems Analysts	$68,300	31.4%	56,000
13. Computer Software Engineers, Applications	$77,090	48.4%	54,000
14. Sales Representatives, Agricultural	$60,760	14.4%	47,000
15. Sales Representatives, Chemical and Pharmaceutical	$60,760	14.4%	47,000
16. Sales Representatives, Electrical/Electronic	$60,760	14.4%	47,000
17. Sales Representatives, Instruments	$60,760	14.4%	47,000
18. Sales Representatives, Mechanical Equipment and Supplies	$60,760	14.4%	47,000
19. Sales Representatives, Medical	$60,760	14.4%	47,000
20. Network Systems and Data Communications Analysts	$61,750	54.6%	43,000
21. Anesthesiologists	more than $145,600	24.0%	41,000
22. Family and General Practitioners	$140,400	24.0%	41,000
23. Internists, General	more than $145,600	24.0%	41,000
24. Obstetricians and Gynecologists	more than $145,600	24.0%	41,000
25. Pediatricians, General	$136,600	24.0%	41,000
26. Psychiatrists	more than $145,600	24.0%	41,000
27. Surgeons	more than $145,600	24.0%	41,000
28. Lawyers	$98,930	15.0%	40,000
29. Sales Managers	$87,580	19.7%	40,000
30. Chief Executives	$142,440	14.9%	38,000
31. First-Line Supervisors/Managers of Non-Retail Sales Workers	$61,970	1.9%	38,000
32. Government Service Executives	$142,440	14.9%	38,000
33. Private Sector Executives	$142,440	14.9%	38,000
34. Loan Officers	$49,440	8.3%	38,000
35. Computer Software Engineers, Systems Software	$82,120	43.0%	37,000
36. Sales Agents, Financial Services	$67,130	11.5%	37,000
37. Sales Agents, Securities and Commodities	$67,130	11.5%	37,000
38. Computer Security Specialists	$59,930	38.4%	34,000
39. Network and Computer Systems Administrators	$59,930	38.4%	34,000
40. First-Line Supervisors/Managers of Mechanics, Installers, and Repairers	$51,980	12.4%	33,000
41. Medical and Health Services Managers	$69,700	22.8%	33,000
42. Educational, Vocational, and School Counselors	$46,440	14.8%	32,000
43. Computer Programmers	$63,420	2.0%	28,000
44. Construction Managers	$72,260	10.4%	28,000

The 100 Best-Paying Jobs with the Most Openings

Job	Annual Earnings	Percent Growth	Annual Openings
45. Financial Analysts	$63,860	17.3%	28,000
46. Education Administrators, Elementary and Secondary School	$75,400	10.4%	27,000
47. Administrative Services Managers	$64,020	16.9%	25,000
48. Computer and Information Systems Managers	$96,520	25.9%	25,000
49. Marketing Managers	$92,680	20.8%	23,000
50. First-Line Supervisors/Managers of Transportation and Material-Moving Machine and Vehicle Operators	$47,530	15.3%	22,000
51. Central Office and PBX Installers and Repairers	$50,620	–4.9%	21,000
52. Communication Equipment Mechanics, Installers, and Repairers	$50,620	–4.9%	21,000
53. Frame Wirers, Central Office	$50,620	–4.9%	21,000
54. Station Installers and Repairers, Telephone	$50,620	–4.9%	21,000
55. Telecommunications Facility Examiners	$50,620	–4.9%	21,000
56. Agricultural Crop Farm Managers	$51,160	4.0%	20,000
57. Fish Hatchery Managers	$51,160	4.0%	20,000
58. Nursery and Greenhouse Managers	$51,160	4.0%	20,000
59. Market Research Analysts	$57,300	19.6%	20,000
60. Civil Engineers	$66,190	16.5%	19,000
61. Postal Service Mail Carriers	$46,330	0.0%	19,000
62. Purchasing Agents, Except Wholesale, Retail, and Farm Products	$49,030	8.1%	19,000
63. Calibration and Instrumentation Technicians	$48,040	9.8%	18,000
64. Electrical Engineering Technicians	$48,040	9.8%	18,000
65. Electronics Engineering Technicians	$48,040	9.8%	18,000
66. Education Administrators, Postsecondary	$70,350	21.3%	18,000
67. Coroners	$49,360	11.6%	17,000
68. Environmental Compliance Inspectors	$49,360	11.6%	17,000
69. Equal Opportunity Representatives and Officers	$49,360	11.6%	17,000
70. Government Property Inspectors and Investigators	$49,360	11.6%	17,000
71. Licensing Examiners and Inspectors	$49,360	11.6%	17,000
72. Pressure Vessel Inspectors	$49,360	11.6%	17,000
73. Dental Hygienists	$60,890	43.3%	17,000
74. Personal Financial Advisors	$63,500	25.9%	17,000
75. Social and Community Service Managers	$49,500	25.5%	17,000
76. Pharmacists	$89,820	24.6%	16,000
77. Compensation, Benefits, and Job Analysis Specialists	$48,870	20.4%	15,000
78. Cost Estimators	$52,020	18.2%	15,000

(continued)

(continued)

The 100 Best-Paying Jobs with the Most Openings

Job	Annual Earnings	Percent Growth	Annual Openings
79. Engineering Managers	$100,760	13.0%	15,000
80. Instructional Coordinators	$50,430	27.5%	15,000
81. Medical Scientists, Except Epidemiologists	$61,730	34.1%	15,000
82. Storage and Distribution Managers	$69,120	12.7%	15,000
83. Transportation Managers	$69,120	12.7%	15,000
84. Caption Writers	$46,420	17.7%	14,000
85. Copy Writers	$46,420	17.7%	14,000
86. Creative Writers	$46,420	17.7%	14,000
87. Poets and Lyricists	$46,420	17.7%	14,000
88. Medical and Clinical Laboratory Technologists	$47,710	20.5%	14,000
89. Multi-Media Artists and Animators	$50,290	14.1%	14,000
90. Industrial Engineers	$66,670	16.0%	13,000
91. Industrial Production Managers	$75,580	0.8%	13,000
92. Insurance Underwriters	$51,270	8.0%	13,000
93. Physical Therapists	$63,080	36.7%	13,000
94. Electrical Engineers	$73,510	11.8%	12,000
95. Real Estate Brokers	$57,190	7.8%	12,000
96. Aircraft Body and Bonded Structure Repairers	$47,310	13.4%	11,000
97. Aircraft Engine Specialists	$47,310	13.4%	11,000
98. Airframe-and-Power-Plant Mechanics	$47,310	13.4%	11,000
99. Directors—Stage, Motion Pictures, Television, and Radio	$53,860	16.6%	11,000
100. Producers	$53,860	16.6%	11,000

Jobs 5 and 6 share 157,000 job openings. Jobs 10 and 11 share 57,000 job openings. Jobs 14, 15, 16, 17, 18, and 19 share 47,000 job openings. Jobs 21, 22, 23, 24, 25, 26, and 27 share 41,000 job openings. Jobs 30, 32, and 33 share 38,000 job openings. Jobs 36 and 37 share 37,000 job openings. Jobs 38 and 39 share 34,000 job openings. Jobs 51, 52, 53, 54, and 55 share 21,000 job openings. Jobs 56, 57, and 58 share 20,000 job openings. Jobs 63, 64, and 65 share 18,000 job openings. Jobs 68, 69, 70, 71, and 72 share 17,000 job openings with each other and with another job not included in this list. Jobs 82 and 83 share 15,000 job openings. Jobs 84, 85, 86, and 87 share 14,000 job openings. Jobs 96, 97, and 98 share 11,000 job openings. Jobs 99 and 100 share 11,000 with each other and with three other jobs not included in this list.

20 Jobs with a Few "Star" Earners

Some occupations have a very unequal distribution of pay, with a few "star" earners and a lot of low earners. For example, for every Mariah Carey or Johnny Depp, there are thousands of other singers and actors who don't earn even minimum wage from performing. If you are interested in a career that has the potential for a big payoff even though the competition is keen, you may want to scan the following list.

This list is different from the previous lists in that it is not based solely on the median wage—which marks the point where half of the workers earn more, half less. Our focus here is not on the *middle* of the wage distribution; instead, we're looking at the *high* end for a few extremely high earners. The way we identify those occupations is to look instead at the *mean* earnings figure and how this differs from the median. The mean is the algebraic average, so if the mean is a lot higher than the median, it means that a few "star" earners are pulling up the average. (They are doing the same thing that high-achieving students do to grades when they "ruin the curve" for average students.)

Here is an example that explains what we're doing. Let's say we're looking at an occupation with only seven workers, and this is how their earnings are distributed:

Worker	Annual Earnings
A	$10,000
B	$20,000
C	$30,000
D	$40,000 (median: half earn more than D, half less)
E	$50,000
F	$60,000
G	$70,000

The median wage is $40,000, and if you do the math you'll find that $40,000 is also the mean (average) wage. That makes sense because the wages are distributed very evenly here. But let's say that worker G suddenly becomes a star and earns $400,000. The median does not change, but the mean now soars to $87,143. Having a star earner in the mix of workers creates a big gap between the median and the mean.

So to compile the following list we identified all the jobs among the 250 best for which the mean wage figure was at least 14 percent higher than the median, and we ordered them by the size of the difference, expressed as a percentage of the mean wage. It may not surprise you to find a number of entertainment-related jobs near the top of the list. (Musicians, Singers, Actors, and Dancers would probably be in this list as well if annual wage figures were available.) But did you realize that some business jobs also have star earners? Some medical specialties may also have outstanding earners (think of Hollywood plastic surgeons), but because we were unable to obtain a median wage figure for these occupations (other than "over $145,600"), we could not do the math to determine whether they belong here.

20 Jobs with a Few "Star" Earners

Job	Percent by Which Mean Annual Earnings Exceed Median	Earnings	Percent Growth	Annual Openings
1. Real Estate Brokers	25.7%	$57,190	7.8%	12,000
2. Sales Agents, Financial Services	23.7%	$67,130	11.5%	37,000
3. Sales Agents, Securities and Commodities	23.7%	$67,130	11.5%	37,000
4. Personal Financial Advisors	23.5%	$63,500	25.9%	17,000
5. Agents and Business Managers of Artists, Performers, and Athletes	23.2%	$53,800	11.8%	2,000
6. Directors—Stage, Motion Pictures, Television, and Radio	21.9%	$53,860	16.6%	11,000
7. Producers	21.9%	$53,860	16.6%	11,000
8. Program Directors	21.9%	$53,860	16.6%	11,000
9. Talent Directors	21.9%	$53,860	16.6%	11,000
10. Technical Directors/Managers	21.9%	$53,860	16.6%	11,000
11. Chiropractors	18.1%	$67,200	22.4%	4,000
12. Loan Officers	16.7%	$49,440	8.3%	38,000
13. First-Line Supervisors/Managers of Non-Retail Sales Workers	15.9%	$61,970	1.9%	38,000
14. Funeral Directors	15.3%	$47,630	6.7%	3,000
15. Sales Representatives, Wholesale and Manufacturing, Except Technical and Scientific Products	15.3%	$47,380	12.9%	169,000
16. Advertising and Promotions Managers	15.2%	$68,860	20.3%	9,000
17. Commercial Pilots	14.9%	$55,810	16.8%	2,000
18. General and Operations Managers	14.6%	$81,480	17.0%	208,000
19. Sociologists	14.5%	$52,760	4.7%	fewer than 500
20. Film and Video Editors	14.2%	$46,930	18.6%	3,000

Jobs 2 and 3 share 37,000 job openings. Jobs 6, 7, 8, 9, and 10 share 11,000 job openings.

39 Jobs in Which Almost Everyone Is Well-Paid

Maybe you're a person who doesn't like to take chances, and you're not confident you have the star power needed to soar above the other earners in your career. This list features occupations in which even comparatively low-paid workers are doing fine. Specifically, the workers who earn at the 10th percentile (meaning that 90 percent of the workers in the occupation earn more than they do) *still* earn at least $46,300, which means they earn more than 75 percent of all American wage-earners. They are ordered by the earnings of the workers at the 10th percentile.

39 Jobs in Which Almost Everyone Is Well-Paid

Job	Annual Earnings of "Low-Paid" Workers	Average Annual Earnings	Percent Growth	Annual Openings
1. Surgeons	$116,560 ....more than	$145,600	24.0%	41,000
2. Anesthesiologists	$108,040 ....more than	$145,600	24.0%	41,000
3. Obstetricians and Gynecologists	$95,960 ....more than	$145,600	24.0%	41,000
4. Internists, General	$88,790 ....more than	$145,600	24.0%	41,000
5. Orthodontists	$73,300 ....more than	$145,600	12.8%	1,000
6. Pediatricians, General	$66,520	$136,600	24.0%	41,000
7. Engineering Managers	$65,150	$100,760	13.0%	15,000
8. Oral and Maxillofacial Surgeons	$64,930 ....more than	$145,600	16.2%	....fewer than 500
9. Dentists, General	$64,770	$125,300	13.5%	7,000
10. Pharmacists	$64,350	$89,820	24.6%	16,000
11. Psychiatrists	$63,820 ....more than	$145,600	24.0%	41,000
12. Nuclear Engineers	$63,760	$88,290	7.3%	1,000
13. Prosthodontists	$63,310 ....more than	$145,600	13.6%	....fewer than 500
14. Air Traffic Controllers	$60,340	$107,590	14.3%	2,000
15. Chief Executives	$59,990	$142,440	14.9%	38,000
16. Government Service Executives	$59,990	$142,440	14.9%	38,000
17. Private Sector Executives	$59,990	$142,440	14.9%	38,000
18. Computer and Information Systems Managers	$57,300	$96,520	25.9%	25,000
19. Aerospace Engineers	$57,250	$84,090	8.3%	6,000
20. Family and General Practitioners	$56,680	$140,400	24.0%	41,000
21. Computer Hardware Engineers	$52,470	$84,420	10.1%	5,000
22. Computer Software Engineers, Systems Software	$51,890	$82,120	43.0%	37,000
23. Airline Pilots, Copilots, and Flight Engineers	$51,540	$138,170	17.2%	7,000
24. Petroleum Engineers	$51,410	$93,000	–0.1%	1,000
25. Nuclear Power Reactor Operators	$51,370	$66,230	–0.5%	1,000
26. Natural Sciences Managers	$50,260	$93,090	13.6%	5,000
27. Electronics Engineers, Except Computer	$50,090	$78,030	9.7%	11,000
28. Astronomers	$49,920	$104,670	10.4%	....fewer than 500
29. Education Administrators, Elementary and Secondary School	$49,540	$75,400	10.4%	27,000
30. Chemical Engineers	$49,350	$77,140	10.6%	3,000
31. Lawyers	$49,180	$98,930	15.0%	40,000
32. Physicists	$49,070	$89,810	7.0%	1,000
33. Industrial-Organizational Psychologists	$48,950	$84,690	20.4%	....fewer than 500
34. Marketing Managers	$48,590	$92,680	20.8%	23,000

(continued)

(continued)

39 Jobs in Which Almost Everyone Is Well-Paid

Job	Annual Earnings of "Low-Paid" Workers	Average Annual Earnings	Percent Growth	Annual Openings
35. Financial Managers, Branch or Department	$47,910	$86,280	14.8%	63,000
36. Treasurers, Controllers, and Chief Financial Officers	$47,910	$86,280	14.8%	63,000
37. Electrical Engineers	$47,750	$73,510	11.8%	12,000
38. Computer Software Engineers, Applications	$47,370	$77,090	48.4%	54,000
39. Industrial Production Managers	$46,300	$75,580	0.8%	13,000

Jobs 1, 2, 3, 4, 6, 11, and 20 share 41,000 job openings. Jobs 15, 16, and 17 share 38,000 job openings.

Jobs and Industries in Which Earnings Average More Than $100,000

Earning a good income is not just a question of getting into the right occupation; it also helps to get into the right industry. In some industries, the balance of supply and demand works out to produce higher salaries, particularly when an industry is growing so fast that skilled workers are in short supply. Fortunately, the Department of Labor's Occupational Earnings Survey (OES) reports wages not just by occupation, but also by industry, so we were able to compile industry-specific earnings figures for the 250 jobs in this book. Having done so, we found almost 500 combinations of job and industry where workers earn an average of over $100,000 per year.

We didn't want any items on this list to reflect a handful of freakishly high earners. For example, Lawyers who are working in the Beverage and Tobacco Product Manufacturing industry earn an average of over $145,600, compared to the average of $97,420 that Lawyers earn in *all* industries. But there are only about 50 of these superstar Lawyers fighting off lawsuits directed at tobacco companies and brewers. Therefore, we limited the list to instances of industries that employ more than 1,000 workers in the occupation. (We made two exceptions to this rule by including Astronomers and Prosthodontists, two tiny occupations with a total workforce of fewer than 10,000 each.) The jobs and the industries employing the high earners for each job are ordered alphabetically.

(For more information about industries, see *40 Best Fields for Your Career* by Mike Farr and Laurence Shatkin, Ph.D., published by JIST.)

Jobs and Industries in Which Earnings Average More Than $100,000

Job	Industries in Which Average Earnings Are More Than $100,000 per Year
Air Traffic Controllers	Federal, State, and Local Government
Airline Pilots, Copilots, and Flight Engineers	Air Transportation
Anesthesiologists	Ambulatory Health Care Services
Astronomers	Federal, State, and Local Government
Chief Executives	Accommodation; Administrative and Support Services; Ambulatory Health Care Services; Amusement, Gambling, and Recreation Industries; Broadcasting (Except Internet); Building Material and Garden Equipment and Supplies Dealers; Chemical Manufacturing; Computer and Electronic Product Manufacturing; Construction of Buildings; Credit Intermediation and Related Activities; Educational Services; Electrical Equipment, Appliance, and Component Manufacturing; Electronics and Appliance Stores; Fabricated Metal Product Manufacturing; Food Manufacturing; Furniture and Home Furnishings Stores; Furniture and Related Product Manufacturing; Health and Personal Care Stores; Heavy and Civil Engineering Construction; Hospitals; Insurance Carriers and Related Activities; Internet Service Providers, Web Search Portals, and Data Processing Services; Machinery Manufacturing; Management of Companies and Enterprises; Merchant Wholesalers, Durable Goods; Merchant Wholesalers, Nondurable Goods; Miscellaneous Manufacturing; Miscellaneous Store Retailers; Motion Picture and Sound Recording Industries; Motor Vehicle and Parts Dealers; Nonmetallic Mineral Product Manufacturing; Nonstore Retailers; Performing Arts, Spectator Sports, and Related Industries; Personal and Laundry Services; Plastics and Rubber Products Manufacturing; Primary Metal Manufacturing; Printing and Related Support Activities; Professional, Scientific, and Technical Services; Publishing Industries (Except Internet); Real Estate; Religious, Grantmaking, Civic, Professional, and Similar Organizations; Rental and Leasing Services; Repair and Maintenance; Securities, Commodity Contracts, and Other Financial Investments and Related Activities; Specialty Trade Contractors; Support Activities for Transportation; Telecommunications; Transportation Equipment Manufacturing; Truck Transportation; Utilities; Waste Management and Remediation Services; Wholesale Electronic Markets and Agents and Brokers; Wood Product Manufacturing

(continued)

(continued)

Jobs and Industries in Which Earnings Average More Than $100,000

Job	Industries in Which Average Earnings Are More Than $100,000 per Year
Computer and Information Systems Managers	Computer and Electronic Product Manufacturing; Internet Service Providers, Web Search Portals, and Data Processing Services; Management of Companies and Enterprises; Professional, Scientific, and Technical Services; Publishing Industries (Except Internet); Securities, Commodity Contracts, and Other Financial Investments and Related Activities; Telecommunications; Transportation Equipment Manufacturing
Dentists, General	Ambulatory Health Care Services
Engineering Managers	Administrative and Support Services; Computer and Electronic Product Manufacturing; Management of Companies and Enterprises; Merchant Wholesalers, Durable Goods; Oil and Gas Extraction; Professional, Scientific, and Technical Services; Telecommunications; Transportation Equipment Manufacturing
Family and General Practitioners	Ambulatory Health Care Services; Federal, State, and Local Government; Hospitals
Financial Managers, Branch or Department	Computer and Electronic Product Manufacturing; Funds, Trusts, and Other Financial Vehicles; Securities, Commodity Contracts, and Other Financial Investments and Related Activities
General and Operations Managers	Chemical Manufacturing; Computer and Electronic Product Manufacturing; Electrical Equipment, Appliance, and Component Manufacturing; Insurance Carriers and Related Activities; Internet Service Providers, Web Search Portals, and Data Processing Services; Lessors of Nonfinancial Intangible Assets (Except Copyrighted Works); Management of Companies and Enterprises; Oil and Gas Extraction; Paper Manufacturing; Petroleum and Coal Products Manufacturing; Professional, Scientific, and Technical Services; Publishing Industries (Except Internet); Securities, Commodity Contracts, and Other Financial Investments and Related Activities Telecommunications
Geologists	Oil and Gas Extraction
Government Service Executives	Accommodation; Administrative and Support Services; Ambulatory Health Care Services; Amusement, Gambling, and Recreation Industries; Broadcasting (Except Internet); Building Material and Garden Equipment and Supplies Dealers; Chemical Manufacturing; Computer and Electronic Product Manufacturing; Construction of Buildings; Credit Intermediation and Related Activities; Educational Services;

Jobs and Industries in Which Earnings Average More Than $100,000

Job	Industries in Which Average Earnings Are More Than $100,000 per Year
	Electrical Equipment, Appliance, and Component Manufacturing; Electronics and Appliance Stores; Fabricated Metal Product Manufacturing; Food Manufacturing; Furniture and Home Furnishings Stores; Furniture and Related Product Manufacturing; Health and Personal Care Stores; Heavy and Civil Engineering Construction; Hospitals; Insurance Carriers and Related Activities; Internet Service Providers, Web Search Portals, and Data Processing Services; Machinery Manufacturing; Management of Companies and Enterprises; Merchant Wholesalers, Durable Goods; Merchant Wholesalers, Nondurable Goods; Miscellaneous Manufacturing; Miscellaneous Store Retailers; Motion Picture and Sound Recording Industries; Motor Vehicle and Parts Dealers; Nonmetallic Mineral Product Manufacturing; Nonstore Retailers; Performing Arts, Spectator Sports, and Related Industries; Personal and Laundry Services; Plastics and Rubber Products Manufacturing; Primary Metal Manufacturing; Printing and Related Support Activities; Professional, Scientific, and Technical Services; Publishing Industries (Except Internet); Real Estate; Religious, Grantmaking, Civic, Professional, and Similar Organizations; Rental and Leasing Services; Repair and Maintenance; Securities, Commodity Contracts, and Other Financial Investments and Related Activities; Specialty Trade Contractors; Support Activities for Transportation; Telecommunications; Transportation Equipment Manufacturing; Truck Transportation; Utilities; Waste Management and Remediation Services; Wholesale Electronic Markets and Agents and Brokers; Wood Product Manufacturing
Internists, General	Ambulatory Health Care Services; Hospitals
Lawyers	Chemical Manufacturing; Computer and Electronic Product Manufacturing; Credit Intermediation and Related Activities; Management of Companies and Enterprises; Professional, Scientific, and Technical Services; Real Estate; Securities, Commodity Contracts, and Other Financial Investments and Related Activities; Telecommunications
Marketing Managers	Chemical Manufacturing; Computer and Electronic Product Manufacturing; Internet Service Providers, Web Search Portals, and Data Processing Services; Merchant Wholesalers, Durable Goods; Professional, Scientific, and Technical Services; Publishing Industries (Except Internet); Securities, Commodity Contracts, and Other Financial Investments and Related Activities

(continued)

(continued)

Jobs and Industries in Which Earnings Average More Than $100,000

Job	Industries in Which Average Earnings Are More Than $100,000 per Year
Natural Sciences Managers	Chemical Manufacturing; Professional, Scientific, and Technical Services
Obstetricians and Gynecologists	Ambulatory Health Care Services; Hospitals
Oral and Maxillofacial Surgeons	Ambulatory Health Care Services
Orthodontists	Ambulatory Health Care Services
Pediatricians, General	Ambulatory Health Care Services; Hospitals
Petroleum Engineers	Oil and Gas Extraction
Podiatrists	Ambulatory Health Care Services
Private Sector Executives	Accommodation; Administrative and Support Services; Ambulatory Health Care Services; Amusement, Gambling, and Recreation Industries; Broadcasting (Except Internet); Building Material and Garden Equipment and Supplies Dealers; Chemical Manufacturing; Computer and Electronic Product Manufacturing; Construction of Buildings; Credit Intermediation and Related Activities; Educational Services; Electrical Equipment, Appliance, and Component Manufacturing; Electronics and Appliance Stores; Fabricated Metal Product Manufacturing; Food Manufacturing; Furniture and Home Furnishings Stores; Furniture and Related Product Manufacturing; Health and Personal Care Stores; Heavy and Civil Engineering Construction; Hospitals; Insurance Carriers and Related Activities; Internet Service Providers, Web Search Portals, and Data Processing Services; Machinery Manufacturing; Management of Companies and Enterprises; Merchant Wholesalers, Durable Goods; Merchant Wholesalers, Nondurable Goods; Miscellaneous Manufacturing; Miscellaneous Store Retailers; Motion Picture and Sound Recording Industries; Motor Vehicle and Parts Dealers; Nonmetallic Mineral Product Manufacturing; Nonstore Retailers; Performing Arts, Spectator Sports, and Related Industries; Personal and Laundry Services; Plastics and Rubber Products Manufacturing; Primary Metal Manufacturing; Printing and Related Support Activities; Professional, Scientific, and Technical Services; Publishing Industries (Except Internet); Real Estate; Religious, Grantmaking, Civic, Professional, and Similar Organizations; Rental and Leasing Services; Repair and Maintenance; Securities, Commodity Contracts, and Other Financial Investments and Related Activities; Specialty Trade Contractors; Support Activities for Transportation; Telecommunications; Transportation

Jobs and Industries in Which Earnings Average More Than $100,000

Job	Industries in Which Average Earnings Are More Than $100,000 per Year
	Equipment Manufacturing; Truck Transportation; Utilities; Waste Management and Remediation Services; Wholesale Electronic Markets and Agents and Brokers; Wood Product Manufacturing
Prosthodontists	Ambulatory Health Care Services
Psychiatrists	Ambulatory Health Care Services; Federal, State, and Local Government; Hospitals
Sales Engineers	Publishing Industries (Except Internet)
Sales Managers	Broadcasting (Except Internet); Chemical Manufacturing; Computer and Electronic Product Manufacturing; Insurance Carriers and Related Activities; Internet Service Providers, Web Search Portals, and Data Processing Services; Professional, Scientific, and Technical Services; Securities, Commodity Contracts, and Other Financial Investments and Related Activities; Wholesale Electronic Markets and Agents and Brokers
Surgeons	Ambulatory Health Care Services; Hospitals
Treasurers, Controllers, and Chief Financial Officers	Computer and Electronic Product Manufacturing; Funds, Trusts, and Other Financial Vehicles; Securities, Commodity Contracts, and Other Financial Investments and Related Activities

Jobs and Metropolitan Areas Where Earnings Average More Than $100,000

Sometimes the best way to boost your pay is to pull up stakes and move to a region of the country where wages are higher. To be sure, sometimes high-wage localities also have a high cost of living, meaning that your improved earnings will put you into a higher tax bracket without buying you a more comfortable lifestyle.

But in other cases you can genuinely improve your circumstances by relocating. For example, for industries that involve a lot of collaborative work, businesses tend to cluster in certain geographical areas (think of Hollywood for the movies, Nashville for music, or Silicon Valley for high tech). Workers who live in such hubs of collaborative activity often can be more productive and thus more able to achieve an affluent standard of living than workers who are located elsewhere. On the other hand, for jobs where people tend to work solo (think of Dentists or Massage Therapists), the reverse is often true—workers can earn more if they move to a region where there are few colleagues and therefore little competition.

If you are thinking of relocating to improve your earnings, some other factors you should consider are the amount and cost of the commuting you may have to do. The time and expense of commuting can effectively erode your earning power. For example, let's say you're earning $1,200 per week for 40 hours of work, which equals $30 per hour. If your daily commute to and from work takes an hour each way, you're actually devoting 50 hours per week to your work, which means you are effectively earning $24 per hour. After you also subtract your costs for gasoline, tolls, and the wear and tear on your vehicle, your job in your new location actually may not be paying you more than your old job in your old location. So the relationship between the location of your job and your earnings can be a complex matter.

To create the following list, we analyzed the OES figures for the earnings of the 250 best-paying jobs in various metropolitan areas and identified those combinations where workers are earning an average of above $100,000. We did not include instances where fewer than 1,000 workers are employed in a metropolitan area unless the workers in this area represent more than three percent of the national workforce for the occupation. The jobs are ordered alphabetically.

Jobs and Metropolitan Areas Where Earnings Average More Than $100,000

Occupation	Metropolitan Area(s) Where Average Earnings Are More Than $100,000 per Year
Administrative Law Judges, Adjudicators, and Hearing Officers	Los Angeles–Long Beach–Santa Ana, CA; Washington–Arlington–Alexandria, DC–VA–MD–WV
Advertising and Promotions Managers	New York–Northern New Jersey–Long Island, NY–NJ–PA
Aerospace Engineers	Washington–Arlington–Alexandria, DC–VA–MD–WV
Air Traffic Controllers	Atlanta–Sandy Springs–Marietta, GA; Chicago–Naperville–Joliet, IL–IN–WI; Los Angeles–Long Beach–Santa Ana, CA; New York–Northern New Jersey–Long Island, NY–NJ–PA; Washington–Arlington–Alexandria, DC–VA–MD–WV
Airline Pilots, Copilots, and Flight Engineers	Anchorage, AK; Boston–Cambridge–Quincy, MA–NH; Chicago–Naperville–Joliet, IL–IN–WI; Denver–Aurora, CO; Los Angeles–Long Beach–Santa Ana, CA; Washington–Arlington–Alexandria, DC–VA–MD–WV
Anesthesiologists	Houston–Sugar Land–Baytown, TX; New York–Northern New Jersey–Long Island, NY–NJ–PA
Astronomers	Boston–Cambridge–Quincy, MA–NH; Washington–Arlington–Alexandria, DC–VA–MD–WV
Chief Executives	Albany–Schenectady–Troy, NY; Atlanta–Sandy Springs–Marietta, GA; Austin–Round Rock, TX; Baltimore–Towson, MD; Birmingham–Hoover, AL; Boston–Cambridge–Quincy,

Jobs and Metropolitan Areas Where Earnings Average More Than $100,000

Occupation	Metropolitan Area(s) Where Average Earnings Are More Than $100,000 per Year
	MA–NH; Buffalo–Niagara Falls, NY; Charleston–North Charleston, SC; Chicago–Naperville–Joliet, IL–IN–WI; Cincinnati–Middletown, OH–KY–IN; Cleveland–Elyria–Mentor, OH; Columbia, SC; Columbus, OH; Dallas–Fort Worth–Arlington, TX; Denver–Aurora, CO; Detroit–Warren–Livonia, MI; Grand Rapids–Wyoming, MI; Greenville, SC; Houston–Sugar Land–Baytown, TX; Indianapolis–Carmel, IN; Jackson, MS; Jacksonville, FL; Kansas City, MO–KS; Los Angeles–Long Beach–Santa Ana, CA; Louisville–Jefferson County, KY–IN; Memphis, TN–MS–AR; Miami–Fort Lauderdale–Miami Beach, FL; Milwaukee–Waukesha–West Allis, WI; Minneapolis–St. Paul–Bloomington, MN–WI; Nashville–Davidson–Murfreesboro, TN; New York–Northern New Jersey–Long Island, NY–NJ–PA; Oklahoma City, OK; Orlando–Kissimmee, FL; Philadelphia–Camden–Wilmington, PA–NJ–DE–MD; Phoenix–Mesa–Scottsdale, AZ; Pittsburgh, PA; Providence–Fall River–Warwick, RI–MA; Riverside–San Bernardino–Ontario, CA; Rochester, NY; Sacramento–Arden–Arcade–Roseville, CA; Salt Lake City, UT; San Antonio, TX; San Diego–Carlsbad–San Marcos, CA; San Francisco–Oakland–Fremont, CA; San Jose–Sunnyvale–Santa Clara, CA; Seattle–Tacoma–Bellevue, WA; Springfield, MA–CT; St. Louis, MO–IL; Tampa–St. Petersburg–Clearwater, FL; Tucson, AZ; Washington–Arlington–Alexandria, DC–VA–MD–WV; Worcester, MA–CT
Computer and Information Systems Managers	Austin–Round Rock, TX; Baltimore–Towson, MD; Boston–Cambridge–Quincy, MA–NH; Bridgeport–Stamford–Norwalk, CT; Charlotte–Gastonia–Concord, NC–SC; Dallas–Fort Worth–Arlington, TX; Denver–Aurora, CO; Los Angeles–Long Beach–Santa Ana, CA; Minneapolis–St. Paul–Bloomington, MN–WI; New York–Northern New Jersey–Long Island, NY–NJ–PA; Philadelphia–Camden–Wilmington, PA–NJ–DE–MD; San Francisco–Oakland–Fremont, CA; San Jose–Sunnyvale–Santa Clara, CA; Seattle–Tacoma–Bellevue, WA; Washington–Arlington–Alexandria, DC–VA–MD–WV
Computer Hardware Engineers	Boulder, CO; San Jose–Sunnyvale–Santa Clara, CA
Computer Software Engineers, Systems Software	San Jose–Sunnyvale–Santa Clara, CA
Construction Managers	New York–Northern New Jersey–Long Island, NY–NJ–PA; Seattle–Tacoma–Bellevue, WA

(continued)

(continued)

Jobs and Metropolitan Areas Where Earnings Average More Than $100,000

Occupation	Metropolitan Area(s) Where Average Earnings Are More Than $100,000 per Year
Dentists, General	Atlanta–Sandy Springs–Marietta, GA; Boston–Cambridge–Quincy, MA–NH; Dallas–Fort Worth–Arlington, TX; Denver–Aurora, CO; Detroit–Warren–Livonia, MI; Houston–Sugar Land–Baytown, TX; Los Angeles–Long Beach–Santa Ana, CA; Miami–Fort Lauderdale–Miami Beach, FL; New York–Northern New Jersey–Long Island, NY–NJ–PA; Philadelphia–Camden–Wilmington, PA–NJ–DE–MD; Phoenix–Mesa–Scottsdale, AZ; Washington–Arlington–Alexandria, DC–VA–MD–WV
Education Administrators, Elementary and Secondary School	San Diego–Carlsbad–San Marcos, CA
Engineering Managers	Albuquerque, NM; Austin–Round Rock, TX; Baltimore–Towson, MD; Boston–Cambridge–Quincy, MA–NH; Dallas–Fort Worth–Arlington, TX; Denver–Aurora, CO; Detroit–Warren–Livonia, MI; Hartford–West Hartford–East Hartford, CT; Houston–Sugar Land–Baytown, TX; Huntsville, AL; Los Angeles–Long Beach–Santa Ana, CA; Minneapolis–St. Paul–Bloomington, MN–WI; New York–Northern New Jersey–Long Island, NY–NJ–PA; Philadelphia–Camden–Wilmington, PA–NJ–DE–MD; Phoenix–Mesa–Scottsdale, AZ; Portland–Vancouver–Beaverton, OR–WA; Sacramento–Arden–Arcade–Roseville, CA; San Diego–Carlsbad–San Marcos, CA; San Francisco–Oakland–Fremont, CA; San Jose–Sunnyvale–Santa Clara, CA; Seattle–Tacoma–Bellevue, WA; Washington–Arlington–Alexandria, DC–VA–MD–WV
Family and General Practitioners	Austin–Round Rock, TX; Baltimore–Towson, MD; Dallas–Fort Worth–Arlington, TX; Detroit–Warren–Livonia, MI; Miami–Fort Lauderdale–Miami Beach, FL; Minneapolis–St. Paul–Bloomington, MN–WI; New York–Northern New Jersey–Long Island, NY–NJ–PA; Philadelphia–Camden–Wilmington, PA–NJ–DE–MD; Phoenix–Mesa–Scottsdale, AZ; Pittsburgh, PA; San Francisco–Oakland–Fremont, CA; Tampa–St. Petersburg–Clearwater, FL; Washington–Arlington–Alexandria, DC–VA–MD–WV
Financial Analysts	Bridgeport–Stamford–Norwalk, CT
Financial Managers, Branch or Department	Boston–Cambridge–Quincy, MA–NH; Bridgeport–Stamford–Norwalk, CT; Milwaukee–Waukesha–West Allis, WI; New York–Northern New Jersey–Long Island, NY–NJ–PA;

Jobs and Metropolitan Areas Where Earnings Average More Than $100,000

Occupation	Metropolitan Area(s) Where Average Earnings Are More Than $100,000 per Year
	San Francisco–Oakland–Fremont, CA; San Jose–Sunnyvale–Santa Clara, CA; Trenton–Ewing, NJ
General and Operations Managers	Bridgeport–Stamford–Norwalk, CT; Hartford–West Hartford–East Hartford, CT; New York–Northern New Jersey–Long Island, NY–NJ–PA; San Francisco–Oakland–Fremont, CA; San Jose–Sunnyvale–Santa Clara, CA; Seattle–Tacoma–Bellevue, WA; Trenton–Ewing, NJ; Washington–Arlington–Alexandria, DC–VA–MD–WV
Geologists	Houston–Sugar Land–Baytown, TX
Government Service Executives	Albany–Schenectady–Troy, NY; Atlanta–Sandy Springs–Marietta, GA; Austin–Round Rock, TX; Baltimore–Towson, MD; Birmingham–Hoover, AL; Boston–Cambridge–Quincy, MA–NH; Buffalo–Niagara Falls, NY; Charleston–North Charleston, SC; Chicago–Naperville–Joliet, IL–IN–WI; Cincinnati–Middletown, OH–KY–IN; Cleveland–Elyria–Mentor, OH; Columbia, SC; Columbus, OH; Dallas–Fort Worth–Arlington, TX; Denver–Aurora, CO; Detroit–Warren–Livonia, MI; Grand Rapids–Wyoming, MI; Greenville, SC; Houston–Sugar Land–Baytown, TX; Indianapolis–Carmel, IN; Jackson, MS; Jacksonville, FL; Kansas City, MO–KS; Los Angeles–Long Beach–Santa Ana, CA; Louisville–Jefferson County, KY–IN; Memphis, TN–MS–AR; Miami–Fort Lauderdale–Miami Beach, FL; Milwaukee–Waukesha–West Allis, WI; Minneapolis–St. Paul–Bloomington, MN–WI; Nashville–Davidson–Murfreesboro, TN; New York–Northern New Jersey–Long Island, NY–NJ–PA; Oklahoma City, OK; Orlando–Kissimmee, FL; Philadelphia–Camden–Wilmington, PA–NJ–DE–MD; Phoenix–Mesa–Scottsdale, AZ; Pittsburgh, PA; Providence–Fall River–Warwick, RI–MA; Riverside–San Bernardino–Ontario, CA; Rochester, NY; Sacramento–Arden–Arcade–Roseville, CA; Salt Lake City, UT; San Antonio, TX; San Diego–Carlsbad–San Marcos, CA; San Francisco–Oakland–Fremont, CA; SanJose–Sunnyvale–Santa Clara, CA; Seattle–Tacoma–Bellevue, WA; Springfield, MA–CT; St. Louis, MO–IL; Tampa–St. Petersburg–Clearwater, FL; Tucson, AZ; Washington–Arlington–Alexandria, DC–VA–MD–WV; Worcester, MA–CT
Industrial Production Managers	San Jose–Sunnyvale–Santa Clara, CA
Internists, General	Atlanta–Sandy Springs–Marietta, GA; Chicago–Naperville–Joliet, IL–IN–WI; Detroit–Warren–Livonia,

(continued)

(continued)

Jobs and Metropolitan Areas Where Earnings Average More Than $100,000	
Occupation	**Metropolitan Area(s) Where Average Earnings Are More Than $100,000 per Year**
	MI; Los Angeles–Long Beach–Santa Ana, CA; New York–Northern New Jersey–Long Island, NY–NJ–PA
Judges, Magistrate Judges, and Magistrates	New York–Northern New Jersey–Long Island, NY–NJ–PA
Lawyers	Atlanta–Sandy Springs–Marietta, GA; Boston–Cambridge–Quincy, MA–NH; Bridgeport–Stamford–Norwalk, CT; Chicago–Naperville–Joliet, IL–IN–WI; Dallas–Fort Worth–Arlington, TX; Hartford–West Hartford–East Hartford, CT; Houston–Sugar Land–Baytown, TX; Las Vegas–Paradise, NV; Los Angeles–Long Beach–Santa Ana, CA; Minneapolis–St. Paul–Bloomington, MN–WI; New York–Northern New Jersey–Long Island, NY–NJ–PA; Riverside–San Bernardino–Ontario, CA; San Diego–Carlsbad–San Marcos, CA; San Francisco–Oakland–Fremont, CA; San Jose–Sunnyvale–Santa Clara, CA; St. Louis, MO–IL; Virginia Beach–Norfolk–Newport News, VA–NC; Washington–Arlington–Alexandria, DC–VA–MD–WV
Marketing Managers	Austin–Round Rock, TX; Boston–Cambridge–Quincy, MA–NH; Bridgeport–Stamford–Norwalk, CT; Houston–Sugar Land–Baytown, TX; Los Angeles–Long Beach–Santa Ana, CA; Minneapolis–St. Paul–Bloomington, MN–WI; New York–Northern New Jersey–Long Island, NY–NJ–PA; San Diego–Carlsbad–San Marcos, CA; San Francisco–Oakland–Fremont, CA; San Jose–Sunnyvale–Santa Clara, CA; Seattle–Tacoma–Bellevue, WA
Natural Sciences Managers	New York–Northern New Jersey–Long Island, NY–NJ–PA; San Diego–Carlsbad–San Marcos, CA; San Francisco–Oakland–Fremont, CA; Washington–Arlington–Alexandria, DC–VA–MD–WV
Obstetricians and Gynecologists	Atlanta–Sandy Springs–Marietta, GA; Chicago–Naperville–Joliet, IL–IN–WI; Dallas–Fort Worth–Arlington, TX; New York–Northern New Jersey–Long Island, NY–NJ–PA; Washington–Arlington–Alexandria, DC–VA–MD–WV
Optometrists	New York–Northern New Jersey–Long Island, NY–NJ–PA
Oral and Maxillofacial Surgeons	Boston–Cambridge–Quincy, MA–NH
Pediatricians, General	Los Angeles–Long Beach–Santa Ana, CA; New York–Northern New Jersey–Long Island, NY–NJ–PA; Washington–Arlington–Alexandria, DC–VA–MD–WV
Petroleum Engineers	Houston–Sugar Land–Baytown, TX

Jobs and Metropolitan Areas Where Earnings Average More Than $100,000

Occupation	Metropolitan Area(s) Where Average Earnings Are More Than $100,000 per Year
Pharmacists	Los Angeles–Long Beach–Santa Ana, CA; Riverside–San Bernardino–Ontario, CA; Sacramento–Arden–Arcade–Roseville, CA; San Diego–Carlsbad–San Marcos, CA; San Francisco–Oakland–Fremont, CA; San Jose–Sunnyvale–Santa Clara, CA
Physicists	Los Angeles–Long Beach–Santa Ana, CA; Washington–Arlington–Alexandria, DC–VA–MD–WV
Podiatrists	Miami–Fort Lauderdale–Miami Beach, FL
Private Sector Executives	Albany–Schenectady–Troy, NY; Atlanta–Sandy Springs–Marietta, GA; Austin–Round Rock, TX; Baltimore–Towson, MD; Birmingham–Hoover, AL; Boston–Cambridge–Quincy, MA–NH; Buffalo–Niagara Falls, NY; Charleston–North Charleston, SC; Chicago–Naperville–Joliet, IL–IN–WI; Cincinnati–Middletown, OH–KY–IN; Cleveland–Elyria–Mentor, OH; Columbia, SC; Columbus, OH; Dallas–Fort Worth–Arlington, TX; Denver–Aurora, CO; Detroit–Warren–Livonia, MI; Grand Rapids–Wyoming, MI; Greenville, SC; Houston–Sugar Land–Baytown, TX; Indianapolis–Carmel, IN; Jackson, MS; Jacksonville, FL; Kansas City, MO–KS; Los Angeles–Long Beach–Santa Ana, CA; Louisville–Jefferson County, KY–IN; Memphis, TN–MS–AR; Miami–Fort Lauderdale–Miami Beach, FL; Milwaukee–Waukesha–West Allis, WI; Minneapolis–St. Paul–Bloomington, MN–WI; Nashville–Davidson–Murfreesboro, TN; New York–Northern New Jersey–Long Island, NY–NJ–PA; Oklahoma City, OK; Orlando–Kissimmee, FL; Philadelphia–Camden–Wilmington, PA–NJ–DE–MD; Phoenix–Mesa–Scottsdale, AZ; Pittsburgh, PA; Providence–Fall River–Warwick, RI–MA; Riverside–San Bernardino–Ontario, CA; Rochester, NY; Sacramento–Arden–Arcade–Roseville, CA; Salt Lake City, UT; San Antonio, TX; San Diego–Carlsbad–San Marcos, CA; San Francisco–Oakland–Fremont, CA; San Jose–Sunnyvale–Santa Clara, CA; Seattle–Tacoma–Bellevue, WA; Springfield, MA–CT; St. Louis, MO–IL; Tampa–St. Petersburg–Clearwater, FL; Tucson, AZ; Washington–Arlington–Alexandria, DC–VA–MD–WV; Worcester, MA–CT
Prosthodontists	Washington–Arlington–Alexandria, DC–VA–MD–WV
Psychiatrists	New York–Northern New Jersey–Long Island, NY–NJ–PA; Philadelphia–Camden–Wilmington, PA–NJ–DE–MD
Public Relations Managers	New York–Northern New Jersey–Long Island, NY–NJ–PA

(continued)

(continued)

Jobs and Metropolitan Areas Where Earnings Average More Than $100,000

Occupation	Metropolitan Area(s) Where Average Earnings Are More Than $100,000 per Year
Purchasing Managers	Washington–Arlington–Alexandria, DC–VA–MD–WV
Sales Agents, Financial Services	Bridgeport–Stamford–Norwalk, CT
Sales Agents, Securities and Commodities	Bridgeport–Stamford–Norwalk, CT
Sales Managers	Boston–Cambridge–Quincy, MA–NH; Bridgeport–Stamford–Norwalk, CT; Denver–Aurora, CO; Hartford–West Hartford–East Hartford, CT; Jacksonville, FL; Miami–Fort Lauderdale–Miami Beach, FL; Milwaukee–Waukesha–West Allis, WI; Minneapolis–St. Paul–Bloomington, MN–WI; New York–Northern New Jersey–Long Island, NY–NJ–PA; Oxnard–Thousand Oaks–Ventura, CA; San Francisco–Oakland–Fremont, CA; San Jose–Sunnyvale–Santa Clara, CA; Seattle–Tacoma–Bellevue, WA
Surgeons	Chicago–Naperville–Joliet, IL–IN–WI; Los Angeles–Long Beach–Santa Ana, CA; Minneapolis–St. Paul–Bloomington, MN–WI; New York–Northern New Jersey–Long Island, NY–NJ–PA; Philadelphia–Camden–Wilmington, PA–NJ–DE–MD
Treasurers, Controllers, and Chief Financial Officers	Boston–Cambridge–Quincy, MA–NH; Bridgeport–Stamford–Norwalk, CT; Milwaukee–Waukesha– West Allis, WI; New York–Northern New Jersey–Long Island, NY–NJ–PA; San Francisco–Oakland–Fremont, CA; San Jose–Sunnyvale–Santa Clara, CA; Trenton–Ewing, NJ

Jobs in Which Women's Average Earnings Are Not Greatly Lower Than Men's

You probably have read about how female workers tend to earn less than males in the same occupation. The reason for this wage difference is the subject of a lot of controversy—is it discrimination, the "mommy track" lifestyle choices of some women (which may include part-time work or periods of absence from the workforce), or some combination of factors? Some researchers have identified jobs where women actually earn more than men, and others have pointed to benefits (most notably maternity leave) that help offset the differences in pay. But in plain dollar terms, the decennial Census and the Current Population Survey seem to show that in most occupations women can expect to earn less than men.

If you're looking for a high-paying job and you are a woman—or a man who feels more comfortable in an environment where pay is equitable—you may want to know which jobs have the smallest gap between the dollar earnings of men and women. With that goal in mind, we used Census 2000 figures to identify the subset of the 250 best-paying jobs in which women's earnings were at least 70 percent of men's. (Sad to say, 70 percent is a "good" ratio.) Unlike the OES figures that we use in other parts of this book, the Census 2000 figures are based on total *weekly* earnings. Although these figures are also a few years older than the figures that we use elsewhere, trends in male-female wage differences are slow to change, so the female-to-male *ratio* for an occupation is probably still pretty close. Nevertheless, to avoid implying more precision than actually exists, we rounded the percentage figures to the nearest whole numbers. You also should know that Census figures were available for only 97 of the 250 best-paying jobs, so some jobs that do not appear here may actually have a good female-to-male wage ratio. Don't assume that a job has a bad ratio just because it doesn't appear on this list.

Jobs in Which Women's Average Earnings Are Not Greatly Lower Than Men's

Job	Ratio of Female to Male Earnings	Annual Earnings, Both Sexes
1. Sociologists	132%	$52,760
2. Sales Engineers	115%	$74,200
3. Engineering Managers	89%	$100,760
4. Avionics Technicians	88%	$46,630
5. Nuclear Equipment Operation Technicians	87%	$61,120
6. Nuclear Monitoring Technicians	87%	$61,120
7. Aircraft Body and Bonded Structure Repairers	85%	$47,310
8. Aircraft Engine Specialists	85%	$47,310
9. Airframe-and-Power-Plant Mechanics	85%	$47,310
10. First-Line Supervisors/Managers of Mechanics, Installers, and Repairers	84%	$51,980
11. Computer Security Specialists	83%	$59,930
12. Forest Fire Fighting and Prevention Supervisors	83%	$60,840
13. Municipal Fire Fighting and Prevention Supervisors	83%	$60,840
14. Network and Computer Systems Administrators	83%	$59,930
15. Urban and Regional Planners	82%	$55,170
16. Atmospheric and Space Scientists	81%	$73,940
17. Coroners	81%	$49,360
18. Environmental Compliance Inspectors	81%	$49,360
19. Equal Opportunity Representatives and Officers	81%	$49,360
20. First-Line Supervisors/Managers of Police and Detectives	81%	$65,570
21. Government Property Inspectors and Investigators	81%	$49,360
22. Licensing Examiners and Inspectors	81%	$49,360

(continued)

(continued)

Jobs in Which Women's Average Earnings Are Not Greatly Lower Than Men's

Job	Ratio of Female to Male Earnings	Annual Earnings, Both Sexes
23. Pressure Vessel Inspectors	81%	$49,360
24. Aerospace Engineers	80%	$84,090
25. Librarians	80%	$47,400
26. Mechanical Engineers	80%	$67,590
27. Postal Service Clerks	80%	$48,310
28. Technical Writers	80%	$55,160
29. Computer Programmers	79%	$63,420
30. Environmental Engineers	79%	$68,090
31. Occupational Therapists	79%	$56,860
32. Storage and Distribution Managers	79%	$69,120
33. Transportation Managers	79%	$69,120
34. Child Support, Missing Persons, and Unemployment Insurance Fraud Investigators	78%	$55,790
35. Criminal Investigators and Special Agents	78%	$55,790
36. First-Line Supervisors and Manager/Supervisors—Construction Trades Workers	78%	$51,970
37. First-Line Supervisors and Manager/Supervisors—Extractive Workers	78%	$51,970
38. First-Line Supervisors/Managers of Correctional Officers	78%	$48,570
39. Immigration and Customs Inspectors	78%	$55,790
40. Police Detectives	78%	$55,790
41. Police Identification and Records Officers	78%	$55,790
42. Operations Research Analysts	77%	$62,180
43. Postal Service Mail Carriers	76%	$46,330
44. Civil Engineers	75%	$66,190
45. Computer and Information Systems Managers	75%	$96,520
46. Administrative Services Managers	74%	$64,020
47. Audiologists	73%	$53,490
48. Credit Analysts	73%	$50,370
49. Network Systems and Data Communications Analysts	73%	$61,750
50. Purchasing Agents, Except Wholesale, Retail, and Farm Products	73%	$49,030
51. Speech-Language Pathologists	73%	$54,880
52. Economists	72%	$73,690
53. Logisticians	72%	$60,110
54. Biomedical Engineers	71%	$71,840

Jobs in Which Women's Average Earnings Are Not Greatly Lower Than Men's

Job	Ratio of Female to Male Earnings	Annual Earnings, Both Sexes
55. Budget Analysts	71%	$58,910
56. Industrial Production Managers	71%	$75,580
57. Chemical Engineers	70%	$77,140
58. Database Administrators	70%	$63,250
59. Directors—Stage, Motion Pictures, Television, and Radio	70%	$53,860
60. Materials Engineers	70%	$69,660
61. Nuclear Engineers	70%	$88,290
62. Pharmacists	70%	$89,820
63. Producers	70%	$53,860
64. Program Directors	70%	$53,860
65. Registered Nurses	70%	$54,670
66. Talent Directors	70%	$53,860
67. Technical Directors/Managers	70%	$53,860

Best-Paying Jobs with a High Percentage of Workers Age 16–24, Workers Age 55 and Over, Part-Time Workers, Self-Employed Workers, Women, and Men

The data we used to create this book included information that allowed us to compile more-specialized sets of lists that include high percentages of younger workers, older workers, part-time workers, self-employed workers, women, and men. As with the other lists, these lists are based on the jobs included in the list of 250 best-paying jobs.

For each group, we set a minimum figure that defines when a job has a high percentage of workers in that group. Then for each group we created three lists that consist only of best-paying jobs that exceed that cutoff figure. For example, the best jobs lists for younger workers include

◎ Best-Paying Jobs for Workers Age 16–24 (this list is ordered by level of earnings and includes all jobs that exceeded the cutoff figure)

◎ Best-Paying Jobs with the Fastest Growth for Workers Age 16–24 (this list is ordered by growth rate and includes the top 25)

○ Best-Paying Jobs with the Most Openings for Workers Age 16–24 (this list is ordered by the number of openings and includes the top 25)

We hope you find these lists interesting and useful. Do note that we are not suggesting that you should use the lists to limit your choices. For example, many jobs with a high percentage of women would provide excellent opportunities for, and should be considered by, men who find them interesting.

Best-Paying Jobs with a High Percentage of Workers Age 16–24

Workers age 16–24 are employed in virtually all major occupations, but they are concentrated in entry-level, part-time, seasonal, or service jobs. This makes sense in that many young workers have not yet settled into careers or are working while going to school. The jobs they get tend to be relatively easy to obtain but have relatively low wages.

For that reason, although workers age 16–24 make up 14 percent of the total workforce, in the 250 *high-paying* jobs they make up only 4.8 percent of the workforce. We decided that a job with only eight percent of young workers has a comparatively high concentration and used that figure as the cutoff point in assembling the following list. A total of 29 occupations exceeded this cutoff.

The jobs on this list are a very diverse set because there are several different reasons why young people would have a relatively large presence in a high-paying occupation. In many cases, the occupation is small and growing very rapidly—almost as if the occupation were just invented—and therefore it has a large contingent of young workers. Two examples are Agents and Business Managers of Artists, Performers, and Athletes and Orthotists and Prosthetists. In the business jobs listed here, workers who have gained experience tend to get promoted out of the job and into management.

If you're a young person, the important point to glean from this list is that there are a good number of high-paying jobs where your age is not a barrier to entry.

Best-Paying Jobs for Workers Age 16–24

Job	Percent Workers 16–24	Annual Earnings	Percent Growth	Annual Openings
1. Astronomers	8.7%	$104,670	10.4%	fewer than 500
2. Physicists	8.7%	$89,810	7.0%	1,000
3. Actuaries	13.0%	$81,640	23.2%	3,000
4. Atmospheric and Space Scientists	8.3%	$73,940	16.5%	1,000
5. Physician Assistants	12.9%	$72,030	49.6%	10,000
6. Administrative Services Managers	8.0%	$64,020	16.9%	25,000

Best-Paying Jobs for Workers Age 16–24

Job	Percent Workers 16–24	Annual Earnings	Percent Growth	Annual Openings
7. Network Systems and Data Communications Analysts	8.7%	$61,750	54.6%	43,000
8. Fashion Designers	8.7%	$60,860	8.4%	2,000
9. Technical Writers	8.2%	$55,160	23.2%	5,000
10. Directors—Stage, Motion Pictures, Television, and Radio	9.5%	$53,860	16.6%	11,000
11. Producers	9.5%	$53,860	16.6%	11,000
12. Program Directors	9.5%	$53,860	16.6%	11,000
13. Talent Directors	9.5%	$53,860	16.6%	11,000
14. Technical Directors/Managers	9.5%	$53,860	16.6%	11,000
15. Agents and Business Managers of Artists, Performers, and Athletes	13.9%	$53,800	11.8%	2,000
16. Orthotists and Prosthetists	8.2%	$53,760	18.0%	fewer than 500
17. Occupational Health and Safety Specialists	8.2%	$53,710	12.4%	3,000
18. Sociologists	20.0%	$52,760	4.7%	fewer than 500
19. Commercial and Industrial Designers	8.7%	$52,200	10.8%	7,000
20. Credit Analysts	10.3%	$50,370	3.6%	3,000
21. Loan Officers	8.7%	$49,440	8.3%	38,000
22. Cartographers and Photogrammetrists	9.4%	$48,250	15.3%	1,000
23. Boilermakers	9.1%	$48,050	8.7%	2,000
24. Medical and Clinical Laboratory Technologists	9.9%	$47,710	20.5%	14,000
25. First-Line Supervisors/Managers of Transportation and Material-Moving Machine and Vehicle Operators	8.6%	$47,530	15.3%	22,000
26. Film and Video Editors	13.8%	$46,930	18.6%	3,000
27. Flight Attendants	9.5%	$46,680	16.3%	7,000
28. Purchasing Agents and Buyers, Farm Products	14.3%	$46,680	7.0%	2,000
29. Educational, Vocational, and School Counselors	10.0%	$46,440	14.8%	32,000

Jobs 10, 11, 12, 13, and 14 share 11,000 job openings.

Best-Paying Jobs with the Fastest Growth for Workers Age 16–24

Job	Percent Workers 16–24	Annual Earnings	Percent Growth	Annual Openings
1. Network Systems and Data Communications Analysts	8.7%	$61,750	54.6%	43,000
2. Physician Assistants	12.9%	$72,030	49.6%	10,000

(continued)

(continued)

Best-Paying Jobs with the Fastest Growth for Workers Age 16–24

Job	Percent Workers 16–24	Annual Earnings	Percent Growth	Annual Openings
3. Technical Writers	8.2%	$55,160	23.2%	5,000
4. Actuaries	13.0%	$81,640	23.2%	3,000
5. Medical and Clinical Laboratory Technologists	9.9%	$47,710	20.5%	14,000
6. Film and Video Editors	13.8%	$46,930	18.6%	3,000
7. Orthotists and Prosthetists	8.2%	$53,760	18.0%	fewer than 500
8. Administrative Services Managers	8.0%	$64,020	16.9%	25,000
9. Directors—Stage, Motion Pictures, Television, and Radio	9.5%	$53,860	16.6%	11,000
10. Producers	9.5%	$53,860	16.6%	11,000
11. Program Directors	9.5%	$53,860	16.6%	11,000
12. Talent Directors	9.5%	$53,860	16.6%	11,000
13. Technical Directors/Managers	9.5%	$53,860	16.6%	11,000
14. Atmospheric and Space Scientists	8.3%	$73,940	16.5%	1,000
15. Flight Attendants	9.5%	$46,680	16.3%	7,000
16. Cartographers and Photogrammetrists	9.4%	$48,250	15.3%	1,000
17. First-Line Supervisors/Managers of Transportation and Material-Moving Machine and Vehicle Operators	8.6%	$47,530	15.3%	22,000
18. Educational, Vocational, and School Counselors	10.0%	$46,440	14.8%	32,000
19. Occupational Health and Safety Specialists	8.2%	$53,710	12.4%	3,000
20. Agents and Business Managers of Artists, Performers, and Athletes	13.9%	$53,800	11.8%	2,000
21. Commercial and Industrial Designers	8.7%	$52,200	10.8%	7,000
22. Astronomers	8.7%	$104,670	10.4%	fewer than 500
23. Boilermakers	9.1%	$48,050	8.7%	2,000
24. Fashion Designers	8.7%	$60,860	8.4%	2,000
25. Loan Officers	8.7%	$49,440	8.3%	38,000

Jobs 9, 10, 11, 12, and 13 share 11,000 job openings.

Best-Paying Jobs with the Most Openings for Workers Age 16–24

Job	Percent Workers 16–24	Annual Earnings	Percent Growth	Annual Openings
1. Network Systems and Data Communications Analysts	8.7%	$61,750	54.6%	43,000
2. Loan Officers	8.7%	$49,440	8.3%	38,000
3. Educational, Vocational, and School Counselors	10.0%	$46,440	14.8%	32,000

Best-Paying Jobs with the Most Openings for Workers Age 16–24

Job	Percent Workers 16–24	Annual Earnings	Percent Growth	Annual Openings
4. Administrative Services Managers	8.0%	$64,020	16.9%	25,000
5. First-Line Supervisors/Managers of Transportation and Material-Moving Machine and Vehicle Operators	8.6%	$47,530	15.3%	22,000
6. Medical and Clinical Laboratory Technologists	9.9%	$47,710	20.5%	14,000
7. Directors—Stage, Motion Pictures, Television, and Radio	9.5%	$53,860	16.6%	11,000
8. Producers	9.5%	$53,860	16.6%	11,000
9. Program Directors	9.5%	$53,860	16.6%	11,000
10. Talent Directors	9.5%	$53,860	16.6%	11,000
11. Technical Directors/Managers	9.5%	$53,860	16.6%	11,000
12. Physician Assistants	12.9%	$72,030	49.6%	10,000
13. Commercial and Industrial Designers	8.7%	$52,200	10.8%	7,000
14. Flight Attendants	9.5%	$46,680	16.3%	7,000
15. Technical Writers	8.2%	$55,160	23.2%	5,000
16. Actuaries	13.0%	$81,640	23.2%	3,000
17. Credit Analysts	10.3%	$50,370	3.6%	3,000
18. Film and Video Editors	13.8%	$46,930	18.6%	3,000
19. Occupational Health and Safety Specialists	8.2%	$53,710	12.4%	3,000
20. Agents and Business Managers of Artists, Performers, and Athletes	13.9%	$53,800	11.8%	2,000
21. Boilermakers	9.1%	$48,050	8.7%	2,000
22. Fashion Designers	8.7%	$60,860	8.4%	2,000
23. Purchasing Agents and Buyers, Farm Products	14.3%	$46,680	7.0%	2,000
24. Atmospheric and Space Scientists	8.3%	$73,940	16.5%	1,000
25. Cartographers and Photogrammetrists	9.4%	$48,250	15.3%	1,000

Jobs 7, 8, 9, 10, and 11 share 11,000 job openings.

Best-Paying Jobs with a High Percentage of Workers Age 55 and Over

Older workers have had more years to gain experience and education and thus more often qualify for better-paying jobs. As a result, although workers age 55 and over make up about 17.2 percent of the labor market, among the 250 best-paying jobs they are more heavily represented. Therefore we included occupations in this list if the percent of workers 55 and over was 20 percent or higher. A total of 69 jobs met this criterion and form the basis of this group of lists.

One use for these lists is to help you identify careers that might be interesting as you decide to change careers or approach retirement. Some occupations on the lists may be attractive to older workers wanting part-time work to supplement their retirement income. For example, we think that the job of Technical Writers is appealing because the job pays well, can be done less than full time and on a flexible schedule, and lends itself to self-employment. Other occupations on the lists (such as Judges, Magistrate Judges, and Magistrates) take many years of training and experience. After a person is established in that career, the person often works in that occupation until retirement. This low job turnover rate may be reflected in the small number of job openings expected for several of the occupations near the top of the list. Another factor that many of the jobs have in common is low physical demands.

Best-Paying Jobs for Workers Age 55 and Over

Job	Percent Workers 55 and Over	Annual Earnings	Percent Growth	Annual Openings
1. Anesthesiologists	20.0% more than	$145,600	24.0%	41,000
2. Internists, General	20.0% more than	$145,600	24.0%	41,000
3. Obstetricians and Gynecologists	20.0% more than	$145,600	24.0%	41,000
4. Oral and Maxillofacial Surgeons	30.5% more than	$145,600	16.2%	fewer than 500
5. Orthodontists	30.5% more than	$145,600	12.8%	1,000
6. Prosthodontists	30.5% more than	$145,600	13.6%	fewer than 500
7. Psychiatrists	20.0% more than	$145,600	24.0%	41,000
8. Surgeons	20.0% more than	$145,600	24.0%	41,000
9. Chief Executives	27.3%	$142,440	14.9%	38,000
10. Government Service Executives	27.3%	$142,440	14.9%	38,000
11. Private Sector Executives	27.3%	$142,440	14.9%	38,000
12. Family and General Practitioners	20.0%	$140,400	24.0%	41,000
13. Pediatricians, General	20.0%	$136,600	24.0%	41,000
14. Dentists, General	30.5%	$125,300	13.5%	7,000
15. Astronomers	30.4%	$104,670	10.4%	fewer than 500
16. Engineering Managers	22.6%	$100,760	13.0%	15,000
17. Podiatrists	25.0%	$100,550	16.2%	1,000
18. Lawyers	23.3%	$98,930	15.0%	40,000
19. Judges, Magistrate Judges, and Magistrates	34.4%	$97,570	6.9%	1,000
20. Natural Sciences Managers	25.0%	$93,090	13.6%	5,000
21. Pharmacists	24.5%	$89,820	24.6%	16,000
22. Physicists	30.4%	$89,810	7.0%	1,000
23. Nuclear Engineers	23.1%	$88,290	7.3%	1,000
24. Optometrists	21.9%	$88,040	19.7%	2,000
25. Industrial-Organizational Psychologists	31.9%	$84,690	20.4%	fewer than 500
26. Political Scientists	23.3%	$84,100	7.3%	fewer than 500
27. Education Administrators, Elementary and Secondary School	23.4%	$75,400	10.4%	27,000

Best-Paying Jobs for Workers Age 55 and Over

Job	Percent Workers 55 and Over	Annual Earnings	Percent Growth	Annual Openings
28. Economists	24.0%	$73,690	5.6%	1,000
29. Administrative Law Judges, Adjudicators, and Hearing Officers	34.4%	$70,680	10.1%	1,000
30. Education Administrators, Postsecondary	23.4%	$70,350	21.3%	18,000
31. Veterinarians	25.9%	$68,910	17.4%	8,000
32. Management Analysts	27.6%	$66,380	20.1%	82,000
33. Administrative Services Managers	23.0%	$64,020	16.9%	25,000
34. Art Directors	23.9%	$63,950	11.5%	10,000
35. Geographers	23.3%	$63,550	6.8%	fewer than 500
36. Financial Examiners	23.1%	$63,090	9.5%	3,000
37. Architects, Except Landscape and Naval	21.3%	$62,850	17.3%	7,000
38. Forest Fire Fighting and Prevention Supervisors	23.3%	$60,840	21.1%	4,000
39. Municipal Fire Fighting and Prevention Supervisors	23.3%	$60,840	21.1%	4,000
40. Gaming Managers	20.0%	$59,940	22.6%	1,000
41. Budget Analysts	20.4%	$58,910	13.5%	6,000
42. Real Estate Brokers	33.4%	$57,190	7.8%	12,000
43. Clinical Psychologists	31.9%	$57,170	19.1%	10,000
44. Counseling Psychologists	31.9%	$57,170	19.1%	10,000
45. School Psychologists	31.9%	$57,170	19.1%	10,000
46. Locomotive Engineers	21.3%	$55,520	−2.5%	2,000
47. Technical Writers	26.5%	$55,160	23.2%	5,000
48. Teachers, Postsecondary	25.4%	$55,100	32.2%	329,000
49. Arbitrators, Mediators, and Conciliators	34.4%	$54,360	15.5%	fewer than 500
50. Landscape Architects	21.3%	$54,220	19.4%	1,000
51. Postmasters and Mail Superintendents	28.9%	$52,710	0.0%	2,000
52. Cost Estimators	20.4%	$52,020	18.2%	15,000
53. Agricultural Crop Farm Managers	27.6%	$51,160	4.0%	20,000
54. Fish Hatchery Managers	27.6%	$51,160	4.0%	20,000
55. Nursery and Greenhouse Managers	27.6%	$51,160	4.0%	20,000
56. Instructional Coordinators	26.9%	$50,430	27.5%	15,000
57. Multi-Media Artists and Animators	23.9%	$50,290	14.1%	14,000
58. Railroad Yard Workers	27.3%	$49,700	−38.5%	1,000
59. Train Crew Members	27.3%	$49,700	−38.5%	1,000
60. Social and Community Service Managers	25.0%	$49,500	25.5%	17,000

(continued)

(continued)

Best-Paying Jobs for Workers Age 55 and Over

Job	Percent Workers 55 and Over	Annual Earnings	Percent Growth	Annual Openings
61. Purchasing Agents, Except Wholesale, Retail, and Farm Products	20.0%	$49,030	8.1%	19,000
62. Transit and Railroad Police	20.0%	$48,850	9.2%	fewer than 500
63. Funeral Directors	32.6%	$47,630	6.7%	3,000
64. Subway and Streetcar Operators	27.3%	$47,500	13.7%	1,000
65. Librarians	29.5%	$47,400	4.9%	8,000
66. Caption Writers	25.3%	$46,420	17.7%	14,000
67. Copy Writers	25.3%	$46,420	17.7%	14,000
68. Creative Writers	25.3%	$46,420	17.7%	14,000
69. Poets and Lyricists	25.3%	$46,420	17.7%	14,000

Jobs 1, 2, 3, 7, 8, 12, and 13 share 41,000 job openings. Jobs 9, 10, and 11 share 38,000 job openings. Jobs 38 and 39 share 4,000 job openings. Jobs 43, 44, and 45 share 10,000 job openings. Job 46 shares 2,000 job openings with two other jobs not included in this list. Jobs 53, 54, and 55 share 20,000 job openings. Jobs 58 and 59 share 1,000 job openings. Jobs 66, 67, 68, and 69 share 14,000 job openings.

Best-Paying Jobs with the Fastest Growth for Workers Age 55 and Over

Job	Percent Workers 55 and Over	Annual Earnings	Percent Growth	Annual Openings
1. Teachers, Postsecondary	25.4%	$55,100	32.2%	329,000
2. Instructional Coordinators	26.9%	$50,430	27.5%	15,000
3. Social and Community Service Managers	25.0%	$49,500	25.5%	17,000
4. Pharmacists	24.5%	$89,820	24.6%	16,000
5. Anesthesiologists	20.0%	more than $145,600	24.0%	41,000
6. Family and General Practitioners	20.0%	$140,400	24.0%	41,000
7. Internists, General	20.0%	more than $145,600	24.0%	41,000
8. Obstetricians and Gynecologists	20.0%	more than $145,600	24.0%	41,000
9. Pediatricians, General	20.0%	$136,600	24.0%	41,000
10. Psychiatrists	20.0%	more than $145,600	24.0%	41,000
11. Surgeons	20.0%	more than $145,600	24.0%	41,000
12. Technical Writers	26.5%	$55,160	23.2%	5,000
13. Gaming Managers	20.0%	$59,940	22.6%	1,000
14. Education Administrators, Postsecondary	23.4%	$70,350	21.3%	18,000
15. Forest Fire Fighting and Prevention Supervisors	23.3%	$60,840	21.1%	4,000
16. Municipal Fire Fighting and Prevention Supervisors	23.3%	$60,840	21.1%	4,000

Best-Paying Jobs with the Fastest Growth for Workers Age 55 and Over

Job	Percent Workers 55 and Over	Annual Earnings	Percent Growth	Annual Openings
17. Industrial-Organizational Psychologists	31.9%	$84,690	20.4%	fewer than 500
18. Management Analysts	27.6%	$66,380	20.1%	82,000
19. Optometrists	21.9%	$88,040	19.7%	2,000
20. Landscape Architects	21.3%	$54,220	19.4%	1,000
21. Clinical Psychologists	31.9%	$57,170	19.1%	10,000
22. Counseling Psychologists	31.9%	$57,170	19.1%	10,000
23. School Psychologists	31.9%	$57,170	19.1%	10,000
24. Cost Estimators	20.4%	$52,020	18.2%	15,000
25. Caption Writers	25.3%	$46,420	17.7%	14,000

Jobs 5, 6, 7, 8, 9, 10, and 11 share 41,000 job openings. Jobs 15 and 16 share 4,000 job openings. Jobs 21, 22, and 23 share 10,000 job openings. Job 25 shares 14,000 jobs with three other jobs not included in this list.

Best-Paying Jobs with the Most Openings for Workers Age 55 and Over

Job	Percent Workers 55 and Over	Annual Earnings	Percent Growth	Annual Openings
1. Teachers, Postsecondary	25.4%	$55,100	32.2%	329,000
2. Management Analysts	27.6%	$66,380	20.1%	82,000
3. Anesthesiologists	20.0%	more than $145,600	24.0%	41,000
4. Family and General Practitioners	20.0%	$140,400	24.0%	41,000
5. Internists, General	20.0%	more than $145,600	24.0%	41,000
6. Obstetricians and Gynecologists	20.0%	more than $145,600	24.0%	41,000
7. Pediatricians, General	20.0%	$136,600	24.0%	41,000
8. Psychiatrists	20.0%	more than $145,600	24.0%	41,000
9. Surgeons	20.0%	more than $145,600	24.0%	41,000
10. Lawyers	23.3%	$98,930	15.0%	40,000
11. Chief Executives	27.3%	$142,440	14.9%	38,000
12. Government Service Executives	27.3%	$142,440	14.9%	38,000
13. Private Sector Executives	27.3%	$142,440	14.9%	38,000
14. Education Administrators, Elementary and Secondary School	23.4%	$75,400	10.4%	27,000
15. Administrative Services Managers	23.0%	$64,020	16.9%	25,000
16. Agricultural Crop Farm Managers	27.6%	$51,160	4.0%	20,000
17. Fish Hatchery Managers	27.6%	$51,160	4.0%	20,000
18. Nursery and Greenhouse Managers	27.6%	$51,160	4.0%	20,000

(continued)

(continued)

Best-Paying Jobs with the Most Openings for Workers Age 55 and Over

Job	Percent Workers 55 and Over	Annual Earnings	Percent Growth	Annual Openings
19. Purchasing Agents, Except Wholesale, Retail, and Farm Products	20.0%	$49,030	8.1%	19,000
20. Education Administrators, Postsecondary	23.4%	$70,350	21.3%	18,000
21. Social and Community Service Managers	25.0%	$49,500	25.5%	17,000
22. Pharmacists	24.5%	$89,820	24.6%	16,000
23. Cost Estimators	20.4%	$52,020	18.2%	15,000
24. Engineering Managers	22.6%	$100,760	13.0%	15,000
25. Instructional Coordinators	26.9%	$50,430	27.5%	15,000

Jobs 3, 4, 5, 6, 7, 8, and 9 share 41,000 job openings. Jobs 11, 12, and 13 share 38,000 job openings. Jobs 16, 17, and 18 share 20,000 job openings.

Best-Paying Jobs with a High Percentage of Part-Time Workers

About 21 percent of workers are employed part-time, but many of them are in low-wage jobs. High-wage jobs are notorious for requiring full-time commitment and sometimes long hours in the office. For that reason, part-time workers are not heavily employed in the 250 best-paying jobs, and for the following lists we defined a "high" percentage of part-time workers as 10 percent or more. A total of 60 jobs met this criterion and are the basis for this group of lists.

The good news is that despite the general trend, there are many opportunities for part-time work within high-paying jobs. The opportunities tend to be best in fields where workers have some kind of professional credential—an advanced degree, a certification, or a license that entitles the holder to premium pay. Often it is necessary to establish yourself as a full-time worker before you can shift to a part-time work arrangement.

Best-Paying Jobs for Part-Time Workers

Job	Percent Part-Time Workers	Annual Earnings	Percent Growth	Annual Openings
1. Oral and Maxillofacial Surgeons	22.6%	more than $145,600	16.2%	fewer than 500
2. Orthodontists	22.6%	more than $145,600	12.8%	1,000
3. Prosthodontists	22.6%	more than $145,600	13.6%	fewer than 500
4. Airline Pilots, Copilots, and Flight Engineers	14.7%	$138,170	17.2%	7,000
5. Dentists, General	22.6%	$125,300	13.5%	7,000

Best-Paying Jobs for Part-Time Workers

Job	Percent Part-Time Workers	Annual Earnings	Percent Growth	Annual Openings
6. Podiatrists	22.4%	$100,550	16.2%	1,000
7. Pharmacists	21.2%	$89,820	24.6%	16,000
8. Optometrists	16.3%	$88,040	19.7%	2,000
9. Industrial-Organizational Psychologists	23.3%	$84,690	20.4%	fewer than 500
10. Political Scientists	15.6%	$84,100	7.3%	fewer than 500
11. Physician Assistants	16.3%	$72,030	49.6%	10,000
12. Veterinarians	11.2%	$68,910	17.4%	8,000
13. Chiropractors	20.7%	$67,200	22.4%	4,000
14. Management Analysts	18.6%	$66,380	20.1%	82,000
15. Art Directors	30.4%	$63,950	11.5%	10,000
16. Geographers	15.6%	$63,550	6.8%	fewer than 500
17. Physical Therapists	24.8%	$63,080	36.7%	13,000
18. Statisticians	10.7%	$62,450	4.6%	2,000
19. Dental Hygienists	56.0%	$60,890	43.3%	17,000
20. Fashion Designers	21.2%	$60,860	8.4%	2,000
21. Nuclear Medicine Technologists	17.2%	$59,670	21.5%	2,000
22. Market Research Analysts	14.2%	$57,300	19.6%	20,000
23. Real Estate Brokers	18.7%	$57,190	7.8%	12,000
24. Clinical Psychologists	23.3%	$57,170	19.1%	10,000
25. Counseling Psychologists	23.3%	$57,170	19.1%	10,000
26. School Psychologists	23.3%	$57,170	19.1%	10,000
27. Occupational Therapists	29.4%	$56,860	33.6%	7,000
28. Commercial Pilots	14.7%	$55,810	16.8%	2,000
29. Urban and Regional Planners	10.2%	$55,170	15.2%	3,000
30. Speech-Language Pathologists	29.9%	$54,880	14.6%	5,000
31. Registered Nurses	24.1%	$54,670	29.4%	229,000
32. Plant Scientists	10.3%	$54,530	13.9%	1,000
33. Soil Scientists	10.3%	$54,530	13.9%	1,000
34. Diagnostic Medical Sonographers	17.2%	$54,370	34.8%	5,000
35. Agents and Business Managers of Artists, Performers, and Athletes	25.3%	$53,800	11.8%	2,000
36. Orthotists and Prosthetists	18.3%	$53,760	18.0%	fewer than 500
37. Audiologists	30.8%	$53,490	9.1%	fewer than 500
38. Ship Engineers	16.7%	$52,780	12.7%	1,000
39. Accountants	10.3%	$52,210	22.4%	157,000
40. Auditors	10.3%	$52,210	22.4%	157,000

(continued)

(continued)

Best-Paying Jobs for Part-Time Workers

Job	Percent Part-Time Workers	Annual Earnings	Percent Growth	Annual Openings
41. Commercial and Industrial Designers	21.2%	$52,200	10.8%	7,000
42. Food Scientists and Technologists	10.3%	$51,440	10.9%	1,000
43. Agricultural Crop Farm Managers	13.1%	$51,160	4.0%	20,000
44. Fish Hatchery Managers	13.1%	$51,160	4.0%	20,000
45. Nursery and Greenhouse Managers	13.1%	$51,160	4.0%	20,000
46. Instructional Coordinators	23.4%	$50,430	27.5%	15,000
47. Multi-Media Artists and Animators	30.4%	$50,290	14.1%	14,000
48. Social and Community Service Managers	12.5%	$49,500	25.5%	17,000
49. Pile-Driver Operators	16.7%	$48,900	11.9%	fewer than 500
50. Medical and Clinical Laboratory Technologists	17.1%	$47,710	20.5%	14,000
51. Librarians	22.3%	$47,400	4.9%	8,000
52. Film and Video Editors	27.6%	$46,930	18.6%	3,000
53. Special Education Teachers, Secondary School	10.5%	$46,820	17.9%	11,000
54. Flight Attendants	28.3%	$46,680	16.3%	7,000
55. Purchasing Agents and Buyers, Farm Products	10.1%	$46,680	7.0%	2,000
56. Educational, Vocational, and School Counselors	16.5%	$46,440	14.8%	32,000
57. Caption Writers	30.2%	$46,420	17.7%	14,000
58. Copy Writers	30.2%	$46,420	17.7%	14,000
59. Creative Writers	30.2%	$46,420	17.7%	14,000
60. Poets and Lyricists	30.2%	$46,420	17.7%	14,000

Jobs 24, 25, and 26 share 10,000 job openings. Jobs 32 and 33 share 1,000 job openings. Jobs 39 and 40 share 157,000 job openings. Jobs 43, 44, and 45 share 20,000 job openings. Jobs 57, 58, 59, and 60 share 14,000 job openings.

Best-Paying Jobs with the Fastest Growth for Part-Time Workers

Job	Percent Part-Time Workers	Annual Earnings	Percent Growth	Annual Openings
1. Physician Assistants	16.3%	$72,030	49.6%	10,000
2. Dental Hygienists	56.0%	$60,890	43.3%	17,000
3. Physical Therapists	24.8%	$63,080	36.7%	13,000
4. Diagnostic Medical Sonographers	17.2%	$54,370	34.8%	5,000
5. Occupational Therapists	29.4%	$56,860	33.6%	7,000
6. Registered Nurses	24.1%	$54,670	29.4%	229,000
7. Instructional Coordinators	23.4%	$50,430	27.5%	15,000
8. Social and Community Service Managers	12.5%	$49,500	25.5%	17,000

Best-Paying Jobs with the Fastest Growth for Part-Time Workers

Job	Percent Part-Time Workers	Annual Earnings	Percent Growth	Annual Openings
9. Pharmacists	21.2%	$89,820	24.6%	16,000
10. Accountants	10.3%	$52,210	22.4%	157,000
11. Auditors	10.3%	$52,210	22.4%	157,000
12. Chiropractors	20.7%	$67,200	22.4%	4,000
13. Nuclear Medicine Technologists	17.2%	$59,670	21.5%	2,000
14. Medical and Clinical Laboratory Technologists	17.1%	$47,710	20.5%	14,000
15. Industrial-Organizational Psychologists	23.3%	$84,690	20.4%	fewer than 500
16. Management Analysts	18.6%	$66,380	20.1%	82,000
17. Optometrists	16.3%	$88,040	19.7%	2,000
18. Market Research Analysts	14.2%	$57,300	19.6%	20,000
19. Clinical Psychologists	23.3%	$57,170	19.1%	10,000
20. Counseling Psychologists	23.3%	$57,170	19.1%	10,000
21. School Psychologists	23.3%	$57,170	19.1%	10,000
22. Film and Video Editors	27.6%	$46,930	18.6%	3,000
23. Orthotists and Prosthetists	18.3%	$53,760	18.0%	fewer than 500
24. Special Education Teachers, Secondary School	10.5%	$46,820	17.9%	11,000
25. Caption Writers	30.2%	$46,420	17.7%	14,000

Jobs 10 and 11 share 157,000 job openings. Jobs 19, 20, and 21 share 10,000 job openings. Job 25 shares 14,000 job openings with three other jobs not included in this list.

Best-Paying Jobs with the Most Openings for Part-Time Workers

Job	Percent Part-Time Workers	Annual Earnings	Percent Growth	Annual Openings
1. Registered Nurses	24.1%	$54,670	29.4%	229,000
2. Accountants	10.3%	$52,210	22.4%	157,000
3. Auditors	10.3%	$52,210	22.4%	157,000
4. Management Analysts	18.6%	$66,380	20.1%	82,000
5. Educational, Vocational, and School Counselors	16.5%	$46,440	14.8%	32,000
6. Agricultural Crop Farm Managers	13.1%	$51,160	4.0%	20,000
7. Fish Hatchery Managers	13.1%	$51,160	4.0%	20,000
8. Nursery and Greenhouse Managers	13.1%	$51,160	4.0%	20,000
9. Market Research Analysts	14.2%	$57,300	19.6%	20,000
10. Dental Hygienists	56.0%	$60,890	43.3%	17,000
11. Social and Community Service Managers	12.5%	$49,500	25.5%	17,000

(continued)

(continued)

Best-Paying Jobs with the Most Openings for Part-Time Workers

Job	Percent Part-Time Workers	Annual Earnings	Percent Growth	Annual Openings
12. Pharmacists	21.2%	$89,820	24.6%	16,000
13. Instructional Coordinators	23.4%	$50,430	27.5%	15,000
14. Caption Writers	30.2%	$46,420	17.7%	14,000
15. Copy Writers	30.2%	$46,420	17.7%	14,000
16. Creative Writers	30.2%	$46,420	17.7%	14,000
17. Poets and Lyricists	30.2%	$46,420	17.7%	14,000
18. Medical and Clinical Laboratory Technologists	17.1%	$47,710	20.5%	14,000
19. Multi-Media Artists and Animators	30.4%	$50,290	14.1%	14,000
20. Physical Therapists	24.8%	$63,080	36.7%	13,000
21. Real Estate Brokers	18.7%	$57,190	7.8%	12,000
22. Special Education Teachers, Secondary School	10.5%	$46,820	17.9%	11,000
23. Art Directors	30.4%	$63,950	11.5%	10,000
24. Clinical Psychologists	23.3%	$57,170	19.1%	10,000
25. Counseling Psychologists	23.3%	$57,170	19.1%	10,000

Jobs 2 and 3 share 157,000 job openings. Jobs 6, 7, and 8 share 20,000 job openings. Jobs 14, 15, 16, and 17 share 14,000 job openings. Jobs 24 and 25 share 10,000 job openings with each other and with another job not included in this list.

Best-Paying Jobs with a High Percentage of Self-Employed Workers

About 7.5 percent of all working people are self-employed or own their own unincorporated business, and this is a common work arrangement among high-paying occupations. For example, many health-care professionals own their own practices, and many artists and designers own their own studios.

The jobs in the lists in this section all have 10 percent or more self-employed workers. Fifty-one jobs met this requirement. In these lists you will find many of the same jobs that appear in the lists of jobs with a lot of part-time workers—jobs that require professional status or certification. But there are also several jobs in other fields, such as the arts, business, and construction. While the lists do not include data on age and gender, older workers and women make up a rapidly growing part of the self-employed population. For example, some highly experienced older workers set up consulting and other small businesses following a layoff or as an alternative to full retirement. Large numbers of women are forming small businesses or creating self-employment opportunities as an alternative to traditional employment.

Best-Paying Jobs for Self-Employed Workers

Job	Percent Self-Employed Workers	Annual Earnings	Percent Growth	Annual Openings
1. Oral and Maxillofacial Surgeons	15.7% more than	$145,600	16.2%	fewer than 500
2. Orthodontists	35.9% more than	$145,600	12.8%	1,000
3. Prosthodontists	38.2% more than	$145,600	13.6%	fewer than 500
4. Chief Executives	16.2%	$142,440	14.9%	38,000
5. Government Service Executives	16.2%	$142,440	14.9%	38,000
6. Private Sector Executives	16.2%	$142,440	14.9%	38,000
7. Dentists, General	30.7%	$125,300	13.5%	7,000
8. Podiatrists	19.8%	$100,550	16.2%	1,000
9. Lawyers	24.1%	$98,930	15.0%	40,000
10. Optometrists	27.4%	$88,040	19.7%	2,000
11. Industrial-Organizational Psychologists	37.6%	$84,690	20.4%	fewer than 500
12. Construction Managers	54.2%	$72,260	10.4%	28,000
13. Veterinarians	20.7%	$68,910	17.4%	8,000
14. Chiropractors	49.2%	$67,200	22.4%	4,000
15. Sales Agents, Financial Services	12.5%	$67,130	11.5%	37,000
16. Sales Agents, Securities and Commodities	12.5%	$67,130	11.5%	37,000
17. Management Analysts	24.7%	$66,380	20.1%	82,000
18. Art Directors	55.8%	$63,950	11.5%	10,000
19. Personal Financial Advisors	38.9%	$63,500	25.9%	17,000
20. Architects, Except Landscape and Naval	20.1%	$62,850	17.3%	7,000
21. First-Line Supervisors/Managers of Non-Retail Sales Workers	37.1%	$61,970	1.9%	38,000
22. Network Systems and Data Communications Analysts	19.9%	$61,750	54.6%	43,000
23. Fashion Designers	26.5%	$60,860	8.4%	2,000
24. Real Estate Brokers	59.9%	$57,190	7.8%	12,000
25. Clinical Psychologists	38.2%	$57,170	19.1%	10,000
26. Counseling Psychologists	38.2%	$57,170	19.1%	10,000
27. School Psychologists	38.2%	$57,170	19.1%	10,000
28. Plant Scientists	35.9%	$54,530	13.9%	1,000
29. Soil Scientists	35.9%	$54,530	13.9%	1,000
30. Landscape Architects	23.7%	$54,220	19.4%	1,000
31. Directors—Stage, Motion Pictures, Television, and Radio	30.4%	$53,860	16.6%	11,000
32. Producers	30.4%	$53,860	16.6%	11,000

(continued)

(continued)

Best-Paying Jobs for Self-Employed Workers

Job	Percent Self-Employed Workers	Annual Earnings	Percent Growth	Annual Openings
33. Program Directors	30.4%	$53,860	16.6%	11,000
34. Talent Directors	30.4%	$53,860	16.6%	11,000
35. Technical Directors/Managers	30.4%	$53,860	16.6%	11,000
36. Agents and Business Managers of Artists, Performers, and Athletes	39.3%	$53,800	11.8%	2,000
37. Orthotists and Prosthetists	14.4%	$53,760	18.0%	fewer than 500
38. Sociologists	11.7%	$52,760	4.7%	fewer than 500
39. Accountants	10.9%	$52,210	22.4%	157,000
40. Auditors	10.9%	$52,210	22.4%	157,000
41. Commercial and Industrial Designers	30.1%	$52,200	10.8%	7,000
42. First-Line Supervisors and Manager/Supervisors—Construction Trades Workers	24.7%	$51,970	10.9%	57,000
43. First-Line Supervisors and Manager/Supervisors—Extractive Workers	24.7%	$51,970	10.9%	57,000
44. Food Scientists and Technologists	28.8%	$51,440	10.9%	1,000
45. Multi-Media Artists and Animators	60.8%	$50,290	14.1%	14,000
46. Funeral Directors	19.7%	$47,630	6.7%	3,000
47. Film and Video Editors	18.2%	$46,930	18.6%	3,000
48. Caption Writers	67.7%	$46,420	17.7%	14,000
49. Copy Writers	67.7%	$46,420	17.7%	14,000
50. Creative Writers	67.7%	$46,420	17.7%	14,000
51. Poets and Lyricists	67.7%	$46,420	17.7%	14,000

Jobs 4, 5, and 6 share 38,000 job openings. Jobs 15 and 16 share 37,000 job openings. Jobs 25, 26, and 27 share 10,000 job openings. Jobs 28 and 29 share 1,000 job openings. Jobs 31, 32, 33, 34, and 35 share 11,000 job openings. Jobs 39 and 40 share 157,000 job openings. Jobs 42 and 43 share 57,000 job openings. Jobs 48, 49, 50, and 51 share 14,000 job openings.

Best-Paying Jobs with the Fastest Growth for Self-Employed Workers

Job	Percent Self-Employed Workers	Annual Earnings	Percent Growth	Annual Openings
1. Network Systems and Data Communications Analysts	19.9%	$61,750	54.6%	43,000
2. Personal Financial Advisors	38.9%	$63,500	25.9%	17,000
3. Accountants	10.9%	$52,210	22.4%	157,000

Best-Paying Jobs with the Fastest Growth for Self-Employed Workers

Job	Percent Self-Employed Workers	Annual Earnings	Percent Growth	Annual Openings
4. Auditors	10.9%	$52,210	22.4%	157,000
5. Chiropractors	49.2%	$67,200	22.4%	4,000
6. Industrial-Organizational Psychologists	37.6%	$84,690	20.4%	fewer than 500
7. Management Analysts	24.7%	$66,380	20.1%	82,000
8. Optometrists	27.4%	$88,040	19.7%	2,000
9. Landscape Architects	23.7%	$54,220	19.4%	1,000
10. Clinical Psychologists	38.2%	$57,170	19.1%	10,000
11. Counseling Psychologists	38.2%	$57,170	19.1%	10,000
12. School Psychologists	38.2%	$57,170	19.1%	10,000
13. Film and Video Editors	18.2%	$46,930	18.6%	3,000
14. Orthotists and Prosthetists	14.4%	$53,760	18.0%	fewer than 500
15. Caption Writers	67.7%	$46,420	17.7%	14,000
16. Copy Writers	67.7%	$46,420	17.7%	14,000
17. Creative Writers	67.7%	$46,420	17.7%	14,000
18. Poets and Lyricists	67.7%	$46,420	17.7%	14,000
19. Veterinarians	20.7%	$68,910	17.4%	8,000
20. Architects, Except Landscape and Naval	20.1%	$62,850	17.3%	7,000
21. Directors—Stage, Motion Pictures, Television, and Radio	30.4%	$53,860	16.6%	11,000
22. Producers	30.4%	$53,860	16.6%	11,000
23. Program Directors	30.4%	$53,860	16.6%	11,000
24. Talent Directors	30.4%	$53,860	16.6%	11,000
25. Technical Directors/Managers	30.4%	$53,860	16.6%	11,000

Jobs 3 and 4 share 157,000 job openings. Jobs 10, 11 and 12 share 10,000 job openings. Jobs 15, 16, 17, and 18 share 14,000 job openings. Jobs 22, 23, 24, and 25 share 11,000 job openings.

Best-Paying Jobs with the Most Openings for Self-Employed Workers

Job	Percent Self-Employed Workers	Annual Earnings	Percent Growth	Annual Openings
1. Accountants	10.9%	$52,210	22.4%	157,000
2. Auditors	10.9%	$52,210	22.4%	157,000
3. Management Analysts	24.7%	$66,380	20.1%	82,000

(continued)

(continued)

Best-Paying Jobs with the Most Openings for Self-Employed Workers

Job	Percent Self-Employed Workers	Annual Earnings	Percent Growth	Annual Openings
4. First-Line Supervisors and Manager/ Supervisors—Construction Trades Workers	24.7%	$51,970	10.9%	57,000
5. First-Line Supervisors and Manager/ Supervisors—Extractive Workers	24.7%	$51,970	10.9%	57,000
6. Network Systems and Data Communications Analysts	19.9%	$61,750	54.6%	43,000
7. Lawyers	24.1%	$98,930	15.0%	40,000
8. First-Line Supervisors/Managers of Non-Retail Sales Workers	37.1%	$61,970	1.9%	38,000
9. Chief Executives	16.2%	$142,440	14.9%	38,000
10. Government Service Executives	16.2%	$142,440	14.9%	38,000
11. Private Sector Executives	16.2%	$142,440	14.9%	38,000
12. Sales Agents, Financial Services	12.5%	$67,130	11.5%	37,000
13. Sales Agents, Securities and Commodities	12.5%	$67,130	11.5%	37,000
14. Construction Managers	54.2%	$72,260	10.4%	28,000
15. Personal Financial Advisors	38.9%	$63,500	25.9%	17,000
16. Caption Writers	67.7%	$46,420	17.7%	14,000
17. Copy Writers	67.7%	$46,420	17.7%	14,000
18. Creative Writers	67.7%	$46,420	17.7%	14,000
19. Poets and Lyricists	67.7%	$46,420	17.7%	14,000
20. Multi-Media Artists and Animators	60.8%	$50,290	14.1%	14,000
21. Real Estate Brokers	59.9%	$57,190	7.8%	12,000
22. Directors—Stage, Motion Pictures, Television, and Radio	30.4%	$53,860	16.6%	11,000
23. Producers	30.4%	$53,860	16.6%	11,000
24. Program Directors	30.4%	$53,860	16.6%	11,000
25. Talent Directors	30.4%	$53,860	16.6%	11,000

Jobs 1 and 2 share 157,000 job openings. Jobs 4 and 5 share 57,000 job openings. Jobs 9, 10, and 11 share 38,000 job openings. Jobs 12 and 13 share 37,000 job openings. Jobs 16, 17, 18, and 19 share 14,000 job openings. Jobs 22, 23, 24, and 25 share 11,000 job openings with each other and with another job not included in this list.

Best-Paying Jobs with a High Percentage of Women

To create the three lists that follow, we sorted the 250 best-paying jobs according to the percentages of women and men in the workforce. We knew we would create some controversy when we first included the best jobs lists with high percentages (more than 70 percent) of men and women. But these lists are not meant to restrict women or men from considering job options; one reason for including these lists is exactly the opposite. We hope the lists will help people see possibilities that they might not otherwise have considered.

The fact is that jobs with high percentages of women or high percentages of men offer good opportunities for both men and women if they want to do one of these jobs. So we suggest that women browse the lists of jobs that employ high percentages of men and that men browse the lists of jobs with high percentages of women. All of the jobs pay well, and women or men who are interested in them and who have or can obtain the necessary education and training should consider them.

An interesting and unfortunate tidbit to bring up at your next party is that workers in the jobs listed here with the highest percentage of women have average earnings of $54,226, compared to $85,464 for workers in the jobs with the highest percentage of men. But earnings don't tell the whole story. We computed the average growth of the jobs with the highest percentage of women and found a growth rate of 27.7 percent, compared to 16.4 percent for the jobs with the highest percentage of men. This discrepancy reinforces the idea that men have had more problems than women in adapting to an economy dominated by service and information-based jobs. Many women may simply be better prepared for these jobs, possessing more appropriate skills for the jobs that are now growing rapidly.

Best-Paying Jobs with a High Percentage of Women

Job	Percent Women	Annual Earnings	Percent Growth	Annual Openings
1. Physical Therapists	70.4%	$63,080	36.7%	13,000
2. Dental Hygienists	97.7%	$60,890	43.3%	17,000
3. Nuclear Medicine Technologists	71.7%	$59,670	21.5%	2,000
4. Occupational Therapists	90.0%	$56,860	33.6%	7,000
5. Speech-Language Pathologists	95.1%	$54,880	14.6%	5,000
6. Registered Nurses	92.4%	$54,670	29.4%	229,000
7. Diagnostic Medical Sonographers	71.7%	$54,370	34.8%	5,000
8. Audiologists	76.7%	$53,490	9.1%	fewer than 500
9. Medical and Clinical Laboratory Technologists	73.9%	$47,710	20.5%	14,000
10. Librarians	82.6%	$47,400	4.9%	8,000
11. Special Education Teachers, Secondary School	86.6%	$46,820	17.9%	11,000
12. Flight Attendants	78.7%	$46,680	16.3%	7,000

Best-Paying Jobs with the Fastest Growth with a High Percentage of Women

Job	Percent Women	Annual Earnings	Percent Growth	Annual Openings
1. Dental Hygienists	97.7%	$60,890	43.3%	17,000
2. Physical Therapists	70.4%	$63,080	36.7%	13,000
3. Diagnostic Medical Sonographers	71.7%	$54,370	34.8%	5,000
4. Occupational Therapists	90.0%	$56,860	33.6%	7,000
5. Registered Nurses	92.4%	$54,670	29.4%	229,000
6. Nuclear Medicine Technologists	71.7%	$59,670	21.5%	2,000
7. Medical and Clinical Laboratory Technologists	73.9%	$47,710	20.5%	14,000
8. Special Education Teachers, Secondary School	86.6%	$46,820	17.9%	11,000
9. Flight Attendants	78.7%	$46,680	16.3%	7,000
10. Speech-Language Pathologists	95.1%	$54,880	14.6%	5,000
11. Audiologists	76.7%	$53,490	9.1%	fewer than 500
12. Librarians	82.6%	$47,400	4.9%	8,000

Best-Paying Jobs with the Most Openings with a High Percentage of Women

Job	Percent Women	Annual Earnings	Percent Growth	Annual Openings
1. Registered Nurses	92.4%	$54,670	29.4%	229,000
2. Dental Hygienists	97.7%	$60,890	43.3%	17,000
3. Medical and Clinical Laboratory Technologists	73.9%	$47,710	20.5%	14,000
4. Physical Therapists	70.4%	$63,080	36.7%	13,000
5. Special Education Teachers, Secondary School	86.6%	$46,820	17.9%	11,000
6. Librarians	82.6%	$47,400	4.9%	8,000
7. Flight Attendants	78.7%	$46,680	16.3%	7,000
8. Occupational Therapists	90.0%	$56,860	33.6%	7,000
9. Diagnostic Medical Sonographers	71.7%	$54,370	34.8%	5,000
10. Speech-Language Pathologists	95.1%	$54,880	14.6%	5,000
11. Nuclear Medicine Technologists	71.7%	$59,670	21.5%	2,000
12. Audiologists	76.7%	$53,490	9.1%	fewer than 500

Best-Paying Jobs with a High Percentage of Men

We suggest you read the introductory material in the "Best-Paying Jobs with a High Percentage of Women" section to better understand the purpose of publishing the following lists. As we state in that section, we are not suggesting that the best jobs lists for men include the only jobs that men should consider.

For example, there is a strong demand for Registered Nurses, a job that employs a high percentage of women, so the few workers available are recruited aggressively and often find jobs quickly. Just as women should consider careers typically held by men, many men should consider career opportunities usually associated with women. This is particularly true now because occupations with high percentages of women workers are growing more rapidly than occupations in our similar lists for men.

In the best-paying jobs list for men, note that many of the top jobs—once you look below the professional-level health-care jobs—are in the business and technology fields and many are at the managerial level, whereas almost all of the primarily female jobs are in the health-care field and none are at the managerial level. This difference confirms the concerns of many educators, counselors, and social advocates about sexual stereotyping of occupations. In many cases, both men and women would be well advised to consider occupations typically held by the opposite sex.

Job	Percent Men	Annual Earnings	Percent Growth	Annual Openings
1. Prosthodontists	82.1%....more than	$145,600	13.6%	....fewer than 500
2. Orthodontists	82.1%....more than	$145,600	12.8%	1,000
3. Oral and Maxillofacial Surgeons	82.1%....more than	$145,600	16.2%	....fewer than 500
4. Internists, General	73.2%....more than	$145,600	24.0%	41,000
5. Anesthesiologists	73.2%....more than	$145,600	24.0%	41,000
6. Psychiatrists	73.2%....more than	$145,600	24.0%	41,000
7. Obstetricians and Gynecologists	73.2%....more than	$145,600	24.0%	41,000
8. Surgeons	73.2%....more than	$145,600	24.0%	41,000
9. Government Service Executives	81.2%	$142,440	14.9%	38,000
10. Private Sector Executives	81.2%	$142,440	14.9%	38,000
11. Chief Executives	81.2%	$142,440	14.9%	38,000
12. Family and General Practitioners	73.2%	$140,400	24.0%	41,000
13. Airline Pilots, Copilots, and Flight Engineers	96.1%	$138,170	17.2%	7,000
14. Pediatricians, General	73.2%	$136,600	24.0%	41,000
15. Dentists, General	82.1%	$125,300	13.5%	7,000

(continued)

(continued)

Best-Paying Jobs with a High Percentage of Men

Job	Percent Men	Annual Earnings	Percent Growth	Annual Openings
16. Air Traffic Controllers	81.6%	$107,590	14.3%	2,000
17. Astronomers	86.1%	$104,670	10.4%	fewer than 500
18. Engineering Managers	93.4%	$100,760	13.0%	15,000
19. Podiatrists	84.2%	$100,550	16.2%	1,000
20. Lawyers	71.3%	$98,930	15.0%	40,000
21. Computer and Information Systems Managers	70.3%	$96,520	25.9%	25,000
22. Petroleum Engineers	93.7%	$93,000	–0.1%	1,000
23. Physicists	86.1%	$89,810	7.0%	1,000
24. Nuclear Engineers	91.4%	$88,290	7.3%	1,000
25. Optometrists	72.4%	$88,040	19.7%	2,000
26. Computer Hardware Engineers	83.7%	$84,420	10.1%	5,000
27. Aerospace Engineers	90.9%	$84,090	8.3%	6,000
28. Computer Software Engineers, Systems Software	75.4%	$82,120	43.0%	37,000
29. General and Operations Managers	73.7%	$81,480	17.0%	208,000
30. Electronics Engineers, Except Computer	91.3%	$78,030	9.7%	11,000
31. Chemical Engineers	85.6%	$77,140	10.6%	3,000
32. Computer Software Engineers, Applications	75.4%	$77,090	48.4%	54,000
33. Industrial Production Managers	83.4%	$75,580	0.8%	13,000
34. Sales Engineers	94.0%	$74,200	14.0%	8,000
35. Atmospheric and Space Scientists	87.1%	$73,940	16.5%	1,000
36. Electrical Engineers	91.3%	$73,510	11.8%	12,000
37. Marine Architects	94.9%	$72,920	8.5%	fewer than 500
38. Marine Engineers	94.9%	$72,920	8.5%	fewer than 500
39. Construction Managers	93.2%	$72,260	10.4%	28,000
40. Biomedical Engineers	89.6%	$71,840	30.7%	1,000
41. Geologists	75.8%	$71,640	8.3%	2,000
42. Materials Engineers	88.0%	$69,660	12.2%	2,000
43. Transportation Managers	82.9%	$69,120	12.7%	15,000
44. Storage and Distribution Managers	82.9%	$69,120	12.7%	15,000
45. Environmental Engineers	77.8%	$68,090	30.0%	5,000
46. Mechanical Engineers	93.4%	$67,590	11.1%	11,000
47. Chiropractors	77.8%	$67,200	22.4%	4,000
48. Industrial Engineers	83.4%	$66,670	16.0%	13,000
49. Nuclear Power Reactor Operators	92.6%	$66,230	–0.5%	1,000
50. Civil Engineers	89.9%	$66,190	16.5%	19,000

Best-Paying Jobs with a High Percentage of Men

Job	Percent Men	Annual Earnings	Percent Growth	Annual Openings
51. First-Line Supervisors/Managers of Police and Detectives	87.2%	$65,570	15.5%	9,000
52. Industrial Safety and Health Engineers	83.4%	$65,210	13.4%	2,000
53. Product Safety Engineers	83.4%	$65,210	13.4%	2,000
54. Fire-Prevention and Protection Engineers	83.4%	$65,210	13.4%	2,000
55. Agricultural Engineers	89.6%	$64,890	12.0%	fewer than 500
56. Hydrologists	75.8%	$63,820	31.6%	1,000
57. Computer Programmers	72.5%	$63,420	2.0%	28,000
58. Architects, Except Landscape and Naval	79.7%	$62,850	17.3%	7,000
59. Network Systems and Data Communications Analysts	73.5%	$61,750	54.6%	43,000
60. Municipal Fire Fighting and Prevention Supervisors	97.0%	$60,840	21.1%	4,000
61. Forest Fire Fighting and Prevention Supervisors	97.0%	$60,840	21.1%	4,000
62. Sales Representatives, Instruments	73.9%	$60,760	14.4%	47,000
63. Sales Representatives, Agricultural	73.9%	$60,760	14.4%	47,000
64. Sales Representatives, Chemical and Pharmaceutical	73.9%	$60,760	14.4%	47,000
65. Sales Representatives, Electrical/Electronic	73.9%	$60,760	14.4%	47,000
66. Sales Representatives, Medical	73.9%	$60,760	14.4%	47,000
67. Sales Representatives, Mechanical Equipment and Supplies	73.9%	$60,760	14.4%	47,000
68. Network and Computer Systems Administrators	76.7%	$59,930	38.4%	34,000
69. Computer Security Specialists	76.7%	$59,930	38.4%	34,000
70. Elevator Installers and Repairers	98.6%	$59,190	14.8%	3,000
71. Power Distributors and Dispatchers	92.6%	$59,160	0.0%	1,000
72. Commercial Pilots	96.1%	$55,810	16.8%	2,000
73. Police Detectives	79.0%	$55,790	16.3%	9,000
74. Police Identification and Records Officers	79.0%	$55,790	16.3%	9,000
75. Criminal Investigators and Special Agents	79.0%	$55,790	16.3%	9,000
76. Child Support, Missing Persons, and Unemployment Insurance Fraud Investigators	79.0%	$55,790	16.3%	9,000
77. Immigration and Customs Inspectors	79.0%	$55,790	16.3%	9,000
78. Locomotive Engineers	96.0%	$55,520	–2.5%	2,000
79. Electrical and Electronics Repairers, Powerhouse, Substation, and Relay	94.1%	$54,970	–0.4%	2,000
80. Plant Scientists	73.9%	$54,530	13.9%	1,000

(continued)

(continued)

Best-Paying Jobs with a High Percentage of Men

Job	Percent Men	Annual Earnings	Percent Growth	Annual Openings
81. Soil Scientists	73.9%	$54,530	13.9%	1,000
82. Landscape Architects	79.7%	$54,220	19.4%	1,000
83. Railroad Conductors and Yardmasters	94.1%	$54,040	20.3%	3,000
84. Park Naturalists	85.3%	$53,350	6.3%	2,000
85. Range Managers	85.3%	$53,350	6.3%	2,000
86. Soil Conservationists	85.3%	$53,350	6.3%	2,000
87. Power Generating Plant Operators, Except Auxiliary Equipment Operators	92.6%	$53,170	–0.4%	5,000
88. Auxiliary Equipment Operators, Power	92.6%	$53,170	–0.4%	5,000
89. Ship Engineers	98.4%	$52,780	12.7%	1,000
90. Environmental Scientists and Specialists, Including Health	75.8%	$52,630	17.1%	8,000
91. Aerospace Engineering and Operations Technicians	80.9%	$52,450	8.5%	1,000
92. Cost Estimators	88.0%	$52,020	18.2%	15,000
93. First-Line Supervisors/Managers of Mechanics, Installers, and Repairers	91.8%	$51,980	12.4%	33,000
94. First-Line Supervisors and Manager/ Supervisors—Construction Trades Workers	97.2%	$51,970	10.9%	57,000
95. First-Line Supervisors and Manager/ Supervisors—Extractive Workers	97.2%	$51,970	10.9%	57,000
96. Gas Distribution Plant Operators	92.6%	$51,920	7.7%	2,000
97. Gas Processing Plant Operators	92.6%	$51,920	7.7%	2,000
98. Food Scientists and Technologists	73.9%	$51,440	10.9%	1,000
99. Fish Hatchery Managers	85.5%	$51,160	4.0%	20,000
100. Agricultural Crop Farm Managers	85.5%	$51,160	4.0%	20,000
101. Nursery and Greenhouse Managers	85.5%	$51,160	4.0%	20,000
102. Petroleum Pump System Operators	92.6%	$51,060	–8.6%	6,000
103. Petroleum Refinery and Control Panel Operators	92.6%	$51,060	–8.6%	6,000
104. Gaugers	92.6%	$51,060	–8.6%	6,000
105. Pilots, Ship	97.1%	$50,940	4.8%	2,000
106. Ship and Boat Captains	97.1%	$50,940	4.8%	2,000
107. Mates—Ship, Boat, and Barge	97.1%	$50,940	4.8%	2,000
108. Station Installers and Repairers, Telephone	87.0%	$50,620	–4.9%	21,000
109. Central Office and PBX Installers and Repairers	87.0%	$50,620	–4.9%	21,000
110. Frame Wirers, Central Office	87.0%	$50,620	–4.9%	21,000
111. Telecommunications Facility Examiners	87.0%	$50,620	–4.9%	21,000

Best-Paying Jobs with a High Percentage of Men

Job	Percent Men	Annual Earnings	Percent Growth	Annual Openings
112. Communication Equipment Mechanics, Installers, and Repairers	87.0%	$50,620	–4.9%	21,000
113. Electrical Power-Line Installers and Repairers	97.3%	$50,150	2.5%	11,000
114. Train Crew Members	96.9%	$49,700	–38.5%	1,000
115. Railroad Yard Workers	96.9%	$49,700	–38.5%	1,000
116. Freight Inspectors	83.8%	$49,490	11.4%	2,000
117. Railroad Inspectors	83.8%	$49,490	11.4%	2,000
118. Motor Vehicle Inspectors	83.8%	$49,490	11.4%	2,000
119. Public Transportation Inspectors	83.8%	$49,490	11.4%	2,000
120. Aviation Inspectors	83.8%	$49,490	11.4%	2,000
121. Marine Cargo Inspectors	83.8%	$49,490	11.4%	2,000
122. Signal and Track Switch Repairers	92.9%	$49,200	2.3%	1,000
123. Pile-Driver Operators	97.8%	$48,900	11.9%	fewer than 500
124. Transit and Railroad Police	86.9%	$48,850	9.2%	fewer than 500
125. Foresters	85.3%	$48,670	6.7%	1,000
126. First-Line Supervisors/Managers of Correctional Officers	74.3%	$48,570	9.4%	2,000
127. Cartographers and Photogrammetrists	82.0%	$48,250	15.3%	1,000
128. Boilermakers	96.8%	$48,050	8.7%	2,000
129. Electronics Engineering Technicians	80.9%	$48,040	9.8%	18,000
130. Electrical Engineering Technicians	80.9%	$48,040	9.8%	18,000
131. Calibration and Instrumentation Technicians	80.9%	$48,040	9.8%	18,000
132. Funeral Directors	82.7%	$47,630	6.7%	3,000
133. First-Line Supervisors/Managers of Transportation and Material-Moving Machine and Vehicle Operators	81.2%	$47,530	15.3%	22,000
134. Subway and Streetcar Operators	91.0%	$47,500	13.7%	1,000
135. Sales Representatives, Wholesale and Manufacturing, Except Technical and Scientific Products	73.9%	$47,380	12.9%	169,000
136. Airframe-and-Power-Plant Mechanics	95.1%	$47,310	13.4%	11,000
137. Aircraft Engine Specialists	95.1%	$47,310	13.4%	11,000
138. Aircraft Body and Bonded Structure Repairers	95.1%	$47,310	13.4%	11,000
139. Film and Video Editors	81.1%	$46,930	18.6%	3,000
140. Chemical Plant and System Operators	92.6%	$46,710	–17.7%	8,000

(continued)

(continued)

Best-Paying Jobs with a High Percentage of Men

Job	Percent Men	Annual Earnings	Percent Growth	Annual Openings
141. Purchasing Agents and Buyers, Farm Products	79.3%	$46,680	7.0%	2,000
142. Avionics Technicians	88.9%	$46,630	9.1%	2,000

Jobs 4, 5, 6, 7, 8, 12, and 14 share 41,000 job openings. Jobs 9, 10, and 11 share 38,000 job openings. Jobs 37 and 38 share fewer than 500 job openings. Jobs 43 and 44 share 15,000 job openings. Jobs 52, 53, and 54 share 2,000 job openings. Jobs 60 and 61 share 4,000 job openings. Jobs 62, 63, 64, 65, 66, and 67 share 47,000 job openings. Jobs 68 and 69 share 34,000 job openings. Jobs 73, 74, 75, 76, and 77 share 9,000 job openings. Job 78 shares 2,000 job openings with two other jobs not included in this list. Jobs 80 and 81 share 34,000 job openings. Jobs 84, 85, and 86 share 2,000 job openings. Jobs 87 and 88 share 5,000 job openings. Jobs 94 and 95 share 57,000 job openings. Jobs 96 and 97 share 2,000 job openings. Jobs 99, 100, and 101 share 20,000 job openings. Jobs 102, 103, and 104 share 6,000 job openings. Jobs 105, 106, and 107 share 2,000 job openings. Jobs 108, 109, 110, 111, and 112 share 21,000 job openings. Jobs 114 and 115 share 1,000 job openings. Jobs 116, 117, 118, 119, 120, and 121 share 2,000 job openings. Jobs 129, 130, and 131 share 18,000 job openings. Jobs 136, 137, and 138 share 11,000 job openings.

Best-Paying Jobs with the Fastest Growth with a High Percentage of Men

Job	Percent Men	Annual Earnings	Percent Growth	Annual Openings
1. Network Systems and Data Communications Analysts	73.5%	$61,750	54.6%	43,000
2. Computer Software Engineers, Applications	75.4%	$77,090	48.4%	54,000
3. Computer Software Engineers, Systems Software	75.4%	$82,120	43.0%	37,000
4. Computer Security Specialists	76.7%	$59,930	38.4%	34,000
5. Network and Computer Systems Administrators	76.7%	$59,930	38.4%	34,000
6. Hydrologists	75.8%	$63,820	31.6%	1,000
7. Biomedical Engineers	89.6%	$71,840	30.7%	1,000
8. Environmental Engineers	77.8%	$68,090	30.0%	5,000
9. Computer and Information Systems Managers	70.3%	$96,520	25.9%	25,000
10. Family and General Practitioners	73.2%	$140,400	24.0%	41,000
11. Internists, General	73.2%	more than $145,600	24.0%	41,000
12. Obstetricians and Gynecologists	73.2%	more than $145,600	24.0%	41,000
13. Pediatricians, General	73.2%	$136,600	24.0%	41,000
14. Psychiatrists	73.2%	more than $145,600	24.0%	41,000
15. Surgeons	73.2%	more than $145,600	24.0%	41,000
16. Anesthesiologists	73.2%	more than $145,600	24.0%	41,000
17. Chiropractors	77.8%	$67,200	22.4%	4,000
18. Forest Fire Fighting and Prevention Supervisors	97.0%	$60,840	21.1%	4,000
19. Municipal Fire Fighting and Prevention Supervisors	97.0%	$60,840	21.1%	4,000
20. Railroad Conductors and Yardmasters	94.1%	$54,040	20.3%	3,000

Best-Paying Jobs with the Fastest Growth with a High Percentage of Men

Job	Percent Men	Annual Earnings	Percent Growth	Annual Openings
21. Optometrists	72.4%	$88,040	19.7%	2,000
22. Landscape Architects	79.7%	$54,220	19.4%	1,000
23. Film and Video Editors	81.1%	$46,930	18.6%	3,000
24. Cost Estimators	88.0%	$52,020	18.2%	15,000
25. Architects, Except Landscape and Naval	79.7%	$62,850	17.3%	7,000

Jobs 4 and 5 share 34,000 job openings. Jobs 10, 11, 12, 13, 14, 15, and 16 share 41,000 job openings. Jobs 18 and 19 share 4,000 job openings.

Best-Paying Jobs with the Most Openings with a High Percentage of Men

Job	Percent Men	Annual Earnings	Percent Growth	Annual Openings
1. General and Operations Managers	73.7%	$81,480	17.0%	208,000
2. Sales Representatives, Wholesale and Manufacturing, Except Technical and Scientific Products	73.9%	$47,380	12.9%	169,000
3. First-Line Supervisors and Manager/Supervisors—Construction Trades Workers	97.2%	$51,970	10.9%	57,000
4. First-Line Supervisors and Manager/Supervisors—Extractive Workers	97.2%	$51,970	10.9%	57,000
5. Computer Software Engineers, Applications	75.4%	$77,090	48.4%	54,000
6. Sales Representatives, Agricultural	73.9%	$60,760	14.4%	47,000
7. Sales Representatives, Chemical and Pharmaceutical	73.9%	$60,760	14.4%	47,000
8. Sales Representatives, Electrical/Electronic	73.9%	$60,760	14.4%	47,000
9. Sales Representatives, Instruments	73.9%	$60,760	14.4%	47,000
10. Sales Representatives, Mechanical Equipment and Supplies	73.9%	$60,760	14.4%	47,000
11. Sales Representatives, Medical	73.9%	$60,760	14.4%	47,000
12. Network Systems and Data Communications Analysts	73.5%	$61,750	54.6%	43,000
13. Anesthesiologists	73.2%	more than $145,600	24.0%	41,000
14. Family and General Practitioners	73.2%	$140,400	24.0%	41,000
15. Internists, General	73.2%	more than $145,600	24.0%	41,000
16. Obstetricians and Gynecologists	73.2%	more than $145,600	24.0%	41,000
17. Pediatricians, General	73.2%	$136,600	24.0%	41,000
18. Psychiatrists	73.2%	more than $145,600	24.0%	41,000

(continued)

(continued)

Best-Paying Jobs with the Most Openings with a High Percentage of Men

Job	Percent Men	Annual Earnings	Percent Growth	Annual Openings
19. Surgeons	73.2% ....more than	$145,600	24.0%	41,000
20. Lawyers	71.3%	$98,930	15.0%	40,000
21. Chief Executives	81.2%	$142,440	14.9%	38,000
22. Government Service Executives	81.2%	$142,440	14.9%	38,000
23. Private Sector Executives	81.2%	$142,440	14.9%	38,000
24. Computer Software Engineers, Systems Software	75.4%	$82,120	43.0%	37,000
25. Computer Security Specialists	76.7%	$59,930	38.4%	34,000

Jobs 3 and 4 share 57,000 job openings. Jobs 6, 7, 8, 9, 10, and 11 share 47,000 job openings. Jobs 13, 14, 15, 16, 17, 18, and 19 share 47,000 job openings. Jobs 21, 22, and 23 share 38,000 job openings. Job 25 shares 34,000 job openings with another job not included in this list.

Best-Paying Jobs Lists Based on Levels of Education, Training, and Experience

The lists in this section separate the 250 jobs that met our criteria for this book into lists based on the education or training typically required for entry. Unlike many of the other lists, these lists are not broken down into separate lists for highest pay, growth, or number of openings. Instead, we provided one list that includes all the best-paying occupations in our database that fit into each of the education levels and ranked the occupations by their earnings. Where jobs have equal earnings, we ordered them alphabetically.

You can use these lists in a variety of ways. For example, they can help you identify a high-paying job with higher potential but with a similar level of education to the job you now hold.

You can also use these lists to figure out additional job possibilities that would open up if you were to get additional training, education, or work experience. For example, maybe you are a high school graduate working in the transportation field and want to advance to a high-paying job. There are many jobs in this field at all levels of education. You can identify the job you're interested in and the related training you need so you can move ahead in the your field.

The lists of jobs by education should also help you when you're planning your education. For example, you might be thinking about a job in the business field, but you aren't sure what kind of work you want to do. The lists show that a job as a Sales Representative requires moderate-term on-the-job training and pays $60,760, while a job as a Loan Officer requires a bachelor's degree but pays less—$49,440. If you want higher earnings without lengthy training, this information might make a difference in your choice.

As you review these lists, doubtless you will notice that the lists grow more crowded and feature higher-paying jobs as the amount of training or education increases. It is a basic fact of the labor market that the highest-paying jobs tend to require considerable preparation. Nevertheless, if you want to minimize the time, expense, and commitment of preparing for a career, you will find several high-paying jobs with lots of openings in the first few lists.

The Education Levels

Here are brief descriptions used by the U.S. Department of Labor for the training and education levels used in the lists that follow:

- **Short-term on-the-job training**—It is possible to work in these occupations and achieve an average level of performance within a few days or weeks through on-the-job training.

- **Moderate-term on-the-job training**—Occupations that require this type of training can be performed adequately after a 1- to 12-month period of combined on-the-job and informal training. Typically, untrained workers observe experienced workers performing tasks and are gradually moved into progressively more difficult assignments.

- **Long-term on-the-job training**—This type of job requires more than 12 months of on-the-job training or combined work experience and formal classroom instruction. This includes occupations that use formal apprenticeships for training workers that may take up to four years. It also includes intensive occupation-specific, employer-sponsored training like police academies. Furthermore, it includes occupations that require natural talent that must be developed over many years.

- **Work experience in a related occupation**—This type of job requires a worker to have experience—usually several years of experience—in a related occupation (such as Police Detectives, who are selected based on their experience as Police Patrol Officers).

- **Postsecondary vocational training**—This requirement involves training that lasts at least a few months but usually less than one year. In a few instances, there may be as many as four years of training.

- **Associate degree**—This degree typically requires two years of full-time academic work beyond high school.

- **Bachelor's degree**—A bachelor's degree usually requires 120 to 130 semester hours to complete. A full-time student usually takes four to five years to complete a bachelor's degree, depending on the complexity of courses. Traditionally, people have thought of the bachelor's degree as a four-year degree. There are some bachelor's degrees—like the Bachelor of Architecture—that are considered a first professional degree and take five or more years to complete.

- **Work experience plus degree**—Some jobs require work experience in a related job in addition to a degree. For example, almost all managers have worked in a related job before being promoted into a management position. Most of the jobs in this group require a four-year bachelor's degree, although some require an associate degree or a master's degree.

- **Master's degree**—This degree usually requires 33 to 60 semester hours beyond the bachelor's degree. The academic master's degrees—such as a Master of Arts in Political

Science—usually require 33 to 36 hours. A first professional degree at the master's level—such as a Master of Social Work—requires almost two years of full-time work.

◎ **Doctoral degree**—The doctoral degree prepares students for careers that consist primarily of theory development, research, and/or college teaching. This type of degree is typically the Doctor of Philosophy (Ph.D.) or Doctor of Education (Ed.D.). Normally, a requirement for a doctoral degree is the completion of a master's degree plus an additional two to three years of full-time coursework and a one- to two-semester research project and paper called the dissertation. It usually takes four to five years beyond the bachelor's degree to complete a doctoral degree.

◎ **First professional degree**—Some professional degrees require three or more years of full-time academic study beyond the bachelor's degree. A professional degree prepares students for a specific profession. It uses theory and research to teach practical applications in a professional occupation. Examples of this type of degree are Doctor of Medicine (M.D.) for physicians, Doctor of Ministry (D.Min.) for clergy, and Juris Doctor (J.D.) for attorneys.

Another Warning About the Data

We warned you in the introduction to use caution in interpreting the data we use, and we want to do it again here. The occupational data we use is the most accurate available anywhere, but it has its limitations. For example, the education or training requirements for entry into a job are those typically required as a minimum—but some people working in those jobs may have considerably more or different credentials. For example, most Registered Nurses now have a four-year bachelor's degree, although the two-year associate degree is the minimum level of training this job requires.

In a similar way, people with jobs that require long-term on-the-job training typically earn more than people with jobs that require moderate-term on-the-job training. However, some people with moderate-term on-the-job training do earn more than the average for the highest-paying occupations listed in this book. On the other hand, some people with long-term on-the-job training earn much less than the average shown in this book—this is particularly true early in a person's career.

So as you browse the lists that follow, please use them as a way to be encouraged rather than discouraged. Education and training are very important for success in the labor market of the future, but so are ability, drive, initiative, and, yes, luck.

Having said this, we encourage you to get as much education and training as you can. It used to be that you got your schooling and never went back, but this is not a good attitude to have now. You will probably need to continue learning new things throughout your working life. You can do so by going to school, and this is a good thing for many people to do. But there are also many other ways to learn, such as workshops, certification programs, employer training, professional conferences, Internet training, reading related books and magazines, and many others. Upgrading your computer and other technical skills is particularly important in our rapidly changing workplace, and you avoid doing so at your peril.

As one of our grandfathers used to say, "The harder you work, the luckier you get." It is just as true now as it was then.

Best-Paying Jobs Requiring Short-Term On-the-Job Training

Job	Annual Earnings	Percent Growth	Annual Openings
1. Postal Service Clerks	$48,310	0.0%	4,000
2. Postal Service Mail Carriers	$46,330	0.0%	19,000

Best-Paying Jobs Requiring Moderate-Term On-the-Job Training

Job	Annual Earnings	Percent Growth	Annual Openings
1. Sales Representatives, Agricultural	$60,760	14.4%	47,000
2. Sales Representatives, Chemical and Pharmaceutical	$60,760	14.4%	47,000
3. Sales Representatives, Electrical/Electronic	$60,760	14.4%	47,000
4. Sales Representatives, Instruments	$60,760	14.4%	47,000
5. Sales Representatives, Mechanical Equipment and Supplies	$60,760	14.4%	47,000
6. Sales Representatives, Medical	$60,760	14.4%	47,000
7. Signal and Track Switch Repairers	$49,200	2.3%	1,000
8. Pile-Driver Operators	$48,900	11.9%	fewer than 500
9. Subway and Streetcar Operators	$47,500	13.7%	1,000
10. Sales Representatives, Wholesale and Manufacturing, Except Technical and Scientific Products	$47,380	12.9%	169,000
11. Caption Writers	$46,420	17.7%	14,000

Jobs 1, 2, 3, 4, 5, and 6 share 47,000 job openings. Job 11 shares 14,000 job openings with three other jobs not included in this list.

Best-Paying Jobs Requiring Long-Term On-the-Job Training

Job	Annual Earnings	Percent Growth	Annual Openings
1. Air Traffic Controllers	$107,590	14.3%	2,000
2. Nuclear Power Reactor Operators	$66,230	–0.5%	1,000
3. Elevator Installers and Repairers	$59,190	14.8%	3,000
4. Power Distributors and Dispatchers	$59,160	0.0%	1,000
5. Talent Directors	$53,860	16.6%	11,000
6. Technical Directors/Managers	$53,860	16.6%	11,000

(continued)

(continued)

Best-Paying Jobs Requiring Long-Term On-the-Job Training

Job	Annual Earnings	Percent Growth	Annual Openings
7. Auxiliary Equipment Operators, Power	$53,170	–0.4%	5,000
8. Power Generating Plant Operators, Except Auxiliary Equipment Operators	$53,170	–0.4%	5,000
9. Gas Distribution Plant Operators	$51,920	7.7%	2,000
10. Gas Processing Plant Operators	$51,920	7.7%	2,000
11. Gaugers	$51,060	–8.6%	6,000
12. Petroleum Pump System Operators	$51,060	–8.6%	6,000
13. Petroleum Refinery and Control Panel Operators	$51,060	–8.6%	6,000
14. Central Office and PBX Installers and Repairers	$50,620	–4.9%	21,000
15. Communication Equipment Mechanics, Installers, and Repairers	$50,620	–4.9%	21,000
16. Frame Wirers, Central Office	$50,620	–4.9%	21,000
17. Station Installers and Repairers, Telephone	$50,620	–4.9%	21,000
18. Telecommunications Facility Examiners	$50,620	–4.9%	21,000
19. Electrical Power-Line Installers and Repairers	$50,150	2.5%	11,000
20. Environmental Compliance Inspectors	$49,360	11.6%	17,000
21. Equal Opportunity Representatives and Officers	$49,360	11.6%	17,000
22. Government Property Inspectors and Investigators	$49,360	11.6%	17,000
23. Licensing Examiners and Inspectors	$49,360	11.6%	17,000
24. Pressure Vessel Inspectors	$49,360	11.6%	17,000
25. Transit and Railroad Police	$48,850	9.2%	fewer than 500
26. Insurance Appraisers, Auto Damage	$48,090	16.6%	2,000
27. Boilermakers	$48,050	8.7%	2,000
28. Chemical Plant and System Operators	$46,710	–17.7%	8,000
29. Flight Attendants	$46,680	16.3%	7,000

Jobs 5 and 6 share 11,000 job openings with each other and with three other jobs not included in this list. Jobs 7 and 8 share 5,000 job openings. Jobs 9 and 10 share 2,000 job openings. Jobs 11, 12, and 13 share 6,000 job openings. Jobs 14, 15, 16, 17, and 18 share 21,000 job openings. Jobs 20, 21, 22, 23, and 24 share 17,000 job openings with each other and with another job not included in this list.

Best-Paying Jobs Requiring Work Experience in a Related Occupation

Job	Annual Earnings	Percent Growth	Annual Openings
1. Industrial Production Managers	$75,580	0.8%	13,000
2. Storage and Distribution Managers	$69,120	12.7%	15,000
3. Transportation Managers	$69,120	12.7%	15,000

Best-Paying Jobs Requiring Work Experience in a Related Occupation

Job	Annual Earnings	Percent Growth	Annual Openings
4. First-Line Supervisors/Managers of Police and Detectives	$65,570	15.5%	9,000
5. First-Line Supervisors/Managers of Non-Retail Sales Workers	$61,970	1.9%	38,000
6. Forest Fire Fighting and Prevention Supervisors	$60,840	21.1%	4,000
7. Municipal Fire Fighting and Prevention Supervisors	$60,840	21.1%	4,000
8. Gaming Managers	$59,940	22.6%	1,000
9. Real Estate Brokers	$57,190	7.8%	12,000
10. Child Support, Missing Persons, and Unemployment Insurance Fraud Investigators	$55,790	16.3%	9,000
11. Criminal Investigators and Special Agents	$55,790	16.3%	9,000
12. Immigration and Customs Inspectors	$55,790	16.3%	9,000
13. Police Detectives	$55,790	16.3%	9,000
14. Police Identification and Records Officers	$55,790	16.3%	9,000
15. Locomotive Engineers	$55,520	–2.5%	2,000
16. Railroad Conductors and Yardmasters	$54,040	20.3%	3,000
17. Postmasters and Mail Superintendents	$52,710	0.0%	2,000
18. Cost Estimators	$52,020	18.2%	15,000
19. First-Line Supervisors/Managers of Mechanics, Installers, and Repairers	$51,980	12.4%	33,000
20. First-Line Supervisors and Manager/Supervisors—Construction Trades Workers	$51,970	10.9%	57,000
21. First-Line Supervisors and Manager/Supervisors—Extractive Workers	$51,970	10.9%	57,000
22. Mates—Ship, Boat, and Barge	$50,940	4.8%	2,000
23. Pilots, Ship	$50,940	4.8%	2,000
24. Ship and Boat Captains	$50,940	4.8%	2,000
25. Railroad Yard Workers	$49,700	–38.5%	1,000
26. Train Crew Members	$49,700	–38.5%	1,000
27. Aviation Inspectors	$49,490	11.4%	2,000
28. Freight Inspectors	$49,490	11.4%	2,000
29. Marine Cargo Inspectors	$49,490	11.4%	2,000
30. Motor Vehicle Inspectors	$49,490	11.4%	2,000
31. Public Transportation Inspectors	$49,490	11.4%	2,000
32. Railroad Inspectors	$49,490	11.4%	2,000
33. Coroners	$49,360	11.6%	17,000
34. Purchasing Agents, Except Wholesale, Retail, and Farm Products	$49,030	8.1%	19,000

(continued)

(continued)

Best-Paying Jobs Requiring Work Experience in a Related Occupation

Job	Annual Earnings	Percent Growth	Annual Openings
35. First-Line Supervisors/Managers of Correctional Officers	$48,570	9.4%	2,000
36. First-Line Supervisors/Managers of Transportation and Material-Moving Machine and Vehicle Operators	$47,530	15.3%	22,000
37. Purchasing Agents and Buyers, Farm Products	$46,680	7.0%	2,000

Jobs 2 and 3 share 15,000 job openings. Jobs 6 and 7 share 4,000 job openings. Jobs 10, 11, 12, 13, and 14 share 9,000 job openings. Job 15 shares 2,000 job openings with two other jobs not included in this list. Jobs 20 and 21 share 57,000 job openings. Jobs 22, 23, and 24 share 2,000 job openings. Jobs 25 and 26 share 1,000 job openings. Jobs 27, 28, 29, 30, 31, and 32 share 2,000 job openings. Job 33 shares 17,000 job openings with five other jobs not included in this list.

Best-Paying Jobs Requiring Postsecondary Vocational Training

Job	Annual Earnings	Percent Growth	Annual Openings
1. Commercial Pilots	$55,810	16.8%	2,000
2. Electrical and Electronics Repairers, Powerhouse, Substation, and Relay	$54,970	–0.4%	2,000
3. Ship Engineers	$52,780	12.7%	1,000
4. Aircraft Body and Bonded Structure Repairers	$47,310	13.4%	11,000
5. Aircraft Engine Specialists	$47,310	13.4%	11,000
6. Airframe-and-Power-Plant Mechanics	$47,310	13.4%	11,000
7. Avionics Technicians	$46,630	9.1%	2,000

Jobs 4, 5, and 6 share 11,000 job openings.

Best-Paying Jobs Requiring an Associate Degree

Job	Annual Earnings	Percent Growth	Annual Openings
1. Radiation Therapists	$62,340	26.3%	1,000
2. Nuclear Equipment Operation Technicians	$61,120	13.7%	1,000
3. Nuclear Monitoring Technicians	$61,120	13.7%	1,000
4. Dental Hygienists	$60,890	43.3%	17,000
5. Nuclear Medicine Technologists	$59,670	21.5%	2,000
6. Registered Nurses	$54,670	29.4%	229,000
7. Diagnostic Medical Sonographers	$54,370	34.8%	5,000
8. Aerospace Engineering and Operations Technicians	$52,450	8.5%	1,000

Best-Paying Jobs Requiring an Associate Degree

Job	Annual Earnings	Percent Growth	Annual Openings
9. Calibration and Instrumentation Technicians	$48,040	9.8%	18,000
10. Electrical Engineering Technicians	$48,040	9.8%	18,000
11. Electronics Engineering Technicians	$48,040	9.8%	18,000
12. Funeral Directors	$47,630	6.7%	3,000

Jobs 2 and 3 share 1,000 job openings. Jobs 9, 10, and 11 share 18,000 job openings.

Best-Paying Jobs Requiring a Bachelor's Degree

Job	Annual Earnings	Percent Growth	Annual Openings
1. Airline Pilots, Copilots, and Flight Engineers	$138,170	17.2%	7,000
2. Petroleum Engineers	$93,000	−0.1%	1,000
3. Nuclear Engineers	$88,290	7.3%	1,000
4. Computer Hardware Engineers	$84,420	10.1%	5,000
5. Aerospace Engineers	$84,090	8.3%	6,000
6. Computer Software Engineers, Systems Software	$82,120	43.0%	37,000
7. Electronics Engineers, Except Computer	$78,030	9.7%	11,000
8. Chemical Engineers	$77,140	10.6%	3,000
9. Computer Software Engineers, Applications	$77,090	48.4%	54,000
10. Sales Engineers	$74,200	14.0%	8,000
11. Atmospheric and Space Scientists	$73,940	16.5%	1,000
12. Electrical Engineers	$73,510	11.8%	12,000
13. Marine Architects	$72,920	8.5%	fewer than 500
14. Marine Engineers	$72,920	8.5%	fewer than 500
15. Construction Managers	$72,260	10.4%	28,000
16. Physician Assistants	$72,030	49.6%	10,000
17. Biomedical Engineers	$71,840	30.7%	1,000
18. Materials Scientists	$71,450	8.0%	fewer than 500
19. Materials Engineers	$69,660	12.2%	2,000
20. Computer Systems Analysts	$68,300	31.4%	56,000
21. Environmental Engineers	$68,090	30.0%	5,000
22. Mechanical Engineers	$67,590	11.1%	11,000
23. Sales Agents, Financial Services	$67,130	11.5%	37,000
24. Sales Agents, Securities and Commodities	$67,130	11.5%	37,000

(continued)

(continued)

Best-Paying Jobs Requiring a Bachelor's Degree

Job	Annual Earnings	Percent Growth	Annual Openings
25. Industrial Engineers	$66,670	16.0%	13,000
26. Civil Engineers	$66,190	16.5%	19,000
27. Fire-Prevention and Protection Engineers	$65,210	13.4%	2,000
28. Industrial Safety and Health Engineers	$65,210	13.4%	2,000
29. Product Safety Engineers	$65,210	13.4%	2,000
30. Agricultural Engineers	$64,890	12.0%	fewer than 500
31. Financial Analysts	$63,860	17.3%	28,000
32. Personal Financial Advisors	$63,500	25.9%	17,000
33. Computer Programmers	$63,420	2.0%	28,000
34. Database Administrators	$63,250	38.2%	9,000
35. Financial Examiners	$63,090	9.5%	3,000
36. Architects, Except Landscape and Naval	$62,850	17.3%	7,000
37. Network Systems and Data Communications Analysts	$61,750	54.6%	43,000
38. Fashion Designers	$60,860	8.4%	2,000
39. Logisticians	$60,110	13.2%	7,000
40. Computer Security Specialists	$59,930	38.4%	34,000
41. Network and Computer Systems Administrators	$59,930	38.4%	34,000
42. Budget Analysts	$58,910	13.5%	6,000
43. Chemists	$57,890	7.3%	5,000
44. Occupational Therapists	$56,860	33.6%	7,000
45. Technical Writers	$55,160	23.2%	5,000
46. Plant Scientists	$54,530	13.9%	1,000
47. Soil Scientists	$54,530	13.9%	1,000
48. Landscape Architects	$54,220	19.4%	1,000
49. Orthotists and Prosthetists	$53,760	18.0%	fewer than 500
50. Park Naturalists	$53,350	6.3%	2,000
51. Range Managers	$53,350	6.3%	2,000
52. Soil Conservationists	$53,350	6.3%	2,000
53. Accountants	$52,210	22.4%	157,000
54. Auditors	$52,210	22.4%	157,000
55. Commercial and Industrial Designers	$52,200	10.8%	7,000
56. Food Scientists and Technologists	$51,440	10.9%	1,000
57. Insurance Underwriters	$51,270	8.0%	13,000
58. Credit Analysts	$50,370	3.6%	3,000
59. Multi-Media Artists and Animators	$50,290	14.1%	14,000
60. Social and Community Service Managers	$49,500	25.5%	17,000

Best-Paying Jobs Requiring a Bachelor's Degree

Job	Annual Earnings	Percent Growth	Annual Openings
61. Loan Officers	$49,440	8.3%	38,000
62. Compensation, Benefits, and Job Analysis Specialists	$48,870	20.4%	15,000
63. Foresters	$48,670	6.7%	1,000
64. Cartographers and Photogrammetrists	$48,250	15.3%	1,000
65. Medical and Clinical Laboratory Technologists	$47,710	20.5%	14,000
66. Film and Video Editors	$46,930	18.6%	3,000
67. Special Education Teachers, Secondary School	$46,820	17.9%	11,000
68. Copy Writers	$46,420	17.7%	14,000
69. Creative Writers	$46,420	17.7%	14,000
70. Poets and Lyricists	$46,420	17.7%	14,000

Jobs 13 and 14 share fewer than 500 job openings. Jobs 23 and 24 share 37,000 job openings. Jobs 27, 28, and 29 share 2,000 job openings. Jobs 40 and 41 share 34,000 job openings. Jobs 46 and 47 share 34,000 job openings. Jobs 50, 51, and 52 share 2,000 job openings. Jobs 53 and 54 share 157,000 job openings. Jobs 68, 69, and 70 share 14,000 job openings.

Best-Paying Jobs Requiring Work Experience Plus Degree

Job	Annual Earnings	Percent Growth	Annual Openings
1. Chief Executives	$142,440	14.9%	38,000
2. Government Service Executives	$142,440	14.9%	38,000
3. Private Sector Executives	$142,440	14.9%	38,000
4. Engineering Managers	$100,760	13.0%	15,000
5. Judges, Magistrate Judges, and Magistrates	$97,570	6.9%	1,000
6. Computer and Information Systems Managers	$96,520	25.9%	25,000
7. Natural Sciences Managers	$93,090	13.6%	5,000
8. Marketing Managers	$92,680	20.8%	23,000
9. Sales Managers	$87,580	19.7%	40,000
10. Financial Managers, Branch or Department	$86,280	14.8%	63,000
11. Treasurers, Controllers, and Chief Financial Officers	$86,280	14.8%	63,000
12. Actuaries	$81,640	23.2%	3,000
13. General and Operations Managers	$81,480	17.0%	208,000
14. Public Relations Managers	$76,450	21.7%	5,000
15. Purchasing Managers	$76,270	7.0%	8,000
16. Education Administrators, Elementary and Secondary School	$75,400	10.4%	27,000
17. Training and Development Managers	$74,180	25.9%	3,000
18. Administrative Law Judges, Adjudicators, and Hearing Officers	$70,680	10.1%	1,000

(continued)

(continued)

Best-Paying Jobs Requiring Work Experience Plus Degree

Job	Annual Earnings	Percent Growth	Annual Openings
19. Education Administrators, Postsecondary	$70,350	21.3%	18,000
20. Medical and Health Services Managers	$69,700	22.8%	33,000
21. Compensation and Benefits Managers	$69,130	21.5%	4,000
22. Advertising and Promotions Managers	$68,860	20.3%	9,000
23. Management Analysts	$66,380	20.1%	82,000
24. Administrative Services Managers	$64,020	16.9%	25,000
25. Art Directors	$63,950	11.5%	10,000
26. Arbitrators, Mediators, and Conciliators	$54,360	15.5%	fewer than 500
27. Directors—Stage, Motion Pictures, Television, and Radio	$53,860	16.6%	11,000
28. Producers	$53,860	16.6%	11,000
29. Program Directors	$53,860	16.6%	11,000
30. Agents and Business Managers of Artists, Performers, and Athletes	$53,800	11.8%	2,000
31. Agricultural Crop Farm Managers	$51,160	4.0%	20,000
32. Fish Hatchery Managers	$51,160	4.0%	20,000
33. Nursery and Greenhouse Managers	$51,160	4.0%	20,000
34. Vocational Education Teachers, Secondary School	$47,090	9.1%	10,000

Jobs 1, 2, and 3 share 38,000 job openings. Jobs 27, 28, and 29 share 11,000 job openings with each other and with two other jobs not included in this list. Jobs 31, 32, and 33 share 20,000 job openings.

Best-Paying Jobs Requiring a Master's Degree

Job	Annual Earnings	Percent Growth	Annual Openings
1. Industrial-Organizational Psychologists	$84,690	20.4%	fewer than 500
2. Political Scientists	$84,100	7.3%	fewer than 500
3. Economists	$73,690	5.6%	1,000
4. Geologists	$71,640	8.3%	2,000
5. Hydrologists	$63,820	31.6%	1,000
6. Geographers	$63,550	6.8%	fewer than 500
7. Physical Therapists	$63,080	36.7%	13,000
8. Statisticians	$62,450	4.6%	2,000
9. Operations Research Analysts	$62,180	8.4%	7,000
10. Market Research Analysts	$57,300	19.6%	20,000
11. Urban and Regional Planners	$55,170	15.2%	3,000

Best-Paying Jobs Requiring a Master's Degree

Job	Annual Earnings	Percent Growth	Annual Openings
12. Teachers, Postsecondary	$55,100	32.2%	329,000
13. Speech-Language Pathologists	$54,880	14.6%	5,000
14. Occupational Health and Safety Specialists	$53,710	12.4%	3,000
15. Audiologists	$53,490	9.1%	fewer than 500
16. Sociologists	$52,760	4.7%	fewer than 500
17. Environmental Scientists and Specialists, Including Health	$52,630	17.1%	8,000
18. Instructional Coordinators	$50,430	27.5%	15,000
19. Librarians	$47,400	4.9%	8,000
20. Educational, Vocational, and School Counselors	$46,440	14.8%	32,000

Best-Paying Jobs Requiring a Doctoral Degree

Job	Annual Earnings	Percent Growth	Annual Openings
1. Astronomers	$104,670	10.4%	fewer than 500
2. Physicists	$89,810	7.0%	1,000
3. Biochemists	$71,000	21.0%	1,000
4. Biophysicists	$71,000	21.0%	1,000
5. Medical Scientists, Except Epidemiologists	$61,730	34.1%	15,000
6. Clinical Psychologists	$57,170	19.1%	10,000
7. Counseling Psychologists	$57,170	19.1%	10,000
8. School Psychologists	$57,170	19.1%	10,000
9. Microbiologists	$56,870	17.2%	1,000
10. Epidemiologists	$52,170	26.2%	1,000
11. Zoologists and Wildlife Biologists	$52,050	13.0%	1,000

Jobs 3 and 4 share 1,000 job openings. Jobs 6, 7, and 8 share 10,000 job openings.

Best-Paying Jobs Requiring a First Professional Degree

Job	Annual Earnings	Percent Growth	Annual Openings
1. Anesthesiologists	more than $145,600	24.0%	41,000
2. Internists, General	more than $145,600	24.0%	41,000
3. Obstetricians and Gynecologists	more than $145,600	24.0%	41,000

(continued)

(continued)

Best-Paying Jobs Requiring a First Professional Degree

Job	Annual Earnings	Percent Growth	Annual Openings
4. Oral and Maxillofacial Surgeons	more than $145,600	16.2%	fewer than 500
5. Orthodontists	more than $145,600	12.8%	1,000
6. Prosthodontists	more than $145,600	13.6%	fewer than 500
7. Psychiatrists	more than $145,600	24.0%	41,000
8. Surgeons	more than $145,600	24.0%	41,000
9. Family and General Practitioners	$140,400	24.0%	41,000
10. Pediatricians, General	$136,600	24.0%	41,000
11. Dentists, General	$125,300	13.5%	7,000
12. Podiatrists	$100,550	16.2%	1,000
13. Lawyers	$98,930	15.0%	40,000
14. Pharmacists	$89,820	24.6%	16,000
15. Optometrists	$88,040	19.7%	2,000
16. Veterinarians	$68,910	17.4%	8,000
17. Chiropractors	$67,200	22.4%	4,000

Jobs 1, 2, 3, 7, 8, 9, and 10 share 41,000 job openings.

Best-Paying Jobs Lists Based on Interests

This group of lists organizes the 250 best-paying jobs into 16 interest areas. You can use these lists to identify jobs quickly based on your interests.

Find the interest area or areas that appeal to you most. Then review the jobs in those areas to identify jobs you want to explore in more detail and look up their descriptions in Part II. You can also review interest areas where you have had past experience, education, or training to see if other jobs in those areas would meet your current requirements.

Within each interest area, jobs are listed in order of their earnings, from highest to lowest. As in the previous lists, jobs that have equal earnings are ordered alphabetically.

Note: The 16 interest areas used in these lists are those used in the *New Guide for Occupational Exploration,* Fourth Edition, published by JIST. The original *GOE* was developed by the U.S. Department of Labor as an intuitive way to assist in career exploration. The 16 interest areas used in the *New GOE* are based on the 16 career clusters that were developed by the U.S. Department of Education's Office of Vocational and Adult Education around 1999 and that presently are being used by many states to organize their career-oriented programs and career information.

Descriptions for the 16 Interest Areas

Brief descriptions for the 16 interest areas we use in the lists follow. The descriptions are from the *New Guide for Occupational Exploration,* Fourth Edition. Some of them refer to jobs (as examples) that aren't included in this book.

Also note that we put each of the 250 best-paying jobs into only one interest area list, the one it fit into best. However, many jobs could be included in more than one list, so consider reviewing a variety of these interest areas to find jobs that you might otherwise overlook.

- **Agriculture and Natural Resources:** *An interest in working with plants, animals, forests, or mineral resources for agriculture, horticulture, conservation, extraction, and other purposes.* You can satisfy this interest by working in farming, landscaping, forestry, fishing, mining, and related fields. You may like doing physical work outdoors, such as on a farm or ranch, in a forest, or on a drilling rig. If you have scientific curiosity, you could study plants and animals or analyze biological or rock samples in a lab. If you have management ability, you could own, operate, or manage a fish hatchery, a landscaping business, or a greenhouse.

- **Architecture and Construction:** *An interest in designing, assembling, and maintaining components of buildings and other structures.* You may want to be part of the team of architects, drafters, and others who design buildings and render the plans. If construction interests you, you can find fulfillment in the many building projects that are being undertaken at all times. If you like to organize and plan, you can find careers in managing these projects. Or you can play a more direct role in putting up and finishing buildings by doing jobs such as plumbing, carpentry, masonry, painting, or roofing, either as a skilled craftsworker or as a helper. You can prepare the building site by operating heavy equipment or install, maintain, and repair vital building equipment and systems such as electricity and heating.

- **Arts and Communication:** *An interest in creatively expressing feelings or ideas, in communicating news or information, or in performing.* You can satisfy this interest in creative, verbal, or performing activities. For example, if you enjoy literature, perhaps writing or editing would appeal to you. Journalism and public relations are other fields for people who like to use their writing or speaking skills. Do you prefer to work in the performing arts? If so, you could direct or perform in drama, music, or dance. If you especially enjoy the visual arts, you could create paintings, sculpture, or ceramics or design products or visual displays. A flair for technology might lead you to specialize in photography, broadcast production, or dispatching.

- **Business and Administration:** *An interest in making a business organization or function run smoothly.* You can satisfy this interest by working in a position of leadership or by specializing in a function that contributes to the overall effort in a business, a nonprofit organization, or a government agency. If you especially enjoy working with people, you may find fulfillment from working in human resources. An interest in numbers may lead you to consider accounting, finance, budgeting, billing, or financial record-keeping. A job as an administrative assistant may interest you if you like a variety of work in a busy environment. If you are good with details and word processing, you may enjoy a job as a secretary or data entry keyer. Or perhaps you would do well as the manager of a business.

⊙ **Education and Training:** *An interest in helping people learn.* You can satisfy this interest by teaching students, who may be preschoolers, retirees, or any age in between. You may specialize in a particular academic field or work with learners of a particular age, with a particular interest, or with a particular learning problem. Working in a library or museum may give you an opportunity to expand people's understanding of the world.

⊙ **Finance and Insurance:** *An interest in helping businesses and people be assured of a financially secure future.* You can satisfy this interest by working in a financial or insurance business in a leadership or support role. If you like gathering and analyzing information, you may find fulfillment as an insurance adjuster or financial analyst. Or you may deal with information at the clerical level as a banking or insurance clerk or in person-to-person situations providing customer service. Another way to interact with people is to sell financial or insurance services that will meet their needs.

⊙ **Government and Public Administration:** *An interest in helping a government agency serve the needs of the public.* You can satisfy this interest by working in a position of leadership or by specializing in a function that contributes to the role of government. You may help protect the public by working as an inspector or examiner to enforce standards. If you enjoy using clerical skills, you may work as a clerk in a law court or government office. Or perhaps you prefer the top-down perspective of a government executive or urban planner.

⊙ **Health Science:** *An interest in helping people and animals be healthy.* You can satisfy this interest by working in a health care team as a doctor, therapist, or nurse. You might specialize in one of the many different parts of the body (such as the teeth or eyes) or in one of the many different types of care. Or you may wish to be a generalist who deals with the whole patient. If you like technology, you might find satisfaction working with X rays or new methods of diagnosis. You might work with healthy people, helping them eat right. If you enjoy working with animals, you might care for them and keep them healthy.

⊙ **Hospitality, Tourism, and Recreation:** *An interest in catering to the personal wishes and needs of others so that they may enjoy a clean environment, good food and drink, comfortable lodging away from home, and recreation.* You can satisfy this interest by providing services for the convenience, care, and pampering of others in hotels, restaurants, airplanes, beauty parlors, and so on. You may wish to use your love of cooking as a chef. If you like working with people, you may wish to provide personal services by being a travel guide, a flight attendant, a concierge, a hairdresser, or a waiter. You may wish to work in cleaning and building services if you like a clean environment. If you enjoy sports or games, you may work for an athletic team or casino.

⊙ **Human Service:** *An interest in improving people's social, mental, emotional, or spiritual well-being.* You can satisfy this interest as a counselor, social worker, or religious worker who helps people sort out their complicated lives or solve personal problems. You may work as a caretaker for very young people or the elderly. Or you may interview people to help identify the social services they need.

◉ **Information Technology:** _An interest in designing, developing, managing, and supporting information systems._ You can satisfy this interest by working with hardware, software, multimedia, or integrated systems. If you like to use your organizational skills, you might work as an administrator of a system or database. Or you can solve complex problems as a software engineer or systems analyst. If you enjoy getting your hands on the hardware, you might find work servicing computers, peripherals, and information-intense machines such as cash registers and ATMs.

◉ **Law and Public Safety:** _An interest in upholding people's rights or in protecting people and property by using authority, inspecting, or investigating._ You can satisfy this interest by working in law, law enforcement, fire fighting, the military, and related fields. For example, if you enjoy mental challenge and intrigue, you could investigate crimes or fires for a living. If you enjoy working with verbal skills and research skills, you may want to defend citizens in court or research deeds, wills, and other legal documents. If you want to help people in critical situations, you may want to fight fires, work as a police officer, or become a paramedic. Or, if you want more routine work in public safety, perhaps a job in guarding, patrolling, or inspecting would appeal to you. If you have management ability, you could seek a leadership position in law enforcement and the protective services. Work in the military gives you a chance to use technical and leadership skills while serving your country.

◉ **Manufacturing:** _An interest in processing materials into intermediate or final products or maintaining and repairing products by using machines or hand tools._ You can satisfy this interest by working in one of many industries that mass-produce goods or by working for a utility that distributes electric power or other resources. You may enjoy manual work, using your hands or hand tools in highly skilled jobs such as assembling engines or electronic equipment. If you enjoy making machines run efficiently or fixing them when they break down, you could seek a job installing or repairing such devices as copiers, aircraft engines, cars, or watches. Perhaps you prefer to set up or operate machines that are used to manufacture products made of food, glass, or paper. You may enjoy cutting and grinding metal and plastic parts to desired shapes and measurements. Or you may wish to operate equipment in systems that provide water and process wastewater. You may like inspecting, sorting, counting, or weighing products. Another option is to work with your hands and machinery to move boxes and freight in a warehouse. If leadership appeals to you, you could manage people engaged in production and repair.

◉ **Retail and Wholesale Sales and Service:** _An interest in bringing others to a particular point of view by personal persuasion and by sales and promotional techniques._ You can satisfy this interest in a variety of jobs that involve persuasion and selling. If you like using your knowledge of science, you may enjoy selling pharmaceutical, medical, or electronic products or services. Real estate offers several kinds of sales jobs as well. If you like speaking on the phone, you could work as a telemarketer. Or you may enjoy selling apparel and other merchandise in a retail setting. If you prefer to help people, you may want a job in customer service.

◉ **Scientific Research, Engineering, and Mathematics:** _An interest in discovering, collecting, and analyzing information about the natural world; in applying scientific research findings to problems in medicine, the life sciences, human behavior, and the natural sciences; in_ *imagining and manipulating quantitative data; and in applying technology to manufacturing, transportation, and other economic activities.* You can satisfy this interest by working with the knowledge and processes of the sciences. You may enjoy researching and developing new knowledge in mathematics, or perhaps solving problems in the physical, life, or social sciences would appeal to you. You may wish to study engineering and help create new machines, processes, and structures. If you want to work with scientific equipment and procedures, you could seek a job in a research or testing laboratory.

- **Transportation, Distribution, and Logistics:** *An interest in operations that move people or materials.* You can satisfy this interest by managing a transportation service, by helping vehicles keep on their assigned schedules and routes, or by driving or piloting a vehicle. If you enjoy taking responsibility, perhaps managing a rail line would appeal to you. If you work well with details and can take pressure on the job, you might consider being an air traffic controller. Or would you rather get out on the highway, on the water, or up in the air? If so, then you could drive a truck from state to state, be employed on a ship, or fly a crop duster over a cornfield. If you prefer to stay closer to home, you could drive a delivery van, taxi, or school bus. You can use your physical strength to load freight and arrange it so it gets to its destination in one piece.

Best-Paying Jobs for People Interested in Agriculture and Natural Resources

Job	Annual Earnings	Percent Growth	Annual Openings
1. Petroleum Engineers	$93,000	–0.1%	1,000
2. Environmental Engineers	$68,090	30.0%	5,000
3. Agricultural Engineers	$64,890	12.0%	fewer than 500
4. Plant Scientists	$54,530	13.9%	1,000
5. Soil Scientists	$54,530	13.9%	1,000
6. Park Naturalists	$53,350	6.3%	2,000
7. Range Managers	$53,350	6.3%	2,000
8. Soil Conservationists	$53,350	6.3%	2,000
9. Zoologists and Wildlife Biologists	$52,050	13.0%	1,000
10. First-Line Supervisors and Manager/Supervisors—Extractive Workers	$51,970	10.9%	57,000
11. Food Scientists and Technologists	$51,440	10.9%	1,000
12. Agricultural Crop Farm Managers	$51,160	4.0%	20,000
13. Fish Hatchery Managers	$51,160	4.0%	20,000
14. Nursery and Greenhouse Managers	$51,160	4.0%	20,000
15. Foresters	$48,670	6.7%	1,000
16. Purchasing Agents and Buyers, Farm Products	$46,680	7.0%	2,000

Jobs 4 and 5 share 34,000 job openings. Jobs 6, 7, and 8 share 2,000 job openings. Job 10 shares 57,000 job openings with another job not included in this list. Jobs 12, 13, and 14 share 20,000 job openings.

Best-Paying Jobs for People Interested in Architecture and Construction

Job	Annual Earnings	Percent Growth	Annual Openings
1. Construction Managers	$72,260	10.4%	28,000
2. Architects, Except Landscape and Naval	$62,850	17.3%	7,000
3. Elevator Installers and Repairers	$59,190	14.8%	3,000
4. Electrical and Electronics Repairers, Powerhouse, Substation, and Relay	$54,970	–0.4%	2,000
5. Landscape Architects	$54,220	19.4%	1,000
6. First-Line Supervisors and Manager/Supervisors—Construction Trades Workers	$51,970	10.9%	57,000
7. Central Office and PBX Installers and Repairers	$50,620	–4.9%	21,000
8. Communication Equipment Mechanics, Installers, and Repairers	$50,620	–4.9%	21,000
9. Frame Wirers, Central Office	$50,620	–4.9%	21,000
10. Station Installers and Repairers, Telephone	$50,620	–4.9%	21,000
11. Telecommunications Facility Examiners	$50,620	–4.9%	21,000
12. Electrical Power-Line Installers and Repairers	$50,150	2.5%	11,000
13. Pile-Driver Operators	$48,900	11.9%	fewer than 500
14. Boilermakers	$48,050	8.7%	2,000

Job 6 shares 57,000 job openings with another job not included in this list. Jobs 7, 8, 9, 10, and 11 share 21,000 job openings.

Best-Paying Jobs for People Interested in Arts and Communication

Job	Annual Earnings	Percent Growth	Annual Openings
1. Air Traffic Controllers	$107,590	14.3%	2,000
2. Public Relations Managers	$76,450	21.7%	5,000
3. Art Directors	$63,950	11.5%	10,000
4. Fashion Designers	$60,860	8.4%	2,000
5. Technical Writers	$55,160	23.2%	5,000
6. Directors—Stage, Motion Pictures, Television, and Radio	$53,860	16.6%	11,000
7. Producers	$53,860	16.6%	11,000
8. Program Directors	$53,860	16.6%	11,000
9. Talent Directors	$53,860	16.6%	11,000
10. Technical Directors/Managers	$53,860	16.6%	11,000
11. Agents and Business Managers of Artists, Performers, and Athletes	$53,800	11.8%	2,000
12. Commercial and Industrial Designers	$52,200	10.8%	7,000
13. Multi-Media Artists and Animators	$50,290	14.1%	14,000

(continued)

(continued)

Best-Paying Jobs for People Interested in Arts and Communication

Job	Annual Earnings	Percent Growth	Annual Openings
14. Film and Video Editors	$46,930	18.6%	3,000
15. Caption Writers	$46,420	17.7%	14,000
16. Copy Writers	$46,420	17.7%	14,000
17. Creative Writers	$46,420	17.7%	14,000
18. Poets and Lyricists	$46,420	17.7%	14,000

Jobs 6, 7, 8, 9, and 10 share 11,000 job openings. Jobs 15, 16, 17, and 18 share 14,000 job openings.

Best-Paying Jobs for People Interested in Business and Administration

Job	Annual Earnings	Percent Growth	Annual Openings
1. Chief Executives	$142,440	14.9%	38,000
2. Private Sector Executives	$142,440	14.9%	38,000
3. General and Operations Managers	$81,480	17.0%	208,000
4. Training and Development Managers	$74,180	25.9%	3,000
5. Compensation and Benefits Managers	$69,130	21.5%	4,000
6. Management Analysts	$66,380	20.1%	82,000
7. Administrative Services Managers	$64,020	16.9%	25,000
8. Operations Research Analysts	$62,180	8.4%	7,000
9. Logisticians	$60,110	13.2%	7,000
10. Budget Analysts	$58,910	13.5%	6,000
11. Accountants	$52,210	22.4%	157,000
12. Auditors	$52,210	22.4%	157,000
13. Compensation, Benefits, and Job Analysis Specialists	$48,870	20.4%	15,000
14. Postal Service Clerks	$48,310	0.0%	4,000

Jobs 1 and 2 share 38,000 job openings with each other and with another job not included in this list. Jobs 11 and 12 share 157,000 job openings.

Best-Paying Jobs for People Interested in Education and Training

Job	Annual Earnings	Percent Growth	Annual Openings
1. Education Administrators, Elementary and Secondary School	$75,400	10.4%	27,000
2. Education Administrators, Postsecondary	$70,350	21.3%	18,000

Best-Paying Jobs for People Interested in Education and Training

Job	Annual Earnings	Percent Growth	Annual Openings
3. Teachers, Postsecondary	$55,100	32.2%	329,000
4. Instructional Coordinators	$50,430	27.5%	15,000
5. Librarians	$47,400	4.9%	8,000
6. Vocational Education Teachers, Secondary School	$47,090	9.1%	10,000
7. Special Education Teachers, Secondary School	$46,820	17.9%	11,000
8. Educational, Vocational, and School Counselors	$46,440	14.8%	32,000

Best-Paying Jobs for People Interested in Finance and Insurance

Job	Annual Earnings	Percent Growth	Annual Openings
1. Financial Managers, Branch or Department	$86,280	14.8%	63,000
2. Treasurers, Controllers, and Chief Financial Officers	$86,280	14.8%	63,000
3. Sales Agents, Financial Services	$67,130	11.5%	37,000
4. Sales Agents, Securities and Commodities	$67,130	11.5%	37,000
5. Financial Analysts	$63,860	17.3%	28,000
6. Personal Financial Advisors	$63,500	25.9%	17,000
7. Market Research Analysts	$57,300	19.6%	20,000
8. Cost Estimators	$52,020	18.2%	15,000
9. Insurance Underwriters	$51,270	8.0%	13,000
10. Credit Analysts	$50,370	3.6%	3,000
11. Loan Officers	$49,440	8.3%	38,000
12. Insurance Appraisers, Auto Damage	$48,090	16.6%	2,000

Jobs 3 and 4 share 37,000 job openings.

Best-Paying Jobs for People Interested in Government and Public Administration

Job	Annual Earnings	Percent Growth	Annual Openings
1. Government Service Executives	$142,440	14.9%	38,000
2. Financial Examiners	$63,090	9.5%	3,000
3. Nuclear Monitoring Technicians	$61,120	13.7%	1,000
4. Child Support, Missing Persons, and Unemployment Insurance Fraud Investigators	$55,790	16.3%	9,000

(continued)

(continued)

Best-Paying Jobs for People Interested in Government and Public Administration

Job	Annual Earnings	Percent Growth	Annual Openings
5. Immigration and Customs Inspectors	$55,790	16.3%	9,000
6. Urban and Regional Planners	$55,170	15.2%	3,000
7. Occupational Health and Safety Specialists	$53,710	12.4%	3,000
8. Social and Community Service Managers	$49,500	25.5%	17,000
9. Aviation Inspectors	$49,490	11.4%	2,000
10. Marine Cargo Inspectors	$49,490	11.4%	2,000
11. Motor Vehicle Inspectors	$49,490	11.4%	2,000
12. Railroad Inspectors	$49,490	11.4%	2,000
13. Environmental Compliance Inspectors	$49,360	11.6%	17,000
14. Equal Opportunity Representatives and Officers	$49,360	11.6%	17,000
15. Government Property Inspectors and Investigators	$49,360	11.6%	17,000
16. Licensing Examiners and Inspectors	$49,360	11.6%	17,000
17. Pressure Vessel Inspectors	$49,360	11.6%	17,000

Job 1 shares 38,000 job openings with two other jobs not included in this list. Job 3 shares 1,000 job openings with another job not included in this list. Jobs 4 and 5 share 9,000 job openings with each other and with three other jobs not included in this list. Jobs 9, 10, 11, and 12 share 2,000 job openings with each other and with two other jobs not included in this list. Jobs 13, 14, 15, 16, and 17 share 17,000 job openings with each other and with another job not included in this list.

Best-Paying Jobs for People Interested in Health Science

Job	Annual Earnings	Percent Growth	Annual Openings
1. Anesthesiologists	more than $145,600	24.0%	41,000
2. Internists, General	more than $145,600	24.0%	41,000
3. Obstetricians and Gynecologists	more than $145,600	24.0%	41,000
4. Oral and Maxillofacial Surgeons	more than $145,600	16.2%	fewer than 500
5. Orthodontists	more than $145,600	12.8%	1,000
6. Prosthodontists	more than $145,600	13.6%	fewer than 500
7. Psychiatrists	more than $145,600	24.0%	41,000
8. Surgeons	more than $145,600	24.0%	41,000
9. Family and General Practitioners	$140,400	24.0%	41,000
10. Pediatricians, General	$136,600	24.0%	41,000
11. Dentists, General	$125,300	13.5%	7,000
12. Podiatrists	$100,550	16.2%	1,000

Best-Paying Jobs for People Interested in Health Science

Job	Annual Earnings	Percent Growth	Annual Openings
13. Pharmacists	$89,820	24.6%	16,000
14. Optometrists	$88,040	19.7%	2,000
15. Physician Assistants	$72,030	49.6%	10,000
16. Medical and Health Services Managers	$69,700	22.8%	33,000
17. Veterinarians	$68,910	17.4%	8,000
18. Chiropractors	$67,200	22.4%	4,000
19. Physical Therapists	$63,080	36.7%	13,000
20. Radiation Therapists	$62,340	26.3%	1,000
21. Dental Hygienists	$60,890	43.3%	17,000
22. Nuclear Medicine Technologists	$59,670	21.5%	2,000
23. Occupational Therapists	$56,860	33.6%	7,000
24. Speech-Language Pathologists	$54,880	14.6%	5,000
25. Registered Nurses	$54,670	29.4%	229,000
26. Diagnostic Medical Sonographers	$54,370	34.8%	5,000
27. Orthotists and Prosthetists	$53,760	18.0%	fewer than 500
28. Audiologists	$53,490	9.1%	fewer than 500
29. Coroners	$49,360	11.6%	17,000
30. Medical and Clinical Laboratory Technologists	$47,710	20.5%	14,000

Jobs 1, 2, 3, 7, 8, 9, and 10 share 41,000 job openings. Job 29 shares 17,000 job openings with five other jobs not included in this list.

Best-Paying Jobs for People Interested in Hospitality, Tourism, and Recreation

Job	Annual Earnings	Percent Growth	Annual Openings
1. Gaming Managers	$59,940	22.6%	1,000
2. Flight Attendants	$46,680	16.3%	7,000

Best-Paying Jobs for People Interested in Human Service

Job	Annual Earnings	Percent Growth	Annual Openings
1. Clinical Psychologists	$57,170	19.1%	10,000
2. Counseling Psychologists	$57,170	19.1%	10,000

Jobs 1 and 2 share 10,000 job openings with each other and with another job not included in this list.

Best-Paying Jobs for People Interested in Information Technology

Job	Annual Earnings	Percent Growth	Annual Openings
1. Computer and Information Systems Managers	$96,520	25.9%	25,000
2. Computer Software Engineers, Systems Software	$82,120	43.0%	37,000
3. Computer Software Engineers, Applications	$77,090	48.4%	54,000
4. Computer Systems Analysts	$68,300	31.4%	56,000
5. Computer Programmers	$63,420	2.0%	28,000
6. Database Administrators	$63,250	38.2%	9,000
7. Network Systems and Data Communications Analysts	$61,750	54.6%	43,000
8. Computer Security Specialists	$59,930	38.4%	34,000
9. Network and Computer Systems Administrators	$59,930	38.4%	34,000

Jobs 8 and 9 share 34,000 job openings.

Best-Paying Jobs for People Interested in Law and Public Safety

Job	Annual Earnings	Percent Growth	Annual Openings
1. Lawyers	$98,930	15.0%	40,000
2. Judges, Magistrate Judges, and Magistrates	$97,570	6.9%	1,000
3. Administrative Law Judges, Adjudicators, and Hearing Officers	$70,680	10.1%	1,000
4. First-Line Supervisors/Managers of Police and Detectives	$65,570	15.5%	9,000
5. Forest Fire Fighting and Prevention Supervisors	$60,840	21.1%	4,000
6. Municipal Fire Fighting and Prevention Supervisors	$60,840	21.1%	4,000
7. Criminal Investigators and Special Agents	$55,790	16.3%	9,000
8. Police Detectives	$55,790	16.3%	9,000
9. Police Identification and Records Officers	$55,790	16.3%	9,000
10. Arbitrators, Mediators, and Conciliators	$54,360	15.5%	fewer than 500
11. Transit and Railroad Police	$48,850	9.2%	fewer than 500
12. First-Line Supervisors/Managers of Correctional Officers	$48,570	9.4%	2,000

Jobs 5 and 6 share 4,000 job openings. Jobs 7, 8, and 9 share 9,000 job openings with each other and with two other jobs not included in this list.

Best-Paying Jobs for People Interested in Manufacturing

Job	Annual Earnings	Percent Growth	Annual Openings
1. Industrial Production Managers	$75,580	0.8%	13,000
2. Nuclear Power Reactor Operators	$66,230	–0.5%	1,000
3. Power Distributors and Dispatchers	$59,160	0.0%	1,000
4. Auxiliary Equipment Operators, Power	$53,170	–0.4%	5,000
5. Power Generating Plant Operators, Except Auxiliary Equipment Operators	$53,170	–0.4%	5,000
6. Ship Engineers	$52,780	12.7%	1,000
7. First-Line Supervisors/Managers of Mechanics, Installers, and Repairers	$51,980	12.4%	33,000
8. Gas Distribution Plant Operators	$51,920	7.7%	2,000
9. Gas Processing Plant Operators	$51,920	7.7%	2,000
10. Gaugers	$51,060	–8.6%	6,000
11. Petroleum Pump System Operators	$51,060	–8.6%	6,000
12. Petroleum Refinery and Control Panel Operators	$51,060	–8.6%	6,000
13. Signal and Track Switch Repairers	$49,200	2.3%	1,000
14. Aircraft Body and Bonded Structure Repairers	$47,310	13.4%	11,000
15. Aircraft Engine Specialists	$47,310	13.4%	11,000
16. Airframe-and-Power-Plant Mechanics	$47,310	13.4%	11,000
17. Chemical Plant and System Operators	$46,710	–17.7%	8,000
18. Avionics Technicians	$46,630	9.1%	2,000

Jobs 8 and 9 share 2,000 job openings. Jobs 10, 11, and 12 share 6,000 job openings. Jobs 14, 15, and 16 share 11,000 job openings.

Best-Paying Jobs for People Interested in Retail and Wholesale Sales and Service

Job	Annual Earnings	Percent Growth	Annual Openings
1. Marketing Managers	$92,680	20.8%	23,000
2. Sales Managers	$87,580	19.7%	40,000
3. Purchasing Managers	$76,270	7.0%	8,000
4. Sales Engineers	$74,200	14.0%	8,000
5. Advertising and Promotions Managers	$68,860	20.3%	9,000
6. First-Line Supervisors/Managers of Non-Retail Sales Workers	$61,970	1.9%	38,000
7. Sales Representatives, Agricultural	$60,760	14.4%	47,000
8. Sales Representatives, Chemical and Pharmaceutical	$60,760	14.4%	47,000

(continued)

(continued)

Best-Paying Jobs for People Interested in Retail and Wholesale Sales and Service

Job	Annual Earnings	Percent Growth	Annual Openings
9. Sales Representatives, Electrical/Electronic	$60,760	14.4%	47,000
10. Sales Representatives, Instruments	$60,760	14.4%	47,000
11. Sales Representatives, Mechanical Equipment and Supplies	$60,760	14.4%	47,000
12. Sales Representatives, Medical	$60,760	14.4%	47,000
13. Real Estate Brokers	$57,190	7.8%	12,000
14. Purchasing Agents, Except Wholesale, Retail, and Farm Products	$49,030	8.1%	19,000
15. Funeral Directors	$47,630	6.7%	3,000
16. Sales Representatives, Wholesale and Manufacturing, Except Technical and Scientific Products	$47,380	12.9%	169,000

Jobs 7, 8, 9, 10, 11, and 12 share 47,000 job openings.

Best-Paying Jobs for People Interested in Scientific Research, Engineering, and Mathematics

Job	Annual Earnings	Percent Growth	Annual Openings
1. Astronomers	$104,670	10.4%	fewer than 500
2. Engineering Managers	$100,760	13.0%	15,000
3. Natural Sciences Managers	$93,090	13.6%	5,000
4. Physicists	$89,810	7.0%	1,000
5. Nuclear Engineers	$88,290	7.3%	1,000
6. Industrial-Organizational Psychologists	$84,690	20.4%	fewer than 500
7. Computer Hardware Engineers	$84,420	10.1%	5,000
8. Political Scientists	$84,100	7.3%	fewer than 500
9. Aerospace Engineers	$84,090	8.3%	6,000
10. Actuaries	$81,640	23.2%	3,000
11. Electronics Engineers, Except Computer	$78,030	9.7%	11,000
12. Chemical Engineers	$77,140	10.6%	3,000
13. Atmospheric and Space Scientists	$73,940	16.5%	1,000
14. Economists	$73,690	5.6%	1,000
15. Electrical Engineers	$73,510	11.8%	12,000
16. Marine Architects	$72,920	8.5%	fewer than 500

Best-Paying Jobs for People Interested in Scientific Research, Engineering, and Mathematics

Job	Annual Earnings	Percent Growth	Annual Openings
17. Marine Engineers	$72,920	8.5%	fewer than 500
18. Biomedical Engineers	$71,840	30.7%	1,000
19. Geologists	$71,640	8.3%	2,000
20. Materials Scientists	$71,450	8.0%	fewer than 500
21. Biochemists	$71,000	21.0%	1,000
22. Biophysicists	$71,000	21.0%	1,000
23. Materials Engineers	$69,660	12.2%	2,000
24. Mechanical Engineers	$67,590	11.1%	11,000
25. Industrial Engineers	$66,670	16.0%	13,000
26. Civil Engineers	$66,190	16.5%	19,000
27. Fire-Prevention and Protection Engineers	$65,210	13.4%	2,000
28. Industrial Safety and Health Engineers	$65,210	13.4%	2,000
29. Product Safety Engineers	$65,210	13.4%	2,000
30. Hydrologists	$63,820	31.6%	1,000
31. Geographers	$63,550	6.8%	fewer than 500
32. Statisticians	$62,450	4.6%	2,000
33. Medical Scientists, Except Epidemiologists	$61,730	34.1%	15,000
34. Nuclear Equipment Operation Technicians	$61,120	13.7%	1,000
35. Chemists	$57,890	7.3%	5,000
36. School Psychologists	$57,170	19.1%	10,000
37. Microbiologists	$56,870	17.2%	1,000
38. Sociologists	$52,760	4.7%	fewer than 500
39. Environmental Scientists and Specialists, Including Health	$52,630	17.1%	8,000
40. Aerospace Engineering and Operations Technicians	$52,450	8.5%	1,000
41. Epidemiologists	$52,170	26.2%	1,000
42. Cartographers and Photogrammetrists	$48,250	15.3%	1,000
43. Calibration and Instrumentation Technicians	$48,040	9.8%	18,000
44. Electrical Engineering Technicians	$48,040	9.8%	18,000
45. Electronics Engineering Technicians	$48,040	9.8%	18,000

Jobs 16 and 17 share fewer than 500 job openings. Jobs 21 and 22 share 1,000 job openings. Jobs 27, 28, and 29 share 2,000 job openings. Job 34 shares 1,000 job openings with another job not included in this list. Job 36 shares 10,000 job openings with two other jobs not included in this list. Jobs 43, 44, and 45 share 18,000 job openings.

Best-Paying Jobs for People Interested in Transportation, Distribution, and Logistics

Job	Annual Earnings	Percent Growth	Annual Openings
1. Airline Pilots, Copilots, and Flight Engineers	$138,170	17.2%	7,000
2. Storage and Distribution Managers	$69,120	12.7%	15,000
3. Transportation Managers	$69,120	12.7%	15,000
4. Commercial Pilots	$55,810	16.8%	2,000
5. Locomotive Engineers	$55,520	−2.5%	2,000
6. Railroad Conductors and Yardmasters	$54,040	20.3%	3,000
7. Postmasters and Mail Superintendents	$52,710	0.0%	2,000
8. Mates—Ship, Boat, and Barge	$50,940	4.8%	2,000
9. Pilots, Ship	$50,940	4.8%	2,000
10. Ship and Boat Captains	$50,940	4.8%	2,000
11. Railroad Yard Workers	$49,700	−38.5%	1,000
12. Train Crew Members	$49,700	−38.5%	1,000
13. Freight Inspectors	$49,490	11.4%	2,000
14. Public Transportation Inspectors	$49,490	11.4%	2,000
15. First-Line Supervisors/Managers of Transportation and Material-Moving Machine and Vehicle Operators	$47,530	15.3%	22,000
16. Subway and Streetcar Operators	$47,500	13.7%	1,000
17. Postal Service Mail Carriers	$46,330	0.0%	19,000

Jobs 2 and 3 share 15,000 job openings. Job 5 shares 2,000 job openings with two other jobs not included in this list. Jobs 8, 9, and 10 share 2,000 job openings. Jobs 11 and 12 share 1,000 job openings. Jobs 13 and 14 share 2,000 job openings with each other and with four other jobs not included in this list.

Best-Paying Jobs Lists Based on Personality Types

These lists organize the 250 best-paying jobs into groups matching six personality types. The personality types are Realistic, Investigative, Artistic, Social, Enterprising, and Conventional. This system was developed by John L. Holland and is used in the *Self Directed Search (SDS)* and other career assessment inventories and information systems.

If you have used one of these career inventories or systems, the lists will help you identify jobs that most closely match these personality types. Even if you have not used one of these systems, the concept of personality types and the jobs that are related to them can help you identify jobs that most closely match the type of person you are.

We've ranked the best-paying jobs within each personality type based on their earnings, following alphabetical order when earnings of jobs are equal. As in the section with job lists for education levels, there is only one list for each personality type. Note that each job is listed in the one personality type it most closely matches, even though it might also fit into others. (The only exception is Teachers, Postsecondary, which is included in several lists because the various postsecondary teaching occupations fall into several personality types. A footnote lists the specific postsecondary teaching occupations for each personality type.) Consider reviewing the jobs for more than one personality type so you don't overlook possible jobs that would interest you. Also, note that we did not have data to crosswalk 10 of the 250 best-paying jobs to their related personality type, so some of the best-paying jobs do not appear on the lists in this section.

Following are brief descriptions for each of the six personality types used in the lists. Select the two or three descriptions that most closely resemble you and then use the lists to identify jobs that best fit these personality types.

Descriptions of the Six Personality Types

- **Realistic:** These occupations frequently involve work activities that include practical, hands-on problems and solutions. They often deal with plants; animals; and real-world materials like wood, tools, and machinery. Many of the occupations require working outside and do not involve a lot of paperwork or working closely with others.

- **Investigative:** These occupations frequently involve working with ideas and require an extensive amount of thinking. These occupations can involve searching for facts and figuring out problems mentally.

- **Artistic:** These occupations frequently involve working with forms, designs, and patterns. They often require self-expression, and the work can be done without following a clear set of rules.

- **Social:** These occupations frequently involve working with, communicating with, and teaching people. These occupations often involve helping or providing service to others.

- **Enterprising:** These occupations frequently involve starting up and carrying out projects. These occupations can involve leading people and making many decisions. They sometimes require risk taking and often deal with business.

- **Conventional:** These occupations frequently involve following set procedures and routines. These occupations can include working with data and details more than with ideas. Usually there is a clear line of authority to follow.

Best-Paying Jobs for People with a Realistic Personality Type

Job	Annual Earnings	Percent Growth	Annual Openings
1. Airline Pilots, Copilots, and Flight Engineers	$138,170	17.2%	7,000
2. Petroleum Engineers	$93,000	–0.1%	1,000
3. Marine Architects	$72,920	8.5%	fewer than 500

(continued)

(continued)

Best-Paying Jobs for People with a Realistic Personality Type

Job	Annual Earnings	Percent Growth	Annual Openings
4. Marine Engineers	$72,920	8.5%	fewer than 500
5. Mechanical Engineers	$67,590	11.1%	11,000
6. Nuclear Power Reactor Operators	$66,230	–0.5%	1,000
7. Civil Engineers	$66,190	16.5%	19,000
8. Nuclear Equipment Operation Technicians	$61,120	13.7%	1,000
9. Nuclear Monitoring Technicians	$61,120	13.7%	1,000
10. Forest Fire Fighting and Prevention Supervisors	$60,840	21.1%	4,000
11. Municipal Fire Fighting and Prevention Supervisors	$60,840	21.1%	4,000
12. Elevator Installers and Repairers	$59,190	14.8%	3,000
13. Power Distributors and Dispatchers	$59,160	0.0%	1,000
14. Commercial Pilots	$55,810	16.8%	2,000
15. Locomotive Engineers	$55,520	–2.5%	2,000
16. Electrical and Electronics Repairers, Powerhouse, Substation, and Relay	$54,970	–0.4%	2,000
17. Railroad Conductors and Yardmasters	$54,040	20.3%	3,000
18. Technical Directors/Managers	$53,860	16.6%	11,000
19. Auxiliary Equipment Operators, Power	$53,170	–0.4%	5,000
20. Power Generating Plant Operators, Except Auxiliary Equipment Operators	$53,170	–0.4%	5,000
21. Ship Engineers	$52,780	12.7%	1,000
22. Gas Distribution Plant Operators	$51,920	7.7%	2,000
23. Gas Processing Plant Operators	$51,920	7.7%	2,000
24. Gaugers	$51,060	–8.6%	6,000
25. Petroleum Pump System Operators	$51,060	–8.6%	6,000
26. Petroleum Refinery and Control Panel Operators	$51,060	–8.6%	6,000
27. Mates—Ship, Boat, and Barge	$50,940	4.8%	2,000
28. Pilots, Ship	$50,940	4.8%	2,000
29. Central Office and PBX Installers and Repairers	$50,620	–4.9%	21,000
30. Communication Equipment Mechanics, Installers, and Repairers	$50,620	–4.9%	21,000
31. Frame Wirers, Central Office	$50,620	–4.9%	21,000
32. Station Installers and Repairers, Telephone	$50,620	–4.9%	21,000
33. Telecommunications Facility Examiners	$50,620	–4.9%	21,000
34. Electrical Power-Line Installers and Repairers	$50,150	2.5%	11,000
35. Railroad Yard Workers	$49,700	–38.5%	1,000
36. Train Crew Members	$49,700	–38.5%	1,000
37. Aviation Inspectors	$49,490	11.4%	2,000

Best-Paying Jobs for People with a Realistic Personality Type

Job	Annual Earnings	Percent Growth	Annual Openings
38. Motor Vehicle Inspectors	$49,490	11.4%	2,000
39. Railroad Inspectors	$49,490	11.4%	2,000
40. Pressure Vessel Inspectors	$49,360	11.6%	17,000
41. Signal and Track Switch Repairers	$49,200	2.3%	1,000
42. Pile-Driver Operators	$48,900	11.9%	fewer than 500
43. Foresters	$48,670	6.7%	1,000
44. Boilermakers	$48,050	8.7%	2,000
45. Calibration and Instrumentation Technicians	$48,040	9.8%	18,000
46. Electrical Engineering Technicians	$48,040	9.8%	18,000
47. Electronics Engineering Technicians	$48,040	9.8%	18,000
48. Subway and Streetcar Operators	$47,500	13.7%	1,000
49. Aircraft Body and Bonded Structure Repairers	$47,310	13.4%	11,000
50. Aircraft Engine Specialists	$47,310	13.4%	11,000
51. Airframe-and-Power-Plant Mechanics	$47,310	13.4%	11,000
52. Chemical Plant and System Operators	$46,710	−17.7%	8,000
53. Avionics Technicians	$46,630	9.1%	2,000

Jobs 3 and 4 share fewer than 500 job openings. Jobs 8 and 9 share 1,000 job openings. Jobs 10 and 11 share 4,000 job openings. Job 15 shares 2,000 job openings with two other jobs not included in this list. Job 18 shares 11,000 job openings with four other jobs not included in this list. Jobs 19 and 20 share 5,000 job openings. Jobs 22 and 23 share 2,000 job openings. Jobs 24, 25, and 26 share 6,000 job openings. Jobs 27 and 28 share 2,000 job openings with each other and with another job not included in this list. Jobs 29, 30, 31, 32, and 33 share 21,000 job openings. Jobs 35 and 36 share 1,000 job openings. Jobs 37, 38, and 39 share 2,000 job openings with each other and with three other jobs not included in this list. Job 40 shares 17,000 job openings with five other jobs not included in this list. Jobs 45, 46, and 47 share 18,000 job openings. Jobs 49, 50, and 51 share 11,000 job openings.

Best-Paying Jobs for People with an Investigative Personality Type

Job	Annual Earnings	Percent Growth	Annual Openings
1. Anesthesiologists	more than $145,600	24.0%	41,000
2. Internists, General	more than $145,600	24.0%	41,000
3. Obstetricians and Gynecologists	more than $145,600	24.0%	41,000
4. Oral and Maxillofacial Surgeons	more than $145,600	16.2%	fewer than 500
5. Orthodontists	more than $145,600	12.8%	1,000
6. Prosthodontists	more than $145,600	13.6%	fewer than 500
7. Psychiatrists	more than $145,600	24.0%	41,000
8. Surgeons	more than $145,600	24.0%	41,000

(continued)

Best-Paying Jobs for People with an Investigative Personality Type

Job	Annual Earnings	Percent Growth	Annual Openings
9. Family and General Practitioners	$140,400	24.0%	41,000
10. Pediatricians, General	$136,600	24.0%	41,000
11. Dentists, General	$125,300	13.5%	7,000
12. Astronomers	$104,670	10.4%	fewer than 500
13. Natural Sciences Managers	$93,090	13.6%	5,000
14. Pharmacists	$89,820	24.6%	16,000
15. Physicists	$89,810	7.0%	1,000
16. Nuclear Engineers	$88,290	7.3%	1,000
17. Optometrists	$88,040	19.7%	2,000
18. Industrial-Organizational Psychologists	$84,690	20.4%	fewer than 500
19. Computer Hardware Engineers	$84,420	10.1%	5,000
20. Political Scientists	$84,100	7.3%	fewer than 500
21. Aerospace Engineers	$84,090	8.3%	6,000
22. Computer Software Engineers, Systems Software	$82,120	43.0%	37,000
23. Electronics Engineers, Except Computer	$78,030	9.7%	11,000
24. Chemical Engineers	$77,140	10.6%	3,000
25. Computer Software Engineers, Applications	$77,090	48.4%	54,000
26. Atmospheric and Space Scientists	$73,940	16.5%	1,000
27. Economists	$73,690	5.6%	1,000
28. Electrical Engineers	$73,510	11.8%	12,000
29. Physician Assistants	$72,030	49.6%	10,000
30. Geologists	$71,640	8.3%	2,000
31. Materials Scientists	$71,450	8.0%	fewer than 500
32. Biochemists	$71,000	21.0%	1,000
33. Biophysicists	$71,000	21.0%	1,000
34. Materials Engineers	$69,660	12.2%	2,000
35. Veterinarians	$68,910	17.4%	8,000
36. Computer Systems Analysts	$68,300	31.4%	56,000
37. Chiropractors	$67,200	22.4%	4,000
38. Fire-Prevention and Protection Engineers	$65,210	13.4%	2,000
39. Industrial Safety and Health Engineers	$65,210	13.4%	2,000
40. Product Safety Engineers	$65,210	13.4%	2,000
41. Agricultural Engineers	$64,890	12.0%	fewer than 500
42. Financial Analysts	$63,860	17.3%	28,000
43. Hydrologists	$63,820	31.6%	1,000
44. Geographers	$63,550	6.8%	fewer than 500
45. Computer Programmers	$63,420	2.0%	28,000

Best-Paying Jobs for People with an Investigative Personality Type

Job	Annual Earnings	Percent Growth	Annual Openings
46. Database Administrators	$63,250	38.2%	9,000
47. Statisticians	$62,450	4.6%	2,000
48. Operations Research Analysts	$62,180	8.4%	7,000
49. Network Systems and Data Communications Analysts	$61,750	54.6%	43,000
50. Medical Scientists, Except Epidemiologists	$61,730	34.1%	15,000
51. Computer Security Specialists	$59,930	38.4%	34,000
52. Nuclear Medicine Technologists	$59,670	21.5%	2,000
53. Chemists	$57,890	7.3%	5,000
54. Market Research Analysts	$57,300	19.6%	20,000
55. Clinical Psychologists	$57,170	19.1%	10,000
56. School Psychologists	$57,170	19.1%	10,000
57. Microbiologists	$56,870	17.2%	1,000
58. Urban and Regional Planners	$55,170	15.2%	3,000
59. Teachers, Postsecondary	$55,100	32.2%	329,000
60. Plant Scientists	$54,530	13.9%	1,000
61. Soil Scientists	$54,530	13.9%	1,000
62. Range Managers	$53,350	6.3%	2,000
63. Soil Conservationists	$53,350	6.3%	2,000
64. Sociologists	$52,760	4.7%	fewer than 500
65. Environmental Scientists and Specialists, Including Health	$52,630	17.1%	8,000
66. Aerospace Engineering and Operations Technicians	$52,450	8.5%	1,000
67. Epidemiologists	$52,170	26.2%	1,000
68. Zoologists and Wildlife Biologists	$52,050	13.0%	1,000
69. Food Scientists and Technologists	$51,440	10.9%	1,000
70. Coroners	$49,360	11.6%	17,000
71. Environmental Compliance Inspectors	$49,360	11.6%	17,000
72. Compensation, Benefits, and Job Analysis Specialists	$48,870	20.4%	15,000
73. Medical and Clinical Laboratory Technologists	$47,710	20.5%	14,000

Jobs 1, 2, 3, 7, 8, 9, and 10 share 41,000 job openings. Jobs 32 and 33 share 1,000 job openings. Jobs 38, 39, and 40 share 2,000 job openings. Job 51 shares 34,000 job openings with another job not included in this list. Jobs 55 and 56 share 10,000 job openings with each other and with another job not included in this list. Jobs 60 and 61 share 34,000 job openings. Jobs 62 and 63 share 2,000 job openings with each other and with another job not included in this list. Jobs 70 and 71 share 17,000 job openings with each other and with three other jobs not included in this list.

Teachers, Postsecondary, is listed here because the following jobs are associated with the Investigative personality type: Agricultural Sciences Teachers, Postsecondary; Biological Science Teachers, Postsecondary; Chemistry Teachers, Postsecondary; Computer Science Teachers, Postsecondary; Engineering Teachers, Postsecondary; Forestry and Conservation Science Teachers, Postsecondary; Health Specialties Teachers, Postsecondary; Mathematical Science Teachers, Postsecondary; and Physics Teachers, Postsecondary.

Best-Paying Jobs for People with an Artistic Personality Type

Job	Annual Earnings	Percent Growth	Annual Openings
1. Advertising and Promotions Managers	$68,860	20.3%	9,000
2. Art Directors	$63,950	11.5%	10,000
3. Architects, Except Landscape and Naval	$62,850	17.3%	7,000
4. Fashion Designers	$60,860	8.4%	2,000
5. Technical Writers	$55,160	23.2%	5,000
6. Teachers, Postsecondary	$55,100	32.2%	329,000
7. Landscape Architects	$54,220	19.4%	1,000
8. Directors—Stage, Motion Pictures, Television, and Radio	$53,860	16.6%	11,000
9. Producers	$53,860	16.6%	11,000
10. Talent Directors	$53,860	16.6%	11,000
11. Commercial and Industrial Designers	$52,200	10.8%	7,000
12. Librarians	$47,400	4.9%	8,000
13. Film and Video Editors	$46,930	18.6%	3,000
14. Caption Writers	$46,420	17.7%	14,000
15. Copy Writers	$46,420	17.7%	14,000
16. Creative Writers	$46,420	17.7%	14,000
17. Poets and Lyricists	$46,420	17.7%	14,000

Jobs 8, 9, and 10 share 11,000 job openings with each other and with two other jobs not included in this list. Jobs 14, 15, 16, and 17 share 14,000 job openings.

Teachers, Postsecondary, is listed here because the following jobs are associated with the Artistic personality type: Art, Drama, and Music Teachers, Postsecondary; English Language and Literature Teachers, Postsecondary; and Foreign Language and Literature Teachers, Postsecondary.

Best-Paying Jobs for People with a Social Personality Type

Job	Annual Earnings	Percent Growth	Annual Openings
1. Podiatrists	$100,550	16.2%	1,000
2. Education Administrators, Elementary and Secondary School	$75,400	10.4%	27,000
3. Personal Financial Advisors	$63,500	25.9%	17,000
4. Physical Therapists	$63,080	36.7%	13,000
5. Radiation Therapists	$62,340	26.3%	1,000
6. Dental Hygienists	$60,890	43.3%	17,000
7. Counseling Psychologists	$57,170	19.1%	10,000
8. Occupational Therapists	$56,860	33.6%	7,000
9. Teachers, Postsecondary	$55,100	32.2%	329,000
10. Speech-Language Pathologists	$54,880	14.6%	5,000

Best-Paying Jobs for People with a Social Personality Type

Job	Annual Earnings	Percent Growth	Annual Openings
11. Registered Nurses	$54,670	29.4%	229,000
12. Orthotists and Prosthetists	$53,760	18.0%	fewer than 500
13. Occupational Health and Safety Specialists	$53,710	12.4%	3,000
14. Audiologists	$53,490	9.1%	fewer than 500
15. Park Naturalists	$53,350	6.3%	2,000
16. Instructional Coordinators	$50,430	27.5%	15,000
17. Social and Community Service Managers	$49,500	25.5%	17,000
18. Equal Opportunity Representatives and Officers	$49,360	11.6%	17,000
19. Vocational Education Teachers, Secondary School	$47,090	9.1%	10,000
20. Special Education Teachers, Secondary School	$46,820	17.9%	11,000
21. Educational, Vocational, and School Counselors	$46,440	14.8%	32,000

Job 7 shares 10,000 job openings with two other jobs not included in this list. Job 15 shares 2,000 job openings with two other jobs not included in this list. Job 18 shares 17,000 job openings with five other jobs not included in this list.

Teachers, Postsecondary, is listed here because the following jobs are associated with the Social personality type: Anthropology and Archeology Teachers, Postsecondary; Area, Ethnic, and Cultural Studies Teachers, Postsecondary; Economics Teachers, Postsecondary; History Teachers, Postsecondary; Nursing Instructors and Teachers, Postsecondary; Political Science Teachers, Postsecondary; Psychology Teachers, Postsecondary; and Sociology Teachers, Postsecondary.

Best-Paying Jobs for People with an Enterprising Personality Type

Job	Annual Earnings	Percent Growth	Annual Openings
1. Government Service Executives	$142,440	14.9%	38,000
2. Private Sector Executives	$142,440	14.9%	38,000
3. Engineering Managers	$100,760	13.0%	15,000
4. Lawyers	$98,930	15.0%	40,000
5. Judges, Magistrate Judges, and Magistrates	$97,570	6.9%	1,000
6. Computer and Information Systems Managers	$96,520	25.9%	25,000
7. Marketing Managers	$92,680	20.8%	23,000
8. Sales Managers	$87,580	19.7%	40,000
9. Financial Managers, Branch or Department	$86,280	14.8%	63,000
10. Treasurers, Controllers, and Chief Financial Officers	$86,280	14.8%	63,000
11. Purchasing Managers	$76,270	7.0%	8,000
12. Industrial Production Managers	$75,580	0.8%	13,000
13. Sales Engineers	$74,200	14.0%	8,000
14. Training and Development Managers	$74,180	25.9%	3,000

(continued)

(continued)

Best-Paying Jobs for People with an Enterprising Personality Type

Job	Annual Earnings	Percent Growth	Annual Openings
15. Construction Managers	$72,260	10.4%	28,000
16. Administrative Law Judges, Adjudicators, and Hearing Officers	$70,680	10.1%	1,000
17. Education Administrators, Postsecondary	$70,350	21.3%	18,000
18. Medical and Health Services Managers	$69,700	22.8%	33,000
19. Compensation and Benefits Managers	$69,130	21.5%	4,000
20. Storage and Distribution Managers	$69,120	12.7%	15,000
21. Transportation Managers	$69,120	12.7%	15,000
22. Sales Agents, Financial Services	$67,130	11.5%	37,000
23. Sales Agents, Securities and Commodities	$67,130	11.5%	37,000
24. Industrial Engineers	$66,670	16.0%	13,000
25. Management Analysts	$66,380	20.1%	82,000
26. First-Line Supervisors/Managers of Police and Detectives	$65,570	15.5%	9,000
27. Administrative Services Managers	$64,020	16.9%	25,000
28. Financial Examiners	$63,090	9.5%	3,000
29. First-Line Supervisors/Managers of Non-Retail Sales Workers	$61,970	1.9%	38,000
30. Sales Representatives, Agricultural	$60,760	14.4%	47,000
31. Sales Representatives, Chemical and Pharmaceutical	$60,760	14.4%	47,000
32. Sales Representatives, Electrical/Electronic	$60,760	14.4%	47,000
33. Sales Representatives, Instruments	$60,760	14.4%	47,000
34. Sales Representatives, Mechanical Equipment and Supplies	$60,760	14.4%	47,000
35. Sales Representatives, Medical	$60,760	14.4%	47,000
36. Gaming Managers	$59,940	22.6%	1,000
37. Child Support, Missing Persons, and Unemployment Insurance Fraud Investigators	$55,790	16.3%	9,000
38. Criminal Investigators and Special Agents	$55,790	16.3%	9,000
39. Police Detectives	$55,790	16.3%	9,000
40. Arbitrators, Mediators, and Conciliators	$54,360	15.5%	fewer than 500
41. Program Directors	$53,860	16.6%	11,000
42. Agents and Business Managers of Artists, Performers, and Athletes	$53,800	11.8%	2,000
43. Postmasters and Mail Superintendents	$52,710	0.0%	2,000
44. First-Line Supervisors/Managers of Mechanics, Installers, and Repairers	$51,980	12.4%	33,000
45. First-Line Supervisors and Manager/Supervisors—Construction Trades Workers	$51,970	10.9%	57,000
46. First-Line Supervisors and Manager/Supervisors—Extractive Workers	$51,970	10.9%	57,000

Best-Paying Jobs for People with an Enterprising Personality Type

Job	Annual Earnings	Percent Growth	Annual Openings
47. Agricultural Crop Farm Managers	$51,160	4.0%	20,000
48. Fish Hatchery Managers	$51,160	4.0%	20,000
49. Nursery and Greenhouse Managers	$51,160	4.0%	20,000
50. Ship and Boat Captains	$50,940	4.8%	2,000
51. Public Transportation Inspectors	$49,490	11.4%	2,000
52. Loan Officers	$49,440	8.3%	38,000
53. Government Property Inspectors and Investigators	$49,360	11.6%	17,000
54. Purchasing Agents, Except Wholesale, Retail, and Farm Products	$49,030	8.1%	19,000
55. Transit and Railroad Police	$48,850	9.2%	fewer than 500
56. Funeral Directors	$47,630	6.7%	3,000
57. First-Line Supervisors/Managers of Transportation and Material-Moving Machine and Vehicle Operators	$47,530	15.3%	22,000
58. Sales Representatives, Wholesale and Manufacturing, Except Technical and Scientific Products	$47,380	12.9%	169,000
59. Flight Attendants	$46,680	16.3%	7,000
60. Purchasing Agents and Buyers, Farm Products	$46,680	7.0%	2,000

Jobs 1 and 2 share 38,000 job openings with each other and with another job not included in this list. Jobs 20 and 21 share 15,000 job openings. Jobs 22 and 23 share 37,000 job openings. Jobs 30, 31, 32, 33, 34, and 35 share 47,000 job openings. Jobs 37, 38, and 39 share 9,000 job openings with each other and with two other jobs not included in this list. Job 41 shares 11,000 job openings with four other jobs not included in this list. Jobs 45 and 46 share 57,000 job openings. Jobs 47, 48, and 49 share 20,000 job openings. Job 50 shares 2,000 job openings with two other jobs not included in this list. Job 51 shares 17,000 job openings with five other jobs not included in this list.

Best-Paying Jobs for People with a Conventional Personality Type

Job	Annual Earnings	Percent Growth	Annual Openings
1. Air Traffic Controllers	$107,590	14.3%	2,000
2. Actuaries	$81,640	23.2%	3,000
3. Budget Analysts	$58,910	13.5%	6,000
4. Immigration and Customs Inspectors	$55,790	16.3%	9,000
5. Police Identification and Records Officers	$55,790	16.3%	9,000
6. Accountants	$52,210	22.4%	157,000
7. Auditors	$52,210	22.4%	157,000
8. Cost Estimators	$52,020	18.2%	15,000
9. Insurance Underwriters	$51,270	8.0%	13,000
10. Credit Analysts	$50,370	3.6%	3,000

(continued)

(continued)

Best-Paying Jobs for People with a Conventional Personality Type

Job	Annual Earnings	Percent Growth	Annual Openings
11. Freight Inspectors	$49,490	11.4%	2,000
12. Marine Cargo Inspectors	$49,490	11.4%	2,000
13. Licensing Examiners and Inspectors	$49,360	11.6%	17,000
14. Postal Service Clerks	$48,310	0.0%	4,000
15. Cartographers and Photogrammetrists	$48,250	15.3%	1,000
16. Insurance Appraisers, Auto Damage	$48,090	16.6%	2,000
17. Postal Service Mail Carriers	$46,330	0.0%	19,000

Jobs 4 and 5 share 9,000 job openings with three other jobs not included in this list. Jobs 6 and 7 share 157,000 job openings. Jobs 11 and 12 share 2,000 job openings with each other and with four other jobs not included in this list. Job 13 shares 17,000 job openings with five other jobs not included in this list.

PART II

Descriptions of the Best-Paying Jobs

This part provides descriptions for all the jobs included in one or more of the lists in Part I. The Introduction gives more details on how to use and interpret the job descriptions, but here is some additional information:

- Job descriptions are arranged in alphabetical order by job title. This approach allows you to find a description quickly if you know its correct title from one of the lists in Part I.

- If you are using this section to browse for interesting options, we suggest you begin with the Table of Contents. Part I features many interesting lists that will help you identify job titles to explore in more detail. If you have not browsed the lists in Part I, consider spending some time there. The lists are interesting and will help you identify job titles you can find described in the material that follows. The job titles in Part II are also listed in the Table of Contents.

- Each description lists the most important skills required by the job. If the name of any skill is not meaningful to you, turn to the appendix for a complete definition. The appendix also discusses which skills are most closely associated with high-paying jobs.

- We include descriptions for the many specific jobs that we included under the single job title of Postsecondary Teachers in the lists in Part I. These more-specific job titles include Agricultural Sciences Teachers, Postsecondary; Anthropology and Archeology Teachers, Postsecondary; Architecture Teachers, Postsecondary; Area, Ethnic, and Cultural Studies Teachers, Postsecondary; Art, Drama, and Music Teachers, Postsecondary; Atmospheric, Earth, Marine, and Space Sciences Teachers, Postsecondary; Biological Science Teachers, Postsecondary; Business Teachers, Postsecondary; Chemistry Teachers, Postsecondary; Communications Teachers, Postsecondary; Computer Science Teachers, Postsecondary; Criminal Justice and Law Enforcement Teachers, Postsecondary; Economics Teachers, Postsecondary; Education Teachers, Postsecondary; Engineering Teachers, Postsecondary; English Language and Literature Teachers, Postsecondary; Environmental Science Teachers, Postsecondary; Foreign Language and Literature Teachers, Postsecondary; Forestry and Conservation Science Teachers, Postsecondary; Geography Teachers, Postsecondary; Graduate Teaching Assistants; Health Specialties Teachers, Postsecondary; History Teachers,

Postsecondary; Home Economics Teachers, Postsecondary; Law Teachers, Postsecondary; Library Science Teachers, Postsecondary; Mathematical Science Teachers, Postsecondary; Nursing Instructors and Teachers, Postsecondary; Philosophy and Religion Teachers, Postsecondary; Physics Teachers, Postsecondary; Political Science Teachers, Postsecondary; Psychology Teachers, Postsecondary; Recreation and Fitness Studies Teachers, Postsecondary; Social Work Teachers, Postsecondary; Sociology Teachers, Postsecondary; and Vocational Education Teachers, Postsecondary.

Accountants

- Annual Earnings: $52,210
- Growth: 22.4%
- Annual Job Openings: 157,000
- Self-Employed: 10.9%
- Part-Time: 10.3%
- Education/Training Required: Bachelor's degree

The job openings listed here are shared with Auditors.

Industries in Which Income Is Highest

Industry	Average Annual Wage	Number Employed
Securities, Commodity Contracts, and Other Financial Investments and Related Activities	$58,790	20,390
Clothing and Clothing Accessories Stores	$57,590	2,840
Computer and Electronic Product Manufacturing	$56,690	13,950
Publishing Industries (Except Internet)	$56,580	9,580
Utilities	$56,140	6,890

Metropolitan Areas Where Income Is Highest

Metropolitan Area	Average Annual Wage	Number Employed
Bridgeport–Stamford–Norwalk, CT	$65,720	6,930
San Jose–Sunnyvale–Santa Clara, CA	$65,050	8,590
New York–Northern New Jersey–Long Island, NY–NJ–PA	$65,050	92,350
Danbury, CT	$64,550	830
Bremerton–Silverdale, WA	$63,970	300

Analyze financial information and prepare financial reports to determine or maintain record of assets, liabilities, profit and loss, tax liability, or other financial activities within an organization. Prepare, examine, and analyze accounting records, financial statements, and other financial reports to assess accuracy, completeness, and conformance to reporting and procedural standards. Compute taxes owed and prepare tax returns, ensuring compliance with payment, reporting, and other tax requirements.

Analyze business operations, trends, costs, revenues, financial commitments, and obligations to project future revenues and expenses or to provide advice. Report to management regarding the finances of establishment. Establish tables of accounts and assign entries to proper accounts. Develop, maintain, and analyze budgets, preparing periodic reports that compare budgeted costs to actual costs. Develop, implement, modify, and document recordkeeping and accounting systems, making use of current computer technology. Prepare forms and manuals for accounting and bookkeeping personnel and direct their work activities. Survey operations to ascertain accounting needs and to recommend, develop, and maintain solutions to business and financial problems. Work as Internal Revenue Service agents. Advise management about issues such as resource utilization, tax strategies, and the assumptions underlying budget forecasts. Provide internal and external auditing services for businesses and individuals. Advise clients in areas such as compensation, employee health care benefits, the design of accounting and data processing systems, and long-range tax and estate plans. Investigate bankruptcies and other complex financial transactions and prepare reports summarizing the findings. Represent clients before taxing authorities and provide support during litigation involving financial issues. Appraise, evaluate, and inventory real property and equipment, recording information such as the property's description, value, and location. Maintain and examine the records of government agencies. **SKILLS**—Management of Financial Resources; Systems Analysis; Systems Evaluation; Operations Analysis; Judgment and Decision Making; Time Management; Programming; Monitoring.

GOE—Interest Area: 04. Business and Administration. **Work Group:** 04.05. Accounting, Auditing, and Analytical Support. **PERSONALITY TYPE:** Conventional. Conventional occupations frequently involve following set procedures and routines. These occupations can include working with data and details more than with ideas. Usually there is a clear line of authority to follow.

EDUCATION/TRAINING PROGRAMS—Accounting; Accounting and Business/Management; Accounting and Computer Science; Accounting and Finance. **RELATED KNOWLEDGE/COURSES**—**Economics and Accounting:** Knowledge of economic and accounting principles and practices, the financial markets, banking, and the analysis and reporting of financial data. **Clerical Practices:** Knowledge of administrative and clerical procedures and systems such as word processing, managing files and records, stenography and transcription, designing forms, and other office procedures and terminology. **Mathematics:** Knowledge of arithmetic, algebra, geometry, calculus, and statistics and their applications. **Law and Government:** Knowledge of laws, legal codes, court procedures, precedents, government regulations, executive orders, agency rules, and the democratic political process. **Customer and Personal Service:** Knowledge of principles and processes for providing customer and personal services. This includes customer needs assessment, meeting quality standards for services, and evaluation of customer satisfaction. **Computers and Electronics:** Knowledge of circuit boards, processors, chips, electronic equipment, and computer hardware and software, including applications and programming.

Actuaries

◎ Annual Earnings: $81,640
◎ Growth: 23.2%
◎ Annual Job Openings: 3,000
◎ Self-Employed: 0.0%
◎ Part-Time: 3.7%
◎ Education/Training Required: Work experience plus degree

Industries in Which Income Is Highest

Industry	Average Annual Wage	Number Employed
Professional, Scientific, and Technical Services	$94,080	3,710
Insurance Carriers and Related Activities	$80,900	9,220
Management of Companies and Enterprises	$70,380	1,230

Metropolitan Areas Where Income Is Highest

Metropolitan Area	Average Annual Wage	Number Employed
Austin–Round Rock, TX	$105,160	150
St. Louis, MO–IL	$100,650	240
New York–Northern New Jersey–Long Island, NY–NJ–PA	$98,870	1,640
Dallas–Fort Worth–Arlington, TX	$96,630	560
Milwaukee–Waukesha–West Allis, WI	$93,200	220

Analyze statistical data, such as mortality, accident, sickness, disability, and retirement rates, and construct probability tables to forecast risk and liability for payment of future benefits. May ascertain premium rates required and cash reserves necessary to ensure payment of future benefits. Ascertain premium rates required and cash reserves and liabilities necessary to ensure payment of future benefits. Analyze statistical information to estimate mortality, accident, sickness, disability, and retirement rates. Design, review, and help administer insurance, annuity, and pension plans, determining financial soundness and calculating premiums. Collaborate with programmers, underwriters, accounts, claims experts, and senior management to help companies develop plans for new lines of business or improving existing business. Determine or help determine company policy and explain complex technical matters to company executives, government officials, shareholders, policyholders, and/or the public. Testify before public agencies on proposed legislation affecting businesses. Provide advice to clients on a contract basis, working as a consultant. Testify in court as expert witness or to provide legal evidence on matters such as the value of potential lifetime earnings of a person who is disabled or killed in an accident. Construct probability tables for events such as fires, natural disasters, and unemployment, based on analysis of statistical data and other pertinent information. Determine policy contract provisions for each type of insurance. **SKILLS**—Programming; Mathematics; Active Learning; Complex Problem Solving; Operations Analysis; Critical Thinking; Coordination; Monitoring.

GOE—Interest Area: 15. Scientific Research, Engineering, and Mathematics. **Work Group:** 15.06. Mathematics and Data Analysis. **PERSONALITY TYPE:** Conventional. Conventional occupations frequently involve following set procedures and routines.

These occupations can include working with data and details more than with ideas. Usually there is a clear line of authority to follow.

EDUCATION/TRAINING PROGRAM—Actuarial Science. **RELATED KNOWLEDGE/COURSES**— **Mathematics:** Knowledge of arithmetic, algebra, geometry, calculus, and statistics and their applications. **Economics and Accounting:** Knowledge of economic and accounting principles and practices, the financial markets, banking, and the analysis and reporting of financial data. **Sales and Marketing:** Knowledge of principles and methods for showing, promoting, and selling products or services. This includes marketing strategy and tactics, product demonstration, sales techniques, and sales control systems. **Computers and Electronics:** Knowledge of circuit boards, processors, chips, electronic equipment, and computer hardware and software, including applications and programming. **Personnel and Human Resources:** Knowledge of principles and procedures for personnel recruitment, selection, training, compensation and benefits, labor relations and negotiation, and personnel information systems. **Administration and Management:** Knowledge of business and management principles involved in strategic planning, resource allocation, human resources modeling, leadership technique, production methods, and coordination of people and resources.

Administrative Law Judges, Adjudicators, and Hearing Officers

- Annual Earnings: $70,680
- Growth: 10.1%
- Annual Job Openings: 1,000
- Self-Employed: 0.0%
- Part-Time: No data available
- Education/Training Required: Work experience plus degree

Industries in Which Income Is Highest

Industry	Average Annual Wage	Number Employed
Federal, State, and Local Government	$70,670	15,340

Metropolitan Areas Where Income Is Highest

Metropolitan Area	Average Annual Wage	Number Employed
Washington–Arlington–Alexandria, DC–VA–MD–WV	$116,430	770
Sacramento–Arden–Arcade–Roseville, CA	$104,140	230
San Diego–Carlsbad–San Marcos, CA	$103,940	150
Riverside–San Bernardino–Ontario, CA	$103,470	50
San Francisco–Oakland–Fremont, CA	$103,380	280

Conduct hearings to decide or recommend decisions on claims concerning government programs or other government-related matters and prepare decisions. Determine penalties or the existence and the amount of liability or recommend the acceptance or rejection of claims or compromise settlements. Prepare written opinions and decisions. Review and evaluate data on documents such as claim applications, birth or death certificates, and physician or employer records. Research and analyze laws, regulations, policies, and precedent decisions to prepare for hearings and to determine conclusions. Confer with individuals or organizations involved in cases in order to obtain relevant information. Recommend the acceptance or rejection of claims or compromise settlements according to laws, regulations, policies, and precedent decisions. Explain to claimants how they can appeal rulings that go against them. Monitor and direct the activities of trials and hearings to ensure that they are conducted fairly and that courts administer justice while safeguarding the legal rights of all involved parties. Authorize payment of valid claims and determine method of payment. Conduct hearings to review and decide claims regarding issues such as social program eligibility, environmental protection, and enforcement of health and safety regulations. Rule on exceptions, motions, and admissibility of evidence. Determine existence and amount of liability according to current laws, administrative and judicial precedents, and available evidence. Issue subpoenas and administer oaths in preparation for formal hearings. **SKILLS—** Social Perceptiveness; Time Management; Active Listening; Judgment and Decision Making; Critical Thinking; Reading Comprehension; Writing; Active Learning.

GOE—Interest Area: 12. Law and Public Safety. **Work Group:** 12.02. Legal Practice and Justice Administration. **PERSONALITY TYPE:** Enterprising. Enterprising occupations frequently involve starting up and carrying out projects. These occupations can involve leading people and making many decisions. They sometimes require risk taking and often deal with business.

EDUCATION/TRAINING PROGRAMS—Law (LL.B., J.D.); Law, Legal Services, and Legal Studies, Other; Legal Studies, General. **RELATED KNOWLEDGE/COURSES—Law and Government:** Knowledge of laws, legal codes, court procedures, precedents, government regulations, executive orders, agency rules, and the democratic political process. **Psychology:** Knowledge of human behavior and performance; individual differences in ability, personality, and interests; learning and motivation; psychological research methods; and the assessment and treatment of behavioral and affective disorders. **Customer and Personal Service:** Knowledge of principles and processes for providing customer and personal services. This includes customer needs assessment, meeting quality standards for services, and evaluation of customer satisfaction. **Medicine and Dentistry:** Knowledge of the information and techniques needed to diagnose and treat human injuries, diseases, and deformities. This includes symptoms, treatment alternatives, drug properties and interactions, and preventive health-care measures. **Therapy and Counseling:** Knowledge of principles, methods, and procedures for diagnosis, treatment, and rehabilitation of physical and mental dysfunctions and for career counseling and guidance. **Computers and Electronics:** Knowledge of circuit boards, processors, chips, electronic equipment, and computer hardware and software, including applications and programming.

Administrative Services Managers

- Annual Earnings: $64,020
- Growth: 16.9%
- Annual Job Openings: 25,000
- Self-Employed: 0.2%
- Part-Time: 5.7%
- Education/Training Required: Work experience plus degree

Industries in Which Income Is Highest

Industry	Average Annual Wage	Number Employed
Securities, Commodity Contracts, and Other Financial Investments and Related Activities	$84,190	4,150
Transportation Equipment Manufacturing	$83,210	1,060
Telecommunications	$82,560	2,010
Computer and Electronic Product Manufacturing	$80,670	2,980
Utilities	$78,120	1,860

Metropolitan Areas Where Income Is Highest

Metropolitan Area	Average Annual Wage	Number Employed
Kennewick–Richland–Pasco, WA	$88,360	130
Danbury, CT	$88,260	150
Yakima, WA	$87,510	110
Trenton–Ewing, NJ	$85,670	740
New York–Northern New Jersey–Long Island, NY–NJ–PA	$85,440	19,190

Plan, direct, or coordinate supportive services of an organization, such as recordkeeping, mail distribution, telephone operator/receptionist, and other office support services. May oversee facilities planning and maintenance and custodial operations. Monitor the facility to ensure that it remains safe, secure, and well-maintained. Direct or coordinate the supportive services department of a business, agency, or organization. Set goals and deadlines for the department. Prepare and review operational reports and schedules to ensure accuracy and efficiency. Analyze internal processes and recommend and implement procedural or policy changes to improve operations, such as supply changes or the disposal of records. Acquire, distribute, and store supplies. Plan, administer and control budgets for contracts, equipment, and supplies. Oversee construction and renovation projects to improve efficiency and to ensure that facilities meet environmental, health, and security standards and comply with government regulations. Hire and terminate clerical and administrative personnel. Oversee the maintenance and repair of machinery, equipment, and electrical and mechanical systems. Manage leasing of facility space. **SKILLS**—Management of Personnel Resources; Management of Financial Resources; Service Orientation; Coordination; Programming; Monitoring; Social Perceptiveness; Speaking.

GOE—Interest Area: 04. Business and Administration. **Work Group:** 04.02. Managerial Work in Business Detail. **PERSONALITY TYPE:** Enterprising. Enterprising occupations frequently involve starting up and carrying out projects. These occupations can involve leading people and making many decisions. They sometimes require risk taking and often deal with business.

EDUCATION/TRAINING PROGRAMS— Business Administration/Management; Business/ Commerce, General; Medical Staff Services Technology/Technician; Medical/Health Management and Clinical Assistant/Specialist; Public Administration; Purchasing, Procurement/Acquisitions, and Contracts Management; Transportation/Transportation Management. **RELATED KNOWLEDGE/COURSES**— **Personnel and Human Resources:** Knowledge of principles and procedures for personnel recruitment, selection, training, compensation and benefits, labor relations and negotiation, and personnel information systems. **Clerical Practices:** Knowledge of administrative and clerical procedures and systems such as word processing, managing files and records, stenography and transcription, designing forms, and other office procedures and terminology. **Economics and Accounting:** Knowledge of economic and accounting principles and practices, the financial markets, banking, and the analysis and reporting of financial data. **Customer and Personal Service:** Knowledge of principles and processes for providing customer and personal services. This includes customer needs assessment, meeting quality standards for services, and

evaluation of customer satisfaction. **Administration and Management:** Knowledge of business and management principles involved in strategic planning, resource allocation, human resources modeling, leadership technique, production methods, and coordination of people and resources. **Public Safety and Security:** Knowledge of relevant equipment, policies, procedures, and strategies to promote effective local, state, or national security operations for the protection of people, data, property, and institutions.

Advertising and Promotions Managers

- ◎ Annual Earnings: $68,860
- ◎ Growth: 20.3%
- ◎ Annual Job Openings: 9,000
- ◎ Self-Employed: 6.7%
- ◎ Part-Time: 5.0%
- ◎ Education/Training Required: Work experience plus degree

Industries in Which Income Is Highest

Industry	Average Annual Wage	Number Employed
Professional, Scientific, and Technical Services	$90,380	8,890
Management of Companies and Enterprises	$78,640	3,570
Publishing Industries (Except Internet)	$71,050	3,550
Merchant Wholesalers, Nondurable Goods	$69,030	2,720
Broadcasting (Except Internet)	$66,290	2,270

Metropolitan Areas Where Income Is Highest

Metropolitan Area	Average Annual Wage	Number Employed
Trenton–Ewing, NJ	More than $146,500	50
New York–Northern New Jersey–Long Island, NY–NJ–PA	$111,780	4,820
Oxnard–Thousand Oaks–Ventura, CA	$99,130	170
Lansing–East Lansing, MI	$99,100	70
Detroit–Warren–Livonia, MI	$97,440	510

Plan and direct advertising policies and programs or produce collateral materials, such as posters, contests, coupons, or giveaways, to create extra interest in the purchase of a product or service for a department or an entire organization or on an account basis. Prepare budgets and submit estimates for program costs as part of campaign plan development. Plan and prepare advertising and promotional material to increase sales of products or services, working with customers, company officials, sales departments, and advertising agencies. Assist with annual budget development. Inspect layouts and advertising copy and edit scripts, audiotapes and videotapes, and other promotional material for adherence to specifications. Coordinate activities of departments such as sales, graphic arts, media, finance, and research. Prepare and negotiate advertising and sales contracts. Identify and develop contacts for promotional campaigns and industry programs that meet identified buyer targets such as dealers, distributors, or consumers. Gather and organize information to plan advertising campaigns. Confer with department heads and/or staff to discuss topics such as contracts, selection of advertising media, or product to be advertised. Confer with clients to provide marketing or technical advice. Monitor and analyze sales promotion results to determine cost-effectiveness of promotion campaigns. Read trade journals and professional literature to stay informed on trends, innovations, and changes that affect media planning. Formulate plans to extend business with established accounts and to transact business as agent for advertising accounts. Provide presentation and product demonstration support during the introduction of new products and services to field staff and customers. Direct, motivate, and monitor the mobilization of a campaign team to advance campaign goals. Plan and execute advertising policies and strategies for organizations. Track program budgets and expenses and campaign response rates to evaluate each campaign based on program objectives and industry norms. Assemble and communicate with a strong, diverse coalition of organizations and/or public figures, securing their cooperation, support and action, to further campaign goals. Train and direct workers engaged in developing and producing advertisements. Coordinate with the media to disseminate advertising. **SKILLS**—Management of Financial Resources; Service Orientation; Persuasion; Time Management; Negotiation; Coordination; Management of Personnel Resources; Monitoring.

GOE—Interest Area: 14. Retail and Wholesale Sales and Service. **Work Group:** 14.01. Managerial Work in Retail/Wholesale Sales and Service. **PERSONALITY TYPE:** Artistic. Artistic occupations frequently involve working with forms, designs, and patterns. They often require self-expression, and the work can be done without following a clear set of rules.

EDUCATION/TRAINING PROGRAMS—Advertising; Marketing/Marketing Management, General; Public Relations/Image Management. **RELATED KNOWLEDGE/COURSES—Sales and Marketing:** Knowledge of principles and methods for showing, promoting, and selling products or services. This includes marketing strategy and tactics, product demonstration, sales techniques, and sales control systems. **Design:** Knowledge of design techniques, tools, and principles involved in production of precision technical plans, blueprints, drawings, and models. **Customer and Personal Service:** Knowledge of principles and processes for providing customer and personal services. This includes customer needs assessment, meeting quality standards for services, and evaluation of customer satisfaction. **Fine Arts:** Knowledge of the theory and techniques required to compose, produce, and perform works of music, dance, visual arts, drama, and sculpture. **Production and Processing:** Knowledge of raw materials, production processes, quality control, costs, and other techniques for maximizing the effective manufacture and distribution of goods. **Communications and Media:** Knowledge of media production, communication, and dissemination techniques and methods. This includes alternative ways to inform and entertain via written, oral, and visual media.

Aerospace Engineering and Operations Technicians

- Annual Earnings: $52,450
- Growth: 8.5%
- Annual Job Openings: 1,000
- Self-Employed: 0.5%
- Part-Time: 6.8%
- Education/Training Required: Associate degree

Industries in Which Income Is Highest

Industry	Average Annual Wage	Number Employed
Air Transportation	$65,450	380
Professional, Scientific, and Technical Services	$58,970	1,890
Transportation Equipment Manufacturing	$51,200	5,370
Management of Companies and Enterprises	$50,000	60
Computer and Electronic Product Manufacturing	$48,680	890

Metropolitan Areas Where Income Is Highest

Metropolitan Area	Average Annual Wage	Number Employed
Seattle–Tacoma–Bellevue, WA	$74,570	330
Huntsville, AL	$67,550	190
Minneapolis–St. Paul–Bloomington, MN–WI	$65,530	130
Washington–Arlington–Alexandria, DC–VA–MD–WV	$60,780	130
Tulsa, OK	$55,990	230

Operate, install, calibrate, and maintain integrated computer/communications systems consoles; simulators; and other data acquisition, test, and measurement instruments and equipment to launch, track, position, and evaluate air and space vehicles. May record and interpret test data. Adjust, repair, or replace faulty components of test setups and equipment. Construct and maintain test facilities for aircraft parts and systems, according to specifications. Fabricate and install parts and systems to be tested in test equipment, using hand tools, power tools, and test instruments. Identify required data, data acquisition plans, and test parameters, setting up equipment to conform to these specifications. Inspect, diagnose, maintain, and operate test setups and equipment to detect malfunctions. Operate and calibrate computer systems and devices to comply with test requirements and to perform data acquisition and analysis. Test aircraft systems under simulated operational conditions, performing systems readiness tests and pre- and post-operational checkouts, to establish design or fabrication parameters. Confer with engineering personnel regarding details and implications of test procedures and results. Exchange cooling system components in various vehicles. Finish vehicle instrumentation and deinstrumentation. Record and interpret test data on parts, assemblies, and mechanisms. **SKILLS—** Science; Programming; Equipment Maintenance; Installation; Mathematics; Operation Monitoring; Repairing; Quality Control Analysis.

GOE—Interest Area: 15. Scientific Research, Engineering, and Mathematics. **Work Group:** 15.09. Engineering Technology. **PERSONALITY TYPE:** Investigative. Investigative occupations frequently involve working with ideas and require an extensive amount of thinking. These occupations can involve searching for facts and figuring out problems mentally.

EDUCATION/TRAINING PROGRAM—Aeronautical/Aerospace Engineering Technology/Technician. **RELATED KNOWLEDGE/COURSES— Engineering and Technology:** Knowledge of the practical application of engineering science and technology. This includes applying principles, techniques, procedures, and equipment to the design and production of various goods and services. **Computers and Electronics:** Knowledge of circuit boards, processors, chips, electronic equipment, and computer hardware and software, including applications and programming. **Physics:** Knowledge and prediction of physical principles and laws and their interrelationships and applications to understanding fluid, material, and atmospheric dynamics and mechanical, electrical, atomic, and subatomic structures and processes. **Mechanical Devices:** Knowledge of machines and tools, including their designs, uses, repair, and maintenance. **Mathematics:** Knowledge of arithmetic, algebra, geometry, calculus, and statistics and their applications.

Aerospace Engineers

- Annual Earnings: $84,090
- Growth: 8.3%
- Annual Job Openings: 6,000
- Self-Employed: 0.0%
- Part-Time: 2.7%
- Education/Training Required: Bachelor's degree

Industries in Which Income Is Highest

Industry	Average Annual Wage	Number Employed
Federal, State, and Local Government	$94,810	7,700
Professional, Scientific, and Technical Services	$89,410	13,740
Computer and Electronic Product Manufacturing	$87,670	14,170
Management of Companies and Enterprises	$81,950	1,490
Transportation Equipment Manufacturing	$80,440	40,880

Metropolitan Areas Where Income Is Highest

Metropolitan Area	Average Annual Wage	Number Employed
Washington–Arlington–Alexandria, DC–VA–MD–WV	$104,980	3,650
Chicago–Naperville–Joliet, IL–IN–WI	$96,140	80
Cleveland–Elyria–Mentor, OH	$95,980	460
Oxnard–Thousand Oaks–Ventura, CA	$95,500	110
Virginia Beach–Norfolk–Newport News, VA–NC	$95,460	1,000

Perform a variety of engineering work in designing, constructing, and testing aircraft, missiles, and spacecraft. May conduct basic and applied research to evaluate adaptability of materials and equipment to aircraft design and manufacture. May recommend improvements in testing equipment and techniques. Formulate conceptual design of aeronautical or aerospace products or systems to meet customer requirements. Direct and coordinate activities of engineering or technical personnel designing, fabricating, modifying, or testing aircraft or aerospace products. Develop design criteria for aeronautical or aerospace products or systems, including testing methods, production costs, quality standards, and completion dates. Plan and conduct experimental, environmental, operational, and stress tests on models and prototypes of aircraft and aerospace systems and equipment. Evaluate product data and design from inspections and reports for conformance to engineering principles, customer requirements, and quality standards. Formulate mathematical models or other methods of computer analysis to develop, evaluate, or modify design according to customer engineering requirements. Write technical reports and other documentation, such as handbooks and bulletins, for use by engineering staff, management, and customers. Analyze project requests and proposals and engineering data to determine feasibility, productibility, cost, and production time of aerospace or aeronautical product. Review performance reports and documentation from customers and field engineers and inspect malfunctioning or damaged products to determine problem. Direct research and development programs. Evaluate and approve selection of vendors by study of past performance and new advertisements. Plan and coordinate activities concerned with investigating and resolving customers' reports of technical problems with aircraft or aerospace vehicles. Maintain records of performance reports for future reference. **SKILLS**—Systems Evaluation; Systems Analysis; Science; Persuasion; Judgment and Decision Making; Management of Personnel Resources; Technology Design; Time Management.

GOE—Interest Area: 15. Scientific Research, Engineering, and Mathematics. **Work Group:** 15.07. Research and Design Engineering. **PERSONALITY TYPE:** Investigative. Investigative occupations frequently involve working with ideas and require an extensive amount of thinking. These occupations can involve searching for facts and figuring out problems mentally.

EDUCATION/TRAINING PROGRAM—Aerospace, Aeronautical, and Astronautical Engineering. **RELATED KNOWLEDGE/COURSES—Engineering and Technology:** Knowledge of the practical application of engineering science and technology. This includes applying principles, techniques, procedures, and equipment to the design and production of various goods and services. **Design:** Knowledge of design techniques, tools, and principles involved in production of precision technical plans, blueprints, drawings, and models. **Physics:** Knowledge and prediction of physical principles and laws and their interrelationships and applications to understanding fluid, material, and atmospheric dynamics and mechanical, electrical, atomic, and subatomic structures and processes. **Mechanical Devices:** Knowledge of machines and tools, including their designs, uses, repair, and maintenance. **Computers and Electronics:** Knowledge of circuit boards, processors, chips, electronic equipment, and computer hardware and software, including applications and programming. **Mathematics:** Knowledge of arithmetic, algebra, geometry, calculus, and statistics and their applications.

Agents and Business Managers of Artists, Performers, and Athletes

◎ Annual Earnings: $53,800
◎ Growth: 11.8%
◎ Annual Job Openings: 2,000
◎ Self-Employed: 39.3%
◎ Part-Time: 25.3%
◎ Education/Training Required: Work experience plus degree

Industries in Which Income Is Highest

Industry	Average Annual Wage	Number Employed
Performing Arts, Spectator Sports, and Related Industries	$57,530	8,270

Metropolitan Areas Where Income Is Highest

Metropolitan Area	Average Annual Wage	Number Employed
New York–Northern New Jersey–Long Island, NY–NJ–PA	$81,940	1,800
Seattle–Tacoma–Bellevue, WA	$62,440	50
Los Angeles–Long Beach–Santa Ana, CA	$59,710	2,800
Phoenix–Mesa–Scottsdale, AZ	$59,100	270
Philadelphia–Camden–Wilmington, PA–NJ–DE–MD	$57,800	80

Represent and promote artists, performers, and athletes to prospective employers. May handle contract negotiation and other business matters for clients. Arrange meetings concerning issues involving their clients. Collect fees, commissions, or other payments according to contract terms. Conduct auditions or interviews in order to evaluate potential clients. Confer with clients to develop strategies for their careers and to explain actions taken on their behalf. Develop contacts with individuals and organizations and apply effective strategies and techniques to ensure their clients' success. Keep informed of industry trends and deals. Manage business and financial affairs for clients, such as arranging travel and lodging, selling tickets, and directing marketing and advertising activities. Negotiate with managers, promoters, union officials, and other persons regarding clients' contractual rights and obligations. Obtain information about and/or inspect performance facilities, equipment, and accommodations to ensure that they meet specifications. Schedule promotional or performance engagements for clients. Advise clients on financial and legal matters such as investments and taxes. Hire trainers or coaches to advise clients on performance matters such as training techniques or performance presentations. Prepare periodic accounting statements for clients. **SKILLS**—Negotiation; Management of Financial Resources; Management of Personnel Resources; Time Management; Service Orientation; Speaking; Systems Evaluation; Systems Analysis.

GOE—Interest Area: 03. Arts and Communication. **Work Group:** 03.01. Managerial Work in Arts and Communication. **PERSONALITY TYPE:** Enterprising. Enterprising occupations frequently involve starting up and carrying out projects. These occupations can involve leading people and making many decisions. They sometimes require risk taking and often deal with business.

EDUCATION/TRAINING PROGRAMS—Arts Management; Purchasing, Procurement/Acquisitions, and Contracts Management. **RELATED KNOWLEDGE/COURSES—Sales and Marketing:** Knowledge of principles and methods for showing, promoting, and selling products or services. This includes marketing strategy and tactics, product demonstration, sales techniques, and sales control systems. **Economics and Accounting:** Knowledge of economic and accounting principles and practices, the financial markets, banking, and the analysis and reporting of financial data. **Personnel and Human Resources:** Knowledge of principles and procedures for personnel recruitment, selection, training, compensation and benefits, labor relations and negotiation, and personnel information systems. **Administration and Management:** Knowledge of business and management principles involved in strategic planning, resource allocation, human resources modeling, leadership technique, production methods, and coordination of people and resources. **Fine Arts:** Knowledge of the theory and techniques required to compose, produce, and perform works of music, dance, visual arts, drama, and sculpture. **Law and Government:** Knowledge of laws, legal codes, court procedures, precedents, government regulations, executive orders, agency rules, and the democratic political process.

Agricultural Crop Farm Managers

- Annual Earnings: $51,160
- Growth: 4.0%
- Annual Job Openings: 20,000
- Self-Employed: 0.0%
- Part-Time: 13.1%
- Education/Training Required: Work experience plus degree

The job openings listed here are shared with Nursery and Greenhouse Managers and Fish Hatchery Managers.

Industries in Which Income Is Highest

Industry	Average Annual Wage	Number Employed
Food Manufacturing	$57,140	90
Merchant Wholesalers, Nondurable Goods	$54,690	290
Administrative and Support Services	$54,540	160
Management of Companies and Enterprises	$52,780	70
Educational Services	$52,690	190

Metropolitan Areas Where Income Is Highest

Metropolitan Area	Average Annual Wage	Number Employed
New York–Northern New Jersey–Long Island, NY–NJ–PA	$76,240	50
Stockton, CA	$72,420	30
Riverside–San Bernardino–Ontario, CA	$67,640	40
Washington–Arlington–Alexandria, DC–VA–MD–WV	$64,020	30
Portland–Vancouver–Beaverton, OR–WA	$60,170	30

Direct and coordinate, through subordinate supervisory personnel, activities of workers engaged in agricultural crop production for corporations, cooperatives, or other owners. Negotiates with bank officials to obtain credit from bank. Evaluates financial statements and makes budget proposals. Directs and coordinates worker activities, such as planting, irrigation, chemical application, harvesting, grading, payroll, and recordkeeping. Contracts with farmers or independent owners for raising of crops or for management of crop production. Coordinates growing activities with those of engineering, equipment maintenance, packing houses, and other related departments. Analyzes market conditions to determine acreage allocations. Confers with purchasers and arranges for sale of crops. Records information, such as production, farm management practices, and parent stock, and prepares financial and operational reports. Determines procedural changes in drying, grading, storage, and shipment for greater efficiency and accuracy. Analyzes soil to determine type and quantity of fertilizer required for maximum production. Inspects equipment to ensure proper functioning. Inspects orchards and fields to determine maturity dates of crops or to estimate potential crop damage from weather. Plans and directs development and production of hybrid plant varieties with high yield or disease and insect-resistant characteristics. Purchases machinery, equipment, and supplies, such as tractors, seed, fertilizer, and chemicals. Hires, discharges, transfers, and promotes workers; enforces safety regulations; and interprets policies. **SKILLS**—Management of Financial Resources; Management of Personnel Resources; Management of Material Resources; Negotiation; Coordination; Systems Analysis; Systems Evaluation; Writing.

GOE—Interest Area: 01. Agriculture and Natural Resources. **Work Group:** 01.01. Managerial Work in Agriculture and Natural Resources. **PERSONALITY TYPE:** Enterprising. Enterprising occupations frequently involve starting up and carrying out projects. These occupations can involve leading people and making many decisions. They sometimes require risk taking and often deal with business.

EDUCATION/TRAINING PROGRAMS— Agribusiness/Agricultural Business Operations; Agricultural Animal Breeding; Agricultural Business and Management, General; Agricultural Business and

Management, Other; Agricultural Production Operations, General; Agricultural Production Operations, Other; Agronomy and Crop Science; Animal Nutrition; Animal Sciences, General; Animal/Livestock Husbandry and Production; Crop Production; Dairy Husbandry and Production; Dairy Science; Farm/Farm and Ranch Management; others. **RELATED KNOWLEDGE/COURSES—Food Production:** Knowledge of techniques and equipment for planting, growing, and harvesting food products (both plant and animal) for consumption, including storage/handling techniques. **Economics and Accounting:** Knowledge of economic and accounting principles and practices, the financial markets, banking, and the analysis and reporting of financial data. **Administration and Management:** Knowledge of business and management principles involved in strategic planning, resource allocation, human resources modeling, leadership technique, production methods, and coordination of people and resources. **Production and Processing:** Knowledge of raw materials, production processes, quality control, costs, and other techniques for maximizing the effective manufacture and distribution of goods. **Personnel and Human Resources:** Knowledge of principles and procedures for personnel recruitment, selection, training, compensation and benefits, labor relations and negotiation, and personnel information systems. **Mathematics:** Knowledge of arithmetic, algebra, geometry, calculus, and statistics and their applications.

Agricultural Engineers

- ◎ Annual Earnings: $64,890
- ◎ Growth: 12.0%
- ◎ Annual Job Openings: fewer than 500
- ◎ Self-Employed: 0.0%
- ◎ Part-Time: 0.0%
- ◎ Education/Training Required: Bachelor's degree

Industries in Which Income Is Highest

Industry	Average Annual Wage	Number Employed
Merchant Wholesalers, Nondurable Goods	$75,720	170
Professional, Scientific, and Technical Services	$71,780	760
Beverage and Tobacco Product Manufacturing	$69,680	110
Food Manufacturing	$65,810	710
Federal, State, and Local Government	$59,680	590

Metropolitan Areas Where Income Is Highest

Metropolitan Area	Average Annual Wage	Number Employed
Wichita, KS	$59,730	30
Minneapolis–St. Paul–Bloomington, MN–WI	$59,430	30

Apply knowledge of engineering technology and biological science to agricultural problems concerned with power and machinery, electrification, structures, soil and water conservation, and processing of agricultural products. Visit sites to observe environmental problems, to consult with contractors, and/or to monitor construction activities. Design agricultural machinery components and equipment, using computer-aided design technology. Test agricultural machinery and equipment to ensure adequate performance. Design structures for crop storage, animal shelter and loading, and animal and crop processing and supervise their construction. Provide advice on water quality and issues related to pollution management, river control, and ground and surface water resources. Conduct educational programs that provide farmers or farm cooperative members with information that can help them improve agricultural productivity. Discuss plans with clients, contractors, consultants, and other engineers so that they can be evaluated and necessary changes made. Supervise food processing or manufacturing plant operations. Design and supervise environmental and land reclamation projects in agriculture and related industries. Plan and direct construction of rural electric-power distribution systems and irrigation, drainage, and flood control systems for soil and water conservation. Design food processing plants and related mechanical systems. Prepare reports, sketches, working drawings, specifications, proposals, and budgets for proposed sites or systems. Meet with clients, such as district or regional councils, farmers, and developers, to discuss their needs. Design sensing, measuring, and recording devices and other instrumentation used to study plant or animal life. **SKILLS**—Programming; Science; Technology Design; Management of Financial Resources; Operations Analysis; Management of Material Resources; Mathematics; Systems Analysis.

GOE—Interest Area: 01. Agriculture and Natural Resources. **Work Group:** 01.02. Resource Science/Engineering for Plants, Animals, and the Environment. **PERSONALITY TYPE:** Investigative. Investigative occupations frequently involve working with ideas and require an extensive amount of thinking. These occupations can involve searching for facts and figuring out problems mentally.

EDUCATION/TRAINING   PROGRAM— Agricultural/Biological Engineering and Bioengineering. **RELATED KNOWLEDGE/COURSES—Food Production:** Knowledge of techniques and equipment for planting, growing, and harvesting food products (both plant and animal) for consumption, including storage/handling techniques. **Design:** Knowledge of design techniques, tools, and principles involved in production of precision technical plans, blueprints, drawings, and models. **Engineering and Technology:** Knowledge of the practical application of engineering science and technology. This includes applying principles, techniques, procedures, and equipment to the design and production of various goods and services. **Physics:** Knowledge and prediction of physical principles and laws and their interrelationships and applications to understanding fluid, material, and atmospheric dynamics and mechanical, electrical, atomic, and subatomic structures and processes. **Biology:** Knowledge of plant and animal organisms and their tissues, cells, functions, interdependencies, and interactions with each other and the environment. **Building and Construction:** Knowledge of the materials, methods, and tools involved in the construction or repair of houses, buildings, or other structures such as highways and roads.

Agricultural Sciences Teachers, Postsecondary

- Annual Earnings: $71,330
- Growth: 32.2%
- Annual Job Openings: 329,000
- Self-Employed: 0.4%
- Part-Time: 27.3%
- Education/Training Required: Master's degree

Our sources did not provide separate job openings data for this occupation. The job openings listed here are shared with 35 other postsecondary teaching occupations. For a complete list, see the beginning of this section.

Industries in Which Income Is Highest

Industry	Average Annual Wage	Number Employed
Educational Services	$71,400	11,430

Metropolitan Areas Where Income Is Highest

Metropolitan Area	Average Annual Wage	Number Employed
Miami–Fort Lauderdale–Miami Beach, FL	$68,260	50
San Francisco–Oakland–Fremont, CA	$67,860	250

Teach courses in the agricultural sciences. Includes teachers of agronomy, dairy sciences, fisheries management, horticultural sciences, poultry sciences, range management, and agricultural soil conservation. Prepare course materials such as syllabi, homework assignments, and handouts. Evaluate and grade students' class work, laboratory work, assignments, and papers. Keep abreast of developments in their field by reading current literature, talking with colleagues, and participating in professional conferences. Prepare and deliver lectures to undergraduate and/or graduate students on topics such as crop production, plant genetics, and soil chemistry. Initiate, facilitate, and moderate classroom discussions. Conduct research in a particular field of knowledge and publish findings in professional journals, books, and/or electronic media. Supervise laboratory sessions and field work and coordinate laboratory operations. Supervise undergraduate and/or graduate teaching, internship, and research work. Compile, administer, and grade examinations or assign this work to others. Advise students on academic and vocational curricula and on career issues. Plan, evaluate, and revise curricula, course content, and course materials and methods of instruction. Maintain student attendance records, grades, and other required records. Write grant proposals to procure external research funding. Collaborate with colleagues to address teaching and research issues. Maintain regularly scheduled office hours in order to advise and assist students. Participate in student recruitment, registration, and placement activities. Select and obtain materials and supplies such as textbooks and laboratory equipment. Act as advisers to student organizations. Participate in campus and community events. Serve on academic or administrative committees that deal with institutional policies, departmental matters, and academic issues. Provide professional consulting services to government and/or industry. Perform administrative duties such as serving as department head. **SKILLS**—Science; Instructing; Management of Financial Resources; Writing; Active Learning; Reading Comprehension; Learning Strategies; Persuasion.

GOE—Interest Area: 05. Education and Training. **Work Group:** 05.03. Postsecondary and Adult Teaching and Instructing. **PERSONALITY TYPE:** Investigative. Investigative occupations frequently involve working with ideas and require an extensive amount of thinking. These occupations can involve searching for facts and figuring out problems mentally.

EDUCATION/TRAINING PROGRAMS— Agribusiness/Agricultural Business Operations; Agricultural and Food Products Processing, General; Agricultural and Horticultural Plant Breeding; Agricultural Animal Breeding; Agricultural Business and Management, General; Agricultural Business and Management, Other; Agricultural Economics; Agricultural Mechanization, General; Agricultural Mechanization, Other; Agricultural Power Machinery

Operation; Agricultural Production Operations, General; Agricultural Production Operations, Other; others. **RELATED KNOWLEDGE/COURSES— Biology:** Knowledge of plant and animal organisms and their tissues, cells, functions, interdependencies, and interactions with each other and the environment. **Education and Training:** Knowledge of principles and methods for curriculum and training design, teaching and instruction for individuals and groups, and the measurement of training effects. **Food Production:** Knowledge of techniques and equipment for planting, growing, and harvesting food products (both plant and animal) for consumption, including storage/handling techniques. **Geography:** Knowledge of principles and methods for describing the features of land, sea, and air masses, including their physical characteristics; locations; interrelationships; and distribution of plant, animal, and human life. **Chemistry:** Knowledge of the chemical composition, structure, and properties of substances and of the chemical processes and transformations that they undergo. This includes uses of chemicals, their danger signs, production techniques, and disposal methods. **English Language:** Knowledge of the structure and content of the English language, including the meaning and spelling of words, rules of composition, and grammar.

Air Traffic Controllers

- Annual Earnings: $107,590
- Growth: 14.3%
- Annual Job Openings: 2,000
- Self-Employed: 1.8%
- Part-Time: 1.4%
- Education/Training Required: Long-term on-the-job training

Industries in Which Income Is Highest

Industry	Average Annual Wage	Number Employed
Federal, State, and Local Government	$111,950	19,660
Support Activities for Transportation	$52,930	1,040

Metropolitan Areas Where Income Is Highest

Metropolitan Area	Average Annual Wage	Number Employed
Houston–Sugar Land–Baytown, TX	$130,970	570
Sacramento–Arden–Arcade–Roseville, CA	$129,190	230
New York–Northern New Jersey–Long Island, NY–NJ–PA	$129,100	900
Atlanta–Sandy Springs–Marietta, GA	$128,780	670
San Francisco–Oakland–Fremont, CA	$127,400	390

Control air traffic on and within vicinity of airport and movement of air traffic between altitude sectors and control centers according to established procedures and policies. Authorize, regulate, and control commercial airline flights according to government or company regulations to expedite and ensure flight safety. Organize flight plans and traffic management plans to prepare for planes about to enter assigned airspace. Provide flight path changes or directions to emergency landing fields for pilots traveling in bad weather or in emergency situations. Compile information about flights from flight plans, pilot reports, radar, and observations. Relay to control centers such air traffic information as courses, altitudes, and expected arrival times. Transfer control of departing flights to traffic control centers and accept control of arriving flights. Complete daily activity reports and keep records of messages from aircraft. Initiate and coordinate searches for missing aircraft. Inspect, adjust, and control radio equipment and airport lights. Review records and reports for clarity and completeness and maintain records and reports as required under federal law. Alert airport emergency services in cases of emergency and when aircraft are experiencing difficulties. Analyze factors such as weather reports, fuel requirements, and maps in order to determine air routes. Check conditions and traffic at different altitudes in response to pilots' requests for altitude changes. Conduct pre-flight briefings on weather conditions, suggested routes, altitudes, indications of turbulence, and other flight safety information. Contact pilots by radio to provide meteorological, navigational, and other information. Determine the timing and procedures for flight vector changes. Direct ground traffic, including taxiing aircraft, maintenance and baggage vehicles, and airport workers. Direct pilots to runways when space is available or direct them to maintain a traffic pattern until there is space for them to land. Inform pilots about nearby planes as well as potentially hazardous conditions such as weather, speed and direction of wind, and visibility problems. Issue landing and take-off authorizations and instructions. Maintain radio and telephone contact with adjacent control towers, terminal control units, and other area control centers in order to coordinate aircraft movement. Monitor aircraft within a specific airspace, using radar, computer equipment, and visual references. **SKILLS**—Operation and Control; Operation Monitoring; Active Listening; Coordination; Critical Thinking; Systems Analysis; Judgment and Decision Making; Active Learning.

GOE—Interest Area: 03. Arts and Communication. **Work Group:** 03.10. Communications Technology. **PERSONALITY TYPE:** Conventional. Conventional occupations frequently involve following set procedures and routines. These occupations can include working with data and details more than with ideas. Usually there is a clear line of authority to follow.

EDUCATION/TRAINING PROGRAM—Air Traffic Controller. **RELATED KNOWLEDGE/COURSES—Transportation:** Knowledge of principles and methods for moving people or goods by air, rail, sea, or road, including the relative costs and benefits. **Physics:** Knowledge and prediction of physical principles and laws and their interrelationships and applications to understanding fluid, material, and atmospheric dynamics and mechanical, electrical, atomic, and subatomic structures and processes. **Telecommunications:** Knowledge of transmission, broadcasting, switching, control, and operation of telecommunications systems. **Geography:** Knowledge of principles and methods for describing the features of land, sea, and air masses, including their physical characteristics; locations; interrelationships; and distribution of plant, animal, and human life. **Computers and Electronics:** Knowledge of circuit boards, processors, chips, electronic equipment, and computer hardware and software, including applications and programming. **Engineering and Technology:** Knowledge of the practical application of engineering science and technology. This includes applying principles, techniques, procedures, and equipment to the design and production of various goods and services.

Aircraft Body and Bonded Structure Repairers

- Annual Earnings: $47,310
- Growth: 13.4%
- Annual Job Openings: 11,000
- Self-Employed: 3.0%
- Part-Time: 2.1%
- Education/Training Required: Postsecondary vocational training

The job openings listed here are shared with Aircraft Engine Specialists and Airframe-and-Power-Plant Mechanics.

Industries in Which Income Is Highest

Industry	Average Annual Wage	Number Employed
Couriers and Messengers	$73,330	4,700
Air Transportation	$56,040	40,930
Federal, State, and Local Government	$47,660	17,040
Administrative and Support Services	$44,410	1,520
Transportation Equipment Manufacturing	$43,810	18,400

Metropolitan Areas Where Income Is Highest

Metropolitan Area	Average Annual Wage	Number Employed
Seattle–Tacoma–Bellevue, WA	$60,150	3,990
Vallejo–Fairfield, CA	$57,520	140
Honolulu, HI	$57,110	610
Indianapolis–Carmel, IN	$56,900	1,070
Houston–Sugar Land–Baytown, TX	$55,950	2,490

Repair body or structure of aircraft according to specifications. Reinstalls repaired or replacement parts for subsequent riveting or welding, using clamps and wrenches. Repairs or fabricates defective section or part, using metal fabricating machines, saws, brakes, shears, and grinders. Reads work orders, blueprints, and specifications or examines sample or damaged part or structure to determine repair or fabrication procedures and sequence of operations. Communicates with other workers to fit and align heavy parts or expedite processing of repair parts. Removes or cuts out defective part or drills holes to gain access to internal defect or damage, using drill and punch. Locates and marks dimension and reference lines on defective or replacement part, using templates, scribes, compass, and steel rule. Trims and shapes replacement section to specified size and fits and secures section in place, using adhesives, hand tools, and power tools. Cleans, strips, primes, and sands structural surfaces and materials prior to bonding. Spreads plastic film over area to be repaired to prevent damage to surrounding area. Cures bonded structure, using portable or stationary curing equipment. **SKILLS**—Installation; Repairing; Equipment Maintenance; Equipment Selection; Mathematics; Operation and Control.

GOE—Interest Area: 13. Manufacturing. **Work Group:** 13.14. Vehicle and Facility Mechanical Work. **PERSONALITY TYPE:** Realistic. Realistic occupations frequently involve work activities that include practical, hands-on problems and solutions. They often deal with plants, animals, and real-world materials like wood, tools, and machinery. Many of the occupations require working outside and do not involve a lot of paperwork or working closely with others.

EDUCATION/TRAINING PROGRAMS—Agricultural Mechanics and Equipment/Machine Technology; Airframe Mechanics and Aircraft Maintenance Technology/Technician. **RELATED KNOWLEDGE/COURSES—Mechanical Devices:** Knowledge of machines and tools, including their designs, uses, repair, and maintenance. **Building and Construction:** Knowledge of the materials, methods, and tools involved in the construction or repair of houses, buildings, or other structures such as highways and roads. **Design:** Knowledge of design techniques, tools, and principles involved in production of precision technical plans, blueprints, drawings, and models. **Engineering and Technology:** Knowledge of the practical application of engineering science and technology. This includes applying principles, techniques, procedures, and equipment to the design and production of various goods and services. **Production and Processing:** Knowledge of raw materials, production processes, quality control, costs, and other techniques for maximizing the effective manufacture and distribution of goods. **Physics:** Knowledge and prediction of physical principles and laws and their interrelationships and applications to understanding fluid, material, and atmospheric dynamics and mechanical, electrical, atomic, and subatomic structures and processes.

Aircraft Engine Specialists

- Annual Earnings: $47,310
- Growth: 13.4%
- Annual Job Openings: 11,000
- Self-Employed: 3.0%
- Part-Time: 2.1%
- Education/Training Required: Postsecondary vocational training

The job openings listed here are shared with Aircraft Body and Bonded Structure Repairers and Airframe-and-Power-Plant Mechanics.

Industries in Which Income Is Highest

Industry	Average Annual Wage	Number Employed
Couriers and Messengers	$73,330	4,700
Air Transportation	$56,040	40,930
Federal, State, and Local Government	$47,660	17,040
Administrative and Support Services	$44,410	1,520
Transportation Equipment Manufacturing	$43,810	18,400

Metropolitan Areas Where Income Is Highest

Metropolitan Area	Average Annual Wage	Number Employed
Seattle–Tacoma–Bellevue, WA	$60,150	3,990
Vallejo–Fairfield, CA	$57,520	140
Honolulu, HI	$57,110	610
Indianapolis–Carmel, IN	$56,900	1,070
Houston–Sugar Land–Baytown, TX	$55,950	2,490

Repair and maintain the operating condition of aircraft engines. Includes helicopter engine mechanics. Replaces or repairs worn, defective, or damaged components, using hand tools, gauges, and testing equipment. Tests engine operation, using test equipment such as ignition analyzer, compression checker, distributor timer, and ammeter, to identify malfunction. Listens to operating engine to detect and diagnose malfunctions, such as sticking or burned valves. Reassembles engine and installs engine in aircraft. Disassembles and inspects engine parts, such as turbine blades and cylinders, for wear, warping, cracks, and leaks. Removes engine from aircraft, using hoist or forklift truck. Services, repairs, and rebuilds aircraft structures, such as wings, fuselage, rigging, and surface and hydraulic controls, using hand or power tools and equipment. Adjusts, repairs, or replaces electrical wiring system and aircraft accessories. Reads and interprets manufacturers' maintenance manuals, service bulletins, and other specifications to determine feasibility and methods of repair. Services and maintains aircraft and related apparatus by performing activities such as flushing crankcase, cleaning screens, and lubricating moving parts. **SKILLS**—Equipment Maintenance; Repairing; Installation; Troubleshooting; Operation Monitoring; Quality Control Analysis; Judgment and Decision Making; Systems Analysis.

GOE—Interest Area: 13. Manufacturing. **Work Group:** 13.14. Vehicle and Facility Mechanical Work. **PERSONALITY TYPE:** Realistic. Realistic occupations frequently involve work activities that include practical, hands-on problems and solutions. They often deal with plants, animals, and real-world materials like wood, tools, and machinery. Many of the occupations require working outside and do not involve a lot of paperwork or working closely with others.

EDUCATION/TRAINING PROGRAMS—Agricultural Mechanics and Equipment/Machine Technology; Aircraft Powerplant Technology/Technician. **RELATED KNOWLEDGE/COURSES—Mechanical Devices:** Knowledge of machines and tools, including their designs, uses, repair, and maintenance. **Engineering and Technology:** Knowledge of the practical application of engineering science and technology. This includes applying principles, techniques, procedures, and equipment to the design and production of various goods and services. **Physics:** Knowledge and prediction of physical principles and laws and their interrelationships and applications to understanding fluid, material, and atmospheric dynamics and mechanical, electrical, atomic, and subatomic structures and processes. **Mathematics:** Knowledge of arithmetic, algebra, geometry, calculus, and statistics and their applications.

Airframe-and-Power-Plant Mechanics

- Annual Earnings: $47,310
- Growth: 13.4%
- Annual Job Openings: 11,000
- Self-Employed: 3.0%
- Part-Time: 2.1%
- Education/Training Required: Postsecondary vocational training

The job openings listed here are shared with Aircraft Body and Bonded Structure Repairers and Aircraft Engine Specialists.

Industries in Which Income Is Highest

Industry	Average Annual Wage	Number Employed
Couriers and Messengers	$73,330	4,700
Air Transportation	$56,040	40,930
Federal, State, and Local Government	$47,660	17,040
Administrative and Support Services	$44,410	1,520
Transportation Equipment Manufacturing	$43,810	18,400

Metropolitan Areas Where Income Is Highest

Metropolitan Area	Average Annual Wage	Number Employed
Seattle–Tacoma–Bellevue, WA	$60,150	3,990
Vallejo–Fairfield, CA	$57,520	140
Honolulu, HI	$57,110	610
Indianapolis–Carmel, IN	$56,900	1,070
Houston–Sugar Land–Baytown, TX	$55,950	2,490

Inspect, test, repair, maintain, and service aircraft. Adjusts, aligns, and calibrates aircraft systems, using hand tools, gauges, and test equipment. Examines and inspects engines or other components for cracks, breaks, or leaks. Disassembles and inspects parts for wear, warping, or other defects. Assembles and installs electrical, plumbing, mechanical, hydraulic, and structural components and accessories, using hand tools and power tools. Services and maintains aircraft systems by performing tasks such as flushing crankcase, cleaning screens, greasing moving parts, and checking brakes. Repairs, replaces, and rebuilds aircraft structures, functional components, and parts, such as wings and fuselage, rigging, and hydraulic units. Tests engine and system operations, using testing equipment, and listens to engine sounds to detect and diagnose malfunctions. Removes engine from aircraft or installs engine, using hoist or forklift truck. Modifies aircraft structures, space vehicles, systems, or components, following drawings, engineering orders, and technical publications. Reads and interprets aircraft maintenance manuals and specifications to determine feasibility and method of repairing or replacing malfunctioning or damaged components. **SKILLS—** Equipment Maintenance; Installation; Repairing; Operation Monitoring; Troubleshooting; Quality Control Analysis; Science; Equipment Selection.

GOE—Interest Area: 13. Manufacturing. **Work Group:** 13.14. Vehicle and Facility Mechanical Work. **PERSONALITY TYPE:** Realistic. Realistic occupations frequently involve work activities that include practical, hands-on problems and solutions. They often deal with plants, animals, and real-world materials like wood, tools, and machinery. Many of the occupations require working outside and do not involve a lot of paperwork or working closely with others.

EDUCATION/TRAINING PROGRAMS— Agricultural Mechanics and Equipment/Machine Technology; Aircraft Powerplant Technology/ Technician; Airframe Mechanics and Aircraft Maintenance Technology/Technician. **RELATED KNOWLEDGE/COURSES—Mechanical Devices:** Knowledge of machines and tools, including their designs, uses, repair, and maintenance. **Building and Construction:** Knowledge of the materials, methods, and tools involved in the construction or repair of houses, buildings, or other structures such as highways and roads. **Engineering and Technology:** Knowledge of the practical application of engineering science and technology. This includes applying principles, techniques, procedures, and equipment to the design and production of various goods and services. **Design:** Knowledge of design techniques, tools, and principles involved in production of precision technical plans, blueprints, drawings, and models. **Physics:** Knowledge and prediction of physical principles and laws and their interrelationships and applications to understanding fluid, material, and atmospheric dynamics and mechanical, electrical, atomic, and subatomic structures and processes.

Airline Pilots, Copilots, and Flight Engineers

- Annual Earnings: $138,170
- Growth: 17.2%
- Annual Job Openings: 7,000
- Self-Employed: 2.4%
- Part-Time: 14.7%
- Education/Training Required: Bachelor's degree

Industries in Which Income Is Highest

Industry	Average Annual Wage	Number Employed
Air Transportation	More than $146,500	69,410
Federal, State, and Local Government	$84,470	2,780

Metropolitan Areas Where Income Is Highest

Metropolitan Area	Average Annual Wage	Number Employed
Anchorage, AK	More than $146,500	1,040
Boston–Cambridge–Quincy, MA–NH	More than $146,500	1,090
Los Angeles–Long Beach–Santa Ana, CA	More than $146,500	2,490
Chicago–Naperville–Joliet, IL–IN–WI	$144,510	6,280
Washington–Arlington–Alexandria, DC–VA–MD–WV	$122,030	3,030

Pilot and navigate the flight of multi-engine aircraft in regularly scheduled service for the transport of passengers and cargo. Requires Federal Air Transport rating and certification in specific aircraft type used. Test and evaluate the performance of new aircraft. Use instrumentation to guide flights when visibility is poor. Brief crews about flight details such as destinations, duties, and responsibilities. Check passenger and cargo distributions and fuel amounts to ensure that weight and balance specifications are met. Choose routes, altitudes, and speeds that will provide the fastest, safest, and smoothest flights. Confer with flight dispatchers and weather forecasters to keep abreast of flight conditions. Contact control towers for takeoff clearances, arrival instructions, and other information, using radio equipment. Coordinate flight activities with ground crews and air-traffic control and inform crew members of flight and test procedures. Direct activities of aircraft crews during flights. File instrument flight plans with air traffic control to ensure that flights are coordinated with other air traffic. Inspect aircraft for defects and malfunctions according to pre-flight checklists. Make announcements regarding flights, using public address systems. Monitor engine operation, fuel consumption, and functioning of aircraft systems during flights. Monitor gauges, warning devices, and control panels to verify aircraft performance and to regulate engine speed. Order changes in fuel supplies, loads, routes, or schedules to ensure safety of flights. Plan and formulate flight activities and test schedules and prepare flight evaluation reports. Respond to and report in-flight emergencies and malfunctions. Start engines, operate controls, and pilot airplanes to transport passengers, mail, or freight while adhering to flight plans, regulations, and procedures. Steer aircraft along planned routes with the assistance of autopilot and flight management computers. Work as part of a flight team with other crew members, especially during takeoffs and landings. Conduct in-flight tests and evaluations at specified altitudes and in all types of weather in order to determine the receptivity and other characteristics of equipment and systems. Evaluate other pilots or pilot-license applicants for proficiency. **SKILLS—** Operation and Control; Operation Monitoring; Science; Instructing; Systems Evaluation; Systems Analysis; Coordination; Judgment and Decision Making.

GOE—Interest Area: 16. Transportation, Distribution, and Logistics. **Work Group:** 16.02. Air Vehicle Operation. **PERSONALITY TYPE:** Realistic. Realistic occupations frequently involve work activities that include practical, hands-on problems and solutions. They often deal with plants, animals, and real-world materials like wood, tools, and machinery. Many of the occupations require working outside and do not involve a lot of paperwork or working closely with others.

EDUCATION/TRAINING   PROGRAMS— Airline/Commercial/Professional Pilot and Flight Crew; Flight Instructor. **RELATED KNOWLEDGE/ COURSES—Transportation:** Knowledge of principles and methods for moving people or goods by air, rail, sea, or road, including the relative costs and benefits. **Geography:** Knowledge of principles and methods for describing the features of land, sea, and air masses, including their physical characteristics; locations; interrelationships; and distribution of plant, animal, and human life. **Education and Training:** Knowledge of principles and methods for curriculum and training design, teaching and instruction for individuals and groups, and the measurement of training effects. **Mechanical Devices:** Knowledge of machines and tools, including their designs, uses, repair, and maintenance. **Public Safety and Security:** Knowledge of relevant equipment, policies, procedures, and strategies to promote effective local, state, or national security operations for the protection of people, data, property, and institutions. **Physics:** Knowledge and prediction of physical principles and laws and their interrelationships and applications to understanding fluid, material, and atmospheric dynamics and mechanical, electrical, atomic, and subatomic structures and processes.

Anesthesiologists

- Annual Earnings: More than $146,500
- Growth: 24.0%
- Annual Job Openings: 41,000
- Self-Employed: 11.0%
- Part-Time: 9.6%
- Education/Training Required: First professional degree

The job openings listed here are shared with Family and General Practitioners; Internists, General; Obstetricians and Gynecologists; Pediatricians, General; Psychiatrists; and Surgeons.

Industries in Which Income Is Highest

Industry	Average Annual Wage	Number Employed
Ambulatory Health Care Services	More than $146,500	24,220

Metropolitan Areas Where Income Is Highest

Metropolitan Area	Average Annual Wage	Number Employed
Houston–Sugar Land–Baytown, TX	More than $146,500	2,300
New York–Northern New Jersey–Long Island, NY–NJ–PA	More than $146,500	1,170
Los Angeles–Long Beach–Santa Ana, CA	More than $146,500	730
Orlando–Kissimmee, FL	More than $146,500	380
St. Louis, MO–IL	More than $146,500	210

Administer anesthetics during surgery or other medical procedures. Administer anesthetic or sedation during medical procedures, using local, intravenous, spinal, or caudal methods. Monitor patient before, during, and after anesthesia and counteract adverse reactions or complications. Provide and maintain life support and airway management and help prepare patients for emergency surgery. Record type and amount of anesthesia and patient condition throughout procedure. Examine patient; obtain medical history; and use diagnostic tests to determine risk during surgical, obstetrical, and other medical procedures. Position patient on operating table to maximize patient comfort and surgical accessibility. Decide when patients have recovered or stabilized enough to be sent to another room or ward or to be sent home following outpatient surgery. Coordinate administration of anesthetics with surgeons during operation. Confer with other medical professionals to determine type and method of anesthetic or sedation to render patient insensible to pain. Coordinate and direct work of nurses, medical technicians, and other health care providers. Order laboratory tests, X rays, and other diagnostic procedures. Diagnose illnesses, using examinations, tests, and reports. Manage anesthesiological services, coordinating them with other medical activities and formulating plans and procedures. Provide medical care and consultation in many settings, prescribing medication and treatment and referring patients for surgery. Inform students and staff of types and methods of anesthesia administration, signs of complications, and emergency methods to counteract reactions. Schedule and maintain use of surgical suite, including operating, wash-up, and waiting rooms and anesthetic and sterilizing equipment. Instruct individuals and groups on ways to preserve health and prevent disease. **SKILLS**—Operation Monitoring; Science;

Operation and Control; Judgment and Decision Making; Social Perceptiveness; Monitoring; Complex Problem Solving; Critical Thinking.

GOE—Interest Area: 08. Health Science. **Work Group:** 08.02. Medicine and Surgery. **PERSONALITY TYPE:** Investigative. Investigative occupations frequently involve working with ideas and require an extensive amount of thinking. These occupations can involve searching for facts and figuring out problems mentally.

EDUCATION/TRAINING PROGRAMS— Anesthesiology; Critical Care Anesthesiology. **RELATED KNOWLEDGE/COURSES—Medicine and Dentistry:** Knowledge of the information and techniques needed to diagnose and treat human injuries, diseases, and deformities. This includes symptoms, treatment alternatives, drug properties and interactions, and preventive health-care measures. **Biology:** Knowledge of plant and animal organisms and their tissues, cells, functions, interdependencies, and interactions with each other and the environment. **Psychology:** Knowledge of human behavior and performance; individual differences in ability, personality, and interests; learning and motivation; psychological research methods; and the assessment and treatment of behavioral and affective disorders. **Chemistry:** Knowledge of the chemical composition, structure, and properties of substances and of the chemical processes and transformations that they undergo. This includes uses of chemicals, their danger signs, production techniques, and disposal methods. **Customer and Personal Service:** Knowledge of principles and processes for providing customer and personal services. This includes customer needs assessment, meeting quality standards for services, and evaluation of customer satisfaction. **Physics:** Knowledge and prediction of physical principles and laws and their interrelationships and applications to understanding fluid, material, and atmospheric dynamics and mechanical, electrical, atomic, and subatomic structures and processes.

Anthropology and Archeology Teachers, Postsecondary

- Annual Earnings: $60,710
- Growth: 32.2%
- Annual Job Openings: 329,000
- Self-Employed: 0.4%
- Part-Time: 27.3%
- Education/Training Required: Master's degree

Our sources did not provide separate job openings data for this occupation. The job openings listed here are shared with 35 other postsecondary teaching occupations. For a complete list, see the beginning of this section.

Industries in Which Income Is Highest

Industry	Average Annual Wage	Number Employed
Educational Services	$60,710	5,320

Metropolitan Areas Where Income Is Highest

Metropolitan Area	Average Annual Wage	Number Employed
Rochester, NY	$105,740	70
Riverside–San Bernardino–Ontario, CA	$78,200	40
New York–Northern New Jersey–Long Island, NY–NJ–PA	$72,870	240
Philadelphia–Camden–Wilmington, PA–NJ–DE–MD	$72,260	290
Boston–Cambridge–Quincy, MA–NH	$71,560	130

Teach courses in anthropology or archeology. Conduct research in a particular field of knowledge and publish findings in professional journals, books, and/or electronic media. Keep abreast of developments in their field by reading current literature, talking with colleagues, and participating in professional conferences. Prepare and deliver lectures to undergraduate and/or graduate students on topics such as research methods, urban anthropology, and language and culture. Evaluate and grade students' class work, assignments, and papers. Initiate, facilitate, and moderate classroom discussions. Write grant proposals to procure external research funding. Supervise undergraduate and/or graduate teaching, internship, and research work. Prepare course materials such as syllabi, homework assignments, and handouts. Compile, administer, and grade examinations or assign this work to others. Supervise students' laboratory or field work. Plan, evaluate, and revise curricula, course content, and course materials and methods of instruction. Advise students on academic and vocational curricula, career issues, and laboratory and field research. Maintain student attendance records, grades, and other required records. Maintain regularly scheduled office hours in order to advise and assist students. Collaborate with colleagues to address teaching and research issues. Compile bibliographies of specialized materials for outside reading assignments. Perform administrative duties such as serving as department head. Select and obtain materials and supplies such as textbooks and laboratory equipment. Serve on academic or administrative committees that deal with institutional policies, departmental matters, and academic issues. Participate in student recruitment, registration, and placement activities. **SKILLS**—Instructing; Writing; Critical Thinking; Active Learning; Science; Reading Comprehension; Learning Strategies; Management of Financial Resources.

GOE—Interest Area: 05. Education and Training. **Work Group:** 05.03. Postsecondary and Adult Teaching and Instructing. **PERSONALITY TYPE:** Social. Social occupations frequently involve working with, communicating with, and teaching people. These occupations often involve helping or providing service to others.

EDUCATION/TRAINING PROGRAMS—Anthropology; Archeology; Physical Anthropology; Social Science Teacher Education. **RELATED KNOWLEDGE/COURSES—Sociology and Anthropology:** Knowledge of group behavior and dynamics, societal trends and influences, human migrations, ethnicity, and cultures and their history and origins. **History and Archeology:** Knowledge of historical events and their causes, indicators, and effects on civilizations and cultures. **Geography:** Knowledge of principles and methods for describing the features of land, sea, and air masses, including their physical characteristics; locations; interrelationships; and distribution of plant, animal, and human life. **Foreign Language:** Knowledge of the structure and

content of a foreign (non-English) language, including the meaning and spelling of words, rules of composition and grammar, and pronunciation. **Philosophy and Theology:** Knowledge of different philosophical systems and religions. This includes their basic principles, values, ethics, ways of thinking, customs, and practices and their impact on human culture. **Education and Training:** Knowledge of principles and methods for curriculum and training design, teaching and instruction for individuals and groups, and the measurement of training effects.

Arbitrators, Mediators, and Conciliators

- Annual Earnings: $54,360
- Growth: 15.5%
- Annual Job Openings: fewer than 500
- Self-Employed: 0.0%
- Part-Time: No data available
- Education/Training Required: Work experience plus degree

Industries in Which Income Is Highest

Industry	Average Annual Wage	Number Employed
Religious, Grantmaking, Civic, Professional, and Similar Organizations	$57,130	1,100
Professional, Scientific, and Technical Services	$56,630	1,300
Educational Services	$54,920	110
Insurance Carriers and Related Activities	$53,990	350
Merchant Wholesalers, Durable Goods	$51,980	40

Metropolitan Areas Where Income Is Highest

Metropolitan Area	Average Annual Wage	Number Employed
Washington–Arlington–Alexandria, DC–VA–MD–WV	$88,660	250
Detroit–Warren–Livonia, MI	$83,590	100
Los Angeles–Long Beach–Santa Ana, CA	$72,730	160
Hartford–West Hartford–East Hartford, CT	$72,510	50
Des Moines–West Des Moines, IA	$67,750	50

Facilitate negotiation and conflict resolution through dialogue. Resolve conflicts outside of the court system by mutual consent of parties involved. Prepare written opinions and decisions regarding cases. Rule on exceptions, motions, and admissibility of evidence. Conduct studies of appeals procedures in order to ensure adherence to legal requirements and to facilitate disposition of cases. Organize and deliver public presentations about mediation to organizations such as community agencies and schools. Analyze evidence and apply relevant laws, regulations, policies, and precedents in order to reach conclusions. Arrange and conduct hearings to obtain information and evidence relative to disposition of claims. Conduct initial meetings with disputants to outline the arbitration process, settle procedural matters such as fees, and determine details such as witness numbers and time requirements. Confer with disputants to clarify issues, identify underlying concerns, and develop an understanding of their respective needs and interests. Interview claimants, agents, or witnesses to obtain information about disputed issues. Participate in court proceedings. Prepare settlement agreements for disputants to sign. Recommend acceptance or rejection of compromise settlement offers. Research laws, regulations, policies, and precedent decisions to prepare for hearings. Review and evaluate information from documents such as claim applications, birth or death certificates, and physician or employer records. Set up appointments for parties to meet for mediation. Use mediation techniques to facilitate communication between disputants, to further parties' understanding of different perspectives, and to guide parties toward mutual agreement. Authorize payment of valid claims. Determine existence and amount of liability according to evidence, laws, and administrative and judicial precedents. Issue subpoenas and administer oaths to prepare for formal hearings. Notify claimants of denied claims and appeal rights. **SKILLS**—Judgment and Decision Making; Active Listening; Critical Thinking; Writing; Reading Comprehension; Speaking; Active Learning; Negotiation.

GOE—Interest Area: 12. Law and Public Safety. **Work Group:** 12.02. Legal Practice and Justice Administration. **PERSONALITY TYPE:** Enterprising. Enterprising occupations frequently involve starting up and carrying out projects. These occupations can involve leading people and making many decisions. They sometimes require risk taking and often deal with business.

EDUCATION/TRAINING PROGRAMS—Law (LL.B., J.D.); Law, Legal Services, and Legal Studies, Other; Legal Studies, General. **RELATED KNOWLEDGE/COURSES—Law and Government:** Knowledge of laws, legal codes, court procedures, precedents, government regulations, executive orders, agency rules, and the democratic political process. **Psychology:** Knowledge of human behavior and performance; individual differences in ability, personality, and interests; learning and motivation; psychological research methods; and the assessment and treatment of behavioral and affective disorders. **Administration and Management:** Knowledge of business and management principles involved in strategic planning, resource allocation, human resources modeling, leadership technique, production methods, and coordination of people and resources. **English Language:** Knowledge of the structure and content of the English language, including the meaning and spelling of words, rules of composition, and grammar.

Architects, Except Landscape and Naval

- Annual Earnings: $62,850
- Growth: 17.3%
- Annual Job Openings: 7,000
- Self-Employed: 20.1%
- Part-Time: 9.2%
- Education/Training Required: Bachelor's degree

Industries in Which Income Is Highest

Industry	Average Annual Wage	Number Employed
Federal, State, and Local Government	$71,990	3,870
Management of Companies and Enterprises	$69,730	1,010
Construction of Buildings	$63,980	4,130
Educational Services	$63,210	1,010
Professional, Scientific, and Technical Services	$62,150	83,970

Metropolitan Areas Where Income Is Highest

Metropolitan Area	Average Annual Wage	Number Employed
Poughkeepsie–Newburgh– Middletown, NY	$81,620	120
Santa Barbara–Santa Maria, CA	$81,370	130
Beaumont–Port Arthur, TX	$80,790	120
San Diego–Carlsbad–San Marcos, CA	$77,040	960
Anchorage, AK	$76,700	200

Plan and design structures, such as private residences, office buildings, theaters, factories, and other structural property. Prepare information regarding design, structure specifications, materials, color, equipment, estimated costs, and construction time. Consult with client to determine functional and spatial requirements of structure. Direct activities of workers engaged in preparing drawings and specification documents. Plan layout of project. Prepare contract documents for building contractors. Prepare scale drawings. Integrate engineering element into unified design. Conduct periodic on-site observation of work during construction to monitor compliance with plans. Administer construction contracts. Represent client in obtaining bids and awarding construction contracts. **SKILLS**—Operations Analysis; Management of Financial Resources; Management of Personnel Resources; Coordination; Complex Problem Solving; Negotiation; Persuasion; Active Listening.

GOE—Interest Area: 02. Architecture and Construction. **Work Group:** 02.02. Architectural Design. **PERSONALITY TYPE:** Artistic. Artistic occupations frequently involve working with forms, designs, and patterns. They often require self-expression, and the work can be done without following a clear set of rules.

EDUCATION/TRAINING PROGRAMS— Architectural History and Criticism; Architecture (BArch, BA/BS, MArch, MA/MS, PhD); Architecture and Related Programs, Other; Environmental Design/ Architecture. **RELATED KNOWLEDGE/ COURSES—Building and Construction:** Knowledge of the materials, methods, and tools involved in the construction or repair of houses, buildings, or other structures such as highways and roads. **Design:** Knowledge of design techniques, tools, and principles involved in production of precision technical plans, blueprints, drawings, and models. **Engineering and Technology:** Knowledge of the practical application of engineering science and technology. This includes applying principles, techniques, procedures, and equipment to the design and production of various goods and services. **Fine Arts:** Knowledge of the theory and techniques required to compose, produce, and perform works of music, dance, visual arts, drama, and sculpture. **Law and Government:** Knowledge of laws, legal codes, court procedures, precedents, government regulations, executive orders, agency rules, and the democratic political process. **Public Safety and Security:** Knowledge of relevant equipment, policies, procedures, and strategies to promote effective local, state, or national security operations for the protection of people, data, property, and institutions.

Architecture Teachers, Postsecondary

- Annual Earnings: $62,270
- Growth: 32.2%
- Annual Job Openings: 329,000
- Self-Employed: 0.4%
- Part-Time: 27.3%
- Education/Training Required: Master's degree

Our sources did not provide separate job openings data for this occupation. The job openings listed here are shared with 35 other postsecondary teaching occupations. For a complete list, see the beginning of this section.

Industries in Which Income Is Highest

Industry	Average Annual Wage	Number Employed
Educational Services	$62,400	6,070

Metropolitan Areas Where Income Is Highest

Metropolitan Area	Average Annual Wage	Number Employed
Boston–Cambridge–Quincy, MA–NH	$84,310	180
Providence–Fall River–Warwick, RI–MA	$72,300	110
San Francisco–Oakland–Fremont, CA	$65,830	300
Miami–Fort Lauderdale–Miami Beach, FL	$64,840	50
Milwaukee–Waukesha–West Allis, WI	$63,880	60

Teach courses in architecture and architectural design, such as architectural environmental design, interior architecture/design, and landscape architecture. Evaluate and grade students' work, including work performed in design studios. Prepare and deliver lectures to undergraduate and/or graduate students on topics such as architectural design methods, aesthetics and design, and structures and materials. Prepare course materials such as syllabi, homework assignments, and handouts. Initiate, facilitate, and moderate classroom discussions. Plan, evaluate, and revise curricula, course content, and course materials and methods of instruction. Keep abreast of developments in their field by reading current literature, talking with colleagues, and participating in professional conferences. Maintain student attendance records, grades, and other required records. Maintain regularly scheduled office hours in order to advise and assist students. Compile, administer, and grade examinations or assign this work to others. Conduct research in a particular field of knowledge and publish findings in professional journals, books, and/or electronic media. Supervise undergraduate and/or graduate teaching, internship, and research work. Advise students on academic and vocational curricula and on career issues. Collaborate with colleagues to address teaching and research issues. Compile bibliographies of specialized materials for outside reading assignments. Serve on academic or administrative committees that deal with institutional policies, departmental matters, and academic issues. Participate in student recruitment, registration, and placement activities. Select and obtain materials and supplies such as textbooks and laboratory equipment. Write grant proposals to procure external research funding. Provide professional consulting services to government and/or industry. Perform administrative duties such as serving as department head. **SKILLS—** Instructing; Technology Design; Writing; Operations Analysis; Learning Strategies; Active Learning; Critical Thinking; Persuasion.

GOE—Interest Area: 05. Education and Training. **Work Group:** 05.03. Postsecondary and Adult Teaching and Instructing. **PERSONALITY TYPE:** No data available.

EDUCATION/TRAINING PROGRAMS— Architectural Engineering; Architecture (BArch, BA/BS, MArch, MA/MS, PhD); City/Urban, Community, and Regional Planning; Environmental Design/Architecture; Interior Architecture; Landscape Architecture (BS, BSLA, BLA, MSLA, MLA, PhD); Teacher Education and Professional Development, Specific Subject Areas, Other. **RELATED KNOWLEDGE/COURSES—Fine Arts:** Knowledge of the theory and techniques required to compose, produce, and perform works of music, dance, visual arts, drama, and sculpture. **Design:** Knowledge of design techniques, tools, and principles involved in production of precision technical plans, blueprints, drawings, and models. **Building and Construction:** Knowledge of the materials, methods, and tools involved in the construction or repair of houses, buildings, or other structures such as highways and roads. **History and Archeology:** Knowledge of historical events and their causes, indicators, and effects on civilizations and cultures. **Education and Training:** Knowledge of principles and methods for curriculum and training design, teaching and instruction for individuals and groups, and the measurement of training effects. **Philosophy and Theology:** Knowledge of different philosophical systems and religions. This includes their basic principles, values, ethics, ways of thinking, customs, and practices and their impact on human culture.

Area, Ethnic, and Cultural Studies Teachers, Postsecondary

- Annual Earnings: $55,610
- Growth: 32.2%
- Annual Job Openings: 329,000
- Self-Employed: 0.4%
- Part-Time: 27.3%
- Education/Training Required: Master's degree

Our sources did not provide separate job openings data for this occupation. The job openings listed here are shared with 35 other postsecondary teaching occupations. For a complete list, see the beginning of this section.

Industries in Which Income Is Highest

Industry	Average Annual Wage	Number Employed
Educational Services	$55,730	7,870

Metropolitan Areas Where Income Is Highest

Metropolitan Area	Average Annual Wage	Number Employed
Columbus, OH	$77,640	50
Philadelphia–Camden–Wilmington, PA–NJ–DE–MD	$70,220	260
Boston–Cambridge–Quincy, MA–NH	$61,480	420
Los Angeles–Long Beach–Santa Ana, CA	$61,360	310
Honolulu, HI	$59,910	180

Teach courses pertaining to the culture and development of an area (e.g., Latin America), an ethnic group, or any other group (e.g., women's studies, urban affairs). Keep abreast of developments in their field by reading current literature, talking with colleagues, and participating in professional conferences. Conduct research in a particular field of knowledge and publish findings in professional journals, books, and/or electronic media. Evaluate and grade students' class work, assignments, and papers. Prepare course materials such as syllabi, homework assignments, and handouts. Prepare and deliver lectures to undergraduate and/or graduate students on topics such as race and ethnic relations, gender studies, and cross-cultural perspectives. Initiate, facilitate, and moderate classroom discussions. Compile, administer, and grade examinations or assign this work to others. Maintain regularly scheduled office hours in order to advise and assist students. Plan, evaluate, and revise curricula, course content, and course materials and methods of instruction. Maintain student attendance records, grades, and other required records. Advise students on academic and vocational curricula and on career issues. Supervise undergraduate and/or graduate teaching, internship,

and research work. Collaborate with colleagues to address teaching and research issues. Select and obtain materials and supplies such as textbooks. Serve on academic or administrative committees that deal with institutional policies, departmental matters, and academic issues. Compile bibliographies of specialized materials for outside reading assignments. Write grant proposals to procure external research funding. Participate in campus and community events. Participate in student recruitment, registration, and placement activities. Act as advisers to student organizations. Incorporate experiential/site visit components into courses. Perform administrative duties such as serving as department head. **SKILLS**—Writing; Instructing; Critical Thinking; Persuasion; Active Learning; Learning Strategies; Social Perceptiveness; Speaking.

GOE—Interest Area: 05. Education and Training. **Work Group:** 05.03. Postsecondary and Adult Teaching and Instructing. **PERSONALITY TYPE:** Social. Social occupations frequently involve working with, communicating with, and teaching people. These occupations often involve helping or providing service to others.

EDUCATION/TRAINING PROGRAMS—African Studies; African-American/Black Studies; American Indian/Native American Studies; American/United States Studies/Civilization; Area Studies, Other; Area, Ethnic, Cultural, and Gender Studies, Other; Asian Studies/Civilization; Asian-American Studies; Balkans Studies; Baltic Studies; Canadian Studies; Caribbean Studies; Central/Middle and Eastern European Studies; Chinese Studies; Commonwealth Studies; East Asian Studies; Ethnic, Cultural Minority, and Gender Studies, Other; others. **RELATED KNOWLEDGE/COURSES—History and Archeology:** Knowledge of historical events and their causes, indicators, and effects on civilizations and cultures. **Sociology and Anthropology:** Knowledge of group behavior and dynamics, societal trends and influences, human migrations, ethnicity, and cultures and their history and origins. **Foreign Language:** Knowledge of the structure and content of a foreign (non-English) language, including the meaning and spelling of words, rules of composition and grammar, and pronunciation. **Philosophy and Theology:** Knowledge of different philosophical systems and religions. This includes their basic principles, values, ethics, ways of thinking, customs, and practices and their impact on human culture. **Education and Training:** Knowledge of principles and methods for curriculum and training design, teaching and instruction for individuals and groups, and the measurement of training effects. **Geography:** Knowledge of principles and methods for describing the features of land, sea, and air masses, including their physical characteristics; locations; interrelationships; and distribution of plant, animal, and human life.

Art Directors

- Annual Earnings: $63,950
- Growth: 11.5%
- Annual Job Openings: 10,000
- Self-Employed: 55.8%
- Part-Time: 30.4%
- Education/Training Required: Work experience plus degree

Industries in Which Income Is Highest

Industry	Average Annual Wage	Number Employed
Management of Companies and Enterprises	$75,650	1,360
Professional, Scientific, and Technical Services	$68,580	14,820
Motion Picture and Sound Recording Industries	$59,840	1,010
Publishing Industries (Except Internet)	$56,920	5,090
Printing and Related Support Activities	$51,530	1,040

Metropolitan Areas Where Income Is Highest

Metropolitan Area	Average Annual Wage	Number Employed
San Jose–Sunnyvale–Santa Clara, CA	$95,970	230
Trenton–Ewing, NJ	$93,910	110
San Francisco–Oakland–Fremont, CA	$93,030	1,010
New York–Northern New Jersey–Long Island, NY–NJ–PA	$87,820	5,210
Bridgeport–Stamford–Norwalk, CT	$77,310	260

Formulate design concepts and presentation approaches and direct workers engaged in art work, layout design, and copy writing for visual communications media, such as magazines, books, newspapers, and packaging. Formulate basic layout design or presentation approach and specify material details, such as style and size of type, photographs, graphics, animation, video, and sound. Review and approve proofs of printed copy and art and copy materials developed by staff members. Manage own accounts and projects, working within budget and scheduling requirements. Confer with creative, art, copy-writing, or production department heads to discuss client requirements and presentation concepts and to coordinate creative activities. Present final layouts to clients for approval. Confer with clients to determine objectives; budget; background information; and presentation approaches, styles, and techniques. Hire, train, and direct staff members who develop design concepts into art layouts or who prepare layouts for printing. Work with creative directors to develop design solutions. Review illustrative material to determine if it conforms to standards and specifications. Attend photo shoots and printing sessions to ensure that the products needed are obtained. Create custom illustrations or other graphic elements. Mark up, paste, and complete layouts and write typography instructions to prepare materials for typesetting or printing. Negotiate with printers and estimators to determine what services will be performed. Conceptualize and help design interfaces for multimedia games, products, and devices. **SKILLS**—Coordination; Negotiation; Persuasion; Management of Financial Resources; Service Orientation; Operations Analysis; Instructing; Management of Personnel Resources.

GOE—Interest Area: 03. Arts and Communication. **Work Group:** 03.01. Managerial Work in Arts and Communication. **PERSONALITY TYPE:** Artistic. Artistic occupations frequently involve working with forms, designs, and patterns. They often require self-expression, and the work can be done without following a clear set of rules.

EDUCATION/TRAINING   PROGRAMS—Graphic Design; Intermedia/Multimedia. **RELATED KNOWLEDGE/COURSES—Design:** Knowledge of design techniques, tools, and principles involved in production of precision technical plans, blueprints, drawings, and models. **Fine Arts:** Knowledge of the theory and techniques required to compose, produce, and perform works of music, dance, visual arts, drama, and sculpture. **Computers and Electronics:** Knowledge of circuit boards, processors, chips, electronic equipment, and computer hardware and software, including applications and programming. **Communi-**

cations and Media: Knowledge of media production, communication, and dissemination techniques and methods. This includes alternative ways to inform and entertain via written, oral, and visual media. **Production and Processing:** Knowledge of raw materials, production processes, quality control, costs, and other techniques for maximizing the effective manufacture and distribution of goods. **Education and Training:** Knowledge of principles and methods for curriculum and training design, teaching and instruction for individuals and groups, and the measurement of training effects.

Art, Drama, and Music Teachers, Postsecondary

- Annual Earnings: $51,240
- Growth: 32.2%
- Annual Job Openings: 329,000
- Self-Employed: 0.4%
- Part-Time: 27.3%
- Education/Training Required: Master's degree

Our sources did not provide separate job openings data for this occupation. The job openings listed here are shared with 35 other postsecondary teaching occupations. For a complete list, see the beginning of this section.

Industries in Which Income Is Highest

Industry	Average Annual Wage	Number Employed
Educational Services	$51,200	68,340

Metropolitan Areas Where Income Is Highest

Metropolitan Area	Average Annual Wage	Number Employed
San Francisco–Oakland–Fremont, CA	$81,190	1,120
Providence–Fall River–Warwick, RI–MA	$69,690	570
Riverside–San Bernardino–Ontario, CA	$69,490	410
San Diego–Carlsbad–San Marcos, CA	$64,590	650
Birmingham–Hoover, AL	$63,780	210

Teach courses in drama, music, and the arts, including fine and applied art, such as painting and sculpture, or design and crafts. Evaluate and grade students' class work, performances, projects, assignments, and papers. Explain and demonstrate artistic techniques. Prepare students for performances, exams, or assessments. Prepare and deliver lectures to undergraduate and/or graduate students on topics such as acting techniques, fundamentals of music, and art history. Organize performance groups and direct their rehearsals. Prepare course materials such as syllabi, homework assignments, and handouts. Initiate, facilitate, and moderate classroom discussions. Keep abreast of developments in their field by reading current literature, talking with colleagues, and participating in professional conferences. Advise students on academic and vocational curricula and on career issues. Maintain student attendance records, grades, and other required records. Conduct research in a particular field of knowledge and publish findings in professional journals, books, and/or electronic media. Supervise undergraduate and/or graduate teaching, internship, and research work. Plan, evaluate, and revise curricula, course content, and course materials and methods of instruction. Maintain regularly scheduled office hours in order to advise and assist students. Compile, administer, and grade examinations or assign this work to others. Participate in student recruitment, registration, and placement activities. Select and obtain materials and supplies such as textbooks and performance pieces. Collaborate with colleagues to address teaching and research issues. Serve on academic or administrative committees that deal with institutional policies, departmental matters, and academic issues. Participate in campus and community events. Keep students informed of community events such as plays and concerts. Compile bibliographies of specialized materials for outside reading assignments. Display students' work in schools, galleries, and exhibitions. Perform administrative duties such as serving as department head. **SKILLS**—Instructing; Social Perceptiveness; Persuasion; Speaking; Learning Strategies; Active Listening; Critical Thinking; Active Learning.

GOE—Interest Area: 05. Education and Training. **Work Group:** 05.03. Postsecondary and Adult Teaching and Instructing. **PERSONALITY TYPE:** Artistic. Artistic occupations frequently involve working with forms, designs, and patterns. They often require self-expression, and the work can be done without following a clear set of rules.

EDUCATION/TRAINING PROGRAMS—Art History, Criticism, and Conservation; Art/Art Studies, General; Arts Management; Ceramic Arts and Ceramics; Cinematography and Film/Video Production; Commercial Photography; Conducting; Crafts/Craft Design, Folk Art, and Artisanry; Dance, General; Design and Applied Arts, Other; Design and Visual Communications, General; Directing and Theatrical Production; Drama and Dramatics/Theatre Arts, General; Dramatic/Theatre Arts and Stagecraft, Other; Fashion/Apparel Design; others. **RELATED KNOWLEDGE/COURSES—Fine Arts:** Knowledge of the theory and techniques required to compose, produce, and perform works of music, dance, visual arts, drama, and sculpture. **Education and Training:** Knowledge of principles and methods for curriculum and training design, teaching and instruction for individuals and groups, and the measurement of training effects. **History and Archeology:** Knowledge of historical events and their causes, indicators, and effects on civilizations and cultures. **Philosophy and Theology:** Knowledge of different philosophical systems and religions. This includes their basic principles, values, ethics, ways of thinking, customs, and practices and their impact on human culture. **English Language:** Knowledge of the structure and content of the English language, including the meaning and spelling of words, rules of composition, and grammar. **Communications and Media:** Knowledge of media production, communication, and dissemination techniques and methods. This includes alternative ways to inform and entertain via written, oral, and visual media.

Astronomers

- ◎ Annual Earnings: $104,670
- ◎ Growth: 10.4%
- ◎ Annual Job Openings: fewer than 500
- ◎ Self-Employed: 0.0%
- ◎ Part-Time: 8.0%
- ◎ Education/Training Required: Doctoral degree

Industries in Which Income Is Highest

Industry	Average Annual Wage	Number Employed
Federal, State, and Local Government	$112,220	450
Educational Services	$72,480	290

Metropolitan Areas Where Income Is Highest

Metropolitan Area	Average Annual Wage	Number Employed
Washington–Arlington–Alexandria, DC–VA–MD–WV	$116,710	390
Boston–Cambridge–Quincy, MA–NH	$116,180	80

Observe, research, and interpret celestial and astronomical phenomena to increase basic knowledge and apply such information to practical problems. Study celestial phenomena, using a variety of ground-based and space-borne telescopes and scientific instruments. Analyze research data to determine its significance, using computers. Present research findings at scientific conferences and in papers written for scientific journals. Measure radio, infrared, gamma, and X-ray emissions from extraterrestrial sources. Develop theories based on personal observations or on observations and theories of other astronomers. Raise funds for scientific research. Collaborate with other astronomers to carry out research projects. Develop instrumentation and software for astronomical observation and analysis. Teach astronomy or astrophysics. Develop and modify astronomy-related programs for public presentation. Calculate orbits and determine sizes, shapes, brightness, and motions of different celestial bodies. **SKILLS**— Science; Programming; Mathematics; Complex Problem Solving; Active Learning; Critical Thinking; Technology Design; Persuasion.

GOE—Interest Area: 15. Scientific Research, Engineering, and Mathematics. **Work Group:** 15.02. Physical Sciences. **PERSONALITY TYPE:** Investigative. Investigative occupations frequently involve working with ideas and require an extensive amount of thinking. These occupations can involve searching for facts and figuring out problems mentally.

EDUCATION/TRAINING PROGRAMS— Astronomy; Astronomy and Astrophysics, Other; Astrophysics; Planetary Astronomy and Science.

RELATED KNOWLEDGE/COURSES—Physics: Knowledge and prediction of physical principles and laws and their interrelationships and applications to understanding fluid, material, and atmospheric dynamics and mechanical, electrical, atomic, and subatomic structures and processes. **Mathematics:** Knowledge of arithmetic, algebra, geometry, calculus, and statistics and their applications. **Engineering and Technology:** Knowledge of the practical application of engineering science and technology. This includes applying principles, techniques, procedures, and equipment to the design and production of various goods and services. **Computers and Electronics:** Knowledge of circuit boards, processors, chips, electronic equipment, and computer hardware and software, including applications and programming. **Chemistry:** Knowledge of the chemical composition, structure, and properties of substances and of the chemical processes and transformations that they undergo. This includes uses of chemicals, their danger signs, production techniques, and disposal methods. **Education and Training:** Knowledge of principles and methods for curriculum and training design, teaching and instruction for individuals and groups, and the measurement of training effects.

Atmospheric and Space Scientists

- Annual Earnings: $73,940
- Growth: 16.5%
- Annual Job Openings: 1,000
- Self-Employed: 0.0%
- Part-Time: 4.3%
- Education/Training Required: Bachelor's degree

Industries in Which Income Is Highest

Industry	Average Annual Wage	Number Employed
Computer and Electronic Product Manufacturing	$95,710	110
Federal, State, and Local Government	$80,790	2,870
Broadcasting (Except Internet)	$67,800	540
Air Transportation	$67,290	70
Professional, Scientific, and Technical Services	$63,290	2,780

Metropolitan Areas Where Income Is Highest

Metropolitan Area	Average Annual Wage	Number Employed
Washington–Arlington–Alexandria, DC–VA–MD–WV	$89,640	380
New York–Northern New Jersey– Long Island, NY–NJ–PA	$89,130	90
Honolulu, HI	$86,570	50
Cleveland–Elyria–Mentor, OH	$83,300	40
Atlanta–Sandy Springs–Marietta, GA	$83,000	60

Investigate atmospheric phenomena and interpret meteorological data gathered by surface and air stations, satellites, and radar to prepare reports and forecasts for public and other uses. Collect and analyze historical climate information such as precipitation and temperature records in order to help predict future weather and climate trends. Conduct basic or applied meteorological research into the processes and determinants of atmospheric phenomena, weather, and climate. Conduct numerical simulations of climate conditions in order to understand and predict global and regional weather patterns. Gather data from sources such as surface and upper air stations, satellites, weather bureaus, and radar for use in meteorological reports and forecasts. Operate computer graphic equipment to produce weather reports and maps for analysis, distribution, or use in weather broadcasts. Prepare forecasts and briefings to meet the needs of industry, business, government, and other groups. Study and interpret data, reports, maps, photographs, and charts to predict long- and short-range weather conditions, using computer models and knowledge of climate theory, physics, and mathematics. Apply meteorological knowledge to problems in areas including agriculture, pollution control, and water management and to issues such as global warming or ozone depletion. Broadcast weather conditions, forecasts, and severe weather warnings to the public via television, radio, and the Internet and/or provide this information to the news media. Collect air samples from planes and ships over land and sea to study atmospheric composition. Consult with agencies, professionals, or researchers regarding the use and interpretation of climatological information. Design and develop new equipment and methods for meteorological data collection, remote sensing, or related applications. Develop and use weather forecasting tools such as mathematical and computer models. Measure wind, temperature, and humidity in the upper atmosphere, using weather balloons. Research and analyze the impact of industrial projects and pollution on climate, air quality, and weather phenomena. Direct forecasting services at weather stations or at radio or television broadcasting facilities. Make scientific presentations and publish reports, articles, or texts. **SKILLS**—Science; Management of Personnel Resources; Active Learning; Systems Analysis; Critical Thinking; Speaking; Judgment and Decision Making; Complex Problem Solving.

GOE—Interest Area: 15. Scientific Research, Engineering, and Mathematics. **Work Group:** 15.02. Physical Sciences. **PERSONALITY TYPE:** Investigative. Investigative occupations frequently involve working with ideas and require an extensive amount of thinking. These occupations can involve searching for facts and figuring out problems mentally.

EDUCATION/TRAINING PROGRAMS—Atmospheric Chemistry and Climatology; Atmospheric Physics and Dynamics; Atmospheric Sciences and Meteorology, General; Atmospheric Sciences and Meteorology, Other; Meteorology. **RELATED KNOWLEDGE/COURSES—Physics:** Knowledge and prediction of physical principles and laws and their interrelationships and applications to understanding fluid, material, and atmospheric dynamics and mechanical, electrical, atomic, and subatomic structures and processes. **Geography:** Knowledge of principles and methods for describing the features of land, sea, and air masses, including their physical characteristics; locations; interrelationships; and distribution of plant, animal, and human life. **Communications and Media:** Knowledge of media production, communication, and dissemination techniques and methods. This includes alternative ways to inform and entertain via written, oral, and visual media. **Telecommunications:** Knowledge of transmission, broadcasting, switching, control, and operation of telecommunications systems. **Administration and Management:** Knowledge of business and management principles involved in strategic planning, resource allocation, human resources modeling, leadership technique, production methods, and coordination of people and resources. **Mathematics:** Knowledge of arithmetic, algebra, geometry, calculus, and statistics and their applications.

Atmospheric, Earth, Marine, and Space Sciences Teachers, Postsecondary

- Annual Earnings: $65,720
- Growth: 32.2%
- Annual Job Openings: 329,000
- Self-Employed: 0.4%
- Part-Time: 27.3%
- Education/Training Required: Master's degree

Our sources did not provide separate job openings data for this occupation. The job openings listed here are shared with 35 other postsecondary teaching occupations. For a complete list, see the beginning of this section.

Industries in Which Income Is Highest

Industry	Average Annual Wage	Number Employed
Educational Services	$65,030	8,640

Metropolitan Areas Where Income Is Highest

Metropolitan Area	Average Annual Wage	Number Employed
Boston–Cambridge–Quincy, MA–NH	$97,900	200
Philadelphia–Camden–Wilmington, PA–NJ–DE–MD	$80,890	260
Denver–Aurora, CO	$74,620	90
Pittsburgh, PA	$74,530	60
Riverside–San Bernardino–Ontario, CA	$71,670	40

Teach courses in the physical sciences, except chemistry and physics. Conduct research in a particular field of knowledge and publish findings in professional journals, books, and/or electronic media. Write grant proposals to procure external research funding. Keep abreast of developments in their field by reading current literature, talking with colleagues, and participating in professional conferences. Supervise undergraduate and/or graduate teaching, internship, and research work. Prepare and deliver lectures to undergraduate and/or graduate students on topics such as structural geology, micrometeorology, and atmospheric thermodynamics. Supervise laboratory work and field work. Evaluate and grade students' class work, assignments, and papers. Prepare course materials such as syllabi, homework assignments, and handouts. Collaborate with colleagues to address teaching and research issues. Compile, administer, and grade examinations or assign this work to others. Plan, evaluate, and revise curricula, course content, and course materials and methods of instruction. Initiate, facilitate, and moderate classroom discussions. Maintain regularly scheduled office hours in order to advise and assist students. Advise students on academic and vocational curricula and on career issues. Maintain student attendance records, grades, and other required records. Participate in student recruitment, registration, and placement activities. Perform administrative duties such as serving as department head. Select and obtain materials and supplies such as textbooks and laboratory equipment. Serve on academic or administrative committees that deal with institutional policies, departmental matters, and academic issues. Compile bibliographies of specialized materials for outside reading assignments. **SKILLS**—Science; Programming; Instructing; Management of Financial Resources; Active Learning; Mathematics; Complex Problem Solving; Writing.

GOE—Interest Area: 05. Education and Training. **Work Group:** 05.03. Postsecondary and Adult Teaching and Instructing. **PERSONALITY TYPE:** No data available.

EDUCATION/TRAINING PROGRAMS— Acoustics; Astronomy; Astrophysics; Atmospheric Chemistry and Climatology; Atmospheric Physics and Dynamics; Atmospheric Sciences and Meteorology, General; Atmospheric Sciences and Meteorology, Other; Atomic/Molecular Physics; Elementary Particle Physics; Geochemistry; Geochemistry and Petrology; Geological and Earth Sciences/Geosciences, Other; Geology/Earth Science, General; Geophysics and Seismology; Hydrology and Water Resources Science; Meteorology; Nuclear Physics; others. **RELATED KNOWLEDGE/COURSES—Physics:** Knowledge and prediction of physical principles and laws and their interrelationships and applications to understanding fluid, material, and atmospheric dynamics and mechanical, electrical, atomic, and subatomic structures and processes. **Geography:** Knowledge of

principles and methods for describing the features of land, sea, and air masses, including their physical characteristics; locations; interrelationships; and distribution of plant, animal, and human life. **Education and Training:** Knowledge of principles and methods for curriculum and training design, teaching and instruction for individuals and groups, and the measurement of training effects. **Mathematics:** Knowledge of arithmetic, algebra, geometry, calculus, and statistics and their applications. **Chemistry:** Knowledge of the chemical composition, structure, and properties of substances and of the chemical processes and transformations that they undergo. This includes uses of chemicals, their danger signs, production techniques, and disposal methods. **Biology:** Knowledge of plant and animal organisms and their tissues, cells, functions, interdependencies, and interactions with each other and the environment.

Audiologists

- Annual Earnings: $53,490
- Growth: 9.1%
- Annual Job Openings: fewer than 500
- Self-Employed: 1.4%
- Part-Time: 30.8%
- Education/Training Required: Master's degree

Industries in Which Income Is Highest

Industry	Average Annual Wage	Number Employed
Hospitals	$54,880	1,720
Ambulatory Health Care Services	$54,030	5,000
Health and Personal Care Stores	$51,650	1,550
Educational Services	$51,220	1,350

Metropolitan Areas Where Income Is Highest

Metropolitan Area	Average Annual Wage	Number Employed
Tampa–St. Petersburg–Clearwater, FL	$74,060	60
Washington–Arlington–Alexandria, DC–VA–MD–WV	$70,390	400
Milwaukee–Waukesha–West Allis, WI	$65,580	80
Seattle–Tacoma–Bellevue, WA	$63,720	130
Omaha–Council Bluffs, NE–IA	$63,520	120

Assess and treat persons with hearing and related disorders. May fit hearing aids and provide auditory training. May perform research related to hearing problems. Evaluate hearing and speech/language disorders to determine diagnoses and courses of treatment. Administer hearing or speech/language evaluations, tests, or examinations to patients to collect information on type and degree of impairment, using specialized instruments and electronic equipment. Fit and dispense assistive devices, such as hearing aids. Maintain client records at all stages, including initial evaluation and discharge. Refer clients to additional medical or educational services if needed. Counsel and instruct clients in techniques to improve hearing or speech impairment, including sign language or lip-reading. Monitor clients' progress and discharge them from treatment when goals have been attained. Plan and conduct treatment programs for clients' hearing or speech problems, consulting with physicians, nurses, psychologists, and other health care personnel as necessary. Recommend assistive devices according to clients' needs or nature of impairments. Participate in conferences or training to update or share knowledge of new hearing or speech disorder treatment methods or technologies. Instruct clients, parents, teachers, or employers in how to avoid behavior patterns that lead to miscommunication. Examine and clean patients' ear canals. Advise educators or other medical staff on speech or hearing topics. Educate and supervise audiology students and health care personnel. Fit and tune cochlear implants, providing rehabilitation for adjustment to listening with implant amplification systems. Work with multi-disciplinary teams to assess and rehabilitate recipients of implanted hearing devices. Develop and supervise hearing screening programs. **SKILLS**—Social Perceptiveness; Service Orientation; Persuasion; Instructing; Active Learning; Science; Learning Strategies; Reading Comprehension.

GOE—**Interest Area:** 08. Health Science. **Work Group:** 08.07. Medical Therapy. **PERSONALITY TYPE:** Social. Social occupations frequently involve working with, communicating with, and teaching people. These occupations often involve helping or providing service to others.

EDUCATION/TRAINING PROGRAMS—Audiology/Audiologist and Hearing Sciences; Audiology/Audiologist and Speech-Language Pathology/Pathologist; Communication Disorders Sciences and Services, Other; Communication Disorders, General. **RELATED KNOWLEDGE/COURSES**—**Therapy and Counseling:** Knowledge of principles, methods, and procedures for diagnosis, treatment, and rehabilitation of physical and mental dysfunctions and for career counseling and guidance. **Medicine and Dentistry:** Knowledge of the information and techniques needed to diagnose and treat human injuries, diseases, and deformities. This includes symptoms, treatment alternatives, drug properties and interactions, and preventive health-care measures. **Customer and Personal Service:** Knowledge of principles and processes for providing customer and personal services. This includes customer needs assessment, meeting quality standards for services, and evaluation of customer satisfaction. **Psychology:** Knowledge of human behavior and performance; individual differences in ability, personality, and interests; learning and motivation; psychological research methods; and the assessment and treatment of behavioral and affective disorders. **Sales and Marketing:** Knowledge of principles and methods for showing, promoting, and selling products or services. This includes marketing strategy and tactics, product demonstration, sales techniques, and sales control systems. **Education and Training:** Knowledge of principles and methods for curriculum and training design, teaching and instruction for individuals and groups, and the measurement of training effects.

Auditors

- Annual Earnings: $52,210
- Growth: 22.4%
- Annual Job Openings: 157,000
- Self-Employed: 10.9%
- Part-Time: 10.3%
- Education/Training Required: Bachelor's degree

The job openings listed here are shared with Accountants.

Industries in Which Income Is Highest

Industry	Average Annual Wage	Number Employed
Securities, Commodity Contracts, and Other Financial Investments and Related Activities	$58,790	20,390
Clothing and Clothing Accessories Stores	$57,590	2,840
Computer and Electronic Product Manufacturing	$56,690	13,950
Publishing Industries (Except Internet)	$56,580	9,580
Utilities	$56,140	6,890

Metropolitan Areas Where Income Is Highest

Metropolitan Area	Average Annual Wage	Number Employed
Bridgeport–Stamford–Norwalk, CT	$65,720	6,930
San Jose–Sunnyvale–Santa Clara, CA	$65,050	8,590
New York–Northern New Jersey–Long Island, NY–NJ–PA	$65,050	92,350
Danbury, CT	$64,550	830
Bremerton–Silverdale, WA	$63,970	300

Examine and analyze accounting records to determine financial status of establishment and prepare financial reports concerning operating procedures. Collect and analyze data to detect deficient controls; duplicated effort; extravagance; fraud; or non-compliance with laws, regulations, and management policies. Report to management about asset utilization and audit results and recommend changes in operations and financial activities. Prepare detailed reports on audit findings. Review data about material assets, net worth, liabilities, capital stock, surplus, income, and expenditures. Inspect account books and accounting systems for efficiency, effectiveness, and use of accepted accounting procedures to record transactions. Examine and evaluate financial and information systems, recommending controls to ensure system reliability and data integrity. Supervise auditing of establishments and determine scope of investigation required. Prepare, analyze, and verify annual reports, financial statements, and other records, using accepted accounting and statistical procedures to assess financial condition and facilitate financial planning. Confer with company officials about financial and regulatory matters. Inspect cash on hand, notes receivable and

payable, negotiable securities, and canceled checks to confirm records are accurate. Examine inventory to verify journal and ledger entries. Examine whether the organization's objectives are reflected in its management activities and whether employees understand the objectives. Examine records and interview workers to ensure recording of transactions and compliance with laws and regulations. Direct activities of personnel engaged in filing, recording, compiling, and transmitting financial records. Produce up-to-the-minute information, using internal computer systems, to allow management to base decisions on actual, not historical, data. Conduct pre-implementation audits to determine if systems and programs under development will work as planned. **SKILLS**—Management of Financial Resources; Time Management; Writing; Instructing; Negotiation; Service Orientation; Persuasion; Mathematics.

GOE—Interest Area: 04. Business and Administration. **Work Group:** 04.05. Accounting, Auditing, and Analytical Support. **PERSONALITY TYPE:** Conventional. Conventional occupations frequently involve following set procedures and routines. These occupations can include working with data and details more than with ideas. Usually there is a clear line of authority to follow.

EDUCATION/TRAINING PROGRAMS—Accounting; Accounting and Business/Management; Accounting and Computer Science; Accounting and Finance; Auditing. **RELATED KNOWLEDGE/COURSES—Economics and Accounting:** Knowledge of economic and accounting principles and practices, the financial markets, banking, and the analysis and reporting of financial data. **Sales and Marketing:** Knowledge of principles and methods for showing, promoting, and selling products or services. This includes marketing strategy and tactics, product demonstration, sales techniques, and sales control systems. **Customer and Personal Service:** Knowledge of principles and processes for providing customer and personal services. This includes customer needs assessment, meeting quality standards for services, and evaluation of customer satisfaction. **Mathematics:** Knowledge of arithmetic, algebra, geometry, calculus, and statistics and their applications. **Law and Government:** Knowledge of laws, legal codes, court procedures, precedents, government regulations, executive orders, agency rules, and the democratic political process. **Computers and Electronics:** Knowledge of circuit boards, processors, chips, electronic equipment, and computer hardware and software, including applications and programming.

Auxiliary Equipment Operators, Power

- Annual Earnings: $53,170
- Growth: –0.4%
- Annual Job Openings: 5,000
- Self-Employed: 0.0%
- Part-Time: 1.5%
- Education/Training Required: Long-term on-the-job training

The job openings listed here are shared with Power Generating Plant Operators, Except Auxiliary Equipment Operators.

Industries in Which Income Is Highest

Industry	Average Annual Wage	Number Employed
Utilities	$55,330	23,660
Federal, State, and Local Government	$45,480	5,460

Metropolitan Areas Where Income Is Highest

Metropolitan Area	Average Annual Wage	Number Employed
Buffalo–Niagara Falls, NY	$66,950	150
Fresno, CA	$66,040	60
Albany–Schenectady–Troy, NY	$65,810	230
New York–Northern New Jersey–Long Island, NY–NJ–PA	$65,570	1,680
Riverside–San Bernardino–Ontario, CA	$65,310	470

Control and maintain auxiliary equipment, such as pumps, fans, compressors, condensers, feedwater heaters, filters, and chlorinators, that supply water, fuel, lubricants, air, and auxiliary power for turbines, generators, boilers, and other power-generating plant facilities. Tends portable or stationary high pressure boilers that supply heat or power for engines, turbines, and steam-powered equipment. Opens and closes valves and switches in sequence upon signal from other worker to start or shut down auxiliary units. Tightens leaking gland and pipe joints and reports need for major equipment repairs. Cleans and lubricates equipment and collects oil, water, and electrolyte samples for laboratory analysis to prevent equipment failure or deterioration. Assists in making electrical repairs. Reads gauges to verify that units are operating at specified capacity and listens for sounds warning of mechanical malfunction. Replenishes electrolyte in batteries and oil in voltage transformers and resets tripped electric relays. **SKILLS**—Operation Monitoring; Operation and Control; Equipment Maintenance; Repairing; Troubleshooting.

GOE—Interest Area: 13. Manufacturing. **Work Group:** 13.16. Utility Operation and Energy Distribution. **PERSONALITY TYPE:** Realistic. Realistic occupations frequently involve work activities that include practical, hands-on problems and solutions. They often deal with plants, animals, and real-world materials like wood, tools, and machinery. Many of the occupations require working outside and do not involve a lot of paperwork or working closely with others.

EDUCATION/TRAINING PROGRAM—No data available. **RELATED KNOWLEDGE/COURSES**—**Mechanical Devices:** Knowledge of machines and tools, including their designs, uses, repair, and maintenance. **Engineering and Technology:** Knowledge of the practical application of engineering science and technology. This includes applying principles, techniques, procedures, and equipment to the design and production of various goods and services.

Aviation Inspectors

- Annual Earnings: $49,490
- Growth: 11.4%
- Annual Job Openings: 2,000
- Self-Employed: 1.9%
- Part-Time: 2.2%
- Education/Training Required: Work experience in a related occupation

The job openings listed here are shared with Freight Inspectors, Marine Cargo Inspectors, Motor Vehicle

Inspectors, Public Transportation Inspectors, and Railroad Inspectors.

Industries in Which Income Is Highest

Industry	Average Annual Wage	Number Employed
Air Transportation	$67,590	1,460
Transportation Equipment Manufacturing	$55,200	1,100
Federal, State, and Local Government	$54,510	10,960
Rail Transportation	$45,840	2,680
Support Activities for Transportation	$37,870	4,350

Metropolitan Areas Where Income Is Highest

Metropolitan Area	Average Annual Wage	Number Employed
Washington–Arlington–Alexandria, DC–VA–MD–WV	$96,800	360
Oklahoma City, OK	$91,650	130
Milwaukee–Waukesha–West Allis, WI	$84,510	50
Miami–Fort Lauderdale–Miami Beach, FL	$84,490	680
Louisville–Jefferson County, KY–IN	$81,260	80

Inspect aircraft, maintenance procedures, air navigational aids, air traffic controls, and communications equipment to ensure conformance with federal safety regulations. Analyze training programs and conduct oral and written examinations to ensure the competency of persons operating, installing, and repairing aircraft equipment. Approve or deny issuance of certificates of airworthiness. Conduct flight test programs to test equipment, instruments, and systems under a variety of conditions, using both manual and automatic controls. Examine landing gear; tires; and exteriors of fuselage, wings, and engines for evidence of damage or corrosion and to determine whether repairs are needed. Examine maintenance records and flight logs to determine if service and maintenance checks and overhauls were performed at prescribed intervals. Inspect new, repaired, or modified aircraft to identify damage or defects and to assess airworthiness and conformance to standards, using checklists, hand tools, and test instruments. Inspect work of aircraft mechanics performing maintenance, modification, or repair and overhaul of aircraft and aircraft mechanical systems in order to ensure adherence to standards and procedures. Prepare and maintain detailed repair, inspection, investigation, and certification records and reports. Recommend replacement, repair, or modification of aircraft equipment. Start aircraft and observe gauges, meters, and other instruments to detect evidence of malfunctions. Examine aircraft access plates and doors for security. Investigate air accidents and complaints to determine causes. Issue pilots' licenses to individuals meeting standards. Observe flight activities of pilots to assess flying skills and to ensure conformance to flight and safety regulations. Recommend changes in rules, policies, standards, and regulations based on knowledge of operating conditions, aircraft improvements, and other factors. Schedule and coordinate in-flight testing programs with ground crews and air traffic control to ensure availability of ground tracking, equipment monitoring, and related services. **SKILLS**—Operation Monitoring; Quality Control Analysis; Science; Systems Analysis; Systems Evaluation; Writing; Critical Thinking; Judgment and Decision Making.

GOE—Interest Area: 07. Government and Public Administration. **Work Group:** 07.03. Regulations Enforcement. **PERSONALITY TYPE:** Realistic. Realistic occupations frequently involve work activities that include practical, hands-on problems and solutions. They often deal with plants, animals, and real-world materials like wood, tools, and machinery. Many of the occupations require working outside and do not involve a lot of paperwork or working closely with others.

EDUCATION/TRAINING PROGRAM—No data available. **RELATED KNOWLEDGE/COURSES— Engineering and Technology:** Knowledge of the practical application of engineering science and technology. This includes applying principles, techniques, procedures, and equipment to the design and production of various goods and services. **Mechanical Devices:** Knowledge of machines and tools, including their designs, uses, repair, and maintenance. **Public Safety and Security:** Knowledge of relevant equipment, policies, procedures, and strategies to promote effective local, state, or national security operations for the protection of people, data, property, and institutions. **Physics:** Knowledge and prediction of physical principles and laws and their interrelationships and applications to understanding fluid, material, and atmospheric dynamics and mechanical, electrical, atomic, and subatomic structures and processes. **Law**

and Government: Knowledge of laws, legal codes, court procedures, precedents, government regulations, executive orders, agency rules, and the democratic political process. **Education and Training:** Knowledge of principles and methods for curriculum and training design, teaching and instruction for individuals and groups, and the measurement of training effects.

Avionics Technicians

- ◎ Annual Earnings: $46,630
- ◎ Growth: 9.1%
- ◎ Annual Job Openings: 2,000
- ◎ Self-Employed: 0.0%
- ◎ Part-Time: 0.0%
- ◎ Education/Training Required: Postsecondary vocational training

Industries in Which Income Is Highest

Industry	Average Annual Wage	Number Employed
Transportation Equipment Manufacturing	$47,790	4,730
Federal, State, and Local Government	$45,880	8,340
Support Activities for Transportation	$40,890	3,470

Metropolitan Areas Where Income Is Highest

Metropolitan Area	Average Annual Wage	Number Employed
Honolulu, HI	$60,190	170
Anchorage, AK	$59,550	70
Atlanta–Sandy Springs–Marietta, GA	$53,370	190
Seattle–Tacoma–Bellevue, WA	$52,510	350
Salt Lake City, UT	$52,480	60

Install, inspect, test, adjust, or repair avionics equipment, such as radar, radio, navigation, and missile control systems, in aircraft or space vehicles. Adjust, repair, or replace malfunctioning components or assemblies, using hand tools and/or soldering irons. Assemble components such as switches, electrical controls, and junction boxes, using hand tools and soldering irons. Connect components to assemblies such as radio systems, instruments, magnetos, inverters, and in-flight refueling systems, using hand tools and soldering irons. Install electrical and electronic components, assemblies, and systems in aircraft, using hand tools, power tools, and/or soldering irons. Interpret flight test data in order to diagnose malfunctions and systemic performance problems. Lay out installation of aircraft assemblies and systems, following documentation such as blueprints, manuals, and wiring diagrams. Test and troubleshoot instruments, components, and assemblies, using circuit testers, oscilloscopes, and voltmeters. Assemble prototypes or models of circuits, instruments, and systems so that they can be used for testing. Coordinate work with that of engineers, technicians, and other aircraft maintenance personnel. Fabricate parts and test aids as required. Keep records of maintenance and repair work. Operate computer-aided drafting and design applications to design avionics system modifications. Set up and operate ground support and test equipment to perform functional flight tests of electrical and electronic systems. **SKILLS**—Repairing; Installation; Operation Monitoring; Equipment Maintenance; Troubleshooting; Science; Operation and Control; Quality Control Analysis.

GOE—Interest Area: 13. Manufacturing. **Work Group:** 13.12. Electrical and Electronic Repair. **PERSONALITY TYPE:** Realistic. Realistic occupations frequently involve work activities that include practical, hands-on problems and solutions. They often deal with plants, animals, and real-world materials like wood, tools, and machinery. Many of the occupations require working outside and do not involve a lot of paperwork or working closely with others.

EDUCATION/TRAINING PROGRAMS—Airframe Mechanics and Aircraft Maintenance Technology/Technician; Avionics Maintenance and Technology/Technician. **RELATED KNOWLEDGE/ COURSES—Computers and Electronics:** Knowledge of circuit boards, processors, chips, electronic equipment, and computer hardware and software, including applications and programming. **Physics:** Knowledge and prediction of physical principles and laws and their interrelationships and applications to understanding fluid, material, and atmospheric dynamics and mechanical, electrical, atomic, and subatomic structures and processes. **Design:** Knowledge of design techniques, tools, and principles involved in production of precision technical plans, blueprints, drawings, and models. **Engineering and Technology:** Knowledge of the practical application of engineering science and technology. This includes applying principles, techniques, procedures, and equipment to the design and production of various goods and services. **Mechanical Devices:** Knowledge of machines and tools, including their designs, uses, repair, and maintenance. **Public Safety and Security:** Knowledge of relevant equipment, policies, procedures, and strategies to promote effective local, state, or national security operations for the protection of people, data, property, and institutions.

Biochemists

- ◎ Annual Earnings: $71,000
- ◎ Growth: 21.0%
- ◎ Annual Job Openings: 1,000
- ◎ Self-Employed: 2.7%
- ◎ Part-Time: 8.6%
- ◎ Education/Training Required: Doctoral degree

The job openings listed here are shared with Biophysicists.

Industries in Which Income Is Highest

Industry	Average Annual Wage	Number Employed
Chemical Manufacturing	$77,370	4,930
Professional, Scientific, and Technical Services	$73,320	8,740
Educational Services	$42,020	1,140

Metropolitan Areas Where Income Is Highest

Metropolitan Area	Average Annual Wage	Number Employed
Atlanta–Sandy Springs–Marietta, GA	$102,560	60
Boston–Cambridge–Quincy, MA–NH	$87,060	1,290
Philadelphia–Camden–Wilmington, PA–NJ–DE–MD	$79,250	790
San Jose–Sunnyvale–Santa Clara, CA	$78,610	160
San Francisco–Oakland–Fremont, CA	$77,950	1,190

Research or study chemical composition and processes of living organisms that affect vital processes such as growth and aging to determine chemical actions and effects on organisms such as the action of foods, drugs, or other substances on body functions and tissues. Studies chemistry of living processes, such as cell development, breathing, and digestion, and living energy changes, such as growth, aging, and death. Researches methods of transferring characteristics, such as resistance to disease, from one organism to another. Examines chemical aspects of formation of antibodies and researches chemistry of cells and blood corpuscles. Develops and executes tests to detect disease, genetic disorders, or other abnormalities. Develops and tests new drugs and medications used for commercial distribution. Designs and builds laboratory equipment needed for special research projects. Analyzes foods to determine nutritional value and effects of cooking, canning, and processing on this value. Cleans, purifies, refines, and otherwise prepares pharmaceutical compounds for commercial distribution. Prepares reports and recommendations based upon research outcomes. Develops methods to process, store, and use food, drugs, and chemical compounds. Isolates, analyzes, and identifies hormones, vitamins, allergens, minerals, and enzymes and determines their effects on body functions. Researches and determines chemical action of substances such as drugs, serums, hormones, and food on tissues and vital processes. **SKILLS**—Science; Programming; Writing; Reading Comprehension; Active Learning; Mathematics; Critical Thinking; Equipment Selection.

GOE—Interest Area: 15. Scientific Research, Engineering, and Mathematics. **Work Group:** 15.03. Life Sciences. **PERSONALITY TYPE:** Investigative. Investigative occupations frequently involve working with ideas and require an extensive amount of thinking. These occupations can involve searching for facts and figuring out problems mentally.

EDUCATION/TRAINING PROGRAMS—Biochemistry; Biochemistry/Biophysics and Molecular Biology; Cell/Cellular Biology and Anatomical Sciences, Other; Molecular Biochemistry; Soil Microbiology. **RELATED KNOWLEDGE/COURSES**—**Biology:** Knowledge of plant and animal organisms and their tissues, cells, functions, interdependencies, and interactions with each other and the environment. **Chemistry:** Knowledge of the chemical composition, structure, and properties of substances and of the chemical processes and transformations that they undergo. This includes uses of chemicals, their danger signs, production techniques, and disposal methods. **Building and Construction:** Knowledge of the materials, methods, and tools involved in the construction or repair of houses, buildings, or other structures such as highways and roads. **Mathematics:** Knowledge of arithmetic, algebra, geometry, calculus, and statistics and their applications.

Biological Science Teachers, Postsecondary

- ⊚ Annual Earnings: $63,570
- ⊚ Growth: 32.2%
- ⊚ Annual Job Openings: 329,000
- ⊚ Self-Employed: 0.4%
- ⊚ Part-Time: 27.3%
- ⊚ Education/Training Required: Master's degree

Our sources did not provide separate job openings data for this occupation. The job openings listed here are shared with 35 other postsecondary teaching occupations. For a complete list, see the beginning of this section.

Industries in Which Income Is Highest

Industry	Average Annual Wage	Number Employed
Educational Services	$63,580	58,750

Metropolitan Areas Where Income Is Highest

Metropolitan Area	Average Annual Wage	Number Employed
Boston–Cambridge–Quincy, MA–NH	$110,080	1,310
San Francisco–Oakland–Fremont, CA	$84,670	870
Riverside–San Bernardino–Ontario, CA	$81,240	210
Durham, NC	$80,360	330
Los Angeles–Long Beach–Santa Ana, CA	$78,900	820

Teach courses in biological sciences. Prepare and deliver lectures to undergraduate and/or graduate students on topics such as molecular biology, marine biology, and botany. Evaluate and grade students' class work, laboratory work, assignments, and papers. Prepare course materials such as syllabi, homework assignments, and handouts. Compile, administer, and grade examinations or assign this work to others. Supervise students' laboratory work. Keep abreast of developments in their field by reading current literature, talking with colleagues, and participating in professional conferences. Maintain student attendance records, grades, and other required records. Initiate, facilitate, and moderate classroom discussions. Plan, evaluate, and revise curricula, course content, and course materials and methods of instruction. Advise students on academic and vocational curricula and on career issues. Maintain regularly scheduled office hours in order to advise and assist students. Supervise undergraduate and/or graduate teaching, internship, and research work. Select and obtain materials and supplies such as textbooks and laboratory equipment. Collaborate with colleagues to address teaching and research issues. Conduct research in a particular field of knowledge and publish findings in professional journals, books, and/or electronic media. Serve on academic or administrative committees that deal with institutional policies, departmental matters, and academic issues. Participate in student recruitment, registration, and placement activities. Write grant proposals to procure external research funding. Perform administrative duties such as serving as department head. **SKILLS—** Science; Instructing; Learning Strategies; Writing; Active Learning; Reading Comprehension; Critical Thinking; Speaking.

GOE—Interest Area: 05. Education and Training. **Work Group:** 05.03. Postsecondary and Adult Teaching and Instructing. **PERSONALITY TYPE:** Investigative. Investigative occupations frequently involve working with ideas and require an extensive amount of thinking. These occupations can involve searching for facts and figuring out problems mentally.

EDUCATION/TRAINING PROGRAMS—Anatomy; Animal Physiology; Biochemistry; Biological and Biomedical Sciences, Other; Biology/Biological Sciences, General; Biometry/Biometrics; Biophysics; Biotechnology; Botany/Plant Biology; Cell/Cellular

Biology and Histology; Ecology; Ecology, Evolution, and Systematics, Other; Entomology; Evolutionary Biology; Immunology; Marine Biology and Biological Oceanography; Microbiology, General; Molecular Biology; Neuroscience; Nutrition Sciences; Parasitology; Pathology/Exper. Pathology; others. **RELATED KNOWLEDGE/COURSES—Biology:** Knowledge of plant and animal organisms and their tissues, cells, functions, interdependencies, and interactions with each other and the environment. **Education and Training:** Knowledge of principles and methods for curriculum and training design, teaching and instruction for individuals and groups, and the measurement of training effects. **Chemistry:** Knowledge of the chemical composition, structure, and properties of substances and of the chemical processes and transformations that they undergo. This includes uses of chemicals, their danger signs, production techniques, and disposal methods. **English Language:** Knowledge of the structure and content of the English language, including the meaning and spelling of words, rules of composition, and grammar. **Medicine and Dentistry:** Knowledge of the information and techniques needed to diagnose and treat human injuries, diseases, and deformities. This includes symptoms, treatment alternatives, drug properties and interactions, and preventive health-care measures. **Geography:** Knowledge of principles and methods for describing the features of land, sea, and air masses, including their physical characteristics; locations; interrelationships; and distribution of plant, animal, and human life.

Biomedical Engineers

- Annual Earnings: $71,840
- Growth: 30.7%
- Annual Job Openings: 1,000
- Self-Employed: 7.2%
- Part-Time: 0.0%
- Education/Training Required: Bachelor's degree

Industries in Which Income Is Highest

Industry	Average Annual Wage	Number Employed
Professional, Scientific, and Technical Services	$81,040	3,080
Chemical Manufacturing	$75,960	2,040
Computer and Electronic Product Manufacturing	$72,590	1,350
Miscellaneous Manufacturing	$71,920	2,170
Hospitals	$52,540	1,520

Metropolitan Areas Where Income Is Highest

Metropolitan Area	Average Annual Wage	Number Employed
San Jose–Sunnyvale–Santa Clara, CA	$124,260	330
Boston–Cambridge–Quincy, MA–NH	$84,720	1,230
Milwaukee–Waukesha–West Allis, WI	$82,960	130
San Diego–Carlsbad–San Marcos, CA	$82,830	290
Seattle–Tacoma–Bellevue, WA	$81,150	410

Apply knowledge of engineering, biology, and biomechanical principles to the design, development, and evaluation of biological and health systems and products, such as artificial organs, prostheses, instrumentation, medical information systems, and health management and care delivery systems. Analyze new medical procedures in order to forecast likely outcomes. Design and deliver technology to assist people with disabilities. Develop new applications for energy sources, such as using nuclear power for biomedical implants. Diagnose and interpret bioelectric data, using signal processing techniques. Teach biomedical engineering or disseminate knowledge about field through writing or consulting. Advise and assist in the application of instrumentation in clinical environments. Conduct research, along with life scientists, chemists, and medical scientists, on the engineering aspects of the biological systems of humans and animals. Design and develop medical diagnostic and clinical instrumentation, equipment, and procedures, utilizing the principles of engineering and bio-behavioral sciences. Develop models or computer simulations of human bio-behavioral systems in order to obtain data for measuring or controlling life processes. Evaluate the safety, efficiency, and effectiveness of biomedical equipment. Install, adjust, maintain, and/or repair biomedical equipment. Research new materials to be used for products such as implanted artificial organs. Adapt or design computer hardware or software for medical science uses. Advise hospital administrators on the planning, acquisition, and use of medical equipment. **SKILLS**—No data available.

GOE—**Interest Area:** 15. Scientific Research, Engineering, and Mathematics. **Work Group:** 15.07. Research and Design Engineering. **PERSONALITY TYPE:** No data available.

EDUCATION/TRAINING PROGRAM—Biomedical/Medical Engineering. **RELATED KNOWLEDGE/COURSES**—No data available.

Biophysicists

- ◎ Annual Earnings: $71,000
- ◎ Growth: 21.0%
- ◎ Annual Job Openings: 1,000
- ◎ Self-Employed: 2.7%
- ◎ Part-Time: 8.6%
- ◎ Education/Training Required: Doctoral degree

The job openings listed here are shared with Biochemists.

Industries in Which Income Is Highest

Industry	Average Annual Wage	Number Employed
Chemical Manufacturing	$77,370	4,930
Professional, Scientific, and Technical Services	$73,320	8,740
Educational Services	$42,020	1,140

Metropolitan Areas Where Income Is Highest

Metropolitan Area	Average Annual Wage	Number Employed
Atlanta–Sandy Springs–Marietta, GA	$102,560	60
Boston–Cambridge–Quincy, MA–NH	$87,060	1,290
Philadelphia–Camden–Wilmington, PA–NJ–DE–MD	$79,250	790
San Jose–Sunnyvale–Santa Clara, CA	$78,610	160
San Francisco–Oakland–Fremont, CA	$77,950	1,190

Research or study physical principles of living cells and organisms, their electrical and mechanical energy, and related phenomena. Studies absorption of light by chlorophyll in photosynthesis or by pigments of eye involved in vision. Researches cancer treatment, using radiation and nuclear particles. Analyzes functions of electronic and human brains, such as learning, thinking, and memory. Investigates dynamics of seeing and hearing. Studies spatial configuration of submicroscopic molecules, such as proteins, using X-ray and electron microscope. Researches manner in which characteristics of plants and animals are carried through successive generations. Investigates damage to cells and tissues caused by X rays and nuclear particles. Researches transformation of substances in cells, using atomic isotopes. Studies physical principles of living cells and organisms and their electrical and mechanical energy. Investigates transmission of electrical impulses along nerves and muscles. **SKILLS**—Science; Reading Comprehension; Writing; Mathematics; Active Learning; Complex Problem Solving; Critical Thinking; Systems Analysis.

GOE—**Interest Area:** 15. Scientific Research, Engineering, and Mathematics. **Work Group:** 15.03. Life Sciences. **PERSONALITY TYPE:** Investigative. Investigative occupations frequently involve working with ideas and require an extensive amount of thinking. These occupations can involve searching for facts and figuring out problems mentally.

EDUCATION/TRAINING PROGRAMS—Biochemistry/Biophysics and Molecular Biology; Biophysics; Cell/Cellular Biology and Anatomical Sciences, Other; Molecular Biophysics; Soil Microbiology. **RELATED KNOWLEDGE/COURSES**—**Biology:** Knowledge of plant and animal organisms and their tissues, cells, functions, interdependencies, and interactions with each other and the environment. **Physics:** Knowledge and prediction of physical principles and laws and their interrelationships and applications to understanding fluid, material, and atmospheric dynamics and mechanical, electrical, atomic, and subatomic structures and processes. **Chemistry:** Knowledge of the chemical composition, structure, and properties of substances and of the chemical processes and transformations that they undergo. This includes uses of chemicals, their danger signs, production techniques, and disposal methods. **Mathematics:** Knowledge of arithmetic, algebra, geometry, calculus, and statistics and their applications.

Boilermakers

- Annual Earnings: $48,050
- Growth: 8.7%
- Annual Job Openings: 2,000
- Self-Employed: 0.0%
- Part-Time: 0.0%
- Education/Training Required: Long-term on-the-job training

Industries in Which Income Is Highest

Industry	Average Annual Wage	Number Employed
Construction of Buildings	$51,750	3,910
Specialty Trade Contractors	$50,300	6,390
Heavy and Civil Engineering Construction	$48,040	1,880
Fabricated Metal Product Manufacturing	$41,440	1,350

Metropolitan Areas Where Income Is Highest

Metropolitan Area	Average Annual Wage	Number Employed
New York–Northern New Jersey–Long Island, NY–NJ–PA	$70,760	610
Chicago–Naperville–Joliet, IL–IN–WI	$67,510	1,080
San Francisco–Oakland–Fremont, CA	$65,380	240
Kansas City, MO–KS	$63,700	670
Peoria, IL	$60,790	50

Construct, assemble, maintain, and repair stationary steam boilers and boiler house auxiliaries. Align structures or plate sections to assemble boiler frame tanks or vats, following blueprints. Work involves use of hand and power tools, plumb bobs, levels, wedges, dogs, or turnbuckles. Assist in testing assembled vessels. Direct cleaning of boilers and boiler furnaces. Inspect and repair boiler fittings, such as safety valves, regulators, automatic-control mechanisms, water columns, and auxiliary machines. Position, align, and secure structural parts and related assemblies to boiler frames, tanks, or vats of pressure vessels, following blueprints. Repair or replace defective pressure vessel parts, such as safety valves and regulators, using torches, jacks, caulking hammers, power saws, threading dies, welding equipment, and metalworking machinery. Shape seams, joints, and irregular edges of pressure vessel sections and structural parts in order to attain specified fit of parts, using cutting torches, hammers, files, and metalworking machines. Straighten or reshape bent pressure vessel plates and structure parts, using hammers, jacks, and torches. Study blueprints to determine locations, relationships, and dimensions of parts. Assemble large vessels in an on-site fabrication shop prior to installation in order to ensure proper fit. Attach rigging and signal crane or hoist operators to lift heavy frame and plate sections and other parts into place. Clean pressure vessel equipment, using scrapers, wire brushes, and cleaning solvents. Shape and fabricate parts, such as stacks, uptakes, and chutes, in order to adapt pressure vessels, heat exchangers, and piping to premises, using heavy-metalworking machines such as brakes, rolls, and drill presses. Bell, bead with power hammers, or weld pressure vessel tube ends in order to ensure leakproof joints. Bolt or arc-weld pressure vessel structures and parts together, using wrenches and welding equipment. Examine boilers, pressure vessels, tanks, and vats to locate defects such as leaks, weak spots, and defective sections so that they can be repaired. Inspect assembled vessels and individual components, such as tubes, fittings, valves, controls, and auxiliary mechanisms, to locate any defects. Install manholes, handholes, taps, tubes, valves, gauges, and feedwater connections in drums of water tube boilers, using hand tools. Install refractory bricks and other heat-resistant materials in fireboxes of pressure vessels. Lay out plate, sheet steel, or other heavy metal and locate and mark bending and cutting lines, using protractors, compasses, and drawing instruments or templates. **SKILLS**—Installation; Repairing; Equipment Maintenance; Quality Control Analysis; Troubleshooting; Systems Analysis; Operation Monitoring; Operation and Control.

GOE—Interest Area: 02. Architecture and Construction. **Work Group:** 02.04. Construction Crafts. **PERSONALITY TYPE:** Realistic. Realistic occupations frequently involve work activities that include practical, hands-on problems and solutions. They often deal with plants, animals, and real-world materials like wood, tools, and machinery. Many of the occupations require working outside and do not involve a lot of paperwork or working closely with others.

EDUCATION/TRAINING PROGRAM—Boilermaking/Boilermaker. **RELATED KNOWL-**

EDGE/COURSES—Building and Construction: Knowledge of the materials, methods, and tools involved in the construction or repair of houses, buildings, or other structures such as highways and roads. **Mechanical Devices:** Knowledge of machines and tools, including their designs, uses, repair, and maintenance. **Engineering and Technology:** Knowledge of the practical application of engineering science and technology. This includes applying principles, techniques, procedures, and equipment to the design and production of various goods and services. **Physics:** Knowledge and prediction of physical principles and laws and their interrelationships and applications to understanding fluid, material, and atmospheric dynamics and mechanical, electrical, atomic, and subatomic structures and processes. **Design:** Knowledge of design techniques, tools, and principles involved in production of precision technical plans, blueprints, drawings, and models. **Public Safety and Security:** Knowledge of relevant equipment, policies, procedures, and strategies to promote effective local, state, or national security operations for the protection of people, data, property, and institutions.

Budget Analysts

- Annual Earnings: $58,910
- Growth: 13.5%
- Annual Job Openings: 6,000
- Self-Employed: 2.0%
- Part-Time: 4.7%
- Education/Training Required: Bachelor's degree

Industries in Which Income Is Highest

Industry	Average Annual Wage	Number Employed
Computer and Electronic Product Manufacturing	$72,860	2,200
Professional, Scientific, and Technical Services	$64,080	5,280
Management of Companies and Enterprises	$63,070	3,110
Federal, State, and Local Government	$58,450	24,270
Insurance Carriers and Related Activities	$55,950	1,360

Metropolitan Areas Where Income Is Highest

Metropolitan Area	Average Annual Wage	Number Employed
San Jose–Sunnyvale–Santa Clara, CA	$80,720	1,000
Kennewick–Richland–Pasco, WA	$77,320	100
Washington–Arlington–Alexandria, DC–VA–MD–WV	$75,950	4,970
San Francisco–Oakland–Fremont, CA	$74,880	1,020
Oxnard–Thousand Oaks–Ventura, CA	$68,840	230

Examine budget estimates for completeness, accuracy, and conformance with procedures and regulations. Analyze budgeting and accounting reports for the purpose of maintaining expenditure controls. Analyze monthly department budgeting and accounting reports to maintain expenditure controls. Direct the preparation of regular and special budget reports. Consult with managers to ensure that budget adjustments are made in accordance with program changes. Match appropriations for specific programs with appropriations for broader programs, including items for emergency funds. Provide advice and technical assistance with cost analysis, fiscal allocation, and budget preparation. Summarize budgets and submit recommendations for the approval or disapproval of funds requests. Seek new ways to improve efficiency and increase profits. Review operating budgets to analyze trends affecting budget needs. Examine budget estimates for completeness, accuracy, and conformance with procedures and regulations. Perform cost-benefits analyses to compare operating programs, review financial requests, and explore alternative financing methods. Interpret budget directives and establish policies for carrying out directives. Compile and analyze accounting records and other data to determine the financial resources required to implement a program. Testify before examining and fund-granting authorities, clarifying and promoting the proposed budgets. **SKILLS**—Management of Financial Resources; Operations Analysis; Mathematics; Service Orientation; Time Management; Complex Problem Solving; Active Learning; Persuasion.

GOE—Interest Area: 04. Business and Administration. **Work Group:** 04.05. Accounting, Auditing, and Analytical Support. **PERSONALITY TYPE:** Conventional. Conventional occupations frequently involve following set procedures and routines. These occupations can include working with data and details more than with ideas. Usually there is a clear line of authority to follow.

EDUCATION/TRAINING PROGRAMS—
Accounting; Finance, General. **RELATED KNOWL-EDGE/COURSES—Economics and Accounting:** Knowledge of economic and accounting principles and practices, the financial markets, banking, and the analysis and reporting of financial data. **Administration and Management:** Knowledge of business and management principles involved in strategic planning, resource allocation, human resources modeling, leadership technique, production methods, and coordination of people and resources. **Computers and Electronics:** Knowledge of circuit boards, processors, chips, electronic equipment, and computer hardware and software, including applications and programming. **Clerical Practices:** Knowledge of administrative and clerical procedures and systems such as word processing, managing files and records, stenography and transcription, designing forms, and other office procedures and terminology. **Personnel and Human Resources:** Knowledge of principles and procedures for personnel recruitment, selection, training, compensation and benefits, labor relations and negotiation, and personnel information systems. **Mathematics:** Knowledge of arithmetic, algebra, geometry, calculus, and statistics and their applications.

Business Teachers, Postsecondary

- ◎ Annual Earnings: $59,210
- ◎ Growth: 32.2%
- ◎ Annual Job Openings: 329,000
- ◎ Self-Employed: 0.4%
- ◎ Part-Time: 27.3%
- ◎ Education/Training Required: Master's degree

Our sources did not provide separate job openings data for this occupation. The job openings listed here are shared with 35 other postsecondary teaching occupations. For a complete list, see the beginning of this section.

Industries in Which Income Is Highest

Industry	Average Annual Wage	Number Employed
Educational Services	$59,260	67,210

Metropolitan Areas Where Income Is Highest

Metropolitan Area	Average Annual Wage	Number Employed
Durham, NC	$109,240	530
San Jose–Sunnyvale–Santa Clara, CA	$105,390	220
Gainesville, FL	$101,570	220
Boston–Cambridge–Quincy, MA–NH	$100,640	1,610
New Haven, CT	$85,090	240

Teach courses in business administration and management, such as accounting, finance, human resources, labor relations, marketing, and operations research. Prepare and deliver lectures to undergraduate and/or graduate students on topics such as financial accounting, principles of marketing, and operations management. Evaluate and grade students' class work, assignments, and papers. Compile, administer, and grade examinations or assign this work to others. Prepare course materials such as syllabi, homework assignments, and handouts. Maintain student attendance records, grades, and other required records. Initiate, facilitate, and moderate classroom discussions. Plan, evaluate, and revise curricula, course content, and course materials and methods of instruction. Maintain regularly scheduled office hours in order to advise and assist students. Keep abreast of developments in their field by reading current literature, talking with colleagues, and participating in professional organizations and conferences. Advise students on academic and vocational curricula and on career issues. Select and obtain materials and supplies such as textbooks. Collaborate with colleagues to address teaching and research issues. Collaborate with members of the business community to improve programs, to develop new programs, and to provide student access to learning opportunities such as internships. Participate in student recruitment, registration, and placement activities. Serve on academic or administrative committees that deal with institutional policies, departmental matters, and academic issues. Participate in campus and community events. Compile bibliographies of specialized materials for outside reading assignments. Perform administrative duties such as serving as department head. Supervise undergraduate and/or graduate teaching, internship, and research work. Conduct research in a particular field of knowledge and publish findings in professional journals, books, and/or electronic media. Act as advisers to student organizations. **SKILLS**—Instructing; Learning Strategies; Monitoring; Writing; Active Learning; Persuasion; Time Management; Social Perceptiveness.

GOE—Interest Area: 05. Education and Training. **Work Group:** 05.03. Postsecondary and Adult Teaching and Instructing. **PERSONALITY TYPE:** No data available.

EDUCATION/TRAINING PROGRAMS— Accounting; Actuarial Science; Business Administration/Management; Business Statistics; Business Teacher Education; Business/Commerce, General; Business/Corporate Communications; Entrepreneurship/Entrepreneurial Studies; Finance, General; Financial Planning and Services; Franchising and Franchise Operations; Human Resources Management/ Personnel Administration, General; Insurance; Internat. Business/Trade/Commerce; International Finance; International Mktg.; Investments and Securities; others. **RELATED KNOWLEDGE/ COURSES—Education and Training:** Knowledge of principles and methods for curriculum and training design, teaching and instruction for individuals and groups, and the measurement of training effects. **Economics and Accounting:** Knowledge of economic and accounting principles and practices, the financial markets, banking, and the analysis and reporting of financial data. **Sales and Marketing:** Knowledge of principles and methods for showing, promoting, and selling products or services. This includes marketing strategy and tactics, product demonstration, sales techniques, and sales control systems. **English Language:** Knowledge of the structure and content of the English language, including the meaning and spelling of words, rules of composition, and grammar. **Personnel and Human Resources:** Knowledge of principles and procedures for personnel recruitment, selection, training, compensation and benefits, labor relations and negotiation, and personnel information systems. **Sociology and Anthropology:** Knowledge of group behavior and dynamics, societal trends and influences, human migrations, ethnicity, and cultures and their history and origins.

Calibration and Instrumentation Technicians

- ◎ Annual Earnings: $48,040
- ◎ Growth: 9.8%
- ◎ Annual Job Openings: 18,000
- ◎ Self-Employed: 0.4%
- ◎ Part-Time: 6.8%
- ◎ Education/Training Required: Associate degree

The job openings listed here are shared with Electrical Engineering Technicians and Electronics Engineering Technicians.

Industries in Which Income Is Highest

Industry	Average Annual Wage	Number Employed
Federal, State, and Local Government	$59,050	13,940
Utilities	$55,890	7,660
Transportation Equipment Manufacturing	$52,760	4,020
Telecommunications	$51,480	12,170
Internet Service Providers, Web Search Portals, and Data Processing Services	$51,250	1,360

Metropolitan Areas Where Income Is Highest

Metropolitan Area	Average Annual Wage	Number Employed
Bakersfield, CA	$68,210	630
Bremerton–Silverdale, WA	$65,220	220
Dover, DE	$64,060	50
Anchorage, AK	$61,110	200
Oxnard–Thousand Oaks–Ventura, CA	$59,770	930

Develop, test, calibrate, operate, and repair electrical, mechanical, electromechanical, electrohydraulic, or electronic measuring and recording instruments, apparatus, and equipment. Plans sequence of testing and calibration program for instruments and equipment according to blueprints, schematics, technical manuals, and other specifications. Performs preventative and corrective maintenance of test apparatus and peripheral equipment. Confers with engineers, supervisor, and other technical workers to assist with equipment installation, maintenance, and repair techniques. Analyzes and converts test data, using mathematical formulas, and reports results and proposed modifications. Sets up test equipment and conducts tests on performance and reliability of mechanical, structural, or electromechanical equipment. Selects sensing, telemetering, and recording instrumentation and circuitry. Disassembles and reassembles instruments and equipment, using hand tools, and inspects instruments and equipment for defects. Sketches plans for developing jigs, fixtures, instruments, and related nonstandard apparatus. Modifies performance and operation of component parts and circuitry to specifications, using test equipment and precision instruments. **SKILLS**—Technology Design; Equipment Maintenance; Quality Control Analysis; Science; Equipment Selection; Installation; Troubleshooting; Operation Monitoring.

GOE—Interest Area: 15. Scientific Research, Engineering, and Mathematics. **Work Group:** 15.09. Engineering Technology. **PERSONALITY TYPE:** Realistic. Realistic occupations frequently involve work activities that include practical, hands-on problems and solutions. They often deal with plants, animals, and real-world materials like wood, tools, and machinery. Many of the occupations require working outside and do not involve a lot of paperwork or working closely with others.

EDUCATION/TRAINING PROGRAMS—Computer Engineering Technology/Technician; Electrical and Electronic Engineering Technologies/Technicians, Other; Electrical, Electronic, and Communications Engineering Technology/Technician; Telecommunications Technology/Technician. **RELATED KNOWLEDGE/COURSES—Design:** Knowledge of design techniques, tools, and principles involved in production of precision technical plans, blueprints, drawings, and models. **Mathematics:** Knowledge of arithmetic, algebra, geometry, calculus, and statistics and their applications. **Engineering and Technology:** Knowledge of the practical application of engineering science and technology. This includes applying principles, techniques, procedures, and equipment to the design and production of various goods and services. **Computers and Electronics:** Knowledge of circuit boards, processors, chips, electronic equipment, and computer

hardware and software, including applications and programming. **Mechanical Devices:** Knowledge of machines and tools, including their designs, uses, repair, and maintenance. **Physics:** Knowledge and prediction of physical principles and laws and their interrelationships and applications to understanding fluid, material, and atmospheric dynamics and mechanical, electrical, atomic, and subatomic structures and processes.

Caption Writers

- Annual Earnings: $46,420
- Growth: 17.7%
- Annual Job Openings: 14,000
- Self-Employed: 67.7%
- Part-Time: 30.2%
- Education/Training Required: Moderate-term on-the-job training

The job openings listed here are shared with Copy Writers, Creative Writers, and Poets and Lyricists.

Industries in Which Income Is Highest

Industry	Average Annual Wage	Number Employed
Motion Picture and Sound Recording Industries	$59,250	1,520
Federal, State, and Local Government	$58,640	1,710
Professional, Scientific, and Technical Services	$49,680	10,870
Religious, Grantmaking, Civic, Professional, and Similar Organizations	$49,100	4,330
Broadcasting (Except Internet)	$43,550	2,920

Metropolitan Areas Where Income Is Highest

Metropolitan Area	Average Annual Wage	Number Employed
Santa Barbara–Santa Maria, CA	$103,570	50
Austin–Round Rock, TX	$72,780	400
San Francisco–Oakland–Fremont, CA	$68,370	730
Los Angeles–Long Beach–Santa Ana, CA	$63,330	2,670
Raleigh–Cary, NC	$63,130	60

Write caption phrases of dialogue for hearing-impaired and foreign language–speaking viewers of movie or television productions. Writes captions to describe music and background noises. Watches production and reviews captions simultaneously to determine which caption phrases require editing. Enters commands to synchronize captions with dialogue and place on the screen. Translates foreign-language dialogue into English-language captions or English-dialogue into foreign-language captions. Operates computerized captioning system for movies or television productions for hearing-impaired and foreign language–speaking viewers. Oversees encoding of captions to master tape of television production. Discusses captions with directors or producers of movie and television productions. Edits translations for correctness of grammar, punctuation, and clarity of expression. **SKILLS**—Writing; Operation and Control.

GOE—Interest Area: 03. Arts and Communication. **Work Group:** 03.03. News, Broadcasting, and Public Relations. **PERSONALITY TYPE:** Artistic. Artistic occupations frequently involve working with forms, designs, and patterns. They often require self-expression, and the work can be done without following a clear set of rules.

EDUCATION/TRAINING PROGRAMS—Communications Studies/Speech Communication and Rhetoric; English Composition; Journalism; Mass Communications/Media Studies. **RELATED KNOWLEDGE/COURSES—Foreign Language:** Knowledge of the structure and content of a foreign (non-English) language, including the meaning and spelling of words, rules of composition and grammar, and pronunciation. **Communications and Media:** Knowledge of media production, communication, and dissemination techniques and methods. This includes alternative ways to inform and entertain via written, oral, and visual media. **English Language:** Knowledge of the structure and content of the English language, including the meaning and spelling of words, rules of composition, and grammar. **Computers and Electronics:** Knowledge of circuit boards, processors, chips, electronic equipment, and computer hardware and software, including applications and programming.

Cartographers and Photogrammetrists

- Annual Earnings: $48,250
- Growth: 15.3%
- Annual Job Openings: 1,000
- Self-Employed: 2.9%
- Part-Time: 9.6%
- Education/Training Required: Bachelor's degree

Industries in Which Income Is Highest

Industry	Average Annual Wage	Number Employed
Federal, State, and Local Government	$53,210	3,770
Professional, Scientific, and Technical Services	$45,710	6,080

Metropolitan Areas Where Income Is Highest

Metropolitan Area	Average Annual Wage	Number Employed
Houston–Sugar Land–Baytown, TX	$76,090	190
Washington–Arlington–Alexandria, DC–VA–MD–WV	$68,080	1,320
Trenton–Ewing, NJ	$66,410	50
Denver–Aurora, CO	$60,150	530
Seattle–Tacoma–Bellevue, WA	$58,320	250

Collect, analyze, and interpret geographic information provided by geodetic surveys, aerial photographs, and satellite data. Research, study, and prepare maps and other spatial data in digital or graphic form for legal, social, political, educational, and design purposes. May work with Geographic Information Systems (GIS). May design and evaluate algorithms, data structures, and user interfaces for GIS and mapping systems. Identify, scale, and orient geodetic points, elevations, and other planimetric or topographic features, applying standard mathematical formulas. Collect information about specific features of the Earth, using aerial photography and other digital remote sensing techniques. Revise existing maps and charts, making all necessary corrections and adjustments. Compile data required for map preparation, including aerial photographs, survey notes, records, reports, and original maps. Inspect final compositions in order to ensure completeness and accuracy. Determine map content and layout, as well as production specifications such as scale, size, projection, and colors, and direct production in order to ensure that specifications are followed. Examine and analyze data from ground surveys, reports, aerial photographs, and satellite images in order to prepare topographic maps, aerial-photograph mosaics, and related charts. Select aerial photographic and remote sensing techniques and plotting equipment needed to meet required standards of accuracy. Delineate aerial photographic detail, such as control points, hydrography, topography, and cultural features, using precision stereoplotting apparatus or drafting instruments. Build and update digital databases. Prepare and alter trace maps, charts, tables, detailed drawings, and three-dimensional optical models of terrain, using stereoscopic plotting and computer graphics equipment. Determine guidelines that specify which source material is acceptable for use. Study legal records in order to establish boundaries of local, national, and international properties. Travel over photographed areas in order to observe, identify, record, and verify all relevant features. **SKILLS**—Active Learning; Technology Design; Science; Mathematics; Troubleshooting; Reading Comprehension; Critical Thinking; Complex Problem Solving.

GOE—Interest Area: 15. Scientific Research, Engineering, and Mathematics. **Work Group:** 15.09. Engineering Technology. **PERSONALITY TYPE:** Conventional. Conventional occupations frequently involve following set procedures and routines. These occupations can include working with data and details more than with ideas. Usually there is a clear line of authority to follow.

EDUCATION/TRAINING   PROGRAMS— Cartography; Surveying Technology/Surveying. **RELATED KNOWLEDGE/COURSES—Geography:** Knowledge of principles and methods for describing the features of land, sea, and air masses, including their physical characteristics; locations; interrelationships; and distribution of plant, animal, and human life. **Design:** Knowledge of design techniques, tools, and principles involved in production of precision technical plans, blueprints, drawings, and models. **Computers and Electronics:** Knowledge of

circuit boards, processors, chips, electronic equipment, and computer hardware and software, including applications and programming. **Engineering and Technology:** Knowledge of the practical application of engineering science and technology. This includes applying principles, techniques, procedures, and equipment to the design and production of various goods and services. **Production and Processing:** Knowledge of raw materials, production processes, quality control, costs, and other techniques for maximizing the effective manufacture and distribution of goods. **Mathematics:** Knowledge of arithmetic, algebra, geometry, calculus, and statistics and their applications.

Central Office and PBX Installers and Repairers

- Annual Earnings: $50,620
- Growth: –4.9%
- Annual Job Openings: 21,000
- Self-Employed: 6.6%
- Part-Time: 4.8%
- Education/Training Required: Long-term on-the-job training

The job openings listed here are shared with Communication Equipment Mechanics, Installers, and Repairers; Frame Wirers, Central Office; Station Installers and Repairers, Telephone; and Telecommunications Facility Examiners.

Industries in Which Income Is Highest

Industry	Average Annual Wage	Number Employed
Telecommunications	$52,170	136,200
Management of Companies and Enterprises	$51,670	2,520
Professional, Scientific, and Technical Services	$51,100	5,810
Wholesale Electronic Markets and Agents and Brokers	$48,990	1,400
Administrative and Support Services	$48,780	3,780

Metropolitan Areas Where Income Is Highest

Metropolitan Area	Average Annual Wage	Number Employed
Atlantic City, NJ	$68,240	50
Trenton–Ewing, NJ	$64,750	280
New York–Northern New Jersey–Long Island, NY–NJ–PA	$62,120	15,460
Rochester, NY	$61,530	620
State College, PA	$59,690	80

Test, analyze, and repair telephone or telegraph circuits and equipment at a central office location, using test meters and hand tools. Analyze and repair defects in communications equipment on customers' premises, using circuit diagrams, polarity probes, meters, and a telephone test set. May install equipment. Tests circuits and components of malfunctioning telecommunication equipment to isolate source of malfunction, using test instruments and circuit diagrams. Analyzes test readings, computer printouts, and trouble reports to determine method of repair. Tests and adjusts installed equipment to ensure circuit continuity and operational performance, using test instruments. Connects wires to equipment, using hand tools, soldering iron, or wire wrap gun. Installs preassembled or partially assembled switching equipment, switchboards, wiring frames, and power apparatus according to floor plans. Retests repaired equipment to ensure that malfunction has been corrected. Repairs or replaces defective components, such as switches, relays, amplifiers, and circuit boards, using hand tools and soldering iron. Removes and remakes connections on wire distributing frame to change circuit layout, following diagrams. Routes cables and trunklines from entry points to specified equipment, following diagrams. Enters codes to correct programming of electronic switching systems. **SKILLS—** Repairing; Installation; Troubleshooting; Technology Design; Operation Monitoring; Science; Equipment Maintenance; Quality Control Analysis.

GOE—Interest Area: 02. Architecture and Construction. **Work Group:** 02.05. Systems and Equipment Installation, Maintenance, and Repair. **PERSONALITY TYPE:** Realistic. Realistic occupations frequently involve work activities that include practical, hands-on problems and solutions. They often deal with plants, animals, and real-world materials like wood, tools, and machinery. Many of the occupations require working outside and do not involve a lot of paperwork or working closely with others.

EDUCATION/TRAINING PROGRAM— Communications Systems Installation and Repair Technology. **RELATED KNOWLEDGE/ COURSES—Telecommunications:** Knowledge of transmission, broadcasting, switching, control, and operation of telecommunications systems. **Computers and Electronics:** Knowledge of circuit boards, processors, chips, electronic equipment, and computer hardware and software, including applications and programming. **Design:** Knowledge of design techniques, tools, and principles involved in production of precision technical plans, blueprints, drawings, and models. **Engineering and Technology:** Knowledge of the practical application of engineering science and technology. This includes applying principles, techniques, procedures, and equipment to the design and production of various goods and services.

Chemical Engineers

- Annual Earnings: $77,140
- Growth: 10.6%
- Annual Job Openings: 3,000
- Self-Employed: 0.0%
- Part-Time: 4.6%
- Education/Training Required: Bachelor's degree

Industries in Which Income Is Highest

Industry	Average Annual Wage	Number Employed
Petroleum and Coal Products Manufacturing	$83,380	1,590
Professional, Scientific, and Technical Services	$79,680	7,790
Federal, State, and Local Government	$78,820	1,290
Chemical Manufacturing	$77,550	9,030
Computer and Electronic Product Manufacturing	$76,050	1,170

Metropolitan Areas Where Income Is Highest

Metropolitan Area	Average Annual Wage	Number Employed
Beaumont–Port Arthur, TX	$96,570	360
Virginia Beach–Norfolk–Newport News, VA–NC	$94,070	120
San Jose–Sunnyvale–Santa Clara, CA	$90,290	220
Kennewick–Richland–Pasco, WA	$88,580	170
Bridgeport–Stamford–Norwalk, CT	$88,510	70

Design chemical plant equipment and devise processes for manufacturing chemicals and products, such as gasoline, synthetic rubber, plastics, detergents, cement, paper, and pulp, by applying principles and technology of chemistry, physics, and engineering. Perform tests throughout stages of production to determine degree of control over variables, including temperature, density, specific gravity, and pressure. Develop safety procedures to be employed by workers operating equipment or working in close proximity to ongoing chemical reactions. Determine most effective arrangement of operations, such as mixing, crushing, heat transfer, distillation, and drying. Prepare estimate of production costs and production progress reports for management. Direct activities of workers who operate or who are engaged in constructing and improving absorption, evaporation, or electromagnetic equipment. Perform laboratory studies of steps in manufacture of new product and test proposed process in small-scale operation (pilot plant). Develop processes to separate components of liquids or gases or generate electrical currents, using controlled chemical processes. Conduct research to develop new and improved chemical manufacturing processes. Design measurement and control systems for chemical plants based on data collected in laboratory experiments and in pilot plant operations. **SKILLS**—Science; Technology Design; Troubleshooting; Programming; Systems Analysis; Mathematics; Operations Analysis; Systems Evaluation.

GOE—**Interest Area:** 15. Scientific Research, Engineering, and Mathematics. **Work Group:** 15.07. Research and Design Engineering. **PERSONALITY TYPE:** Investigative. Investigative occupations frequently involve working with ideas and require an extensive amount of thinking. These occupations can involve searching for facts and figuring out problems mentally.

EDUCATION/TRAINING PROGRAM—Chemical Engineering. **RELATED KNOWLEDGE/ COURSES**—**Chemistry:** Knowledge of the chemical composition, structure, and properties of substances and of the chemical processes and transformations that they undergo. This includes uses of chemicals, their danger signs, production techniques, and disposal methods. **Engineering and Technology:** Knowledge of the practical application of engineering science and technology. This includes applying principles, techniques, procedures, and equipment to the design and production of various goods and services. **Physics:** Knowledge and prediction of physical principles and laws and their interrelationships and applications to understanding fluid, material, and atmospheric dynamics and mechanical, electrical, atomic, and subatomic structures and processes. **Design:** Knowledge of design techniques, tools, and principles involved in production of precision technical plans, blueprints, drawings, and models. **Production and Processing:** Knowledge of raw materials, production processes, quality control, costs, and other techniques for maximizing the effective manufacture and distribution of goods. **Mathematics:** Knowledge of arithmetic, algebra, geometry, calculus, and statistics and their applications.

Chemical Plant and System Operators

- Annual Earnings: $46,710
- Growth: –17.7%
- Annual Job Openings: 8,000
- Self-Employed: 0.1%
- Part-Time: 0.8%
- Education/Training Required: Long-term on-the-job training

Industries in Which Income Is Highest

Industry	Average Annual Wage	Number Employed
Petroleum and Coal Products Manufacturing	$53,240	1,460
Paper Manufacturing	$48,650	1,390
Chemical Manufacturing	$46,520	53,610

Metropolitan Areas Where Income Is Highest

Metropolitan Area	Average Annual Wage	Number Employed
Cedar Rapids, IA	$56,250	60
Corpus Christi, TX	$56,050	260
Houston–Sugar Land–Baytown, TX	$55,090	5,740
Beaumont–Port Arthur, TX	$54,160	1,710
Victoria, TX	$53,980	1,290

Control or operate an entire chemical process or system of machines. Record operating data such as process conditions, test results, and instrument readings. Regulate or shut down equipment during emergency situations as directed by supervisory personnel. Start pumps to wash and rinse reactor vessels; to exhaust gases and vapors; to regulate the flow of oil, steam, air, and perfume to towers; and to add products to converter or blending vessels. Turn valves to regulate flow of products or byproducts through agitator tanks, storage drums, or neutralizer tanks. Confer with technical and supervisory personnel to report or resolve conditions affecting safety, efficiency, and product quality. Defrost frozen valves, using steam hoses. Direct workers engaged in operating machinery that regulates the flow of materials and products. Inspect operating units such as towers, soap-spray storage tanks, scrubbers, collectors, and driers to ensure that all are functioning and to maintain maximum efficiency. Repair and replace damaged equipment. Supervise the cleaning of towers, strainers, and spray tips. Calculate material requirements or yields according to formulas. Control or operate chemical processes or systems of machines, using panelboards, control boards, or semi-automatic equipment. Draw samples of products and conduct quality control tests in order to monitor processing and to ensure that standards are met. Gauge tank levels, using calibrated rods. Interpret chemical reactions visible through sight glasses or on television monitors and review laboratory test reports for process adjustments. Monitor recording instruments, flowmeters, panel lights, and other indicators, and listen for warning signals, in order to verify conformity of process conditions. Move control settings to make necessary adjustments on equipment units affecting speeds of chemical reactions, quality, and yields. Notify maintenance, stationary-engineering, and other auxiliary personnel to correct equipment malfunctions and to adjust power, steam, water, or air supplies. Patrol work areas to ensure that solutions in tanks and troughs are not in danger of overflowing. **SKILLS—** Operation Monitoring; Operation and Control; Science; Troubleshooting; Systems Analysis; Quality Control Analysis; Mathematics; Systems Evaluation.

GOE—Interest Area: 13. Manufacturing. **Work Group:** 13.16. Utility Operation and Energy Distribution. **PERSONALITY TYPE:** Realistic. Realistic occupations frequently involve work activities that include practical, hands-on problems and solutions. They often deal with plants, animals, and real-world materials like wood, tools, and machinery. Many of the occupations require working outside and do not involve a lot of paperwork or working closely with others.

EDUCATION/TRAINING PROGRAM— Chemical Technology/Technician. **RELATED KNOWLEDGE/COURSES—Chemistry:** Knowledge of the chemical composition, structure, and properties of substances and of the chemical processes and transformations that they undergo. This includes uses of chemicals, their danger signs, production techniques, and disposal methods. **Production and Processing:** Knowledge of raw materials, production processes, quality control, costs, and other techniques for maximizing the effective manufacture and distribution of goods. **Mechanical Devices:** Knowledge of machines and tools, including their designs, uses, repair, and maintenance. **Engineering and Technology:** Knowledge of the practical application of engineering science and technology. This includes applying principles, techniques, procedures, and equipment to the design and production of various goods and services. **Public Safety and Security:** Knowledge of relevant equipment, policies, procedures, and strategies to promote effective local, state, or national security operations for the protection of people, data, property, and institutions. **Mathematics:** Knowledge of arithmetic, algebra, geometry, calculus, and statistics and their applications.

Chemistry Teachers, Postsecondary

- Annual Earnings: $58,060
- Growth: 32.2%
- Annual Job Openings: 329,000
- Self-Employed: 0.4%
- Part-Time: 27.3%
- Education/Training Required: Master's degree

Our sources did not provide separate job openings data for this occupation. The job openings listed here are shared with 35 other postsecondary teaching occupations. For a complete list, see the beginning of this section.

Industries in Which Income Is Highest

Industry	Average Annual Wage	Number Employed
Educational Services	$58,010	18,940

Metropolitan Areas Where Income Is Highest

Metropolitan Area	Average Annual Wage	Number Employed
College Station–Bryan, TX	$105,940	100
Durham, NC	$81,350	160
San Francisco–Oakland–Fremont, CA	$76,530	310
Riverside–San Bernardino–Ontario, CA	$75,170	130
Boston–Cambridge–Quincy, MA–NH	$74,560	430

Teach courses pertaining to the chemical and physical properties and compositional changes of substances. Work may include instruction in the methods of qualitative and quantitative chemical analysis. Includes both teachers primarily engaged in teaching and those who do a combination of both teaching and research. Prepare and deliver lectures to undergraduate and/or graduate students on topics such as organic chemistry, analytical chemistry, and chemical separation. Supervise students' laboratory work. Evaluate and grade students' class work, laboratory performance, assignments, and papers. Compile, administer, and grade examinations or assign this work to others. Maintain student attendance records, grades, and other required records. Prepare course materials such as syllabi, homework assignments, and handouts. Maintain regularly scheduled office hours in order to advise and assist students. Plan, evaluate, and revise curricula, course content, and course materials and methods of instruction. Supervise undergraduate and/or graduate teaching, internship, and research work. Keep abreast of developments in their field by reading current literature, talking with colleagues, and participating in professional conferences. Initiate, facilitate, and moderate classroom discussions. Select and obtain materials and supplies such as textbooks and laboratory equipment. Conduct research in a particular field of knowledge and publish findings in professional journals, books and/or electronic media. Advise students on academic and vocational curricula and on career issues. Collaborate with colleagues to address teaching and research issues. Serve on academic or administrative committees that deal with institutional policies, departmental matters, and academic issues. Write grant proposals to procure external research funding. Participate in student recruitment, registration, and placement activities. Prepare and submit required reports related to instruction. Perform administrative duties such as serving as a department head. **SKILLS**—Science; Instructing; Active Learning; Mathematics; Writing; Learning Strategies; Reading Comprehension; Critical Thinking.

GOE—Interest Area: 05. Education and Training. **Work Group:** 05.03. Postsecondary and Adult Teaching and Instructing. **PERSONALITY TYPE:** Investigative. Investigative occupations frequently involve working with ideas and require an extensive amount of thinking. These occupations can involve searching for facts and figuring out problems mentally.

EDUCATION/TRAINING PROGRAMS—Analytical Chemistry; Chemical Physics; Chemistry, General; Chemistry, Other; Geochemistry; Inorganic Chemistry; Organic Chemistry; Physical and Theoretical Chemistry; Polymer Chemistry. **RELATED KNOWLEDGE/COURSES—Chemistry:** Knowledge of the chemical composition, structure, and properties of substances and of the chemical processes and transformations that they undergo. This includes uses of chemicals, their danger signs, production techniques, and disposal methods. **Education and Training:** Knowledge of principles and methods for curriculum and training design, teaching and instruction for individuals and groups, and the measurement of training effects. **Biology:** Knowledge of plant and animal organisms and their tissues, cells, functions, interdependencies, and interactions with each other and the environment. **Physics:** Knowledge and prediction of physical principles and laws and their interrelationships and applications to understanding fluid, material, and atmospheric dynamics and mechanical, electrical, atomic, and subatomic structures and processes. **Mathematics:** Knowledge of arithmetic, algebra, geometry, calculus, and statistics and their applications. **English Language:** Knowledge of the structure and content of the English language, including the meaning and spelling of words, rules of composition, and grammar.

Chemists

- Annual Earnings: $57,890
- Growth: 7.3%
- Annual Job Openings: 5,000
- Self-Employed: 0.4%
- Part-Time: 6.6%
- Education/Training Required: Bachelor's degree

Industries in Which Income Is Highest

Industry	Average Annual Wage	Number Employed
Federal, State, and Local Government	$68,000	9,600
Management of Companies and Enterprises	$66,330	2,330
Merchant Wholesalers, Nondurable Goods	$60,130	1,660
Chemical Manufacturing	$58,260	26,310
Administrative and Support Services	$56,010	1,440

Metropolitan Areas Where Income Is Highest

Metropolitan Area	Average Annual Wage	Number Employed
Indianapolis–Carmel, IN	$97,220	1,120
Washington–Arlington–Alexandria, DC–VA–MD–WV	$87,630	3,010
Bakersfield, CA	$81,660	130
Boulder, CO	$81,020	480
Oxnard–Thousand Oaks–Ventura, CA	$76,750	250

Conduct qualitative and quantitative chemical analyses or chemical experiments in laboratories for quality or process control or to develop new products or knowledge. Analyze organic and inorganic compounds to determine chemical and physical properties, composition, structure, relationships, and reactions, utilizing chromatography, spectroscopy, and spectrophotometry techniques. Develop, improve, and customize products, equipment, formulas, processes, and analytical methods. Compile and analyze test information to determine process or equipment operating efficiency and to diagnose malfunctions. Confer with scientists and engineers to conduct analyses of research projects, interpret test results, or develop nonstandard tests. Direct, coordinate, and advise personnel in test procedures for analyzing components and physical properties of materials. Induce changes in composition of substances by introducing heat, light, energy, and chemical catalysts for quantitative and qualitative analysis. Write technical papers and reports and prepare standards and specifications for processes, facilities, products, and tests. Study effects of various methods of processing, preserving, and packaging on composition and properties of foods. Prepare test solutions, compounds, and reagents for laboratory personnel to conduct test. **SKILLS**—Science; Quality Control Analysis; Technology Design; Management of Financial Resources; Operation Monitoring; Time Management; Management of Material Resources; Equipment Selection.

GOE—Interest Area: 15. Scientific Research, Engineering, and Mathematics. **Work Group:** 15.02. Physical Sciences. **PERSONALITY TYPE:** Investigative. Investigative occupations frequently involve working with ideas and require an extensive amount of thinking. These occupations can involve searching for facts and figuring out problems mentally.

EDUCATION/TRAINING PROGRAMS—Analytical Chemistry; Chemical Physics; Chemistry, General; Chemistry, Other; Inorganic Chemistry; Organic Chemistry; Physical and Theoretical Chemistry; Polymer Chemistry. **RELATED KNOWLEDGE/COURSES—Chemistry:** Knowledge of the chemical composition, structure, and properties of substances and of the chemical processes and transformations that they undergo. This includes uses of chemicals, their danger signs, production techniques, and disposal methods. **Mathematics:** Knowledge of arithmetic, algebra, geometry, calculus, and statistics and their applications. **Engineering and Technology:** Knowledge of the practical application of engineering science and technology. This includes applying principles, techniques, procedures, and equipment to the design and production of various goods and services. **Education and Training:** Knowledge of principles and methods for curriculum and training design, teaching and instruction for individuals and groups, and the measurement of training effects. **Computers and Electronics:** Knowledge of circuit boards, processors, chips, electronic equipment, and computer hardware and software, including applications and programming. **Production and Processing:** Knowledge of raw materials, production processes, quality control, costs, and other techniques for maximizing the effective manufacture and distribution of goods.

Chief Executives

- ◎ Annual Earnings: $142,440
- ◎ Growth: 14.9%
- ◎ Annual Job Openings: 38,000
- ◎ Self-Employed: 16.2%
- ◎ Part-Time: 6.8%
- ◎ Education/Training Required: Work experience plus degree

The job openings listed here are shared with Government Service Executives and Private Sector Executives.

Industries in Which Income Is Highest

Industry	Average Annual Wage	Number Employed
Plastics and Rubber Products Manufacturing	More than $146,500	2,340
Printing and Related Support Activities	More than $146,500	2,320
Machinery Manufacturing	More than $146,500	4,870
Primary Metal Manufacturing	More than $146,500	1,240
Telecommunications	More than $146,500	1,280

Metropolitan Areas Where Income Is Highest

Metropolitan Area	Average Annual Wage	Number Employed
Boston–Cambridge–Quincy, MA–NH	More than $146,500	17,530
New York–Northern New Jersey–Long Island, NY–NJ–PA	More than $146,500	15,260
Chicago–Naperville–Joilet, IL–IN–WI	More than $146,500	14,910
Los Angeles–Long Beach–Santa Ana, CA	More than $146,500	13,510
Atlanta–Sandy Springs–Marietta, GA	More than $146,500	11,950

Determine and formulate policies and provide the overall direction of companies or private and public sector organizations within the guidelines set up by a board of directors or similar governing body. Plan, direct, or coordinate operational activities at the highest level of management with the help of subordinate executives and staff managers. Analyze operations to evaluate performance of a company and its staff in meeting objectives and to determine areas of potential cost reduction, program improvement, or policy change. Appoint department heads or managers and assign or delegate responsibilities to them. Confer with board members, organization officials, and staff members to discuss issues, coordinate activities, and resolve problems. Coordinate the development and implementation of budgetary control systems, record-keeping systems, and other administrative control processes. Direct and coordinate an organization's financial and budget activities in order to fund operations, maximize investments, and increase efficiency. Direct human resources activities, including the approval of human resource plans and activities, the selection of directors and other high-level staff, and establishment and organization of major departments. Direct, plan, and implement policies, objectives, and activities of organizations or businesses in order to ensure continuing operations, to maximize returns on investments, and to increase productivity. Establish departmental responsibilities and coordinate functions among departments and sites. Implement corrective action plans to solve organizational or departmental problems. Prepare and present reports concerning activities, expenses, budgets, government statutes and rulings, and other items affecting businesses or program services. Preside over or serve on boards of directors, management committees, or other governing boards. Represent organizations and promote their objectives at official functions or delegate representatives to do so. Serve as liaisons between organizations,

C

shareholders, and outside organizations. Administer programs for selection of sites, construction of buildings, and provision of equipment and supplies. Attend and participate in meetings of municipal councils and council committees. Deliver speeches, write articles, and present information at meetings or conventions in order to promote services, exchange ideas, and accomplish objectives. Direct and conduct studies and research on issues affecting areas of responsibility. **SKILLS**—No data available.

GOE—Interest Area: 04. Business and Administration. **Work Group:** 04.01. Managerial Work in General Business. **PERSONALITY TYPE:** No data available.

EDUCATION/TRAINING PROGRAMS—Business Administration/Management; Business/Commerce, General; Entrepreneurship/Entrepreneurial Studies; International Business/Trade/Commerce; Public Administration; Public Administration and Services, Other; Public Policy Analysis; Transportation/Transportation Management. **RELATED KNOWLEDGE/COURSES**—No data available.

Child Support, Missing Persons, and Unemployment Insurance Fraud Investigators

- Annual Earnings: $55,790
- Growth: 16.3%
- Annual Job Openings: 9,000
- Self-Employed: 0.0%
- Part-Time: 2.9%
- Education/Training Required: Work experience in a related occupation

The job openings listed here are shared with Criminal Investigators and Special Agents; Immigration and Customs Inspectors; Police Detectives; and Police Identification and Records Officers.

Industries in Which Income Is Highest

Industry	Average Annual Wage	Number Employed
Federal, State, and Local Government	$55,790	84,720

Metropolitan Areas Where Income Is Highest

Metropolitan Area	Average Annual Wage	Number Employed
Washington–Arlington–Alexandria, DC–VA–MD–WV	$79,180	4,270
Trenton–Ewing, NJ	$78,420	260
Chicago–Naperville–Joliet, IL–IN–WI	$76,080	3,170
Springfield, IL	$74,260	50
Oxnard–Thousand Oaks–Ventura, CA	$73,250	80

Conduct investigations to locate, arrest, and return fugitives and persons wanted for non-payment of support payments and unemployment insurance fraud and to locate missing persons. Serves warrants and makes arrests to return persons sought in connection with crimes or for non-payment of child support. Computes amount of child support payments. Testifies in court to present evidence regarding cases. Examines medical and dental X rays, fingerprints, and other information to identify bodies held in morgue. Examines case file to determine that divorce decree and court-ordered judgment for payment are in order. Completes reports to document information acquired during criminal and child support cases and actions taken. Monitors child support payments awarded by court to ensure compliance and enforcement of child support laws. Determines types of court jurisdiction, according to facts and circumstances surrounding case, and files court action. Confers with prosecuting attorney to prepare court case and with court clerk to obtain arrest warrant and schedule court date. Interviews client to obtain information such as relocation of absent parent, amount of child support awarded, and names of witnesses. Interviews and discusses case with parent charged with nonpayment of support to resolve issues in lieu of filing court proceedings. Reviews files and criminal records to develop possible leads, such as previous addresses and aliases. Prepares file indicating data such as wage records of accused, witnesses, and blood test results. Obtains extradition papers to bring about return of fugitive. Contacts employers, neighbors, relatives, and law enforcement agencies to locate person sought and verify information gathered about case. **SKILLS**—Speaking; Active Listening; Critical Thinking; Writing; Judgment and Decision Making; Reading Comprehension; Persuasion; Systems Evaluation.

GOE—Interest Area: 07. Government and Public Administration. **Work Group:** 07.03. Regulations Enforcement. **PERSONALITY TYPE:** Enterprising. Enterprising occupations frequently involve starting up and carrying out projects. These occupations can involve leading people and making many decisions. They sometimes require risk taking and often deal with business.

EDUCATION/TRAINING PROGRAMS— Criminal Justice/Police Science; Criminalistics and Criminal Science. **RELATED KNOWLEDGE/ COURSES—Law and Government:** Knowledge of laws, legal codes, court procedures, precedents, government regulations, executive orders, agency rules, and the democratic political process. **Public Safety and Security:** Knowledge of relevant equipment, policies, procedures, and strategies to promote effective local, state, or national security operations for the protection of people, data, property, and institutions. **Economics and Accounting:** Knowledge of economic and accounting principles and practices, the financial markets, banking, and the analysis and reporting of financial data. **English Language:** Knowledge of the structure and content of the English language, including the meaning and spelling of words, rules of composition, and grammar. **Mathematics:** Knowledge of arithmetic, algebra, geometry, calculus, and statistics and their applications. **Clerical Practices:** Knowledge of administrative and clerical procedures and systems such as word processing, managing files and records, stenography and transcription, designing forms, and other office procedures and terminology.

Chiropractors

- Annual Earnings: $67,200
- Growth: 22.4%
- Annual Job Openings: 4,000
- Self-Employed: 49.2%
- Part-Time: 20.7%
- Education/Training Required: First professional degree

Industries in Which Income Is Highest

Industry	Average Annual Wage	Number Employed
Ambulatory Health Care Services	$67,700	23,590

Metropolitan Areas Where Income Is Highest

Metropolitan Area	Average Annual Wage	Number Employed
Milwaukee–Waukesha–West Allis, WI	More than $146,500	220
Washington–Arlington–Alexandria, DC–VA–MD–WV	More than $146,500	350
Las Vegas–Paradise, NV	$128,040	150
Sioux Falls, SD	$105,230	50
Phoenix–Mesa–Scottsdale, AZ	$100,530	520

Adjust spinal column and other articulations of the body to correct abnormalities of the human body believed to be caused by interference with the nervous system. Examine patient to determine nature and extent of disorder. Manipulate spine or other involved area. May utilize supplementary measures, such as exercise, rest, water, light, heat, and nutritional therapy. Perform a series of manual adjustments to the spine, or other articulations of the body, in order to correct the musculoskeletal system. Evaluate the functioning of the neuromuscularskeletal system and the spine, using systems of chiropractic diagnosis. Diagnose health problems by reviewing patients' health and medical histories; questioning, observing, and examining patients; and interpreting X rays. Maintain accurate case histories of patients. Advise patients about recommended courses of treatment. Obtain and record patients' medical histories.

Analyze X rays in order to locate the sources of patients' difficulties and to rule out fractures or diseases as sources of problems. Counsel patients about nutrition, exercise, sleeping habits, stress management, and other matters. Arrange for diagnostic X rays to be taken. Consult with and refer patients to appropriate health practitioners when necessary. Suggest and apply the use of supports such as straps, tapes, bandages, and braces if necessary. **SKILLS**—Social Perceptiveness; Persuasion; Management of Financial Resources; Service Orientation; Science; Critical Thinking; Active Listening; Instructing.

GOE—Interest Area: 08. Health Science. **Work Group:** 08.04. Health Specialties. **PERSONALITY TYPE:** Investigative. Investigative occupations frequently involve working with ideas and require an extensive amount of thinking. These occupations can involve searching for facts and figuring out problems mentally.

EDUCATION/TRAINING PROGRAM—Chiropractic (DC). **RELATED KNOWLEDGE/COURSES—Medicine and Dentistry:** Knowledge of the information and techniques needed to diagnose and treat human injuries, diseases, and deformities. This includes symptoms, treatment alternatives, drug properties and interactions, and preventive health-care measures. **Therapy and Counseling:** Knowledge of principles, methods, and procedures for diagnosis, treatment, and rehabilitation of physical and mental dysfunctions and for career counseling and guidance. **Biology:** Knowledge of plant and animal organisms and their tissues, cells, functions, interdependencies, and interactions with each other and the environment. **Psychology:** Knowledge of human behavior and performance; individual differences in ability, personality, and interests; learning and motivation; psychological research methods; and the assessment and treatment of behavioral and affective disorders. **Sales and Marketing:** Knowledge of principles and methods for showing, promoting, and selling products or services. This includes marketing strategy and tactics, product demonstration, sales techniques, and sales control systems. **Customer and Personal Service:** Knowledge of principles and processes for providing customer and personal services. This includes customer needs assessment, meeting quality standards for services, and evaluation of customer satisfaction.

Civil Engineers

- Annual Earnings: $66,190
- Growth: 16.5%
- Annual Job Openings: 19,000
- Self-Employed: 4.9%
- Part-Time: 3.5%
- Education/Training Required: Bachelor's degree

Industries in Which Income Is Highest

Industry	Average Annual Wage	Number Employed
Management of Companies and Enterprises	$68,520	2,330
Administrative and Support Services	$68,040	3,330
Utilities	$67,510	2,350
Federal, State, and Local Government	$66,390	69,120
Professional, Scientific, and Technical Services	$66,330	121,810

Metropolitan Areas Where Income Is Highest

Metropolitan Area	Average Annual Wage	Number Employed
San Jose–Sunnyvale–Santa Clara, CA	$82,910	2,450
Winchester, VA–WV	$82,010	100
Odessa, TX	$79,780	70
Las Vegas–Paradise, NV	$78,780	1,690
Midland, TX	$77,840	90

Perform engineering duties in planning, designing, and overseeing construction and maintenance of building structures and facilities, such as roads, railroads, airports, bridges, harbors, channels, dams, irrigation projects, pipelines, power plants, water and sewage systems, and waste disposal units. Includes architectural, structural, traffic, ocean, and geo-technical engineers. Analyze survey reports, maps, drawings, blueprints, aerial photography, and other topographical or geologic data to plan projects. Plan and design transportation or hydraulic systems and structures, following construction and government standards and using design software and drawing tools. Compute load and grade requirements, water flow rates, and material stress factors to determine design specifications. Inspect project sites to monitor progress and ensure conformance to design specifications and safety or sanitation standards. Direct construction, operations, and maintenance activities at project site. Direct or participate in surveying to lay out installations and establish reference points, grades, and elevations to guide construction. Estimate quantities and cost of materials, equipment, or labor to determine project feasibility. Prepare or present public reports, such as bid proposals, deeds, environmental impact statements, and property and right-of-way descriptions. Test soils and materials to determine the adequacy and strength of foundations, concrete, asphalt, or steel. Provide technical advice regarding design, construction, or program modifications and structural repairs to industrial and managerial personnel. **SKILLS**—Science; Persuasion; Coordination; Mathematics; Negotiation; Operations Analysis; Instructing; Complex Problem Solving.

GOE—Interest Area: 15. Scientific Research, Engineering, and Mathematics. **Work Group:** 15.07. Research and Design Engineering. **PERSONALITY TYPE:** Realistic. Realistic occupations frequently involve work activities that include practical, hands-on problems and solutions. They often deal with plants, animals, and real-world materials like wood, tools, and machinery. Many of the occupations require working outside and do not involve a lot of paperwork or working closely with others.

EDUCATION/TRAINING PROGRAMS—Civil Engineering, General; Civil Engineering, Other; Transportation and Highway Engineering; Water Resources Engineering. **RELATED KNOWLEDGE/COURSES—Engineering and Technology:** Knowledge of the practical application of engineering science and technology. This includes applying principles, techniques, procedures, and equipment to the design and production of various goods and services. **Design:** Knowledge of design techniques, tools, and principles involved in production of precision technical plans, blueprints, drawings, and models. **Building and Construction:** Knowledge of the materials, methods, and tools involved in the construction or repair of houses, buildings, or other structures such as highways and roads. **Mathematics:** Knowledge of arithmetic, algebra, geometry, calculus, and statistics and their applications. **Customer and Personal Service:** Knowledge of principles and processes for providing customer and personal services.

This includes customer needs assessment, meeting quality standards for services, and evaluation of customer satisfaction. **Physics:** Knowledge and prediction of physical principles and laws and their interrelationships and applications to understanding fluid, material, and atmospheric dynamics and mechanical, electrical, atomic, and subatomic structures and processes.

Clinical Psychologists

- Annual Earnings: $57,170
- Growth: 19.1%
- Annual Job Openings: 10,000
- Self-Employed: 38.2%
- Part-Time: 23.3%
- Education/Training Required: Doctoral degree

The job openings listed here are shared with Counseling Psychologists and School Psychologists.

Industries in Which Income Is Highest

Industry	Average Annual Wage	Number Employed
Hospitals	$61,740	8,950
Ambulatory Health Care Services	$60,260	21,730
Educational Services	$57,730	45,870
Federal, State, and Local Government	$57,260	9,190
Social Assistance	$45,800	8,020

Metropolitan Areas Where Income Is Highest

Metropolitan Area	Average Annual Wage	Number Employed
Napa, CA	$91,830	190
Salinas, CA	$83,160	170
Ogden–Clearfield, UT	$81,730	150
Trenton–Ewing, NJ	$81,710	270
Jonesboro, AR	$81,400	70

Diagnose or evaluate mental and emotional disorders of individuals through observation, interview, and psychological tests and formulate and administer programs of treatment. Consult reference material such as textbooks, manuals, and journals in order to identify symptoms, to make diagnoses, and to develop approaches to treatment. Counsel individuals and groups regarding problems such as stress, substance abuse, and family situations in order to modify behavior and/or to improve personal, social, and vocational adjustment. Develop and implement individual treatment plans, specifying type, frequency, intensity, and duration of therapy. Discuss the treatment of problems with clients. Evaluate the effectiveness of counseling or treatments and the accuracy and completeness of diagnoses and then modify plans and diagnoses as necessary. Identify psychological, emotional, or behavioral issues and diagnose disorders, using information obtained from interviews, tests, records, and reference materials. Interact with clients to assist them in gaining insight, defining goals, and planning action to achieve effective personal, social, educational, and vocational development and adjustment. Observe individuals at play, in group interactions, or in other contexts to detect indications of mental deficiency, abnormal behavior, or maladjustment. Obtain and study medical, psychological, social, and family histories by interviewing individuals, couples, or families and by reviewing records. Provide occupational, educational, and other information to individuals so that they can make educational and vocational plans. Select, administer, score, and interpret psychological tests in order to obtain information on individuals' intelligence, achievements, interests, and personalities. Utilize a variety of treatment methods, such as psychotherapy, hypnosis, behavior modification, stress reduction therapy, psychodrama, and play therapy. Maintain current knowledge of relevant research. Plan, supervise, and conduct psychological research and write papers describing research results. Refer clients to other specialists, institutions, or support services as necessary. Write reports on clients and maintain required paperwork. Develop, direct, and participate in training programs for staff and students. **SKILLS—** Social Perceptiveness; Active Listening; Systems Evaluation; Persuasion; Systems Analysis; Science; Speaking; Complex Problem Solving.

GOE—Interest Area: 10. Human Service. **Work Group:** 10.01. Counseling and Social Work. **PERSONALITY TYPE:** Investigative. Investigative occupations frequently involve working with ideas and require an extensive amount of thinking. These occupations can involve searching for facts and figuring out problems mentally.

EDUCATION/TRAINING PROGRAMS— Clinical Child Psychology; Clinical Psychology; Counseling Psychology; Developmental and Child Psychology; Psychoanalysis and Psychotherapy; Psychology, General; School Psychology. **RELATED KNOWLEDGE/COURSES—Therapy and Counseling:** Knowledge of principles, methods, and procedures for diagnosis, treatment, and rehabilitation of physical and mental dysfunctions and for career counseling and guidance. **Psychology:** Knowledge of human behavior and performance; individual differences in ability, personality, and interests; learning and motivation; psychological research methods; and the assessment and treatment of behavioral and affective disorders. **Administration and Management:** Knowledge of business and management principles involved in strategic planning, resource allocation, human resources modeling, leadership technique, production methods, and coordination of people and resources. **Biology:** Knowledge of plant and animal organisms and their tissues, cells, functions, interdependencies, and interactions with each other and the environment. **Sociology and Anthropology:** Knowledge of group behavior and dynamics, societal trends and influences, human migrations, ethnicity, and cultures and their history and origins. **Customer and Personal Service:** Knowledge of principles and processes for providing customer and personal services. This includes customer needs assessment, meeting quality standards for services, and evaluation of customer satisfaction.

Commercial and Industrial Designers

- Annual Earnings: $52,200
- Growth: 10.8%
- Annual Job Openings: 7,000
- Self-Employed: 30.1%
- Part-Time: 21.2%
- Education/Training Required: Bachelor's degree

Industries in Which Income Is Highest

Industry	Average Annual Wage	Number Employed
Administrative and Support Services	$65,450	1,000
Transportation Equipment Manufacturing	$61,210	2,610
Management of Companies and Enterprises	$59,010	1,480
Professional, Scientific, and Technical Services	$57,220	9,780
Machinery Manufacturing	$50,850	1,750

Metropolitan Areas Where Income Is Highest

Metropolitan Area	Average Annual Wage	Number Employed
Oxnard–Thousand Oaks–Ventura, CA	$87,090	110
Detroit–Warren–Livonia, MI	$72,900	4,410
San Jose–Sunnyvale–Santa Clara, CA	$71,260	230
Ann Arbor, MI	$69,610	100
Syracuse, NY	$63,990	220

Develop and design manufactured products, such as cars, home appliances, and children's toys. Combine artistic talent with research on product use, marketing, and materials to create the most functional and appealing product design. Prepare sketches of ideas, detailed drawings, illustrations, artwork, and/or blueprints, using drafting instruments, paints and brushes, or computer-aided design equipment. Direct and coordinate the fabrication of models or samples and the drafting of working drawings and specification sheets from sketches. Modify and refine designs, using working models, to conform with customer specifications, production limitations, or changes in design trends. Coordinate the look and function of product lines. Confer with engineering, marketing, production, and/or sales departments, or with customers, to establish and evaluate design concepts for manufactured products. Present designs and reports to customers or design committees for approval and discuss need for modification. Evaluate feasibility of design ideas, based on factors such as appearance, safety, function, serviceability, budget, production costs/methods, and market characteristics. Read publications, attend showings, and study competing products and design styles and motifs to obtain perspective

and generate design concepts. Research production specifications, costs, production materials, and manufacturing methods and provide cost estimates and itemized production requirements. Design graphic material for use as ornamentation, illustration, or advertising on manufactured materials and packaging or containers. Develop manufacturing procedures and monitor the manufacture of their designs in a factory to improve operations and product quality. Supervise assistants' work throughout the design process. Fabricate models or samples in paper, wood, glass, fabric, plastic, metal, or other materials, using hand and/or power tools. Investigate product characteristics such as the product's safety and handling qualities; its market appeal; how efficiently it can be produced; and ways of distributing, using, and maintaining it. Develop industrial standards and regulatory guidelines. Participate in new product planning or market research, including studying the potential need for new products. **SKILLS**—Technology Design; Operations Analysis; Troubleshooting; Time Management; Quality Control Analysis; Coordination; Systems Evaluation; Installation.

GOE—Interest Area: 03. Arts and Communication. **Work Group:** 03.05. Design. **PERSONALITY TYPE:** Artistic. Artistic occupations frequently involve working with forms, designs, and patterns. They often require self-expression, and the work can be done without following a clear set of rules.

EDUCATION/TRAINING PROGRAMS—Commercial and Advertising Art; Design and Applied Arts, Other; Design and Visual Communications, General; Industrial Design. **RELATED KNOWLEDGE/COURSES—Design:** Knowledge of design techniques, tools, and principles involved in production of precision technical plans, blueprints, drawings, and models. **Engineering and Technology:** Knowledge of the practical application of engineering science and technology. This includes applying principles, techniques, procedures, and equipment to the design and production of various goods and services. **Mathematics:** Knowledge of arithmetic, algebra, geometry, calculus, and statistics and their applications. **Clerical Practices:** Knowledge of administrative and clerical procedures and systems such as word processing, managing files and records, stenography and transcription, designing forms, and other office procedures and terminology. **Computers and Electronics:** Knowledge of circuit boards, processors, chips, electronic equipment, and computer hardware and software, including applications and programming. **Production and Processing:** Knowledge of raw materials, production processes, quality control, costs, and other techniques for maximizing the effective manufacture and distribution of goods.

Commercial Pilots

- Annual Earnings: $55,810
- Growth: 16.8%
- Annual Job Openings: 2,000
- Self-Employed: 2.5%
- Part-Time: 14.7%
- Education/Training Required: Postsecondary vocational training

Industries in Which Income Is Highest

Industry	Average Annual Wage	Number Employed
Air Transportation	$61,470	7,670
Ambulatory Health Care Services	$54,070	1,140
Support Activities for Transportation	$50,770	3,030
Support Activities for Agriculture and Forestry	$47,240	1,270
Educational Services	$40,900	4,710

Metropolitan Areas Where Income Is Highest

Metropolitan Area	Average Annual Wage	Number Employed
Palm Bay–Melbourne–Titusville, FL	$116,300	160
Evansville, IN–KY	$96,070	90
New York–Northern New Jersey–Long Island, NY–NJ–PA	$87,080	710
Anchorage, AK	$78,260	250
Minneapolis–St. Paul–Bloomington, MN–WI	$78,040	180

Pilot and navigate the flight of small fixed- or rotary-winged aircraft, primarily for the transport of cargo and passengers. Requires commercial rating. Check aircraft prior to flights to ensure that the engines, controls, instruments, and other systems are functioning properly. Check baggage or cargo to ensure that it has been loaded correctly. Choose routes, altitudes, and speeds that will provide the fastest, safest, and smoothest flights. Consider airport altitudes, outside temperatures, plane weights, and wind speeds and directions in order to calculate the speed needed to become airborne. Contact control towers for takeoff clearances, arrival instructions, and other information, using radio equipment. Coordinate flight activities with ground crews and air-traffic control and inform crew members of flight and test procedures. File instrument flight plans with air traffic control so that flights can be coordinated with other air traffic. Monitor engine operation, fuel consumption, and functioning of aircraft systems during flights. Obtain and review data such as load weights, fuel supplies, weather conditions, and flight schedules in order to determine flight plans and to see if changes might be necessary. Order changes in fuel supplies, loads, routes, or schedules to ensure safety of flights. Plan and formulate flight activities and test schedules and prepare flight evaluation reports. Plan flights, following government and company regulations, using aeronautical charts and navigation instruments. Request changes in altitudes or routes as circumstances dictate. Start engines, operate controls, and pilot airplanes to transport passengers, mail, or freight, while adhering to flight plans, regulations, and procedures. Use instrumentation to pilot aircraft when visibility is poor. Check the flight performance of new and experimental planes. Conduct in-flight tests and evaluations at specified altitudes and in all types of weather in order to determine the receptivity and other characteristics of equipment and systems. Co-pilot aircraft or perform captain's duties if required. Fly with other pilots or pilot-license applicants to evaluate their proficiency. Instruct other pilots and student pilots in aircraft operations. Perform minor aircraft maintenance and repair work or arrange for major maintenance. **SKILLS—** Operation and Control; Operation Monitoring; Science; Instructing; Systems Evaluation; Systems Analysis; Coordination; Judgment and Decision Making.

GOE—Interest Area: 16. Transportation, Distribution, and Logistics. **Work Group:** 16.02. Air Vehicle Operation. **PERSONALITY TYPE:** Realistic. Realistic occupations frequently involve work activities that include practical, hands-on problems and solutions. They often deal with plants, animals, and real-world materials like wood, tools, and machinery. Many of the occupations require working outside and do not involve a lot of paperwork or working closely with others.

EDUCATION/TRAINING PROGRAMS—Airline/Commercial/Professional Pilot and Flight Crew; Flight Instructor. **RELATED KNOWLEDGE/ COURSES**—**Transportation:** Knowledge of principles and methods for moving people or goods by air, rail, sea, or road, including the relative costs and benefits. **Geography:** Knowledge of principles and methods for describing the features of land, sea, and air masses, including their physical characteristics; locations; interrelationships; and distribution of plant, animal, and human life. **Education and Training:** Knowledge of principles and methods for curriculum and training design, teaching and instruction for individuals and groups, and the measurement of training effects. **Mechanical Devices:** Knowledge of machines and tools, including their designs, uses, repair, and maintenance. **Public Safety and Security:** Knowledge of relevant equipment, policies, procedures, and strategies to promote effective local, state, or national security operations for the protection of people, data, property, and institutions. **Physics:** Knowledge and prediction of physical principles and laws and their interrelationships and applications to understanding fluid, material, and atmospheric dynamics and mechanical, electrical, atomic, and subatomic structures and processes.

Communication Equipment Mechanics, Installers, and Repairers

- ◉ Annual Earnings: $50,620
- ◉ Growth: -4.9%
- ◉ Annual Job Openings: 21,000
- ◉ Self-Employed: 6.6%
- ◉ Part-Time: 4.8%
- ◉ Education/Training Required: Long-term on-the-job training

The job openings listed here are shared with Central Office and PBX Installers and Repairers; Frame Wirers, Central Office; Station Installers and Repairers, Telephone; and Telecommunications Facility Examiners.

Industries in Which Income Is Highest

Industry	Average Annual Wage	Number Employed
Telecommunications	$52,170	136,200
Management of Companies and Enterprises	$51,670	2,520
Professional, Scientific, and Technical Services	$51,100	5,810
Wholesale Electronic Markets and Agents and Brokers	$48,990	1,400
Administrative and Support Services	$48,780	3,780

Metropolitan Areas Where Income Is Highest

Metropolitan Area	Average Annual Wage	Number Employed
Atlantic City, NJ	$68,240	50
Trenton–Ewing, NJ	$64,750	280
New York–Northern New Jersey–Long Island, NY–NJ–PA	$62,120	15,460
Rochester, NY	$61,530	620
State College, PA	$59,690	80

Install, maintain, test, and repair communication cables and equipment. Adjusts or modifies equipment in accordance with customer request or to enhance performance of equipment. Performs routine maintenance on equipment, which includes adjustment, repair, and painting. Measures, cuts, splices, connects, solders, and installs wires and cables. Examines and tests malfunctioning equipment to determine defects, using blueprints and electrical measuring instruments. Tests installed equipment for conformance to specifications, using test equipment. Assembles and installs communication equipment, such as data communication lines and equipment, computer systems, and antennas and towers, using hand tools. Repairs, replaces, or adjusts defective components. Disassembles equipment to adjust, repair, or replace parts, using hand tools. Evaluates quality of performance of installed equipment by observance and using test equipment. Digs holes or trenches. Answers customers' inquiries or complaints. Cleans and maintains tools, test equipment, and motor vehicle. Communicates with base, using telephone or two-way radio to receive instructions or technical advice or to report unauthorized use of equipment. Demonstrates equipment and instructs customer in use of equipment. Determines viability of site through observation and discusses site location and construction requirements with customer. Measures distance from landmarks to identify exact installation site. Climbs poles and ladders; constructs pole, roof mounts, or reinforcements; and mixes concrete to enable equipment installation. Plans layout and installation of data communications equipment. Reviews work orders, building permits, manufacturer's instructions, and ordinances to move, change, install, repair, or remove communication equipment. **SKILLS**—Repairing; Installation; Troubleshooting; Equipment Maintenance; Quality Control Analysis; Technology Design; Operation Monitoring; Operation and Control.

GOE—Interest Area: 02. Architecture and Construction. **Work Group:** 02.05. Systems and Equipment Installation, Maintenance, and Repair. **PERSONALITY TYPE:** Realistic. Realistic occupations frequently involve work activities that include practical, hands-on problems and solutions. They often deal with plants, animals, and real-world materials like wood, tools, and machinery. Many of the occupations require working outside and do not involve a lot of paperwork or working closely with others.

EDUCATION/TRAINING PROGRAM—Communications Systems Installation and Repair Technology. **RELATED KNOWLEDGE/COURSES—Telecommunications:** Knowledge of transmission, broadcasting, switching, control, and operation of telecommunications systems. **Computers and Electronics:** Knowledge of circuit boards, processors, chips, electronic equipment, and computer hardware and software, including applications and programming. **Design:** Knowledge of design techniques, tools, and principles involved in production of precision technical plans, blueprints, drawings, and models. **Mechanical Devices:** Knowledge of machines and tools, including their designs, uses, repair, and maintenance.

Communications Teachers, Postsecondary

- Annual Earnings: $50,890
- Growth: 32.2%
- Annual Job Openings: 329,000
- Self-Employed: 0.4%
- Part-Time: 27.3%
- Education/Training Required: Master's degree

Our sources did not provide separate job openings data for this occupation. The job openings listed here are shared with 35 other postsecondary teaching occupations. For a complete list, see the beginning of this section.

Industries in Which Income Is Highest

Industry	Average Annual Wage	Number Employed
Educational Services	$50,890	22,300

Metropolitan Areas Where Income Is Highest

Metropolitan Area	Average Annual Wage	Number Employed
San Diego–Carlsbad–San Marcos, CA	$76,390	180
Los Angeles–Long Beach–Santa Ana, CA	$69,140	1,110
Riverside–San Bernardino–Ontario, CA	$67,700	140
Providence–Fall River–Warwick, RI–MA	$63,630	90
Wichita, KS	$63,090	60

Teach courses in communications, such as organizational communications, public relations, radio/television broadcasting, and journalism. Evaluate and grade students' class work, assignments, and papers. Prepare course materials such as syllabi, homework assignments, and handouts. Initiate, facilitate, and moderate classroom discussions. Prepare and deliver lectures to undergraduate and/or graduate students on topics such as public speaking, media criticism, and oral traditions. Compile, administer, and grade examinations or assign this work to others. Maintain student attendance records, grades, and other required records. Plan, evaluate, and revise curricula, course content, and course materials and methods of instruction. Maintain regularly scheduled office hours in order to advise and assist students. Keep abreast of developments in their field by reading current literature, talking with colleagues, and participating in professional conferences. Advise students on academic and vocational curricula and on career issues. Supervise undergraduate and/or graduate teaching, internship, and research work. Select and obtain materials and supplies such as textbooks. Collaborate with colleagues to address teaching and research issues. Conduct research in a particular field of knowledge and publish findings in professional journals, books, and/or electronic media. Participate in student recruitment, registration, and placement activities. Serve on academic or administrative committees that deal with institutional policies, departmental matters, and academic issues. Compile bibliographies of specialized materials for outside reading assignments. Act as advisers to student organizations. Participate in campus and community events. Perform administrative duties such as serving as department head. **SKILLS**—Instructing; Persuasion; Learning Strategies; Writing; Social Perceptiveness; Monitoring; Active Learning; Critical Thinking.

GOE—Interest Area: 05. Education and Training. **Work Group:** 05.03. Postsecondary and Adult Teaching and Instructing. **PERSONALITY TYPE:** No data available.

EDUCATION/TRAINING PROGRAMS— Advertising; Broadcast Journalism; Communications Studies/Speech Communication and Rhetoric; Communications, Journalism, and Related Fields, Other; Digital Communications and Media/Multimedia; Health Communications; Journalism; Journalism, Other; Mass Communications/Media Studies; Political Communications; Public Relations/Image Management; Radio and Television. **RELATED KNOWLEDGE/COURSES—Education and Training:** Knowledge of principles and methods for curriculum and training design, teaching and instruction for individuals and groups, and the measurement of training effects. **Communications and Media:** Knowledge of media production, communication, and

dissemination techniques and methods. This includes alternative ways to inform and entertain via written, oral, and visual media. **English Language:** Knowledge of the structure and content of the English language, including the meaning and spelling of words, rules of composition, and grammar. **Philosophy and Theology:** Knowledge of different philosophical systems and religions. This includes their basic principles, values, ethics, ways of thinking, customs, and practices and their impact on human culture. **Sociology and Anthropology:** Knowledge of group behavior and dynamics, societal trends and influences, human migrations, ethnicity, and cultures and their history and origins. **History and Archeology:** Knowledge of historical events and their causes, indicators, and effects on civilizations and cultures.

Compensation and Benefits Managers

- Annual Earnings: $69,130
- Growth: 21.5%
- Annual Job Openings: 4,000
- Self-Employed: 1.2%
- Part-Time: 3.6%
- Education/Training Required: Work experience plus degree

Industries in Which Income Is Highest

Industry	Annual Wage	Average Number Employed
Computer and Electronic Product Manufacturing	$85,000	1,110
Management of Companies and Enterprises	$80,800	5,840
Insurance Carriers and Related Activities	$77,950	2,130
Professional, Scientific, and Technical Services	$75,930	5,240
Credit Intermediation and Related Activities	$72,220	2,440

Metropolitan Areas Where Income Is Highest

Metropolitan Area	Average Annual Wage	Number Employed
Bridgeport–Stamford–Norwalk, CT	$103,300	200
Minneapolis–St. Paul–Bloomington, MN–WI	$97,050	440
Columbus, OH	$96,160	310
New York–Northern New Jersey–Long Island, NY–NJ–PA	$93,650	3,590
Danbury, CT	$92,870	50

Plan, direct, or coordinate compensation and benefits activities and staff of an organization. Advise management on such matters as equal employment opportunity, sexual harassment, and discrimination. Direct preparation and distribution of written and verbal information to inform employees of benefits, compensation, and personnel policies. Administer, direct, and review employee benefit programs, including the integration of benefit programs following mergers and acquisitions. Plan and conduct new employee orientations to foster positive attitude toward organizational objectives. Plan, direct, supervise, and coordinate work activities of subordinates and staff relating to employment, compensation, labor relations, and employee relations. Identify and implement benefits to increase the quality of life for employees by working with brokers and researching benefits issues. Design, evaluate, and modify benefits policies to ensure that programs are current, competitive, and in compliance with legal requirements. Analyze compensation policies, government regulations, and prevailing wage rates to develop competitive compensation plan. Formulate policies, procedures, and programs for recruitment, testing, placement, classification, orientation, benefits and compensation, and labor and industrial relations. Mediate between benefits providers and employees, such as by assisting in handling employees' benefits-related questions or taking suggestions. Fulfill all reporting requirements of all relevant government rules and regulations, including the Employee Retirement Income Security Act (ERISA). Maintain records and compile statistical reports concerning personnel-related data such as hires, transfers, performance appraisals, and absenteeism rates. Analyze statistical data and reports to identify and determine causes of personnel problems and develop recommendations for improvement of organization's personnel policies and practices. Develop methods to improve employment policies, processes, and practices and recommend changes to management. Negotiate bargaining agreements. Investigate and report on industrial accidents for insurance carriers. Represent organization at personnel-related hearings and investigations. **SKILLS—** Management of Personnel Resources; Management of Financial Resources; Social Perceptiveness; Time Management; Management of Material Resources; Monitoring; Instructing; Negotiation.

GOE—Interest Area: 04. Business and Administration. **Work Group:** 04.01. Managerial Work in General Business. **PERSONALITY TYPE:** Enterprising. Enterprising occupations frequently involve starting up and carrying out projects. These occupations can involve leading people and making many decisions. They sometimes require risk taking and often deal with business.

EDUCATION/TRAINING PROGRAMS— Human Resources Management/Personnel Administration, General; Labor and Industrial Relations. **RELATED KNOWLEDGE/COURSES— Personnel and Human Resources:** Knowledge of principles and procedures for personnel recruitment, selection, training, compensation and benefits, labor relations and negotiation, and personnel information systems. **Clerical Practices:** Knowledge of administrative and clerical procedures and systems such as word processing, managing files and records, stenography and transcription, designing forms, and other office procedures and terminology. **Economics and Accounting:** Knowledge of economic and accounting principles and practices, the financial markets, banking, and the analysis and reporting of financial data. **Administration and Management:** Knowledge of business and management principles involved in strategic planning, resource allocation, human resources modeling, leadership technique, production methods, and coordination of people and resources. **Education and Training:** Knowledge of principles and methods for curriculum and training design, teaching and instruction for individuals and groups, and the measurement of training effects. **Law and Government:** Knowledge of laws, legal codes, court procedures, precedents, government regulations, executive orders, agency rules, and the democratic political process.

Compensation, Benefits, and Job Analysis Specialists

- Annual Earnings: $48,870
- Growth: 20.4%
- Annual Job Openings: 15,000
- Self-Employed: 2.7%
- Part-Time: 7.7%
- Education/Training Required: Bachelor's degree

Industries in Which Income Is Highest

Industry	Average Annual Wage	Number Employed
Telecommunications	$58,420	1,110
Computer and Electronic Product Manufacturing	$56,490	1,770
Professional, Scientific, and Technical Services	$54,970	9,780
Transportation Equipment Manufacturing	$53,690	1,190
Management of Companies and Enterprises	$53,290	10,380

Metropolitan Areas Where Income Is Highest

Metropolitan Area	Average Annual Wage	Number Employed
Altoona, PA	$64,200	50
San Jose–Sunnyvale–Santa Clara, CA	$63,750	780
Bridgeport–Stamford–Norwalk, CT	$58,740	440
New York–Northern New Jersey–Long Island, NY–NJ–PA	$58,500	10,900
New Haven, CT	$58,400	200

Conduct programs of compensation and benefits and job analysis for employer. May specialize in specific areas, such as position classification and pension programs. Evaluate job positions, determining classification, exempt or non-exempt status, and salary. Ensure company compliance with federal and state laws, including reporting requirements. Advise managers and employees on state and federal employment regulations, collective agreements, benefit and compensation policies, personnel procedures, and classification programs. Plan, develop, evaluate, improve, and communicate methods and techniques for selecting, promoting, compensating, evaluating, and training workers. Provide advice on the resolution of classification and salary complaints. Prepare occupational classifications, job descriptions, and salary scales. Assist in preparing and maintaining personnel records and handbooks. Prepare reports, such as organization and flow charts and career path reports, to summarize job analysis and evaluation and compensation analysis information. Administer employee insurance, pension, and savings plans, working with insurance brokers and plan carriers. Negotiate collective agreements on behalf of employers or workers and mediate labor disputes and grievances. Develop, implement, administer, and evaluate personnel and labor relations programs, including performance appraisal, affirmative action, and employment equity programs. Perform multifactor data and cost analyses that may be used in areas such as support of collective bargaining agreements. Research employee benefit and health and safety practices and recommend changes or modifications to existing policies. Analyze organizational, occupational, and industrial data to facilitate organizational functions and provide technical information to business, industry, and government. Advise staff of individuals' qualifications. Assess need for and develop job analysis instruments and materials. Review occupational data on Alien Employment Certification Applications to determine the appropriate occupational title and code; provide local offices with information about immigration and occupations. Research job and worker requirements, structural and functional relationships among jobs and occupations, and occupational trends. **SKILLS**—Service Orientation; Persuasion; Coordination; Negotiation; Management of Financial Resources; Judgment and Decision Making; Social Perceptiveness; Active Listening.

GOE—Interest Area: 04. Business and Administration. **Work Group:** 04.03. Human Resources Support. **PERSONALITY TYPE:** Investigative. Investigative occupations frequently involve working with ideas and require an extensive amount of thinking. These occupations can involve searching for facts and figuring out problems mentally.

EDUCATION/TRAINING PROGRAMS— Human Resources Management/Personnel Administration, General; Labor and Industrial Relations. **RELATED KNOWLEDGE/COURSES—**

Personnel and Human Resources: Knowledge of principles and procedures for personnel recruitment, selection, training, compensation and benefits, labor relations and negotiation, and personnel information systems. **Clerical Practices:** Knowledge of administrative and clerical procedures and systems such as word processing, managing files and records, stenography and transcription, designing forms, and other office procedures and terminology. **Customer and Personal Service:** Knowledge of principles and processes for providing customer and personal services. This includes customer needs assessment, meeting quality standards for services, and evaluation of customer satisfaction. **Administration and Management:** Knowledge of business and management principles involved in strategic planning, resource allocation, human resources modeling, leadership technique, production methods, and coordination of people and resources. **Education and Training:** Knowledge of principles and methods for curriculum and training design, teaching and instruction for individuals and groups, and the measurement of training effects. **English Language:** Knowledge of the structure and content of the English language, including the meaning and spelling of words, rules of composition, and grammar.

Computer and Information Systems Managers

- Annual Earnings: $96,520
- Growth: 25.9%
- Annual Job Openings: 25,000
- Self-Employed: 1.2%
- Part-Time: 3.3%
- Education/Training Required: Work experience plus degree

Industries in Which Income Is Highest

Industry	Average Annual Wage	Number Employed
Securities, Commodity Contracts, and Other Financial Investments and Related Activities	$116,360	7,230
Computer and Electronic Product Manufacturing	$110,120	9,270
Publishing Industries (Except Internet)	$106,740	10,930
Professional, Scientific, and Technical Services	$103,980	63,710
Management of Companies and Enterprises	$102,480	21,060

Metropolitan Areas Where Income Is Highest

Metropolitan Area	Average Annual Wage	Number Employed
San Jose–Sunnyvale–Santa Clara, CA	$134,440	5,700
New York–Northern New Jersey–Long Island, NY–NJ–PA	$123,020	24,250
San Francisco–Oakland–Fremont, CA	$120,530	7,900
Bridgeport–Stamford–Norwalk, CT	$118,920	1,430
Winchester, VA–WV	$118,400	50

Plan, direct, or coordinate activities in such fields as electronic data processing, information systems, systems analysis, and computer programming. Manage backup, security, and user help systems. Consult with users, management, vendors, and technicians to assess computing needs and system requirements. Direct daily operations of department, analyzing workflow, establishing priorities, developing standards, and setting deadlines. Assign and review the work of systems analysts, programmers, and other computer-related workers. Stay abreast of advances in technology. Develop computer information resources, providing for data security and control, strategic computing, and disaster recovery. Review and approve all systems charts and programs prior to their implementation. Evaluate the organization's technology use and needs and recommend improvements, such as hardware and software upgrades. Control operational budget and expenditures. Meet with department heads, managers, supervisors, vendors, and others to solicit cooperation and resolve problems. Develop and interpret organizational goals, policies, and procedures. Recruit, hire, train, and supervise staff and/or participate in staffing decisions. Review project plans in order to plan and coordinate project activity. Evaluate data processing proposals to assess project feasibility and requirements. Prepare and review operational reports or project progress reports. Purchase necessary equipment. **SKILLS**—Management of Financial Resources; Programming; Operations Analysis; Negotiation; Systems Analysis; Management of Material Resources; Persuasion; Systems Evaluation.

GOE—Interest Area: 11. Information Technology. **Work Group:** 11.01. Managerial Work in Information Technology. **PERSONALITY TYPE:** Enterprising. Enterprising occupations frequently involve starting up and carrying out projects. These occupations can involve leading people and making many decisions. They sometimes require risk taking and often deal with business.

EDUCATION/TRAINING PROGRAMS—Computer and Information Sciences, General; Computer Science; Information Resources Management/CIO Training; Information Science/Studies; Knowledge Management; Management Information Systems, General; Operations Management and Supervision; System Administration/Administrator. **RELATED KNOWLEDGE/COURSES—Clerical Practices:** Knowledge of administrative and clerical procedures and systems such as word processing, managing files and records, stenography and transcription, designing forms, and other office procedures and terminology. **Computers and Electronics:** Knowledge of circuit boards, processors, chips, electronic equipment, and computer hardware and software, including applications and programming. **Economics and Accounting:** Knowledge of economic and accounting principles and practices, the financial markets, banking, and the analysis and reporting of financial data. **Engineering and Technology:** Knowledge of the practical application of engineering science and technology. This includes applying principles, techniques, procedures, and equipment to the design and production of various goods and services. **Design:** Knowledge of design techniques, tools, and principles involved in production of precision technical plans, blueprints, drawings, and models. **Administration and Management:** Knowledge of business and management principles involved in strategic planning, resource allocation, human resources modeling, leadership technique, production methods, and coordination of people and resources.

Computer Hardware Engineers

- Annual Earnings: $84,420
- Growth: 10.1%
- Annual Job Openings: 5,000
- Self-Employed: 0.8%
- Part-Time: 4.1%
- Education/Training Required: Bachelor's degree

Industries in Which Income Is Highest

Industry	Average Annual Wage	Number Employed
Computer and Electronic Product Manufacturing	$87,480	34,990
Internet Service Providers, Web Search Portals, and Data Processing Services	$87,240	1,560
Merchant Wholesalers, Durable Goods	$85,010	4,360
Professional, Scientific, and Technical Services	$84,130	20,820
Federal, State, and Local Government	$83,800	4,000

Metropolitan Areas Where Income Is Highest

Metropolitan Area	Average Annual Wage	Number Employed
Boulder, CO	$103,780	1,570
Worcester, MA–CT	$101,310	250
San Jose–Sunnyvale–Santa Clara, CA	$100,860	9,710
Santa Cruz–Watsonville, CA	$98,220	60
Colorado Springs, CO	$97,150	570

Research, design, develop, and test computer or computer-related equipment for commercial, industrial, military, or scientific use. May supervise the manufacturing and installation of computer or computer-related equipment and components. Update knowledge and skills to keep up with rapid advancements in computer technology. Provide technical support to designers, marketing and sales departments, suppliers, engineers, and other team members throughout the product development and implementation process. Test and verify hardware and support peripherals to ensure that they meet specifications and requirements, analyzing and recording test data. Monitor functioning of equipment and make necessary modifications to ensure system operates in conformance with specifications. Analyze information to determine, recommend, and plan layout, including type of computers and peripheral equipment modifications. Build, test, and modify product prototypes, using working models or theoretical models constructed using computer simulation. Analyze user needs and recommend appropriate hardware. Direct technicians, engineering designers, or other technical support personnel as needed. Confer with engineering staff and consult specifications to evaluate interface between hardware and software and operational and performance requirements of overall system. Select hardware and material, assuring compliance with specifications and product requirements. Store, retrieve, and manipulate data for analysis of system capabilities and requirements. Write detailed functional specifications that document the hardware development process and support hardware introduction. Specify power supply requirements and configuration, drawing on system performance expectations and design specifications. Provide training and support to system designers and users. Assemble and modify existing pieces of equipment to meet special needs. Evaluate factors such as reporting formats required, cost constraints, and need for security restrictions to determine hardware configuration. Design and develop computer hardware and support peripherals, including central processing units (CPUs), support logic, microprocessors, custom integrated circuits, and printers and disk drives. **SKILLS**—Programming; Troubleshooting; Systems Analysis; Operations Analysis; Systems Evaluation; Technology Design; Judgment and Decision Making; Quality Control Analysis.

GOE—Interest Area: 15. Scientific Research, Engineering, and Mathematics. **Work Group:** 15.07. Research and Design Engineering. **PERSONALITY TYPE:** Investigative. Investigative occupations frequently involve working with ideas and require an extensive amount of thinking. These occupations can involve searching for facts and figuring out problems mentally.

EDUCATION/TRAINING PROGRAMS—Computer Engineering, General; Computer Hardware Engineering. **RELATED KNOWLEDGE/**

COURSES—Computers and Electronics: Knowledge of circuit boards, processors, chips, electronic equipment, and computer hardware and software, including applications and programming. **Engineering and Technology:** Knowledge of the practical application of engineering science and technology. This includes applying principles, techniques, procedures, and equipment to the design and production of various goods and services. **Design:** Knowledge of design techniques, tools, and principles involved in production of precision technical plans, blueprints, drawings, and models. **Telecommunications:** Knowledge of transmission, broadcasting, switching, control, and operation of telecommunications systems. **Education and Training:** Knowledge of principles and methods for curriculum and training design, teaching and instruction for individuals and groups, and the measurement of training effects. **Mathematics:** Knowledge of arithmetic, algebra, geometry, calculus, and statistics and their applications.

Computer Programmers

- Annual Earnings: $63,420
- Growth: 2.0%
- Annual Job Openings: 28,000
- Self-Employed: 4.5%
- Part-Time: 6.2%
- Education/Training Required: Bachelor's degree

Industries in Which Income Is Highest

Industry	Average Annual Wage	Number Employed
Securities, Commodity Contracts, and Other Financial Investments and Related Activities	$74,600	5,960
Publishing Industries (Except Internet)	$74,010	21,640
Computer and Electronic Product Manufacturing	$71,360	8,350
Merchant Wholesalers, Durable Goods	$69,740	17,900
Credit Intermediation and Related Activities	$67,880	10,610

Metropolitan Areas Where Income Is Highest

Metropolitan Area	Average Annual Wage	Number Employed
San Jose–Sunnyvale–Santa Clara, CA	$86,400	5,460
Monroe, LA	$82,890	130
Winston–Salem, NC	$81,870	830
Poughkeepsie–Newburgh–Middletown, NY	$81,210	800
Waterbury, CT	$80,910	110

Convert project specifications and statements of problems and procedures to detailed logical flow charts for coding into computer language. Develop and write computer programs to store, locate, and retrieve specific documents, data, and information. May program Web sites. Correct errors by making appropriate changes and then rechecking the program to ensure that the desired results are produced. Conduct trial runs of programs and software applications to be sure that they will produce the desired information and that the instructions are correct. Compile and write documentation of program development and subsequent revisions, inserting comments in the coded instructions so others can understand the program. Write, update, and maintain computer programs or software packages to handle specific jobs, such as tracking inventory, storing or retrieving data, or controlling other equipment. Consult with managerial, engineering, and technical personnel to clarify program intent, identify problems, and suggest changes. Perform or direct revision, repair, or expansion of existing programs to increase operating efficiency or adapt to new requirements. Write, analyze, review, and rewrite programs, using workflow chart and diagram and applying knowledge of computer capabilities, subject matter, and symbolic logic. Write or contribute to instructions or manuals to guide end users. Investigate whether networks, workstations, the central processing unit of the system, and/or peripheral equipment are responding to a program's instructions. Prepare detailed workflow charts and diagrams that describe input, output, and logical operation and convert them into a series of instructions coded in a computer language. Perform systems analysis and programming tasks to maintain and control the use of computer systems software as a systems programmer. Consult with and assist computer operators or system analysts to define and resolve problems in running computer programs. Assign, coordinate, and review work and activities of programming personnel. **SKILLS—** Programming; Operations Analysis; Technology Design; Troubleshooting; Systems Analysis; Critical Thinking; Complex Problem Solving; Installation.

GOE—Interest Area: 11. Information Technology. **Work Group:** 11.02. Information Technology Specialties. **PERSONALITY TYPE:** Investigative. Investigative occupations frequently involve working with ideas and require an extensive amount of thinking. These occupations can involve searching for facts and figuring out problems mentally.

EDUCATION/TRAINING PROGRAMS—Artificial Intelligence and Robotics; Bioinformatics; Computer Graphics; Computer Programming, Specific Applications; Computer Programming, Vendor/Product Certification; Computer Programming/Programmer, General; E-Commerce/Electronic Commerce; Management Information Systems, General; Medical Informatics; Medical Office Computer Specialist/Assistant; Web Page, Digital/Multimedia, and Information Resources Design; Web/Multimedia Management and Webmaster. **RELATED KNOWLEDGE/COURSES—Computers and Electronics:** Knowledge of circuit boards, processors, chips, electronic equipment, and computer hardware and software, including applications and programming. **Design:** Knowledge of design techniques, tools, and principles involved in production of precision technical plans, blueprints, drawings, and models. **Mathematics:** Knowledge of arithmetic, algebra, geometry, calculus, and statistics and their applications. **Economics and Accounting:** Knowledge of economic and accounting principles and practices, the financial markets, banking, and the analysis and reporting of financial data. **Telecommunications:** Knowledge of transmission, broadcasting, switching, control, and operation of telecommunications systems. **Engineering and Technology:** Knowledge of the practical application of engineering science and technology. This includes applying principles, techniques, procedures, and equipment to the design and production of various goods and services.

Computer Science Teachers, Postsecondary

- Annual Earnings: $54,270
- Growth: 32.2%
- Annual Job Openings: 329,000
- Self-Employed: 0.4%
- Part-Time: 27.3%
- Education/Training Required: Master's degree

Our sources did not provide separate job openings data for this occupation. The job openings listed here are shared with 35 other postsecondary teaching occupations. For a complete list, see the beginning of this section.

Industries in Which Income Is Highest

Industry	Average Annual Wage	Number Employed
Educational Services	$54,300	38,350

Metropolitan Areas Where Income Is Highest

Metropolitan Area	Average Annual Wage	Number Employed
Durham, NC	$84,330	140
Salt Lake City, UT	$82,020	120
Boston–Cambridge–Quincy, MA–NH	$82,020	780
Worcester, MA–CT	$79,030	60
San Francisco–Oakland–Fremont, CA	$78,810	1,040

Teach courses in computer science. May specialize in a field of computer science, such as the design and function of computers or operations and research analysis. Evaluate and grade students' class work, laboratory work, assignments, and papers. Maintain student attendance records, grades, and other required records. Prepare and deliver lectures to undergraduate and/or graduate students on topics such as programming, data structures, and software design. Prepare course materials such as syllabi, homework assignments, and handouts. Compile, administer, and grade examinations or assign this work to others. Keep abreast of developments in their field by reading current literature, talking with colleagues, and participating in professional conferences. Initiate, facilitate, and moderate classroom discussions. Plan, evaluate, and revise curricula, course content, and course materials and methods of instruction. Supervise students' laboratory work. Maintain regularly scheduled office hours in order to advise and assist students. Select and obtain materials and supplies such as textbooks and laboratory equipment. Advise students on academic and vocational curricula and on career issues. Participate in student recruitment, registration, and placement activities. Collaborate with colleagues to address teaching and research issues. Serve on academic or administrative committees that deal with institutional policies, departmental matters, and academic issues. Act as advisers to student organizations. Supervise undergraduate and/or graduate teaching, internship, and research work. Perform administrative duties such as serving as department head. Conduct research in a particular field of knowledge and publish findings in professional journals, books, and/or electronic media. Direct research of other teachers or of graduate students working for advanced academic degrees. **SKILLS**—Programming; Instructing; Learning Strategies; Technology Design; Active Learning; Operations Analysis; Complex Problem Solving; Critical Thinking.

GOE—Interest Area: 05. Education and Training. **Work Group:** 05.03. Postsecondary and Adult Teaching and Instructing. **PERSONALITY TYPE:** Investigative. Investigative occupations frequently involve working with ideas and require an extensive amount of thinking. These occupations can involve searching for facts and figuring out problems mentally.

EDUCATION/TRAINING PROGRAMS—Computer and Information Sciences, General; Computer Programming/Programmer, General; Computer Science; Computer Systems Analysis/Analyst; Information Science/Studies. **RELATED KNOWLEDGE/COURSES—Education and Training:** Knowledge of principles and methods for curriculum and training design, teaching and instruction for individuals and groups, and the measurement of training effects. **Computers and Electronics:** Knowledge of circuit boards, processors, chips, electronic equipment, and computer hardware and software, including applications and programming. **Telecommunications:** Knowledge of transmission, broadcasting, switching, control, and operation of telecommunications systems.

Mathematics: Knowledge of arithmetic, algebra, geometry, calculus, and statistics and their applications. **English Language:** Knowledge of the structure and content of the English language, including the meaning and spelling of words, rules of composition, and grammar. **Engineering and Technology:** Knowledge of the practical application of engineering science and technology. This includes applying principles, techniques, procedures, and equipment to the design and production of various goods and services.

Computer Security Specialists

- Annual Earnings: $59,930
- Growth: 38.4%
- Annual Job Openings: 34,000
- Self-Employed: 0.6%
- Part-Time: No data available
- Education/Training Required: Bachelor's degree

The job openings listed here are shared with Network and Computer Systems Administrators.

Industries in Which Income Is Highest

Industry	Average Annual Wage	Number Employed
Securities, Commodity Contracts, and Other Financial Investments and Related Activities	$69,660	5,390
Telecommunications	$66,740	13,610
Chemical Manufacturing	$66,430	1,310
Computer and Electronic Product Manufacturing	$65,730	6,620
Transportation Equipment Manufacturing	$65,350	2,180

Metropolitan Areas Where Income Is Highest

Metropolitan Area	Average Annual Wage	Number Employed
San Jose–Sunnyvale–Santa Clara, CA	$85,960	3,910
San Francisco–Oakland–Fremont, CA	$75,970	5,880
New York–Northern New Jersey–Long Island, NY–NJ–PA	$74,630	20,100
Leominster–Fitchburg–Gardner, MA	$72,620	90
Danbury, CT	$72,070	120

Plan, coordinate, and implement security measures for information systems to regulate access to computer data files and prevent unauthorized modification, destruction, or disclosure of information. Train users and promote security awareness to ensure system security and to improve server and network efficiency. Develop plans to safeguard computer files against accidental or unauthorized modification, destruction, or disclosure and to meet emergency data processing needs. Confer with users to discuss issues such as computer data access needs, security violations, and programming changes. Monitor current reports of computer viruses to determine when to update virus protection systems. Modify computer security files to incorporate new software, correct errors, or change individual access status. Coordinate implementation of computer system plan with establishment personnel and outside vendors. Monitor use of data files and regulate access to safeguard information in computer files. Perform risk assessments and execute tests of data processing system to ensure functioning of data processing activities and security measures. Encrypt data transmissions and erect firewalls to conceal confidential information as it is being transmitted and to keep out tainted digital transfers. Document computer security and emergency measures policies, procedures, and tests. Review violations of computer security procedures and discuss procedures with violators to ensure violations are not repeated. **SKILLS**—Systems Evaluation; Systems Analysis; Programming; Troubleshooting; Management of Material Resources; Operations Analysis; Management of Financial Resources; Active Learning.

GOE—Interest Area: 11. Information Technology. **Work Group:** 11.02. Information Technology Specialties. **PERSONALITY TYPE:** Investigative. Investigative occupations frequently involve working with ideas

250 Best-Paying Jobs © JIST Works

189

and require an extensive amount of thinking. These occupations can involve searching for facts and figuring out problems mentally.

EDUCATION/TRAINING PROGRAM— Computer and Information Systems Security. **RELATED KNOWLEDGE/COURSES— Computers and Electronics:** Knowledge of circuit boards, processors, chips, electronic equipment, and computer hardware and software, including applications and programming. **Telecommunications:** Knowledge of transmission, broadcasting, switching, control, and operation of telecommunications systems. **Education and Training:** Knowledge of principles and methods for curriculum and training design, teaching and instruction for individuals and groups, and the measurement of training effects. **Design:** Knowledge of design techniques, tools, and principles involved in production of precision technical plans, blueprints, drawings, and models. **Engineering and Technology:** Knowledge of the practical application of engineering science and technology. This includes applying principles, techniques, procedures, and equipment to the design and production of various goods and services. **Customer and Personal Service:** Knowledge of principles and processes for providing customer and personal services. This includes customer needs assessment, meeting quality standards for services, and evaluation of customer satisfaction.

Computer Software Engineers, Applications

- ⊚ Annual Earnings: $77,090
- ⊚ Growth: 48.4%
- ⊚ Annual Job Openings: 54,000
- ⊚ Self-Employed: 2.4%
- ⊚ Part-Time: 2.7%
- ⊚ Education/Training Required: Bachelor's degree

Industries in Which Income Is Highest

Industry	Average Annual Wage	Number Employed
Securities, Commodity Contracts, and Other Financial Investments and Related Activities	$87,250	12,080
Computer and Electronic Product Manufacturing	$86,300	41,800
Transportation Equipment Manufacturing	$81,190	10,590
Publishing Industries (Except Internet)	$80,290	44,490
Chemical Manufacturing	$80,070	1,790

Metropolitan Areas Where Income Is Highest

Metropolitan Area	Average Annual Wage	Number Employed
Santa Rosa–Petaluma, CA	$99,280	760
San Jose–Sunnyvale–Santa Clara, CA	$97,200	22,470
Salinas, CA	$90,300	150
San Francisco–Oakland–Fremont, CA	$89,810	19,410
Modesto, CA	$89,350	130

Develop, create, and modify general computer applications software or specialized utility programs. Analyze user needs and develop software solutions. Design software or customize software for client use with the aim of optimizing operational efficiency. May analyze and design databases within an application area, working individually or coordinating database development as part of a team. Confer with systems analysts, engineers, programmers and others to design system and to obtain information on project limitations and capabilities, performance requirements and interfaces. Modify existing software to correct errors, allow it to adapt to new hardware, or to improve its performance. Analyze user needs and software requirements to determine feasibility of design within time and cost constraints. Consult with customers about software system design and maintenance. Coordinate software system installation and monitor equipment functioning to ensure specifications are met. Design, develop and modify software systems, using scientific analysis and mathematical models to predict and measure outcome and consequences of design. Develop and direct software system testing and validation procedures, programming, and documentation. Analyze information to determine, recommend, and plan computer specifications and layouts, and peripheral equipment modifications. Supervise the work of programmers, technologists and technicians and other engineering and scientific personnel. Obtain and evaluate information on factors such as reporting formats required, costs, and security needs to determine hardware configuration. Determine system performance standards. Train users to use new or modified equipment. Store, retrieve, and manipulate data for analysis of system capabilities and requirements. **SKILLS**—Programming; Troubleshooting; Technology Design; Systems Analysis; Quality Control Analysis; Operations Analysis; Complex Problem Solving; Critical Thinking.

GOE—Interest Area: 11. Information Technology. **Work Group:** 11.02. Information Technology Specialties. **PERSONALITY TYPE:** Investigative. Investigative occupations frequently involve working with ideas and require an extensive amount of thinking. These occupations can involve searching for facts and figuring out problems mentally.

EDUCATION/TRAINING PROGRAMS—Artificial Intelligence and Robotics; Bioinformatics; Computer Engineering Technologies/Technicians, Other; Computer Engineering, General; Computer Science; Computer Software Engineering; Information Technology; Medical Illustration and Informatics, Other; Medical Informatics. **RELATED KNOWLEDGE/COURSES—Computers and Electronics:** Knowledge of circuit boards, processors, chips, electronic equipment, and computer hardware and software, including applications and programming. **Telecommunications:** Knowledge of transmission, broadcasting, switching, control, and operation of telecommunications systems. **Engineering and Technology:** Knowledge of the practical application of engineering science and technology. This includes applying principles, techniques, procedures, and equipment to the design and production of various goods and services. **Design:** Knowledge of design techniques, tools, and principles involved in production of precision technical plans, blueprints, drawings, and models. **Mathematics:** Knowledge of arithmetic, algebra, geometry, calculus, and statistics and their applications. **English Language:** Knowledge of the structure and content of the English language, including the meaning and spelling of words, rules of composition, and grammar.

Computer Software Engineers, Systems Software

- Annual Earnings: $82,120
- Growth: 43.0%
- Annual Job Openings: 37,000
- Self-Employed: 2.4%
- Part-Time: 2.7%
- Education/Training Required: Bachelor's degree

Industries in Which Income Is Highest

Industry	Average Annual Wage	Number Employed
Computer and Electronic Product Manufacturing	$86,830	43,960
Merchant Wholesalers, Durable Goods	$84,960	13,650
Publishing Industries (Except Internet)	$84,820	22,000
Wholesale Electronic Markets and Agents and Brokers	$84,770	2,050
Securities, Commodity Contracts, and Other Financial Investments and Related Activities	$84,360	4,440

Metropolitan Areas Where Income Is Highest

Metropolitan Area	Average Annual Wage	Number Employed
San Jose–Sunnyvale–Santa Clara, CA	$103,520	13,480
Baltimore–Towson, MD	$95,110	4,960
San Francisco–Oakland–Fremont, CA	$94,030	9,520
Boulder, CO	$93,890	1,520
New York–Northern New Jersey–Long Island, NY–NJ–PA	$91,490	24,770

Research, design, develop, and test operating systems-level software, compilers, and network distribution software for medical, industrial, military, communications, aerospace, business, scientific, and general computing applications. Set operational specifications and formulate and analyze software requirements. Apply principles and techniques of computer science, engineering, and

mathematical analysis. Modify existing software to correct errors, to adapt it to new hardware or to upgrade interfaces and improve performance. Design and develop software systems, using scientific analysis and mathematical models to predict and measure outcome and consequences of design. Consult with engineering staff to evaluate interface between hardware and software, develop specifications and performance requirements and resolve customer problems. Analyze information to determine, recommend and plan installation of a new system or modification of an existing system. Develop and direct software system testing and validation procedures. Direct software programming and development of documentation. Consult with customers and/or other departments on project status, proposals and technical issues such as software system design and maintenance. Advise customer about, or perform, maintenance of software system. Coordinate installation of software system. Monitor functioning of equipment to ensure system operates in conformance with specifications. Store, retrieve, and manipulate data for analysis of system capabilities and requirements. Confer with data processing and project managers to obtain information on limitations and capabilities for data processing projects. Prepare reports and correspondence concerning project specifications, activities and status. Evaluate factors such as reporting formats required, cost constraints, and need for security restrictions to determine hardware configuration. Supervise and assign work to programmers, designers, technologists and technicians and other engineering and scientific personnel. Train users to use new or modified equipment. Utilize microcontrollers to develop control signals, implement control algorithms and measure process variables such as temperatures, pressures and positions. **SKILLS—** Programming; Technology Design; Systems Analysis; Troubleshooting; Complex Problem Solving; Operations Analysis; Active Learning; Mathematics.

GOE—Interest Area: 11. Information Technology. **Work Group:** 11.02. Information Technology Specialties. **PERSONALITY TYPE:** Investigative. Investigative occupations frequently involve working with ideas and require an extensive amount of thinking. These occupations can involve searching for facts and figuring out problems mentally.

EDUCATION/TRAINING PROGRAMS—Artificial Intelligence and Robotics; Computer Engineering Technologies/Technicians, Other; Computer Engineering, General; Computer Science; Information

Science/Studies; Information Technology. **RELATED KNOWLEDGE/COURSES—Computers and Electronics:** Knowledge of circuit boards, processors, chips, electronic equipment, and computer hardware and software, including applications and programming. **Design:** Knowledge of design techniques, tools, and principles involved in production of precision technical plans, blueprints, drawings, and models. **Engineering and Technology:** Knowledge of the practical application of engineering science and technology. This includes applying principles, techniques, procedures, and equipment to the design and production of various goods and services. **Telecommunications:** Knowledge of transmission, broadcasting, switching, control, and operation of telecommunications systems. **Education and Training:** Knowledge of principles and methods for curriculum and training design, teaching and instruction for individuals and groups, and the measurement of training effects. **Mathematics:** Knowledge of arithmetic, algebra, geometry, calculus, and statistics and their applications.

Computer Systems Analysts

◎ Annual Earnings: $68,300
◎ Growth: 31.4%
◎ Annual Job Openings: 56,000
◎ Self-Employed: 5.0%
◎ Part-Time: 6.5%
◎ Education/Training Required: Bachelor's degree

Industries in Which Income Is Highest

Industry	Average Annual Wage	Number Employed
Securities, Commodity Contracts, and Other Financial Investments and Related Activities	$76,550	8,930
Merchant Wholesalers, Durable Goods	$74,710	22,650
Chemical Manufacturing	$72,730	4,540
Computer and Electronic Product Manufacturing	$72,380	13,250
Utilities	$71,850	4,410

Metropolitan Areas Where Income Is Highest

Metropolitan Area	Average Annual Wage	Number Employed
Atlantic City, NJ	$85,270	540
San Jose–Sunnyvale–Santa Clara, CA	$82,590	5,370
Oxnard–Thousand Oaks–Ventura, CA	$80,440	1,260
San Francisco–Oakland–Fremont, CA	$79,470	11,180
Washington–Arlington–Alexandria, DC–VA–MD–WV	$79,240	43,860

Analyze science, engineering, business, and all other data processing problems for application to electronic data processing systems. Analyze user requirements, procedures, and problems to automate or improve existing systems and review computer system capabilities, workflow, and scheduling limitations. May analyze or recommend commercially available software. May supervise computer programmers. Provide staff and users with assistance solving computer related problems, such as malfunctions and program problems. Test, maintain, and monitor computer programs and systems, including coordinating the installation of computer programs and systems. Use object-oriented programming languages, as well as client/server applications development processes and multimedia and Internet technology. Confer with clients regarding the nature of the information processing or computation needs a computer program is to address. Coordinate and link the computer systems within an organization to increase compatibility and so information can be shared. Consult with management to ensure agreement on system principles. Expand or modify system to serve new purposes or improve work flow. Interview or survey workers, observe job performance and/or perform the job in order to determine what information is processed and how it is processed. Determine computer software or hardware needed to set up or alter system. Train staff and users to work with computer systems and programs. Analyze information processing or computation needs and plan and design computer systems, using techniques such as structured analysis, data modeling and information engineering. Assess the usefulness of pre-developed application packages and adapt them to a user environment. Define the goals of the system and devise flow charts and diagrams describing logical operational steps of programs. Develop, document and revise system design procedures, test procedures, and quality standards. Review and analyze computer printouts and performance indicators to locate code problems, and correct errors by correcting codes. Recommend new equipment or software packages. Read manuals, periodicals, and technical reports to learn how to develop programs that meet staff and user requirements. Supervise computer programmers or other systems analysts or serve as project leaders for particular systems projects. Utilize the computer in the analysis and solution of business problems such as development of integrated production and inventory control and cost analysis systems. **SKILLS**—Installation; Quality Control Analysis; Troubleshooting; Programming; Technology Design; Systems Analysis; Time Management; Operations Analysis.

GOE—Interest Area: 11. Information Technology. **Work Group:** 11.02. Information Technology Specialties. **PERSONALITY TYPE:** Investigative. Investigative occupations frequently involve working with ideas and require an extensive amount of thinking. These occupations can involve searching for facts and figuring out problems mentally.

EDUCATION/TRAINING PROGRAMS—Computer and Information Sciences, General; Computer Systems Analysis/Analyst; Information Technology; Web/Multimedia Management and Webmaster. **RELATED KNOWLEDGE/COURSES**—**Computers and Electronics:** Knowledge of circuit boards, processors, chips, electronic equipment, and computer hardware and software, including applications and programming. **Design:** Knowledge of design techniques, tools, and principles involved in production of precision technical plans, blueprints, drawings, and models. **Telecommunications:** Knowledge of transmission, broadcasting, switching, control, and operation of telecommunications systems. **Customer and Personal Service:** Knowledge of principles and processes for providing customer and personal services. This includes customer needs assessment, meeting quality standards for services, and evaluation of customer satisfaction. **Education and Training:** Knowledge of principles and methods for curriculum and training design, teaching and instruction for individuals and groups, and the measurement of training effects. **Law and Government:** Knowledge of laws, legal codes, court procedures, precedents, government regulations, executive orders, agency rules, and the democratic political process.

Construction Managers

- Annual Earnings: $72,260
- Growth: 10.4%
- Annual Job Openings: 28,000
- Self-Employed: 54.2%
- Part-Time: 5.5%
- Education/Training Required: Bachelor's degree

Industries in Which Income Is Highest

Industry	Average Annual Wage	Number Employed
Management of Companies and Enterprises	$83,570	2,360
Real Estate	$81,340	3,690
Professional, Scientific, and Technical Services	$76,460	9,490
Administrative and Support Services	$74,710	1,860
Heavy and Civil Engineering Construction	$74,450	22,050

Metropolitan Areas Where Income Is Highest

Metropolitan Area	Average Annual Wage	Number Employed
Rockford, IL	$106,850	110
Bridgeport–Stamford–Norwalk, CT	$104,490	520
New York–Northern New Jersey–Long Island, NY–NJ–PA	$104,170	13,040
Ocala, FL	$103,150	170
Santa Rosa–Petaluma, CA	$101,370	230

Plan, direct, coordinate, or budget, usually through subordinate supervisory personnel, activities concerned with the construction and maintenance of structures, facilities, and systems. Participate in the conceptual development of a construction project and oversee its organization, scheduling, and implementation. Confer with supervisory personnel, owners, contractors, and design professionals to discuss and resolve matters such as work procedures, complaints, and construction problems. Plan, organize, and direct activities concerned with the construction and maintenance of structures, facilities, and systems. Schedule the project in logical steps and

budget time required to meet deadlines. Determine labor requirements and dispatch workers to construction sites. Inspect and review projects to monitor compliance with building and safety codes, and other regulations. Interpret and explain plans and contract terms to administrative staff, workers, and clients, representing the owner or developer. Prepare contracts and negotiate revisions, changes and additions to contractual agreements with architects, consultants, clients, suppliers and subcontractors. Obtain all necessary permits and licenses. Direct and supervise workers. Study job specifications to determine appropriate construction methods. Select, contract, and oversee workers who complete specific pieces of the project, such as painting or plumbing. Requisition supplies and materials to complete construction projects. Prepare and submit budget estimates and progress and cost tracking reports. Develop and implement quality control programs. Take actions to deal with the results of delays, bad weather, or emergencies at construction site. Investigate damage, accidents, or delays at construction sites, to ensure that proper procedures are being carried out. Evaluate construction methods and determine cost-effectiveness of plans, using computers. **SKILLS**—Installation; Repairing; Troubleshooting; Coordination; Negotiation; Management of Material Resources; Management of Financial Resources; Instructing.

GOE—Interest Area: 02. Architecture and Construction. **Work Group:** 02.01. Managerial Work in Architecture and Construction. **PERSONALITY TYPE:** Enterprising. Enterprising occupations frequently involve starting up and carrying out projects. These occupations can involve leading people and making many decisions. They sometimes require risk taking and often deal with business.

EDUCATION/TRAINING PROGRAMS—Business Administration/Management; Business/Commerce, General; Construction Engineering Technology/Technician; Operations Management and Supervision. **RELATED KNOWLEDGE/COURSES—Building and Construction:** Knowledge of the materials, methods, and tools involved in the construction or repair of houses, buildings, or other structures such as highways and roads. **Design:** Knowledge of design techniques, tools, and principles involved in production of precision technical plans, blueprints, drawings, and models. **Administration and Management:** Knowledge of business and management principles involved in strategic planning, resource allocation, human resources modeling, leadership technique, production methods, and coordination of people and resources. **Mechanical Devices:** Knowledge of machines and tools, including their designs, uses, repair, and maintenance. **Public Safety and Security:** Knowledge of relevant equipment, policies, procedures, and strategies to promote effective local, state, or national security operations for the protection of people, data, property, and institutions. **Sales and Marketing:** Knowledge of principles and methods for showing, promoting, and selling products or services. This includes marketing strategy and tactics, product demonstration, sales techniques, and sales control systems.

Copy Writers

- ◎ Annual Earnings: $46,420
- ◎ Growth: 17.7%
- ◎ Annual Job Openings: 14,000
- ◎ Self-Employed: 67.7%
- ◎ Part-Time: 30.2%
- ◎ Education/Training Required: Bachelor's degree

The job openings listed here are shared with Caption Writers; Creative Writers; and Poets and Lyricists.

Industries in Which Income Is Highest

Industry	Average Annual Wage	Number Employed
Motion Picture and Sound Recording Industries	$59,250	1,520
Federal, State, and Local Government	$58,640	1,710
Professional, Scientific, and Technical Services	$49,680	10,870
Religious, Grantmaking, Civic, Professional, and Similar Organizations	$49,100	4,330
Broadcasting (Except Internet)	$43,550	2,920

Metropolitan Areas Where Income Is Highest

Metropolitan Area	Average Annual Wage	Number Employed
Santa Barbara–Santa Maria, CA	$103,570	50
Austin–Round Rock, TX	$72,780	400
San Francisco–Oakland–Fremont, CA	$68,370	730
Los Angeles–Long Beach–Santa Ana, CA	$63,330	2,670
Raleigh–Cary, NC	$63,130	60

Write advertising copy for use by publication or broadcast media to promote sale of goods and services. Write advertising copy for use by publication, broadcast or internet media to promote the sale of goods and services. Present drafts and ideas to clients. Discuss with the client the product, advertising themes and methods, and any changes that should be made in advertising copy. Vary language and tone of messages based on product and medium. Consult with sales, media and marketing representatives to obtain information on product or service and discuss style and length of advertising copy. Edit or rewrite existing copy as necessary, and submit copy for approval by supervisor. Write to customers in their terms and on their level so that the advertiser's sales message is more readily received. Write articles, bulletins, sales letters, speeches, and other related informative, marketing and promotional material. Invent names for products and write the slogans that appear on packaging, brochures and other promotional material. Review advertising trends, consumer surveys, and other data regarding marketing of goods and services to determine the best way to promote products. Develop advertising campaigns for a wide range of clients, working with an advertising agency's creative director and art director to determine the best way to present advertising information. Conduct research and interviews to determine which of a product's selling features should be promoted. **SKILLS**—Persuasion; Time Management; Instructing; Negotiation; Technology Design; Coordination; Active Listening; Critical Thinking.

GOE—Interest Area: 03. Arts and Communication. **Work Group:** 03.02. Writing and Editing. **PERSONALITY TYPE:** Artistic. Artistic occupations frequently involve working with forms, designs, and patterns. They often require self-expression, and the work can be done without following a clear set of rules.

EDUCATION/TRAINING PROGRAMS—Communications Studies/Speech Communication and Rhetoric; English Composition; Journalism; Mass Communications/Media Studies. **RELATED KNOWLEDGE/COURSES—Sales and Marketing:** Knowledge of principles and methods for showing, promoting, and selling products or services. This includes marketing strategy and tactics, product demonstration, sales techniques, and sales control systems. **Communications and Media:** Knowledge of media production, communication, and dissemination techniques and methods. This includes alternative ways to inform and entertain via written, oral, and visual media. **Sociology and Anthropology:** Knowledge of group behavior and dynamics, societal trends and influences, human migrations, ethnicity, and cultures and their history and origins. **English Language:** Knowledge of the structure and content of the English language, including the meaning and spelling of words, rules of composition, and grammar. **Computers and Electronics:** Knowledge of circuit boards, processors, chips, electronic equipment, and computer hardware and software, including applications and programming. **Psychology:** Knowledge of human behavior and performance; individual differences in ability, personality, and interests; learning and motivation; psychological research methods; and the assessment and treatment of behavioral and affective disorders.

Coroners

- Annual Earnings: $49,360
- Growth: 11.6%
- Annual Job Openings: 17,000
- Self-Employed: 0.0%
- Part-Time: 5.1%
- Education/Training Required: Work experience in a related occupation

The job openings listed here are shared with Environmental Compliance Inspectors; Equal Opportunity Representatives and Officers; Government Property Inspectors and Investigators; Licensing Examiners and Inspectors; and Pressure Vessel Inspectors.

Industries in Which Income Is Highest

Industry	Average Annual Wage	Number Employed
Postal Service	$72,700	1,710
Utilities	$66,390	1,310
Securities, Commodity Contracts, and Other Financial Investments and Related Activities	$64,490	5,130
Computer and Electronic Product Manufacturing	$59,540	1,390
Telecommunications	$59,310	2,620

Metropolitan Areas Where Income Is Highest

Metropolitan Area	Average Annual Wage	Number Employed
Kankakee–Bradley, IL	$81,020	170
Brunswick, GA	$79,710	340
San Jose–Sunnyvale–Santa Clara, CA	$67,550	930
San Francisco–Oakland–Fremont, CA	$64,010	3,320
Santa Rosa–Petaluma, CA	$63,660	410

Direct activities such as autopsies, pathological and toxicological analyses, and inquests relating to the investigation of deaths occurring within a legal jurisdiction to determine cause of death or to fix responsibility for accidental, violent, or unexplained deaths. Collect and document any pertinent medical history information. Complete death certificates, including the assignment of a cause and manner of death. Complete reports and forms required to finalize cases. Direct activities of workers who conduct autopsies, perform pathological and toxicological analyses, and prepare documents for permanent records. Inquire into the cause, manner, and circumstances of human deaths, and establish the identities of deceased persons. Interview persons present at death scenes to obtain information useful in determining the manner of death. Observe and record the positions and conditions of bodies and of related evidence. Observe, record, and preserve any objects or personal property related to deaths, including objects such as medication containers and suicide notes. Perform medico-legal examinations and autopsies, conducting preliminary examinations of the body in order to identify victims, to locate signs of trauma, and to identify factors that would indicate time of death. Testify at inquests, hearings, and court trials. Arrange for the next of kin to be notified of deaths. Collect wills, burial instructions, and other documentation needed for investigations and for handling of the remains. Confer with officials of public health and law enforcement agencies in order to coordinate interdepartmental activities. Coordinate the release of personal effects to authorized persons, and facilitate the disposition of unclaimed corpses and personal effects. Inventory personal effects, such as jewelry or wallets, that are recovered from bodies. Locate and document information regarding the next of kin, including their relationship to the deceased and the status of notification attempts. Provide information concerning the circumstances of death to relatives of the deceased. Remove or supervise removal of bodies from death scenes, using the proper equipment and supplies, and arrange for transportation to morgues. Witness and certify deaths that are the result of a judicial order. Record the disposition of minor children, as well as details of arrangements made for their care. **SKILLS**—Science; Speaking; Reading Comprehension; Writing; Critical Thinking; Mathematics; Management of Personnel Resources; Complex Problem Solving.

GOE—Interest Area: 08. Health Science. **Work Group:** 08.01. Managerial Work in Medical and Health Services. **PERSONALITY TYPE:** Investigative. Investigative occupations frequently involve working with ideas and require an extensive amount of thinking. These occupations can involve searching for facts and figuring out problems mentally.

EDUCATION/TRAINING PROGRAM—No data available. **RELATED KNOWLEDGE/COURSES**— **Medicine and Dentistry:** Knowledge of the information and techniques needed to diagnose and treat human injuries, diseases, and deformities. This includes symptoms, treatment alternatives, drug properties and interactions, and preventive health-care measures. **Biology:** Knowledge of plant and animal organisms and their tissues, cells, functions, interdependencies, and interactions with each other and the environment. **Chemistry:** Knowledge of the chemical composition, structure, and properties of substances and of the chemical processes and transformations that they undergo. This includes uses of chemicals, their danger signs, production techniques, and disposal methods. **Administration and Management:** Knowledge of business and management principles involved

in strategic planning, resource allocation, human resources modeling, leadership technique, production methods, and coordination of people and resources. **Law and Government:** Knowledge of laws, legal codes, court procedures, precedents, government regulations, executive orders, agency rules, and the democratic political process. **Public Safety and Security:** Knowledge of relevant equipment, policies, procedures, and strategies to promote effective local, state, or national security operations for the protection of people, data, property, and institutions.

Cost Estimators

- Annual Earnings: $52,020
- Growth: 18.2%
- Annual Job Openings: 15,000
- Self-Employed: 2.2%
- Part-Time: 6.3%
- Education/Training Required: Work experience in a related occupation

Industries in Which Income Is Highest

Industry	Average Annual Wage	Number Employed
Waste Management and Remediation Services	$58,920	1,390
Professional, Scientific, and Technical Services	$58,550	7,380
Transportation Equipment Manufacturing	$58,420	3,150
Computer and Electronic Product Manufacturing	$58,170	1,650
Heavy and Civil Engineering Construction	$57,420	11,910

Metropolitan Areas Where Income Is Highest

Metropolitan Area	Average Annual Wage	Number Employed
Kennewick–Richland–Pasco, WA	$69,060	240
Salinas, CA	$69,010	160
Anchorage, AK	$68,260	250
San Francisco–Oakland–Fremont, CA	$66,700	3,160
San Jose–Sunnyvale–Santa Clara, CA	$66,220	1,290

Prepare cost estimates for product manufacturing, construction projects, or services to aid management in bidding on or determining price of product or service. May specialize according to particular service performed or type of product manufactured. Analyze blueprints and other documentation to prepare time, cost, materials, and labor estimates. Assess cost effectiveness of products, projects or services, tracking actual costs relative to bids as the project develops. Consult with clients, vendors, personnel in other departments or construction foremen to discuss and formulate estimates and resolve issues. Confer with engineers, architects, owners, contractors and subcontractors on changes and adjustments to cost estimates. Prepare estimates used by management for purposes such as planning, organizing, and scheduling work. Prepare estimates for use in selecting vendors or subcontractors. Review material and labor requirements, to decide whether it is more cost-effective to produce or purchase components. Prepare cost and expenditure statements and other necessary documentation at regular intervals for the duration of the project. Prepare and maintain a directory of suppliers, contractors and subcontractors. Set up cost monitoring and reporting systems and procedures. Establish and maintain tendering process, and conduct negotiations. Conduct special studies to develop and establish standard hour and related cost data or to effect cost reduction. Visit site and record information about access, drainage and topography, and availability of services such as water and electricity. **SKILLS—** Management of Financial Resources; Negotiation; Management of Personnel Resources; Mathematics; Coordination; Persuasion; Active Listening; Time Management.

GOE—Interest Area: 06. Finance and Insurance. **Work Group:** 06.02. Finance/Insurance Investigation and Analysis. **PERSONALITY TYPE:** Conventional. Conventional occupations frequently involve following set procedures and routines. These occupations can include working with data and details more than with ideas. Usually there is a clear line of authority to follow.

EDUCATION/TRAINING PROGRAMS— Business Administration/Management; Business/Commerce, General; Construction Engineering; Construction Engineering Technology/Technician; Manufacturing Engineering; Materials Engineering; Mechanical Engineering. **RELATED KNOWLEDGE/COURSES—Administration and**

Management: Knowledge of business and management principles involved in strategic planning, resource allocation, human resources modeling, leadership technique, production methods, and coordination of people and resources. **Economics and Accounting:** Knowledge of economic and accounting principles and practices, the financial markets, banking, and the analysis and reporting of financial data. **Sales and Marketing:** Knowledge of principles and methods for showing, promoting, and selling products or services. This includes marketing strategy and tactics, product demonstration, sales techniques, and sales control systems. **Production and Processing:** Knowledge of raw materials, production processes, quality control, costs, and other techniques for maximizing the effective manufacture and distribution of goods. **Clerical Practices:** Knowledge of administrative and clerical procedures and systems such as word processing, managing files and records, stenography and transcription, designing forms, and other office procedures and terminology. **Personnel and Human Resources:** Knowledge of principles and procedures for personnel recruitment, selection, training, compensation and benefits, labor relations and negotiation, and personnel information systems.

Counseling Psychologists

- Annual Earnings: $57,170
- Growth: 19.1%
- Annual Job Openings: 10,000
- Self-Employed: 38.2%
- Part-Time: 23.3%
- Education/Training Required: Doctoral degree

The job openings listed here are shared with Clinical Psychologists and School Psychologists.

Industries in Which Income Is Highest

Industry	Average Annual Wage	Number Employed
Hospitals	$61,740	8,950
Ambulatory Health Care Services	$60,260	21,730
Educational Services	$57,730	45,870
Federal, State, and Local Government	$57,260	9,190
Social Assistance	$45,800	8,020

Metropolitan Areas Where Income Is Highest

Metropolitan Area	Average Annual Wage	Number Employed
Napa, CA	$91,830	190
Salinas, CA	$83,160	170
Ogden–Clearfield, UT	$81,730	150
Trenton–Ewing, NJ	$81,710	270
Jonesboro, AR	$81,400	70

Assess and evaluate individuals' problems through the use of case history, interview, and observation and provide individual or group counseling services to assist individuals in achieving more effective personal, social, educational, and vocational development and adjustment. Evaluate the results of counseling methods to determine the reliability and validity of treatments. Select, administer, and interpret psychological tests to assess intelligence, aptitudes, abilities, or interests. Consult with other professionals to discuss therapies, treatments, counseling resources, or techniques, and to share occupational information. Refer clients to specialists or to other institutions for non-counseling treatment of problems. Conduct research to develop or improve diagnostic or therapeutic counseling techniques. Provide consulting services to schools, social service agencies, and businesses. Advise clients on how they could be helped by counseling. Analyze data such as interview notes, test results, and reference manuals in order to identify symptoms, and to diagnose the nature of clients' problems. Collect information about individuals or clients, using interviews, case histories, observational techniques, and other assessment methods. Counsel individuals, groups, or families to help them understand problems, define goals, and develop realistic action plans. Develop therapeutic and treatment plans based on clients' interests, abilities, and needs. **SKILLS**—Social Perceptiveness; Active Listening; Learning Strategies; Persuasion; Reading Comprehension; Critical Thinking; Active Learning; Science.

GOE—Interest Area: 10. Human Service. **Work Group:** 10.01. Counseling and Social Work. **PERSONALITY TYPE:** Social. Social occupations frequently involve working with, communicating with, and teaching people. These occupations often involve helping or providing service to others.

EDUCATION/TRAINING PROGRAMS—Clinical Child Psycology; Clinical Psychology; Counseling Psychology; Developmental and Child Psychology; Psychoanalysis and Psychotherapy; Psychology, General; School Psychology. **RELATED KNOWLEDGE/COURSES—Therapy and Counseling:** Knowledge of principles, methods, and procedures for diagnosis, treatment, and rehabilitation of physical and mental dysfunctions and for career counseling and guidance. **Psychology:** Knowledge of human behavior and performance; individual differences in ability, personality, and interests; learning and motivation; psychological research methods; and the assessment and treatment of behavioral and affective disorders. **Sociology and Anthropology:** Knowledge of group behavior and dynamics, societal trends and influences, human migrations, ethnicity, and cultures and their history and origins. **Mathematics:** Knowledge of arithmetic, algebra, geometry, calculus, and statistics and their applications. **Education and Training:** Knowledge of principles and methods for curriculum and training design, teaching and instruction for individuals and groups, and the measurement of training effects.

Creative Writers

- Annual Earnings: $46,420
- Growth: 17.7%
- Annual Job Openings: 14,000
- Self-Employed: 67.7%
- Part-Time: 30.2%
- Education/Training Required: Bachelor's degree

The job openings listed here are shared with Caption Writers; Copy Writers; and Poets and Lyricists.

Industries in Which Income Is Highest

Industry	Average Annual Wage	Number Employed
Motion Picture and Sound Recording Industries	$59,250	1,520
Federal, State, and Local Government	$58,640	1,710
Professional, Scientific, and Technical Services	$49,680	10,870
Religious, Grantmaking, Civic, Professional, and Similar Organizations	$49,100	4,330
Broadcasting (Except Internet)	$43,550	2,920

Metropolitan Areas Where Income Is Highest

Metropolitan Area	Average Annual Wage	Number Employed
Santa Barbara–Santa Maria, CA	$103,570	50
Austin–Round Rock, TX	$72,780	400
San Francisco–Oakland–Fremont, CA	$68,370	730
Los Angeles–Long Beach–Santa Ana, CA	$63,330	2,670
Raleigh–Cary, NC	$63,130	60

Create original written works, such as plays or prose, for publication or performance. Selects subject or theme for writing project based on personal interest and writing specialty, or assignment from publisher, client, producer, or director. Develops factors, such as theme, plot, characterization, psychological analysis, historical environment, action, and dialogue, to create material. Writes humorous material for publication or performance, such as comedy routines, gags, comedy shows, or scripts for entertainers. Writes fiction or nonfiction prose work, such as short story, novel, biography, article, descriptive or critical analysis, or essay. Writes play or script for moving pictures or television, based on original ideas or adapted from fictional, historical, or narrative sources. Organizes material for project, plans arrangement or outline, and writes synopsis. Collaborates with other writers on specific projects. Confers with client, publisher, or producer to discuss development changes or revisions. Conducts research to obtain factual information and authentic detail, utilizing sources such as newspaper accounts, diaries, and interviews. Reviews, submits for approval, and revises written material to meet personal standards and satisfy needs of client, publisher,

director, or producer. **SKILLS**—Writing; Reading Comprehension; Coordination; Critical Thinking; Complex Problem Solving.

GOE—Interest Area: 03. Arts and Communication. **Work Group:** 03.02. Writing and Editing. **PERSONALITY TYPE:** Artistic. Artistic occupations frequently involve working with forms, designs, and patterns. They often require self-expression, and the work can be done without following a clear set of rules.

EDUCATION/TRAINING PROGRAMS—Communications Studies/Speech Communication and Rhetoric; Creative Writing; English Composition; Family and Consumer Sciences/Human Sciences Communications; Mass Communications/Media Studies; Playwriting and Screenwriting. **RELATED KNOWLEDGE/COURSES—Communications and Media:** Knowledge of media production, communication, and dissemination techniques and methods. This includes alternative ways to inform and entertain via written, oral, and visual media. **English Language:** Knowledge of the structure and content of the English language, including the meaning and spelling of words, rules of composition, and grammar. **Fine Arts:** Knowledge of the theory and techniques required to compose, produce, and perform works of music, dance, visual arts, drama, and sculpture. **Computers and Electronics:** Knowledge of circuit boards, processors, chips, electronic equipment, and computer hardware and software, including applications and programming.

Credit Analysts

- Annual Earnings: $50,370
- Growth: 3.6%
- Annual Job Openings: 3,000
- Self-Employed: 0.0%
- Part-Time: 4.1%
- Education/Training Required: Bachelor's degree

Industries in Which Income Is Highest

Industry	Average Annual Wage	Number Employed
Motor Vehicle and Parts Dealers	$67,810	7,830
Securities, Commodity Contracts, and Other Financial Investments and Related Activities	$63,250	2,310
Professional, Scientific, and Technical Services	$59,070	1,370
Merchant Wholesalers, Durable Goods	$48,510	1,620
Credit Intermediation and Related Activities	$48,190	31,810

Metropolitan Areas Where Income Is Highest

Metropolitan Area	Average Annual Wage	Number Employed
Cape Coral–Fort Myers, FL	$78,880	60
Bridgeport–Stamford–Norwalk, CT	$76,010	290
Little Rock–North Little Rock, AR	$74,760	170
San Francisco–Oakland–Fremont, CA	$69,440	1,230
San Jose–Sunnyvale–Santa Clara, CA	$65,940	500

Analyze current credit data and financial statements of individuals or firms to determine the degree of risk involved in extending credit or lending money. Prepare reports with this credit information for use in decision-making. Analyze credit data and financial statements to determine the degree of risk involved in extending credit or lending money. Prepare reports that include the degree of risk involved in extending credit or lending money. Evaluate customer records and recommend payment plans based on earnings, savings data, payment history, and purchase activity. Confer with credit association and other business representatives to exchange credit information. Complete loan applications, including credit analyses and summaries of loan requests, and submit to loan committees for approval. Generate financial ratios, using computer programs, to evaluate customers' financial status. Review individual or commercial customer files to identify and select delinquent accounts for collection. Compare liquidity, profitability, and credit histories of establishments being evaluated with those of similar establishments in the same industries and geographic locations. Consult with customers to resolve complaints and verify financial and credit transactions. Analyze financial data such as income growth, quality of management, and market share to determine expected profitability of loans. **SKILLS**—Speaking; Writing; Negotiation; Active Listening; Instructing; Social Perceptiveness; Operations Analysis; Monitoring.

GOE—Interest Area: 06. Finance and Insurance. **Work Group:** 06.02. Finance/Insurance Investigation and Analysis. **PERSONALITY TYPE:** Conventional. Conventional occupations frequently involve following set procedures and routines. These occupations can include working with data and details more than with ideas. Usually there is a clear line of authority to follow.

EDUCATION/TRAINING   PROGRAMS—Accounting; Credit Management; Finance, General. **RELATED KNOWLEDGE/COURSES—Economics and Accounting:** Knowledge of economic and accounting principles and practices, the financial markets, banking, and the analysis and reporting of financial data. **Clerical Practices:** Knowledge of administrative and clerical procedures and systems such as word processing, managing files and records, stenography and transcription, designing forms, and other office procedures and terminology. **Mathematics:** Knowledge of arithmetic, algebra, geometry, calculus, and statistics and their applications. **Customer and Personal Service:** Knowledge of principles and processes for providing customer and personal services. This includes customer needs assessment, meeting quality standards for services, and evaluation of customer satisfaction. **Administration and Management:** Knowledge of business and management principles involved in strategic planning, resource allocation, human resources modeling, leadership technique, production methods, and coordination of people and resources. **Law and Government:** Knowledge of laws, legal codes, court procedures, precedents, government regulations, executive orders, agency rules, and the democratic political process.

Criminal Investigators and Special Agents

- Annual Earnings: $55,790
- Growth: 16.3%
- Annual Job Openings: 9,000
- Self-Employed: 0.0%
- Part-Time: 2.9%
- Education/Training Required: Work experience in a related occupation

The job openings listed here are shared with Child Support, Missing Persons, and Unemployment Insurance Fraud Investigators; Immigration and Customs Inspectors; Police Detectives; and Police Identification and Records Officers.

Industries in Which Income Is Highest

Industry	Average Annual Wage	Number Employed
Federal, State, and Local Government	$55,790	84,720

Metropolitan Areas Where Income Is Highest

Metropolitan Area	Average Annual Wage	Number Employed
Washington–Arlington–Alexandria, DC–VA–MD–WV	$79,180	4,270
Trenton–Ewing, NJ	$78,420	260
Chicago–Naperville–Joliet, IL–IN–WI	$76,080	3,170
Springfield, IL	$74,260	50
Oxnard–Thousand Oaks–Ventura, CA	$73,250	80

Investigate alleged or suspected criminal violations of Federal, state, or local laws to determine if evidence is sufficient to recommend prosecution. Obtain and verify evidence by interviewing and observing suspects and witnesses, or by analyzing records. Record evidence and documents, using equipment such as cameras and photocopy machines. Examine records in order to locate links in chains of evidence or information. Prepare reports that detail investigation findings. Collaborate with other offices and agencies in order to exchange information and coordinate activities. Determine scope, timing, and direction of investigations. Testify before grand juries concerning criminal activity investigations. Analyze evidence in laboratories, or in the field. Investigate organized crime, public corruption, financial crime, copyright infringement, civil rights violations, bank robbery, extortion, kidnapping, and other violations of federal or state statutes. Identify case issues and evidence needed, based on analysis of charges, complaints, or allegations of law violations. Obtain and use search and arrest warrants. Serve subpoenas or other official papers. Collaborate with other authorities on activities such as surveillance, transcription and research. Develop relationships with informants in order to obtain information related to cases. Search for and collect evidence such as fingerprints, using investigative equipment. Collect and record physical information about arrested suspects, including fingerprints, height and weight measurements, and photographs. Compare crime scene fingerprints with those from suspects or fingerprint files to identify perpetrators, using computers. Administer counter-terrorism and counter-narcotics reward programs. Provide protection for individuals such as government leaders, political candidates and visiting foreign dignitaries. Perform undercover assignments and maintain surveillance, including monitoring authorized wiretaps. Manage security programs designed to protect personnel, facilities, and information. Issue security clearances. **SKILLS**—Negotiation; Service Orientation; Persuasion; Judgment and Decision Making; Programming; Operations Analysis; Instructing; Social Perceptiveness.

GOE—Interest Area: 12. Law and Public Safety. **Work Group:** 12.04. Law Enforcement and Public Safety. **PERSONALITY TYPE:** Enterprising. Enterprising occupations frequently involve starting up and carrying out projects. These occupations can involve leading people and making many decisions. They sometimes require risk taking and often deal with business.

EDUCATION/TRAINING PROGRAMS—Criminal Justice/Police Science; Criminalistics and Criminal Science. **RELATED KNOWLEDGE/COURSES**—**Law and Government:** Knowledge of laws, legal codes, court procedures, precedents, government regulations, executive orders, agency rules, and the democratic political process. **Psychology:** Knowledge of human behavior and performance; individual differences in ability, personality, and interests; learning and motivation; psychological research methods; and the assessment and treatment of behavioral and affective disorders. **Public Safety and Security:** Knowledge of relevant equipment, policies, procedures, and strategies to promote effective local, state, or national security operations for the protection of people, data, property, and institutions. **Geography:** Knowledge of principles and methods for describing the features of land, sea, and air masses, including their physical characteristics; locations; interrelationships; and distribution of plant, animal, and human life. **Clerical Practices:** Knowledge of administrative and clerical procedures and systems such as word processing, managing files and records, stenography and transcription, designing forms, and other office procedures and terminology. **Sociology and Anthropology:** Knowledge of group behavior and dynamics, societal trends and influences, human migrations, ethnicity, and cultures and their history and origins.

Criminal Justice and Law Enforcement Teachers, Postsecondary

- Annual Earnings: $49,240
- Growth: 32.2%
- Annual Job Openings: 329,000
- Self-Employed: 0.4%
- Part-Time: 27.3%
- Education/Training Required: Master's degree

Our sources did not provide separate job openings data for this occupation. The job openings listed here are shared with 35 other postsecondary teaching occupations. For a complete list, see the beginning of this section.

Industries in Which Income Is Highest

Industry	Average Annual Wage	Number Employed
Educational Services	$49,350	9,710
Federal, State, and Local Government	$34,250	90

Metropolitan Areas Where Income Is Highest

Metropolitan Area	Average Annual Wage	Number Employed
Sacramento–Arden–Arcade–Roseville, CA	$67,890	90
Los Angeles–Long Beach–Santa Ana, CA	$66,160	360
San Francisco–Oakland–Fremont, CA	$58,660	220
St. Louis, MO–IL	$57,830	120
Miami–Fort Lauderdale–Miami Beach, FL	$56,400	80

Teach courses in criminal justice, corrections, and law enforcement administration. Initiate, facilitate, and moderate classroom discussions. Keep abreast of developments in their field by reading current literature, talking with colleagues, and participating in professional conferences. Evaluate and grade students' class work, assignments, and papers. Compile, administer, and grade examinations or assign this work to others. Prepare and deliver lectures to undergraduate and/or graduate students on topics such as criminal law, defensive policing, and investigation techniques. Prepare course materials such as syllabi, homework assignments, and handouts. Conduct research in a particular field of knowledge and publish findings in professional journals, books, and/or electronic media. Plan, evaluate, and revise curricula, course content, and course materials and methods of instruction. Supervise undergraduate and/or graduate teaching, internship, and research work. Maintain student attendance records, grades, and other required records. Select and obtain materials and supplies such as textbooks. Advise students on academic and vocational curricula and on career issues. Maintain regularly scheduled office hours in order to advise and assist students. Collaborate with colleagues to address teaching and research issues. Write grant proposals to procure external research funding. Serve on academic or administrative committees that deal with institutional policies, departmental matters, and academic issues. Compile bibliographies of specialized materials for outside reading assignments. Participate in student recruitment, registration, and placement activities. Provide professional consulting services to government and/or industry. Perform administrative duties such as serving as department head. **SKILLS**—Instructing; Critical Thinking; Writing; Active Learning; Persuasion; Learning Strategies; Time Management; Speaking.

GOE—**Interest Area:** 05. Education and Training. **Work Group:** 05.03. Postsecondary and Adult Teaching and Instructing. **PERSONALITY TYPE:** No data available.

EDUCATION/TRAINING PROGRAMS— Corrections; Corrections Administration; Corrections and Criminal Justice, Other; Criminal Justice/Law Enforcement Administration; Criminal Justice/Police Science; Criminal Justice/Safety Studies; Criminalistics and Criminal Science; Forensic Science and Technology; Juvenile Corrections; Security and Loss Prevention Services; Teacher Education and Professional Development, Specific Subject Areas, Other. **RELATED KNOWLEDGE/COURSES—Sociology and Anthropology:** Knowledge of group behavior and dynamics, societal trends and influences, human migrations, ethnicity, and cultures and their history and origins. **Philosophy and Theology:** Knowledge of different philosophical systems and religions. This includes their basic principles, values, ethics, ways of thinking, customs, and practices and their impact on human culture. **Education and Training:** Knowledge of principles and methods for curriculum and training design, teaching and instruction for individuals and groups, and the measurement of training effects. **Law and Government:** Knowledge of laws, legal codes, court procedures, precedents, government regulations, executive orders, agency rules, and the democratic political process. **History and Archeology:** Knowledge of historical events and their causes, indicators, and effects on civilizations and cultures. **English Language:** Knowledge of the structure and content of the English language, including the meaning and spelling of words, rules of composition, and grammar.

Database Administrators

- Annual Earnings: $63,250
- Growth: 38.2%
- Annual Job Openings: 9,000
- Self-Employed: 0.5%
- Part-Time: 5.2%
- Education/Training Required: Bachelor's degree

Industries in Which Income Is Highest

Industry	Average Annual Wage	Number Employed
Securities, Commodity Contracts, and Other Financial Investments and Related Activities	$78,510	3,060
Computer and Electronic Product Manufacturing	$67,570	3,580
Insurance Carriers and Related Activities	$67,440	5,600
Internet Service Providers, Web Search Portals, and Data Processing Services	$67,120	3,860
Professional, Scientific, and Technical Services	$66,690	25,220

Metropolitan Areas Where Income Is Highest

Metropolitan Area	Average Annual Wage	Number Employed
Danbury, CT	$89,980	80
San Jose–Sunnyvale–Santa Clara, CA	$82,170	1,210
Trenton–Ewing, NJ	$78,720	220
San Francisco–Oakland–Fremont, CA	$78,540	2,470
Seattle–Tacoma–Bellevue, WA	$75,610	1,930

Coordinate changes to computer databases, test and implement the database applying knowledge of database management systems. May plan, coordinate, and implement security measures to safeguard computer databases. Develop standards and guidelines to guide the use and acquisition of software and to protect vulnerable information. Modify existing databases and database management systems or direct programmers and analysts to make changes. Test programs or databases, correct errors and make necessary modifications. Plan, coordinate and implement security measures to safeguard information in computer files against accidental or unauthorized damage, modification or disclosure. Approve, schedule, plan, and supervise the installation and testing of new products and improvements to computer systems, such as the installation of new databases. Train users and answer questions. Establish and calculate optimum values for database parameters, using manuals and calculator.

Specify users and user access levels for each segment of database. Develop data model describing data elements and how they are used, following procedures and using pen, template or computer software. Develop methods for integrating different products so they work properly together, such as customizing commercial databases to fit specific needs. Review project requests describing database user needs to estimate time and cost required to accomplish project. Review procedures in database management system manuals for making changes to database. Work as part of a project team to coordinate database development and determine project scope and limitations. Select and enter codes to monitor database performance and to create production database. Identify and evaluate industry trends in database systems to serve as a source of information and advice for upper management. Write and code logical and physical database descriptions and specify identifiers of database to management system or direct others in coding descriptions. Review workflow charts developed by programmer analyst to understand tasks computer will perform, such as updating records. Revise company definition of data as defined in data dictionary. **SKILLS—**Troubleshooting; Persuasion; Operations Analysis; Systems Evaluation; Systems Analysis; Management of Personnel Resources; Programming; Instructing.

GOE—Interest Area: 11. Information Technology. **Work Group:** 11.02. Information Technology Specialties. **PERSONALITY TYPE:** Investigative. Investigative occupations frequently involve working with ideas and require an extensive amount of thinking. These occupations can involve searching for facts and figuring out problems mentally.

EDUCATION/TRAINING PROGRAMS—Computer and Information Sciences, General; Computer and Information Systems Security; Computer Systems Analysis/Analyst; Data Modeling/Warehousing and Database Administration; Management Information Systems, General. **RELATED KNOWLEDGE/COURSES—Computers and Electronics:** Knowledge of circuit boards, processors, chips, electronic equipment, and computer hardware and software, including applications and programming. **Economics and Accounting:** Knowledge of economic and accounting principles and practices, the financial markets, banking, and the analysis and reporting of financial data. **Clerical Practices:** Knowledge of administrative and clerical procedures and systems such as word processing, managing files and records, stenography and transcription, designing forms, and other office procedures and terminology. **Customer and Personal Service:** Knowledge of principles and processes for providing customer and personal services. This includes customer needs assessment, meeting quality standards for services, and evaluation of customer satisfaction. **Administration and Management:** Knowledge of business and management principles involved in strategic planning, resource allocation, human resources modeling, leadership technique, production methods, and coordination of people and resources. **Education and Training:** Knowledge of principles and methods for curriculum and training design, teaching and instruction for individuals and groups, and the measurement of training effects.

Dental Hygienists

- Annual Earnings: $60,890
- Growth: 43.3%
- Annual Job Openings: 17,000
- Self-Employed: 0.3%
- Part-Time: 56.0%
- Education/Training Required: Associate degree

Industries in Which Income Is Highest

Industry	Average Annual Wage	Number Employed
Administrative and Support Services	$70,930	1,560
Ambulatory Health Care Services	$61,010	157,150
Federal, State, and Local Government	$45,590	1,050

Metropolitan Areas Where Income Is Highest

Metropolitan Area	Average Annual Wage	Number Employed
Santa Rosa–Petaluma, CA	$102,730	290
Modesto, CA	$96,640	290
Sacramento–Arden–Arcade–Roseville, CA	$89,110	1,440
San Francisco–Oakland–Fremont, CA	$87,700	3,700
San Diego–Carlsbad–San Marcos, CA	$86,850	1,090

Clean teeth and examine oral areas, head, and neck for signs of oral disease. May educate patients on oral hygiene, take and develop X rays, or apply fluoride or sealants. Clean calcareous deposits, accretions, and stains from teeth and beneath margins of gums, using dental instruments. Feel and visually examine gums for sores and signs of disease. Chart conditions of decay and disease for diagnosis and treatment by dentist. Feel lymph nodes under patient's chin to detect swelling or tenderness that could indicate presence of oral cancer. Apply fluorides and other cavity preventing agents to arrest dental decay. Examine gums, using probes, to locate periodontal recessed gums and signs of gum disease. Expose and develop X-ray film. Provide clinical services and health education to improve and maintain oral health of school children. Remove excess cement from coronal surfaces of teeth. Make impressions for study casts. Place, carve, and finish amalgam restorations. Administer local anesthetic agents. Conduct dental health clinics for community groups to augment services of dentist. **SKILLS**—Active Learning; Time Management; Persuasion; Social Perceptiveness; Instructing; Learning Strategies; Reading Comprehension; Service Orientation.

GOE—Interest Area: 08. Health Science. **Work Group:** 08.03. Dentistry. **PERSONALITY TYPE:** Social. Social occupations frequently involve working with, communicating with, and teaching people. These occupations often involve helping or providing service to others.

EDUCATION/TRAINING PROGRAM—Dental Hygiene/Hygienist. **RELATED KNOWLEDGE/ COURSES—Biology:** Knowledge of plant and animal organisms and their tissues, cells, functions, interdependencies, and interactions with each other and the environment. **Medicine and Dentistry:** Knowledge of the information and techniques needed to diagnose and treat human injuries, diseases, and deformities. This includes symptoms, treatment alternatives, drug properties and interactions, and preventive health-care measures. **Chemistry:** Knowledge of the chemical composition, structure, and properties of substances and of the chemical processes and transformations that they undergo. This includes uses of chemicals, their danger signs, production techniques, and disposal methods. **Psychology:** Knowledge of human behavior and performance; individual differences in ability, personality, and interests; learning and motivation; psychological research methods; and the assessment and

treatment of behavioral and affective disorders. **Customer and Personal Service:** Knowledge of principles and processes for providing customer and personal services. This includes customer needs assessment, meeting quality standards for services, and evaluation of customer satisfaction. **Sales and Marketing:** Knowledge of principles and methods for showing, promoting, and selling products or services. This includes marketing strategy and tactics, product demonstration, sales techniques, and sales control systems.

Dentists, General

- Annual Earnings: $125,300
- Growth: 13.5%
- Annual Job Openings: 7,000
- Self-Employed: 30.7%
- Part-Time: 22.6%
- Education/Training Required: First professional degree

Industries in Which Income Is Highest

Industry	Average Annual Wage	Number Employed
Ambulatory Health Care Services	$128,750	81,440
Federal, State, and Local Government	$99,360	2,780

Metropolitan Areas Where Income Is Highest

Metropolitan Area	Average Annual Wage	Number Employed
Houston–Sugar Land–Baytown, TX	More than $146,500	1,600
Dallas–Fort Worth–Arlington, TX	More than $146,500	1,330
Atlanta–Sandy Springs–Marietta, GA	More than $146,500	1,310
Denver–Aurora, CO	More than $146,500	1,010
St. Louis, MO–IL	More than $146,500	970

Diagnose and treat diseases, injuries, and malformations of teeth and gums and related oral structures. May treat diseases of nerve, pulp, and other dental tissues affecting vitality of teeth. Use masks, gloves and safety glasses to protect themselves and their patients from infectious diseases. Administer anesthetics to limit the amount of pain experienced by patients during procedures. Examine teeth, gums, and related tissues, using dental instruments, X rays, and other diagnostic equipment, to evaluate dental health, diagnose diseases or abnormalities, and plan appropriate treatments. Formulate plan of treatment for patient's teeth and mouth tissue. Use air turbine and hand instruments, dental appliances and surgical implements. Advise and instruct patients regarding preventive dental care, the causes and treatment of dental problems, and oral health care services. Design, make, and fit prosthodontic appliances such as space maintainers, bridges, and dentures, or write fabrication instructions or prescriptions for denturists and dental technicians. Diagnose and treat diseases, injuries, and malformations of teeth, gums and related oral structures, and provide preventive and corrective services. Fill pulp chamber and canal with endodontic materials. Write prescriptions for antibiotics and other medications. Analyze and evaluate dental needs to determine changes and trends in patterns of dental disease. Treat exposure of pulp by pulp capping, removal of pulp from pulp chamber, or root canal, using dental instruments. Eliminate irritating margins of fillings and correct occlusions, using dental instruments. Perform oral and periodontal surgery on the jaw or mouth. Remove diseased tissue using surgical instruments. Apply fluoride and sealants to teeth. Manage business, employing and supervising staff and handling paperwork and insurance claims. Bleach, clean or polish teeth to restore natural color. Plan, organize, and maintain dental health programs. Produce and evaluate dental health educational materials. **SKILLS**—Science; Management of Financial Resources; Management of Material Resources; Complex Problem Solving; Service Orientation; Persuasion; Management of Personnel Resources; Equipment Selection.

GOE—Interest Area: 08. Health Science. **Work Group:** 08.03. Dentistry. **PERSONALITY TYPE:** Investigative. Investigative occupations frequently involve working with ideas and require an extensive amount of thinking. These occupations can involve searching for facts and figuring out problems mentally.

EDUCATION/TRAINING PROGRAMS—Advanced General Dentistry (Cert, MS, PhD) ; Dental Public Health and Education (Cert, MS/MPH, PhD/DPH) ; Dental Public Health Specialty; Dentistry (DDS, DMD); Pediatric Dentistry/Pedodontics (Cert, MS, PhD); Pedodontics Specialty. **RELATED**

KNOWLEDGE/COURSES—Medicine and Dentistry: Knowledge of the information and techniques needed to diagnose and treat human injuries, diseases, and deformities. This includes symptoms, treatment alternatives, drug properties and interactions, and preventive health-care measures. **Biology:** Knowledge of plant and animal organisms and their tissues, cells, functions, interdependencies, and interactions with each other and the environment. **Psychology:** Knowledge of human behavior and performance; individual differences in ability, personality, and interests; learning and motivation; psychological research methods; and the assessment and treatment of behavioral and affective disorders. **Personnel and Human Resources:** Knowledge of principles and procedures for personnel recruitment, selection, training, compensation and benefits, labor relations and negotiation, and personnel information systems. **Chemistry:** Knowledge of the chemical composition, structure, and properties of substances and of the chemical processes and transformations that they undergo. This includes uses of chemicals, their danger signs, production techniques, and disposal methods. **Sales and Marketing:** Knowledge of principles and methods for showing, promoting, and selling products or services. This includes marketing strategy and tactics, product demonstration, sales techniques, and sales control systems.

Diagnostic Medical Sonographers

- Annual Earnings: $54,370
- Growth: 34.8%
- Annual Job Openings: 5,000
- Self-Employed: 0.4%
- Part-Time: 17.2%
- Education/Training Required: Associate degree

Industries in Which Income Is Highest

Industry	Average Annual Wage	Number Employed
Ambulatory Health Care Services	$54,450	17,080
Hospitals	$54,190	25,500

Metropolitan Areas Where Income Is Highest

Metropolitan Area	Average Annual Wage	Number Employed
San Jose–Sunnyvale–Santa Clara, CA	$81,960	170
Milwaukee–Waukesha–West Allis, WI	$71,300	330
Bridgeport–Stamford–Norwalk, CT	$70,990	130
San Francisco–Oakland–Fremont, CA	$69,270	320
Tucson, AZ	$68,370	100

Produce ultrasonic recordings of internal organs for use by physicians. Decide which images to include, looking for differences between healthy and pathological areas. Observe screen during scan to ensure that image produced is satisfactory for diagnostic purposes, making adjustments to equipment as required. Observe and care for patients throughout examinations to ensure their safety and comfort. Provide sonogram and oral or written summary of technical findings to physician for use in medical diagnosis. Operate ultrasound equipment to produce and record images of the motion, shape and composition of blood, organs, tissues and bodily masses such as fluid accumulations. Select appropriate equipment settings and adjust patient positions to obtain the best sites and angles. Determine whether scope of exam should be extended, based on findings. Process and code film from procedures and complete appropriate documentation. Obtain and record accurate patient history, including prior test results and information from physical examinations. Prepare patient for exam by explaining procedure, transferring them to ultrasound table, scrubbing skin and applying gel, and positioning them properly. Record and store suitable images, using camera unit connected to the ultrasound equipment. Coordinate work with physicians and other health-care team members, including providing assistance during invasive procedures. Maintain records that include patient information, sonographs and interpretations, files of correspondence, publications and regulations, and quality assurance records (e.g., pathology, biopsy, post-operative reports). Perform legal and ethical duties including preparing safety and accident reports, obtaining written consent from patient to perform invasive procedures, and reporting symptoms of abuse and neglect. Supervise and train students and other medical sonographers. Maintain stock and supplies, preparing supplies for special examinations and ordering supplies when necessary. Clean, check and maintain sonographic equipment, submitting maintenance requests or performing minor repairs as necessary. Perform clerical duties such as scheduling exams and special procedures, keeping records and archiving computerized images. **SKILLS**—Social Perceptiveness; Reading Comprehension; Learning Strategies; Instructing; Operation and Control; Active Learning; Active Listening; Service Orientation.

GOE—Interest Area: 08. Health Science. **Work Group:** 08.06. Medical Technology. **PERSONALITY TYPE:** No data available.

EDUCATION/TRAINING PROGRAMS—Allied Health Diagnostic, Intervention, and Treatment Professions, Other; Diagnostic Medical Sonography/Sonographer and Ultrasound Technician. **RELATED KNOWLEDGE/COURSES—Medicine and Dentistry:** Knowledge of the information and techniques needed to diagnose and treat human injuries, diseases, and deformities. This includes symptoms, treatment alternatives, drug properties and interactions, and preventive health-care measures. **Biology:** Knowledge of plant and animal organisms and their tissues, cells, functions, interdependencies, and interactions with each other and the environment. **Physics:** Knowledge and prediction of physical principles and laws and their interrelationships and applications to understanding fluid, material, and atmospheric dynamics and mechanical, electrical, atomic, and subatomic structures and processes. **Education and Training:** Knowledge of principles and methods for curriculum and training design, teaching and instruction for individuals and groups, and the measurement of training effects. **Customer and Personal Service:** Knowledge of principles and processes for providing customer and personal services. This includes customer needs assessment, meeting quality standards for services, and evaluation of customer satisfaction. **Therapy and Counseling:** Knowledge of principles, methods, and procedures for diagnosis, treatment, and rehabilitation of physical and mental dysfunctions and for career counseling and guidance.

Directors—Stage, Motion Pictures, Television, and Radio

- Annual Earnings: $53,860
- Growth: 16.6%
- Annual Job Openings: 11,000
- Self-Employed: 30.4%
- Part-Time: 8.4%
- Education/Training Required: Work experience plus degree

The job openings listed here are shared with Producers, Program Directors, Talent Directors, and Technical Directors/Managers.

Industries in Which Income Is Highest

Industry	Average Annual Wage	Number Employed
Motion Picture and Sound Recording Industries	$70,820	16,180
Professional, Scientific, and Technical Services	$69,870	3,100
Federal, State, and Local Government	$55,810	1,690
Broadcasting (Except Internet)	$48,650	23,240
Educational Services	$44,150	2,950

Metropolitan Areas Where Income Is Highest

Metropolitan Area	Average Annual Wage	Number Employed
Bridgeport–Stamford–Norwalk, CT	$98,420	150
New York–Northern New Jersey–Long Island, NY–NJ–PA	$81,710	10,130
San Francisco–Oakland–Fremont, CA	$79,980	1,300
Los Angeles–Long Beach–Santa Ana, CA	$72,210	9,760
Buffalo–Niagara Falls, NY	$66,330	170

Interpret script, conduct rehearsals, and direct activities of cast and technical crew for stage, motion pictures, television, or radio programs. Direct live broadcasts, films and recordings, or non-broadcast programming for public entertainment or education. Supervise and coordinate the work of camera, lighting, design, and sound crewmembers. Study and research scripts in order to determine how they should be directed. Cut and edit film or tape in order to integrate component parts into desired sequences. Collaborate with film and sound editors during the post-production process as films are edited and soundtracks are added. Confer with technical directors, managers, crew members, and writers to discuss details of production, such as photography, script, music, sets, and costumes. Plan details such as framing, composition, camera movement, sound, and actor movement for each shot or scene. Communicate to actors the approach, characterization, and movement needed for each scene in such a way that rehearsals and takes are minimized. Establish pace of programs and sequences of scenes according to time requirements and cast and set accessibility. Choose settings and locations for films and determine how scenes will be shot in these settings. Identify and approve equipment and elements required for productions, such as scenery, lights, props, costumes, choreography, and music. Compile scripts, program notes, and other material related to productions. Perform producers' duties such as securing financial backing, establishing and administering budgets, and recruiting cast and crew. Select plays or scripts for production, and determine how material should be interpreted and performed. Compile cue words and phrases, and cue announcers, cast members, and technicians during performances. Consult with writers, producers, and/or actors about script changes, or "workshop" scripts, through rehearsal with writers and actors to create final drafts. Review film daily in order to check on work in progress and to plan for future filming. Collaborate with producers in order to hire crewmembers such as art directors, cinematographers, and costumer designers. Interpret stage-set diagrams to determine stage layouts, and supervise placement of equipment and scenery. **SKILLS**—Management of Personnel Resources; Time Management; Judgment and Decision Making; Active Listening; Critical Thinking; Operations Analysis; Speaking; Active Learning.

GOE—Interest Area: 03. Arts and Communication. **Work Group:** 03.06. Drama. **PERSONALITY TYPE:** Artistic. Artistic occupations frequently involve working with forms, designs, and patterns. They often require self-expression, and the work can be done without following a clear set of rules.

EDUCATION/TRAINING PROGRAMS— Cinematography and Film/Video Production; Directing and Theatrical Production; Directing and Theatrical Production; Drama and Dramatics/Theatre Arts, General; Dramatic/Theatre Arts and Stagecraft, Other; Film/Cinema Studies; Radio and Television; Theatre/Theatre Arts Management. **RELATED KNOWLEDGE/COURSES—Communications and Media:** Knowledge of media production, communication, and dissemination techniques and methods. This includes alternative ways to inform and entertain via written, oral, and visual media. **Telecommunications:** Knowledge of transmission, broadcasting, switching, control, and operation of telecommunications systems. **Fine Arts:** Knowledge of the theory and techniques required to compose, produce, and perform works of music, dance, visual arts, drama, and sculpture. **Computers and Electronics:** Knowledge of circuit boards, processors, chips, electronic equipment, and computer hardware and software, including applications and programming. **Geography:** Knowledge of principles and methods for describing the features of land, sea, and air masses, including their physical characteristics; locations; interrelationships; and distribution of plant, animal, and human life. **Education and Training:** Knowledge of principles and methods for curriculum and training design, teaching and instruction for individuals and groups, and the measurement of training effects.

Economics Teachers, Postsecondary

- Annual Earnings: $68,910
- Growth: 32.2%
- Annual Job Openings: 329,000
- Self-Employed: 0.4%
- Part-Time: 27.3%
- Education/Training Required: Master's degree

Our sources did not provide separate job openings data for this occupation. The job openings listed here are shared with 35 other postsecondary teaching occupations. For a complete list, see the beginning of this section.

Industries in Which Income Is Highest

Industry	Average Annual Wage	Number Employed
Educational Services	$68,900	12,670

Metropolitan Areas Where Income Is Highest

Metropolitan Area	Average Annual Wage	Number Employed
Durham, NC	$104,100	130
Providence–Fall River–Warwick, RI–MA	$88,000	90
San Diego–Carlsbad–San Marcos, CA	$85,120	130
San Francisco–Oakland–Fremont, CA	$82,730	300
Boston–Cambridge–Quincy, MA–NH	$82,570	390

Teach courses in economics. Prepare and deliver lectures to undergraduate and/or graduate students on topics such as econometrics, price theory, and macroeconomics. Prepare course materials such as syllabi, homework assignments, and handouts. Evaluate and grade students' class work, assignments, and papers. Compile, administer, and grade examinations or assign this work to others. Keep abreast of developments in their field by reading current literature, talking with colleagues, and participating in professional conferences. Maintain student attendance records, grades, and other required records. Initiate, facilitate, and moderate classroom discussions. Maintain regularly scheduled office hours in order to advise and assist students. Select and obtain materials and supplies such as textbooks. Plan, evaluate, and revise curricula, course content, and course materials and methods of instruction. Conduct research in a particular field of knowledge and publish findings in professional journals, books, and/or electronic media. Supervise undergraduate and/or graduate teaching, internship, and research work. Advise students on academic and vocational curricula and on career issues. Serve on academic or administrative committees that deal with institutional policies, departmental matters, and academic issues. Collaborate with colleagues to address teaching and research issues. Compile bibliographies of specialized materials for outside reading assignments. Participate in student recruitment, registration, and placement activities. Perform administrative duties such as serving as department head. **SKILLS**—Instructing; Writing; Mathematics; Speaking; Critical Thinking; Reading Comprehension; Learning Strategies; Persuasion.

GOE—Interest Area: 05. Education and Training. **Work Group:** 05.03. Postsecondary and Adult Teaching and Instructing. **PERSONALITY TYPE:** Social. Social occupations frequently involve working with, communicating with, and teaching people. These occupations often involve helping or providing service to others.

EDUCATION/TRAINING PROGRAMS—Applied Economics; Business/Managerial Economics; Development Economics and International Development; Econometrics and Quantitative Economics; Economics, General; Economics, Other; International Economics; Social Science Teacher Education. **RELATED KNOWLEDGE/COURSES—Economics and Accounting:** Knowledge of economic and accounting principles and practices, the financial markets, banking, and the analysis and reporting of financial data. **Education and Training:** Knowledge of principles and methods for curriculum and training design, teaching and instruction for individuals and groups, and the measurement of training effects. **History and Archeology:** Knowledge of historical events and their causes, indicators, and effects on civilizations and cultures. **Mathematics:** Knowledge of arithmetic, algebra, geometry, calculus, and statistics and their applications. **English Language:** Knowledge of the structure and content of the English language, including the meaning and spelling of words, rules of composition, and grammar. **Philosophy and Theology:** Knowledge of different philosophical systems and religions. This includes their basic principles, values, ethics, ways of thinking, customs, and practices and their impact on human culture.

Economists

- ◎ Annual Earnings: $73,690
- ◎ Growth: 5.6%
- ◎ Annual Job Openings: 1,000
- ◎ Self-Employed: 0.0%
- ◎ Part-Time: 2.8%
- ◎ Education/Training Required: Master's degree

Industries in Which Income Is Highest

Industry	Average Annual Wage	Number Employed
Professional, Scientific, and Technical Services	$82,490	3,150
Federal, State, and Local Government	$71,270	6,860

Metropolitan Areas Where Income Is Highest

Metropolitan Area	Average Annual Wage	Number Employed
Washington–Arlington–Alexandria, DC–VA–MD–WV	$92,670	4,250
New York–Northern New Jersey–Long Island, NY–NJ–PA	$87,540	350
Tampa–St. Petersburg–Clearwater, FL	$81,140	60
Atlanta–Sandy Springs–Marietta, GA	$79,570	210
San Francisco–Oakland–Fremont, CA	$79,340	300

Conduct research, prepare reports, or formulate plans to aid in solution of economic problems arising from production and distribution of goods and services. May collect and process economic and statistical data using econometric and sampling techniques. Study economic and statistical data in area of specialization, such as finance, labor, or agriculture. Provide advice and consultation on economic relationships to businesses, public and private agencies, and other employers. Compile, analyze, and report data to explain economic phenomena and forecast market trends, applying mathematical models and statistical techniques. Formulate recommendations, policies, or plans to solve economic problems or to interpret markets. Develop economic guidelines and standards and prepare points of view used in forecasting trends and formulating economic policy. Testify at regulatory or legislative hearings concerning the estimated effects of changes in legislation or public policy and present recommendations based on cost-benefit analyses. Supervise research projects and students' study projects. **SKILLS**—Persuasion; Mathematics; Programming; Judgment and Decision Making; Critical Thinking; Complex Problem Solving; Writing; Coordination.

GOE—Interest Area: 15. Scientific Research, Engineering, and Mathematics. **Work Group:** 15.04.

Social Sciences. **PERSONALITY TYPE:** Investigative. Investigative occupations frequently involve working with ideas and require an extensive amount of thinking. These occupations can involve searching for facts and figuring out problems mentally.

EDUCATION/TRAINING PROGRAMS— Agricultural Economics; Applied Economics; Business/Managerial Economics; Development Economics and International Development; Econometrics and Quantitative Economics; Economics, General; Economics, Other; International Economics. **RELATED KNOWLEDGE/COURSES—Economics and Accounting:** Knowledge of economic and accounting principles and practices, the financial markets, banking, and the analysis and reporting of financial data. **Mathematics:** Knowledge of arithmetic, algebra, geometry, calculus, and statistics and their applications. **Sales and Marketing:** Knowledge of principles and methods for showing, promoting, and selling products or services. This includes marketing strategy and tactics, product demonstration, sales techniques, and sales control systems. **Computers and Electronics:** Knowledge of circuit boards, processors, chips, electronic equipment, and computer hardware and software, including applications and programming. **English Language:** Knowledge of the structure and content of the English language, including the meaning and spelling of words, rules of composition, and grammar. **Geography:** Knowledge of principles and methods for describing the features of land, sea, and air masses, including their physical characteristics; locations; interrelationships; and distribution of plant, animal, and human life.

Education Administrators, Elementary and Secondary School

- ◎ Annual Earnings: $75,400
- ◎ Growth: 10.4%
- ◎ Annual Job Openings: 27,000
- ◎ Self-Employed: 3.6%
- ◎ Part-Time: 9.5%
- ◎ Education/Training Required: Work experience plus degree

Industries in Which Income Is Highest

Industry	Average Annual Wage	Number Employed
Educational Services	$75,510	210,280
Federal, State, and Local Government	$73,270	1,610

Metropolitan Areas Where Income Is Highest

Metropolitan Area	Average Annual Wage	Number Employed
Bridgeport–Stamford–Norwalk, CT	$104,500	690
San Diego–Carlsbad–San Marcos, CA	$102,400	1,260
Hartford–West Hartford–East Hartford, CT	$99,960	830
Los Angeles–Long Beach–Santa Ana, CA	$99,540	5,630
New Haven, CT	$98,870	490

Plan, direct, or coordinate the academic, clerical, or auxiliary activities of public or private elementary or secondary level schools. Review and approve new programs, or recommend modifications to existing programs, submitting program proposals for school board approval as necessary. Prepare, maintain, or oversee the preparation/maintenance of attendance, activity, planning, or personnel reports and records. Confer with parents and staff to discuss educational activities, policies, and student behavioral or learning problems. Prepare and submit budget requests and recommendations, or grant proposals to solicit program funding. Direct and coordinate school maintenance services and the use of school facilities. Counsel and provide guidance to students regarding personal, academic, vocational, or behavioral issues. Organize and direct committees of specialists, volunteers, and staff to provide technical and advisory assistance for programs. Teach classes or courses to students. Advocate for new schools to be built, or for existing facilities to be repaired or remodeled. Plan and develop instructional methods and content for educational, vocational, or student activity programs. Develop partnerships with businesses, communities, and other organizations to help meet identified educational needs and to provide school-to-work programs. Direct and coordinate activities of teachers, administrators, and support staff at schools, public agencies, and institutions. Evaluate curricula, teaching methods, and programs to determine their effectiveness, efficiency, and utilization, and to ensure that school activities comply with federal, state, and local regulations. Set educational standards and goals, and help establish policies and procedures to carry them out. Recruit, hire, train, and evaluate primary and supplemental staff. Enforce discipline and attendance rules. Observe teaching methods and examine learning materials in order to evaluate and standardize curricula and teaching techniques, and to determine areas where improvement is needed. Establish, coordinate, and oversee particular programs across school districts, such as programs to evaluate student academic achievement. Review and interpret government codes, and develop programs to ensure adherence to codes and facility safety, security, and maintenance. **SKILLS**—Management of Personnel Resources; Management of Financial Resources; Negotiation; Learning Strategies; Social Perceptiveness; Persuasion; Monitoring; Coordination.

GOE—Interest Area: 05. Education and Training. **Work Group:** 05.01. Managerial Work in Education. **PERSONALITY TYPE:** Social. Social occupations frequently involve working with, communicating with, and teaching people. These occupations often involve helping or providing service to others.

EDUCATION/TRAINING   PROGRAMS— Educational Administration and Supervision, Other; Educational Leadership and Administration, General; Educational, Instructional, and Curriculum Supervision; Elementary and Middle School Administration/Principalship; Secondary School Administration/ Principalship. **RELATED KNOWLEDGE/COURSES—Education and Training:** Knowledge of principles and methods for curriculum and training design, teaching and instruction for individuals and groups, and the measurement of training effects. **Therapy and Counseling:** Knowledge of principles, methods, and procedures for diagnosis, treatment, and rehabilitation of physical and mental dysfunctions and for career counseling and guidance. **Personnel and Human Resources:** Knowledge of principles and procedures for personnel recruitment, selection, training, compensation and benefits, labor relations and negotiation, and personnel information systems. **Psychology:** Knowledge of human behavior and performance; individual differences in ability, personality, and interests; learning and motivation; psychological research methods; and the assessment and treatment of behavioral and affective disorders. **Customer and Personal Service:** Knowledge of principles and processes for providing customer and personal services. This includes customer needs assessment, meeting quality standards

for services, and evaluation of customer satisfaction. **Administration and Management:** Knowledge of business and management principles involved in strategic planning, resource allocation, human resources modeling, leadership technique, production methods, and coordination of people and resources.

Education Administrators, Postsecondary

- Annual Earnings: $70,350
- Growth: 21.3%
- Annual Job Openings: 18,000
- Self-Employed: 3.3%
- Part-Time: 9.5%
- Education/Training Required: Work experience plus degree

Industries in Which Income Is Highest

Industry	Average Annual Wage	Number Employed
Educational Services	$70,290	103,550

Metropolitan Areas Where Income Is Highest

Metropolitan Area	Average Annual Wage	Number Employed
College Station–Bryan, TX	$103,530	180
Burlington–South Burlington, VT	$95,990	120
Amarillo, TX	$95,870	70
Hartford–West Hartford–East Hartford, CT	$94,540	700
Fresno, CA	$91,520	240

Plan, direct, or coordinate research, instructional, student administration and services, and other educational activities at postsecondary institutions, including universities, colleges, and junior and community colleges. Recruit, hire, train, and terminate departmental personnel. Plan, administer, and control budgets, maintain financial records, and produce financial reports. Represent institutions at community and campus events, in meetings with other institution personnel, and during accreditation processes. Participate in faculty and college committee

E

activities. Provide assistance to faculty and staff in duties such as teaching classes, conducting orientation programs, issuing transcripts, and scheduling events. Establish operational policies and procedures and make any necessary modifications, based on analysis of operations, demographics, and other research information. Confer with other academic staff to explain and formulate admission requirements and course credit policies. Appoint individuals to faculty positions, and evaluate their performance. Direct activities of administrative departments such as admissions, registration, and career services. Develop curricula, and recommend curricula revisions and additions. Determine course schedules, and coordinate teaching assignments and room assignments in order to ensure optimum use of buildings and equipment. Consult with government regulatory and licensing agencies in order to ensure the institution's conformance with applicable standards. Direct, coordinate, and evaluate the activities of personnel engaged in administering academic institutions, departments, and/or alumni organizations. Teach courses within their department. Participate in student recruitment, selection, and admission, making admissions recommendations when required to do so. Review student misconduct reports requiring disciplinary action, and counsel students regarding such reports. Supervise coaches. Assess and collect tuition and fees. Direct scholarship, fellowship, and loan programs, performing activities such as selecting recipients and distributing aid. Coordinate the production and dissemination of university publications such as course catalogs and class schedules. Review registration statistics, and consult with faculty officials to develop registration policies. **SKILLS**—Management of Personnel Resources; Management of Financial Resources; Persuasion; Social Perceptiveness; Service Orientation; Coordination; Negotiation; Monitoring.

GOE—Interest Area: 05. Education and Training. **Work Group:** 05.01. Managerial Work in Education. **PERSONALITY TYPE:** Enterprising. Enterprising occupations frequently involve starting up and carrying out projects. These occupations can involve leading people and making many decisions. They sometimes require risk taking and often deal with business.

EDUCATION/TRAINING PROGRAMS— Community College Education; Educational Administration and Supervision, Other; Educational Leadership and Administration, General; Educational,

Instructional, and Curriculum Supervision; Higher Education/Higher Education Administration. **RELATED KNOWLEDGE/COURSES—Education and Training:** Knowledge of principles and methods for curriculum and training design, teaching and instruction for individuals and groups, and the measurement of training effects. **Personnel and Human Resources:** Knowledge of principles and procedures for personnel recruitment, selection, training, compensation and benefits, labor relations and negotiation, and personnel information systems. **Administration and Management:** Knowledge of business and management principles involved in strategic planning, resource allocation, human resources modeling, leadership technique, production methods, and coordination of people and resources. **Customer and Personal Service:** Knowledge of principles and processes for providing customer and personal services. This includes customer needs assessment, meeting quality standards for services, and evaluation of customer satisfaction. **Sociology and Anthropology:** Knowledge of group behavior and dynamics, societal trends and influences, human migrations, ethnicity, and cultures and their history and origins. **English Language:** Knowledge of the structure and content of the English language, including the meaning and spelling of words, rules of composition, and grammar.

Education Teachers, Postsecondary

- Annual Earnings: $50,380
- Growth: 32.2%
- Annual Job Openings: 329,000
- Self-Employed: 0.4%
- Part-Time: 27.3%
- Education/Training Required: Master's degree

Our sources did not provide separate job openings data for this occupation. The job openings listed here are shared with 35 other postsecondary teaching occupations. For a complete list, see the beginning of this section.

Industries in Which Income Is Highest

Industry	Average Annual Wage	Number Employed
Educational Services	$50,390	51,040

Metropolitan Areas Where Income Is Highest

Metropolitan Area	Average Annual Wage	Number Employed
San Diego–Carlsbad–San Marcos, CA	$91,940	380
San Jose–Sunnyvale–Santa Clara, CA	$77,850	170
Providence–Fall River–Warwick, RI–MA	$63,500	90
Riverside–San Bernardino–Ontario, CA	$63,080	250
Springfield, MA–CT	$62,250	180

Teach courses pertaining to education, such as counseling, curriculum, guidance, instruction, teacher education, and teaching English as a second language. Prepare course materials such as syllabi, homework assignments, and handouts. Prepare and deliver lectures to undergraduate and/or graduate students on topics such as children's literature, learning and development, and reading instruction. Initiate, facilitate, and moderate classroom discussions. Evaluate and grade students' class work, assignments, and papers. Plan, evaluate, and revise curricula, course content, and course materials and methods of instruction. Supervise students' fieldwork, internship, and research work. Keep abreast of developments in their field by reading current literature, talking with colleagues, and participating in professional conferences. Advise students on academic and vocational curricula and on career issues. Maintain regularly scheduled office hours in order to advise and assist students. Maintain student attendance records, grades, and other required records. Collaborate with colleagues to address teaching and research issues. Compile, administer, and grade examinations or assign this work to others. Conduct research in a particular field of knowledge and publish findings in professional journals, books, and/or electronic media. Select and obtain materials and supplies such as textbooks. Participate in student recruitment, registration, and placement activities. Advise and instruct teachers employed in school systems, by providing activities such as in-service seminars. Serve on academic or administrative committees that deal with institutional policies, departmental matters, and academic issues. Compile bibliographies of specialized materials for outside reading assignments. Write grant proposals to procure external research funding. Participate in campus and community events. Perform administrative duties such as serving as department head. Act as advisers to student organizations. **SKILLS**—Instructing; Learning Strategies; Writing; Social Perceptiveness; Persuasion; Active Learning; Speaking; Service Orientation.

GOE—Interest Area: 05. Education and Training. **Work Group:** 05.03. Postsecondary and Adult Teaching and Instructing. **PERSONALITY TYPE:** No data available.

EDUCATION/TRAINING PROGRAMS—Agricultural Teacher Education; Art Teacher Education; Biology Teacher Education; Business Teacher Education; Chemistry Teacher Education; Computer Teacher Education; Drama and Dance Teacher Education; Driver and Safety Teacher Education; Education, General; English/Language Arts Teacher Education; Family and Consumer Sciences/Home Economics Teacher Education; Foreign Language Teacher Education; French Language Teacher Education; Geography Teacher Education; others. **RELATED KNOWLEDGE/COURSES—Education and Training:** Knowledge of principles and methods for curriculum and training design, teaching and instruction for individuals and groups, and the measurement of training effects. **Therapy and Counseling:** Knowledge of principles, methods, and procedures for diagnosis, treatment, and rehabilitation of physical and mental dysfunctions and for career counseling and guidance. **Sociology and Anthropology:** Knowledge of group behavior and dynamics, societal trends and influences, human migrations, ethnicity, and cultures and their history and origins. **Philosophy and Theology:** Knowledge of different philosophical systems and religions. This includes their basic principles, values, ethics, ways of thinking, customs, and practices and their impact on human culture. **Psychology:** Knowledge of human behavior and performance; individual differences in ability, personality, and interests; learning and motivation; psychological research methods; and the assessment and treatment of behavioral and affective disorders. **English Language:** Knowledge of the structure and content of the English language, including the meaning and spelling of words, rules of composition, and grammar.

E

Educational, Vocational, and School Counselors

- Annual Earnings: $46,440
- Growth: 14.8%
- Annual Job Openings: 32,000
- Self-Employed: 5.8%
- Part-Time: 16.5%
- Education/Training Required: Master's degree

Industries in Which Income Is Highest

Industry	Average Annual Wage	Number Employed
Educational Services	$49,230	172,080
Federal, State, and Local Government	$46,500	10,650
Religious, Grantmaking, Civic, Professional, and Similar Organizations	$32,290	1,370
Social Assistance	$30,410	20,960
Nursing and Residential Care Facilities	$28,780	4,710

Metropolitan Areas Where Income Is Highest

Metropolitan Area	Average Annual Wage	Number Employed
Bakersfield, CA	$74,140	380
Saginaw–Saginaw Township North, MI	$73,720	110
Visalia–Porterville, CA	$68,610	140
Trenton–Ewing, NJ	$66,630	350
Detroit–Warren–Livonia, MI	$63,610	2,110

Counsel individuals and provide group educational and vocational guidance services. Counsel students regarding educational issues such as course and program selection, class scheduling, school adjustment, truancy, study habits, and career planning. Counsel individuals to help them understand and overcome personal, social, or behavioral problems affecting their educational or vocational situations. Maintain accurate and complete student records as required by laws, district policies, and administrative regulations. Confer with parents or guardians, teachers, other counselors, and administrators to resolve students' behavioral, academic, and other problems. Provide crisis intervention to students when difficult situations occur at schools. Identify cases involving domestic abuse or other family problems affecting students' development. Meet with parents and guardians to discuss their children's progress, and to determine their priorities for their children and their resource needs. Prepare students for later educational experiences by encouraging them to explore learning opportunities and to persevere with challenging tasks. Encourage students and/or parents to seek additional assistance from mental health professionals when necessary. Observe and evaluate students' performance, behavior, social development, and physical health. Enforce all administration policies and rules governing students. Meet with other professionals to discuss individual students' needs and progress. Provide students with information on such topics as college degree programs and admission requirements, financial aid opportunities, trade and technical schools, and apprenticeship programs. Evaluate individuals' abilities, interests, and personality characteristics using tests, records, interviews, and professional sources. Collaborate with teachers and administrators in the development, evaluation, and revision of school programs. Teach classes and present self-help or information sessions on subjects related to education and career planning. Establish and enforce behavioral rules and procedures to maintain order among students. Conduct follow-up interviews with counselees to determine if their needs have been met. **SKILLS**—Social Perceptiveness; Service Orientation; Persuasion; Negotiation; Active Listening; Learning Strategies; Coordination; Instructing.

GOE—Interest Area: 05. Education and Training. **Work Group:** 05.06. Counseling, Health, and Fitness Education. **PERSONALITY TYPE:** Social. Social occupations frequently involve working with, communicating with, and teaching people. These occupations often involve helping or providing service to others.

EDUCATION/TRAINING PROGRAMS—College Student Counseling and Personnel Services; Counselor Education/School Counseling and Guidance Services. **RELATED KNOWLEDGE/COURSES—Therapy and Counseling:** Knowledge of principles, methods, and procedures for diagnosis, treatment, and rehabilitation of physical and mental dysfunctions and for career counseling and guidance. **Psychology:** Knowledge of human behavior and performance; individual differences in ability, personality, and interests; learning and motivation; psychological research methods; and the assessment and treatment of behavioral and affective disorders. **Education and Training:** Knowledge of principles and methods for curriculum and training design, teaching and instruction for individuals and groups, and the measurement of training effects. **Sociology and Anthropology:** Knowledge of group behavior and dynamics, societal trends and influences, human migrations, ethnicity, and cultures and their history and origins. **Customer and Personal Service:** Knowledge of principles and processes for providing customer and personal services. This includes customer needs assessment, meeting quality standards for services, and evaluation of customer satisfaction. **Philosophy and Theology:** Knowledge of different philosophical systems and religions. This includes their basic principles, values, ethics, ways of thinking, customs, and practices and their impact on human culture.

Electrical and Electronics Repairers, Powerhouse, Substation, and Relay

- Annual Earnings: $54,970
- Growth: –0.4%
- Annual Job Openings: 2,000
- Self-Employed: 0.0%
- Part-Time: 0.0%
- Education/Training Required: Postsecondary vocational training

Industries in Which Income Is Highest

Industry	Average Annual Wage	Number Employed
Utilities	$56,290	15,930
Federal, State, and Local Government	$53,120	2,060

Metropolitan Areas Where Income Is Highest

Metropolitan Area	Average Annual Wage	Number Employed
Houston–Sugar Land–Baytown, TX	$74,140	330
Poughkeepsie–Newburgh–Middletown, NY	$66,350	70
St. Louis, MO–IL	$63,360	130
Salt Lake City, UT	$62,940	100
Syracuse, NY	$62,280	150

Inspect, test, repair, or maintain electrical equipment in generating stations, substations, and in-service relays. Analyze test data in order to diagnose malfunctions, to determine performance characteristics of systems, and to evaluate effects of system modifications. Construct, test, maintain, and repair substation relay and control systems. Consult manuals, schematics, wiring diagrams, and engineering personnel in order to troubleshoot and solve equipment problems and to determine optimum equipment functioning. Inspect and test equipment and circuits to identify malfunctions or defects, using wiring diagrams and testing devices such as ohmmeters, voltmeters, or ammeters. Open and close switches to isolate defective relays; then perform adjustments or repairs. Repair, replace, and clean equipment and components such as circuit breakers, brushes, and commutators. Run signal quality and connectivity tests for individual cables, and record results. Disconnect voltage regulators, bolts, and screws, and connect replacement regulators to high-voltage lines. Maintain inventories of spare parts for all equipment, requisitioning parts as necessary. Notify facility personnel of equipment shutdowns. Prepare and maintain records detailing tests, repairs, and maintenance. Schedule and supervise splicing or termination of cables in color-code order. Test insulators and bushings of equipment by inducing voltage across insulation, testing current, and calculating insulation loss. Test oil in circuit breakers and transformers for dielectric strength, refilling oil periodically. Schedule and supervise the construction and testing of special devices and the implementation of unique monitoring or control systems. Set forms and pour concrete footings for installation of heavy equipment. **SKILLS**—Repairing; Equipment Maintenance; Installation; Troubleshooting; Science; Operation Monitoring; Quality Control Analysis; Equipment Selection.

GOE—Interest Area: 02. Architecture and Construction. **Work Group:** 02.05. Systems and Equipment Installation, Maintenance, and Repair. **PERSONALITY TYPE:** Realistic. Realistic occupations frequently involve work activities that include practical, hands-on problems and solutions. They often deal with plants, animals, and real-world materials like wood, tools, and machinery. Many of the occupations require working outside and do not involve a lot of paperwork or working closely with others.

EDUCATION/TRAINING PROGRAM—No data available. **RELATED KNOWLEDGE/COURSES— Computers and Electronics:** Knowledge of circuit boards, processors, chips, electronic equipment, and computer hardware and software, including applications and programming. **Mechanical Devices:** Knowledge of machines and tools, including their designs, uses, repair, and maintenance. **Physics:** Knowledge and prediction of physical principles and laws and their interrelationships and applications to understanding fluid, material, and atmospheric dynamics and mechanical, electrical, atomic, and sub-atomic structures and processes. **Engineering and Technology:** Knowledge of the practical application of engineering science and technology. This includes applying principles, techniques, procedures, and equipment to the design and production of various goods and services. **Mathematics:** Knowledge of arithmetic, algebra, geometry, calculus, and statistics and their applications.

Electrical Engineering Technicians

- Annual Earnings: $48,040
- Growth: 9.8%
- Annual Job Openings: 18,000
- Self-Employed: 0.4%
- Part-Time: 6.8%
- Education/Training Required: Associate degree

The job openings listed here are shared with Calibration and Instrumentation Technicians; and Electronics Engineering Technicians.

Industries in Which Income Is Highest

Industry	Average Annual Wage	Number Employed
Federal, State, and Local Government	$59,050	13,940
Utilities	$55,890	7,660
Transportation Equipment Manufacturing	$52,760	4,020
Telecommunications	$51,480	12,170
Internet Service Providers, Web Search Portals, and Data Processing Services	$51,250	1,360

Metropolitan Areas Where Income Is Highest

Metropolitan Area	Average Annual Wage	Number Employed
Bakersfield, CA	$68,210	630
Bremerton–Silverdale, WA	$65,220	220
Dover, DE	$64,060	50
Anchorage, AK	$61,110	200
Oxnard–Thousand Oaks–Ventura, CA	$59,770	930

Apply electrical theory and related knowledge to test and modify developmental or operational electrical machinery and electrical control equipment and circuitry in industrial or commercial plants and laboratories. Usually work under direction of engineering staff. Provide technical assistance and resolution when electrical or engineering problems are encountered before, during, and after construction. Assemble electrical and electronic systems and prototypes according to engineering data and knowledge of electrical principles, using hand tools and measuring instruments. Install and maintain electrical control systems and solid state equipment. Modify electrical prototypes, parts, assemblies, and systems to correct functional deviations. Set up and operate test equipment to evaluate performance of developmental parts, assemblies, or systems under simulated operating conditions, and record results. Collaborate with electrical engineers and other personnel to identify, define, and solve developmental problems. Build, calibrate, maintain, troubleshoot and repair electrical instruments or testing equipment. Analyze and interpret test information to resolve design-related problems. Write commissioning procedures for electrical installations. Prepare project cost and work-time estimates. Evaluate engineering proposals, shop drawings and design comments for sound electrical engineering practice and conformance with established safety and design criteria, and recommend approval or disapproval. Draw or modify diagrams and write engineering specifications to clarify design details and functional criteria of experimental electronics units. Conduct inspections for quality control and assurance programs, reporting findings and recommendations. Prepare contracts and initiate, review and coordinate modifications to contract specifications and plans throughout the construction process. Plan, schedule and monitor work of support personnel to assist supervisor. Review existing electrical engineering criteria to identify necessary revisions, deletions or amendments to outdated material. Perform supervisory duties such as recommending work assignments, approving leaves and completing performance evaluations. Plan method and sequence of operations for developing and testing experimental electronic and electrical equipment. **SKILLS**—Repairing; Troubleshooting; Installation; Technology Design; Science; Operations Analysis; Equipment Maintenance; Mathematics.

GOE—Interest Area: 15. Scientific Research, Engineering, and Mathematics. **Work Group:** 15.09. Engineering Technology. **PERSONALITY TYPE:** Realistic. Realistic occupations frequently involve work activities that include practical, hands-on problems and solutions. They often deal with plants, animals, and real-world materials like wood, tools, and machinery. Many of the occupations require working outside and do not involve a lot of paperwork or working closely with others.

EDUCATION/TRAINING PROGRAMS—Computer Engineering Technology/Technician; Computer Technology/Computer Systems Technology; Electrical and Electronic Engineering Technologies/Technicians, Other; Electrical, Electronic and Communications Engineering Technology/Technician; Telecommunications Technology/Technician. **RELATED KNOWLEDGE/COURSES—Engineering and Technology:** Knowledge of the practical application of engineering science and technology. This includes applying principles, techniques, procedures, and equipment to the design and production of various goods and services. **Design:** Knowledge of design techniques, tools, and principles involved in production of precision technical plans, blueprints, drawings, and models. **Computers and Electronics:** Knowledge of circuit boards, processors, chips, electronic equipment,

and computer hardware and software, including applications and programming. **Physics:** Knowledge and prediction of physical principles and laws and their interrelationships and applications to understanding fluid, material, and atmospheric dynamics and mechanical, electrical, atomic, and subatomic structures and processes. **Mechanical Devices:** Knowledge of machines and tools, including their designs, uses, repair, and maintenance. **Telecommunications:** Knowledge of transmission, broadcasting, switching, control, and operation of telecommunications systems.

Electrical Engineers

- Annual Earnings: $73,510
- Growth: 11.8%
- Annual Job Openings: 12,000
- Self-Employed: 3.3%
- Part-Time: 2.1%
- Education/Training Required: Bachelor's degree

Industries in Which Income Is Highest

Industry	Average Annual Wage	Number Employed
Computer and Electronic Product Manufacturing	$78,200	32,840
Management of Companies and Enterprises	$77,500	3,240
Utilities	$75,510	11,950
Federal, State, and Local Government	$75,360	7,410
Professional, Scientific, and Technical Services	$74,800	43,790

Metropolitan Areas Where Income Is Highest

Metropolitan Area	Average Annual Wage	Number Employed
San Jose–Sunnyvale–Santa Clara, CA	$92,220	4,560
Anchorage, AK	$88,680	150
Austin–Round Rock, TX	$86,990	2,450
Fort Walton Beach–Crestview–Destin, FL	$86,430	220
Beaumont–Port Arthur, TX	$86,370	170

E

Design, develop, test, or supervise the manufacturing and installation of electrical equipment, components, or systems for commercial, industrial, military, or scientific use. Confer with engineers, customers, and others to discuss existing or potential engineering projects and products. Design, implement, maintain, and improve electrical instruments, equipment, facilities, components, products, and systems for commercial, industrial, and domestic purposes. Operate computer-assisted engineering and design software and equipment to perform engineering tasks. Direct and coordinate manufacturing, construction, installation, maintenance, support, documentation, and testing activities to ensure compliance with specifications, codes, and customer requirements. Perform detailed calculations to compute and establish manufacturing, construction, and installation standards and specifications. Inspect completed installations and observe operations, to ensure conformance to design and equipment specifications and compliance with operational and safety standards. Plan and implement research methodology and procedures to apply principles of electrical theory to engineering projects. Prepare specifications for purchase of materials and equipment. Supervise and train project team members as necessary. Investigate and test vendors' and competitors' products. Oversee project production efforts to assure projects are completed satisfactorily, on time and within budget. Prepare and study technical drawings, specifications of electrical systems, and topographical maps to ensure that installation and operations conform to standards and customer requirements. Investigate customer or public complaints, determine nature and extent of problem, and recommend remedial measures. Plan layout of electric power generating plants and distribution lines and stations. Assist in developing capital project programs for new equipment and major repairs. Develop budgets, estimating labor, material, and construction costs. **SKILLS**—Technology Design; Troubleshooting; Systems Analysis; Science; Systems Evaluation; Complex Problem Solving; Equipment Selection; Management of Material Resources.

GOE—Interest Area: 15. Scientific Research, Engineering, and Mathematics. **Work Group:** 15.07. Research and Design Engineering. **PERSONALITY TYPE:** Investigative. Investigative occupations frequently involve working with ideas and require an extensive amount of thinking. These occupations can involve searching for facts and figuring out problems mentally.

EDUCATION/TRAINING PROGRAM— Electrical, Electronics and Communications Engineering. **RELATED KNOWLEDGE/COURSES— Engineering and Technology:** Knowledge of the practical application of engineering science and technology. This includes applying principles, techniques, procedures, and equipment to the design and production of various goods and services. **Design:** Knowledge of design techniques, tools, and principles involved in production of precision technical plans, blueprints, drawings, and models. **Physics:** Knowledge and prediction of physical principles and laws and their interrelationships and applications to understanding fluid, material, and atmospheric dynamics and mechanical, electrical, atomic, and subatomic structures and processes. **Computers and Electronics:** Knowledge of circuit boards, processors, chips, electronic equipment, and computer hardware and software, including applications and programming. **Mathematics:** Knowledge of arithmetic, algebra, geometry, calculus, and statistics and their applications. **Telecommunications:** Knowledge of transmission, broadcasting, switching, control, and operation of telecommunications systems.

Electrical Power-Line Installers and Repairers

- Annual Earnings: $50,150
- Growth: 2.5%
- Annual Job Openings: 11,000
- Self-Employed: 2.3%
- Part-Time: 1.2%
- Education/Training Required: Long-term on-the-job training

Industries in Which Income Is Highest

Industry	Average Annual Wage	Number Employed
Utilities	$53,080	57,900
Telecommunications	$49,780	8,650
Management of Companies and Enterprises	$49,390	2,330
Federal, State, and Local Government	$48,110	10,440
Specialty Trade Contractors	$43,480	4,410

Metropolitan Areas Where Income Is Highest

Metropolitan Area	Average Annual Wage	Number Employed
Medford, OR	$66,460	120
Kennewick–Richland–Pasco, WA	$65,010	80
Anchorage, AK	$64,930	150
Binghamton, NY	$64,790	80
Minneapolis–St. Paul–Bloomington, MN–WI	$64,250	620

Install or repair cables or wires used in electrical power or distribution systems. May erect poles and light or heavy duty transmission towers. Adhere to safety practices and procedures, such as checking equipment regularly and erecting barriers around work areas. Open switches or attach grounding devices in order to remove electrical hazards from disturbed or fallen lines or to facilitate repairs. Climb poles or use truck-mounted buckets to access equipment. Place insulating or fireproofing materials over conductors and joints. Install, maintain, and repair electrical distribution and transmission systems, including conduits, cables, wires, and related equipment such as transformers, circuit breakers, and switches. Identify defective sectionalizing devices, circuit breakers, fuses, voltage regulators, transformers, switches, relays, or wiring, using wiring diagrams and electrical-testing instruments. Drive vehicles equipped with tools and materials to job sites. Coordinate work assignment preparation and completion with other workers. Inspect and test power lines and auxiliary equipment to locate and identify problems, using reading and testing instruments. String wire conductors and cables between poles, towers, trenches, pylons, and buildings, setting lines in place and using winches to adjust tension. Test conductors, according to electrical diagrams and specifications, to identify corresponding conductors and to prevent incorrect connections. Replace damaged poles with new poles, and straighten the poles. Install watt-hour meters and connect service drops between power lines and consumers' facilities. Attach crossarms, insulators, and auxiliary equipment to poles prior to installing them. Travel in trucks, helicopters, and airplanes to inspect lines for freedom from obstruction and adequacy of insulation. Dig holes using augers, and set poles, using cranes and power equipment. Trim trees that could be hazardous to the functioning of cables or wires. Splice or solder cables together or to overhead transmission lines, customer service lines, or street light lines, using hand tools, epoxies, or specialized equipment. Cut and peel lead sheathing and insulation from defective or newly installed cables and conduits prior to splicing. **SKILLS**—Repairing; Installation; Equipment Maintenance; Troubleshooting; Operation Monitoring; Instructing; Coordination; Management of Personnel Resources.

GOE—Interest Area: 02. Architecture and Construction. **Work Group:** 02.05. Systems and Equipment Installation, Maintenance, and Repair. **PERSONALITY TYPE:** Realistic. Realistic occupations frequently involve work activities that include practical, hands-on problems and solutions. They often deal with plants, animals, and real-world materials like wood, tools, and machinery. Many of the occupations require working outside and do not involve a lot of paperwork or working closely with others.

EDUCATION/TRAINING PROGRAMS—Electrical and Power Transmission Installation/Installer, General; Electrical and Power Transmission Installers, Other; Lineworker. **RELATED KNOWLEDGE/COURSES—Building and Construction:** Knowledge of the materials, methods, and tools involved in the construction or repair of houses, buildings, or other structures such as highways and roads. **Customer and Personal Service:** Knowledge of principles and processes for providing customer and personal services. This includes customer needs assessment, meeting quality standards for services, and evaluation of customer satisfaction. **Mechanical Devices:** Knowledge of machines and tools, including their designs, uses, repair, and maintenance. **Engineering and Technology:** Knowledge of the practical application of engineering science and technology. This includes applying principles, techniques, procedures, and equipment to the design and production of various goods and services. **Transportation:** Knowledge of principles and methods for moving people or goods by air, rail, sea, or road, including the relative costs and benefits. **Design:** Knowledge of design techniques, tools, and principles involved in production of precision technical plans, blueprints, drawings, and models.

Electronics Engineering Technicians

- Annual Earnings: $48,040
- Growth: 9.8%
- Annual Job Openings: 18,000
- Self-Employed: 0.4%
- Part-Time: 6.8%
- Education/Training Required: Associate degree

The job openings listed here are shared with Calibration and Instrumentation Technicians and Electrical Engineering Technicians.

Industries in Which Income Is Highest

Industry	Average Annual Wage	Number Employed
Federal, State, and Local Government	$59,050	13,940
Utilities	$55,890	7,660
Transportation Equipment Manufacturing	$52,760	4,020
Telecommunications	$51,480	12,170
Internet Service Providers, Web Search Portals, and Data Processing Services	$51,250	1,360

Metropolitan Areas Where Income Is Highest

Metropolitan Area	Average Annual Wage	Number Employed
Bakersfield, CA	$68,210	630
Bremerton–Silverdale, WA	$65,220	220
Dover, DE	$64,060	50
Anchorage, AK	$61,110	200
Oxnard–Thousand Oaks–Ventura, CA	$59,770	930

Lay out, build, test, troubleshoot, repair, and modify developmental and production electronic components, parts, equipment, and systems, such as computer equipment, missile control instrumentation, electron tubes, test equipment, and machine tool numerical controls, applying principles and theories of electronics, electrical circuitry, engineering mathematics, electronic and electrical testing, and physics. Usually work under direction of engi-neering staff.** Test electronics units, using standard test equipment, and analyze results to evaluate performance and determine need for adjustment. Perform preventative maintenance and calibration of equipment and systems. Read blueprints, wiring diagrams, schematic drawings, and engineering instructions for assembling electronics units, applying knowledge of electronic theory and components. Identify and resolve equipment malfunctions, working with manufacturers and field representatives as necessary to procure replacement parts. Maintain system logs and manuals to document testing and operation of equipment. Assemble, test, and maintain circuitry or electronic components according to engineering instructions, technical manuals, and knowledge of electronics, using hand and power tools. Adjust and replace defective or improperly functioning circuitry and electronics components, using hand tools and soldering iron. Procure parts and maintain inventory and related documentation. Maintain working knowledge of state-of-the-art tools, software, etc., through reading and/or attending conferences, workshops or other training. Provide user applications and engineering support and recommendations for new and existing equipment with regard to installation, upgrades and enhancement. Write reports and record data on testing techniques, laboratory equipment, and specifications to assist engineers. Provide customer support and education, working with users to identify needs, determine sources of problems and to provide information on product use. Design basic circuitry and draft sketches for clarification of details and design documentation under engineers' direction, using drafting instruments and computer aided design equipment. Build prototypes from rough sketches or plans. Develop and upgrade preventative maintenance procedures for components, equipment, parts and systems. Fabricate parts, such as coils, terminal boards, and chassis, using bench lathes, drills, or other machine tools. Research equipment and component needs, sources, competitive prices, delivery times and ongoing operational costs. **SKILLS**—Repairing; Troubleshooting; Equipment Maintenance; Installation; Technology Design; Operation Monitoring; Systems Evaluation; Programming.

GOE—Interest Area: 15. Scientific Research, Engineering, and Mathematics. **Work Group:** 15.09. Engineering Technology. **PERSONALITY TYPE:** Realistic. Realistic occupations frequently involve work activities that include practical, hands-on problems and solutions. They often deal with plants, animals, and real-world materials like wood, tools, and machinery. Many of the occupations require working outside and do not involve a lot of paperwork or working closely with others.

EDUCATION/TRAINING PROGRAMS— Computer Engineering Technology/Technician; Electrical and Electronic Engineering Technologies/Technicians, Other; Electrical, Electronic and Communications Engineering Technology/Technician; Telecommunications Technology/Technician. **RELATED KNOWLEDGE/COURSES—Engineering and Technology:** Knowledge of the practical application of engineering science and technology. This includes applying principles, techniques, procedures, and equipment to the design and production of various goods and services. **Computers and Electronics:** Knowledge of circuit boards, processors, chips, electronic equipment, and computer hardware and software, including applications and programming. **Mechanical Devices:** Knowledge of machines and tools, including their designs, uses, repair, and maintenance. **Design:** Knowledge of design techniques, tools, and principles involved in production of precision technical plans, blueprints, drawings, and models. **Telecommunications:** Knowledge of transmission, broadcasting, switching, control, and operation of telecommunications systems. **Mathematics:** Knowledge of arithmetic, algebra, geometry, calculus, and statistics and their applications.

Electronics Engineers, Except Computer

- Annual Earnings: $78,030
- Growth: 9.7%
- Annual Job Openings: 11,000
- Self-Employed: 3.2%
- Part-Time: 2.1%
- Education/Training Required: Bachelor's degree

Industries in Which Income Is Highest

Industry	Average Annual Wage	Number Employed
Federal, State, and Local Government	$89,330	19,300
Transportation Equipment Manufacturing	$84,570	1,500
Professional, Scientific, and Technical Services	$82,860	23,520
Management of Companies and Enterprises	$82,150	4,960
Computer and Electronic Product Manufacturing	$78,310	33,910

Metropolitan Areas Where Income Is Highest

Metropolitan Area	Average Annual Wage	Number Employed
Greensboro–High Point, NC	$98,310	220
Santa Barbara–Santa Maria, CA	$95,460	410
Utica–Rome, NY	$94,280	250
Bakersfield, CA	$93,830	610
San Jose–Sunnyvale–Santa Clara, CA	$93,010	7,560

Research, design, develop, and test electronic components and systems for commercial, industrial, military, or scientific use utilizing knowledge of electronic theory and materials properties. Design electronic circuits and components for use in fields such as telecommunications, aerospace guidance and propulsion control, acoustics, or instruments and controls. Design electronic components and software, products and systems for commercial, industrial, medical, military, and scientific applications. Provide technical support and instruction to staff and customers regarding equipment standards, and help solve specific, difficult in-service engineering problems. Operate computer-assisted engineering and design software and equipment to perform engineering tasks. Analyze system requirements, capacity, cost, and customer needs to determine feasibility of project and develop system plan. Confer with engineers, customers, vendors and others to discuss existing and potential engineering projects or products. Review and evaluate work of others, inside and outside the organization, to ensure effectiveness, technical adequacy and compatibility in the resolution of complex engineering problems. Determine material and equipment needs and order supplies. Inspect electronic equipment, instruments, products, and systems to ensure conformance to specifications, safety standards, and applicable codes and regulations. Evaluate operational systems, prototypes and proposals and recommend repair or design modifications based on factors such as environment, service, cost, and system capabilities. Prepare documentation containing information such as confidential descriptions and specifications of proprietary hardware and software, product development and introduction schedules, product costs, and information about product performance weaknesses. Direct and coordinate activities concerned with manufacture, construction, installation, maintenance, operation, and modification of electronic equipment, products, and systems. Develop and perform operational, maintenance, and testing procedures for electronic products, components, equipment, and systems. Plan and develop applications and modifications for electronic properties used in components, products, and systems, to improve technical performance. Prepare engineering sketches and specifications for construction, relocation, and installation of equipment, facilities, products, and systems. Plan and implement research, methodology, and procedures to apply principles of electronic theory to engineering projects. **SKILLS—** Troubleshooting; Technology Design; Operations Analysis; Installation; Science; Complex Problem Solving; Systems Evaluation; Equipment Selection.

GOE—Interest Area: 15. Scientific Research, Engineering, and Mathematics. **Work Group:** 15.07. Research and Design Engineering. **PERSONALITY TYPE:** Investigative. Investigative occupations frequently involve working with ideas and require an extensive amount of thinking. These occupations can involve searching for facts and figuring out problems mentally.

EDUCATION/TRAINING PROGRAM—Electrical, Electronics and Communications Engineering. **RELATED KNOWLEDGE/COURSES—Engineering and Technology:** Knowledge of the practical application of engineering science and technology. This includes applying principles, techniques, procedures, and equipment to the design and production of various goods and services. **Design:** Knowledge of design techniques, tools, and principles involved in production of precision technical plans, blueprints, drawings, and models. **Computers and Electronics:** Knowledge of circuit boards, processors, chips, electronic equipment, and computer hardware and

software, including applications and programming. **Physics:** Knowledge and prediction of physical principles and laws and their interrelationships and applications to understanding fluid, material, and atmospheric dynamics and mechanical, electrical, atomic, and subatomic structures and processes. **Telecommunications:** Knowledge of transmission, broadcasting, switching, control, and operation of telecommunications systems. **Mathematics:** Knowledge of arithmetic, algebra, geometry, calculus, and statistics and their applications.

Elevator Installers and Repairers

- Annual Earnings: $59,190
- Growth: 14.8%
- Annual Job Openings: 3,000
- Self-Employed: 0.4%
- Part-Time: 0.0%
- Education/Training Required: Long-term on-the-job training

Industries in Which Income Is Highest

Industry	Average Annual Wage	Number Employed
Specialty Trade Contractors	$59,880	19,410

Metropolitan Areas Where Income Is Highest

Metropolitan Area	Average Annual Wage	Number Employed
San Francisco–Oakland–Fremont, CA	$78,300	450
Seattle–Tacoma–Bellevue, WA	$74,870	190
Honolulu, HI	$73,160	280
Chicago–Naperville–Joliet, IL–IN–WI	$72,230	750
Cleveland–Elyria–Mentor, OH	$72,070	520

Assemble, install, repair, or maintain electric or hydraulic freight or passenger elevators, escalators, or dumbwaiters. Adjust safety controls, counterweights, door mechanisms, and components such as valves, ratchets, seals, and brake linings. Assemble electrically powered stairs, steel frameworks, and tracks, and install associated motors and electrical wiring. Assemble elevator cars, installing each car's platform, walls, and doors. Assemble, install, repair, and maintain elevators, escalators, moving sidewalks, and dumbwaiters, using hand and power tools, and testing devices such as test lamps, ammeters, and voltmeters. Attach guide shoes and rollers to minimize the lateral motion of cars as they travel through shafts. Bolt or weld steel rails to the walls of shafts to guide elevators, working from scaffolding or platforms. Check that safety regulations and building codes are met, and complete service reports verifying conformance to standards. Connect car frames to counterweights, using steel cables. Connect electrical wiring to control panels and electric motors. Cut prefabricated sections of framework, rails, and other components to specified dimensions. Disassemble defective units, and repair or replace parts such as locks, gears, cables, and electric wiring. Inspect wiring connections, control panel hookups, door installations, and alignments and clearances of cars and hoistways to ensure that equipment will operate properly. Install electrical wires and controls by attaching conduit along shaft walls from floor to floor, then pulling plastic-covered wires through the conduit. Install outer doors and door frames at elevator entrances on each floor of a structure. Locate malfunctions in brakes, motors, switches, and signal and control systems, using test equipment. Maintain log books that detail all repairs and checks performed. Operate elevators to determine power demands, and test power consumption to detect overload factors. Read and interpret blueprints to determine the layout of system components, frameworks, and foundations, and to select installation equipment. Test newly installed equipment to ensure that it meets specifications, such as stopping at floors for set amounts of time. **SKILLS**—Installation; Repairing; Equipment Maintenance; Troubleshooting; Quality Control Analysis; Operation Monitoring; Systems Analysis; Operation and Control.

GOE—Interest Area: 02. Architecture and Construction. **Work Group:** 02.05. Systems and Equipment Installation, Maintenance, and Repair. **PERSONALITY TYPE:** Realistic. Realistic occupations frequently involve work activities that include practical, hands-on problems and solutions. They often deal with plants, animals, and real-world materials like wood, tools, and machinery. Many of the occupations require working outside and do not involve a lot of paperwork or working closely with others.

EDUCATION/TRAINING PROGRAM— Industrial Mechanics and Maintenance Technology. **RELATED KNOWLEDGE/COURSES—Building and Construction:** Knowledge of the materials, methods, and tools involved in the construction or repair of houses, buildings, or other structures such as highways and roads. **Mechanical Devices:** Knowledge of machines and tools, including their designs, uses, repair, and maintenance. **Engineering and Technology:** Knowledge of the practical application of engineering science and technology. This includes applying principles, techniques, procedures, and equipment to the design and production of various goods and services. **Physics:** Knowledge and prediction of physical principles and laws and their interrelationships and applications to understanding fluid, material, and atmospheric dynamics and mechanical, electrical, atomic, and subatomic structures and processes. **Public Safety and Security:** Knowledge of relevant equipment, policies, procedures, and strategies to promote effective local, state, or national security operations for the protection of people, data, property, and institutions. **Computers and Electronics:** Knowledge of circuit boards, processors, chips, electronic equipment, and computer hardware and software, including applications and programming.

Engineering Managers

- Annual Earnings: $100,760
- Growth: 13.0%
- Annual Job Openings: 15,000
- Self-Employed: 0.5%
- Part-Time: 1.2%
- Education/Training Required: Work experience plus degree

Industries in Which Income Is Highest

Industry	Average Annual Wage	Number Employed
Oil and Gas Extraction	$116,960	1,130
Computer and Electronic Product Manufacturing	$115,690	29,440
Merchant Wholesalers, Durable Goods	$105,240	2,540
Professional, Scientific, and Technical Services	$104,350	52,400
Management of Companies and Enterprises	$104,310	8,150

Metropolitan Areas Where Income Is Highest

Metropolitan Area	Average Annual Wage	Number Employed
Baton Rouge, LA	More than $146,500	440
San Jose–Sunnyvale–Santa Clara, CA	$139,820	8,700
Atlantic City, NJ	$128,660	80
Boulder, CO	$124,880	690
San Francisco–Oakland–Fremont, CA	$119,260	4,430

Plan, direct, or coordinate activities in such fields as architecture and engineering or research and development in these fields. Confer with management, production, and marketing staff to discuss project specifications and procedures. Coordinate and direct projects, making detailed plans to accomplish goals and directing the integration of technical activities. Analyze technology, resource needs, and market demand, to plan and assess the feasibility of projects. Plan and direct the installation, testing, operation, maintenance, and repair of facilities and equipment. Direct, review, and approve product design and changes. Recruit employees; assign, direct, and evaluate their work; and oversee the development and maintenance of staff competence. Prepare budgets, bids, and contracts, and direct the negotiation of research contracts. Develop and implement policies, standards and procedures for the engineering and technical work performed in the department, service, laboratory or firm. Perform administrative functions such as reviewing and writing reports, approving expenditures, enforcing rules, and making decisions about the purchase of materials or services. Review and recommend or approve contracts and cost estimates. Present and explain proposals, reports, and findings to clients. Consult or negotiate with clients to prepare project specifications. Set scientific and technical goals within broad outlines provided by top management. Administer highway planning, construction, and maintenance. Direct the engineering of water control, treatment, and distribution projects. Plan, direct, and coordinate survey work with other staff activities, certifying survey work, and writing land legal descriptions. Confer with and report to officials and the public to provide information and solicit support for projects. **SKILLS**—Technology Design; Operations Analysis; Science; Management of Financial Resources; Installation; Negotiation; Persuasion; Mathematics.

GOE—Interest Area: 15. Scientific Research, Engineering, and Mathematics. **Work Group:** 15.01. Managerial Work in Scientific Research, Engineering, and Mathematics. **PERSONALITY TYPE:** Enterprising. Enterprising occupations frequently involve starting up and carrying out projects. These occupations can involve leading people and making many decisions. They sometimes require risk taking and often deal with business.

EDUCATION/TRAINING PROGRAMS—Aerospace, Aeronautical and Astronautical Engineering; Agricultural/Biological Engineering and Bioengineering; Architectural Engineering; Architecture (BArch, BA/BS, MArch, MA/MS, PhD); Biomedical/Medical Engineering; Ceramic Sciences and Engineering; Chemical Engineering; City/Urban, Community and Regional Planning; Civil Engineering, General; Civil Engineering, Other; Computer Engineering, Gen.; Computer Engineering, Other; Computer Hardware Engineering; Computer Software Engineering; others. **RELATED KNOWLEDGE/COURSES**—**Engineering and Technology:** Knowledge of the practical application of engineering science and technology. This includes applying principles, techniques, procedures, and equipment to the design and production of various goods and services. **Design:** Knowledge of design techniques, tools, and principles involved in production of precision technical plans, blueprints, drawings, and models. **Physics:** Knowledge and prediction of physical principles and laws and their interrelationships and applications to understanding fluid, material, and atmospheric dynamics and mechanical, electrical, atomic, and subatomic structures and processes. **Personnel and Human Resources:**

Knowledge of principles and procedures for personnel recruitment, selection, training, compensation and benefits, labor relations and negotiation, and personnel information systems. **Building and Construction:** Knowledge of the materials, methods, and tools involved in the construction or repair of houses, buildings, or other structures such as highways and roads. **Mathematics:** Knowledge of arithmetic, algebra, geometry, calculus, and statistics and their applications.

Engineering Teachers, Postsecondary

- Annual Earnings: $74,540
- Growth: 32.2%
- Annual Job Openings: 329,000
- Self-Employed: 0.4%
- Part-Time: 27.3%
- Education/Training Required: Master's degree

Our sources did not provide separate job openings data for this occupation. The job openings listed here are shared with 35 other postsecondary teaching occupations. For a complete list, see the beginning of this section.

Industries in Which Income Is Highest

Industry	Average Annual Wage	Number Employed
Educational Services	$74,410	34,300

Metropolitan Areas Where Income Is Highest

Metropolitan Area	Average Annual Wage	Number Employed
College Station–Bryan, TX	$116,870	430
Boston–Cambridge–Quincy, MA–NH	$97,360	1,050
Portland–Vancouver–Beaverton, OR–WA	$89,040	120
San Francisco–Oakland–Fremont, CA	$87,980	690
Providence–Fall River–Warwick, RI–MA	$86,310	230

Teach courses pertaining to the application of physical laws and principles of engineering for the development of machines, materials, instruments, processes, and services. Includes teachers of subjects, such as chemical, civil, electrical, industrial, mechanical, mineral, and petroleum engineering. Includes both teachers primarily engaged in teaching and those who do a combination of both teaching and research. Prepare and deliver lectures to undergraduate and/or graduate students on topics such as mechanics, hydraulics, and robotics. Keep abreast of developments in their field by reading current literature, talking with colleagues, and participating in professional conferences. Supervise undergraduate and/or graduate teaching, internship, and research work. Evaluate and grade students' class work, laboratory work, assignments, and papers. Conduct research in a particular field of knowledge and publish findings in professional journals, books, and/or electronic media. Prepare course materials such as syllabi, homework assignments, and handouts. Compile, administer, and grade examinations or assign this work to others. Write grant proposals to procure external research funding. Supervise students' laboratory work. Initiate, facilitate, and moderate class discussions. Maintain regularly scheduled office hours in order to advise and assist students. Plan, evaluate, and revise curricula, course content, and course materials and methods of instruction. Advise students on academic and vocational curricula and on career issues. Maintain student attendance records, grades, and other required records. Collaborate with colleagues to address teaching and research issues. Select and obtain materials and supplies such as textbooks and laboratory equipment. Participate in student recruitment, registration, and placement activities. Serve on academic or administrative committees that deal with institutional policies, departmental matters, and academic issues. Perform administrative duties such as serving as department head. **SKILLS**—Science; Programming; Instructing; Mathematics; Technology Design; Critical Thinking; Active Learning; Complex Problem Solving.

GOE—Interest Area: 05. Education and Training. **Work Group:** 05.03. Postsecondary and Adult Teaching and Instructing. **PERSONALITY TYPE:** Investigative. Investigative occupations frequently involve working with ideas and require an extensive amount of thinking. These occupations can involve searching for facts and figuring out problems mentally.

E

EDUCATION/TRAINING PROGRAMS— Aerospace, Aeronautical and Astronautical Engineering; Agricultural/Biological Engineering and Bioengineering; Architectural Engineering; Biomedical/Medical Engineering; Ceramic Sciences and Engineering; Chemical Engineering; Civil Engineering, General; Civil Engineering, Other; Computer Engineering, General; Computer Engineering, Other; Computer Hardware Engineering; Computer Software Engineering; Construction Engineering; Electrical, Electronics and Communications Engineering; others. **RELATED KNOWLEDGE/COURSES—Engineering and Technology:** Knowledge of the practical application of engineering science and technology. This includes applying principles, techniques, procedures, and equipment to the design and production of various goods and services. **Design:** Knowledge of design techniques, tools, and principles involved in production of precision technical plans, blueprints, drawings, and models. **Physics:** Knowledge and prediction of physical principles and laws and their interrelationships and applications to understanding fluid, material, and atmospheric dynamics and mechanical, electrical, atomic, and subatomic structures and processes. **Education and Training:** Knowledge of principles and methods for curriculum and training design, teaching and instruction for individuals and groups, and the measurement of training effects. **Mathematics:** Knowledge of arithmetic, algebra, geometry, calculus, and statistics and their applications. **Computers and Electronics:** Knowledge of circuit boards, processors, chips, electronic equipment, and computer hardware and software, including applications and programming.

English Language and Literature Teachers, Postsecondary

- Annual Earnings: $49,480
- Growth: 32.2%
- Annual Job Openings: 329,000
- Self-Employed: 0.4%
- Part-Time: 27.3%
- Education/Training Required: Master's degree

Our sources did not provide separate job openings data for this occupation. The job openings listed here are shared with 35 other postsecondary teaching occupations. For a complete list, see the beginning of this section.

Industries in Which Income Is Highest

Industry	Average Annual Wage	Number Employed
Educational Services	$49,530	58,530

Metropolitan Areas Where Income Is Highest

Metropolitan Area	Average Annual Wage	Number Employed
San Jose–Sunnyvale–Santa Clara, CA	$80,260	250
Bakersfield, CA	$72,780	70
San Diego–Carlsbad–San Marcos, CA	$69,870	670
Los Angeles–Long Beach–Santa Ana, CA	$67,810	1,170
Riverside–San Bernardino–Ontario, CA	$66,770	380

Teach courses in English language and literature, including linguistics and comparative literature. Initiate, facilitate, and moderate classroom discussions. Evaluate and grade students' class work, assignments, and papers. Prepare course materials such as syllabi, homework assignments, and handouts. Prepare and deliver lectures to undergraduate and/or graduate students on topics such as poetry, novel structure, and translation and adaptation. Maintain student attendance records, grades, and other required records. Plan, evaluate, and revise curricula, course content, and course materials and methods of instruction. Compile, administer, and grade examinations or assign this work to others. Maintain regularly scheduled office hours in order to advise and assist students. Keep abreast of developments in their field by reading current literature, talking with colleagues, and participating in professional conferences. Select and obtain materials and supplies such as textbooks. Advise students on academic and vocational curricula and on career issues. Conduct research in a particular field of knowledge and publish findings in professional journals, books, and/or electronic media. Collaborate with colleagues to address teaching and research issues.

Serve on academic or administrative committees that deal with institutional policies, departmental matters, and academic issues. Participate in campus and community events. Participate in student recruitment, registration, and placement activities. Compile bibliographies of specialized materials for outside reading assignments. Supervise undergraduate and/or graduate teaching, internship, and research work. Provide assistance to students in college writing centers. Perform administrative duties such as serving as department head. Recruit, train, and supervise student writing instructors. Act as advisers to student organizations. **SKILLS**—Instructing; Learning Strategies; Social Perceptiveness; Persuasion; Writing; Active Learning; Critical Thinking; Reading Comprehension.

GOE—Interest Area: 05. Education and Training. **Work Group:** 05.03. Postsecondary and Adult Teaching and Instructing. **PERSONALITY TYPE:** Artistic. Artistic occupations frequently involve working with forms, designs, and patterns. They often require self-expression, and the work can be done without following a clear set of rules.

EDUCATION/TRAINING PROGRAMS—American Literature (Canadian); American Literature (United States); Comparative Literature; Creative Writing; English Composition; English Language and Literature, General; English Language and Literature/Letters, Other; English Literature (British and Commonwealth); Technical and Business Writing. **RELATED KNOWLEDGE/COURSES**—**Philosophy and Theology:** Knowledge of different philosophical systems and religions. This includes their basic principles, values, ethics, ways of thinking, customs, and practices and their impact on human culture. **Education and Training:** Knowledge of principles and methods for curriculum and training design, teaching and instruction for individuals and groups, and the measurement of training effects. **English Language:** Knowledge of the structure and content of the English language, including the meaning and spelling of words, rules of composition, and grammar. **History and Archeology:** Knowledge of historical events and their causes, indicators, and effects on civilizations and cultures. **Sociology and Anthropology:** Knowledge of group behavior and dynamics, societal trends and influences, human migrations, ethnicity, and cultures and their history and origins. **Communications and Media:** Knowledge of media production, communication, and

dissemination techniques and methods. This includes alternative ways to inform and entertain via written, oral, and visual media.

Environmental Compliance Inspectors

- Annual Earnings: $49,360
- Growth: 11.6%
- Annual Job Openings: 17,000
- Self-Employed: 0.0%
- Part-Time: 5.1%
- Education/Training Required: Long-term on-the-job training

The job openings listed here are shared with Coroners, Equal Opportunity Representatives and Officers, Government Property Inspectors and Investigators, Licensing Examiners and Inspectors, and Pressure Vessel Inspectors.

Industries in Which Income Is Highest

Industry	Average Annual Wage	Number Employed
Postal Service	$72,700	1,710
Utilities	$66,390	1,310
Securities, Commodity Contracts, and Other Financial Investments and Related Activities	$64,490	5,130
Computer and Electronic Product Manufacturing	$59,540	1,390
Telecommunications	$59,310	2,620

Metropolitan Areas Where Income Is Highest

Metropolitan Area	Average Annual Wage	Number Employed
Kankakee–Bradley, IL	$81,020	170
Brunswick, GA	$79,710	340
San Jose–Sunnyvale–Santa Clara, CA	$67,550	930
San Francisco–Oakland–Fremont, CA	$64,010	3,320
Santa Rosa–Petaluma, CA	$63,660	410

E

Inspect and investigate sources of pollution to protect the public and environment and ensure conformance with Federal, State, and local regulations and ordinances. Analyze and implement state, federal or local requirements as necessary to maintain approved pretreatment, pollution prevention, and storm water runoff programs. Conduct research on hazardous waste management projects in order to determine the magnitude of problems, and treatment or disposal alternatives and costs. Determine the nature of code violations and actions to be taken, and issue written notices of violation; participate in enforcement hearings as necessary. Determine sampling locations and methods, and collect water or wastewater samples for analysis, preserving samples with appropriate containers and preservation methods. Determine which sites and violation reports to investigate, and coordinate compliance and enforcement activities with other government agencies. Examine permits, licenses, applications, and records to ensure compliance with licensing requirements. Inform individuals and groups of pollution control regulations and inspection findings, and explain how problems can be corrected. Inspect waste pretreatment, treatment, and disposal facilities and systems for conformance to federal, state, or local regulations. Interview individuals to determine the nature of suspected violations and to obtain evidence of violations. Investigate complaints and suspected violations regarding illegal dumping, pollution, pesticides, product quality, or labeling laws. Learn and observe proper safety precautions, rules, regulations, and practices so that unsafe conditions can be recognized and proper safety protocols implemented. Monitor follow-up actions in cases where violations were found, and review compliance monitoring reports. Observe and record field conditions, gathering, interpreting, and reporting data such as flow meter readings and chemical levels. Perform laboratory tests on samples collected, such as analyzing the content of contaminated wastewater. Prepare, organize, and maintain inspection records. Research and perform calculations related to landscape allowances, discharge volumes, production-based and alternative limits, and wastewater strength classifications, then make recommendations and complete documentation. **SKILLS**—Science; Systems Evaluation; Systems Analysis; Reading Comprehension; Speaking; Negotiation; Critical Thinking; Writing.

GOE—Interest Area: 07. Government and Public Administration. **Work Group:** 07.03. Regulations Enforcement. **PERSONALITY TYPE:** Investigative. Investigative occupations frequently involve working with ideas and require an extensive amount of thinking. These occupations can involve searching for facts and figuring out problems mentally.

EDUCATION/TRAINING PROGRAM—No data available. **RELATED KNOWLEDGE/COURSES**— **Chemistry:** Knowledge of the chemical composition, structure, and properties of substances and of the chemical processes and transformations that they undergo. This includes uses of chemicals, their danger signs, production techniques, and disposal methods. **Public Safety and Security:** Knowledge of relevant equipment, policies, procedures, and strategies to promote effective local, state, or national security operations for the protection of people, data, property, and institutions. **Law and Government:** Knowledge of laws, legal codes, court procedures, precedents, government regulations, executive orders, agency rules, and the democratic political process. **Biology:** Knowledge of plant and animal organisms and their tissues, cells, functions, interdependencies, and interactions with each other and the environment. **Physics:** Knowledge and prediction of physical principles and laws and their interrelationships and applications to understanding fluid, material, and atmospheric dynamics and mechanical, electrical, atomic, and subatomic structures and processes. **Production and Processing:** Knowledge of raw materials, production processes, quality control, costs, and other techniques for maximizing the effective manufacture and distribution of goods.

Environmental Engineers

- Annual Earnings: $68,090
- Growth: 30.0%
- Annual Job Openings: 5,000
- Self-Employed: 0.3%
- Part-Time: 1.8%
- Education/Training Required: Bachelor's degree

Industries in Which Income Is Highest

Industry	Average Annual Wage	Number Employed
Waste Management and Remediation Services	$71,380	2,150
Professional, Scientific, and Technical Services	$67,750	26,690
Federal, State, and Local Government	$66,660	13,790

Metropolitan Areas Where Income Is Highest

Metropolitan Area	Average Annual Wage	Number Employed
Augusta–Richmond County, GA–SC	$86,820	170
Kennewick–Richland–Pasco, WA	$82,600	370
San Jose–Sunnyvale–Santa Clara, CA	$81,190	150
Bakersfield, CA	$80,240	170
San Francisco–Oakland–Fremont, CA	$79,490	1,380

Design, plan, or perform engineering duties in the prevention, control, and remediation of environmental health hazards utilizing various engineering disciplines. Work may include waste treatment, site remediation, or pollution control technology. Prepare, review, and update environmental investigation and recommendation reports. Collaborate with environmental scientists, planners, hazardous waste technicians, engineers, and other specialists, and experts in law and business to address environmental problems. Obtain, update, and maintain plans, permits, and standard operating procedures. Provide technical-level support for environmental remediation and litigation projects, including remediation system design and determination of regulatory applicability. Monitor progress of environmental improvement programs. Inspect industrial and municipal facilities and programs in order to evaluate operational effectiveness and ensure compliance with environmental regulations. Provide administrative support for projects by collecting data, providing project documentation, training staff, and performing other general administrative duties. Develop proposed project objectives and targets, and report to management on progress in attaining them. Advise corporations and government agencies of procedures to follow in cleaning up contaminated sites in order to protect people and the environment. Advise industries and government agencies about environmental policies and standards. Inform company employees and other interested parties of environmental issues. Assess the existing or potential environmental impact of land use projects on air, water, and land. Assist in budget implementation, forecasts, and administration. Develop site-specific health and safety protocols, such as spill contingency plans and methods for loading and transporting waste. Coordinate and manage environmental protection programs and projects, assigning and evaluating work. Serve as liaison with federal, state, and local agencies and officials on issues pertaining to solid and hazardous waste program requirements. Design systems, processes, and equipment for control, management, and remediation of water, air, and soil quality. Prepare hazardous waste manifests and land disposal restriction notifications. Serve on teams conducting multimedia inspections at complex facilities, providing assistance with planning, quality assurance, safety inspection protocols, and sampling. **SKILLS—** Science; Management of Financial Resources; Coordination; Writing; Persuasion; Mathematics; Negotiation; Technology Design.

GOE—Interest Area: 01. Agriculture and Natural Resources. **Work Group:** 01.02. Resource Science/Engineering for Plants, Animals, and the Environment. **PERSONALITY TYPE:** No data available.

EDUCATION/TRAINING PROGRAM— Environmental/Environmental Health Engineering. **RELATED KNOWLEDGE/COURSES—Education and Training:** Knowledge of principles and methods for curriculum and training design, teaching and instruction for individuals and groups, and the measurement of training effects. **Chemistry:** Knowledge of the chemical composition, structure, and properties of substances and of the chemical processes and transformations that they undergo. This includes uses of chemicals, their danger signs, production techniques, and disposal methods. **Biology:** Knowledge of plant and animal organisms and their tissues, cells, functions, interdependencies, and interactions with each other and the environment. **Law and Government:** Knowledge of laws, legal codes, court procedures, precedents, government regulations, executive orders, agency rules, and the democratic political process. **Public Safety and Security:** Knowledge of relevant equipment, policies, procedures, and

E

strategies to promote effective local, state, or national security operations for the protection of people, data, property, and institutions. **Engineering and Technology:** Knowledge of the practical application of engineering science and technology. This includes applying principles, techniques, procedures, and equipment to the design and production of various goods and services.

Environmental Science Teachers, Postsecondary

- Annual Earnings: $60,880
- Growth: 32.2%
- Annual Job Openings: 329,000
- Self-Employed: 0.4%
- Part-Time: 27.3%
- Education/Training Required: Master's degree

Our sources did not provide separate job openings data for this occupation. The job openings listed here are shared with 35 other postsecondary teaching occupations. For a complete list, see the beginning of this section.

Industries in Which Income Is Highest

Industry	Average Annual Wage	Number Employed
Educational Services	$60,630	4,270

Metropolitan Areas Where Income Is Highest

Metropolitan Area	Average Annual Wage	Number Employed
Philadelphia–Camden–Wilmington, PA–NJ–DE–MD	$76,370	200
Minneapolis–St. Paul–Bloomington, MN–WI	$71,520	50
Boston–Cambridge–Quincy, MA–NH	$70,450	100
Chicago–Naperville–Joliet, IL–IN–WI	$66,130	270
New York–Northern New Jersey–Long Island, NY–NJ–PA	$64,300	390

Teach courses in environmental science. Supervise undergraduate and/or graduate teaching, internship, and research work. Conduct research in a particular field of knowledge and publish findings in professional journals, books, and/or electronic media. Keep abreast of developments in their field by reading current literature, talking with colleagues, and participating in professional conferences. Evaluate and grade students' class work, laboratory work, assignments, and papers. Write grant proposals to procure external research funding. Supervise students' laboratory and field work. Prepare course materials such as syllabi, homework assignments, and handouts. Plan, evaluate, and revise curricula, course content, and course materials and methods of instruction. Initiate, facilitate, and moderate classroom discussions. Compile, administer, and grade examinations or assign this work to others. Advise students on academic and vocational curricula and on career issues. Prepare and deliver lectures to undergraduate and/or graduate students on topics such as hazardous waste management, industrial safety, and environmental toxicology. Maintain student attendance records, grades, and other required records. Select and obtain materials and supplies such as textbooks and laboratory equipment. Maintain regularly scheduled office hours in order to advise and assist students. Collaborate with colleagues to address teaching and research issues. Perform administrative duties such as serving as department head. Participate in student recruitment, registration, and placement activities. Provide professional consulting services to government and/or industry. Serve on academic or administrative committees that deal with institutional policies, departmental matters, and academic issues. Compile bibliographies of specialized materials for outside reading assignments. **SKILLS**—Science; Instructing; Writing; Critical Thinking; Active Learning; Reading Comprehension; Management of Financial Resources; Learning Strategies.

GOE—Interest Area: 05. Education and Training. **Work Group:** 05.03. Postsecondary and Adult Teaching and Instructing. **PERSONALITY TYPE:** No data available.

EDUCATION/TRAINING PROGRAMS—Environmental Science; Environmental Studies; Science Teacher Education/General Science Teacher Education. **RELATED KNOWLEDGE/COURSES—Biology:** Knowledge of plant and animal organisms and their tissues, cells, functions, interdependencies, and interactions with each other and the environment. **Geography:** Knowledge of principles and methods for describing the features of land, sea, and air masses, including their physical characteristics; locations; interrelationships; and distribution of plant, animal, and human life. **Education and Training:** Knowledge of principles and methods for curriculum and training design, teaching and instruction for individuals and groups, and the measurement of training effects. **Chemistry:** Knowledge of the chemical composition, structure, and properties of substances and of the chemical processes and transformations that they undergo. This includes uses of chemicals, their danger signs, production techniques, and disposal methods. **English Language:** Knowledge of the structure and content of the English language, including the meaning and spelling of words, rules of composition, and grammar. **History and Archeology:** Knowledge of historical events and their causes, indicators, and effects on civilizations and cultures.

Environmental Scientists and Specialists, Including Health

- ◎ Annual Earnings: $52,630
- ◎ Growth: 17.1%
- ◎ Annual Job Openings: 8,000
- ◎ Self-Employed: 4.2%
- ◎ Part-Time: 5.9%
- ◎ Education/Training Required: Master's degree

Industries in Which Income Is Highest

Industry	Average Annual Wage	Number Employed
Professional, Scientific, and Technical Services	$54,110	28,950
Federal, State, and Local Government	$51,760	33,700
Educational Services	$42,340	3,610

Metropolitan Areas Where Income Is Highest

Metropolitan Area	Average Annual Wage	Number Employed
Kennewick–Richland–Pasco, WA	$80,000	430
Las Vegas–Paradise, NV	$78,340	300
Washington–Arlington–Alexandria, DC–VA–MD–WV	$77,120	3,610
Ann Arbor, MI	$75,830	70
Salinas, CA	$72,730	50

Conduct research or perform investigation for the purpose of identifying, abating, or eliminating sources of pollutants or hazards that affect either the environment or the health of the population. Utilizing knowledge of various scientific disciplines may collect, synthesize, study, report, and take action based on data derived from measurements or observations of air, food, soil, water, and other sources. Conduct environmental audits and inspections, and investigations of violations. Evaluate violations or problems discovered during inspections in order to determine appropriate regulatory actions or to provide advice on the development and prosecution of regulatory cases. Communicate scientific and technical information through oral briefings, written documents, workshops, conferences, and public hearings. Review and implement environmental technical standards, guidelines, policies, and formal regulations that meet all appropriate requirements. Provide technical guidance, support, and oversight to environmental programs, industry, and the public. Provide advice on proper standards and regulations and the development of policies, strategies, and codes of practice for environmental management. Analyze data to determine validity, quality, and scientific significance, and to interpret correlations between human activities and environmental effects. Collect, synthesize, and analyze data derived from pollution emission measurements, atmospheric monitoring, meteorological and mineralogical information, and soil or water samples. Determine data collection methods to be employed in research projects and surveys. Prepare charts or graphs from data samples, and provide summary information on the environmental relevance of the data. Develop the technical portions of legal documents, administrative orders, or consent decrees. Investigate and report on accidents affecting the environment. Monitor environmental

E

impacts of development activities. Supervise environmental technologists and technicians. Develop programs designed to obtain the most productive, non-damaging use of land. Research sources of pollution to determine their effects on the environment and to develop theories or methods of pollution abatement or control. Monitor effects of pollution and land degradation, and recommend means of prevention or control. Design and direct studies to obtain technical environmental information about planned projects. Conduct applied research on topics such as waste control and treatment and pollution control methods. **SKILLS**—Science; Service Orientation; Negotiation; Coordination; Persuasion; Reading Comprehension; Active Learning; Complex Problem Solving.

GOE—Interest Area: 15. Scientific Research, Engineering, and Mathematics. **Work Group:** 15.03. Life Sciences. **PERSONALITY TYPE:** Investigative. Investigative occupations frequently involve working with ideas and require an extensive amount of thinking. These occupations can involve searching for facts and figuring out problems mentally.

EDUCATION/TRAINING   PROGRAMS—Environmental Science; Environmental Studies. **RELATED KNOWLEDGE/COURSES—Biology:** Knowledge of plant and animal organisms and their tissues, cells, functions, interdependencies, and interactions with each other and the environment. **Geography:** Knowledge of principles and methods for describing the features of land, sea, and air masses, including their physical characteristics; locations; interrelationships; and distribution of plant, animal, and human life. **Chemistry:** Knowledge of the chemical composition, structure, and properties of substances and of the chemical processes and transformations that they undergo. This includes uses of chemicals, their danger signs, production techniques, and disposal methods. **Law and Government:** Knowledge of laws, legal codes, court procedures, precedents, government regulations, executive orders, agency rules, and the democratic political process. **Customer and Personal Service:** Knowledge of principles and processes for providing customer and personal services. This includes customer needs assessment, meeting quality standards for services, and evaluation of customer satisfaction. **Education and Training:** Knowledge of principles and methods for curriculum and training design, teaching and instruction for individuals and groups, and the measurement of training effects.

Epidemiologists

- Annual Earnings: $52,170
- Growth: 26.2%
- Annual Job Openings: 1,000
- Self-Employed: 0.4%
- Part-Time: 5.8%
- Education/Training Required: Doctoral degree

Industries in Which Income Is Highest

Industry	Average Annual Wage	Number Employed
Professional, Scientific, and Technical Services	$68,420	310
Ambulatory Health Care Services	$66,130	50
Hospitals	$59,850	550
Religious, Grantmaking, Civic, Professional, and Similar Organizations	$52,070	60
Federal, State, and Local Government	$48,670	2,190

Metropolitan Areas Where Income Is Highest

Metropolitan Area	Average Annual Wage	Number Employed
San Francisco–Oakland–Fremont, CA	$80,270	100
Hartford–West Hartford–East Hartford, CT	$67,460	190
Minneapolis–St. Paul–Bloomington, MN–WI	$62,760	100
Washington–Arlington–Alexandria, DC–VA–MD–WV	$61,730	50
Seattle–Tacoma–Bellevue, WA	$61,090	130

Investigate and describe the determinants and distribution of disease, disability, and other health outcomes and develop the means for prevention and control. Oversee public health programs, including statistical analysis, health care planning, surveillance systems, and public health improvement. Investigate diseases or parasites to determine cause and risk factors, progress, life cycle, or mode of transmission. Plan and direct studies to investigate human or animal disease, preventive methods, and treatments for disease. Plan, administer and evaluate health safety standards and programs to improve public health, conferring with health department, industry personnel, physicians and others. Provide expertise in the design, management and evaluation of study protocols and health status questionnaires, sample selection and analysis. Conduct research to develop methodologies, instrumentation and procedures for medical application, analyzing data and presenting findings. Consult with and advise physicians, educators, researchers, government health officials and others regarding medical applications of sciences, such as physics, biology, and chemistry. Supervise professional, technical and clerical personnel. Identify and analyze public health issues related to foodborne parasitic diseases and their impact on public policies or scientific studies or surveys. Teach principles of medicine and medical and laboratory procedures to physicians, residents, students, and technicians. Standardize drug dosages, methods of immunization, and procedures for manufacture of drugs and medicinal compounds. Prepare and analyze samples to study effects of drugs, gases, pesticides, or microorganisms on cell structure and tissue. **SKILLS**—Science; Programming; Reading Comprehension; Persuasion; Active Learning; Writing; Social Perceptiveness; Complex Problem Solving.

GOE—Interest Area: 15. Scientific Research, Engineering, and Mathematics. **Work Group:** 15.03. Life Sciences. **PERSONALITY TYPE:** Investigative. Investigative occupations frequently involve working with ideas and require an extensive amount of thinking. These occupations can involve searching for facts and figuring out problems mentally.

EDUCATION/TRAINING PROGRAMS—Cell/Cellular Biology and Histology; Epidemiology; Medical Scientist (MS, PhD); This is a broad SOC occupation. For related CIP programs, see detailed O*NET occupations listed below. **RELATED KNOWLEDGE/COURSES—Biology:** Knowledge of plant and animal organisms and their tissues, cells, functions, interdependencies, and interactions with each other and the environment. **Sociology and Anthropology:** Knowledge of group behavior and dynamics, societal trends and influences, human migrations, ethnicity, and cultures and their history and origins. **Medicine and Dentistry:** Knowledge of the information and techniques needed to diagnose and treat human injuries, diseases, and deformities. This includes symptoms, treatment alternatives, drug properties and

interactions, and preventive health-care measures. **Education and Training:** Knowledge of principles and methods for curriculum and training design, teaching and instruction for individuals and groups, and the measurement of training effects. **English Language:** Knowledge of the structure and content of the English language, including the meaning and spelling of words, rules of composition, and grammar. **Computers and Electronics:** Knowledge of circuit boards, processors, chips, electronic equipment, and computer hardware and software, including applications and programming.

Equal Opportunity Representatives and Officers

- Annual Earnings: $49,360
- Growth: 11.6%
- Annual Job Openings: 17,000
- Self-Employed: 0.0%
- Part-Time: 5.1%
- Education/Training Required: Long-term on-the-job training

The job openings listed here are shared with Coroners, Environmental Compliance Inspectors, Government Property Inspectors and Investigators, Licensing Examiners and Inspectors, and Pressure Vessel Inspectors.

Industries in Which Income Is Highest

Industry	Average Annual Wage	Number Employed
Postal Service	$72,700	1,710
Utilities	$66,390	1,310
Securities, Commodity Contracts, and Other Financial Investments and Related Activities	$64,490	5,130
Computer and Electronic Product Manufacturing	$59,540	1,390
Telecommunications	$59,310	2,620

E

Metropolitan Areas Where Income Is Highest

Metropolitan Area	Average Annual Wage	Number Employed
Kankakee–Bradley, IL	$81,020	170
Brunswick, GA	$79,710	340
San Jose–Sunnyvale–Santa Clara, CA	$67,550	930
San Francisco–Oakland–Fremont, CA	$64,010	3,320
Santa Rosa–Petaluma, CA	$63,660	410

Monitor and evaluate compliance with equal opportunity laws, guidelines, and policies to ensure that employment practices and contracting arrangements give equal opportunity without regard to race, religion, color, national origin, sex, age, or disability. Conduct surveys and evaluate findings in order to determine if systematic discrimination exists. Counsel newly hired members of minority and disadvantaged groups, informing them about details of civil rights laws. Interpret civil rights laws and equal opportunity regulations for individuals and employers. Investigate employment practices and alleged violations of laws, in order to document and correct discriminatory factors. Meet with persons involved in equal opportunity complaints in order to verify case information, and to arbitrate and settle disputes. Prepare reports of selection, survey, and other statistics, and recommendations for corrective action. Provide information, technical assistance, and training to supervisors, managers, and employees on topics such as employee supervision, hiring, grievance procedures, and staff development. Review company contracts to determine actions required to meet governmental equal opportunity provisions. Study equal opportunity complaints in order to clarify issues. Act as liaisons between minority placement agencies and employers, or between job search committees and other equal opportunity administrators. Consult with community representatives to develop technical assistance agreements in accordance with governmental regulations. Coordinate, monitor, and revise complaint procedures to ensure timely processing and review of complaints. Develop guidelines for non-discriminatory employment practices, and monitor their implementation and impact. Meet with job search committees or coordinators to explain the role of the equal opportunity coordinator, to provide resources for advertising, and to explain expectations for future contacts. Participate in the recruitment of employees through job fairs, career days, and advertising plans.

Verify that all job descriptions are submitted for review and approval, and that descriptions meet regulatory standards. **SKILLS**—Negotiation; Writing; Speaking; Persuasion; Systems Analysis; Systems Evaluation; Active Listening; Reading Comprehension.

GOE—Interest Area: 07. Government and Public Administration. **Work Group:** 07.03. Regulations Enforcement. **PERSONALITY TYPE:** Social. Social occupations frequently involve working with, communicating with, and teaching people. These occupations often involve helping or providing service to others.

EDUCATION/TRAINING PROGRAM—No data available. **RELATED KNOWLEDGE/COURSES**—**Personnel and Human Resources:** Knowledge of principles and procedures for personnel recruitment, selection, training, compensation and benefits, labor relations and negotiation, and personnel information systems. **Law and Government:** Knowledge of laws, legal codes, court procedures, precedents, government regulations, executive orders, agency rules, and the democratic political process. **English Language:** Knowledge of the structure and content of the English language, including the meaning and spelling of words, rules of composition, and grammar. **Communications and Media:** Knowledge of media production, communication, and dissemination techniques and methods. This includes alternative ways to inform and entertain via written, oral, and visual media. **Mathematics:** Knowledge of arithmetic, algebra, geometry, calculus, and statistics and their applications.

Family and General Practitioners

- Annual Earnings: $140,400
- Growth: 24.0%
- Annual Job Openings: 41,000
- Self-Employed: 11.0%
- Part-Time: 9.6%
- Education/Training Required: First professional degree

The job openings listed here are shared with Anesthesiologists; Internists, General; Obstetricians and Gynecologists; Pediatricians, General; Psychiatrists; and Surgeons.

Industries in Which Income Is Highest

Industry	Average Annual Wage	Number Employed
Ambulatory Health Care Services	More than $146,500	81,590
Hospitals	$135,290	18,470
Federal, State, and Local Government	$101,090	4,980
Educational Services	$44,440	5,230

Metropolitan Areas Where Income Is Highest

Metropolitan Area	Average Annual Wage	Number Employed
Miami–Fort Lauderdale–Miami Beach, FL	More than $146,500	4,780
Dallas–Fort Worth–Arlington, TX	More than $146,500	1,770
Phoenix–Mesa–Scottsdale, AZ	More than $146,500	1,540
San Francisco–Oakland–Fremont, CA	More than $146,500	1,240
Baltimore–Towson, MD	More than $146,500	1,050

Diagnose, treat, and help prevent diseases and injuries that commonly occur in the general population. Prescribe or administer treatment, therapy, medication, vaccination, and other specialized medical care to treat or prevent illness, disease, or injury. Order, perform and interpret tests, and analyze records, reports and examination information to diagnose patients' condition. Monitor the patients' conditions and progress and re-evaluate treatments as necessary. Collect, record, and maintain patient information, such as medical history, reports, and examination results. Explain procedures and discuss test results or prescribed treatments with patients. Advise patients and community members concerning diet, activity, hygiene, and disease prevention. Refer patients to medical specialists or other practitioners when necessary. Direct and coordinate activities of nurses, students, assistants, specialists, therapists, and other medical staff. Coordinate work with nurses, social workers, rehabilitation therapists, pharmacists, psychologists and other health care providers. Deliver babies. Operate on patients to remove, repair, or improve functioning of diseased or injured body parts and systems. Plan, implement, or administer health programs or standards in hospital, business, or community for information, prevention, or treatment of injury or illness. Prepare reports for government or management of birth, death, and disease statistics, workforce evaluations, or medical status of individuals. Conduct research to study anatomy and develop or test medications, treatments, or procedures to prevent or control disease or injury. **SKILLS**—Social Perceptiveness; Persuasion; Science; Service Orientation; Instructing; Reading Comprehension; Complex Problem Solving; Active Learning.

GOE—Interest Area: 08. Health Science. **Work Group:** 08.02. Medicine and Surgery. **PERSONALITY TYPE:** Investigative. Investigative occupations frequently involve working with ideas and require an extensive amount of thinking. These occupations can involve searching for facts and figuring out problems mentally.

EDUCATION/TRAINING PROGRAMS—Family Medicine; Medicine (MD); Osteopathic Medicine/Osteopathy (DO). **RELATED KNOWLEDGE/COURSES—Medicine and Dentistry:** Knowledge of the information and techniques needed to diagnose and treat human injuries, diseases, and deformities. This includes symptoms, treatment alternatives, drug properties and interactions, and preventive health-care measures. **Therapy and Counseling:** Knowledge of principles, methods, and procedures for diagnosis, treatment, and rehabilitation of physical and mental dysfunctions and for career counseling and guidance. **Biology:** Knowledge of plant and animal organisms and their tissues, cells, functions, interdependencies, and interactions with each other and the environment. **Psychology:** Knowledge of human behavior and performance; individual differences in ability, personality, and interests; learning and motivation; psychological research methods; and the assessment and treatment of behavioral and affective disorders. **Customer and Personal Service:** Knowledge of principles and processes for providing customer and personal services. This includes customer needs assessment, meeting quality standards for services, and evaluation of customer satisfaction. **Sociology and Anthropology:** Knowledge of group behavior and dynamics, societal trends and influences, human migrations, ethnicity, and cultures and their history and origins.

Fashion Designers

- Annual Earnings: $60,860
- Growth: 8.4%
- Annual Job Openings: 2,000
- Self-Employed: 26.5%
- Part-Time: 21.2%
- Education/Training Required: Bachelor's degree

Industries in Which Income Is Highest

Industry	Average Annual Wage	Number Employed
Apparel Manufacturing	$68,840	3,740
Management of Companies and Enterprises	$66,420	1,710
Merchant Wholesalers, Nondurable Goods	$58,590	4,430

Metropolitan Areas Where Income Is Highest

Metropolitan Area	Average Annual Wage	Number Employed
New York–Northern New Jersey–Long Island, NY–NJ–PA	$68,990	6,530
St. Louis, MO–IL	$62,610	100
Boston–Cambridge–Quincy, MA–NH	$62,130	590
Seattle–Tacoma–Bellevue, WA	$61,360	160
Philadelphia–Camden–Wilmington, PA–NJ–DE–MD	$57,780	250

Design clothing and accessories. Create original garments or design garments that follow well established fashion trends. May develop the line of color and kinds of materials. Attend fashion shows and review garment magazines and manuals in order to gather information about fashion trends and consumer preferences. Design custom clothing and accessories for individuals, retailers, or theatrical, television, or film productions. Draw patterns for articles designed; then cut patterns, and cut material according to patterns, using measuring instruments and scissors. Examine sample garments on and off models; then modify designs to achieve desired effects. Select materials and production techniques to be used for products. Sketch rough and detailed drawings of apparel or accessories, and write specifications such as color schemes, construction, material types, and accessory requirements. Adapt other designers' ideas for the mass market. Collaborate with other designers to coordinate special products and designs. Confer with sales and management executives or with clients in order to discuss design ideas. Determine prices for styles. Develop a group of products and/or accessories, and market them through venues such as boutiques or mail-order catalogs. Direct and coordinate workers involved in drawing and cutting patterns and constructing samples or finished garments. Identify target markets for designs, looking at factors such as age, gender, and socioeconomic status. Provide sample garments to agents and sales representatives, and arrange for showings of sample garments at sales meetings or fashion shows. Purchase new or used clothing and accessory items as needed to complete designs. Read scripts and consult directors and other production staff in order to develop design concepts and plan productions. Research the styles and periods of clothing needed for film or theatrical productions. Sew together sections of material to form mockups or samples of garments or articles, using sewing equipment. Visit textile showrooms to keep up-to-date on the latest fabrics. Test fabrics or oversee testing so that garment care labels can be created. **SKILLS**—Systems Analysis; Management of Financial Resources; Operations Analysis; Persuasion; Negotiation; Systems Evaluation; Management of Material Resources; Management of Personnel Resources.

GOE—Interest Area: 03. Arts and Communication. **Work Group:** 03.05. Design. **PERSONALITY TYPE:** Artistic. Artistic occupations frequently involve working with forms, designs, and patterns. They often require self-expression, and the work can be done without following a clear set of rules.

EDUCATION/TRAINING PROGRAMS— Apparel and Textile Manufacture; Fashion and Fabric Consultant; Fashion/Apparel Design; Textile Science. **RELATED KNOWLEDGE/COURSES—Fine Arts:** Knowledge of the theory and techniques required to compose, produce, and perform works of music, dance, visual arts, drama, and sculpture. **Design:** Knowledge of design techniques, tools, and principles involved in production of precision technical plans, blueprints, drawings, and models. **Sales and Marketing:** Knowledge of principles and methods for showing, promoting, and selling products or services. This includes marketing strategy and tactics, product demonstration, sales techniques, and sales control systems. **Education and Training:** Knowledge of principles and methods for curriculum and training design, teaching and instruction for individuals and groups, and the measurement of training effects. **Customer and Personal Service:** Knowledge of principles and processes for providing customer and personal services. This includes customer needs assessment, meeting quality standards for services, and evaluation of customer satisfaction.

Film and Video Editors

- ⊚ Annual Earnings: $46,930
- ⊚ Growth: 18.6%
- ⊚ Annual Job Openings: 3,000
- ⊚ Self-Employed: 18.2%
- ⊚ Part-Time: 27.6%
- ⊚ Education/Training Required: Bachelor's degree

Industries in Which Income Is Highest

Industry	Average Annual Wage	Number Employed
Motion Picture and Sound Recording Industries	$52,400	8,930
Broadcasting (Except Internet)	$41,730	3,830

Metropolitan Areas Where Income Is Highest

Metropolitan Area	Average Annual Wage	Number Employed
Las Vegas–Paradise, NV	$92,150	290
Denver–Aurora, CO	$77,540	80
Chicago–Naperville–Joliet, IL–IN–WI	$59,860	270
New York–Northern New Jersey–Long Island, NY–NJ–PA	$58,910	2,580
Rochester, NY	$57,770	50

Edit motion picture soundtracks, film, and video. Cut shot sequences to different angles at specific points in scenes, making each individual cut as fluid and seamless as possible. Study scripts to become familiar with production concepts and requirements. Edit films and videotapes to insert music, dialogue, and sound effects, to arrange films into sequences, and to correct errors, using editing equipment. Select and combine the most effective shots of each scene in order to form a logical and smoothly running story. Mark frames where a particular shot or piece of sound is to begin or end. Determine the specific audio and visual effects and music necessary to complete films. Verify key numbers and time codes on materials. Organize and string together raw footage into a continuous whole according to scripts and/or the instructions of directors and producers. Review assembled films or edited videotapes on screens or monitors in order to determine if corrections are necessary. Program computerized graphic effects. Review footage sequence by sequence in order to become familiar with it before assembling it into a final product. Set up and operate computer editing systems, electronic titling systems, video switching equipment, and digital video effects units in order to produce a final product. Record needed sounds, or obtain them from sound effects libraries. Confer with producers and directors concerning layout or editing approaches needed to increase dramatic or entertainment value of productions. Manipulate plot, score, sound, and graphics to make the parts into a continuous whole, working closely with people in audio, visual, music, optical and/or special effects departments. Supervise and coordinate activities of workers engaged in film editing, assembling, and recording activities. Trim film segments to specified lengths, and reassemble segments in sequences that present stories with maximum effect. Develop post-production models for films. Piece sounds together to develop film soundtracks. Conduct film screenings for directors and members of production staffs. Collaborate with music editors to select appropriate passages of music and develop production scores. **SKILLS**—Equipment Selection; Operations Analysis; Equipment Maintenance; Active Learning; Coordination; Operation and Control; Time Management; Installation.

GOE—Interest Area: 03. Arts and Communication. **Work Group:** 03.09. Media Technology. **PERSONALITY TYPE:** Artistic. Artistic occupations frequently involve working with forms, designs, and patterns. They often require self-expression, and the work can be done without following a clear set of rules.

EDUCATION/TRAINING PROGRAMS—Audiovisual Communications Technologies/Technicians, Other; Cinematography and Film/Video Production; Communications Technology/Technician; Photojournalism; Radio and Television; Radio and

Television Broadcasting Technology/Technician. **RELATED KNOWLEDGE/COURSES—Fine Arts:** Knowledge of the theory and techniques required to compose, produce, and perform works of music, dance, visual arts, drama, and sculpture. **Communications and Media:** Knowledge of media production, communication, and dissemination techniques and methods. This includes alternative ways to inform and entertain via written, oral, and visual media. **Computers and Electronics:** Knowledge of circuit boards, processors, chips, electronic equipment, and computer hardware and software, including applications and programming. **Design:** Knowledge of design techniques, tools, and principles involved in production of precision technical plans, blueprints, drawings, and models. **Education and Training:** Knowledge of principles and methods for curriculum and training design, teaching and instruction for individuals and groups, and the measurement of training effects. **English Language:** Knowledge of the structure and content of the English language, including the meaning and spelling of words, rules of composition, and grammar.

Financial Analysts

- ◎ Annual Earnings: $63,860
- ◎ Growth: 17.3%
- ◎ Annual Job Openings: 28,000
- ◎ Self-Employed: 6.7%
- ◎ Part-Time: 9.7%
- ◎ Education/Training Required: Bachelor's degree

Industries in Which Income Is Highest

Industry	Average Annual Wage	Number Employed
Securities, Commodity Contracts, and Other Financial Investments and Related Activities	$76,260	40,980
Oil and Gas Extraction	$69,140	1,590
Merchant Wholesalers, Durable Goods	$67,740	2,320
Computer and Electronic Product Manufacturing	$67,490	7,580
Utilities	$67,410	1,480

Metropolitan Areas Where Income Is Highest

Metropolitan Area	Average Annual Wage	Number Employed
Bridgeport–Stamford–Norwalk, CT	$104,100	3,000
Lafayette, LA	$91,320	50
Santa Rosa–Petaluma, CA	$85,300	180
San Francisco–Oakland–Fremont, CA	$83,210	4,720
Salinas, CA	$79,190	50

Conduct quantitative analyses of information affecting investment programs of public or private institutions. Assemble spreadsheets and draw charts and graphs used to illustrate technical reports, using computer. Analyze financial information to produce forecasts of business, industry, and economic conditions for use in making investment decisions. Maintain knowledge and stay abreast of developments in the fields of industrial technology, business, finance, and economic theory. Interpret data affecting investment programs, such as price, yield, stability, future trends in investment risks, and economic influences. Monitor fundamental economic, industrial, and corporate developments through the analysis of information obtained from financial publications and services, investment banking firms, government agencies, trade publications, company sources, and personal interviews. Recommend investments and investment timing to companies, investment firm staff, or the investing public. Determine the prices at which securities should be syndicated and offered to the public. Prepare plans of action for investment based on financial analyses. Evaluate and compare the relative quality of various securities in a given industry. Present oral and written reports on general economic trends, individual corporations, and entire industries. Contact brokers and purchase investments for companies, according to company policy. Collaborate with investment bankers to attract new corporate clients to securities firms. **SKILLS**—Management of Financial Resources; Judgment and Decision Making; Time Management; Complex Problem Solving; Active Learning; Programming; Systems Evaluation; Mathematics.

GOE—Interest Area: 06. Finance and Insurance. **Work Group:** 06.02. Finance/Insurance Investigation and Analysis. **PERSONALITY TYPE:** Investigative. Investigative occupations frequently involve working with ideas and require an extensive amount of thinking.

These occupations can involve searching for facts and figuring out problems mentally.

EDUCATION/TRAINING PROGRAMS— Accounting and Business/Management; Accounting and Finance; Finance, General. **RELATED KNOWL-EDGE/COURSES—Economics and Accounting:** Knowledge of economic and accounting principles and practices, the financial markets, banking, and the analysis and reporting of financial data. **Mathematics:** Knowledge of arithmetic, algebra, geometry, calculus, and statistics and their applications. **Law and Government:** Knowledge of laws, legal codes, court procedures, precedents, government regulations, executive orders, agency rules, and the democratic political process. **Administration and Management:** Knowledge of business and management principles involved in strategic planning, resource allocation, human resources modeling, leadership technique, production methods, and coordination of people and resources. **English Language:** Knowledge of the structure and content of the English language, including the meaning and spelling of words, rules of composition, and grammar. **Clerical Practices:** Knowledge of administrative and clerical procedures and systems such as word processing, managing files and records, stenography and transcription, designing forms, and other office procedures and terminology.

Financial Examiners

- ◎ Annual Earnings: $63,090
- ◎ Growth: 9.5%
- ◎ Annual Job Openings: 3,000
- ◎ Self-Employed: 0.0%
- ◎ Part-Time: 0.0%
- ◎ Education/Training Required: Bachelor's degree

Industries in Which Income Is Highest

Industry	Average Annual Wage	Number Employed
Monetary Authorities—Central Bank	$75,060	1,520
Federal, State, and Local Government	$74,370	8,530
Securities, Commodity Contracts, and Other Financial Investments and Related Activities	$60,200	2,660
Insurance Carriers and Related Activities	$52,470	1,450
Credit Intermediation and Related Activities	$51,020	5,470

Metropolitan Areas Where Income Is Highest

Metropolitan Area	Average Annual Wage	Number Employed
Washington–Arlington–Alexandria, DC–VA–MD–WV	$92,870	470
Kansas City, MO–KS	$89,640	320
San Francisco–Oakland–Fremont, CA	$85,170	630
Jackson, MS	$82,150	50
Tampa–St. Petersburg–Clearwater, FL	$81,180	110

Enforce or ensure compliance with laws and regulations governing financial and securities institutions and financial and real estate transactions. May examine, verify correctness of, or establish authenticity of records. Investigate activities of institutions in order to enforce laws and regulations and to ensure legality of transactions and operations or financial solvency. Review and analyze new, proposed, or revised laws, regulations, policies, and procedures in order to interpret their meaning and determine their impact. Plan, supervise, and review work of assigned subordinates. Recommend actions to ensure compliance with laws and regulations, or to protect solvency of institutions. Examine the minutes of meetings of directors, stockholders and committees in order to investigate the specific authority extended at various levels of management. Prepare reports, exhibits and other supporting schedules that detail an institution's safety and soundness, compliance with laws and regulations, and recommended solutions to questionable financial conditions. Review balance sheets, operating income and expense accounts, and loan documentation in order to confirm institution assets and liabilities. Review audit reports of internal and external auditors in order to monitor adequacy of scope of reports or to discover specific weaknesses in internal routines. Train other examiners in the financial examination process. Establish guidelines for procedures and policies that comply with new and revised regulations, and direct their implementation. Direct and participate in formal and informal meetings with bank directors, trustees, senior management, counsels, outside accountants and consultants in order to gather information and discuss findings. Verify and inspect cash reserves, assigned collateral, and bank-owned securities in order to check internal control procedures. Review applications for mergers, acquisitions, establishment of new institutions, acceptance in Federal Reserve System, or registration of securities sales in order to determine their public interest value and conformance to regulations, and recommend acceptance or rejection. Resolve problems concerning the overall financial integrity of banking institutions including loan investment portfolios, capital, earnings, and specific or large troubled accounts. **SKILLS**—Monitoring; Management of Financial Resources; Persuasion; Time Management; Systems Analysis; Quality Control Analysis; Systems Evaluation; Learning Strategies.

GOE—**Interest Area:** 07. Government and Public Administration. **Work Group:** 07.03. Regulations Enforcement. **PERSONALITY TYPE:** Enterprising. Enterprising occupations frequently involve starting up and carrying out projects. These occupations can involve leading people and making many decisions. They sometimes require risk taking and often deal with business.

EDUCATION/TRAINING PROGRAMS— Accounting; Taxation. **RELATED KNOWLEDGE/ COURSES**—**Economics and Accounting:** Knowledge of economic and accounting principles and practices, the financial markets, banking, and the analysis and reporting of financial data. **Law and Government:** Knowledge of laws, legal codes, court procedures, precedents, government regulations, executive orders, agency rules, and the democratic political process. **Clerical Practices:** Knowledge of administrative and clerical procedures and systems such as word processing, managing files and records, stenography and transcription, designing forms, and other office procedures and terminology. **Mathematics:** Knowledge of arithmetic, algebra, geometry, calculus, and statistics and their applications. **Education and Training:** Knowledge of principles and methods for curriculum

and training design, teaching and instruction for individuals and groups, and the measurement of training effects. **Administration and Management:** Knowledge of business and management principles involved in strategic planning, resource allocation, human resources modeling, leadership technique, production methods, and coordination of people and resources.

Financial Managers, Branch or Department

- Annual Earnings: $86,280
- Growth: 14.8%
- Annual Job Openings: 63,000
- Self-Employed: 3.2%
- Part-Time: 4.3%
- Education/Training Required: Work experience plus degree

Industries in Which Income Is Highest

Industry	Average Annual Wage	Number Employed
Securities, Commodity Contracts, and Other Financial Investments and Related Activities	$132,390	31,320
Funds, Trusts, and Other Financial Vehicles	$107,590	1,860
Computer and Electronic Product Manufacturing	$100,940	9,420
Management of Companies and Enterprises	$99,280	37,340
Oil and Gas Extraction	$98,840	2,050

Metropolitan Areas Where Income Is Highest

Metropolitan Area	Average Annual Wage	Number Employed
Bridgeport–Stamford–Norwalk, CT	$125,300	3,070
New York–Northern New Jersey–Long Island, NY–NJ–PA	$125,200	53,490
San Jose–Sunnyvale–Santa Clara, CA	$119,540	6,360
Danbury, CT	$113,680	270
Burlington–South Burlington, VT	$107,760	240

Direct and coordinate financial activities of workers in a branch, office, or department of an establishment, such as branch bank, brokerage firm, risk and insurance department, or credit department. Analyze and classify risks and investments to determine their potential impacts on companies. Approve or reject, or coordinate the approval and rejection of, lines of credit and commercial, real estate, and personal loans. Develop and analyze information to assess the current and future financial status of firms. Establish procedures for custody and control of assets, records, loan collateral, and securities, in order to ensure safekeeping. Evaluate data pertaining to costs in order to plan budgets. Evaluate financial reporting systems, accounting and collection procedures, and investment activities, and make recommendations for changes to procedures, operating systems, budgets, and other financial control functions. Network within communities to find and attract new business. Oversee the flow of cash and financial instruments. Plan, direct, and coordinate risk and insurance programs of establishments to control risks and losses. Plan, direct, and coordinate the activities of workers in branches, offices, or departments of such establishments as branch banks, brokerage firms, risk and insurance departments, or credit departments. Prepare financial and regulatory reports required by laws, regulations, and boards of directors. Prepare operational and risk reports for management analysis. Communicate with stockholders and other investors to provide information, and to raise capital. Direct floor operations of brokerage firm engaged in buying and selling securities at exchange. Direct insurance negotiations, select insurance brokers and carriers, and place insurance. Establish and maintain relationships with individual and business customers, and provide assistance with problems these customers may encounter. Examine, evaluate, and process loan applications. Monitor order flow and transactions that brokerage firm executes on the floor of exchange. Recruit staff members, and oversee training programs. Review collection reports to determine the status of collections and the amounts of outstanding balances. Review reports of securities transactions and price lists in order to analyze market conditions. **SKILLS**—Management of Financial Resources; Management of Personnel Resources; Systems Analysis; Systems Evaluation; Judgment and Decision Making; Writing; Monitoring; Complex Problem Solving.

GOE—Interest Area: 06. Finance and Insurance. **Work Group:** 06.01. Managerial Work in Finance and Insurance. **PERSONALITY TYPE:** Enterprising. Enterprising occupations frequently involve starting up and carrying out projects. These occupations can involve leading people and making many decisions. They sometimes require risk taking and often deal with business.

EDUCATION/TRAINING PROGRAMS— Accounting and Finance; Credit Management; Finance and Financial Management Services, Other; Finance, General; International Finance; Public Finance. **RELATED KNOWLEDGE/COURSES**— **Economics and Accounting:** Knowledge of economic and accounting principles and practices, the financial markets, banking, and the analysis and reporting of financial data. **Administration and Management:** Knowledge of business and management principles involved in strategic planning, resource allocation, human resources modeling, leadership technique, production methods, and coordination of people and resources. **Law and Government:** Knowledge of laws, legal codes, court procedures, precedents, government regulations, executive orders, agency rules, and the democratic political process. **Mathematics:** Knowledge of arithmetic, algebra, geometry, calculus, and statistics and their applications. **Personnel and Human Resources:** Knowledge of principles and procedures for personnel recruitment, selection, training, compensation and benefits, labor relations and negotiation, and personnel information systems. **Psychology:** Knowledge of human behavior and performance; individual differences in ability, personality, and interests; learning and motivation; psychological research methods; and the assessment and treatment of behavioral and affective disorders.

Fire-Prevention and Protection Engineers

- Annual Earnings: $65,210
- Growth: 13.4%
- Annual Job Openings: 2,000
- Self-Employed: 0.5%
- Part-Time: 2.7%
- Education/Training Required: Bachelor's degree

The job openings listed here are shared with Industrial Safety and Health Engineers and Product Safety Engineers.

Industries in Which Income Is Highest

Industry	Average Annual Wage	Number Employed
Transportation Equipment Manufacturing	$70,130	1,160
Professional, Scientific, and Technical Services	$69,370	2,750
Federal, State, and Local Government	$68,740	5,370
Chemical Manufacturing	$65,700	2,990
Construction of Buildings	$57,920	2,080

Metropolitan Areas Where Income Is Highest

Metropolitan Area	Average Annual Wage	Number Employed
San Jose–Sunnyvale–Santa Clara, CA	$84,920	390
Washington–Arlington–Alexandria, DC–VA–MD–WV	$84,880	960
Anchorage, AK	$84,300	70
Durham, NC	$83,530	100
Knoxville, TN	$78,820	130

Research causes of fires, determine fire protection methods, and design or recommend materials or equipment such as structural components or fire-detection equipment to assist organizations in safeguarding life and property against fire, explosion, and related hazards. Advise architects, builders, and other construction personnel on fire prevention equipment and techniques, and on fire code and standard interpretation and compliance. Conduct research on fire retardants and the fire safety of materials and devices. Consult with authorities to discuss safety regulations and to recommend changes as necessary. Design fire detection equipment, alarm systems, and fire extinguishing devices and systems. Determine causes of fires, and ways in which they could have been prevented. Direct the purchase, modification, installation, maintenance, and operation of fire protection systems. Inspect buildings or building designs to determine fire protection system requirements and potential problems in areas such as water supplies, exit locations, and construction materials. Study the relationships between ignition sources and materials to determine how fires start. Attend workshops, seminars, or conferences to present or obtain information regarding fire prevention and protection. Develop plans for the prevention of destruction by fire, wind, and water. Develop training materials, and conduct training sessions on fire protection. Evaluate fire department performance and the laws and regulations affecting fire prevention or fire safety. Prepare and write reports detailing specific fire prevention and protection issues such as work performed and proposed review schedules. **SKILLS—** Technology Design; Operations Analysis; Instructing; Science; Systems Evaluation; Systems Analysis; Quality Control Analysis; Speaking.

GOE—Interest Area: 15. Scientific Research, Engineering, and Mathematics. **Work Group:** 15.08. Industrial and Safety Engineering. **PERSONALITY TYPE:** Investigative. Investigative occupations frequently involve working with ideas and require an extensive amount of thinking. These occupations can involve searching for facts and figuring out problems mentally.

EDUCATION/TRAINING PROGRAM— Environmental/Environmental Health Engineering. **RELATED KNOWLEDGE/COURSES—Public Safety and Security:** Knowledge of relevant equipment, policies, procedures, and strategies to promote effective local, state, or national security operations for the protection of people, data, property, and institutions. **Education and Training:** Knowledge of principles and methods for curriculum and training design, teaching and instruction for individuals and groups, and the measurement of training effects. **Engineering and Technology:** Knowledge of the practical application of engineering science and technology. This includes applying principles, techniques, procedures, and equipment to the design and production of various goods and services. **Chemistry:** Knowledge of the chemical composition, structure, and properties of substances and of the chemical processes and transformations that they undergo. This includes uses of chemicals, their danger signs, production techniques, and disposal methods. **Design:** Knowledge of design techniques, tools, and principles involved in production of precision technical plans, blueprints, drawings, and models. **Law and Government:** Knowledge of laws, legal codes, court procedures, precedents, government regulations, executive orders, agency rules, and the democratic political process.

First-Line Supervisors and Manager/Supervisors— Construction Trades Workers

- Annual Earnings: $51,970
- Growth: 10.9%
- Annual Job Openings: 57,000
- Self-Employed: 24.7%
- Part-Time: 3.8%
- Education/Training Required: Work experience in a related occupation

The job openings listed here are shared with First-Line Supervisors and Manager/Supervisors—Extractive Workers.

Industries in Which Income Is Highest

Industry	Average Annual Wage	Number Employed
Management of Companies and Enterprises	$61,040	2,720
Utilities	$60,910	3,860
Hospitals	$60,340	1,340
Mining (Except Oil and Gas)	$59,500	8,020
Oil and Gas Extraction	$57,520	2,280

Metropolitan Areas Where Income Is Highest

Metropolitan Area	Average Annual Wage	Number Employed
San Jose–Sunnyvale–Santa Clara, CA	$79,250	3,000
San Francisco–Oakland–Fremont, CA	$74,730	8,580
Fairbanks, AK	$74,100	200
Vineland–Millville–Bridgeton, NJ	$72,690	220
New York–Northern New Jersey–Long Island, NY–NJ–PA	$71,400	26,840

Directly supervise and coordinate activities of construction trades workers and their helpers. Manager/Supervisors are generally found in smaller establishments where they perform both superviso- ry and management functions, such as accounting, marketing, and personnel work and may also engage in the same construction trades work as the workers they supervise. Supervises and coordinates activities of construction trades workers. Directs and leads workers engaged in construction activities. Assigns work to employees, using material and worker requirements data. Confers with staff and worker to ensure production and personnel problems are resolved. Suggests and initiates personnel actions, such as promotions, transfers, and hires. Analyzes and resolves worker problems and recommends motivational plans. Examines and inspects work progress, equipment and construction sites to verify safety and ensure that specifications are met. Estimates material and worker requirements to complete job. Reads specifications, such as blueprints and data, to determine construction requirements. Analyzes and plans installation and construction of equipment and structures. Locates, measures, and marks location and placement of structures and equipment. Records information, such as personnel, production, and operational data, on specified forms and reports. Trains workers in construction methods and operation of equipment. Recommends measures to improve production methods and equipment performance to increase efficiency and safety. Assists workers engaged in construction activities, using hand tools and equipment. **SKILLS**—Management of Personnel Resources; Management of Material Resources; Systems Evaluation; Systems Analysis; Time Management; Quality Control Analysis; Persuasion; Management of Financial Resources.

GOE—Interest Area: 02. Architecture and Construction. **Work Group:** 02.01. Managerial Work in Architecture and Construction. **PERSONALITY TYPE:** Enterprising. Enterprising occupations frequently involve starting up and carrying out projects. These occupations can involve leading people and making many decisions. They sometimes require risk taking and often deal with business.

EDUCATION/TRAINING PROGRAMS— Building/Construction Finishing, Management, and Inspection, Other; Building/Construction Site Management/Manager; Building/Construction Trades, Other; Building/Home/Construction Inspection/Inspector; Building/property Maintenance and Management; Carpentry/Carpenter; Concrete Finishing/Concrete Finisher; Drywall Installation/Drywaller; Electrical and Power Transmission Installation/Installer,

General; Electrical and Power Transmission Installers, Other; Electrician; Glazier; Lineworker; others. **RELATED KNOWLEDGE/COURSES—Building and Construction:** Knowledge of the materials, methods, and tools involved in the construction or repair of houses, buildings, or other structures such as highways and roads. **Personnel and Human Resources:** Knowledge of principles and procedures for personnel recruitment, selection, training, compensation and benefits, labor relations and negotiation, and personnel information systems. **Administration and Management:** Knowledge of business and management principles involved in strategic planning, resource allocation, human resources modeling, leadership technique, production methods, and coordination of people and resources. **Design:** Knowledge of design techniques, tools, and principles involved in production of precision technical plans, blueprints, drawings, and models. **Engineering and Technology:** Knowledge of the practical application of engineering science and technology. This includes applying principles, techniques, procedures, and equipment to the design and production of various goods and services.

First-Line Supervisors and Manager/Supervisors—Extractive Workers

- Annual Earnings: $51,970
- Growth: 10.9%
- Annual Job Openings: 57,000
- Self-Employed: 24.7%
- Part-Time: 3.8%
- Education/Training Required: Work experience in a related occupation

The job openings listed here are shared with First-Line Supervisors and Manager/Supervisors—Construction Trades Workers.

Industries in Which Income Is Highest

Industry	Average Annual Wage	Number Employed
Management of Companies and Enterprises	$61,040	2,720
Utilities	$60,910	3,860
Hospitals	$60,340	1,340
Mining (Except Oil and Gas)	$59,500	8,020
Oil and Gas Extraction	$57,520	2,280

Metropolitan Areas Where Income Is Highest

Metropolitan Area	Average Annual Wage	Number Employed
San Jose–Sunnyvale–Santa Clara, CA	$79,250	3,000
San Francisco–Oakland–Fremont, CA	$74,730	8,580
Fairbanks, AK	$74,100	200
Vineland–Millville–Bridgeton, NJ	$72,690	220
New York–Northern New Jersey–Long Island, NY–NJ–PA	$71,400	26,840

Directly supervise and coordinate activities of extractive workers and their helpers. Manager/Supervisors are generally found in smaller establishments where they perform both supervisory and management functions, such as accounting, marketing, and personnel work, and may also engage in the same extractive work as the workers they supervise. Supervises and coordinates activities of workers engaged in the extraction of geological materials. Directs and leads workers engaged in extraction of geological materials. Assigns work to employees, using material and worker requirements data. Confers with staff and workers to ensure production personnel problems are resolved. Analyzes and resolves worker problems and recommends motivational plans. Analyzes and plans extraction process of geological materials. Trains workers in construction methods and operation of equipment. Examines and inspects equipment, site, and materials, to verify specifications are met. Recommends measures to improve production methods and equipment performance to increase efficiency and safety. Suggests and initiates personnel actions, such as promotions, transfers, and hires. Records information, such as personnel, production, and operational data on specified forms. Assists workers engaged in extraction activities, using hand tools and equipment. Locates, measures, and marks, materials and site location, using measuring and marking equipment. Orders materials, supplies and repair of equipment and machinery. **SKILLS**—Management of Personnel Resources; Management of Material Resources; Systems Evaluation; Systems Analysis; Instructing; Operation Monitoring; Coordination; Negotiation.

GOE—Interest Area: 01. Agriculture and Natural Resources. **Work Group:** 01.01. Managerial Work in Agriculture and Natural Resources. **PERSONALITY TYPE:** Enterprising. Enterprising occupations frequently involve starting up and carrying out projects. These occupations can involve leading people and making many decisions. They sometimes require risk taking and often deal with business.

EDUCATION/TRAINING   PROGRAMS— Blasting/Blaster; Well Drilling/Driller. **RELATED KNOWLEDGE/COURSES—Personnel and Human Resources:** Knowledge of principles and procedures for personnel recruitment, selection, training, compensation and benefits, labor relations and negotiation, and personnel information systems. **Administration and Management:** Knowledge of business and management principles involved in strategic planning, resource allocation, human resources modeling, leadership technique, production methods, and coordination of people and resources. **Engineering and Technology:** Knowledge of the practical application of engineering science and technology. This includes applying principles, techniques, procedures, and equipment to the design and production of various goods and services. **Physics:** Knowledge and prediction of physical principles and laws and their interrelationships and applications to understanding fluid, material, and atmospheric dynamics and mechanical, electrical, atomic, and subatomic structures and processes. **Mechanical Devices:** Knowledge of machines and tools, including their designs, uses, repair, and maintenance. **Education and Training:** Knowledge of principles and methods for curriculum and training design, teaching and instruction for individuals and groups, and the measurement of training effects.

First-Line Supervisors/Managers of Correctional Officers

- Annual Earnings: $48,570
- Growth: 9.4%
- Annual Job Openings: 2,000
- Self-Employed: 0.0%
- Part-Time: 0.0%
- Education/Training Required: Work experience in a related occupation

Industries in Which Income Is Highest

Industry	Average Annual Wage	Number Employed
Federal, State, and Local Government	$48,840	36,250
Administrative and Support Services	$35,400	1,070

Metropolitan Areas Where Income Is Highest

Metropolitan Area	Average Annual Wage	Number Employed
Riverside–San Bernardino–Ontario, CA	$70,890	600
Bakersfield, CA	$70,400	410
San Diego–Carlsbad–San Marcos, CA	$65,910	190
Tampa–St. Petersburg–Clearwater, FL	$61,870	170
Minneapolis–St. Paul–Bloomington, MN–WI	$61,600	220

Supervise and coordinate activities of correctional officers and jailers. Transfer and transport offenders on foot, or by driving vehicles such as trailers, vans, and buses. Complete administrative paperwork, and supervise the preparation and maintenance of records, forms, and reports. Conduct roll calls of correctional officers. Develop work and security procedures. Instruct employees, and provide on-the-job training. Maintain knowledge of, comply with, and enforce all institutional policies, rules, procedures, and regulations. Maintain order, discipline, and security within assigned areas in accordance with relevant rules, regulations, policies, and laws. Monitor behavior of subordinates to ensure alert, courteous, and professional behavior toward inmates, parolees, fellow employees, visitors, and the public. Read and review offender information to identify issues that require special attention. Respond to emergencies such as escapes. Restrain, secure, and control offenders, using chemical agents, firearms, and other weapons of force as necessary. Set up employee work schedules. Supervise and direct the work of correctional officers to ensure the safe custody, discipline, and welfare of inmates. Supervise and perform searches of inmates and their quarters to locate contraband items. Supervise activities such as searches, shakedowns, riot control, and institutional tours. Take, receive, and check periodic inmate counts. Carry injured offenders or employees to safety, and provide emergency first aid when necessary. Convey correctional officers' and inmates' complaints to superiors. Examine incoming and outgoing mail to ensure conformance with regulations. Rate behavior of inmates, promoting acceptable attitudes and behaviors to those with low ratings. Resolve problems between inmates. Supervise and provide security for offenders performing tasks such as construction, maintenance, laundry, food service, and other industrial or agricultural operations. **SKILLS—** No data available.

GOE—Interest Area: 12. Law and Public Safety. **Work Group:** 12.01. Managerial Work in Law and Public Safety. **PERSONALITY TYPE:** No data available.

EDUCATION/TRAINING PROGRAMS— Corrections; Corrections Administration. **RELATED KNOWLEDGE/COURSES—No data available.**

First-Line Supervisors/Managers of Mechanics, Installers, and Repairers

- Annual Earnings: $51,980
- Growth: 12.4%
- Annual Job Openings: 33,000
- Self-Employed: 0.3%
- Part-Time: 1.2%
- Education/Training Required: Work experience in a related occupation

Industries in Which Income Is Highest

Industry	Average Annual Wage	Number Employed
Petroleum and Coal Products Manufacturing	$69,070	1,970
Utilities	$65,860	15,300
Telecommunications	$65,080	19,710
Internet Service Providers, Web Search Portals, and Data Processing Services	$64,010	1,000
Transportation Equipment Manufacturing	$62,130	9,070

Metropolitan Areas Where Income Is Highest

Metropolitan Area	Average Annual Wage	Number Employed
Kokomo, IN	$74,360	230
Danbury, CT	$69,940	220
Bremerton–Silverdale, WA	$68,800	620
Monroe, MI	$67,170	130
Bridgeport–Stamford–Norwalk, CT	$67,000	940

Supervise and coordinate the activities of mechanics, installers, and repairers. Determine schedules, sequences, and assignments for work activities, based on work priority, quantity of equipment and skill of personnel. Patrol and monitor work areas and examine tools and equipment in order to detect unsafe conditions or violations of procedures or safety rules. Monitor employees' work levels and review work performance. Examine objects, systems, or facilities; and analyze information to determine needed installations, services, or repairs. Participate in budget preparation and administration, coordinating purchasing and documentation, and monitoring departmental expenditures. Counsel employees about work-related issues and assist employees to correct job-skill deficiencies. Requisition materials and supplies, such as tools, equipment, and replacement parts. Compute estimates and actual costs of factors such as materials, labor, and outside contractors. Interpret specifications, blueprints, and job orders in order to construct templates and lay out reference points for workers. Conduct or arrange for worker training in safety, repair, and maintenance techniques; operational procedures; and equipment use. Investigate accidents and injuries, and prepare reports of findings. Confer with personnel, such as management, engineering, quality control, customer, and union workers' representatives, in order to coordinate work activities, resolve employee grievances, and identify and review resource needs. Recommend or initiate personnel actions, such as hires, promotions, transfers, discharges, and disciplinary measures. Perform skilled repair and maintenance operations, using equipment such as hand and power tools, hydraulic presses and shears, and welding equipment. Compile operational and personnel records, such as time and production records, inventory data, repair and maintenance statistics, and test results. Develop, implement, and evaluate maintenance policies and procedures. Monitor tool inventories and the condition and maintenance of shops in order to ensure adequate working conditions. Inspect, test, and measure completed work, using devices such as hand tools and gauges to verify conformance to standards and repair requirements. **SKILLS**—Management of Personnel Resources; Installation; Repairing; Management of Financial Resources; Management of Material Resources; Equipment Maintenance; Negotiation; Troubleshooting.

GOE—Interest Area: 13. Manufacturing. **Work Group:** 13.01. Managerial Work in Manufacturing. **PERSONALITY TYPE:** Enterprising. Enterprising occupations frequently involve starting up and carrying out projects. These occupations can involve leading people and making many decisions. They sometimes require risk taking and often deal with business.

EDUCATION/TRAINING PROGRAM—Operations Management and Supervision. **RELATED KNOWLEDGE/COURSES—Building and Construction:** Knowledge of the materials, methods, and tools involved in the construction or repair of houses, buildings, or other structures such as highways and roads. **Mechanical Devices:** Knowledge of machines and tools, including their designs, uses, repair, and maintenance. **Personnel and Human Resources:** Knowledge of principles and procedures for personnel recruitment, selection, training, compensation and benefits, labor relations and negotiation, and personnel information systems. **Design:** Knowledge of design techniques, tools, and principles involved in production of precision technical plans, blueprints, drawings, and models. **Administration and Management:** Knowledge of business and management principles involved in strategic planning, resource allocation, human resources modeling, leadership technique, production methods, and coordination of people and

resources. **Engineering and Technology:** Knowledge of the practical application of engineering science and technology. This includes applying principles, techniques, procedures, and equipment to the design and production of various goods and services.

First-Line Supervisors/Managers of Non-Retail Sales Workers

- ◎ Annual Earnings: $61,970
- ◎ Growth: 1.9%
- ◎ Annual Job Openings: 38,000
- ◎ Self-Employed: 37.1%
- ◎ Part-Time: 6.8%
- ◎ Education/Training Required: Work experience in a related occupation

Industries in Which Income Is Highest

Industry	Average Annual Wage	Number Employed
Computer and Electronic Product Manufacturing	$84,410	3,400
Securities, Commodity Contracts, and Other Financial Investments and Related Activities	$80,950	6,270
Wholesale Electronic Markets and Agents and Brokers	$78,910	15,650
Telecommunications	$75,890	7,210
Chemical Manufacturing	$74,880	2,240

Metropolitan Areas Where Income Is Highest

Metropolitan Area	Average Annual Wage	Number Employed
Lebanon, PA	$96,560	70
New York–Northern New Jersey–Long Island, NY–NJ–PA	$92,670	27,060
San Jose–Sunnyvale–Santa Clara, CA	$86,200	1,980
Boulder, CO	$79,680	370
Winchester, VA–WV	$78,250	70

Directly supervise and coordinate activities of sales workers other than retail sales workers. May perform duties, such as budgeting, accounting, and personnel work, in addition to supervisory duties. Coordinate sales promotion activities, and prepare merchandise displays and advertising copy. Examine merchandise to ensure correct pricing and display, and that it functions as advertised. Examine products purchased for resale or received for storage to determine product condition. Formulate pricing policies on merchandise according to profitability requirements. Prepare rental or lease agreements, specifying charges and payment procedures for use of machinery, tools, or other items. Visit retailers and sales representatives to promote products and gather information. Analyze details of sales territories to assess their growth potential, and to set quotas. Direct and supervise employees engaged in sales, inventory-taking, reconciling cash receipts, or performing specific services such as pumping gasoline for customers. Hire, train, and evaluate personnel. Inventory stock, and reorder when inventories drop to specified levels. Keep records pertaining to purchases, sales, and requisitions. Listen to and resolve customer complaints regarding services, products, or personnel. Monitor sales staff performance to ensure that goals are met. Plan and prepare work schedules, and assign employees to specific duties. Prepare sales and inventory reports for management and budget departments. Provide staff with assistance in performing difficult or complicated duties. Attend company meetings to exchange product information and coordinate work activities with other departments. Confer with company officials to develop methods and procedures to increase sales, expand markets, and promote business. **SKILLS**—Management of Personnel Resources; Management of Financial Resources; Management of Material Resources; Systems Evaluation; Systems Analysis; Negotiation; Coordination; Social Perceptiveness.

GOE—Interest Area: 14. Retail and Wholesale Sales and Service. **Work Group:** 14.01. Managerial Work in Retail/Wholesale Sales and Service. **PERSONALITY TYPE:** Enterprising. Enterprising occupations frequently involve starting up and carrying out projects. These occupations can involve leading people and making many decisions. They sometimes require risk taking and often deal with business.

EDUCATION/TRAINING   PROGRAMS— Business, Management, Marketing, and Related Support Services; General Merchandising, Sales, and Related Marketing Operations, Other; Special Products Marketing Operations; Specialized Merchandising, Sales, and Related Marketing Operations, Other. **RELATED KNOWLEDGE/COURSES—Sales and Marketing:** Knowledge of principles and methods for showing, promoting, and selling products or services. This includes marketing strategy and tactics, product demonstration, sales techniques, and sales control systems. **Economics and Accounting:** Knowledge of economic and accounting principles and practices, the financial markets, banking, and the analysis and reporting of financial data. **Personnel and Human Resources:** Knowledge of principles and procedures for personnel recruitment, selection, training, compensation and benefits, labor relations and negotiation, and personnel information systems. **Administration and Management:** Knowledge of business and management principles involved in strategic planning, resource allocation, human resources modeling, leadership technique, production methods, and coordination of people and resources. **Mathematics:** Knowledge of arithmetic, algebra, geometry, calculus, and statistics and their applications. **Customer and Personal Service:** Knowledge of principles and processes for providing customer and personal services. This includes customer needs assessment, meeting quality standards for services, and evaluation of customer satisfaction.

First-Line Supervisors/Managers of Police and Detectives

- Annual Earnings: $65,570
- Growth: 15.5%
- Annual Job Openings: 9,000
- Self-Employed: 0.0%
- Part-Time: 1.4%
- Education/Training Required: Work experience in a related occupation

Industries in Which Income Is Highest

Industry	Average Annual Wage	Number Employed
Federal, State, and Local Government	$65,770	89,380
Educational Services	$54,190	1,570

Metropolitan Areas Where Income Is Highest

Metropolitan Area	Average Annual Wage	Number Employed
San Jose–Sunnyvale–Santa Clara, CA	$108,220	170
San Francisco–Oakland–Fremont, CA	$99,680	870
Trenton–Ewing, NJ	$98,240	270
Brunswick, GA	$93,960	50
Oxnard–Thousand Oaks–Ventura, CA	$93,220	90

Supervise and coordinate activities of members of police force. Explain police operations to subordinates to assist them in performing their job duties. Inform personnel of changes in regulations and policies, implications of new or amended laws, and new techniques of police work. Supervise and coordinate the investigation of criminal cases, offering guidance and expertise to investigators, and ensuring that procedures are conducted in accordance with laws and regulations. Investigate and resolve personnel problems within organization and charges of misconduct against staff. Train staff in proper police work procedures. Maintain logs, prepare reports, and direct the preparation, handling, and maintenance of departmental records. Monitor and evaluate the job performance of subordinates, and authorize promotions and transfers. Direct collection, preparation, and handling of evidence and personal property of prisoners. Develop, implement and revise departmental policies and procedures. Conduct raids and order detention of witnesses and suspects for questioning. Prepare work schedules and assign duties to subordinates. Discipline staff for violation of department rules and regulations. Cooperate with court personnel and officials from other law enforcement agencies and testify in court as necessary. Review contents of written orders to ensure adherence to legal requirements. Inspect facilities, supplies, vehicles, and equipment to ensure conformance to standards. Prepare news releases and respond to police correspondence. Requisition and issue equipment and supplies. Meet with civic, educational, and community groups to develop community programs and events, and to discuss law enforcement subjects. Direct release or transfer of prisoners. Prepare budgets and manage expenditures of department funds. **SKILLS**—Management of Personnel Resources; Persuasion; Negotiation; Social Perceptiveness; Service Orientation; Monitoring; Instructing; Judgment and Decision Making.

GOE—Interest Area: 12. Law and Public Safety. **Work Group:** 12.01. Managerial Work in Law and Public Safety. **PERSONALITY TYPE:** Enterprising. Enterprising occupations frequently involve starting up and carrying out projects. These occupations can involve leading people and making many decisions. They sometimes require risk taking and often deal with business.

EDUCATION/TRAINING   PROGRAMS— Corrections; Criminal Justice/Law Enforcement Administration; Criminal Justice/Safety Studies. **RELATED   KNOWLEDGE/COURSES—Public Safety and Security:** Knowledge of relevant equipment, policies, procedures, and strategies to promote effective local, state, or national security operations for the protection of people, data, property, and institutions. **Psychology:** Knowledge of human behavior and performance; individual differences in ability, personality, and interests; learning and motivation; psychological research methods; and the assessment and treatment of behavioral and affective disorders. **Law and Government:** Knowledge of laws, legal codes, court procedures, precedents, government regulations, executive orders, agency rules, and the democratic political process. **Education and Training:** Knowledge of principles and methods for curriculum and training design, teaching and instruction for individuals and groups, and the measurement of training effects. **Personnel and Human Resources:** Knowledge of principles and procedures for personnel recruitment, selection, training, compensation and benefits, labor relations and negotiation, and personnel information systems. **Customer and Personal Service:** Knowledge of principles and processes for providing customer and personal services. This includes customer needs assessment, meeting quality standards for services, and evaluation of customer satisfaction.

First-Line Supervisors/Managers of Transportation and Material-Moving Machine and Vehicle Operators

- Annual Earnings: $47,530
- Growth: 15.3%
- Annual Job Openings: 22,000
- Self-Employed: 1.3%
- Part-Time: 5.0%
- Education/Training Required: Work experience in a related occupation

Industries in Which Income Is Highest

Industry	Average Annual Wage	Number Employed
Rail Transportation	$60,490	2,860
Postal Service	$58,710	7,920
Federal, State, and Local Government	$57,780	19,100
Couriers and Messengers	$55,870	13,520
Chemical Manufacturing	$50,810	1,130

Metropolitan Areas Where Income Is Highest

Metropolitan Area	Average Annual Wage	Number Employed
Boulder, CO	$72,070	180
Fairbanks, AK	$70,860	50
Anchorage, AK	$66,840	320
Longview, WA	$66,150	90
Olympia, WA	$61,780	180

Directly supervise and coordinate activities of transportation and material-moving machine and vehicle operators and helpers. Enforce safety rules and regulations. Plan work assignments and equipment allocations in order to meet transportation, operations, or production goals. Confer with customers, supervisors, contractors, and other personnel to exchange information and to resolve problems. Direct workers in transportation or related services, such as pumping, moving, storing, and loading/unloading of materials or people. Resolve worker problems, or collaborate with employees to assist in problem resolution. Review orders, production schedules, blueprints, and shipping/receiving notices to determine work sequences and material shipping dates, types, volumes, and destinations. Monitor field work to ensure that it is being performed properly and that materials are being used as they should be. Recommend and implement measures to improve worker motivation, equipment performance, work methods, and customer services. Maintain or verify records of time, materials, expenditures, and crew activities. Interpret transportation and tariff regulations, shipping orders, safety regulations, and company policies and procedures for workers. Explain and demonstrate work tasks to new workers, or assign workers to more experienced workers for further training. Prepare, compile, and submit reports on work activities, operations, production, and work-related accidents. Recommend or implement personnel actions such as employee selection, evaluation, and rewards or disciplinary actions. Requisition needed personnel, supplies, equipment, parts, or repair services. Plan and establish transportation routes. Inspect or test materials, stock, vehicles, equipment, and facilities to ensure that they are safe, free of defects, and meet specifications. Compute and estimate cash, payroll, transportation, personnel, and storage requirements. Dispatch personnel and vehicles in respond to telephone or radio reports of emergencies. Perform or schedule repairs and preventive maintenance of vehicles and other equipment. Examine, measure, and weigh cargo or materials to determine specific handling requirements. Provide workers with assistance in performing tasks such as coupling railroad cars or loading vehicles. **SKILLS—** Management of Personnel Resources; Management of Financial Resources; Social Perceptiveness; Management of Material Resources; Persuasion; Monitoring; Time Management; Negotiation.

GOE—Interest Area: 16. Transportation, Distribution, and Logistics. **Work Group:** 16.01. Managerial Work in Transportation. **PERSONALITY TYPE:** Enterprising. Enterprising occupations frequently involve starting up and carrying out projects. These occupations can involve leading people and making many decisions. They sometimes require risk taking and often deal with business.

EDUCATION/TRAINING PROGRAM—No data available. **RELATED KNOWLEDGE/COURSES— Transportation:** Knowledge of principles and methods for moving people or goods by air, rail, sea, or road, including the relative costs and benefits. **Customer and Personal Service:** Knowledge of principles and processes for providing customer and personal services. This includes customer needs assessment, meeting quality standards for services, and evaluation of customer satisfaction. **Production and Processing:** Knowledge of raw materials, production processes, quality control, costs, and other techniques for maximizing the effective manufacture and distribution of goods. **Personnel and Human Resources:** Knowledge of principles and procedures for personnel recruitment, selection, training, compensation and benefits, labor relations and negotiation, and personnel information systems. **Administration and Management:** Knowledge of business and management principles involved in strategic planning, resource allocation, human resources modeling, leadership technique, production methods, and coordination of people and resources. **Public Safety and Security:** Knowledge of relevant equipment, policies, procedures, and strategies to promote effective local, state, or national security operations for the protection of people, data, property, and institutions.

Fish Hatchery Managers

- Annual Earnings: $51,160
- Growth: 4.0%
- Annual Job Openings: 20,000
- Self-Employed: 0.0%
- Part-Time: 13.1%
- Education/Training Required: Work experience plus degree

The job openings listed here are shared with Agricultural Crop Farm Managers; and Nursery and Greenhouse Managers.

Industries in Which Income Is Highest

Industry	Average Annual Wage	Number Employed
Food Manufacturing	$57,140	90
Merchant Wholesalers, Nondurable Goods	$54,690	290
Administrative and Support Services	$54,540	160
Management of Companies and Enterprises	$52,780	70
Educational Services	$52,690	190

Metropolitan Areas Where Income Is Highest

Metropolitan Area	Average Annual Wage	Number Employed
New York–Northern New Jersey–Long Island, NY–NJ–PA	$76,240	50
Stockton, CA	$72,420	30
Riverside–San Bernardino–Ontario, CA	$67,640	40
Washington–Arlington–Alexandria, DC–VA–MD–WV	$64,020	30
Portland–Vancouver–Beaverton, OR–WA	$60,170	30

Direct and coordinate, through subordinate supervisory personnel, activities of workers engaged in fish hatchery production for corporations, cooperatives, or other owners. Determines, administers, and executes policies relating to administration, standards of hatchery operations, and facility maintenance. Oversees trapping and spawning of fish, egg incubation, and fry rearing, applying knowledge of management and fish culturing techniques. Oversees movement of mature fish to lakes, ponds, streams or commercial tanks. Collects information regarding techniques for collecting, fertilizing, incubating spawn, and treatment of spawn and fry. Accounts for and dispenses funds. Prepares reports required by state and federal laws. Prepares budget reports. Confers with biologists and other fishery personnel to obtain data concerning fish habits, food, and environmental requirements. Approves employment and discharge of employees, signs payrolls, and performs personnel duties. **SKILLS**—Management of Financial Resources; Management of Personnel Resources; Science; Management of Material Resources; Systems Analysis; Writing; Systems Evaluation; Reading Comprehension.

GOE—**Interest Area:** 01. Agriculture and Natural Resources. **Work Group:** 01.01. Managerial Work in Agriculture and Natural Resources. **PERSONALITY TYPE:** Enterprising. Enterprising occupations frequently involve starting up and carrying out projects. These occupations can involve leading people and making many decisions. They sometimes require risk taking and often deal with business.

EDUCATION/TRAINING PROGRAMS—Agribusiness/Agricultural Business Operations; Agricultural Business and Management, General; Agricultural Business and Management, Other; Agricultural Production Operations, General; Agricultural Production Operations, Other; Animal/Livestock Husbandry and Production; Crop Production; Farm/Farm and Ranch Management. **RELATED KNOWLEDGE/COURSES—Food Production:** Knowledge of techniques and equipment for planting, growing, and harvesting food products (both plant and animal) for consumption, including storage/handling techniques. **Administration and Management:** Knowledge of business and management principles involved in strategic planning, resource allocation, human resources modeling, leadership technique, production methods, and coordination of people and resources. **Personnel and Human Resources:** Knowledge of principles and procedures for personnel recruitment, selection, training, compensation and benefits, labor relations and negotiation, and personnel information systems. **Economics and Accounting:** Knowledge of economic and accounting principles and practices, the financial markets, banking, and the analysis and reporting of financial data. **Biology:** Knowledge of plant and animal organisms and their tissues, cells, functions, interdependencies, and interactions with each other and the environment.

Flight Attendants

- Annual Earnings: $46,680
- Growth: 16.3%
- Annual Job Openings: 7,000
- Self-Employed: 0.2%
- Part-Time: 28.3%
- Education/Training Required: Long-term on-the-job training

Industries in Which Income Is Highest

Industry	Average Annual Wage	Number Employed
Air Transportation	$46,640	99,030

Metropolitan Areas Where Income Is Highest

Metropolitan Area	Average Annual Wage	Number Employed
New York–Northern New Jersey–Long Island, NY–NJ–PA	$63,610	13,430
Boston–Cambridge–Quincy, MA–NH	$38,590	2,420
Chicago–Naperville–Joliet, IL–IN–WI	$34,980	10,520

Provide personal services to ensure the safety and comfort of airline passengers during flight. Greet passengers, verify tickets, explain use of safety equipment, and serve food or beverages. Announce and demonstrate safety and emergency procedures such as the use of oxygen masks, seat belts, and life jackets. Answer passengers' questions about flights, aircraft, weather, travel routes and services, arrival times, and/or schedules. Assist passengers in placing carry-on luggage in overhead, garment, or under-seat storage. Assist passengers while entering or disembarking the aircraft. Attend preflight briefings concerning weather, altitudes, routes, emergency procedures, crew coordination, lengths of flights, food and beverage services offered, and numbers of passengers. Check to ensure that food, beverages, blankets, reading material, emergency equipment, and other supplies are aboard and are in adequate supply. Collect money for meals and beverages. Conduct periodic trips through the cabin to ensure passenger comfort, and to distribute reading material, headphones, pillows, playing cards, and blankets. Determine special assistance needs of passengers such as small children, the elderly, or disabled persons. Direct and assist passengers in the event of an emergency, such as directing passengers to evacuate a plane following an emergency landing. Prepare passengers and aircraft for landing, following procedures. Greet passengers boarding aircraft and direct them to assigned seats. Heat and serve prepared foods. Announce flight delays and descent preparations. Sell alcoholic beverages to passengers. Take inventory of headsets, alcoholic beverages, and money collected. Walk aisles of planes to verify that passengers have complied with federal regulations prior to take-offs and landings. Administer first aid to passengers in distress. Inspect and clean cabins, checking for any problems and making sure that cabins are in order. Inspect passenger tickets to verify information and to obtain destination information. Operate audio and video systems. Prepare reports showing places of departure and destination, passenger ticket numbers, meal and beverage inventories, the conditions of cabin equipment, and any problems encountered by passengers. Reassure passengers when situations such as turbulence are encountered. **SKILLS**—Service Orientation; Social Perceptiveness.

GOE—Interest Area: 09. Hospitality, Tourism, and Recreation. **Work Group:** 09.03. Hospitality and Travel Services. **PERSONALITY TYPE:** Enterprising. Enterprising occupations frequently involve starting up and carrying out projects. These occupations can involve leading people and making many decisions. They sometimes require risk taking and often deal with business.

EDUCATION/TRAINING PROGRAM—Airline Flight Attendant. **RELATED KNOWLEDGE/ COURSES—Customer and Personal Service:** Knowledge of principles and processes for providing customer and personal services. This includes customer needs assessment, meeting quality standards for services, and evaluation of customer satisfaction. **Medicine and Dentistry:** Knowledge of the information and techniques needed to diagnose and treat human injuries, diseases, and deformities. This includes symptoms, treatment alternatives, drug properties and interactions, and preventive health-care measures. **Transportation:** Knowledge of principles and methods for moving people or goods by air, rail, sea, or road, including the relative costs and benefits. **Public Safety and Security:** Knowledge of relevant equipment, policies, procedures, and strategies to promote effective local, state, or national security operations for the protection of people, data, property, and institutions.

Food Scientists and Technologists

- Annual Earnings: $51,440
- Growth: 10.9%
- Annual Job Openings: 1,000
- Self-Employed: 28.8%
- Part-Time: 10.3%
- Education/Training Required: Bachelor's degree

Industries in Which Income Is Highest

Industry	Average Annual Wage	Number Employed
Merchant Wholesalers, Nondurable Goods	$71,290	470
Management of Companies and Enterprises	$69,210	500
Professional, Scientific, and Technical Services	$63,100	1,120
Federal, State, and Local Government	$58,860	360
Support Activities for Agriculture and Forestry	$56,820	80

Metropolitan Areas Where Income Is Highest

Metropolitan Area	Average Annual Wage	Number Employed
Washington–Arlington–Alexandria, DC–VA–MD–WV	$84,420	70
Dallas–Fort Worth–Arlington, TX	$81,080	170
Cincinnati–Middletown, OH–KY–IN	$78,420	140
Columbus, OH	$72,690	310
Philadelphia–Camden–Wilmington, PA–NJ–DE–MD	$68,550	50

Use chemistry, microbiology, engineering, and other sciences to study the principles underlying the processing and deterioration of foods; analyze food content to determine levels of vitamins, fat, sugar, and protein; discover new food sources; research ways to make processed foods safe, palatable, and healthful; and apply food science knowledge to determine best ways to process, package, preserve, store, and distribute food. Test new products for flavor, texture, color, nutritional content, and adherence to government and industry standards. Check raw ingredients for maturity or stability for processing, and finished products for safety, quality and nutritional value. Confer with process engineers, plant operators, flavor experts, and packaging and marketing specialists in order to resolve problems in product development. Evaluate food processing and storage operations, and assist in the development of quality assurance programs for such operations. Study methods to improve aspects of foods such as chemical composition, flavor, color, texture, nutritional value, and convenience. Study the structure and composition of food, or the changes foods undergo in storage and processing. Develop new or improved ways of preserving, processing, packaging, storing, and delivering foods, using knowledge of chemistry, microbiology, and other sciences. Develop food standards and production specifications, safety and sanitary regulations, and waste management and water supply specifications. Demonstrate products to clients. Inspect food processing areas in order to ensure compliance with government regulations and standards for sanitation, safety, quality, and waste management standards. Search for substitutes for harmful or undesirable additives, such as nitrites. **SKILLS**—Quality Control Analysis; Science; Troubleshooting; Persuasion; Active Learning; Monitoring; Reading Comprehension; Operations Analysis.

GOE—Interest Area: 01. Agriculture and Natural Resources. **Work Group:** 01.03. Resource Technologies for Plants, Animals, and the Environment. **PERSONALITY TYPE:** Investigative. Investigative occupations frequently involve working with ideas and require an extensive amount of thinking. These occupations can involve searching for facts and figuring out problems mentally.

EDUCATION/TRAINING   PROGRAMS— Agriculture, General; Food Science; Food Technology and Processing; International Agriculture. **RELATED KNOWLEDGE/COURSES—Food   Production:** Knowledge of techniques and equipment for planting, growing, and harvesting food products (both plant and animal) for consumption, including storage/handling techniques. **Chemistry:** Knowledge of the chemical composition, structure, and properties of substances and of the chemical processes and transformations that

they undergo. This includes uses of chemicals, their danger signs, production techniques, and disposal methods. **Production and Processing:** Knowledge of raw materials, production processes, quality control, costs, and other techniques for maximizing the effective manufacture and distribution of goods. **Biology:** Knowledge of plant and animal organisms and their tissues, cells, functions, interdependencies, and interactions with each other and the environment. **Physics:** Knowledge and prediction of physical principles and laws and their interrelationships and applications to understanding fluid, material, and atmospheric dynamics and mechanical, electrical, atomic, and subatomic structures and processes. **Customer and Personal Service:** Knowledge of principles and processes for providing customer and personal services. This includes customer needs assessment, meeting quality standards for services, and evaluation of customer satisfaction.

Foreign Language and Literature Teachers, Postsecondary

- Annual Earnings: $49,570
- Growth: 32.2%
- Annual Job Openings: 329,000
- Self-Employed: 0.4%
- Part-Time: 27.3%
- Education/Training Required: Master's degree

Our sources did not provide separate job openings data for this occupation. The job openings listed here are shared with 35 other postsecondary teaching occupations. For a complete list, see the beginning of this section.

Industries in Which Income Is Highest

Industry	Average Annual Wage	Number Employed
Educational Services	$49,570	23,820

Metropolitan Areas Where Income Is Highest

Metropolitan Area	Average Annual Wage	Number Employed
Riverside–San Bernardino–Ontario, CA	$71,590	130
Springfield, MA–CT	$66,860	130
Sacramento–Arden-Arcade–Roseville, CA	$66,280	80
Pittsburgh, PA	$64,600	270
Providence–Fall River–Warwick, RI–MA	$64,540	130

Teach courses in foreign (i.e., other than English) languages and literature. Evaluate and grade students' class work, assignments, and papers. Prepare course materials such as syllabi, homework assignments, and handouts. Initiate, facilitate, and moderate classroom discussions. Maintain student attendance records, grades, and other required records. Compile, administer, and grade examinations or assign this work to others. Plan, evaluate, and revise curricula, course content, and course materials and methods of instruction. Prepare and deliver lectures to undergraduate and/or graduate students on topics such as how to speak and write a foreign language, and the cultural aspects of areas where a particular language is used. Maintain regularly scheduled office hours in order to advise and assist students. Select and obtain materials and supplies such as textbooks. Keep abreast of developments in their field by reading current literature, talking with colleagues, and participating in professional organizations and activities. Advise students on academic and vocational curricula and on career issues. Conduct research in a particular field of knowledge and publish findings in scholarly journals, books, and/or electronic media. Collaborate with colleagues to address teaching and research issues. Serve on academic or administrative committees that deal with institutional policies, departmental matters, and academic issues. Participate in student recruitment, registration, and placement activities. Compile bibliographies of specialized materials for outside reading assignments. Participate in campus and community events. Act as advisers to student organizations. Perform administrative duties such as serving as department head. Supervise undergraduate and/or graduate teaching, internship, and research work. **SKILLS**—Instructing; Learning Strategies; Persuasion; Social Perceptiveness; Speaking; Writing; Critical Thinking; Reading Comprehension.

GOE—Interest Area: 05. Education and Training. **Work Group:** 05.03. Postsecondary and Adult Teaching and Instructing. **PERSONALITY TYPE:** Artistic. Artistic occupations frequently involve working with forms, designs, and patterns. They often require self-expression, and the work can be done without following a clear set of rules.

EDUCATION/TRAINING PROGRAMS—African Languages, Literatures, and Linguistics; Albanian Language and Literature; American Indian/Native American Languages, Literatures, and Linguistics; Ancient Near Eastern and Biblical Languages, Literatures, and Linguistics; Ancient/Classical Greek Language and Literature; Arabic Language and Literature; others. **RELATED KNOWLEDGE/COURSES—Foreign Language:** Knowledge of the structure and content of a foreign (non-English) language, including the meaning and spelling of words, rules of composition and grammar, and pronunciation. **Philosophy and Theology:** Knowledge of different philosophical systems and religions. This includes their basic principles, values, ethics, ways of thinking, customs, and practices and their impact on human culture. **History and Archeology:** Knowledge of historical events and their causes, indicators, and effects on civilizations and cultures. **Sociology and Anthropology:** Knowledge of group behavior and dynamics, societal trends and influences, human migrations, ethnicity, and cultures and their history and origins. **Education and Training:** Knowledge of principles and methods for curriculum and training design, teaching and instruction for individuals and groups, and the measurement of training effects. **English Language:** Knowledge of the structure and content of the English language, including the meaning and spelling of words, rules of composition, and grammar.

Forest Fire Fighting and Prevention Supervisors

- Annual Earnings: $60,840
- Growth: 21.1%
- Annual Job Openings: 4,000
- Self-Employed: 0.0%
- Part-Time: 0.7%
- Education/Training Required: Work experience in a related occupation

The job openings listed here are shared with Municipal Fire Fighting and Prevention Supervisors.

Industries in Which Income Is Highest

Industry	Average Annual Wage	Number Employed
Federal, State, and Local Government	$61,010	52,470

Metropolitan Areas Where Income Is Highest

Metropolitan Area	Average Annual Wage	Number Employed
San Jose–Sunnyvale–Santa Clara, CA	$107,220	500
San Francisco–Oakland–Fremont, CA	$105,180	900
Miami–Fort Lauderdale–Miami Beach, FL	$79,240	850
Chicago–Naperville–Joliet, IL–IN–WI	$77,150	1,440
Vallejo–Fairfield, CA	$75,840	80

Supervise fire fighters who control and suppress fires in forests or vacant public land. Communicate fire details to superiors, subordinates, and interagency dispatch centers, using two-way radios. Serve as working leader of an engine-, hand-, helicopter-, or prescribed fire crew of three or more firefighters. Maintain fire suppression equipment in good condition, checking equipment periodically in order to ensure that it is ready for use. Evaluate size, location, and condition of forest fires in order to request and dispatch crews and position equipment so fires can be contained safely and effectively. Operate wildland fire engines and hoselays. Monitor prescribed burns to ensure that they are conducted safely and effectively. Direct and supervise prescribed burn projects, and prepare post-burn reports analyzing burn conditions and results. Identify staff training and development needs in order to ensure that appropriate training can be arranged. Maintain knowledge of forest fire laws and fire prevention techniques and tactics. Recommend equipment modifications or new equipment purchases. Perform administrative duties such as compiling and maintaining records, completing forms, preparing reports, and composing correspondence. Recruit and hire forest fire-fighting personnel. Train workers in such skills as parachute jumping, fire suppression, aerial observation, and radio communication, both in the classroom and on the job. Review and evaluate employee performance. Observe fires and crews from air to determine fire-fighting force

requirements and to note changing conditions that will affect fire-fighting efforts. Inspect all stations, uniforms, equipment, and recreation areas in order to ensure compliance with safety standards, taking corrective action as necessary. Schedule employee work assignments, and set work priorities. Regulate open burning by issuing burning permits, inspecting problem sites, issuing citations for violations of laws and ordinances, and educating the public in proper burning practices. Direct investigations of suspected arsons in wildfires, working closely with other investigating agencies. Monitor fire suppression expenditures in order to ensure that they are necessary and reasonable. **SKILLS**— Equipment Maintenance; Management of Personnel Resources; Repairing; Operation Monitoring; Service Orientation; Management of Financial Resources; Management of Material Resources; Troubleshooting.

GOE—Interest Area: 12. Law and Public Safety. **Work Group:** 12.01. Managerial Work in Law and Public Safety. **PERSONALITY TYPE:** Realistic. Realistic occupations frequently involve work activities that include practical, hands-on problems and solutions. They often deal with plants, animals, and real-world materials like wood, tools, and machinery. Many of the occupations require working outside and do not involve a lot of paperwork or working closely with others.

EDUCATION/TRAINING PROGRAMS—Fire Protection and Safety Technology/Technician; Fire Services Administration. **RELATED KNOWLEDGE/ COURSES—Public Safety and Security:** Knowledge of relevant equipment, policies, procedures, and strategies to promote effective local, state, or national security operations for the protection of people, data, property, and institutions. **Customer and Personal Service:** Knowledge of principles and processes for providing customer and personal services. This includes customer needs assessment, meeting quality standards for services, and evaluation of customer satisfaction. **Personnel and Human Resources:** Knowledge of principles and procedures for personnel recruitment, selection, training, compensation and benefits, labor relations and negotiation, and personnel information systems. **Building and Construction:** Knowledge of the materials, methods, and tools involved in the construction or repair of houses, buildings, or other structures such as highways and roads. **Mechanical Devices:** Knowledge of machines and tools, including their designs, uses, repair, and maintenance. **Transportation:** Knowledge of principles and methods for moving people or goods by air, rail, sea, or road, including the relative costs and benefits.

Foresters

- Annual Earnings: $48,670
- Growth: 6.7%
- Annual Job Openings: 1,000
- Self-Employed: 9.1%
- Part-Time: 7.3%
- Education/Training Required: Bachelor's degree

Industries in Which Income Is Highest

Industry	Average Annual Wage	Number Employed
Wood Product Manufacturing	$50,330	1,320
Federal, State, and Local Government	$49,420	6,500

Metropolitan Areas Where Income Is Highest

Metropolitan Area	Average Annual Wage	Number Employed
Washington–Arlington–Alexandria, DC–VA–MD–WV	$81,050	80
Portland–Vancouver–Beaverton, OR–WA	$71,650	140
Redding, CA	$64,280	50
Minneapolis–St. Paul–Bloomington, MN–WI	$63,410	130
Alexandria, LA	$63,050	50

Manage forested lands for economic, recreational, and conservation purposes. May inventory the type, amount, and location of standing timber, appraise the timber's worth, negotiate the purchase, and draw up contracts for procurement. May determine how to conserve wildlife habitats, creek beds, water quality, and soil stability, and how best to comply with environmental regulations. May devise plans for planting and growing new trees, monitor trees for healthy growth, and determine the best time for harvesting. Develop forest management plans for public and privately-owned forested lands. Monitor contract compliance and results of forestry activities to assure adherence to government regulations. Establish short- and long-term plans for management of forest lands and forest resources. Supervise activities of other forestry workers. Choose and prepare sites for new trees, using controlled burning, bulldozers, or herbicides to clear weeds, brush, and logging debris. Plan and supervise forestry projects, such as determining the type, number and placement of trees to be planted, managing tree nurseries, thinning forest and monitoring growth of new seedlings. Negotiate terms and conditions of agreements and contracts for forest harvesting, forest management and leasing of forest lands. Direct, and participate in, forest-fire suppression. Determine methods of cutting and removing timber with minimum waste and environmental damage. Analyze effect of forest conditions on tree growth rates and tree species prevalence and the yield, duration, seed production, growth viability, and germination of different species. Monitor forest-cleared lands to ensure that they are reclaimed to their most suitable end use. Plan and implement projects for conservation of wildlife habitats and soil and water quality. Plan and direct forest surveys and related studies and prepare reports and recommendations. Perform inspections of forests or forest nurseries. Map forest area soils and vegetation to estimate the amount of standing timber and future value and growth. Conduct public educational programs on forest care and conservation. Procure timber from private landowners. Subcontract with loggers or pulpwood cutters for tree removal and to aid in road layout. Plan cutting programs and manage timber sales from harvested areas, assisting companies to achieve production goals. Monitor wildlife populations and assess the impacts of forest operations on population and habitats. Plan and direct construction and maintenance of recreation facilities, fire towers, trails, roads and bridges, ensuring that they comply with guidelines and regulations set for forested public lands. Contact local forest owners and gain permission to take inventory of the type, amount, and location of all standing timber on the property. **SKILLS**—Management of Financial Resources; Science; Coordination; Programming; Time Management; Operations Analysis; Mathematics; Quality Control Analysis.

GOE—Interest Area: 01. Agriculture and Natural Resources. **Work Group:** 01.02. Resource Science/Engineering for Plants, Animals, and the Environment. **PERSONALITY TYPE:** Realistic. Realistic occupations frequently involve work activities that include practical, hands-on problems and solutions. They often deal with plants, animals, and real-world materials like wood, tools, and machinery. Many of the occupations require working outside and do not involve a lot of paperwork or working closely with others.

EDUCATION/TRAINING PROGRAMS—Forest Management/ Forest Resources Management; Forest Resources Production and Management; Forest Sciences; Forestry, General; Forestry, Other; Natural Resources and Conservation, Other; Natural Resources Management and Policy, General; Natural Resources Management and Policy, Other; Natural Resources/ Conservation, General; Urban Forestry; Wood Science and Wood Products/Pulp and Paper Technology. **RELATED KNOWLEDGE/COURSES**—**Biology:** Knowledge of plant and animal organisms and their tissues, cells, functions, interdependencies, and interactions with each other and the environment. **Geography:** Knowledge of principles and methods for describing the features of land, sea, and air masses, including their physical characteristics; locations; interrelationships; and distribution of plant, animal, and human life. **Administration and Management:** Knowledge of business and management principles involved in strategic planning, resource allocation, human resources modeling, leadership technique, production methods, and coordination of people and resources. **Mathematics:** Knowledge of arithmetic, algebra, geometry, calculus, and statistics and their applications. **Computers and Electronics:** Knowledge of circuit boards, processors, chips, electronic equipment, and computer hardware and software, including applications and programming. **Law and Government:** Knowledge of laws, legal codes, court procedures, precedents, government regulations, executive orders, agency rules, and the democratic political process.

Forestry and Conservation Science Teachers, Postsecondary

- Annual Earnings: $64,870
- Growth: 32.2%
- Annual Job Openings: 329,000
- Self-Employed: 0.4%
- Part-Time: 27.3%
- Education/Training Required: Master's degree

Our sources did not provide separate job openings data for this occupation. The job openings listed here are shared with 35 other postsecondary teaching occupations. For a complete list, see the beginning of this section.

Industries in Which Income Is Highest

Industry	Average Annual Wage	Number Employed
Educational Services	$65,170	2,870

Metropolitan Areas Where Income Is Highest

Metropolitan Area	Average Annual Wage	Number Employed
Philadelphia–Camden–Wilmington, PA–NJ–DE–MD	$72,150	100

Teach courses in environmental and conservation science. Conduct research in a particular field of knowledge and publish findings in books, professional journals, and/or electronic media. Keep abreast of developments in their field by reading current literature, talking with colleagues, and participating in professional conferences. Prepare and deliver lectures to undergraduate and/or graduate students on topics such as forest resource policy, forest pathology, and mapping. Evaluate and grade students' class work, assignments, and papers. Write grant proposals to procure external research funding. Supervise undergraduate and/or graduate teaching, internship, and research work. Plan, evaluate, and revise curricula, course content, and course materials and methods of instruction. Prepare course materials such as syllabi, homework assignments, and handouts. Compile, administer, and grade examinations or assign this work to others. Advise students on academic and vocational curricula and on career issues. Initiate, facilitate, and moderate classroom discussions. Supervise students' laboratory and/or field work. Maintain student attendance records, grades, and other required records. Collaborate with colleagues to address teaching and research issues. Maintain regularly scheduled office hours in order to advise and assist students. Select and obtain materials and supplies such as textbooks and laboratory equipment. Participate in student recruitment, registration, and placement activities. Serve on academic or administrative committees that deal with institutional policies, departmental matters, and academic issues. Provide professional consulting services to government and/or industry. Perform administrative duties such as serving as department head. **SKILLS**—Science; Management of Financial Resources; Instructing; Management of Personnel Resources; Writing; Active Learning; Critical Thinking; Time Management.

GOE—Interest Area: 05. Education and Training. **Work Group:** 05.03. Postsecondary and Adult Teaching and Instructing. **PERSONALITY TYPE:** Investigative. Investigative occupations frequently involve working with ideas and require an extensive amount of thinking. These occupations can involve searching for facts and figuring out problems mentally.

EDUCATION/TRAINING PROGRAM—Science Teacher Education/General Science Teacher Education. **RELATED KNOWLEDGE/COURSES—Biology:** Knowledge of plant and animal organisms and their tissues, cells, functions, interdependencies, and interactions with each other and the environment. **Education and Training:** Knowledge of principles and methods for curriculum and training design, teaching and instruction for individuals and groups, and the measurement of training effects. **Geography:** Knowledge of principles and methods for describing the features of land, sea, and air masses, including their physical characteristics; locations; interrelationships; and distribution of plant, animal, and human life. **English Language:** Knowledge of the structure and content of the English language, including the meaning and spelling of words, rules of composition, and grammar. **Mathematics:** Knowledge of arithmetic, algebra, geometry, calculus, and statistics and their applications. **Computers and Electronics:** Knowledge of circuit boards, processors, chips, electronic equipment, and computer hardware and software, including applications and programming.

Frame Wirers, Central Office

- Annual Earnings: $50,620
- Growth: –4.9%
- Annual Job Openings: 21,000
- Self-Employed: 6.6%
- Part-Time: 4.8%
- Education/Training Required: Long-term on-the-job training

The job openings listed here are shared with Central Office and PBX Installers and Repairers; Communication Equipment Mechanics, Installers, and Repairers; Station Installers and Repairers, Telephone; and Telecommunications Facility Examiners.

Industries in Which Income Is Highest

Industry	Average Annual Wage	Number Employed
Telecommunications	$52,170	136,200
Management of Companies and Enterprises	$51,670	2,520
Professional, Scientific, and Technical Services	$51,100	5,810
Wholesale Electronic Markets and Agents and Brokers	$48,990	1,400
Administrative and Support Services	$48,780	3,780

Metropolitan Areas Where Income Is Highest

Metropolitan Area	Average Annual Wage	Number Employed
Atlantic City, NJ	$68,240	50
Trenton–Ewing, NJ	$64,750	280
New York–Northern New Jersey–Long Island, NY–NJ–PA	$62,120	15,460
Rochester, NY	$61,530	620
State College, PA	$59,690	80

Connect wires from telephone lines and cables to distributing frames in telephone company central office, using soldering iron and other hand tools. Strings distributing frames with connecting wires. Tests circuit connections, using voltmeter or ammeter. Assists in locating and correcting malfunction in wiring on distributing frame. Lubricates moving switch parts. Cleans switches and replaces contact points, using vacuum hose, solvents, and hand tools. Removes and remakes connections to change circuit layouts. Solders connections, following diagram or oral instructions. **SKILLS**—Installation; Repairing; Quality Control Analysis; Troubleshooting; Operation Monitoring.

GOE—Interest Area: 02. Architecture and Construction. **Work Group:** 02.05. Systems and Equipment Installation, Maintenance, and Repair. **PERSONALITY TYPE:** Realistic. Realistic occupations frequently involve work activities that include practical, hands-on problems and solutions. They often deal with plants, animals, and real-world materials like wood, tools, and machinery. Many of the occupations require working outside and do not involve a lot of paperwork or working closely with others.

EDUCATION/TRAINING PROGRAM— Communications Systems Installation and Repair Technology. **RELATED KNOWLEDGE/ COURSES—Telecommunications:** Knowledge of transmission, broadcasting, switching, control, and operation of telecommunications systems. **Engineering and Technology:** Knowledge of the practical application of engineering science and technology. This includes applying principles, techniques, procedures, and equipment to the design and production of various goods and services. **Mechanical Devices:** Knowledge of machines and tools, including their designs, uses, repair, and maintenance.

Freight Inspectors

- Annual Earnings: $49,490
- Growth: 11.4%
- Annual Job Openings: 2,000
- Self-Employed: 1.9%
- Part-Time: 2.2%
- Education/Training Required: Work experience in a related occupation

The job openings listed here are shared with Aviation Inspectors, Marine Cargo Inspectors, Motor Vehicle Inspectors, Public Transportation Inspectors, and Railroad Inspectors.

Industries in Which Income Is Highest

Industry	Average Annual Wage	Number Employed
Air Transportation	$67,590	1,460
Transportation Equipment Manufacturing	$55,200	1,100
Federal, State, and Local Government	$54,510	10,960
Rail Transportation	$45,840	2,680
Support Activities for Transportation	$37,870	4,350

Metropolitan Areas Where Income Is Highest

Metropolitan Area	Average Annual Wage	Number Employed
Washington–Arlington–Alexandria, DC–VA–MD–WV	$96,800	360
Oklahoma City, OK	$91,650	130
Milwaukee–Waukesha–West Allis, WI	$84,510	50
Miami–Fort Lauderdale–Miami Beach, FL	$84,490	680
Louisville–Jefferson County, KY–IN	$81,260	80

Inspect freight for proper storage according to specifications. Inspects shipment to ascertain that freight is securely braced and blocked. Observes loading of freight to ensure that crews comply with procedures. Monitors temperature and humidity of freight storage area. Records freight condition and handling, and notifies crews to reload freight or insert additional bracing or packing. Measures height and width of loads that will pass over bridges or through tunnels. Notifies workers of special treatment required for shipments. Prepares and submits report after trip. Posts warning signs on vehicles containing explosives or inflammatory or radioactive materials. **SKILLS**—None met the criteria.

GOE—Interest Area: 16. Transportation, Distribution, and Logistics. **Work Group:** 16.07. Transportation Support Work. **PERSONALITY TYPE:** Conventional. Conventional occupations frequently involve following set procedures and routines. These occupations can include working with data and details more than with ideas. Usually there is a clear line of authority to follow.

EDUCATION/TRAINING PROGRAM—No data available. **RELATED KNOWLEDGE/COURSES— Transportation:** Knowledge of principles and methods for moving people or goods by air, rail, sea, or road, including the relative costs and benefits. **Public Safety and Security:** Knowledge of relevant equipment, policies, procedures, and strategies to promote effective local, state, or national security operations for the protection of people, data, property, and institutions. **Production and Processing:** Knowledge of raw materials, production processes, quality control, costs, and other techniques for maximizing the effective manufacture and distribution of goods.

Funeral Directors

◎ Annual Earnings: $47,630

◎ Growth: 6.7%

◎ Annual Job Openings: 3,000

◎ Self-Employed: 19.7%

◎ Part-Time: 9.4%

◎ Education/Training Required: Associate degree

Industries in Which Income Is Highest

Industry	Average Annual Wage	Number Employed
Personal and Laundry Services	$47,620	21,860

Metropolitan Areas Where Income Is Highest

Metropolitan Area	Average Annual Wage	Number Employed
Salt Lake City, UT	$80,770	70
Providence–Fall River–Warwick, RI–MA	$73,150	120
Canton–Massillon, OH	$71,190	70
Youngstown–Warren–Boardman, OH–PA	$64,370	70
Chicago–Naperville–Joliet, IL–IN–WI	$60,970	730

Perform various tasks to arrange and direct funeral services, such as coordinating transportation of body to mortuary for embalming, interviewing family or other authorized person to arrange details, selecting pallbearers, procuring official for religious rites, and providing transportation for mourners. Consult with families and/or friends of the deceased to arrange funeral details such as obituary notice wording, casket selection, and plans for services. Plan, schedule and coordinate funerals, burials, and cremations,

arranging such details as the time and place of services. Obtain information needed to complete legal documents such as death certificates and burial permits. Oversee the preparation and care of the remains of people who have died. Contact cemeteries to schedule the opening and closing of graves. Provide information on funeral service options, products, and merchandise, and maintain a casket display area. Manage funeral home operations, including hiring and supervising embalmers, funeral attendants, and other staff. Offer counsel and comfort to bereaved families and friends. Close caskets and lead funeral corteges to churches or burial sites. Arrange for clergy members to perform needed services. Provide or arrange transportation between sites for the remains, mourners, pallbearers, clergy, and flowers. Perform embalming duties as necessary. Direct preparations and shipment of bodies for out-of-state burial. Discuss and negotiate pre-arranged funerals with clients. Inform survivors of benefits for which they may be eligible. Maintain financial records, order merchandise, and prepare accounts. Plan placement of caskets at funeral sites, and place and adjust lights, fixtures, and floral displays. Arrange for pallbearers, and inform pallbearers and honorary groups of their duties. Receive and usher people to their seats for services. **SKILLS**—Service Orientation; Social Perceptiveness; Management of Financial Resources; Management of Personnel Resources; Coordination; Negotiation; Management of Material Resources; Time Management.

GOE—Interest Area: 14. Retail and Wholesale Sales and Service. **Work Group:** 14.01. Managerial Work in Retail/Wholesale Sales and Service. **PERSONALITY TYPE:** Enterprising. Enterprising occupations frequently involve starting up and carrying out projects. These occupations can involve leading people and making many decisions. They sometimes require risk taking and often deal with business.

EDUCATION/TRAINING PROGRAMS—Funeral Direction/Service; Funeral Service and Mortuary Science, General. **RELATED KNOWLEDGE/COURSES—Customer and Personal Service:** Knowledge of principles and processes for providing customer and personal services. This includes customer needs assessment, meeting quality standards for services, and evaluation of customer satisfaction. **Therapy and Counseling:** Knowledge of principles, methods, and procedures for diagnosis, treatment, and rehabilitation of physical and mental dysfunctions and for career counseling and guidance. **Philosophy and Theology:**

Knowledge of different philosophical systems and religions. This includes their basic principles, values, ethics, ways of thinking, customs, and practices and their impact on human culture. **Sales and Marketing:** Knowledge of principles and methods for showing, promoting, and selling products or services. This includes marketing strategy and tactics, product demonstration, sales techniques, and sales control systems. **Clerical Practices:** Knowledge of administrative and clerical procedures and systems such as word processing, managing files and records, stenography and transcription, designing forms, and other office procedures and terminology. **Psychology:** Knowledge of human behavior and performance; individual differences in ability, personality, and interests; learning and motivation; psychological research methods; and the assessment and treatment of behavioral and affective disorders.

Gaming Managers

- ◉ Annual Earnings: $59,940
- ◉ Growth: 22.6%
- ◉ Annual Job Openings: 1,000
- ◉ Self-Employed: 4.0.0%
- ◉ Part-Time: 5.3%
- ◉ Education/Training Required: Work experience in a related occupation

Industries in Which Income Is Highest

Industry	Average Annual Wage	Number Employed
Accommodation	$72,920	1,010
Performing Arts, Spectator Sports, and Related Industries	$57,260	110
Federal, State, and Local Government	$56,670	810
Amusement, Gambling, and Recreation Industries	$54,650	1,280

Metropolitan Areas Where Income Is Highest

Metropolitan Area	Average Annual Wage	Number Employed
San Diego–Carlsbad–San Marcos, CA	$87,190	50
Los Angeles–Long Beach–Santa Ana, CA	$85,210	60
Atlantic City, NJ	$79,550	210
Seattle–Tacoma–Bellevue, WA	$75,070	40
Las Vegas–Paradise, NV	$74,470	440

Plan, organize, direct, control, or coordinate gaming operations in a casino. Formulate gaming policies for their area of responsibility. Resolve customer complaints regarding problems such as payout errors. Remove suspected cheaters, such as card counters and other players who may have systems that shift the odds of winning to their favor. Maintain familiarity with all games used at a facility, as well as strategies and tricks employed in those games. Train new workers and evaluate their performance. Circulate among gaming tables to ensure that operations are conducted properly, that dealers follow house rules, and that players are not cheating. Explain and interpret house rules, such as game rules and betting limits. Monitor staffing levels to ensure that games and tables are adequately staffed for each shift, arranging for staff rotations and breaks, and locating substitute employees as necessary. Interview and hire workers. Prepare work schedules and station assignments, and keep attendance records. Direct the distribution of complimentary hotel rooms, meals, and other discounts or free items given to players based on their length of play and betting totals. Establish policies on issues such as the type of gambling offered and the odds, the extension of credit, and the serving of food and beverages. Track supplies of money to tables, and perform any required paperwork. Set and maintain a bank and table limit for each game. Monitor credit extended to players. Review operational expenses, budget estimates, betting accounts, and collection reports for accuracy. Record, collect, and pay off bets, issuing receipts as necessary. Direct workers compiling summary sheets that show wager amounts and payoffs for races and events. Notify board attendants of table vacancies so that waiting patrons can play. **SKILLS—** Management of Personnel Resources; Service Orientation; Management of Financial Resources; Negotiation; Social Perceptiveness; Persuasion; Systems Evaluation; Learning Strategies.

GOE—**Interest Area:** 09. Hospitality, Tourism, and Recreation. **Work Group:** 09.01. Managerial Work in Hospitality and Tourism. **PERSONALITY TYPE:** Enterprising. Enterprising occupations frequently involve starting up and carrying out projects. These occupations can involve leading people and making many decisions. They sometimes require risk taking and often deal with business.

EDUCATION/TRAINING PROGRAM—Personal and Culinary Services, Other. **RELATED KNOWLEDGE/COURSES—Customer and Personal Service:** Knowledge of principles and processes for providing customer and personal services. This includes customer needs assessment, meeting quality standards for services, and evaluation of customer satisfaction. **Sales and Marketing:** Knowledge of principles and methods for showing, promoting, and selling products or services. This includes marketing strategy and tactics, product demonstration, sales techniques, and sales control systems. **Administration and Management:** Knowledge of business and management principles involved in strategic planning, resource allocation, human resources modeling, leadership technique, production methods, and coordination of people and resources. **Personnel and Human Resources:** Knowledge of principles and procedures for personnel recruitment, selection, training, compensation and benefits, labor relations and negotiation, and personnel information systems. **Economics and Accounting:** Knowledge of economic and accounting principles and practices, the financial markets, banking, and the analysis and reporting of financial data. **Education and Training:** Knowledge of principles and methods for curriculum and training design, teaching and instruction for individuals and groups, and the measurement of training effects.

Gas Distribution Plant Operators

- Annual Earnings: $51,920
- Growth: 7.7%
- Annual Job Openings: 2,000
- Self-Employed: 0.1%
- Part-Time: 0.8%
- Education/Training Required: Long-term on-the-job training

The job openings listed here are shared with Gas Processing Plant Operators.

Industries in Which Income Is Highest

Industry	Average Annual Wage	Number Employed
Utilities	$55,000	5,000
Pipeline Transportation	$49,770	3,040
Oil and Gas Extraction	$48,360	1,050

Metropolitan Areas Where Income Is Highest

Metropolitan Area	Average Annual Wage	Number Employed
New York–Northern New Jersey–Long Island, NY–NJ–PA	$66,890	420
Des Moines–West Des Moines, IA	$65,070	60
Washington–Arlington–Alexandria, DC–VA–MD–WV	$52,280	320
Philadelphia–Camden–Wilmington, PA–NJ–DE–MD	$51,650	160
Boston–Cambridge–Quincy, MA–NH	$49,200	210

Control equipment to regulate flow and pressure of gas for utility companies and industrial use. May control distribution of gas for a municipal or industrial plant or a single process in an industrial plant. Controls equipment to regulate flow and pressure of gas to feedlines of boilers, furnaces, and related steam-generating or heating equipment. Observes, records, and reports flow and pressure gauge readings on gas mains and fuel feedlines. Changes charts in recording meters. Determines causes of abnormal pressure variances and makes corrective recommendations, such as installation of pipe to relieve overloading. Determines required governor adjustments, according to customer-demand estimates. Adjusts governors to maintain specified gas pressure and volume. **SKILLS**—Operation and Control; Operation Monitoring; Equipment Maintenance; Operations Analysis; Troubleshooting; Repairing.

GOE—Interest Area: 13. Manufacturing. **Work Group:** 13.16. Utility Operation and Energy Distribution. **PERSONALITY TYPE:** Realistic. Realistic occupations frequently involve work activities that include practical, hands-on problems and solutions. They often deal with plants, animals, and real-world materials like wood, tools, and machinery. Many of the occupations require working outside and do not involve a lot of paperwork or working closely with others.

EDUCATION/TRAINING PROGRAM—No data available. **RELATED KNOWLEDGE/COURSES**— **Mechanical Devices:** Knowledge of machines and tools, including their designs, uses, repair, and maintenance. **Physics:** Knowledge and prediction of physical principles and laws and their interrelationships and applications to understanding fluid, material, and atmospheric dynamics and mechanical, electrical, atomic, and subatomic structures and processes. **Engineering and Technology:** Knowledge of the practical application of engineering science and technology. This includes applying principles, techniques, procedures, and equipment to the design and production of various goods and services. **Production and Processing:** Knowledge of raw materials, production processes, quality control, costs, and other techniques for maximizing the effective manufacture and distribution of goods. **Clerical Practices:** Knowledge of administrative and clerical procedures and systems such as word processing, managing files and records, stenography and transcription, designing forms, and other office procedures and terminology.

Gas Processing Plant Operators

- Annual Earnings: $51,920
- Growth: 7.7%
- Annual Job Openings: 2,000
- Self-Employed: 0.1%
- Part-Time: 0.8%
- Education/Training Required: Long-term on-the-job training

The job openings listed here are shared with Gas Distribution Plant Operators.

Industries in Which Income Is Highest

Industry	Average Annual Wage	Number Employed
Utilities	$55,000	5,000
Pipeline Transportation	$49,770	3,040
Oil and Gas Extraction	$48,360	1,050

Metropolitan Areas Where Income Is Highest

Metropolitan Area	Average Annual Wage	Number Employed
New York–Northern New Jersey–Long Island, NY–NJ–PA	$66,890	420
Des Moines–West Des Moines, IA	$65,070	60
Washington–Arlington–Alexandria, DC–VA–MD–WV	$52,280	320
Philadelphia–Camden–Wilmington, PA–NJ–DE–MD	$51,650	160
Boston–Cambridge–Quincy, MA–NH	$49,200	210

Control equipment, such as compressors, evaporators, heat exchangers, and refrigeration equipment to process gas for utility companies and for industrial use. Controls fractioning columns, compressors, purifying towers, heat exchangers, and related equipment, to extract nitrogen and oxygen from air. Adjusts temperature, pressure, vacuum, level, flow rate, or transfer of gas, according to test results and knowledge of process and equipment. Observes pressure, temperature, level, and flow gauges to ensure standard operation. Reads logsheet to ascertain demand and disposition of product or to detect equipment malfunctions. Records gauge readings and test results. Signals or directs workers tending auxiliary equipment. Cleans and repairs equipment, using hand tools. Calculates gas ratios, using testing apparatus, to detect deviations from specifications. Tests oxygen for purity and moisture content at various stages of process, using burette and moisture meter. Controls operation of compressors, scrubbers, evaporators, and refrigeration equipment to liquefy, compress, or regasify natural gas. **SKILLS**— Operation Monitoring; Repairing; Operation and Control; Equipment Maintenance; Science; Mathematics; Quality Control Analysis; Troubleshooting.

GOE—Interest Area: 13. Manufacturing. **Work Group:** 13.16. Utility Operation and Energy Distribution. **PERSONALITY TYPE:** Realistic. Realistic occupations frequently involve work activities that include practical, hands-on problems and solutions. They often deal with plants, animals, and real-world materials like wood, tools, and machinery. Many of the occupations require working outside and do not involve a lot of paperwork or working closely with others.

EDUCATION/TRAINING PROGRAM—No data available. **RELATED KNOWLEDGE/COURSES**— **Mechanical Devices:** Knowledge of machines and tools, including their designs, uses, repair, and maintenance. **Chemistry:** Knowledge of the chemical composition, structure, and properties of substances and of the chemical processes and transformations that they undergo. This includes uses of chemicals, their danger signs, production techniques, and disposal methods. **Engineering and Technology:** Knowledge of the practical application of engineering science and technology. This includes applying principles, techniques, procedures, and equipment to the design and production of various goods and services. **Production and Processing:** Knowledge of raw materials, production processes, quality control, costs, and other techniques for maximizing the effective manufacture and distribution of goods. **Physics:** Knowledge and prediction of physical principles and laws and their interrelationships and applications to understanding fluid, material, and atmospheric dynamics and mechanical, electrical, atomic, and subatomic structures and processes.

Gaugers

- Annual Earnings: $51,060
- Growth: –8.6%
- Annual Job Openings: 6,000
- Self-Employed: 0.1%
- Part-Time: 0.8%
- Education/Training Required: Long-term on-the-job training

The job openings listed here are shared with Petroleum Pump System Operators; and Petroleum Refinery and Control Panel Operators.

Industries in Which Income Is Highest

Industry	Average Annual Wage	Number Employed
Oil and Gas Extraction	$52,700	8,680
Petroleum and Coal Products Manufacturing	$52,150	21,060
Pipeline Transportation	$50,740	4,530
Support Activities for Mining	$39,420	3,060

Metropolitan Areas Where Income Is Highest

Metropolitan Area	Average Annual Wage	Number Employed
Vallejo–Fairfield, CA	$81,650	90
Los Angeles–Long Beach–Santa Ana, CA	$58,990	1,800
Fairbanks, AK	$58,980	70
Billings, MT	$57,220	420
Denver–Aurora, CO	$55,610	280

Gauge and test oil in storage tanks. Regulate flow of oil into pipelines at wells, tank farms, refineries, and marine and rail terminals, following prescribed standards and regulations. Gauges quality of oil in storage tanks before and after delivery, using calibrated steel tape and conversion. Regulates flow of products into pipelines, using automated pumping equipment. Reads automatic gauges at specified intervals to determine flow rate of oil into or from tanks and amount of oil in tanks. Operates pumps, teletype, and mobile radio. Turns bleeder valves or lowers sample container into tank to obtain oil sample. Lowers thermometer into tanks to obtain temperature reading. Reports leaks or defective valves to maintenance. Tightens connections with wrenches and greases and oils valves, using grease gum and oil can. Inspects pipelines, valves, and flanges to detect malfunctions, such as loose connections and leaks. Clamps seal around valves to secure tanks. Records meter and pressure readings at gas well. Records readings and test results. Calculates test results, using standard formulas. Gauges tank containing petroleum and natural gas byproducts, such as condensate or natural gasoline. Starts pumps and opens valves to regulate flow of oil into and out of tanks, according to delivery schedules. Tests oil to determine amount of bottom sediment, water, and foreign materials, using centrifugal tester. **SKILLS**—Operation Monitoring; Equipment Maintenance; Operation and Control; Science; Mathematics; Quality Control Analysis; Troubleshooting; Repairing.

GOE—Interest Area: 13. Manufacturing. **Work Group:** 13.16. Utility Operation and Energy Distribution. **PERSONALITY TYPE:** Realistic. Realistic occupations frequently involve work activities that include practical, hands-on problems and solutions. They often deal with plants, animals, and real-world materials like wood, tools, and machinery. Many of the occupations require working outside and do not involve a lot of paperwork or working closely with others.

EDUCATION/TRAINING PROGRAM—No data available. **RELATED KNOWLEDGE/COURSES— Mechanical Devices:** Knowledge of machines and tools, including their designs, uses, repair, and maintenance. **Physics:** Knowledge and prediction of physical principles and laws and their interrelationships and applications to understanding fluid, material, and atmospheric dynamics and mechanical, electrical, atomic, and subatomic structures and processes. **Engineering and Technology:** Knowledge of the practical application of engineering science and technology. This includes applying principles, techniques, procedures, and equipment to the design and production of various goods and services. **Production and Processing:** Knowledge of raw materials, production processes, quality control, costs, and other techniques for maximizing the effective manufacture and distribution of goods. **Public Safety and Security:** Knowledge of relevant equipment, policies, procedures, and strategies to promote effective local, state, or national security operations for the protection of people, data, property, and

institutions. **Mathematics:** Knowledge of arithmetic, algebra, geometry, calculus, and statistics and their applications.

General and Operations Managers

- ⌬ Annual Earnings: $81,480
- ⌬ Growth: 17.0%
- ⌬ Annual Job Openings: 208,000
- ⌬ Self-Employed: 0.6%
- ⌬ Part-Time: 3.4%
- ⌬ Education/Training Required: Work experience plus degree

Industries in Which Income Is Highest

Industry	Average Annual Wage	Number Employed
Securities, Commodity Contracts, and Other Financial Investments and Related Activities	$131,530	15,010
Computer and Electronic Product Manufacturing	$118,780	17,650
Oil and Gas Extraction	$112,870	5,210
Professional, Scientific, and Technical Services	$112,090	149,590
Internet Service Providers, Web Search Portals, and Data Processing Services	$110,790	8,160

Metropolitan Areas Where Income Is Highest

Metropolitan Area	Average Annual Wage	Number Employed
Bridgeport–Stamford–Norwalk, CT	$137,760	6,440
New York–Northern New Jersey–Long Island, NY–NJ–PA	$124,400	89,000
Trenton–Ewing, NJ	$123,430	2,040
San Jose–Sunnyvale–Santa Clara, CA	$121,010	14,720
Seattle–Tacoma–Bellevue, WA	$116,870	11,160

Plan, direct, or coordinate the operations of companies or public and private sector organizations. Duties and responsibilities include formulating policies, managing daily operations, and planning

the use of materials and human resources, but are too diverse and general in nature to be classified in any one functional area of management or administration, such as personnel, purchasing, or administrative services. Includes owners and managers who head small business establishments whose duties are primarily managerial. Direct and coordinate activities of businesses or departments concerned with the production, pricing, sales, and/or distribution of products. Manage staff, preparing work schedules and assigning specific duties. Review financial statements, sales and activity reports, and other performance data to measure productivity and goal achievement and to determine areas needing cost reduction and program improvement. Establish and implement departmental policies, goals, objectives, and procedures, conferring with board members, organization officials, and staff members as necessary. Determine staffing requirements, and interview, hire and train new employees, or oversee those personnel processes. Monitor businesses and agencies to ensure that they efficiently and effectively provide needed services while staying within budgetary limits. Oversee activities directly related to making products or providing services. Direct and coordinate organization's financial and budget activities to fund operations, maximize investments, and increase efficiency. Determine goods and services to be sold, and set prices and credit terms, based on forecasts of customer demand. Manage the movement of goods into and out of production facilities. Locate, select, and procure merchandise for resale, representing management in purchase negotiations. Perform sales floor work such as greeting and assisting customers, stocking shelves, and taking inventory. Develop and implement product marketing strategies including advertising campaigns and sales promotions. Plan and direct activities such as sales promotions, coordinating with other department heads as required. Direct non-merchandising departments of businesses, such as advertising and purchasing. SKILLS—Management of Financial Resources; Management of Personnel Resources; Management of Material Resources; Negotiation; Monitoring; Persuasion; Coordination; Social Perceptiveness.

GOE—Interest Area: 04. Business and Administration. Work Group: 04.01. Managerial Work in General Business. PERSONALITY TYPE: No data available.

EDUCATION/TRAINING PROGRAMS—Business Administration/Management; Entrepreneurship/Entrepreneurial Studies; International Business/Trade/

Commerce; Public Administration. RELATED KNOWLEDGE/COURSES—Sales and Marketing: Knowledge of principles and methods for showing, promoting, and selling products or services. This includes marketing strategy and tactics, product demonstration, sales techniques, and sales control systems. Administration and Management: Knowledge of business and management principles involved in strategic planning, resource allocation, human resources modeling, leadership technique, production methods, and coordination of people and resources. Customer and Personal Service: Knowledge of principles and processes for providing customer and personal services. This includes customer needs assessment, meeting quality standards for services, and evaluation of customer satisfaction. Personnel and Human Resources: Knowledge of principles and procedures for personnel recruitment, selection, training, compensation and benefits, labor relations and negotiation, and personnel information systems. Economics and Accounting: Knowledge of economic and accounting principles and practices, the financial markets, banking, and the analysis and reporting of financial data. Law and Government: Knowledge of laws, legal codes, court procedures, precedents, government regulations, executive orders, agency rules, and the democratic political process.

Geographers

- Annual Earnings: $63,550
- Growth: 6.8%
- Annual Job Openings: fewer than 500
- Self-Employed: 4.2%
- Part-Time: 15.6%
- Education/Training Required: Master's degree

Industries in Which Income Is Highest

Industry	Average Annual Wage	Number Employed
Federal, State, and Local Government	$65,060	600
Professional, Scientific, and Technical Services	$55,710	110

Metropolitan Areas Where Income Is Highest

Metropolitan Area	Average Annual Wage	Number Employed
Washington–Arlington–Alexandria, DC–VA–MD–WV	$71,520	210

Study nature and use of areas of earth's surface, relating and interpreting interactions of physical and cultural phenomena. Conduct research on physical aspects of a region, including land forms, climates, soils, plants and animals, and conduct research on the spatial implications of human activities within a given area, including social characteristics, economic activities, and political organization, as well as researching interdependence between regions at scales ranging from local to global. Create and modify maps, graphs, and/or diagrams, using geographical information software and related equipment, and principles of cartography such as coordinate systems, longitude, latitude, elevation, topography, and map scales. Write and present reports of research findings. Develop, operate, and maintain geographical information (GIS) computer systems, including hardware, software, plotters, digitizers, printers, and video cameras. Locate and obtain existing geographic information databases. Analyze geographic distributions of physical and cultural phenomena on local, regional, continental, and/or global scales. Teach geography. Gather and compile geographic data from sources including censuses, field observations, satellite imagery, aerial photographs, and existing maps. Conduct fieldwork at outdoor sites. Study the economic, political, and cultural characteristics of a specific region's population. Provide consulting services in fields including resource development and management, business location and market area analysis, environmental hazards, regional cultural history, and urban social planning. Collect data on physical characteristics of specified areas, such as geological formations, climates, and vegetation, using surveying or meteorological equipment. Provide geographical information systems support to the private and public sectors. **SKILLS**—Programming; Science; Complex Problem Solving; Management of Financial Resources; Writing; Instructing; Critical Thinking; Reading Comprehension.

GOE—Interest Area: 15. Scientific Research, Engineering, and Mathematics. **Work Group:** 15.02. Physical Sciences. **PERSONALITY TYPE:** Investigative. Investigative occupations frequently involve working with ideas and require an extensive amount of thinking. These occupations can involve searching for facts and figuring out problems mentally.

EDUCATION/TRAINING PROGRAM—Geography. **RELATED KNOWLEDGE/COURSES**—**Geography:** Knowledge of principles and methods for describing the features of land, sea, and air masses, including their physical characteristics; locations; interrelationships; and distribution of plant, animal, and human life. **Sociology and Anthropology:** Knowledge of group behavior and dynamics, societal trends and influences, human migrations, ethnicity, and cultures and their history and origins. **History and Archeology:** Knowledge of historical events and their causes, indicators, and effects on civilizations and cultures. **Education and Training:** Knowledge of principles and methods for curriculum and training design, teaching and instruction for individuals and groups, and the measurement of training effects. **Biology:** Knowledge of plant and animal organisms and their tissues, cells, functions, interdependencies, and interactions with each other and the environment. **Philosophy and Theology:** Knowledge of different philosophical systems and religions. This includes their basic principles, values, ethics, ways of thinking, customs, and practices and their impact on human culture.

Geography Teachers, Postsecondary

- Annual Earnings: $57,870
- Growth: 32.2%
- Annual Job Openings: 329,000
- Self-Employed: 0.4%
- Part-Time: 27.3%
- Education/Training Required: Master's degree

Our sources did not provide separate job openings data for this occupation. The job openings listed here are shared with 35 other postsecondary teaching occupations. For a complete list, see the beginning of this section.

Industries in Which Income Is Highest

Industry	Average Annual Wage	Number Employed
Educational Services	$57,880	4,250

Metropolitan Areas Where Income Is Highest

Metropolitan Area	Average Annual Wage	Number Employed
Atlanta–Sandy Springs–Marietta, GA	$75,570	30
San Diego–Carlsbad–San Marcos, CA	$75,360	30
Durham, NC	$71,600	40
Philadelphia–Camden–Wilmington, PA–NJ–DE–MD	$70,040	270
New York–Northern New Jersey–Long Island, NY–NJ–PA	$68,510	30

Teach courses in geography. Prepare and deliver lectures to undergraduate and/or graduate students on topics such as urbanization, environmental systems, and cultural geography. Evaluate and grade students' class work, assignments, and papers. Compile, administer, and grade examinations or assign this work to others. Initiate, facilitate, and moderate classroom discussions. Maintain student attendance records, grades, and other required records. Prepare course materials such as syllabi, homework assignments, and handouts. Keep abreast of developments in their field by reading current literature, talking with colleagues, and participating in professional conferences. Supervise undergraduate and/or graduate teaching, internship, and research work. Plan, evaluate, and revise curricula, course content, and course materials and methods of instruction. Maintain regularly scheduled office hours in order to advise and assist students. Supervise students' laboratory and field work. Conduct research in a particular field of knowledge and publish findings in professional journals, books, and/or electronic media. Collaborate with colleagues to address teaching and research issues. Select and obtain materials and supplies such as textbooks. Advise students on academic and vocational curricula and on career issues. Serve on academic or administrative committees that deal with institutional policies, departmental matters, and academic issues. Participate in student recruitment, registration, and placement activities. Participate in campus and community events. Compile bibliographies of specialized materials for outside reading assignments. Perform administrative duties such as serving as department head. Write grant proposals to procure external research funding. Maintain geographic information systems laboratories, performing duties such as updating software. Perform spatial analysis and modeling, using geographic information system techniques. **SKILLS**—Instructing; Learning Strategies; Writing; Science; Critical Thinking; Active Learning; Speaking; Reading Comprehension.

GOE—Interest Area: 05. Education and Training. **Work Group:** 05.03. Postsecondary and Adult Teaching and Instructing. **PERSONALITY TYPE:** No data available.

EDUCATION/TRAINING PROGRAMS—Geography; Geography Teacher Education. **RELATED KNOWLEDGE/COURSES—Geography:** Knowledge of principles and methods for describing the features of land, sea, and air masses, including their physical characteristics; locations; interrelationships; and distribution of plant, animal, and human life. **Sociology and Anthropology:** Knowledge of group behavior and dynamics, societal trends and influences, human migrations, ethnicity, and cultures and their history and origins. **History and Archeology:** Knowledge of historical events and their causes, indicators, and effects on civilizations and cultures. **Education and Training:** Knowledge of principles and methods for curriculum and training design, teaching and instruction for individuals and groups, and the measurement of training effects. **Philosophy and Theology:** Knowledge of different philosophical systems and religions. This includes their basic principles, values, ethics, ways of thinking, customs, and practices and their impact on human culture. **English Language:** Knowledge of the structure and content of the English language, including the meaning and spelling of words, rules of composition, and grammar.

Geologists

- ◎ Annual Earnings: $71,640
- ◎ Growth: 8.3%
- ◎ Annual Job Openings: 2,000
- ◎ Self-Employed: 5.1%
- ◎ Part-Time: 5.9%
- ◎ Education/Training Required: Master's degree

Industries in Which Income Is Highest

Industry	Average Annual Wage	Number Employed
Oil and Gas Extraction	$102,850	5,680
Support Activities for Mining	$94,550	1,410
Federal, State, and Local Government	$65,400	5,370
Professional, Scientific, and Technical Services	$64,470	12,110
Educational Services	$53,590	1,190

Metropolitan Areas Where Income Is Highest

Metropolitan Area	Average Annual Wage	Number Employed
Houston–Sugar Land–Baytown, TX	$115,880	5,060
Tulsa, OK	$106,100	170
Washington–Arlington–Alexandria, DC–VA–MD–WV	$93,880	890
Oklahoma City, OK	$93,790	470
Denver–Aurora, CO	$91,640	900

Study composition, structure, and history of the earth's crust; examine rocks, minerals, and fossil remains to identify and determine the sequence of processes affecting the development of the earth; apply knowledge of chemistry, physics, biology, and mathematics to explain these phenomena and to help locate mineral and petroleum deposits and underground water resources; prepare geologic reports and maps; and interpret research data to recommend further action for study. Analyze and interpret geological, geochemical, and geophysical information from sources such as survey data, well logs, boreholes, and aerial photos. Plan and conduct geological, geochemical, and geophysical field studies and surveys; sample collection; and drilling and testing programs used to collect data for research and/or application. Investigate the composition, structure, and history of the Earth's crust through the collection, examination, measurement, and classification of soils, minerals, rocks, and fossil remains. Prepare geological maps, cross-sectional diagrams, charts, and reports concerning mineral extraction, land use, and resource management, using results of field work and laboratory research. Locate and estimate probable natural gas, oil, and mineral ore deposits and underground water resources, using aerial photographs, charts, and research and survey results. Assess ground and surface water movement in order to provide advice regarding issues such as waste management, route and site selection, and the restoration of contaminated sites. Identify risks for natural disasters such as mud slides, earthquakes, and volcanic eruptions, and provide advice on ways in which potential damage can be mitigated. Conduct geological and geophysical studies to provide information for use in regional development, site selection, and the development of public works projects. Inspect construction projects in order to analyze engineering problems, applying geological knowledge and using test equipment and drilling machinery. Advise construction firms and government agencies on dam and road construction, foundation design, and land use and resource management. **SKILLS**—Science; Management of Financial Resources; Time Management; Active Learning; Coordination; Persuasion; Critical Thinking; Negotiation.

GOE—Interest Area: 15. Scientific Research, Engineering, and Mathematics. **Work Group:** 15.02. Physical Sciences. **PERSONALITY TYPE:** Investigative. Investigative occupations frequently involve working with ideas and require an extensive amount of thinking. These occupations can involve searching for facts and figuring out problems mentally.

EDUCATION/TRAINING PROGRAMS— Geochemistry; Geochemistry and Petrology; Geological and Earth Sciences/Geosciences, Other; Geology/Earth Science, General; Geophysics and Seismology; Oceanography, Chemical and Physical; Paleontology. **RELATED KNOWLEDGE/COURSES**— **Geography:** Knowledge of principles and methods for describing the features of land, sea, and air masses, including their physical characteristics; locations; interrelationships; and distribution of plant, animal, and human life. **Chemistry:** Knowledge of the chemical composition, structure, and properties of substances and of the chemical processes and transformations that they undergo. This includes uses of chemicals, their danger signs, production techniques, and disposal methods. **Physics:** Knowledge and prediction of physical principles and laws and their interrelationships and applications to understanding fluid, material, and atmospheric dynamics and mechanical, electrical, atomic, and subatomic structures and processes. **Biology:** Knowledge of plant and animal organisms and their tissues, cells, functions, interdependencies, and interactions with each other and the environment. **Engineering and Technology:** Knowledge of the practical application of engineering science and technology. This includes applying principles, techniques, procedures, and equipment to the design and production of various goods and services. **Mathematics:** Knowledge of arithmetic, algebra, geometry, calculus, and statistics and their applications.

Government Property Inspectors and Investigators

◎ Annual Earnings: $49,360
◎ Growth: 11.6%
◎ Annual Job Openings: 17,000
◎ Self-Employed: 0.0%
◎ Part-Time: 5.1%
◎ Education/Training Required: Long-term on-the-job training

The job openings listed here are shared with Coroners, Environmental Compliance Inspectors, Equal Opportunity Representatives and Officers, Licensing Examiners and Inspectors, and Pressure Vessel Inspectors.

Industries in Which Income Is Highest

Industry	Average Annual Wage	Number Employed
Postal Service	$72,700	1,710
Utilities	$66,390	1,310
Securities, Commodity Contracts, and Other Financial Investments and Related Activities	$64,490	5,130
Computer and Electronic Product Manufacturing	$59,540	1,390
Telecommunications	$59,310	2,620

Metropolitan Areas Where Income Is Highest

Metropolitan Area	Average Annual Wage	Number Employed
Kankakee–Bradley, IL	$81,020	170
Brunswick, GA	$79,710	340
San Jose–Sunnyvale–Santa Clara, CA	$67,550	930
San Francisco–Oakland–Fremont, CA	$64,010	3,320
Santa Rosa–Petaluma, CA	$63,660	410

Investigate or inspect government property to ensure compliance with contract agreements and government regulations. Collect, identify, evaluate, and preserve case evidence. Examine records, reports, and documents in order to establish facts and detect discrepancies. Inspect government-owned equipment and materials in the possession of private contractors, in order to ensure compliance with contracts and regulations and to prevent misuse. Inspect manufactured or processed products to ensure compliance with contract specifications and legal requirements. Locate and interview plaintiffs, witnesses, or representatives of business or government in order to gather facts relevant to inspections or alleged violations. Prepare correspondence, reports of inspections or investigations, and recommendations for action. Recommend legal or administrative action to protect government property. Submit samples of products to government laboratories for testing as required. Coordinate with and assist law enforcement agencies in matters of mutual concern. Investigate applications for special licenses or permits, as well as alleged license or permit violations. Testify in court or at administrative proceedings concerning investigation findings. Monitor investigations of suspected offenders to ensure that they are conducted in accordance with constitutional requirements. **SKILLS**—Systems Analysis; Speaking; Negotiation; Judgment and Decision Making; Writing; Systems Evaluation; Reading Comprehension; Critical Thinking.

GOE—Interest Area: 07. Government and Public Administration. **Work Group:** 07.03. Regulations Enforcement. **PERSONALITY TYPE:** Enterprising. Enterprising occupations frequently involve starting up and carrying out projects. These occupations can involve leading people and making many decisions. They sometimes require risk taking and often deal with business.

EDUCATION/TRAINING PROGRAM—No data available. **RELATED KNOWLEDGE/COURSES**— **Law and Government:** Knowledge of laws, legal codes, court procedures, precedents, government regulations, executive orders, agency rules, and the democratic political process. **Personnel and Human Resources:** Knowledge of principles and procedures for personnel recruitment, selection, training, compensation and benefits, labor relations and negotiation, and personnel information systems. **Public Safety and Security:** Knowledge of relevant equipment, policies, procedures, and strategies to promote effective local, state, or national security operations for the protection of people, data, property, and institutions. **English Language:** Knowledge of the structure and content of the English language, including the meaning and spelling of words, rules of composition, and grammar. **Communications and Media:** Knowledge of media production, communication, and dissemination techniques and methods. This includes alternative ways to inform and entertain via written, oral, and visual media. **Mathematics:** Knowledge of arithmetic, algebra, geometry, calculus, and statistics and their applications.

Government Service Executives

- Annual Earnings: $142,440
- Growth: 14.9%
- Annual Job Openings: 38,000
- Self-Employed: 16.2%
- Part-Time: 6.8%
- Education/Training Required: Work experience plus degree

The job openings listed here are shared with Chief Executives and Private Sector Executives.

Industries in Which Income Is Highest

Industry	Average Annual Wage	Number Employed
Performing Arts, Spectator Sports, and Related Industries	More than $146,500	1,450
Nonstore Retailers	More than $146,500	1,420
Utilities	More than $146,500	1,600
Electronics and Appliance Stores	More than $146,500	1,060
Wholesale Electronic Markets and Agents and Brokers	More than $146,500	2,400

Metropolitan Areas Where Income Is Highest

Metropolitan Area	Average Annual Wage	Number Employed
Boston–Cambridge–Quincy, MA–NH	More than $146,500	17,530
New York–Northern New Jersey–Long Island, NY–NJ–PA	More than $146,500	15,260
Chicago–Naperville–Joilet, IL–IN–WI	More than $146,500	14,910
Los Angeles–Long Beach–Santa Ana, CA	More than $146,500	13,510
Atlanta–Sandy Springs–Marietta, GA	More than $146,500	11,950

Determine and formulate policies and provide overall direction of federal, state, local, or international government activities. Plan, direct, and coordinate operational activities at the highest level of

management with the help of subordinate managers. Directs organization charged with administering and monitoring regulated activities to interpret and clarify laws and ensure compliance with laws. Administers, interprets, and explains policies, rules, regulations, and laws to organizations and individuals under authority of commission or applicable legislation. Develops, plans, organizes, and administers policies and procedures for organization to ensure administrative and operational objectives are met. Directs and coordinates activities of workers in public organization to ensure continuing operations, maximize returns on investments, and increase productivity. Negotiates contracts and agreements with federal and state agencies and other organizations and prepares budget for funding and implementation of programs. Implements corrective action plan to solve problems. Reviews and analyzes legislation, laws, and public policy and recommends changes to promote and support interests of general population, as well as special groups. Develops, directs, and coordinates testing, hiring, training, and evaluation of staff personnel. Establishes and maintains comprehensive and current recordkeeping system of activities and operational procedures in business office. Testifies in court, before control or review board, or at legislature. Participates in activities to promote business and expand services, and provides technical assistance in conducting of conferences, seminars, and workshops. Delivers speeches, writes articles, and presents information for organization at meetings or conventions to promote services, exchange ideas, and accomplish objectives. Plans, promotes, organizes, and coordinates public community service program and maintains cooperative working relationships among public and agency participants. Conducts or directs investigations or hearings to resolve complaints and violations of laws. Prepares, reviews, and submits reports concerning activities, expenses, budget, government statutes and rulings, and other items affecting business or program services. Directs, coordinates, and conducts activities between United States Government and foreign entities to provide information to promote international interest and harmony. **SKILLS**—Management of Financial Resources; Systems Evaluation; Systems Analysis; Management of Personnel Resources; Coordination; Judgment and Decision Making; Negotiation; Persuasion.

GOE—Interest Area: 07. Government and Public Administration. **Work Group:** 07.01. Managerial Work in Government and Public Administration. **PERSONALITY TYPE:** Enterprising. Enterprising occupations frequently involve starting up and carrying out projects. These occupations can involve leading people and making many decisions. They sometimes require risk taking and often deal with business.

EDUCATION/TRAINING PROGRAMS—Public Administration; Public Administration and Services, Other; Public Policy Analysis. **RELATED KNOWLEDGE/COURSES—Administration and Management:** Knowledge of business and management principles involved in strategic planning, resource allocation, human resources modeling, leadership technique, production methods, and coordination of people and resources. **Personnel and Human Resources:** Knowledge of principles and procedures for personnel recruitment, selection, training, compensation and benefits, labor relations and negotiation, and personnel information systems. **Law and Government:** Knowledge of laws, legal codes, court procedures, precedents, government regulations, executive orders, agency rules, and the democratic political process. **Economics and Accounting:** Knowledge of economic and accounting principles and practices, the financial markets, banking, and the analysis and reporting of financial data. **Education and Training:** Knowledge of principles and methods for curriculum and training design, teaching and instruction for individuals and groups, and the measurement of training effects. **Psychology:** Knowledge of human behavior and performance; individual differences in ability, personality, and interests; learning and motivation; psychological research methods; and the assessment and treatment of behavioral and affective disorders.

Graduate Teaching Assistants

- ◎ Annual Earnings: $27,340
- ◎ Growth: 32.2%
- ◎ Annual Job Openings: 329,000
- ◎ Self-Employed: 0.4%
- ◎ Part-Time: 27.3%
- ◎ Education/Training Required: Master's degree

Our sources did not provide separate job openings data for this occupation. The job openings listed here are shared with 35 other postsecondary teaching occupations. For a complete list, see the beginning of this section.

Industries in Which Income Is Highest

Industry	Average Annual Wage	Number Employed
Educational Services	$27,350	116,920

Metropolitan Areas Where Income Is Highest

Metropolitan Area	Average Annual Wage	Number Employed
Boston–Cambridge–Quincy, MA–NH	$46,170	2,990
Riverside–San Bernardino–Ontario, CA	$39,340	1,030
Lincoln, NE	$34,520	710
Eugene–Springfield, OR	$31,870	760
Springfield, MA–CT	$28,610	100

Assist department chairperson, faculty members, or other professional staff members in college or university by performing teaching or teaching-related duties, such as teaching lower level courses, developing teaching materials, preparing and giving examinations, and grading examinations or papers. Graduate assistants must be enrolled in a graduate school program. Graduate assistants who primarily perform non-teaching duties, such as laboratory research, should be reported in the occupational category related to the work performed. Evaluate and grade examinations, assignments, and papers, and record grades. Lead discussion sections, tutorials, and laboratory sections. Teach undergraduate level courses. Develop teaching materials such as syllabi, visual aids, answer keys, supplementary notes, and course websites. Attend lectures given by the instructor whom they are assisting. Complete laboratory projects prior to assigning them to students so that any needed modifications can be made. Copy and distribute classroom materials. Demonstrate use of laboratory equipment, and enforce laboratory rules. Inform students of the procedures for completing and submitting class work such as lab reports. Meet with supervisors to discuss students' grades, and to complete required grade-related paperwork. Notify instructors of errors or problems with assignments. Order or obtain materials needed for classes. Prepare and proctor examinations. Return assignments to students in accordance with established deadlines. Schedule and maintain regular office hours to meet with students. Arrange for supervisors to conduct teaching observations; meet with supervisors to receive feedback about teaching performance. Assist faculty members or staff with student conferences. Provide assistance to faculty members or staff with laboratory or field research. Provide instructors with assistance in the use of audiovisual equipment. Provide assistance to library staff in maintaining library collections. **SKILLS**—Instructing; Learning Strategies; Speaking; Science; Reading Comprehension; Writing; Mathematics; Critical Thinking.

GOE—Interest Area: 05. Education and Training. **Work Group:** 05.03. Postsecondary and Adult Teaching and Instructing. **PERSONALITY TYPE:** Social. Social occupations frequently involve working with, communicating with, and teaching people. These occupations often involve helping or providing service to others.

EDUCATION/TRAINING PROGRAM—No data available. **RELATED KNOWLEDGE/COURSES**—**Education and Training:** Knowledge of principles and methods for curriculum and training design, teaching and instruction for individuals and groups, and the measurement of training effects. **English Language:** Knowledge of the structure and content of the English language, including the meaning and spelling of words, rules of composition, and grammar. **Clerical Practices:** Knowledge of administrative and clerical procedures and systems such as word processing, managing files and records, stenography and transcription, designing forms, and other office procedures and terminology. **Administration and Management:** Knowledge of business and management principles involved in strategic planning, resource allocation, human resources modeling, leadership technique, production methods, and coordination of people and resources. **Mathematics:** Knowledge of arithmetic, algebra, geometry, calculus, and statistics and their applications. **Computers and Electronics:** Knowledge of circuit boards, processors, chips, electronic equipment, and computer hardware and software, including applications and programming.

Health Specialties Teachers, Postsecondary

- Annual Earnings: $70,890
- Growth: 32.2%
- Annual Job Openings: 329,000
- Self-Employed: 0.4%
- Part-Time: 27.3%
- Education/Training Required: Master's degree

Our sources did not provide separate job openings data for this occupation. The job openings listed here are shared with 35 other postsecondary teaching occupations. For a complete list, see the beginning of this section.

Industries in Which Income Is Highest

Industry	Average Annual Wage	Number Employed
Educational Services	$71,590	100,740
Hospitals	$64,850	5,570

Metropolitan Areas Where Income Is Highest

Metropolitan Area	Average Annual Wage	Number Employed
Baltimore–Towson, MD	$109,920	3,560
Jacksonville, FL	$102,030	940
San Diego–Carlsbad–San Marcos, CA	$93,290	510
Durham, NC	$92,370	3,940
Houston–Sugar Land–Baytown, TX	$88,590	3,290

Teach courses in health specialties, such as veterinary medicine, dentistry, pharmacy, therapy, laboratory technology, and public health. Initiate, facilitate, and moderate classroom discussions. Keep abreast of developments in their field by reading current literature, talking with colleagues, and participating in professional conferences. Compile, administer, and grade examinations or assign this work to others. Evaluate and grade students' class work, assignments, and papers. Prepare course materials such as syllabi, homework assignments, and handouts. Prepare and deliver lectures to undergraduate and/or graduate students on topics such as public health, stress management, and worksite health promotion. Plan, evaluate, and revise curricula, course content, and course materials and methods of instruction. Supervise undergraduate and/or graduate teaching, internship, and research work. Conduct research in a particular field of knowledge and publish findings in professional journals, books, and/or electronic media. Collaborate with colleagues to address teaching and research issues. Supervise laboratory sessions. Maintain student attendance records, grades, and other required records. Maintain regularly scheduled office hours in order to advise and assist students. Advise students on academic and vocational curricula and on career issues. Participate in student recruitment, registration, and placement activities. Write grant proposals to procure external research funding. Serve on academic or administrative committees that deal with institutional policies, departmental matters, and academic issues. Select and obtain materials and supplies such as textbooks and laboratory equipment. Act as advisers to student organizations. Perform administrative duties such as serving as department head. **SKILLS**—Science; Instructing; Learning Strategies; Writing; Critical Thinking; Reading Comprehension; Time Management; Active Learning.

GOE—Interest Area: 05. Education and Training. **Work Group:** 05.03. Postsecondary and Adult Teaching and Instructing. **PERSONALITY TYPE:** Investigative. Investigative occupations frequently involve working with ideas and require an extensive amount of thinking. These occupations can involve searching for facts and figuring out problems mentally.

EDUCATION/TRAINING PROGRAMS—Allied Health Diagnostic, Intervention, and Treatment Professions, Other; Art Therapy/Therapist; Asian Bodywork Therapy; Audiology/Audiologist and Hearing Sciences; Audiology/Audiologist and Speech-Language Pathology/Pathologist; Biostatistics; Blood Bank Technology Specialist; Cardiovascular Technology/Technologist; Chiropractic (DC); Clinical Laboratory Science/Medical Technology/Technologist; Clinical/Medical Laboratory Technician; others. **RELATED KNOWLEDGE/COURSES—Education and Training:** Knowledge of principles and methods for curriculum and training design, teaching and instruction for individuals and groups, and the measurement of training effects. **Biology:** Knowledge of plant and animal organisms and their tissues, cells, functions, interdependencies, and interactions with each other and the environment. **Medicine and Dentistry:** Knowledge of the information and techniques needed to diagnose and treat human injuries, diseases, and deformities. This includes symptoms, treatment alternatives, drug properties and interactions, and preventive health-care measures. **Therapy and Counseling:** Knowledge of principles, methods, and procedures for diagnosis, treatment, and rehabilitation of physical and mental dysfunctions and for career counseling and guidance. **Sociology and Anthropology:** Knowledge of group behavior and dynamics, societal trends and influences, human migrations, ethnicity, and cultures and their history and origins. **Psychology:** Knowledge of human behavior and performance; individual differences in ability, personality, and interests; learning and motivation; psychological research methods; and the assessment and treatment of behavioral and affective disorders.

History Teachers, Postsecondary

- Annual Earnings: $54,780
- Growth: 32.2%
- Annual Job Openings: 329,000
- Self-Employed: 0.4%
- Part-Time: 27.3%
- Education/Training Required: Master's degree

Our sources did not provide separate job openings data for this occupation. The job openings listed here are shared with 35 other postsecondary teaching occupations. For a complete list, see the beginning of this section.

Industries in Which Income Is Highest

Industry	Average Annual Wage	Number Employed
Educational Services	$54,780	20,510

Metropolitan Areas Where Income Is Highest

Metropolitan Area	Average Annual Wage	Number Employed
Durham, NC	$78,180	160
Providence–Fall River–Warwick, RI–MA	$75,240	160
Rochester, NY	$73,220	130
Springfield, MA–CT	$70,690	80
Honolulu, HI	$70,610	140

Teach courses in human history and historiography. Prepare and deliver lectures to undergraduate and/or graduate students on topics such as ancient history, postwar civilizations, and the history of third-world countries. Evaluate and grade students' class work, assignments, and papers. Prepare course materials such as syllabi, homework assignments, and handouts. Compile, administer, and grade examinations or assign this work to others. Initiate, facilitate, and moderate classroom discussions. Keep abreast of developments in their field by reading current literature, talking with colleagues, and participating in professional conferences. Maintain student attendance records, grades, and other required records. Plan, evaluate, and revise curricula, course content, and course materials and methods of instruction. Maintain regularly scheduled office hours in order to advise and assist students. Conduct research in a particular field of knowledge and publish findings in professional journals, books, and/or electronic media. Select and obtain materials and supplies such as textbooks. Advise students on academic and vocational curricula and on career issues. Collaborate with colleagues to address teaching and research issues. Serve on academic or administrative committees that deal with institutional policies, departmental matters, and academic issues. Participate in campus and community events. Act as advisers to student organizations. Participate in student recruitment, registration, and placement activities. Compile bibliographies of specialized materials for outside reading assignments. Supervise undergraduate and/or graduate teaching, internship, and research work. Perform administrative duties such as serving as department head. **SKILLS—** Instructing; Writing; Learning Strategies; Persuasion; Critical Thinking; Speaking; Social Perceptiveness; Active Learning.

GOE—Interest Area: 05. Education and Training. **Work Group:** 05.03. Postsecondary and Adult

Teaching and Instructing. **PERSONALITY TYPE:** Social. Social occupations frequently involve working with, communicating with, and teaching people. These occupations often involve helping or providing service to others.

EDUCATION/TRAINING PROGRAMS— American History (United States); Asian History; Canadian History; European History; History and Philosophy of Science and Technology; History, General; History, Other; Public/Applied History and Archival Administration. **RELATED KNOWLEDGE/ COURSES—History and Archeology:** Knowledge of historical events and their causes, indicators, and effects on civilizations and cultures. **Philosophy and Theology:** Knowledge of different philosophical systems and religions. This includes their basic principles, values, ethics, ways of thinking, customs, and practices and their impact on human culture. **Geography:** Knowledge of principles and methods for describing the features of land, sea, and air masses, including their physical characteristics; locations; interrelationships; and distribution of plant, animal, and human life. **Education and Training:** Knowledge of principles and methods for curriculum and training design, teaching and instruction for individuals and groups, and the measurement of training effects. **Sociology and Anthropology:** Knowledge of group behavior and dynamics, societal trends and influences, human migrations, ethnicity, and cultures and their history and origins. **English Language:** Knowledge of the structure and content of the English language, including the meaning and spelling of words, rules of composition, and grammar.

Home Economics Teachers, Postsecondary

- Annual Earnings: $48,720
- Growth: 32.2%
- Annual Job Openings: 329,000
- Self-Employed: 0.4%
- Part-Time: 27.3%
- Education/Training Required: Master's degree

Our sources did not provide separate job openings data for this occupation. The job openings listed here are shared with 35 other postsecondary teaching occupations. For a complete list, see the beginning of this section.

Industries in Which Income Is Highest

Industry	Average Annual Wage	Number Employed
Educational Services	$48,830	4,000

Metropolitan Areas Where Income Is Highest

Metropolitan Area	Average Annual Wage	Number Employed
Riverside–San Bernardino–Ontario, CA	$86,410	40
Minneapolis–St. Paul–Bloomington, MN–WI	$65,710	70
Pittsburgh, PA	$60,060	30
Los Angeles–Long Beach–Santa Ana, CA	$56,640	50
St. Louis, MO–IL	$53,520	70

Teach courses in child care, family relations, finance, nutrition, and related subjects as pertaining to home management. Evaluate and grade students' class work, laboratory work, projects, assignments, and papers. Initiate, facilitate, and moderate classroom discussions. Prepare and deliver lectures to undergraduate and/or graduate students on topics such as food science, nutrition, and child care. Prepare course materials such as syllabi, homework assignments, and handouts. Keep abreast of developments in their field by reading current literature, talking with colleagues, and participating in professional conferences. Maintain student attendance records, grades, and other required records. Plan, evaluate, and revise curricula, course content, and course materials and methods of instruction. Compile, administer, and grade examinations or assign this work to others. Advise students on academic and vocational curricula and on career issues. Maintain regularly scheduled office hours in order to advise and assist students. Supervise undergraduate and/or graduate teaching, internship, and research work. Select and obtain materials and supplies such as textbooks. Conduct research in a particular field of knowledge and publish findings in professional journals, books, and/or electronic media. Collaborate with colleagues to address teaching and research issues. Act as advisers to student organizations. Participate in student recruitment, registration, and placement activities. Serve on academic or administrative committees that deal with institutional policies, departmental matters, and academic issues. Participate in campus and community events. Compile bibliographies of specialized materials for outside reading assignments. Perform administrative duties such as serving as department head. Write grant proposals to procure external research funding. Provide professional consulting services to government and/or industry. **SKILLS**—Instructing; Learning Strategies; Writing; Service Orientation; Active Learning; Social Perceptiveness; Persuasion; Negotiation.

GOE—Interest Area: 05. Education and Training. **Work Group:** 05.03. Postsecondary and Adult Teaching and Instructing. **PERSONALITY TYPE:** No data available.

EDUCATION/TRAINING PROGRAMS—Business Family and Consumer Sciences/Human Sciences; Child Care and Support Services Management; Family and Consumer Sciences/Human Sciences, General; Foodservice Systems Administration/Management; Human Development and Family Studies, General. **RELATED KNOWLEDGE/COURSES—Education and Training:** Knowledge of principles and methods for curriculum and training design, teaching and instruction for individuals and groups, and the measurement of training effects. **Philosophy and Theology:** Knowledge of different philosophical systems and religions. This includes their basic principles, values, ethics, ways of thinking, customs, and practices and their impact on human culture. **Sociology and Anthropology:** Knowledge of group behavior and dynamics, societal trends and influences, human migrations, ethnicity, and cultures and their history and origins. **Psychology:** Knowledge of human behavior and performance; individual differences in ability, personality, and interests; learning and motivation; psychological research methods; and the assessment and treatment of behavioral and affective disorders. **Therapy and Counseling:** Knowledge of principles, methods, and procedures for diagnosis, treatment, and rehabilitation of physical and mental dysfunctions and for career counseling and guidance. **English Language:** Knowledge of the structure and content of the English language, including the meaning and spelling of words, rules of composition, and grammar.

Hydrologists

- Annual Earnings: $63,820
- Growth: 31.6%
- Annual Job Openings: 1,000
- Self-Employed: 4.3%
- Part-Time: 5.9%
- Education/Training Required: Master's degree

Industries in Which Income Is Highest

Industry	Average Annual Wage	Number Employed
Utilities	$68,430	40
Religious, Grantmaking, Civic, Professional, and Similar Organizations	$66,430	40
Professional, Scientific, and Technical Services	$64,650	4,000
Federal, State, and Local Government	$63,060	4,170
Educational Services	$55,210	60

Metropolitan Areas Where Income Is Highest

Metropolitan Area	Average Annual Wage	Number Employed
Washington–Arlington–Alexandria, DC–VA–MD–WV	$86,760	250
Las Vegas–Paradise, NV	$86,150	170
San Francisco–Oakland–Fremont, CA	$82,590	320
Boston–Cambridge–Quincy, MA–NH	$81,440	70
Los Angeles–Long Beach–Santa Ana, CA	$80,950	110

Research the distribution, circulation, and physical properties of underground and surface waters; study the form and intensity of precipitation, its rate of infiltration into the soil, movement through the earth, and its return to the ocean and atmosphere. Evaluate research data in terms of its impact on issues such as soil and water conservation, flood control planning, and water supply forecasting. Investigate properties, origins, and activities of glaciers, ice, snow, and permafrost. Measure and graph phenomena such as lake levels, stream flows, and changes in water volumes. Study and analyze the physical aspects of the Earth in terms of the hydrological components, including atmosphere, hydrosphere, and interior structure. Study and document quantities, distribution, disposition, and development of underground and surface waters. Study public water supply issues, including flood and drought risks, water quality, wastewater, and impacts on wetland habitats. Answer questions and provide technical assistance and information to contractors and/or the public regarding issues such as well drilling, code requirements, hydrology, and geology. Collect and analyze water samples as part of field investigations and/or to validate data from automatic monitors. Coordinate and supervise the work of professional and technical staff, including research assistants, technologists, and technicians. Design civil works associated with hydrographic activities, and supervise their construction, installation, and maintenance. Develop or modify methods of conducting hydrologic studies. Draft final reports describing research results, including illustrations, appendices, maps, and other attachments. Evaluate data and provide recommendations regarding the feasibility of municipal projects such as hydroelectric power plants, irrigation systems, flood warning systems and waste treatment facilities. Install, maintain, and calibrate instruments such as those that monitor water levels, rainfall, and sediments. Investigate complaints or conflicts related to the alteration of public waters, gathering information, recommending alternatives, informing participants of progress, and preparing draft orders. Prepare hydrogeologic evaluations of known or suspected hazardous waste sites and land treatment and feedlot facilities. Administer programs designed to ensure the proper sealing of abandoned wells. **SKILLS**—Science; Mathematics; Systems Analysis; Writing; Active Learning; Critical Thinking; Complex Problem Solving; Judgment and Decision Making.

GOE—Interest Area: 15. Scientific Research, Engineering, and Mathematics. **Work Group:** 15.02. Physical Sciences. **PERSONALITY TYPE:** Investigative. Investigative occupations frequently involve working with ideas and require an extensive amount of thinking. These occupations can involve searching for facts and figuring out problems mentally.

EDUCATION/TRAINING PROGRAMS—Geology/Earth Science, General; Hydrology and Water Resources Science; Oceanography, Chemical and Physical. **RELATED KNOWLEDGE/COURSES**—**Physics:** Knowledge and prediction of physical principles and laws and their interrelationships and applications to understanding fluid, material, and atmospheric dynamics and mechanical, electrical, atomic, and subatomic structures and processes. **Geography:** Knowledge of principles and methods for describing the features of land, sea, and air masses, including their physical characteristics; locations; interrelationships; and distribution of plant, animal, and human life. **Mathematics:** Knowledge of arithmetic, algebra, geometry, calculus, and statistics and their applications. **Chemistry:** Knowledge of the chemical composition, structure, and properties of substances and of the chemical processes and transformations that they undergo. This includes uses of chemicals, their danger signs, production techniques, and disposal methods. **History and Archeology:** Knowledge of historical events and their causes, indicators, and effects on civilizations and cultures. **Communications and Media:** Knowledge of media production, communication, and dissemination techniques and methods. This includes alternative ways to inform and entertain via written, oral, and visual media.

Immigration and Customs Inspectors

- Annual Earnings: $55,790
- Growth: 16.3%
- Annual Job Openings: 9,000
- Self-Employed: 0.0%
- Part-Time: 2.9%
- Education/Training Required: Work experience in a related occupation

The job openings listed here are shared with Child Support, Missing Persons, and Unemployment Insurance Fraud Investigators; Criminal Investigators and Special Agents; Police Detectives; and Police Identification and Records Officers.

Industries in Which Income Is Highest

Industry	Average Annual Wage	Number Employed
Federal, State, and Local Government	$55,790	84,720

Metropolitan Areas Where Income Is Highest

Metropolitan Area	Average Annual Wage	Number Employed
Washington–Arlington–Alexandria, DC–VA–MD–WV	$79,180	4,270
Trenton–Ewing, NJ	$78,420	260
Chicago–Naperville–Joliet, IL–IN–WI	$76,080	3,170
Springfield, IL	$74,260	50
Oxnard–Thousand Oaks–Ventura, CA	$73,250	80

Investigate and inspect persons, common carriers, goods, and merchandise, arriving in or departing from the United States or between states to detect violations of immigration and customs laws and regulations. Detain persons found to be in violation of customs or immigration laws, and arrange for legal action such as deportation. Determine duty and taxes to be paid on goods. Examine immigration applications, visas, and passports, and interview persons in order to determine eligibility for admission, residence, and travel in U.S. Inspect cargo, baggage, and personal articles entering or leaving U.S. for compliance with revenue laws and U.S. Customs Service regulations. Interpret and explain laws and regulations to travelers, prospective immigrants, shippers, and manufacturers. Investigate applications for duty refunds, and petition for remission or mitigation of penalties when warranted. Locate and seize contraband, undeclared merchandise, and vehicles, aircraft, or boats that contain such merchandise. Record and report job-related activities, findings, transactions, violations, discrepancies, and decisions. Collect samples of merchandise for examination, appraisal, or testing. Institute civil and criminal prosecutions, and cooperate with other law enforcement agencies in the investigation and prosecution of those in violation of immigration or customs laws. Testify regarding decisions at immigration appeals or in federal court. **SKILLS**—Writing; Speaking; Judgment and Decision Making; Negotiation.

GOE—Interest Area: 07. Government and Public Administration. **Work Group:** 07.03. Regulations Enforcement. **PERSONALITY TYPE:** Conventional.

Conventional occupations frequently involve following set procedures and routines. These occupations can include working with data and details more than with ideas. Usually there is a clear line of authority to follow.

EDUCATION/TRAINING PROGRAMS—Criminal Justice/Police Science; Criminalistics and Criminal Science. **RELATED KNOWLEDGE/COURSES—Law and Government:** Knowledge of laws, legal codes, court procedures, precedents, government regulations, executive orders, agency rules, and the democratic political process. **Geography:** Knowledge of principles and methods for describing the features of land, sea, and air masses, including their physical characteristics; locations; interrelationships; and distribution of plant, animal, and human life. **Public Safety and Security:** Knowledge of relevant equipment, policies, procedures, and strategies to promote effective local, state, or national security operations for the protection of people, data, property, and institutions. **Transportation:** Knowledge of principles and methods for moving people or goods by air, rail, sea, or road, including the relative costs and benefits. **Communications and Media:** Knowledge of media production, communication, and dissemination techniques and methods. This includes alternative ways to inform and entertain via written, oral, and visual media. **Clerical Practices:** Knowledge of administrative and clerical procedures and systems such as word processing, managing files and records, stenography and transcription, designing forms, and other office procedures and terminology.

Industrial Engineers

- Annual Earnings: $66,670
- Growth: 16.0%
- Annual Job Openings: 13,000
- Self-Employed: 0.4%
- Part-Time: 2.7%
- Education/Training Required: Bachelor's degree

Industries in Which Income Is Highest

Industry	Average Annual Wage	Number Employed
Federal, State, and Local Government	$74,690	1,600
Professional, Scientific, and Technical Services	$73,640	23,120
Computer and Electronic Product Manufacturing	$71,900	30,090
Management of Companies and Enterprises	$71,650	7,400
Wholesale Electronic Markets and Agents and Brokers	$71,520	1,650

Metropolitan Areas Where Income Is Highest

Metropolitan Area	Average Annual Wage	Number Employed
San Jose–Sunnyvale–Santa Clara, CA	$92,650	5,330
Bakersfield, CA	$86,120	270
San Francisco–Oakland–Fremont, CA	$83,150	2,210
Santa Cruz–Watsonville, CA	$79,690	90
Tyler, TX	$79,410	60

Design, develop, test, and evaluate integrated systems for managing industrial production processes including human work factors, quality control, inventory control, logistics and material flow, cost analysis, and production coordination. Analyze statistical data and product specifications to determine standards and establish quality and reliability objectives of finished product. Develop manufacturing methods, labor utilization standards, and cost analysis systems to promote efficient staff and facility utilization. Recommend methods for improving utilization of personnel, material, and utilities. Plan and establish sequence of operations to fabricate and assemble parts or products and to promote efficient utilization. Apply statistical methods and perform mathematical calculations to determine manufacturing processes, staff requirements, and production standards. Coordinate quality control objectives and activities to resolve production problems, maximize product reliability, and minimize cost. Confer with vendors, staff, and management personnel regarding purchases, procedures, product specifications, manufacturing capabilities, and project status. Draft and design layout of equipment, materials, and work-space to illustrate maximum efficiency, using drafting tools and computer. Review production schedules, engineering specifications, orders, and related information to obtain knowledge of manufacturing methods, procedures, and activities. Communicate with management and user personnel to develop production and design standards. Estimate production cost and effect of product design changes for management review, action, and control. Formulate sampling procedures and designs and develop forms and instructions for recording, evaluating, and reporting quality and reliability data. Record or oversee recording of information to ensure currency of engineering drawings and documentation of production problems. Study operations sequence, material flow, functional statements, organization charts, and project information to determine worker functions and responsibilities. Direct workers engaged in product measurement, inspection, and testing activities to ensure quality control and reliability. Implement methods and procedures for disposition of discrepant material and defective or damaged parts, and assess cost and responsibility. **SKILLS**—Equipment Selection; Technology Design; Negotiation; Troubleshooting; Judgment and Decision Making; Persuasion; Systems Analysis; Active Learning.

GOE—Interest Area: 15. Scientific Research, Engineering, and Mathematics. **Work Group:** 15.08. Industrial and Safety Engineering. **PERSONALITY TYPE:** Enterprising. Enterprising occupations frequently involve starting up and carrying out projects. These occupations can involve leading people and making many decisions. They sometimes require risk taking and often deal with business.

EDUCATION/TRAINING PROGRAM—Industrial Engineering. **RELATED KNOWLEDGE/COURSES—Design:** Knowledge of design techniques, tools, and principles involved in production of precision technical plans, blueprints, drawings, and models. **Engineering and Technology:** Knowledge of the practical application of engineering science and technology. This includes applying principles, techniques, procedures, and equipment to the design and production of various goods and services. **Production and Processing:** Knowledge of raw materials, production processes, quality control, costs, and other techniques for maximizing the effective manufacture and distribution of goods. **Education and Training:** Knowledge of principles and methods for curriculum and training design, teaching and instruction for individuals and groups, and the measurement of training effects. **Mechanical Devices:** Knowledge of machines and tools, including their designs, uses, repair, and maintenance. **Mathematics:** Knowledge of arithmetic, algebra, geometry, calculus, and statistics and their applications.

Industrial Production Managers

- Annual Earnings: $75,580
- Growth: 0.8%
- Annual Job Openings: 13,000
- Self-Employed: 1.7%
- Part-Time: 2.3%
- Education/Training Required: Work experience in a related occupation

Industries in Which Income Is Highest

Industry	Average Annual Wage	Number Employed
Utilities	$96,970	1,140
Professional, Scientific, and Technical Services	$92,690	3,250
Computer and Electronic Product Manufacturing	$87,470	12,350
Management of Companies and Enterprises	$86,950	5,170
Petroleum and Coal Products Manufacturing	$85,640	1,200

Metropolitan Areas Where Income Is Highest

Metropolitan Area	Average Annual Wage	Number Employed
San Jose–Sunnyvale–Santa Clara, CA	$112,700	2,450
Bridgeport–Stamford–Norwalk, CT	$102,120	540
Boulder, CO	$101,990	200
Austin–Round Rock, TX	$98,320	670
Durham, NC	$97,420	410

Plan, direct, or coordinate the work activities and resources necessary for manufacturing products in accordance with cost, quality, and quantity specifications. Direct and coordinate production, processing, distribution, and marketing activities of industrial organization. Develop budgets and approve expenditures for supplies, materials, and human resources, ensuring that materials, labor and equipment are used efficiently to meet production targets. Review processing schedules and production orders to make decisions concerning inventory requirements, staffing requirements, work procedures, and duty assignments, considering budgetary limitations and time constraints. Review operations and confer with technical or administrative staff to resolve production or processing problems. Hire, train, evaluate, and discharge staff, and resolve personnel grievances. Initiate and coordinate inventory and cost control programs. Prepare and maintain production reports and personnel records. Set and monitor product standards, examining samples of raw products or directing testing during processing, to ensure finished products are of prescribed quality. Develop and implement production tracking and quality control systems, analyzing production, quality control, maintenance, and other operational reports, to detect production problems. Review plans and confer with research and support staff to develop new products and processes. Institute employee suggestion or involvement programs. Coordinate and recommend procedures for facility and equipment maintenance or modification, including the replacement of machines. Maintain current knowledge of the quality control field, relying on current literature pertaining to materials use, technological advances, and statistical studies. Negotiate materials prices with suppliers. **SKILLS—** Management of Material Resources; Management of Personnel Resources; Persuasion; Systems Evaluation; Coordination; Monitoring; Operations Analysis; Time Management.

GOE—Interest Area: 13. Manufacturing. **Work Group:** 13.01. Managerial Work in Manufacturing. **PERSONALITY TYPE:** Enterprising. Enterprising occupations frequently involve starting up and carrying out projects. These occupations can involve leading people and making many decisions. They sometimes require risk taking and often deal with business.

EDUCATION/TRAINING PROGRAMS—Business Administration/Management; Business/Commerce, General; Operations Management and Supervision. **RELATED KNOWLEDGE/COURSES— Production and Processing:** Knowledge of raw materials, production processes, quality control, costs, and other techniques for maximizing the effective manufacture and distribution of goods. **Personnel and Human**

Resources: Knowledge of principles and procedures for personnel recruitment, selection, training, compensation and benefits, labor relations and negotiation, and personnel information systems. **Education and Training:** Knowledge of principles and methods for curriculum and training design, teaching and instruction for individuals and groups, and the measurement of training effects. **Administration and Management:** Knowledge of business and management principles involved in strategic planning, resource allocation, human resources modeling, leadership technique, production methods, and coordination of people and resources. **Mechanical Devices:** Knowledge of machines and tools, including their designs, uses, repair, and maintenance. **Design:** Knowledge of design techniques, tools, and principles involved in production of precision technical plans, blueprints, drawings, and models.

Industrial Safety and Health Engineers

- Annual Earnings: $65,210
- Growth: 13.4%
- Annual Job Openings: 2,000
- Self-Employed: 0.5%
- Part-Time: 2.7%
- Education/Training Required: Bachelor's degree

The job openings listed here are shared with Fire-Prevention and Protection Engineers and Product Safety Engineers.

Industries in Which Income Is Highest

Industry	Average Annual Wage	Number Employed
Transportation Equipment Manufacturing	$70,130	1,160
Professional, Scientific, and Technical Services	$69,370	2,750
Federal, State, and Local Government	$68,740	5,370
Chemical Manufacturing	$65,700	2,990
Construction of Buildings	$57,920	2,080

Metropolitan Areas Where Income Is Highest

Metropolitan Area	Average Annual Wage	Number Employed
San Jose–Sunnyvale–Santa Clara, CA	$84,920	390
Washington–Arlington–Alexandria, DC–VA–MD–WV	$84,880	960
Anchorage, AK	$84,300	70
Durham, NC	$83,530	100
Knoxville, TN	$78,820	130

Plan, implement, and coordinate safety programs, requiring application of engineering principles and technology, to prevent or correct unsafe environmental working conditions. Investigate industrial accidents, injuries, or occupational diseases to determine causes and preventive measures. Report or review findings from accident investigations, facilities inspections, or environmental testing. Maintain and apply knowledge of current policies, regulations, and industrial processes. Inspect facilities, machinery, and safety equipment in order to identify and correct potential hazards, and to ensure safety regulation compliance. Conduct or coordinate worker training in areas such as safety laws and regulations, hazardous condition monitoring, and use of safety equipment. Review employee safety programs to determine their adequacy. Interview employers and employees to obtain information about work environments and workplace incidents. Review plans and specifications for construction of new machinery or equipment in order to determine if all safety requirements have been met. Compile, analyze, and interpret statistical data related to occupational illnesses and accidents. Interpret safety regulations for others interested in industrial safety, such as safety engineers, labor representatives, and safety inspectors. Recommend process and product safety features that will reduce employees' exposure to chemical, physical, and biological work hazards. Conduct or direct testing of air quality, noise, temperature, and/or radiation levels to verify compliance with health and safety regulations. Provide technical advice and guidance to organizations on how to handle health-related problems and make needed changes. Confer with medical professionals to assess health risks and to develop ways to manage health issues and concerns. Install safety devices on machinery, or direct device installation. Maintain liaisons with outside organizations, such as fire departments, mutual aid societies, and rescue teams, so that emergency responses can be facilitated. Evaluate adequacy of actions taken to correct health inspection violations. Write and revise safety regulations and codes. Check floors of plants to ensure that they are strong enough to support heavy machinery. Plan and conduct industrial hygiene research. **SKILLS**—Management of Financial Resources; Persuasion; Science; Systems Analysis; Negotiation; Management of Personnel Resources; Service Orientation; Management of Material Resources.

GOE—Interest Area: 15. Scientific Research, Engineering, and Mathematics. **Work Group:** 15.08. Industrial and Safety Engineering. **PERSONALITY TYPE:** Investigative. Investigative occupations frequently involve working with ideas and require an extensive amount of thinking. These occupations can involve searching for facts and figuring out problems mentally.

EDUCATION/TRAINING PROGRAM— Environmental/Environmental Health Engineering. **RELATED KNOWLEDGE/COURSES— Education and Training:** Knowledge of principles and methods for curriculum and training design, teaching and instruction for individuals and groups, and the measurement of training effects. **Chemistry:** Knowledge of the chemical composition, structure, and properties of substances and of the chemical processes and transformations that they undergo. This includes uses of chemicals, their danger signs, production techniques, and disposal methods. **Building and Construction:** Knowledge of the materials, methods, and tools involved in the construction or repair of houses, buildings, or other structures such as highways and roads. **Public Safety and Security:** Knowledge of relevant equipment, policies, procedures, and strategies to promote effective local, state, or national security operations for the protection of people, data, property, and institutions. **Biology:** Knowledge of plant and animal organisms and their tissues, cells, functions, interdependencies, and interactions with each other and the environment. **Personnel and Human Resources:** Knowledge of principles and procedures for personnel recruitment, selection, training, compensation and benefits, labor relations and negotiation, and personnel information systems.

Industrial-Organizational Psychologists

- Annual Earnings: $84,690
- Growth: 20.4%
- Annual Job Openings: fewer than 500
- Self-Employed: 37.6%
- Part-Time: 23.3%
- Education/Training Required: Master's degree

Industries in Which Income Is Highest

Industry	Average Annual Wage	Number Employed
Professional, Scientific, and Technical Services	$94,650	480
Computer and Electronic Product Manufacturing	$88,340	220
Ambulatory Health Care Services	$85,270	40
Management of Companies and Enterprises	$82,680	40
Educational Services	$68,650	110

Metropolitan Areas Where Income Is Highest

Metropolitan Area	Average Annual Wage	Number Employed
New York–Northern New Jersey–Long Island, NY–NJ–PA	$93,010	120
Washington–Arlington–Alexandria, DC–VA–MD–WV	$72,150	110

Apply principles of psychology to personnel, administration, management, sales, and marketing problems. Activities may include policy planning; employee screening, training and development; and organizational development and analysis. May work with management to reorganize the work setting to improve worker productivity. Develop and implement employee selection and placement programs. Analyze job requirements and content in order to establish criteria for classification, selection, training, and other related personnel functions. Observe and interview workers in order to obtain information about the physical, mental, and educational requirements of jobs as well as information about aspects such as job satisfaction. Write reports on research findings and implications in order to contribute to general knowledge and to suggest potential changes in organizational functioning. Advise management concerning personnel, managerial, and marketing policies and practices and their potential effects on organizational effectiveness and efficiency. Identify training and development needs. Conduct research studies of physical work environments, organizational structures, communication systems, group interactions, morale, and motivation in order to assess organizational functioning. Formulate and implement training programs, applying principles of learning and individual differences. Develop interview techniques, rating scales, and psychological tests used to assess skills, abilities, and interests for the purpose of employee selection, placement, and promotion. Assess employee performance. Study organizational effectiveness, productivity, and efficiency, including the nature of workplace supervision and leadership. Facilitate organizational development and change. Analyze data, using statistical methods and applications, in order to evaluate the outcomes and effectiveness of workplace programs. Counsel workers about job and career-related issues. Study consumers' reactions to new products and package designs, and to advertising efforts, using surveys and tests. Participate in mediation and dispute resolution. **SKILLS**—Management of Personnel Resources; Science; Judgment and Decision Making; Service Orientation; Systems Evaluation; Coordination; Time Management; Learning Strategies.

GOE—Interest Area: 15. Scientific Research, Engineering, and Mathematics. **Work Group:** 15.04. Social Sciences. **PERSONALITY TYPE:** Investigative. Investigative occupations frequently involve working with ideas and require an extensive amount of thinking. These occupations can involve searching for facts and figuring out problems mentally.

EDUCATION/TRAINING PROGRAMS— Industrial and Organizational Psychology; Psychology, General. **RELATED KNOWLEDGE/COURSES— Personnel and Human Resources:** Knowledge of principles and procedures for personnel recruitment, selection, training, compensation and benefits, labor relations and negotiation, and personnel information systems. **Psychology:** Knowledge of human behavior and performance; individual differences in ability, personality, and interests; learning and motivation; psychological research methods; and the assessment and treatment of behavioral and affective disorders. **Education and Training:** Knowledge of principles and

methods for curriculum and training design, teaching and instruction for individuals and groups, and the measurement of training effects. **Sales and Marketing:** Knowledge of principles and methods for showing, promoting, and selling products or services. This includes marketing strategy and tactics, product demonstration, sales techniques, and sales control systems. **Customer and Personal Service:** Knowledge of principles and processes for providing customer and personal services. This includes customer needs assessment, meeting quality standards for services, and evaluation of customer satisfaction. **Sociology and Anthropology:** Knowledge of group behavior and dynamics, societal trends and influences, human migrations, ethnicity, and cultures and their history and origins.

Instructional Coordinators

- Annual Earnings: $50,430
- Growth: 27.5%
- Annual Job Openings: 15,000
- Self-Employed: 3.1%
- Part-Time: 23.4%
- Education/Training Required: Master's degree

Industries in Which Income Is Highest

Industry	Average Annual Wage	Number Employed
Federal, State, and Local Government	$54,730	11,160
Professional, Scientific, and Technical Services	$54,610	2,910
Educational Services	$51,880	84,890
Religious, Grantmaking, Civic, Professional, and Similar Organizations	$40,720	1,480
Social Assistance	$34,530	6,800

Metropolitan Areas Where Income Is Highest

Metropolitan Area	Average Annual Wage	Number Employed
Hartford–West Hartford–East Hartford, CT	$86,070	430
Pittsburgh, PA	$75,300	570
Modesto, CA	$74,660	120
New Haven, CT	$73,210	160
Merced, CA	$72,350	60

Develop instructional material, coordinate educational content, and incorporate current technology in specialized fields that provide guidelines to educators and instructors for developing curricula and conducting courses. Conduct or participate in workshops, committees, and conferences designed to promote the intellectual, social, and physical welfare of students. Plan and conduct teacher training programs and conferences dealing with new classroom procedures, instructional materials and equipment, and teaching aids. Advise teaching and administrative staff in curriculum development, use of materials and equipment, and implementation of state and federal programs and procedures. Recommend, order, or authorize purchase of instructional materials, supplies, equipment, and visual aids designed to meet student educational needs and district standards. Interpret and enforce provisions of state education codes, and rules and regulations of state education boards. Confer with members of educational committees and advisory groups to obtain knowledge of subject areas, and to relate curriculum materials to specific subjects, individual student needs, and occupational areas. Organize production and design of curriculum materials. Research, evaluate, and prepare recommendations on curricula, instructional methods, and materials for school systems. Observe work of teaching staff in order to evaluate performance, and to recommend changes that could strengthen teaching skills. Develop instructional materials to be used by educators and instructors. Prepare grant proposals, budgets, and program policies and goals, or assist in their preparation. Develop tests, questionnaires, and procedures that measure the effectiveness of curricula, and use these tools to determine whether program objectives are being met. Update the content of educational programs to ensure that students are being trained with equipment and processes that are technologically current. Address public audiences to explain program objectives and to elicit support. Advise and teach students. Prepare or approve manuals, guidelines, and reports on state educational policies and practices for distribution to school districts. Develop classroom-based and distance learning training courses, using needs assessments and skill level analyses. Inspect instructional equipment to determine if repairs are needed; authorize necessary repairs. **SKILLS—**Management of Financial Resources; Learning Strategies; Social Perceptiveness; Coordination; Time Management; Monitoring; Persuasion; Management of Personnel Resources.

GOE—Interest Area: 05. Education and Training. **Work Group:** 05.01. Managerial Work in Education. **PERSONALITY TYPE:** Social. Social occupations frequently involve working with, communicating with, and teaching people. These occupations often involve helping or providing service to others.

EDUCATION/TRAINING PROGRAMS—Curriculum and Instruction; Educational/Instructional Media Design. **RELATED KNOWLEDGE/ COURSES—Education and Training:** Knowledge of principles and methods for curriculum and training design, teaching and instruction for individuals and groups, and the measurement of training effects. **Customer and Personal Service:** Knowledge of principles and processes for providing customer and personal services. This includes customer needs assessment, meeting quality standards for services, and evaluation of customer satisfaction. **Personnel and Human Resources:** Knowledge of principles and procedures for personnel recruitment, selection, training, compensation and benefits, labor relations and negotiation, and personnel information systems. **English Language:** Knowledge of the structure and content of the English language, including the meaning and spelling of words, rules of composition, and grammar. **Sociology and Anthropology:** Knowledge of group behavior and dynamics, societal trends and influences, human migrations, ethnicity, and cultures and their history and origins. **Psychology:** Knowledge of human behavior and performance; individual differences in ability, personality, and interests; learning and motivation; psychological research methods; and the assessment and treatment of behavioral and affective disorders.

Insurance Appraisers, Auto Damage

- Annual Earnings: $48,090
- Growth: 16.6%
- Annual Job Openings: 2,000
- Self-Employed: 2.9%
- Part-Time: 5.0%
- Education/Training Required: Long-term on-the-job training

Industries in Which Income Is Highest

Industry	Average Annual Wage	Number Employed
Insurance Carriers and Related Activities	$48,320	11,750

Metropolitan Areas Where Income Is Highest

Metropolitan Area	Average Annual Wage	Number Employed
San Francisco–Oakland–Fremont, CA	$56,000	150
Boston–Cambridge–Quincy, MA–NH	$55,350	480
New Haven, CT	$54,250	50
Portland–Vancouver–Beaverton, OR–WA	$53,480	80
Worcester, MA–CT	$52,350	170

Appraise automobile or other vehicle damage to determine cost of repair for insurance claim settlement and seek agreement with automotive repair shop on cost of repair. Prepare insurance forms to indicate repair cost or cost estimates and recommendations. Estimate parts and labor to repair damage, using standard automotive labor and parts-cost manuals and knowledge of automotive repair. Review repair-cost estimates with automobile-repair shop to secure agreement on cost of repairs. Examine damaged vehicle to determine extent of structural, body, mechanical, electrical, or interior damage. Evaluate practicality of repair as opposed to payment of market value of vehicle before accident. Determine salvage value on total-loss vehicle. Prepare insurance forms to indicate repair-cost estimates and recommendations. Arrange to have damage appraised by another appraiser to resolve disagreement with shop on repair cost. **SKILLS**—Negotiation; Service Orientation; Persuasion; Time Management; Active Listening; Judgment and Decision Making; Speaking; Writing.

GOE—Interest Area: 06. Finance and Insurance. **Work Group:** 06.02. Finance/Insurance Investigation and Analysis. **PERSONALITY TYPE:** Conventional. Conventional occupations frequently involve following set procedures and routines. These occupations can include working with data and details more than with ideas. Usually there is a clear line of authority to follow.

EDUCATION/TRAINING PROGRAM— Insurance. **RELATED KNOWLEDGE/COURS-**

ES—Customer and Personal Service: Knowledge of principles and processes for providing customer and personal services. This includes customer needs assessment, meeting quality standards for services, and evaluation of customer satisfaction. **Law and Government:** Knowledge of laws, legal codes, court procedures, precedents, government regulations, executive orders, agency rules, and the democratic political process. **Computers and Electronics:** Knowledge of circuit boards, processors, chips, electronic equipment, and computer hardware and software, including applications and programming. **Administration and Management:** Knowledge of business and management principles involved in strategic planning, resource allocation, human resources modeling, leadership technique, production methods, and coordination of people and resources. **Transportation:** Knowledge of principles and methods for moving people or goods by air, rail, sea, or road, including the relative costs and benefits. **Medicine and Dentistry:** Knowledge of the information and techniques needed to diagnose and treat human injuries, diseases, and deformities. This includes symptoms, treatment alternatives, drug properties and interactions, and preventive health-care measures.

Insurance Underwriters

- Annual Earnings: $51,270
- Growth: 8.0%
- Annual Job Openings: 13,000
- Self-Employed: 1.0%
- Part-Time: 3.2%
- Education/Training Required: Bachelor's degree

Industries in Which Income Is Highest

Industry	Average Annual Wage	Number Employed
Insurance Carriers and Related Activities	$51,630	85,370
Credit Intermediation and Related Activities	$51,470	5,470
Funds, Trusts, and Other Financial Vehicles	$49,390	1,060
Management of Companies and Enterprises	$46,960	3,940

Metropolitan Areas Where Income Is Highest

Metropolitan Area	Average Annual Wage	Number Employed
Orlando–Kissimmee, FL	$70,720	1,240
Santa Rosa–Petaluma, CA	$69,050	170
Boston–Cambridge–Quincy, MA–NH	$66,830	2,430
San Jose–Sunnyvale–Santa Clara, CA	$65,180	270
New York–Northern New Jersey–Long Island, NY–NJ–PA	$61,870	8,250

Review individual applications for insurance to evaluate degree of risk involved and determine acceptance of applications. Examine documents to determine degree of risk from such factors as applicant financial standing and value and condition of property. Decline excessive risks. Write to field representatives, medical personnel, and others to obtain further information, quote rates, or explain company underwriting policies. Evaluate possibility of losses due to catastrophe or excessive insurance. Decrease value of policy when risk is substandard and specify applicable endorsements or apply rating to ensure safe profitable distribution of risks, using reference materials. Review company records to determine amount of insurance in force on single risk or group of closely related risks. Authorize reinsurance of policy when risk is high. **SKILLS**—Service Orientation; Writing; Learning Strategies; Active Learning; Persuasion; Active Listening; Speaking; Monitoring.

GOE—Interest Area: 06. Finance and Insurance. **Work Group:** 06.02. Finance/Insurance Investigation and Analysis. **PERSONALITY TYPE:** Conventional. Conventional occupations frequently involve following set procedures and routines. These occupations can include working with data and details more than with ideas. Usually there is a clear line of authority to follow.

EDUCATION/TRAINING PROGRAM—Insurance. **RELATED KNOWLEDGE/COURSES—Customer and Personal Service:** Knowledge of principles and processes for providing customer and personal services. This includes customer needs assessment, meeting quality standards for services, and evaluation of customer satisfaction. **Clerical Practices:** Knowledge of administrative and clerical procedures and systems such as word processing, managing files and records, stenography and transcription, designing forms, and other office procedures and terminology. **Sales and Marketing:** Knowledge of principles and methods for showing, promoting, and selling products or services. This includes marketing strategy and tactics, product demonstration, sales techniques, and sales control systems. **Economics and Accounting:** Knowledge of economic and accounting principles and practices, the financial markets, banking, and the analysis and reporting of financial data. **Computers and Electronics:** Knowledge of circuit boards, processors, chips, electronic equipment, and computer hardware and software, including applications and programming. **Law and Government:** Knowledge of laws, legal codes, court procedures, precedents, government regulations, executive orders, agency rules, and the democratic political process.

Internists, General

- ◎ Annual Earnings: More than $146,500
- ◎ Growth: 24.0%
- ◎ Annual Job Openings: 41,000
- ◎ Self-Employed: 11.0%
- ◎ Part-Time: 9.6%
- ◎ Education/Training Required: First professional degree

The job openings listed here are shared with Anesthesiologists; Family and General Practitioners; Obstetricians and Gynecologists; Pediatricians, General; Psychiatrists; and Surgeons.

Industries in Which Income Is Highest

Industry	Average Annual Wage	Number Employed
Ambulatory Health Care Services	More than $146,500	40,360
Hospitals	$130,630	6,500

Metropolitan Areas Where Income Is Highest

Metropolitan Area	Average Annual Wage	Number Employed
New York–Northern New Jersey–Long Island, NY–NJ–PA	More than $146,500	4,360
Los Angeles–Long Beach–Santa Ana, CA	More than $146,500	1,690
Atlanta–Sandy Springs–Marietta, GA	More than $146,500	1,470
Detroit–Warren–Livonia, MI	More than $146,500	1,460
Chicago–Naperville–Joilet, IL–IN–WI	More than $146,500	1,090

Diagnose and provide non-surgical treatment of diseases and injuries of internal organ systems. Provide care mainly for adults who have a wide range of problems associated with the internal organs. Treat internal disorders, such as hypertension, heart disease, diabetes, and problems of the lung, brain, kidney, and gastrointestinal tract. Analyze records, reports, test results, or examination information to diagnose medical condition of patient. Prescribe or administer medication, therapy, and other specialized medical care to treat or prevent illness, disease, or injury. Provide and manage long-term, comprehensive medical care, including diagnosis and non-surgical treatment of diseases, for adult patients in an office or hospital. Manage and treat common health problems, such as infections, influenza and pneumonia, as well as serious, chronic, and complex illnesses, in adolescents, adults, and the elderly. Monitor patients' conditions and progress and re-evaluate treatments as necessary. Collect, record, and maintain patient information, such as medical history, reports, and examination results. Make diagnoses when different illnesses occur together or in situations where the diagnosis may be obscure. Explain procedures and discuss test results or prescribed treatments with patients. Advise patients and community members concerning diet, activity, hygiene, and disease prevention. Refer patient to medical specialist or other practitioner when necessary. Immunize patients to protect them from preventable diseases. Advise surgeon of a patient's risk status and recommend appropriate intervention to minimize risk. Direct and coordinate activities of nurses, students, assistants, specialists, therapists, and other medical staff. Provide consulting services to other doctors caring for patients with special or difficult problems. Operate on patients to remove, repair, or improve functioning of diseased or injured body parts and systems. Plan, implement, or administer health programs in hospitals, businesses, or communities for prevention and treatment of injuries or illnesses. Conduct research to develop or test medications, treatments, or procedures to prevent or control disease or injury. **SKILLS**—Science; Social Perceptiveness; Service Orientation; Persuasion; Judgment and Decision Making; Complex Problem Solving; Instructing; Active Listening.

GOE—Interest Area: 08. Health Science. **Work Group:** 08.02. Medicine and Surgery. **PERSONALITY TYPE:** Investigative. Investigative occupations frequently involve working with ideas and require an extensive amount of thinking. These occupations can involve searching for facts and figuring out problems mentally.

EDUCATION/TRAINING PROGRAMS— Cardiology; Critical Care Medicine; Endocrinology and Metabolism; Gastroenterology; Geriatric Medicine; Hematology; Infectious Disease; Internal Medicine; Nephrology; Neurology; Nuclear Medicine; Oncology; Pulmonary Disease; Rheumatology. **RELATED KNOWLEDGE/COURSES—Medicine and Dentistry:** Knowledge of the information and techniques needed to diagnose and treat human injuries, diseases, and deformities. This includes symptoms, treatment alternatives, drug properties and interactions, and preventive health-care measures. **Biology:** Knowledge of plant and animal organisms and their tissues, cells, functions, interdependencies, and interactions with each other and the environment. **Therapy and Counseling:** Knowledge of principles, methods, and procedures for diagnosis, treatment, and rehabilitation of physical and mental dysfunctions and for career counseling and guidance. **Psychology:** Knowledge of human behavior and performance; individual differences in ability, personality, and interests; learning and motivation; psychological research methods; and the assessment and treatment of behavioral and affective disorders. **Education and Training:** Knowledge of principles and methods for curriculum and training design, teaching and instruction for individuals and groups, and the measurement of training effects. **Chemistry:** Knowledge of the chemical composition, structure, and properties of substances and of the chemical processes and transformations that they undergo. This includes uses of chemicals, their danger signs, production techniques, and disposal methods.

Judges, Magistrate Judges, and Magistrates

- Annual Earnings: $97,570
- Growth: 6.9%
- Annual Job Openings: 1,000
- Self-Employed: 0.0%
- Part-Time: No data available
- Education/Training Required: Work experience plus degree

Industries in Which Income Is Highest

Industry	Average Annual Wage	Number Employed
Federal, State, and Local Government	$97,570	25,330

Metropolitan Areas Where Income Is Highest

Metropolitan Area	Average Annual Wage	Number Employed
Providence–Fall River–Warwick, RI–MA	More than $146,500	100
Kansas City, MO–KS	More than $146,500	150
Chicago–Naperville–Joliet, IL–IN–WI	More than $146,500	750
Sacramento–Arden–Arcade–Roseville, CA	$136,970	110
Las Vegas–Paradise, NV	$135,900	50

Arbitrate, advise, adjudicate, or administer justice in a court of law. May sentence defendant in criminal cases according to government statutes. May determine liability of defendant in civil cases. May issue marriage licenses and perform wedding ceremonies. Instruct juries on applicable laws, direct juries to deduce the facts from the evidence presented, and hear their verdicts. Sentence defendants in criminal cases, on conviction by jury, according to applicable government statutes. Rule on admissibility of evidence and methods of conducting testimony. Preside over hearings and listen to allegations made by plaintiffs to determine whether the evidence supports the charges. Read documents on pleadings and motions to ascertain facts and issues. Interpret and enforce rules of procedure or establish new rules in situations where there are no procedures already established by law. Monitor proceedings to ensure that all applicable rules and procedures are followed. Advise attorneys, juries, litigants, and court personnel regarding conduct, issues, and proceedings. Research legal issues and write opinions on the issues. Conduct preliminary hearings to decide issues such as whether there is reasonable and probable cause to hold defendants in felony cases. Write decisions on cases. Award compensation for damages to litigants in civil cases in relation to findings by juries or by the court. Settle disputes between opposing attorneys. Supervise other judges, court officers, and the court's administrative staff. Impose restrictions upon parties in civil cases until trials can be held. Rule on custody and access disputes, and enforce court orders regarding custody and support of children. Grant divorces and divide assets between spouses. Participate in judicial tribunals to help resolve disputes. **SKILLS—** Judgment and Decision Making; Persuasion; Negotiation; Critical Thinking; Social Perceptiveness; Active Listening; Management of Personnel Resources; Service Orientation.

GOE—Interest Area: 12. Law and Public Safety. **Work Group:** 12.02. Legal Practice and Justice Administration. **PERSONALITY TYPE:** Enterprising. Enterprising occupations frequently involve starting up and carrying out projects. These occupations can involve leading people and making many decisions. They sometimes require risk taking and often deal with business.

EDUCATION/TRAINING PROGRAMS—Law (LL.B., J.D.); Law, Legal Services, and Legal Studies, Other; Legal Studies, General. **RELATED KNOWLEDGE/COURSES—Law and Government:** Knowledge of laws, legal codes, court procedures, precedents, government regulations, executive orders, agency rules, and the democratic political process. **English Language:** Knowledge of the structure and content of the English language, including the meaning and spelling of words, rules of composition, and grammar. **Philosophy and Theology:** Knowledge of different philosophical systems and religions. This includes their basic principles, values, ethics, ways of thinking, customs, and practices and their impact on human culture.

Therapy and Counseling: Knowledge of principles, methods, and procedures for diagnosis, treatment, and rehabilitation of physical and mental dysfunctions and for career counseling and guidance. **Psychology:** Knowledge of human behavior and performance; individual differences in ability, personality, and interests; learning and motivation; psychological research methods; and the assessment and treatment of behavioral and affective disorders. **Public Safety and Security:** Knowledge of relevant equipment, policies, procedures, and strategies to promote effective local, state, or national security operations for the protection of people, data, property, and institutions.

Landscape Architects

- Annual Earnings: $54,220
- Growth: 19.4%
- Annual Job Openings: 1,000
- Self-Employed: 23.7%
- Part-Time: 9.2%
- Education/Training Required: Bachelor's degree

Industries in Which Income Is Highest

Industry	Average Annual Wage	Number Employed
Federal, State, and Local Government	$63,800	1,940
Professional, Scientific, and Technical Services	$54,130	12,860
Administrative and Support Services	$50,080	3,600

Metropolitan Areas Where Income Is Highest

Metropolitan Area	Average Annual Wage	Number Employed
Fresno, CA	$79,620	90
Anchorage, AK	$68,460	60
Jacksonville, FL	$67,290	110
San Diego–Carlsbad–San Marcos, CA	$66,710	610
Albuquerque, NM	$64,920	60

Plan and design land areas for such projects as parks and other recreational facilities, airports, highways, hospitals, schools, land subdivisions, and commercial, industrial, and residential sites. Prepare site plans, specifications, and cost estimates for land development, coordinating arrangement of existing and proposed land features and structures. Confer with clients, engineering personnel, and architects on overall program. Compile and analyze data on conditions, such as location, drainage, and location of structures for environmental reports and landscaping plans. Inspect landscape work to ensure compliance with specifications, approve quality of materials and work, and advise client and construction personnel. **SKILLS**—Operations Analysis; Coordination; Management of Financial Resources; Social Perceptiveness; Persuasion; Complex Problem Solving; Time Management; Mathematics.

GOE—Interest Area: 02. Architecture and Construction. **Work Group:** 02.02. Architectural Design. **PERSONALITY TYPE:** Artistic. Artistic occupations frequently involve working with forms, designs, and patterns. They often require self-expression, and the work can be done without following a clear set of rules.

EDUCATION/TRAINING PROGRAMS—Environmental Design/Architecture; Landscape Architecture (BS, BSLA, BLA, MSLA, MLA, PhD). **RELATED KNOWLEDGE/COURSES—Design:** Knowledge of design techniques, tools, and principles involved in production of precision technical plans, blueprints, drawings, and models. **Building and Construction:** Knowledge of the materials, methods, and tools involved in the construction or repair of houses, buildings, or other structures such as highways and roads. **Geography:** Knowledge of principles and methods for describing the features of land, sea, and air masses, including their physical characteristics; locations; interrelationships; and distribution of plant, animal, and human life. **Biology:** Knowledge of plant and animal organisms and their tissues, cells, functions, interdependencies, and interactions with each other and the environment. **Engineering and Technology:** Knowledge of the practical application of engineering science and technology. This includes applying principles, techniques, procedures, and equipment to the design and production of various goods and services. **Sales and Marketing:** Knowledge of principles and methods for showing, promoting, and selling products or services. This includes marketing strategy and tactics, product demonstration, sales techniques, and sales control systems.

Law Teachers, Postsecondary

- Annual Earnings: $89,790
- Growth: 32.2%
- Annual Job Openings: 329,000
- Self-Employed: 0.4%
- Part-Time: 27.3%
- Education/Training Required: First professional degree

Our sources did not provide separate job openings data for this occupation. The job openings listed here are shared with 35 other postsecondary teaching occupations. For a complete list, see the beginning of this section.

Industries in Which Income Is Highest

Industry	Average Annual Wage	Number Employed
Educational Services	$89,820	13,560

Metropolitan Areas Where Income Is Highest

Metropolitan Area	Average Annual Wage	Number Employed
Tampa–St. Petersburg–Clearwater, FL	More than $146,500	100
Boston–Cambridge–Quincy, MA–NH	$114,180	780
Buffalo–Niagara Falls, NY	$113,800	70
Atlanta–Sandy Springs–Marietta, GA	$110,220	240
New York–Northern New Jersey–Long Island, NY–NJ–PA	$100,130	760

Teach courses in law. Evaluate and grade students' class work, assignments, papers, and oral presentations. Compile, administer, and grade examinations or assign this work to others. Prepare and deliver lectures to undergraduate and/or graduate students on topics such as civil procedure, contracts, and torts. Initiate, facilitate, and moderate classroom discussions. Prepare course materials such as syllabi, homework assignments, and handouts. Keep abreast of developments in their field by reading current literature, talking with colleagues, and participating in professional conferences. Plan, evaluate, and revise curricula, course content, and course materials and methods of instruction. Maintain regularly scheduled office hours in order to advise and assist students. Conduct research in a particular field of knowledge and publish findings in professional journals, books, and/or electronic media. Advise students on academic and vocational curricula and on career issues. Supervise undergraduate and/or graduate teaching, internship, and research work. Select and obtain materials and supplies such as textbooks. Maintain student attendance records, grades, and other required records. Serve on academic or administrative committees that deal with institutional policies, departmental matters, and academic issues. Perform administrative duties such as serving as department head. Collaborate with colleagues to address teaching and research issues. Participate in student recruitment, registration, and placement activities. Compile bibliographies of specialized materials for outside reading assignments. Participate in campus and community events. Act as advisers to student organizations. Assign cases for students to hear and try. **SKILLS—** Instructing; Critical Thinking; Persuasion; Reading Comprehension; Writing; Speaking; Learning Strategies; Active Listening.

GOE—Interest Area: 05. Education and Training. **Work Group:** 05.03. Postsecondary and Adult Teaching and Instructing. **PERSONALITY TYPE:** No data available.

EDUCATION/TRAINING PROGRAM—Law (LL.B., J.D.). **RELATED KNOWLEDGE/ COURSES—Law and Government:** Knowledge of laws, legal codes, court procedures, precedents, government regulations, executive orders, agency rules, and the democratic political process. **Education and Training:** Knowledge of principles and methods for curriculum and training design, teaching and instruction for individuals and groups, and the measurement of training effects. **English Language:** Knowledge of the structure and content of the English language, including the meaning and spelling of words, rules of composition, and grammar. **History and Archeology:** Knowledge of historical events and their causes, indicators, and effects on civilizations and cultures. **Philosophy and Theology:** Knowledge of different philosophical systems and religions. This includes their basic principles, values, ethics, ways of thinking, customs, and practices and their impact on human culture. **Communications and Media:** Knowledge of media production, communication, and dissemination techniques and methods. This includes alternative ways to inform and entertain via written, oral, and visual media.

Lawyers

- Annual Earnings: $98,930
- Growth: 15.0%
- Annual Job Openings: 40,000
- Self-Employed: 24.1%
- Part-Time: 6.9%
- Education/Training Required: First professional degree

Industries in Which Income Is Highest

Industry	Average Annual Wage	Number Employed
Securities, Commodity Contracts, and Other Financial Investments and Related Activities	$137,070	3,900
Computer and Electronic Product Manufacturing	$137,070	1,410
Telecommunications	$131,580	1,190
Chemical Manufacturing	$128,240	1,010
Management of Companies and Enterprises	$124,760	11,920

Metropolitan Areas Where Income Is Highest

Metropolitan Area	Average Annual Wage	Number Employed
Blacksburg–Christiansburg–Radford, VA	More than $146,500	70
Longview, TX	More than $146,500	160
San Jose–Sunnyvale–Santa Clara, CA	More than $146,500	3,970
Santa Cruz–Watsonville, CA	$135,290	250
Oxnard–Thousand Oaks–Ventura, CA	$129,290	990

Represent clients in criminal and civil litigation and other legal proceedings, draw up legal documents, and manage or advise clients on legal transactions. May specialize in a single area or may practice broadly in many areas of law. Advise clients concerning business transactions, claim liability, advisability of prosecuting or defending lawsuits, or legal rights and obligations. Interpret laws, rulings and regulations for individuals and businesses. Analyze the probable outcomes of cases, using knowledge of legal precedents. Present and summarize cases to judges and juries. Evaluate findings and develop strategies and arguments in preparation for presentation of cases. Gather evidence to formulate defense or to initiate legal actions, by such means as interviewing clients and witnesses to ascertain the facts of a case. Represent clients in court or before government agencies. Examine legal data to determine advisability of defending or prosecuting lawsuit. Select jurors, argue motions, meet with judges and question witnesses during the course of a trial. Present evidence to defend clients or prosecute defendants in criminal or civil litigation. Study Constitution, statutes, decisions, regulations, and ordinances of quasi-judicial bodies to determine ramifications for cases. Prepare and draft legal documents, such as wills, deeds, patent applications, mortgages, leases, and contracts. Prepare legal briefs and opinions, and file appeals in state and federal courts of appeal. Negotiate settlements of civil disputes. Confer with colleagues with specialties in appropriate areas of legal issue to establish and verify bases for legal proceedings. Search for and examine public and other legal records to write opinions or establish ownership. Supervise legal assistants. Perform administrative and management functions related to the practice of law. Act as agent, trustee, guardian, or executor for businesses or individuals. Probate wills and represent and advise executors and administrators of estates. Help develop federal and state programs, draft and interpret laws and legislation, and establish enforcement procedures. Work in environmental law, representing public interest groups, waste disposal companies, or construction firms in their dealings with state and federal agencies. **SKILLS**—Persuasion; Negotiation; Critical Thinking; Writing; Judgment and Decision Making; Active Learning; Social Perceptiveness; Speaking.

GOE—Interest Area: 12. Law and Public Safety. **Work Group:** 12.02. Legal Practice and Justice Administration. **PERSONALITY TYPE:** Enterprising. Enterprising occupations frequently involve starting up and carrying out projects. These occupations can involve leading people and making many decisions. They sometimes require risk taking and often deal with business.

EDUCATION/TRAINING PROGRAMS—
Advanced Legal Research/Studies, General (LL.M., M.C.L., M.L.I., M.S.L., J.S.D./S.J.D.); American/U.S. Law/Legal Studies/Jurisprudence (LL.M., M.C.J., J.S.D./S.J.D.); Banking, Corporate, Finance, and Securities Law (LL.M., J.S.D./S.J.D.); Canadian Law/Legal Studies/Jurisprudence (LL.M., M.C.J., J.S.D./S.J.D.); Comparative Law (LL.M., M.C.L., J.S.D./S.J.D.); Energy, Environment, and Natural Resources Law (LL.M., M.S., J.S.D./S.J.D.); Health Law (LL.M., M.J., J.S.D./S.J.D.); others. **RELATED KNOWLEDGE/COURSES—Law and Government:** Knowledge of laws, legal codes, court procedures, precedents, government regulations, executive orders, agency rules, and the democratic political process. **English Language:** Knowledge of the structure and content of the English language, including the meaning and spelling of words, rules of composition, and grammar. **Personnel and Human Resources:** Knowledge of principles and procedures for personnel recruitment, selection, training, compensation and benefits, labor relations and negotiation, and personnel information systems. **Customer and Personal Service:** Knowledge of principles and processes for providing customer and personal services. This includes customer needs assessment, meeting quality standards for services, and evaluation of customer satisfaction. **Administration and Management:** Knowledge of business and management principles involved in strategic planning, resource allocation, human resources modeling, leadership technique, production methods, and coordination of people and resources. **Psychology:** Knowledge of human behavior and performance; individual differences in ability, personality, and interests; learning and motivation; psychological research methods; and the assessment and treatment of behavioral and affective disorders.

Librarians

- Annual Earnings: $47,400
- Growth: 4.9%
- Annual Job Openings: 8,000
- Self-Employed: 0.0%
- Part-Time: 22.3%
- Education/Training Required: Master's degree

Industries in Which Income Is Highest

Industry	Average Annual Wage	Number Employed
Professional, Scientific, and Technical Services	$54,080	3,320
Educational Services	$49,250	87,620
Federal, State, and Local Government	$44,330	43,530
Hospitals	$44,020	1,760
Other Information Services	$41,040	6,100

Metropolitan Areas Where Income Is Highest

Metropolitan Area	Average Annual Wage	Number Employed
Brunswick, GA	$70,020	50
Stockton, CA	$67,590	50
San Jose–Sunnyvale–Santa Clara, CA	$66,790	780
Oxnard–Thousand Oaks–Ventura, CA	$63,200	500
Holland–Grand Haven, MI	$61,060	100

Administer libraries and perform related library services. Work in a variety of settings, including public libraries, schools, colleges and universities, museums, corporations, government agencies, law firms, non-profit organizations, and healthcare providers. Tasks may include selecting, acquiring, cataloguing, classifying, circulating, and maintaining library materials; and furnishing reference, bibliographical, and readers' advisory services. May perform in-depth, strategic research, and synthesize, analyze, edit, and filter information. May set up or work with databases and information systems to catalogue and access information. Search standard reference materials, including on-line sources and the Internet, in order to answer patrons' reference questions. Analyze patrons' requests to determine needed information, and assist in furnishing or locating that information. Teach library patrons to search for information using databases. Keep records of circulation and materials. Supervise budgeting, planning, and personnel activities. Check books in and out of the library. Explain use of library facilities, resources, equipment, and services, and provide information about library policies. Review and evaluate resource material, such as book reviews and catalogs, in order to select and order print, audiovisual, and electronic resources.

Code, classify, and catalog books, publications, films, audiovisual aids, and other library materials based on subject matter or standard library classification systems. Locate unusual or unique information in response to specific requests. Direct and train library staff in duties such as receiving, shelving, researching, cataloging, and equipment use. Respond to customer complaints, taking action as necessary. Organize collections of books, publications, documents, audiovisual aids, and other reference materials for convenient access. Develop library policies and procedures. Evaluate materials to determine outdated or unused items to be discarded. Develop information access aids such as indexes and annotated bibliographies, web pages, electronic pathfinders, and on-line tutorials. Plan and deliver client-centered programs and services such as special services for corporate clients, storytelling for children, newsletters, or programs for special groups. Compile lists of books, periodicals, articles, and audiovisual materials on particular subjects. Arrange for interlibrary loans of materials not available in a particular library. Assemble and arrange display materials. Confer with teachers, parents, and community organizations to develop, plan, and conduct programs in reading, viewing, and communication skills. Compile lists of overdue materials, and notify borrowers that their materials are overdue. **SKILLS**—Management of Financial Resources; Learning Strategies; Persuasion; Service Orientation; Management of Material Resources; Instructing; Monitoring; Social Perceptiveness.

GOE—Interest Area: 05. Education and Training. **Work Group:** 05.04. Library Services. **PERSONALITY TYPE:** Artistic. Artistic occupations frequently involve working with forms, designs, and patterns. They often require self-expression, and the work can be done without following a clear set of rules.

EDUCATION/TRAINING PROGRAMS—Library Science, Other; Library Science/Librarianship; School Librarian/School Library Media Specialist. **RELATED KNOWLEDGE/COURSES—Customer and Personal Service:** Knowledge of principles and processes for providing customer and personal services. This includes customer needs assessment, meeting quality standards for services, and evaluation of customer satisfaction. **Clerical Practices:** Knowledge of administrative and clerical procedures and systems such as word processing, managing files and records, stenography and transcription, designing forms, and other office procedures and terminology. **Personnel and Human Resources:** Knowledge of principles and procedures for personnel recruitment, selection, training, compensation and benefits, labor relations and negotiation, and personnel information systems. **English Language:** Knowledge of the structure and content of the English language, including the meaning and spelling of words, rules of composition, and grammar. **Communications and Media:** Knowledge of media production, communication, and dissemination techniques and methods. This includes alternative ways to inform and entertain via written, oral, and visual media. **Education and Training:** Knowledge of principles and methods for curriculum and training design, teaching and instruction for individuals and groups, and the measurement of training effects.

Library Science Teachers, Postsecondary

- Annual Earnings: $53,810
- Growth: 32.2%
- Annual Job Openings: 329,000
- Self-Employed: 0.4%
- Part-Time: 27.3%
- Education/Training Required: Master's degree

Our sources did not provide separate job openings data for this occupation. The job openings listed here are shared with 35 other postsecondary teaching occupations. For a complete list, see the beginning of this section.

Industries in Which Income Is Highest

Industry	Average Annual Wage	Number Employed
Educational Services	$53,830	3,950

Metropolitan Areas Where Income Is Highest

Metropolitan Area	Average Annual Wage	Number Employed
Kansas City, MO–KS	$72,060	40
Los Angeles–Long Beach–Santa Ana, CA	$69,500	70
Philadelphia–Camden–Wilmington, PA–NJ–DE–MD	$67,370	80
Providence–Fall River–Warwick, RI–MA	$63,390	40
Chicago–Naperville–Joliet, IL–IN–WI	$59,530	510

Teach courses in library science. Prepare course materials such as syllabi, homework assignments, and handouts. Prepare and deliver lectures to undergraduate and/or graduate students on topics such as collection development, archival methods, and indexing and abstracting. Evaluate and grade students' class work, assignments, and papers. Keep abreast of developments in their field by reading current literature, talking with colleagues, and participating in professional conferences. Initiate, facilitate, and moderate classroom discussions. Plan, evaluate, and revise curricula, course content, and course materials and methods of instruction. Conduct research in a particular field of knowledge and publish findings in professional journals, books, and/or electronic media. Maintain student attendance records, grades, and other required records. Collaborate with colleagues to address teaching and research issues. Advise students on academic and vocational curricula and on career issues. Compile, administer, and grade examinations or assign this work to others. Supervise undergraduate and/or graduate teaching, internship, and research work. Maintain regularly scheduled office hours in order to advise and assist students. Write grant proposals to procure external research funding. Select and obtain materials and supplies such as textbooks. Serve on academic or administrative committees that deal with institutional policies, departmental matters, and academic issues. Participate in student recruitment, registration, and placement activities. Compile bibliographies of specialized materials for outside reading assignments. Perform administrative duties such as serving as department head. **SKILLS**—Instructing; Learning Strategies; Writing; Active Learning; Persuasion; Service Orientation; Critical Thinking; Reading Comprehension.

GOE—Interest Area: 05. Education and Training. **Work Group:** 05.03. Postsecondary and Adult

Teaching and Instructing. **PERSONALITY TYPE:** No data available.

EDUCATION/TRAINING PROGRAMS—Library Science/Librarianship; Teacher Education and Professional Development, Specific Subject Areas, Other. **RELATED KNOWLEDGE/COURSES**—**Education and Training:** Knowledge of principles and methods for curriculum and training design, teaching and instruction for individuals and groups, and the measurement of training effects. **English Language:** Knowledge of the structure and content of the English language, including the meaning and spelling of words, rules of composition, and grammar. **Sociology and Anthropology:** Knowledge of group behavior and dynamics, societal trends and influences, human migrations, ethnicity, and cultures and their history and origins. **Communications and Media:** Knowledge of media production, communication, and dissemination techniques and methods. This includes alternative ways to inform and entertain via written, oral, and visual media. **Philosophy and Theology:** Knowledge of different philosophical systems and religions. This includes their basic principles, values, ethics, ways of thinking, customs, and practices and their impact on human culture. **Computers and Electronics:** Knowledge of circuit boards, processors, chips, electronic equipment, and computer hardware and software, including applications and programming.

Licensing Examiners and Inspectors

- Annual Earnings: $49,360
- Growth: 11.6%
- Annual Job Openings: 17,000
- Self-Employed: 0.0%
- Part-Time: 5.1%
- Education/Training Required: Long-term on-the-job training

The job openings listed here are shared with Coroners, Environmental Compliance Inspectors, Equal Opportunity Representatives and Officers, Government Property Inspectors and Investigators, and Pressure Vessel Inspectors.

Industries in Which Income Is Highest

Industry	Average Annual Wage	Number Employed
Postal Service	$72,700	1,710
Utilities	$66,390	1,310
Securities, Commodity Contracts, and Other Financial Investments and Related Activities	$64,490	5,130
Computer and Electronic Product Manufacturing	$59,540	1,390
Telecommunications	$59,310	2,620

Metropolitan Areas Where Income Is Highest

Metropolitan Area	Average Annual Wage	Number Employed
Kankakee–Bradley, IL	$81,020	170
Brunswick, GA	$79,710	340
San Jose–Sunnyvale–Santa Clara, CA	$67,550	930
San Francisco–Oakland–Fremont, CA	$64,010	3,320
Santa Rosa–Petaluma, CA	$63,660	410

Examine, evaluate, and investigate eligibility for, conformity with, or liability under licenses or permits. Administer oral, written, road, or flight tests to license applicants. Advise licensees and other individuals or groups concerning licensing, permit, or passport regulations. Evaluate applications, records, and documents in order to gather information about eligibility or liability issues. Issue licenses to individuals meeting standards. Prepare correspondence to inform concerned parties of licensing decisions and of appeals processes. Prepare reports of activities, evaluations, recommendations, and decisions. Report law or regulation violations to appropriate boards and agencies. Score tests and observe equipment operation and control in order to rate ability of applicants. Confer with and interview officials, technical or professional specialists, and applicants, in order to obtain information or to clarify facts relevant to licensing decisions. Visit establishments to verify that valid licenses and permits are displayed, and that licensing standards are being upheld. Warn violators of infractions or penalties. **SKILLS**—Speaking; Writing; Monitoring; Active Listening; Reading Comprehension; Judgment and Decision Making; Mathematics.

GOE—Interest Area: 07. Government and Public Administration. **Work Group:** 07.03. Regulations Enforcement. **PERSONALITY TYPE:** Conventional. Conventional occupations frequently involve following set procedures and routines. These occupations can include working with data and details more than with ideas. Usually there is a clear line of authority to follow.

EDUCATION/TRAINING PROGRAM—No data available. **RELATED KNOWLEDGE/COURSES**— **Law and Government:** Knowledge of laws, legal codes, court procedures, precedents, government regulations, executive orders, agency rules, and the democratic political process. **Clerical Practices:** Knowledge of administrative and clerical procedures and systems such as word processing, managing files and records, stenography and transcription, designing forms, and other office procedures and terminology. **Communications and Media:** Knowledge of media production, communication, and dissemination techniques and methods. This includes alternative ways to inform and entertain via written, oral, and visual media. **English Language:** Knowledge of the structure and content of the English language, including the meaning and spelling of words, rules of composition, and grammar.

Loan Officers

- Annual Earnings: $49,440
- Growth: 8.3%
- Annual Job Openings: 38,000
- Self-Employed: 2.7%
- Part-Time: 7.3%
- Education/Training Required: Bachelor's degree

Industries in Which Income Is Highest

Industry	Average Annual Wage	Number Employed
Federal, State, and Local Government	$60,810	4,570
Real Estate	$53,760	3,400
Insurance Carriers and Related Activities	$51,620	6,990
Securities, Commodity Contracts, and Other Financial Investments and Related Activities	$51,580	3,370
Management of Companies and Enterprises	$51,180	7,090

Metropolitan Areas Where Income Is Highest

Metropolitan Area	Average Annual Wage	Number Employed
Bridgeport–Stamford–Norwalk, CT	$80,390	1,030
Santa Barbara–Santa Maria, CA	$79,260	430
Norwich–New London, CT–RI	$77,150	160
Boston–Cambridge–Quincy, MA–NH	$72,880	6,650
Salinas, CA	$71,660	260

Evaluate, authorize, or recommend approval of commercial, real estate, or credit loans. Advise borrowers on financial status and methods of payments. Includes mortgage loan officers and agents, collection analysts, loan servicing officers, and loan underwriters. Approve loans within specified limits, and refer loan applications outside those limits to management for approval. Meet with applicants to obtain information for loan applications and to answer questions about the process. Analyze applicants' financial status, credit, and property evaluations to determine feasibility of granting loans. Explain to customers the different types of loans and credit options that are available, as well as the terms of those services. Obtain and compile copies of loan applicants' credit histories, corporate financial statements, and other financial information. Review and update credit and loan files. Review loan agreements to ensure that they are complete and accurate according to policy. Compute payment schedules. Stay abreast of new types of loans and other financial services and products in order to better meet customers' needs. Submit applications to credit analysts for verification and recommendation. Handle customer complaints and take appropriate action to resolve them. Work with clients to identify their financial goals and to find ways of reaching those goals. Confer with underwriters to aid in resolving mortgage application problems. Negotiate payment arrangements with customers who have delinquent loans. Market bank products to individuals and firms, promoting bank services that may meet customers' needs. Supervise loan personnel. Set credit policies, credit lines, procedures and standards in conjunction with senior managers. Provide special services such as investment banking for clients with more specialized needs.

Analyze potential loan markets and develop referral networks in order to locate prospects for loans. Prepare reports to send to customers whose accounts are delinquent, and forward irreconcilable accounts for collector action. Arrange for maintenance and liquidation of delinquent properties. Interview, hire, and train new employees. Petition courts to transfer titles and deeds of collateral to banks. **SKILLS**—Persuasion; Social Perceptiveness; Service Orientation; Instructing; Negotiation; Complex Problem Solving; Learning Strategies; Speaking.

GOE—Interest Area: 06. Finance and Insurance. **Work Group:** 06.02. Finance/Insurance Investigation and Analysis. **PERSONALITY TYPE:** Enterprising. Enterprising occupations frequently involve starting up and carrying out projects. These occupations can involve leading people and making many decisions. They sometimes require risk taking and often deal with business.

EDUCATION/TRAINING PROGRAMS—Credit Management; Finance, General. **RELATED KNOWLEDGE/COURSES—Economics and Accounting:** Knowledge of economic and accounting principles and practices, the financial markets, banking, and the analysis and reporting of financial data. **Sales and Marketing:** Knowledge of principles and methods for showing, promoting, and selling products or services. This includes marketing strategy and tactics, product demonstration, sales techniques, and sales control systems. **Law and Government:** Knowledge of laws, legal codes, court procedures, precedents, government regulations, executive orders, agency rules, and the democratic political process. **Customer and Personal Service:** Knowledge of principles and processes for providing customer and personal services. This includes customer needs assessment, meeting quality standards for services, and evaluation of customer satisfaction. **English Language:** Knowledge of the structure and content of the English language, including the meaning and spelling of words, rules of composition, and grammar. **Personnel and Human Resources:** Knowledge of principles and procedures for personnel recruitment, selection, training, compensation and benefits, labor relations and negotiation, and personnel information systems.

Locomotive Engineers

- Annual Earnings: $55,520
- Growth: –2.5%
- Annual Job Openings: 2,000
- Self-Employed: 0.0%
- Part-Time: 0.9%
- Education/Training Required: Work experience in a related occupation

The job openings listed here are shared with Locomotive Firers; and Rail Yard Engineers, Dinkey Operators, and Hostlers.

Industries in Which Income Is Highest

Industry	Average Annual Wage	Number Employed
Rail Transportation	$56,330	35,410
Federal, State, and Local Government	$50,060	1,210

Metropolitan Areas Where Income Is Highest

Metropolitan Area	Average Annual Wage	Number Employed

No metropolitan area had enough workers to be included here.

Drive electric, diesel-electric, steam, or gas-turbine-electric locomotives to transport passengers or freight. Interpret train orders, electronic or manual signals, and railroad rules and regulations. Receive starting signals from conductors, then move controls such as throttles and air brakes to drive electric, diesel-electric, steam, or gas-turbine-electric locomotives. Call out train signals to assistants in order to verify meanings. Check to ensure that brake examination tests are conducted at shunting stations. Check to ensure that documentation, including procedure manuals and logbooks, is in the driver's cab and available for staff use. Drive diesel-electric rail-detector cars to transport rail-flaw-detecting machines over tracks. Inspect locomotives after runs to detect damaged or defective equipment. Monitor train loading procedures to ensure that freight and rolling stock are loaded or unloaded without damage. Prepare reports regarding any problems encountered, such as accidents, signaling problems, unscheduled stops, or delays. Respond to emergency conditions or breakdowns, following applicable safety procedures and rules. Confer with conductors or traffic control center personnel via radio-phones to issue or receive information concerning stops, delays, or oncoming trains. Inspect locomotives to verify adequate fuel, sand, water, and other supplies before each run, and to check for mechanical problems. Interpret train orders, signals, and railroad rules and regulations that govern the operation of locomotives. Monitor gauges and meters that measure speed, amperage, battery charge, and air pressure in brakelines and in main reservoirs. Observe tracks to detect obstructions. Operate locomotives to transport freight or passengers between stations, and to assemble and disassemble trains within rail yards. **SKILLS**—Operation and Control; Operation Monitoring; Equipment Maintenance; Systems Analysis; Troubleshooting.

GOE—Interest Area: 16. Transportation, Distribution, and Logistics. **Work Group:** 16.04. Rail Vehicle Operation. **PERSONALITY TYPE:** Realistic. Realistic occupations frequently involve work activities that include practical, hands-on problems and solutions. They often deal with plants, animals, and real-world materials like wood, tools, and machinery. Many of the occupations require working outside and do not involve a lot of paperwork or working closely with others.

EDUCATION/TRAINING PROGRAM—Transportation and Materials Moving Services, Other. **RELATED KNOWLEDGE/COURSES**—**Transportation:** Knowledge of principles and methods for moving people or goods by air, rail, sea, or road, including the relative costs and benefits. **Geography:** Knowledge of principles and methods for describing the features of land, sea, and air masses, including their physical characteristics; locations; interrelationships; and distribution of plant, animal, and human life. **Public Safety and Security:** Knowledge of relevant equipment, policies, procedures, and strategies to promote effective local, state, or national security operations for the protection of people, data, property, and institutions. **Mechanical Devices:** Knowledge of machines and tools, including their designs, uses, repair, and maintenance. **Engineering and Technology:** Knowledge of the practical application of engineering science and technology. This includes applying principles, techniques, procedures, and equipment to the design and production of various goods and services.

Logisticians

- Annual Earnings: $60,110
- Growth: 13.2%
- Annual Job Openings: 7,000
- Self-Employed: 0.7%
- Part-Time: 4.0%
- Education/Training Required: Bachelor's degree

Industries in Which Income Is Highest

Industry	Average Annual Wage	Number Employed
Telecommunications	$70,360	1,620
Computer and Electronic Product Manufacturing	$67,300	5,590
Management of Companies and Enterprises	$62,970	4,920
Transportation Equipment Manufacturing	$61,870	5,590
Professional, Scientific, and Technical Services	$61,230	8,770

Metropolitan Areas Where Income Is Highest

Metropolitan Area	Average Annual Wage	Number Employed
Richmond, VA	$81,060	290
Oxnard–Thousand Oaks–Ventura, CA	$77,630	150
Santa Rosa–Petaluma, CA	$75,590	50
Beaumont–Port Arthur, TX	$75,220	70
Hartford–West Hartford–East Hartford, CT	$74,930	150

Analyze and coordinate the logistical functions of a firm or organization. Responsible for the entire life cycle of a product, including acquisition, distribution, internal allocation, delivery, and final disposal of resources. Develop and implement technical project management tools such as plans, schedules, and responsibility and compliance matrices. Develop proposals that include documentation for estimates. Direct and support the compilation and analysis of technical source data necessary for product development. Direct availability and allocation of materials, supplies, and finished products. Direct team activities, establishing task priorities, scheduling and tracking work assignments, providing guidance, and ensuring the availability of resources. Manage the logistical aspects of product life cycles, including coordination or provisioning of samples, and the minimization of obsolescence. Participate in the assessment and review of design alternatives and design change proposal impacts. Perform system life-cycle cost analysis, and develop component studies. Plan, organize, and execute logistics support activities such as maintenance planning, repair analysis, and test equipment recommendations. Provide project management services, including the provision and analysis of technical data. Redesign the movement of goods in order to maximize value and minimize costs. Report project plans, progress, and results. Stay informed of logistics technology advances, and apply appropriate technology in order to improve logistics processes. Collaborate with other departments as necessary to meet customer requirements, to take advantage of sales opportunities or, in the case of shortages, to minimize negative impacts on a business. Develop an understanding of customers' needs, and take actions to ensure that such needs are met. Explain proposed solutions to customers, management, or other interested parties through written proposals and oral presentations. Maintain and develop positive business relationships with a customer's key personnel involved in or directly relevant to a logistics activity. Manage subcontractor activities, reviewing proposals, developing performance specifications, and serving as liaisons between subcontractors and organizations. Protect and control proprietary materials. Review logistics performance with customers against targets, benchmarks and service agreements. **SKILLS**—No data available.

GOE—Interest Area: 04. Business and Administration. **Work Group:** 04.05. Accounting, Auditing, and Analytical Support. **PERSONALITY TYPE:** No data available.

EDUCATION/TRAINING PROGRAMS—Logistics and Materials Management; Operations Management and Supervision; Transportation/Transportation Management. **RELATED KNOWLEDGE/COURSES**—No data available.

Management Analysts

- Annual Earnings: $66,380
- Growth: 20.1%
- Annual Job Openings: 82,000
- Self-Employed: 24.7%
- Part-Time: 18.6%
- Education/Training Required: Work experience plus degree

Industries in Which Income Is Highest

Industry	Average Annual Wage	Number Employed
Merchant Wholesalers, Durable Goods	$85,090	6,550
Professional, Scientific, and Technical Services	$73,990	162,430
Wholesale Electronic Markets and Agents and Brokers	$72,070	1,690
Publishing Industries (Except Internet)	$70,730	5,740
Securities, Commodity Contracts, and Other Financial Investments and Related Activities	$70,410	6,020

Metropolitan Areas Where Income Is Highest

Metropolitan Area	Average Annual Wage	Number Employed
Greeley, CO	$90,720	110
San Jose–Sunnyvale–Santa Clara, CA	$89,280	5,240
Bridgeport–Stamford–Norwalk, CT	$85,700	2,690
Salt Lake City, UT	$83,550	1,210
Orlando–Kissimmee, FL	$81,060	4,530

Conduct organizational studies and evaluations, design systems and procedures, conduct work simplifications and measurement studies, and prepare operations and procedures manuals to assist management in operating more efficiently and effectively. Includes program analysts and management consultants. Gather and organize information on problems or procedures. Analyze data gathered and develop solutions or alternative methods of proceeding. Confer with personnel concerned to ensure successful functioning of newly implemented systems or procedures. Develop and implement records management program for filing, protection, and retrieval of records, and assure compliance with program. Review forms and reports, and confer with management and users about format, distribution, and purpose, and to identify problems and improvements. Interview personnel and conduct on-site observation to ascertain unit functions, work performed, and methods, equipment, and personnel used. Document findings of study and prepare recommendations for implementation of new systems, procedures, or organizational changes. Prepare manuals and train workers in use of new forms, reports, procedures or equipment, according to organizational policy. Design, evaluate, recommend, and approve changes of forms and reports. Plan study of work problems and procedures, such as organizational change, communications, information flow, integrated production methods, inventory control, or cost analysis. **SKILLS**—Management of Financial Resources; Systems Evaluation; Operations Analysis; Installation; Quality Control Analysis; Judgment and Decision Making; Systems Analysis; Service Orientation.

GOE—Interest Area: 04. Business and Administration. **Work Group:** 04.05. Accounting, Auditing, and Analytical Support. **PERSONALITY TYPE:** Enterprising. Enterprising occupations frequently involve starting up and carrying out projects. These occupations can involve leading people and making many decisions. They sometimes require risk taking and often deal with business.

EDUCATION/TRAINING PROGRAMS—Business Administration/Management; Business/Commerce, General. **RELATED KNOWLEDGE/COURSES**— **Customer and Personal Service:** Knowledge of principles and processes for providing customer and personal services. This includes customer needs assessment, meeting quality standards for services, and evaluation of customer satisfaction. **Personnel and Human Resources:** Knowledge of principles and procedures for personnel recruitment, selection, training, compensation and benefits, labor relations and negotiation, and personnel information systems. **Clerical Practices:** Knowledge of administrative and clerical procedures and systems such as word processing, managing files and records, stenography and transcription, designing forms, and other office procedures and terminology. **Sales and Marketing:** Knowledge of principles and methods for showing, promoting, and selling products or services. This includes marketing strategy and tactics, product demonstration, sales techniques, and sales control systems. **Administration and Management:** Knowledge of business and management principles involved in strategic planning, resource allocation, human resources modeling, leadership technique, production methods, and coordination of people and resources. **Economics and Accounting:** Knowledge of economic and accounting principles and practices, the financial markets, banking, and the analysis and reporting of financial data.

Marine Architects

- ◎ Annual Earnings: $72,920
- ◎ Growth: 8.5%
- ◎ Annual Job Openings: fewer than 500
- ◎ Self-Employed: 0.0%
- ◎ Part-Time: 1.9%
- ◎ Education/Training Required: Bachelor's degree

The job openings listed here are shared with Marine Engineers.

Industries in Which Income Is Highest

Industry	Average Annual Wage	Number Employed
Petroleum and Coal Products Manufacturing	$86,960	40
Federal, State, and Local Government	$84,510	900
Water Transportation	$83,720	460
Transportation Equipment Manufacturing	$74,840	620
Support Activities for Transportation	$72,950	360

Metropolitan Areas Where Income Is Highest

Metropolitan Area	Average Annual Wage	Number Employed
Washington–Arlington–Alexandria, DC–VA–MD–WV	$97,030	730
Honolulu, HI	$89,860	80
Houston–Sugar Land–Baytown, TX	$78,410	1,030
Baltimore–Towson, MD	$72,990	60
Philadelphia–Camden–Wilmington, PA–NJ–DE–MD	$70,490	50

Design and oversee construction and repair of marine craft and floating structures such as ships, barges, tugs, dredges, submarines, torpedoes, floats, and buoys. May confer with marine engineers. Oversee construction and testing of prototype in model basin and develop sectional and waterline curves of hull to establish center of gravity, ideal hull form, and buoyancy and stability data. Confer with marine engineering personnel to establish arrangement of boiler room equipment and propulsion machinery, heating and ventilating systems, refrigeration equipment, piping, and other functional equipment. Design complete hull and superstructure according to specifications and test data, in conformity with standards of safety, efficiency, and economy. Design layout of craft interior, including cargo space, passenger compartments, ladder wells, and elevators. Study design proposals and specifications to establish basic characteristics of craft, such as size, weight, speed, propulsion, displacement, and draft. Evaluate performance of craft during dock and sea trials to determine design changes and conformance with national and international standards. **SKILLS—** Quality Control Analysis; Science; Technology Design; Mathematics; Systems Analysis; Active Learning; Systems Evaluation; Monitoring.

GOE—Interest Area: 15. Scientific Research, Engineering, and Mathematics. **Work Group:** 15.07. Research and Design Engineering. **PERSONALITY TYPE:** Realistic. Realistic occupations frequently involve work activities that include practical, hands-on problems and solutions. They often deal with plants, animals, and real-world materials like wood, tools, and machinery. Many of the occupations require working outside and do not involve a lot of paperwork or working closely with others.

EDUCATION/TRAINING PROGRAM—Naval Architecture and Marine Engineering. **RELATED KNOWLEDGE/COURSES—Design:** Knowledge of design techniques, tools, and principles involved in production of precision technical plans, blueprints, drawings, and models. **Physics:** Knowledge and prediction of physical principles and laws and their interrelationships and applications to understanding fluid, material, and atmospheric dynamics and mechanical, electrical, atomic, and subatomic structures and processes. **Engineering and Technology:** Knowledge of the practical application of engineering science and technology. This includes applying principles, techniques, procedures, and equipment to the design and production of various goods and services. **Building and**

Construction: Knowledge of the materials, methods, and tools involved in the construction or repair of houses, buildings, or other structures such as highways and roads. Mathematics: Knowledge of arithmetic, algebra, geometry, calculus, and statistics and their applications. Administration and Management: Knowledge of business and management principles involved in strategic planning, resource allocation, human resources modeling, leadership technique, production methods, and coordination of people and resources.

Marine Cargo Inspectors

- Annual Earnings: $49,490
- Growth: 11.4%
- Annual Job Openings: 2,000
- Self-Employed: 1.9%
- Part-Time: 2.2%
- Education/Training Required: Work experience in a related occupation

The job openings listed here are shared with Aviation Inspectors, Freight Inspectors, Motor Vehicle Inspectors, Public Transportation Inspectors, and Railroad Inspectors.

Industries in Which Income Is Highest

Industry	Average Annual Wage	Number Employed
Air Transportation	$67,590	1,460
Transportation Equipment Manufacturing	$55,200	1,100
Federal, State, and Local Government	$54,510	10,960
Rail Transportation	$45,840	2,680
Support Activities for Transportation	$37,870	4,350

Metropolitan Areas Where Income Is Highest

Metropolitan Area	Average Annual Wage	Number Employed
Washington–Arlington–Alexandria, DC–VA–MD–WV	$96,800	360
Oklahoma City, OK	$91,650	130
Milwaukee–Waukesha–West Allis, WI	$84,510	50
Miami–Fort Lauderdale–Miami Beach, FL	$84,490	680
Louisville–Jefferson County, KY–IN	$81,260	80

Inspect cargoes of seagoing vessels to certify compliance with health and safety regulations in cargo handling and stowage. Examines blueprints of ship and takes physical measurements to determine capacity and depth of vessel in water, using measuring instruments. Writes certificates of admeasurement, listing details, such as design, length, depth, and breadth of vessel, and method of propulsion. Issues certificate of compliance when violations are not detected or recommends remedial procedures to correct deficiencies. Times roll of ship, using stopwatch. Analyzes data, formulates recommendations, and writes reports of findings. Advises crew in techniques of stowing dangerous and heavy cargo, according to knowledge of hazardous cargo. Inspects loaded cargo in holds and cargo handling devices to determine compliance with regulations and need for maintenance. Reads vessel documents to ascertain cargo capabilities according to design and cargo regulations. Calculates gross and net tonnage, hold capacities, volume of stored fuel and water, cargo weight, and ship stability factors, using mathematical formulas. Determines type of license and safety equipment required, and computes applicable tolls and wharfage fees. SKILLS—Mathematics; Systems Evaluation; Writing; Systems Analysis; Judgment and Decision Making; Speaking; Active Listening; Reading Comprehension.

GOE—Interest Area: 07. Government and Public Administration. Work Group: 07.03. Regulations Enforcement. PERSONALITY TYPE: Conventional. Conventional occupations frequently involve following set procedures and routines. These occupations can include working with data and details more than with ideas. Usually there is a clear line of authority to follow.

EDUCATION/TRAINING PROGRAM—No data available. RELATED KNOWLEDGE/COURSES— Public Safety and Security: Knowledge of relevant equipment, policies, procedures, and strategies to promote effective local, state, or national security operations for the protection of people, data, property, and institutions. Transportation: Knowledge of principles and methods for moving people or goods by air, rail, sea, or road, including the relative costs and benefits. Design: Knowledge of design techniques, tools, and principles involved in production of precision technical plans, blueprints, drawings, and models. Mathematics: Knowledge of arithmetic, algebra, geometry, calculus, and statistics and their applications. Physics: Knowledge and prediction of physical principles and laws and their interrelationships and applications to understanding fluid, material, and atmospheric dynamics and mechanical, electrical, atomic, and subatomic structures and processes. **Law and Government:** Knowledge of laws, legal codes, court procedures, precedents, government regulations, executive orders, agency rules, and the democratic political process.

Marine Engineers

- ◎ Annual Earnings: $72,920
- ◎ Growth: 8.5%
- ◎ Annual Job Openings: fewer than 500
- ◎ Self-Employed: 0.0%
- ◎ Part-Time: 1.9%
- ◎ Education/Training Required: Bachelor's degree

The job openings listed here are shared with Marine Architects.

Industries in Which Income Is Highest

Industry	Average Annual Wage	Number Employed
Petroleum and Coal Products Manufacturing	$86,960	40
Federal, State, and Local Government	$84,510	900
Water Transportation	$83,720	460
Transportation Equipment Manufacturing	$74,840	620
Support Activities for Transportation	$72,950	360

Metropolitan Areas Where Income Is Highest

Metropolitan Area	Average Annual Wage	Number Employed
Washington–Arlington–Alexandria, DC–VA–MD–WV	$97,030	730
Honolulu, HI	$89,860	80
Houston–Sugar Land–Baytown, TX	$78,410	1,030
Baltimore–Towson, MD	$72,990	60
Philadelphia–Camden–Wilmington, PA–NJ–DE–MD	$70,490	50

Design, develop, and take responsibility for the installation of ship machinery and related equipment including propulsion machines and power supply systems. Prepare, or direct the preparation of, product or system layouts and detailed drawings and schematics. Inspect marine equipment and machinery in order to draw up work requests and job specifications. Conduct analytical, environmental, operational, or performance studies in order to develop designs for products, such as marine engines, equipment, and structures. Design and oversee testing, installation, and repair of marine apparatus and equipment. Prepare plans, estimates, design and construction schedules, and contract specifications, including any special provisions. Investigate and observe tests on machinery and equipment for compliance with standards. Coordinate activities with regulatory bodies in order to ensure repairs and alterations are at minimum cost, consistent with safety. Conduct environmental, operational, or performance tests on marine machinery and equipment. Prepare technical reports for use by engineering, management, or sales personnel. Maintain contact with, and formulate reports for, contractors and clients in order to ensure completion of work at minimum cost. Evaluate operation of marine equipment during acceptance testing and shakedown cruises. Analyze data in order to determine feasibility of product proposals. Determine conditions under which tests are to be conducted, as well as sequences and phases of test operations. Procure materials needed to repair marine equipment and machinery. Confer with research personnel in order to clarify or resolve problems, and to develop or modify designs. Review work requests, and compare them with previous work completed on ships in order to ensure that costs are economically sound. Act as liaisons between ships' captains and shore personnel in order to ensure that schedules and budgets are maintained, and that ships are operated safely and efficiently. Perform monitoring activities in order to ensure that ships comply with international regulations and standards for life saving equipment and pollution preventatives. Check, test, and maintain automatic controls and alarm systems. Supervise other engineers and crewmembers, and train them for routine and emergency duties. **SKILLS**—Science; Technology Design; Installation; Mathematics; Operations Analysis; Persuasion; Systems Analysis; Troubleshooting.

GOE—Interest Area: 15. Scientific Research, Engineering, and Mathematics. **Work Group:** 15.07. Research and Design Engineering. **PERSONALITY TYPE:** Realistic. Realistic occupations frequently involve work activities that include practical, hands-on problems and solutions. They often deal with plants, animals, and real-world materials like wood, tools, and machinery. Many of the occupations require working outside and do not involve a lot of paperwork or working closely with others.

EDUCATION/TRAINING PROGRAM—Naval Architecture and Marine Engineering. RELATED KNOWLEDGE/COURSES—Design: Knowledge of design techniques, tools, and principles involved in production of precision technical plans, blueprints, drawings, and models. Engineering and Technology: Knowledge of the practical application of engineering science and technology. This includes applying principles, techniques, procedures, and equipment to the design and production of various goods and services. Mechanical Devices: Knowledge of machines and tools, including their designs, uses, repair, and maintenance. Physics: Knowledge and prediction of physical principles and laws and their interrelationships and applications to understanding fluid, material, and atmospheric dynamics and mechanical, electrical, atomic, and subatomic structures and processes. Building and Construction: Knowledge of the materials, methods, and tools involved in the construction or repair of houses, buildings, or other structures such as highways and roads. Computers and Electronics: Knowledge of circuit boards, processors, chips, electronic equipment, and computer hardware and software, including applications and programming.

Market Research Analysts

- Annual Earnings: $57,300
- Growth: 19.6%
- Annual Job Openings: 20,000
- Self-Employed: 7.2%
- Part-Time: 14.2%
- Education/Training Required: Master's degree

Industries in Which Income Is Highest

Industry	Average Annual Wage	Number Employed
Computer and Electronic Product Manufacturing	$77,310	8,310
Transportation Equipment Manufacturing	$76,210	1,810
Utilities	$73,870	1,710
Telecommunications	$73,200	5,920
Securities, Commodity Contracts, and Other Financial Investments and Related Activities	$71,090	7,650

Metropolitan Areas Where Income Is Highest

Metropolitan Area	Average Annual Wage	Number Employed
Durham, NC	$87,210	780
Seattle–Tacoma–Bellevue, WA	$78,150	6,260
San Jose–Sunnyvale–Santa Clara, CA	$76,960	2,690
Austin–Round Rock, TX	$76,920	2,400
Oxnard–Thousand Oaks–Ventura, CA	$76,310	580

Research market conditions in local, regional, or national areas to determine potential sales of a product or service. May gather information on competitors, prices, sales, and methods of marketing and distribution. May use survey results to create a marketing campaign based on regional preferences and buying habits. Collect and analyze data on customer demographics, preferences, needs, and buying habits to identify potential markets and factors affecting product demand. Prepare reports of findings, illustrating data graphically and translating complex findings into written text. Measure and assess customer and employee satisfaction. Forecast and track marketing and sales trends, analyzing collected data. Seek and provide information to help companies determine their position in the marketplace. Measure the effectiveness of marketing, advertising, and communications programs and strategies. Conduct research on consumer opinions and marketing strategies, collaborating with marketing professionals, statisticians, pollsters, and other professionals. Attend staff conferences to provide management with information and proposals concerning the promotion, distribution, design, and pricing of company products or services. Gather data on competitors and analyze their prices, sales, and method of marketing and distribution. Monitor industry statistics and follow trends in trade literature. Devise and evaluate methods and procedures for collecting data (such as surveys, opinion polls, or questionnaires), or arrange to obtain existing data. Develop and implement procedures for identifying advertising needs. Direct trained survey interviewers. **SKILLS**—Persuasion; Negotiation; Coordination; Writing; Time Management; Judgment and Decision Making; Social Perceptiveness; Management of Financial Resources.

GOE—Interest Area: 06. Finance and Insurance. **Work Group:** 06.02. Finance/Insurance Investigation and Analysis. **PERSONALITY TYPE:** Investigative. Investigative occupations frequently involve working with ideas and require an extensive amount of thinking. These occupations can involve searching for facts and figuring out problems mentally.

EDUCATION/TRAINING PROGRAMS—Applied Economics; Business/Managerial Economics; Econometrics and Quantitative Economics; Economics, General; International Economics; Marketing Research. **RELATED KNOWLEDGE/COURSES— Sales and Marketing:** Knowledge of principles and methods for showing, promoting, and selling products or services. This includes marketing strategy and tactics, product demonstration, sales techniques, and sales control systems. **Administration and Management:** Knowledge of business and management principles involved in strategic planning, resource allocation, human resources modeling, leadership technique, production methods, and coordination of people and resources. **Communications and Media:** Knowledge of media production, communication, and dissemination techniques and methods. This includes alternative ways to inform and entertain via written, oral, and visual media. **Economics and Accounting:** Knowledge of economic and accounting principles and practices, the financial markets, banking, and the analysis and reporting of financial data. **Customer and Personal Service:** Knowledge of principles and processes for providing customer and personal services. This includes customer needs assessment, meeting quality standards for services, and evaluation of customer satisfaction. **Education and Training:** Knowledge of principles and methods for curriculum and training design, teaching and instruction for individuals and groups, and the measurement of training effects.

Marketing Managers

- Annual Earnings: $92,680
- Growth: 20.8%
- Annual Job Openings: 23,000
- Self-Employed: 3.6%
- Part-Time: 5.0%
- Education/Training Required: Work experience plus degree

Industries in Which Income Is Highest

Industry	Average Annual Wage	Number Employed
Securities, Commodity Contracts, and Other Financial Investments and Related Activities	$125,160	4,490
Computer and Electronic Product Manufacturing	$112,630	11,760
Internet Service Providers, Web Search Portals, and Data Processing Services	$106,480	2,740
Chemical Manufacturing	$105,650	3,820
Professional, Scientific, and Technical Services	$101,530	29,870

Metropolitan Areas Where Income Is Highest

Metropolitan Area	Average Annual Wage	Number Employed
San Jose–Sunnyvale–Santa Clara, CA	$134,350	6,170
New York–Northern New Jersey–Long Island, NY–NJ–PA	$124,650	15,890
Danbury, CT	$124,500	130
Trenton–Ewing, NJ	$123,470	400
Bridgeport–Stamford–Norwalk, CT	$121,820	1,290

Determine the demand for products and services offered by a firm and its competitors and identify potential customers. Develop pricing strategies with the goal of maximizing the firm's profits or share of the market while ensuring the firm's customers are satisfied. Oversee product development or monitor trends that indicate the need for new products and services. Develop pricing strategies, balancing firm objectives and customer satisfaction. Identify, develop, and evaluate marketing strategy, based on knowledge of establishment objectives, market characteristics, and cost and markup factors. Evaluate the financial aspects of product development, such as budgets, expenditures, research and development appropriations, and return-on-investment and profit-loss projections. Formulate, direct and coordinate marketing activities and policies to promote products and services, working with advertising and promotion managers. Direct the hiring, training, and performance evaluations of marketing and sales staff and oversee their daily activities. Negotiate contracts with vendors and distributors to manage product distribution, establishing distribution networks and developing distribution strategies. Consult with product development personnel on product specifications such as design, color, and packaging. Compile lists describing product or service offerings. Use sales forecasting and strategic planning to ensure the sale and profitability of products, lines, or services, analyzing business developments and monitoring market trends. Select products and accessories to be displayed at trade or special production shows. Confer with legal staff to resolve problems, such as copyright infringement and royalty sharing with outside producers and distributors. Coordinate and participate in promotional activities and trade shows, working with developers, advertisers, and production managers, to market products and services. Advise business and other groups on local, national, and international factors affecting the buying and selling of products and services. Initiate market research studies and analyze their findings. Consult with buying personnel to gain advice regarding the types of products or services expected to be in demand. Conduct economic and commercial surveys to identify potential markets for products and services. **SKILLS**—Management of Financial Resources; Management of Personnel Resources; Negotiation; Operations Analysis; Persuasion; Coordination; Instructing; Learning Strategies.

GOE—Interest Area: 14. Retail and Wholesale Sales and Service. **Work Group:** 14.01. Managerial Work in Retail/Wholesale Sales and Service. **PERSONALITY TYPE:** Enterprising. Enterprising occupations frequently involve starting up and carrying out projects. These occupations can involve leading people and making many decisions. They sometimes require risk taking and often deal with business.

EDUCATION/TRAINING PROGRAMS—Apparel and Textile Marketing Management; Consumer Merchandising/Retailing Management; International Marketing; Marketing Research; Marketing, Other; Marketing/Marketing Management, General. **RELATED KNOWLEDGE/COURSES—Sales and Marketing:** Knowledge of principles and methods for showing, promoting, and selling products or services. This includes marketing strategy and tactics, product demonstration, sales techniques, and sales control systems. **Customer and Personal Service:** Knowledge of principles and processes for providing customer and personal services. This includes customer needs assessment, meeting quality standards for services, and evaluation of customer satisfaction. **Administration and Management:** Knowledge of business and management principles involved in strategic planning, resource allocation, human resources modeling, leadership technique, production methods, and coordination of people and resources. **Personnel and Human Resources:** Knowledge of principles and procedures for personnel recruitment, selection, training, compensation and benefits, labor relations and negotiation, and personnel information systems. **Education and Training:** Knowledge of principles and methods for curriculum and training design, teaching and instruction for individuals and groups, and the measurement of training effects. **Communications and Media:** Knowledge of media production, communication, and dissemination techniques and methods. This includes alternative ways to inform and entertain via written, oral, and visual media.

Materials Engineers

- Annual Earnings: $69,660
- Growth: 12.2%
- Annual Job Openings: 2,000
- Self-Employed: 0.0%
- Part-Time: 2.4%
- Education/Training Required: Bachelor's degree

Industries in Which Income Is Highest

Industry	Average Annual Wage	Number Employed
Federal, State, and Local Government	$85,850	1,540
Transportation Equipment Manufacturing	$78,460	2,790
Professional, Scientific, and Technical Services	$71,240	3,600
Computer and Electronic Product Manufacturing	$69,020	3,470
Primary Metal Manufacturing	$64,830	2,340

Metropolitan Areas Where Income Is Highest

Metropolitan Area	Average Annual Wage	Number Employed
Washington–Arlington–Alexandria, DC–VA–MD–WV	$95,500	380
Dayton, OH	$91,860	340
Baltimore–Towson, MD	$85,190	120
Cleveland–Elyria–Mentor, OH	$83,990	240
Virginia Beach–Norfolk–Newport News, VA–NC	$83,130	60

Evaluate materials and develop machinery and processes to manufacture materials for use in products that must meet specialized design and performance specifications. Develop new uses for known materials. Includes those working with composite materials or specializing in one type of material, such as graphite, metal and metal alloys, ceramics and glass, plastics and polymers, and naturally occurring materials. Guide technical staff engaged in developing materials for specific uses in projected products or devices. Modify properties of metal alloys, using thermal and mechanical treatments. Perform managerial functions such as preparing proposals and budgets, analyzing labor costs, and writing reports. Plan and evaluate new projects, consulting with other engineers and corporate executives as necessary. Remove metals from ores, and refine and alloy them to obtain useful metal. Replicate the characteristics of materials and their components with computers. Supervise the work of technologists, technicians and other engineers and scientists. Sell and service metal products. Teach in colleges and universities. Write for technical magazines, journals, and trade association publications. Analyze product failure data and laboratory test results in order to determine causes of problems and develop solutions. Conduct or supervise tests on raw materials or finished products in order to ensure their quality. Design and direct the testing and/or control of processing procedures. Determine appropriate methods for fabricating and joining materials. Evaluate technical specifications and economic factors relating to process or product design objectives. Monitor material performance and evaluate material deterioration. Plan and implement laboratory operations for the purpose of developing material and fabrication procedures that meet cost, product specification, and performance standards. Review new product plans and make recommendations for material selection based on design objectives, such as strength, weight, heat resistance, electrical conductivity, and cost. Solve problems in a number of engineering fields, such as mechanical, chemical, electrical, civil, nuclear and aerospace. Supervise production and testing processes in industrial settings such as metal refining facilities, smelting or foundry operations, or non-metallic materials production operations. Conduct training sessions on new material products, applications, or manufacturing methods for customers and their employees. Design processing plants and equipment. **SKILLS**—Science; Operations Analysis; Technology Design; Mathematics; Judgment and Decision Making; Systems Evaluation; Complex Problem Solving; Active Learning.

GOE—Interest Area: 15. Scientific Research, Engineering, and Mathematics. **Work Group:** 15.07. Research and Design Engineering. **PERSONALITY TYPE:** Investigative. Investigative occupations frequently involve working with ideas and require an extensive amount of thinking. These occupations can involve searching for facts and figuring out problems mentally.

EDUCATION/TRAINING PROGRAMS—Ceramic Sciences and Engineering; Materials Engineering; Metallurgical Engineering. **RELATED KNOWLEDGE/COURSES**—**Engineering and Technology:** Knowledge of the practical application of engineering science and technology. This includes applying principles, techniques, procedures, and equipment to the design and production of various goods and services. **Design:** Knowledge of design techniques, tools, and principles involved in production of precision technical plans, blueprints, drawings, and models. **Mathematics:** Knowledge of arithmetic, algebra, geometry, calculus, and statistics and their applications. **Production and Processing:** Knowledge of raw materials, production processes, quality control, costs, and other techniques for maximizing the effective manufacture and distribution of goods. **Physics:** Knowledge and prediction of physical principles and laws and their interrelationships and applications to understanding fluid, material, and atmospheric dynamics and mechanical, electrical, atomic, and subatomic structures and processes. **Chemistry:** Knowledge of the chemical composition, structure, and properties of substances and of the chemical processes and transformations that they undergo. This includes uses of chemicals, their danger signs, production techniques, and disposal methods.

Materials Scientists

- Annual Earnings: $71,450
- Growth: 8.0%
- Annual Job Openings: fewer than 500
- Self-Employed: 0.4%
- Part-Time: 6.6%
- Education/Training Required: Bachelor's degree

Industries in Which Income Is Highest

Industry	Average Annual Wage	Number Employed
Federal, State, and Local Government	$96,210	100
Food Manufacturing	$90,180	60
Electrical Equipment, Appliance, and Component Manufacturing	$89,250	50
Computer and Electronic Product Manufacturing	$80,180	320
Plastics and Rubber Products Manufacturing	$78,040	80

Metropolitan Areas Where Income Is Highest

Metropolitan Area	Average Annual Wage	Number Employed
Richmond, VA	$103,760	100
San Jose–Sunnyvale–Santa Clara, CA	$97,140	210
Washington–Arlington–Alexandria, DC–VA–MD–WV	$96,430	80
Boston–Cambridge–Quincy, MA–NH	$90,000	260
Houston–Sugar Land–Baytown, TX	$88,660	150

Research and study the structures and chemical properties of various natural and manmade materials, including metals, alloys, rubber, ceramics, semiconductors, polymers, and glass. Determine ways to strengthen or combine materials or develop new materials with new or specific properties for use in a variety of products and applications. Conduct research into the structures and properties of materials, such as metals, alloys, polymers, and ceramics in order to obtain information that could be used to develop new products or enhance existing ones. Determine ways to strengthen or combine materials, or develop new materials with new or specific properties for use in a variety of products and applications. Devise testing methods to evaluate the effects of various conditions on particular materials. Plan laboratory experiments to confirm feasibility of processes and techniques used in the production of materials having special characteristics. Prepare reports of materials study findings for the use of other scientists and requestors. Recommend materials for reliable performance in various environments. Research methods of processing, forming, and firing materials in order to develop such products as ceramic fillings for teeth, unbreakable dinner plates, and telescope lenses. Study the nature, structure and physical properties of metals and their alloys, and their responses to applied forces. Test material samples for tolerance under tension, compression and shear, to determine the cause of metal failures. Confer with customers in order to determine how materials can be tailored to suit their needs. Monitor production processes in order to ensure that equipment is used efficiently and that projects are completed within appropriate time frames and budgets. Receive molten metal from smelters, and further alloy and refine it in oxygen, open-hearth or other kinds of furnaces. Teach in colleges and universities. Test individual parts and products in order to ensure that manufacturer and governmental quality and safety standards are met. Test metals in order to determine whether they meet specifications of mechanical strength, strength-weight ratio, ductility, magnetic and electrical properties, and resistance to abrasion, corrosion, heat and cold. Visit suppliers of materials or users of products in order to gather specific information. **SKILLS**—Science; Writing; Active Learning; Mathematics; Operations Analysis; Quality Control Analysis; Reading Comprehension; Systems Evaluation.

GOE—Interest Area: 15. Scientific Research, Engineering, and Mathematics. **Work Group:** 15.02. Physical Sciences. **PERSONALITY TYPE:** Investigative. Investigative occupations frequently involve working with ideas and require an extensive amount of thinking. These occupations can involve searching for facts and figuring out problems mentally.

EDUCATION/TRAINING PROGRAM—Materials Science. **RELATED KNOWLEDGE/COURSES**— **Chemistry:** Knowledge of the chemical composition, structure, and properties of substances and of the chemical processes and transformations that they undergo. This includes uses of chemicals, their danger signs, production techniques, and disposal methods. **Physics:** Knowledge and prediction of physical principles and laws and their interrelationships and applications to understanding fluid, material, and atmospheric dynamics and mechanical, electrical, atomic, and subatomic structures and processes. **Engineering and Technology:** Knowledge of the practical application of engineering science and technology. This includes applying principles, techniques, procedures, and equipment to the design and production of various goods and services. **Mathematics:** Knowledge of arithmetic, algebra, geometry, calculus, and statistics and their applications. **Administration and Management:** Knowledge of business and management principles involved in strategic planning, resource allocation, human resources modeling, leadership technique, production methods, and coordination of people and resources. **Communications and Media:** Knowledge of media production, communication, and dissemination techniques and

methods. This includes alternative ways to inform and entertain via written, oral, and visual media.

Mates—Ship, Boat, and Barge

- ◎ Annual Earnings: $50,940
- ◎ Growth: 4.8%
- ◎ Annual Job Openings: 2,000
- ◎ Self-Employed: 5.4%
- ◎ Part-Time: 8.3%
- ◎ Education/Training Required: Work experience in a related occupation

The job openings listed here are shared with Pilots, Ship; and Ship and Boat Captains.

Industries in Which Income Is Highest

Industry	Average Annual Wage	Number Employed
Support Activities for Transportation	$54,490	8,480
Water Transportation	$54,410	9,820
Federal, State, and Local Government	$53,760	1,600
Rental and Leasing Services	$52,030	1,360
Scenic and Sightseeing Transportation	$36,810	2,990

Metropolitan Areas Where Income Is Highest

Metropolitan Area	Average Annual Wage	Number Employed
Baton Rouge, LA	$67,280	470
Bremerton–Silverdale, WA	$66,460	70
New York–Northern New Jersey–Long Island, NY–NJ–PA	$62,450	1,970
Lake Charles, LA	$61,120	210
Seattle–Tacoma–Bellevue, WA	$60,990	850

Supervise and coordinate activities of crew aboard ships, boats, barges, or dredges. Determine geographical positions of ships, using lorans, azimuths of celestial bodies, or computers, and use this information to determine the course and speed of a ship. Inspect equipment such as cargo-handling gear, lifesaving equipment, visual-signaling equipment, and fishing, towing, or dredging gear, in order to detect problems. Observe loading and unloading of cargo and equipment to ensure that handling and storage are performed according to specifications. Observe water from ships' mastheads in order to advise on navigational direction. Steer vessels, utilizing navigational devices such as compasses and sextons, and navigational aids such as lighthouses and buoys. Supervise crew members in the repair or replacement of defective gear and equipment. Supervise crews in cleaning and maintaining decks, superstructures, and bridges. Arrange for ships to be stocked, fueled, and repaired. Assume command of vessels in the event that ships' masters become incapacitated. Participate in activities related to maintenance of vessel security. Stand watches on vessels during specified periods while vessels are under way. **SKILLS—** Management of Personnel Resources; Operation and Control; Repairing; Coordination; Systems Analysis; Operation Monitoring; Systems Evaluation; Equipment Maintenance.

GOE—Interest Area: 16. Transportation, Distribution, and Logistics. **Work Group:** 16.05. Water Vehicle Operation. **PERSONALITY TYPE:** Realistic. Realistic occupations frequently involve work activities that include practical, hands-on problems and solutions. They often deal with plants, animals, and real-world materials like wood, tools, and machinery. Many of the occupations require working outside and do not involve a lot of paperwork or working closely with others.

EDUCATION/TRAINING PROGRAMS— Commercial Fishing; Marine Science/Merchant Marine Officer; Marine Transportation Services, Other. **RELATED KNOWLEDGE/COURSES— Transportation:** Knowledge of principles and methods for moving people or goods by air, rail, sea, or road, including the relative costs and benefits. **Geography:** Knowledge of principles and methods for describing the features of land, sea, and air masses, including their physical characteristics; locations; interrelationships; and distribution of plant, animal, and human life. **Mechanical Devices:** Knowledge of machines and tools, including their designs, uses, repair, and maintenance. **Administration and Management:** Knowledge of business and management principles involved in strategic planning, resource allocation, human resources modeling, leadership technique, production methods, and coordination of people and resources. **Physics:** Knowledge and prediction of physical

principles and laws and their interrelationships and applications to understanding fluid, material, and atmospheric dynamics and mechanical, electrical, atomic, and subatomic structures and processes. **Public Safety and Security:** Knowledge of relevant equipment, policies, procedures, and strategies to promote effective local, state, or national security operations for the protection of people, data, property, and institutions.

Mathematical Science Teachers, Postsecondary

- Annual Earnings: $53,820
- Growth: 32.2%
- Annual Job Openings: 329,000
- Self-Employed: 0.4%
- Part-Time: 27.3%
- Education/Training Required: Master's degree

Our sources did not provide separate job openings data for this occupation. The job openings listed here are shared with 35 other postsecondary teaching occupations. For a complete list, see the beginning of this section.

Industries in Which Income Is Highest

Industry	Average Annual Wage	Number Employed
Educational Services	$53,790	44,520

Metropolitan Areas Where Income Is Highest

Metropolitan Area	Average Annual Wage	Number Employed
San Jose–Sunnyvale–Santa Clara, CA	$85,980	110
Providence–Fall River–Warwick, RI–MA	$79,730	200
Sacramento–Arden–Arcade–Roseville, CA	$78,590	210
San Francisco–Oakland–Fremont, CA	$74,820	810
Riverside–San Bernardino–Ontario, CA	$71,830	270

Teach courses pertaining to mathematical concepts, statistics, and actuarial science and to the application of original and standardized mathematical

techniques in solving specific problems and situations. Evaluate and grade students' class work, assignments, and papers. Compile, administer, and grade examinations or assign this work to others. Prepare and deliver lectures to undergraduate and/or graduate students on topics such as linear algebra, differential equations, and discrete mathematics. Prepare course materials such as syllabi, homework assignments, and handouts. Maintain student attendance records, grades, and other required records. Maintain regularly scheduled office hours in order to advise and assist students. Plan, evaluate, and revise curricula, course content, and course materials and methods of instruction. Initiate, facilitate, and moderate classroom discussions. Select and obtain materials and supplies such as textbooks. Keep abreast of developments in their field by reading current literature, talking with colleagues, and participating in professional conferences. Advise students on academic and vocational curricula and on career issues. Collaborate with colleagues to address teaching and research issues. Serve on academic or administrative committees that deal with institutional policies, departmental matters, and academic issues. Participate in student recruitment, registration, and placement activities. Perform administrative duties such as serving as department head. Conduct research in a particular field of knowledge and publish findings in books, professional journals, and/or electronic media. Supervise undergraduate and/or graduate teaching, internship, and research work. Act as advisers to student organizations. **SKILLS**—Mathematics; Instructing; Learning Strategies; Critical Thinking; Active Learning; Speaking; Persuasion; Complex Problem Solving.

GOE—**Interest Area:** 05. Education and Training. **Work Group:** 05.03. Postsecondary and Adult Teaching and Instructing. **PERSONALITY TYPE:** Investigative. Investigative occupations frequently involve working with ideas and require an extensive amount of thinking. These occupations can involve searching for facts and figuring out problems mentally.

EDUCATION/TRAINING PROGRAMS—Algebra and Number Theory; Analysis and Functional Analysis; Applied Mathematics; Business Statistics; Geometry/Geometric Analysis; Logic; Mathematical Statistics and Probability; Mathematics and Statistics, Other; Mathematics, General; Mathematics, Other; Statistics, General; Topology and Foundations. **RELATED KNOWLEDGE/COURSES**—**Mathematics:** Knowledge of arithmetic, algebra, geometry, calculus, and statistics and their applications. **Education and Training:** Knowledge of principles and methods for curriculum and training design, teaching and instruction for individuals and groups, and the measurement of training effects. **Computers and Electronics:** Knowledge of circuit boards, processors, chips, electronic equipment, and computer hardware and software, including applications and programming. **Physics:** Knowledge and prediction of physical principles and laws and their interrelationships and applications to understanding fluid, material, and atmospheric dynamics and mechanical, electrical, atomic, and subatomic structures and processes. **English Language:** Knowledge of the structure and content of the English language, including the meaning and spelling of words, rules of composition, and grammar. **Psychology:** Knowledge of human behavior and performance; individual differences in ability, personality, and interests; learning and motivation; psychological research methods; and the assessment and treatment of behavioral and affective disorders.

Mechanical Engineers

- Annual Earnings: $67,590
- Growth: 11.1%
- Annual Job Openings: 11,000
- Self-Employed: 2.5%
- Part-Time: No data available
- Education/Training Required: Bachelor's degree

Industries in Which Income Is Highest

Industry	Average Annual Wage	Number Employed
Federal, State, and Local Government	$79,610	11,120
Utilities	$75,420	1,110
Management of Companies and Enterprises	$72,660	3,730
Petroleum and Coal Products Manufacturing	$72,610	1,020
Computer and Electronic Product Manufacturing	$71,690	21,350

Metropolitan Areas Where Income Is Highest

Metropolitan Area	Average Annual Wage	Number Employed
San Jose–Sunnyvale–Santa Clara, CA	$89,930	3,470
Vallejo–Fairfield, CA	$85,790	50
Bakersfield, CA	$85,220	430
Panama City–Lynn Haven, FL	$82,870	340
Santa Rosa–Petaluma, CA	$82,030	260

Perform engineering duties in planning and designing tools, engines, machines, and other mechanically functioning equipment. Oversee installation, operation, maintenance, and repair of such equipment as centralized heat, gas, water, and steam systems. Read and interpret blueprints, technical drawings, schematics, and computer-generated reports. Confer with engineers and other personnel to implement operating procedures, resolve system malfunctions, and provide technical information. Research and analyze customer design proposals, specifications, manuals, and other data to evaluate the feasibility, cost, and maintenance requirements of designs or applications. Specify system components or direct modification of products to ensure conformance with engineering design and performance specifications. Research, design, evaluate, install, operate, and maintain mechanical products, equipment, systems and processes to meet requirements, applying knowledge of engineering principles. Investigate equipment failures and difficulties to diagnose faulty operation, and to make recommendations to maintenance crew. Assist drafters in developing the structural design of products, using drafting tools or computer-assisted design/drafting equipment and software. Provide feedback to design engineers on customer problems and needs. Oversee installation, operation, maintenance, and repair to ensure that machines and equipment are installed and functioning according to specifications. Conduct research that tests and analyzes the feasibility, design, operation and performance of equipment, components and systems. Recommend design modifications to eliminate machine or system malfunctions. Develop and test models of alternate designs and processing methods to assess feasibility, operating condition effects, possible new applications and necessity of modification. Develop, coordinate, and monitor all aspects of production, including selection of manufacturing methods, fabrication, and operation of product designs.

Estimate costs and submit bids for engineering, construction, or extraction projects, and prepare contract documents. Perform personnel functions, such as supervision of production workers, technicians, technologists and other engineers, and design of evaluation programs. Solicit new business and provide technical customer service. Establish and coordinate the maintenance and safety procedures, service schedule, and supply of materials required to maintain machines and equipment in the prescribed condition. **SKILLS—** Science; Operations Analysis; Complex Problem Solving; Installation; Mathematics; Coordination; Judgment and Decision Making; Negotiation.

GOE—Interest Area: 15. Scientific Research, Engineering, and Mathematics. **Work Group:** 15.07. Research and Design Engineering. **PERSONALITY TYPE:** Realistic. Realistic occupations frequently involve work activities that include practical, hands-on problems and solutions. They often deal with plants, animals, and real-world materials like wood, tools, and machinery. Many of the occupations require working outside and do not involve a lot of paperwork or working closely with others.

EDUCATION/TRAINING PROGRAM— Mechanical Engineering. **RELATED KNOWLEDGE/COURSES—Design:** Knowledge of design techniques, tools, and principles involved in production of precision technical plans, blueprints, drawings, and models. **Engineering and Technology:** Knowledge of the practical application of engineering science and technology. This includes applying principles, techniques, procedures, and equipment to the design and production of various goods and services. **Mechanical Devices:** Knowledge of machines and tools, including their designs, uses, repair, and maintenance. **Production and Processing:** Knowledge of raw materials, production processes, quality control, costs, and other techniques for maximizing the effective manufacture and distribution of goods. **Administration and Management:** Knowledge of business and management principles involved in strategic planning, resource allocation, human resources modeling, leadership technique, production methods, and coordination of people and resources. **Physics:** Knowledge and prediction of physical principles and laws and their interrelationships and applications to understanding fluid, material, and atmospheric dynamics and mechanical, electrical, atomic, and subatomic structures and processes.

Medical and Clinical Laboratory Technologists

- ◎ Annual Earnings: $47,710
- ◎ Growth: 20.5%
- ◎ Annual Job Openings: 14,000
- ◎ Self-Employed: 0.1%
- ◎ Part-Time: 17.1%
- ◎ Education/Training Required: Bachelor's degree

Industries in Which Income Is Highest

Industry	Average Annual Wage	Number Employed
Administrative and Support Services	$52,750	1,440
Federal, State, and Local Government	$52,740	6,550
Professional, Scientific, and Technical Services	$49,980	2,030
Hospitals	$47,960	97,270
Ambulatory Health Care Services	$45,850	40,620

Metropolitan Areas Where Income Is Highest

Metropolitan Area	Average Annual Wage	Number Employed
San Jose–Sunnyvale–Santa Clara, CA	$72,750	700
Salinas, CA	$70,070	100
Stockton, CA	$68,770	210
San Francisco–Oakland–Fremont, CA	$67,710	1,590
Santa Rosa–Petaluma, CA	$67,280	100

Perform complex medical laboratory tests for diagnosis, treatment, and prevention of disease. May train or supervise staff. Analyze laboratory findings to check the accuracy of the results. Conduct chemical analysis of body fluids, including blood, urine, and spinal fluid, to determine presence of normal and abnormal components. Operate, calibrate and maintain equipment used in quantitative and qualitative analysis, such as spectrophotometers, calorimeters, flame photometers, and computer-controlled analyzers. Enter data from analysis of medical tests and clinical results into computer for storage. Analyze samples of biological material for chemical content or reaction. Establish and monitor programs to ensure the accuracy of laboratory results. Set up, clean, and maintain laboratory equipment. Provide technical information about test results to physicians, family members and researchers. Supervise, train, and direct lab assistants, medical and clinical laboratory technicians and technologists, and other medical laboratory workers engaged in laboratory testing. Develop, standardize, evaluate, and modify procedures, techniques and tests used in the analysis of specimens and in medical laboratory experiments. Cultivate, isolate, and assist in identifying microbial organisms, and perform various tests on these microorganisms. Study blood samples to determine the number of cells and their morphology, as well as the blood group, type and compatibility for transfusion purposes, using microscopic technique. Obtain, cut, stain, and mount biological material on slides for microscopic study and diagnosis, following standard laboratory procedures. Select and prepare specimen and media for cell culture, using aseptic technique and knowledge of medium components and cell requirements. Conduct medical research under direction of microbiologist or biochemist. Harvest cell cultures at optimum time based on knowledge of cell cycle differences and culture conditions. **SKILLS—** Equipment Maintenance; Operation Monitoring; Quality Control Analysis; Science; Troubleshooting; Operation and Control; Repairing; Instructing.

GOE—Interest Area: 08. Health Science. **Work Group:** 08.06. Medical Technology. **PERSONALITY TYPE:** Investigative. Investigative occupations frequently involve working with ideas and require an extensive amount of thinking. These occupations can involve searching for facts and figuring out problems mentally.

EDUCATION/TRAINING PROGRAMS—Clinical Laboratory Science/Medical Technology/Technologist; Clinical/Medical Laboratory Science and Allied Professions, Other; Clinical/Medical Laboratory Science and Allied Professions, Other; Cytogenetics/Genetics/Clinical Genetics Technology/Technologists; Cytotechnology/Cytotechnologist; Histologic Technology/Histotechnologist; Renal/Dialysis Technologist/Technician. **RELATED KNOWLEDGE/COURSES—Biology:** Knowledge of plant and animal organisms and their tissues, cells, functions, interdependencies, and interactions with each other and the environment. **Chemistry:** Knowledge of the chemical composition, structure, and properties of substances and of the chemical processes and transformations that they undergo. This includes uses of chemicals, their danger signs, production techniques, and disposal methods. **Public Safety and Security:** Knowledge of relevant equipment, policies, procedures, and strategies to promote effective local, state, or national security operations for the protection of people, data, property, and institutions. **Computers and Electronics:** Knowledge of circuit boards, processors, chips, electronic equipment, and computer hardware and software, including applications and programming. **Customer and Personal Service:** Knowledge of principles and processes for providing customer and personal services. This includes customer needs assessment, meeting quality standards for services, and evaluation of customer satisfaction. **Mathematics:** Knowledge of arithmetic, algebra, geometry, calculus, and statistics and their applications.

Medical and Health Services Managers

- Annual Earnings: $69,700
- Growth: 22.8%
- Annual Job Openings: 33,000
- Self-Employed: 5.7%
- Part-Time: 5.8%
- Education/Training Required: Work experience plus degree

Industries in Which Income Is Highest

Industry	Average Annual Wage	Number Employed
Professional, Scientific, and Technical Services	$81,780	2,400
Insurance Carriers and Related Activities	$81,090	4,150
Management of Companies and Enterprises	$78,730	4,560
Educational Services	$76,050	4,790
Hospitals	$73,600	92,650

Metropolitan Areas Where Income Is Highest

Metropolitan Area	Average Annual Wage	Number Employed
San Jose–Sunnyvale–Santa Clara, CA	$95,540	790
Fort Collins–Loveland, CO	$95,120	140
San Francisco–Oakland–Fremont, CA	$95,030	2,500
Seattle–Tacoma–Bellevue, WA	$94,510	1,630
Spokane, WA	$92,510	240

Plan, direct, or coordinate medicine and health services in hospitals, clinics, managed care organizations, public health agencies, or similar organizations. Direct, supervise and evaluate work activities of medical, nursing, technical, clerical, service, maintenance, and other personnel. Establish objectives and evaluative or operational criteria for units they manage. Direct or conduct recruitment, hiring and training of personnel. Develop and maintain computerized record management systems to store and process data, such as personnel activities and information, and to produce reports. Develop and implement organizational policies and procedures for the facility or medical unit. Conduct and administer fiscal operations, including accounting, planning budgets, authorizing expenditures, establishing rates for services, and coordinating financial reporting. Establish work schedules and assignments for staff, according to workload, space and equipment availability. Maintain communication between governing boards, medical staff, and department heads by attending board meetings and coordinating interdepartmental functioning. Monitor the use of diagnostic services, inpatient beds, facilities, and staff to ensure effective use of resources and assess the need for additional staff, equipment, and services. Maintain awareness of advances in medicine, computerized diagnostic and treatment equipment, data processing technology, government regulations, health insurance changes, and financing options. Manage change in integrated health care delivery systems, such as work restructuring, technological innovations, and shifts in the focus of care. Prepare activity reports to inform management of the status and implementation plans of programs, services, and quality initiatives. Plan, implement and administer programs and services in a health care or medical facility, including personnel administration, training, and coordination of medical, nursing and physical plant staff. Consult with medical, business, and community groups to discuss service problems, respond to community needs, enhance public relations, coordinate activities and plans, and promote health programs. Inspect facilities and recommend building or equipment modifications to ensure emergency readiness and compliance to access, safety, and sanitation regulations. **SKILLS**—Management of Personnel Resources; Persuasion; Service Orientation; Management of Material Resources; Management of Financial Resources; Monitoring; Learning Strategies; Social Perceptiveness.

GOE—**Interest Area:** 08. Health Science. **Work Group:** 08.01. Managerial Work in Medical and Health Services. **PERSONALITY TYPE:** Enterprising. Enterprising occupations frequently involve starting up and carrying out projects. These occupations can involve leading people and making many decisions. They sometimes require risk taking and often deal with business.

EDUCATION/TRAINING PROGRAMS— Community Health and Preventive Medicine ; Health and Medical Administrative Services, Other; Health Information/Medical Records Administration/ Administrator; Health Services Administration; Health Unit Manager/Ward Supervisor; Health/Health Care Administration/Management; Hospital and Health Care Facilities Administration/Management; Nursing Administration (MSN, MS, PhD); Public Health, General (MPH, DPH). **RELATED KNOWLEDGE/ COURSES**—**Therapy and Counseling:** Knowledge of principles, methods, and procedures for diagnosis, treatment, and rehabilitation of physical and mental dysfunctions and for career counseling and guidance. **Medicine and Dentistry:** Knowledge of the information and techniques needed to diagnose and treat human injuries, diseases, and deformities. This includes symptoms, treatment alternatives, drug properties and interactions, and preventive health-care measures. **Personnel and Human Resources:** Knowledge of principles and procedures for personnel recruitment, selection, training, compensation and benefits, labor relations and negotiation, and personnel information systems. **Philosophy and Theology:** Knowledge of different philosophical systems and religions. This includes their basic principles, values, ethics, ways of thinking, customs, and practices and their impact on human culture. **Customer and Personal Service:** Knowledge of principles and processes for providing customer and personal services. This includes customer needs assessment, meeting quality standards for services, and evaluation of customer satisfaction. **Psychology:** Knowledge of human behavior and performance; individual differences in ability, personality, and interests; learning and motivation; psychological research methods; and the assessment and treatment of behavioral and affective disorders.

Medical Scientists, Except Epidemiologists

- Annual Earnings: $61,730
- Growth: 34.1%
- Annual Job Openings: 15,000
- Self-Employed: 0.4%
- Part-Time: 5.8%
- Education/Training Required: Doctoral degree

Industries in Which Income Is Highest

Industry	Average Annual Wage	Number Employed
Federal, State, and Local Government	$87,110	2,940
Merchant Wholesalers, Nondurable Goods	$81,880	1,640
Chemical Manufacturing	$76,050	10,390
Professional, Scientific, and Technical Services	$68,500	23,090
Ambulatory Health Care Services	$62,550	4,350

Metropolitan Areas Where Income Is Highest

Metropolitan Area	Average Annual Wage	Number Employed
Atlanta–Sandy Springs–Marietta, GA	$93,110	380
Denver–Aurora, CO	$89,190	390
New Haven, CT	$88,590	540
New Orleans–Metairie–Kenner, LA	$84,390	70
Morgantown, WV	$82,860	80

Conduct research dealing with the understanding of human diseases and the improvement of human health. Engage in clinical investigation or other

research, production, technical writing, or related activities. Conduct research to develop methodologies, instrumentation and procedures for medical application, analyzing data and presenting findings. Plan and direct studies to investigate human or animal disease, preventive methods, and treatments for disease. Follow strict safety procedures when handling toxic materials to avoid contamination. Evaluate effects of drugs, gases, pesticides, parasites, and microorganisms at various levels. Teach principles of medicine and medical and laboratory procedures to physicians, residents, students, and technicians. Prepare and analyze organ, tissue and cell samples to identify toxicity, bacteria, or microorganisms, or to study cell structure. Standardize drug dosages, methods of immunization, and procedures for manufacture of drugs and medicinal compounds. Investigate cause, progress, life cycle, or mode of transmission of diseases or parasites. Confer with health department, industry personnel, physicians, and others to develop health safety standards and public health improvement programs. Study animal and human health and physiological processes. Consult with and advise physicians, educators, researchers, and others regarding medical applications of physics, biology, and chemistry. Use equipment such as atomic absorption spectrometers, electron microscopes, flow cytometers and chromatography systems. **SKILLS**—Science; Management of Financial Resources; Instructing; Judgment and Decision Making; Time Management; Reading Comprehension; Writing; Active Listening.

GOE—Interest Area: 15. Scientific Research, Engineering, and Mathematics. **Work Group:** 15.03. Life Sciences. **PERSONALITY TYPE:** Investigative. Investigative occupations frequently involve working with ideas and require an extensive amount of thinking. These occupations can involve searching for facts and figuring out problems mentally.

EDUCATION/TRAINING PROGRAMS— Anatomy; Biochemistry; Biomedical Sciences, General; Biophysics; Biostatistics; Cardiovascular Science; Cell Physiology; Cell/Cellular Biology and Histology; Endocrinology; Environmental Toxicology; Epidemiology; Exercise Physiology; Human/Medical Genetics; Immunology; Medical Microbiology and Bacteriology; Medical Scientist (MS, PhD); Molecular Biology; Molecular Pharmacology; Molecular Physiology; Molecular Toxicology; Neurobiology and Neurophysiology;

Neuropharmacology; others. **RELATED KNOWLEDGE/COURSES—Biology:** Knowledge of plant and animal organisms and their tissues, cells, functions, interdependencies, and interactions with each other and the environment. **Medicine and Dentistry:** Knowledge of the information and techniques needed to diagnose and treat human injuries, diseases, and deformities. This includes symptoms, treatment alternatives, drug properties and interactions, and preventive health-care measures. **Chemistry:** Knowledge of the chemical composition, structure, and properties of substances and of the chemical processes and transformations that they undergo. This includes uses of chemicals, their danger signs, production techniques, and disposal methods. **Communications and Media:** Knowledge of media production, communication, and dissemination techniques and methods. This includes alternative ways to inform and entertain via written, oral, and visual media. **Personnel and Human Resources:** Knowledge of principles and procedures for personnel recruitment, selection, training, compensation and benefits, labor relations and negotiation, and personnel information systems. **Education and Training:** Knowledge of principles and methods for curriculum and training design, teaching and instruction for individuals and groups, and the measurement of training effects.

Microbiologists

- Annual Earnings: $56,870
- Growth: 17.2%
- Annual Job Openings: 1,000
- Self-Employed: 2.9%
- Part-Time: 8.6%
- Education/Training Required: Doctoral degree

Industries in Which Income Is Highest

Industry	Average Annual Wage	Number Employed
Federal, State, and Local Government	$62,520	4,070
Professional, Scientific, and Technical Services	$58,720	4,820
Chemical Manufacturing	$55,160	3,870
Educational Services	$43,500	1,030

Metropolitan Areas Where Income Is Highest

Metropolitan Area	Average Annual Wage	Number Employed
Washington–Arlington–Alexandria, DC–VA–MD–WV	$82,150	1,310
San Francisco–Oakland–Fremont, CA	$74,710	500
San Jose–Sunnyvale–Santa Clara, CA	$69,600	160
Boulder, CO	$69,470	150
Cincinnati–Middletown, OH–KY–IN	$68,770	80

Investigate the growth, structure, development, and other characteristics of microscopic organisms, such as bacteria, algae, or fungi. Includes medical microbiologists who study the relationship between organisms and disease or the effects of antibiotics on microorganisms. Isolate and make cultures of bacteria or other microorganisms in prescribed media, controlling moisture, aeration, temperature, and nutrition. Perform tests on water, food and the environment to detect harmful microorganisms and to obtain information about sources of pollution and contamination. Examine physiological, morphological, and cultural characteristics, using microscope, to identify and classify microorganisms in human, water, and food specimens. Provide laboratory services for health departments, for community environmental health programs and for physicians needing information for diagnosis and treatment. Observe action of microorganisms upon living tissues of plants, higher animals, and other microorganisms, and on dead organic matter. Investigate the relationship between organisms and disease, including the control of epidemics and the effects of antibiotics on microorganisms. Supervise biological technologists and technicians and other scientists. Study growth, structure, development, and general characteristics of bacteria and other microorganisms to understand their relationship to human, plant, and animal health. Prepare technical reports and recommendations based upon research outcomes. Study the structure and function of human, animal and plant tissues, cells, pathogens and toxins. Use a variety of specialized equipment such as electron microscopes, gas chromatographs and high pressure liquid chromatographs, electrophoresis units, thermocyclers, fluorescence activated cell sorters and phosphoimagers. Conduct chemical analyses of substances, such as acids, alcohols, and enzymes. **SKILLS**—Science; Operation Monitoring; Equipment Maintenance; Repairing; Active Listening; Quality Control Analysis; Instructing; Troubleshooting.

GOE—Interest Area: 15. Scientific Research, Engineering, and Mathematics. **Work Group:** 15.03. Life Sciences. **PERSONALITY TYPE:** Investigative. Investigative occupations frequently involve working with ideas and require an extensive amount of thinking. These occupations can involve searching for facts and figuring out problems mentally.

EDUCATION/TRAINING PROGRAMS—Biochemistry/Biophysics and Molecular Biology; Cell/Cellular Biology and Anatomical Sciences, Other; Microbiology, General; Neuroanatomy; Soil Microbiology; Structural Biology. **RELATED KNOWLEDGE/COURSES—Biology:** Knowledge of plant and animal organisms and their tissues, cells, functions, interdependencies, and interactions with each other and the environment. **Chemistry:** Knowledge of the chemical composition, structure, and properties of substances and of the chemical processes and transformations that they undergo. This includes uses of chemicals, their danger signs, production techniques, and disposal methods. **Clerical Practices:** Knowledge of administrative and clerical procedures and systems such as word processing, managing files and records, stenography and transcription, designing forms, and other office procedures and terminology. **English Language:** Knowledge of the structure and content of the English language, including the meaning and spelling of words, rules of composition, and grammar. **Computers and Electronics:** Knowledge of circuit boards, processors, chips, electronic equipment, and computer hardware and software, including applications and programming. **Administration and Management:** Knowledge of business and management principles involved in strategic planning, resource allocation, human resources modeling, leadership technique, production methods, and coordination of people and resources.

Motor Vehicle Inspectors

- Annual Earnings: $49,490
- Growth: 11.4%
- Annual Job Openings: 2,000
- Self-Employed: 1.9%
- Part-Time: 2.2%
- Education/Training Required: Work experience in a related occupation

The job openings listed here are shared with Aviation Inspectors, Freight Inspectors, Marine Cargo Inspectors, Public Transportation Inspectors, and Railroad Inspectors.

Industries in Which Income Is Highest

Industry	Average Annual Wage	Number Employed
Air Transportation	$67,590	1,460
Transportation Equipment Manufacturing	$55,200	1,100
Federal, State, and Local Government	$54,510	10,960
Rail Transportation	$45,840	2,680
Support Activities for Transportation	$37,870	4,350

Metropolitan Areas Where Income Is Highest

Metropolitan Area	Average Annual Wage	Number Employed
Washington–Arlington–Alexandria, DC–VA–MD–WV	$96,800	360
Oklahoma City, OK	$91,650	130
Milwaukee–Waukesha–West Allis, WI	$84,510	50
Miami–Fort Lauderdale–Miami Beach, FL	$84,490	680
Louisville–Jefferson County, KY–IN	$81,260	80

Inspect automotive vehicles to ensure compliance with governmental regulations and safety standards. Inspects truck accessories, air lines and electric circuits, and reports needed repairs. Examines vehicles for damage, and drives vehicle to detect malfunctions. Tests vehicle components for wear, damage, or improper adjustment, using mechanical or electrical devices.

Applies inspection sticker to vehicles that pass inspection, and rejection sticker to vehicles that fail. Prepares report on each vehicle for follow-up action by owner or police. Prepares and keeps record of vehicles delivered. Positions trailer and drives car onto truck trailer. Notifies authorities of owners having illegal equipment installed on vehicle. Services vehicles with fuel and water. **SKILLS**—Science; Troubleshooting; Quality Control Analysis; Operation Monitoring; Systems Evaluation.

GOE—Interest Area: 07. Government and Public Administration. **Work Group:** 07.03. Regulations Enforcement. **PERSONALITY TYPE:** Realistic. Realistic occupations frequently involve work activities that include practical, hands-on problems and solutions. They often deal with plants, animals, and real-world materials like wood, tools, and machinery. Many of the occupations require working outside and do not involve a lot of paperwork or working closely with others.

EDUCATION/TRAINING PROGRAM—No data available. **RELATED KNOWLEDGE/COURSES**—**Public Safety and Security:** Knowledge of relevant equipment, policies, procedures, and strategies to promote effective local, state, or national security operations for the protection of people, data, property, and institutions. **Mechanical Devices:** Knowledge of machines and tools, including their designs, uses, repair, and maintenance. **Computers and Electronics:** Knowledge of circuit boards, processors, chips, electronic equipment, and computer hardware and software, including applications and programming.

Multi-Media Artists and Animators

- Annual Earnings: $50,290
- Growth: 14.1%
- Annual Job Openings: 14,000
- Self-Employed: 60.8%
- Part-Time: 30.4%
- Education/Training Required: Bachelor's degree

Industries in Which Income Is Highest

Industry	Average Annual Wage	Number Employed
Motion Picture and Sound Recording Industries	$60,550	5,660
Publishing Industries (Except Internet)	$50,460	2,210
Professional, Scientific, and Technical Services	$49,060	9,760
Broadcasting (Except Internet)	$42,010	1,380

Metropolitan Areas Where Income Is Highest

Metropolitan Area	Average Annual Wage	Number Employed
San Francisco–Oakland–Fremont, CA	$69,010	1,110
Los Angeles–Long Beach–Santa Ana, CA	$68,900	4,560
San Diego–Carlsbad–San Marcos, CA	$61,340	430
New York–Northern New Jersey–Long Island, NY–NJ–PA	$57,090	2,680
San Jose–Sunnyvale–Santa Clara, CA	$56,890	90

Create special effects, animation, or other visual images using film, video, computers, or other electronic tools and media for use in products or creations, such as computer games, movies, music videos, and commercials. Design complex graphics and animation, using independent judgment, creativity, and computer equipment. Create two-dimensional and three-dimensional images depicting objects in motion or illustrating a process, using computer animation or modeling programs. Make objects or characters appear lifelike by manipulating light, color, texture, shadow, and transparency, and/or manipulating static images to give the illusion of motion. Assemble, typeset, scan and produce digital camera-ready art or film negatives and printer's proofs. Apply story development, directing, cinematography, and editing to animation to create storyboards that show the flow of the animation and map out key scenes and characters. Script, plan, and create animated narrative sequences under tight deadlines, using computer software and hand drawing techniques. Create basic designs, drawings, and illustrations for product labels, cartons, direct mail, or television. Create pen-and-paper images to be scanned, edited, colored, textured or animated by computer. Develop briefings, brochures, multimedia presentations, web pages, promotional products, technical illustrations, and computer artwork for use in products, technical manuals, literature, newsletters and slide shows. **SKILLS**—Operations Analysis; Technology Design; Time Management; Persuasion; Active Listening; Judgment and Decision Making; Reading Comprehension; Active Learning.

GOE—Interest Area: 03. Arts and Communication. **Work Group:** 03.09. Media Technology. **PERSONALITY TYPE:** No data available.

EDUCATION/TRAINING PROGRAMS—Animation, Interactive Technology, Video Graphics and Special Effects; Drawing; Graphic Design; Intermedia/Multimedia; Painting; Printmaking; Web Page, Digital/Multimedia and Information Resources Design. **RELATED KNOWLEDGE/COURSES**—**Fine Arts:** Knowledge of the theory and techniques required to compose, produce, and perform works of music, dance, visual arts, drama, and sculpture. **Design:** Knowledge of design techniques, tools, and principles involved in production of precision technical plans, blueprints, drawings, and models. **Computers and Electronics:** Knowledge of circuit boards, processors, chips, electronic equipment, and computer hardware and software, including applications and programming. **Communications and Media:** Knowledge of media production, communication, and dissemination techniques and methods. This includes alternative ways to inform and entertain via written, oral, and visual media. **English Language:** Knowledge of the structure and content of the English language, including the meaning and spelling of words, rules of composition, and grammar. **Administration and Management:** Knowledge of business and management principles involved in strategic planning, resource allocation, human resources modeling, leadership technique, production methods, and coordination of people and resources.

Municipal Fire Fighting and Prevention Supervisors

- Annual Earnings: $60,840
- Growth: 21.1%
- Annual Job Openings: 4,000
- Self-Employed: 0.0%
- Part-Time: 0.7%
- Education/Training Required: Work experience in a related occupation

The job openings listed here are shared with Forest Fire Fighting and Prevention Supervisors.

Industries in Which Income Is Highest

Industry	Average Annual Wage	Number Employed
Federal, State, and Local Government	$61,010	52,470

Metropolitan Areas Where Income Is Highest

Metropolitan Area	Average Annual Wage	Number Employed
San Jose–Sunnyvale–Santa Clara, CA	$107,220	500
San Francisco–Oakland–Fremont, CA	$105,180	900
Miami–Fort Lauderdale–Miami Beach, FL	$79,240	850
Chicago–Naperville–Joliet, IL–IN–WI	$77,150	1,440
Vallejo–Fairfield, CA	$75,840	80

Supervise fire fighters who control and extinguish municipal fires, protect life and property, and conduct rescue efforts. Assign firefighters to jobs at strategic locations in order to facilitate rescue of persons and maximize application of extinguishing agents. Provide emergency medical services as required, and perform light to heavy rescue functions at emergencies. Assess nature and extent of fire, condition of building, danger to adjacent buildings, and water supply status in order to determine crew or company requirements. Instruct and drill fire department personnel in assigned duties, including firefighting, medical care, hazardous materials response, fire prevention, and related subjects. Evaluate the performance of assigned firefighting personnel. Direct the training of firefighters, assigning of instructors to training classes, and providing of supervisors with reports on training progress and status. Prepare activity reports listing fire call locations, actions taken, fire types and probable causes, damage estimates, and situation dispositions. Maintain required maps and records. Attend in-service training classes to remain current in knowledge of codes, laws, ordinances, and regulations. Evaluate fire station procedures in order to ensure efficiency and enforcement of departmental regulations. Direct firefighters in station maintenance duties, and participate in these duties. Compile and maintain equipment and personnel records, including accident reports. Direct investigation of cases of suspected arson, hazards, and false alarms and submit reports outlining findings. Recommend personnel actions related to disciplinary procedures, performance, leaves of absence, and grievances. Supervise and participate in the inspection of properties in order to ensure that they are in compliance with applicable fire codes, ordinances, laws, regulations, and standards. Write and submit proposals for repair, modification, or replacement of firefighting equipment. Coordinate the distribution of fire prevention promotional materials. Identify corrective actions needed to bring properties into compliance with applicable fire codes and ordinances and conduct follow-up inspections to see if corrective actions have been taken. **SKILLS—** Management of Personnel Resources; Service Orientation; Equipment Maintenance; Coordination; Operation Monitoring; Management of Material Resources; Judgment and Decision Making; Instructing.

GOE—Interest Area: 12. Law and Public Safety. **Work Group:** 12.01. Managerial Work in Law and Public Safety. **PERSONALITY TYPE:** Realistic. Realistic occupations frequently involve work activities that include practical, hands-on problems and solutions. They often deal with plants, animals, and real-world materials like wood, tools, and machinery. Many of the occupations require working outside and do not involve a lot of paperwork or working closely with others.

EDUCATION/TRAINING PROGRAMS— Fire Protection and Safety Technology/Technician; Fire Services Administration. **RELATED KNOWLEDGE/ COURSES—Public Safety and Security:** Knowledge of relevant equipment, policies, procedures, and strategies to promote effective local, state, or national security operations for the protection of people, data, property, and institutions. **Education and Training:** Knowledge of principles and methods for curriculum and training design, teaching and instruction for individuals and groups, and the measurement of training effects. **Customer and Personal Service:** Knowledge of principles and processes for providing customer and personal services. This includes customer needs assessment, meeting quality standards for services, and evaluation of customer satisfaction. **Building and Construction:** Knowledge of the materials, methods, and tools involved in the construction or repair of houses, buildings, or other structures such as highways and roads. **Medicine and Dentistry:** Knowledge of the information and techniques needed to diagnose and treat human injuries, diseases, and deformities. This includes symptoms, treatment alternatives, drug properties and interactions, and preventive health-care measures. **Psychology:** Knowledge of human behavior and performance; individual differences in ability, personality, and interests; learning and motivation; psychological research methods; and the assessment and treatment of behavioral and affective disorders.

Natural Sciences Managers

- ◉ Annual Earnings: $93,090
- ◉ Growth: 13.6%
- ◉ Annual Job Openings: 5,000
- ◉ Self-Employed: 0.0%
- ◉ Part-Time: 2.7%
- ◉ Education/Training Required: Work experience plus degree

Industries in Which Income Is Highest

Industry	Average Annual Wage	Number Employed
Professional, Scientific, and Technical Services	$107,470	12,910
Chemical Manufacturing	$105,810	4,700
Educational Services	$80,800	1,310
Federal, State, and Local Government	$78,310	16,220

Metropolitan Areas Where Income Is Highest

Metropolitan Area	Average Annual Wage	Number Employed
Boston–Cambridge–Quincy, MA–NH	$141,440	940
San Jose–Sunnyvale–Santa Clara, CA	$138,860	660
Oxnard–Thousand Oaks–Ventura, CA	$134,190	180
New York–Northern New Jersey–Long Island, NY–NJ–PA	$125,980	2,950
San Francisco–Oakland–Fremont, CA	$124,930	1,500

Plan, direct, or coordinate activities in such fields as life sciences, physical sciences, mathematics, statistics, and research and development in these fields. Confer with scientists, engineers, regulators, and others, to plan and review projects, and to provide technical assistance. Develop client relationships and communicate with clients to explain proposals, present research findings, establish specifications or discuss project status. Plan and direct research, development, and production activities. Prepare project proposals. Design and coordinate successive phases of problem analysis, solution proposals, and testing. Review project activities, and prepare and review research, testing, and operational reports. Hire, supervise and evaluate engineers, technicians, researchers and other staff. Determine scientific and technical goals within broad outlines provided by top management and make detailed plans to accomplish these goals. Develop and implement policies, standards and procedures for the architectural, scientific and technical work performed, to ensure regulatory compliance and operations enhancement. Develop innovative technology and train staff for its implementation. Provide for stewardship of plant and animal resources and habitats, studying land use, monitoring animal populations and/or providing shelter, resources, and medical treatment for animals. Conduct own research in field of expertise. Recruit personnel and oversee the development and maintenance of staff competence. Advise and assist in obtaining patents or meeting other legal requirements. **SKILLS**—Science; Active Learning; Management of Personnel Resources; Mathematics; Critical Thinking; Reading Comprehension; Time Management; Complex Problem Solving.

GOE—Interest Area: 15. Scientific Research, Engineering, and Mathematics. **Work Group:** 15.01. Managerial Work in Scientific Research, Engineering, and Mathematics. **PERSONALITY TYPE:** Investigative. Investigative occupations frequently involve working with ideas and require an extensive amount of thinking. These occupations can involve searching for facts and figuring out problems mentally.

EDUCATION/TRAINING PROGRAMS— Acoustics; Algebra and Number Theory; Analysis and Functional Analysis; Analytical Chemistry; Anatomy; Animal Genetics; Animal Physiology; Applied Mathematics; Applied Mathematics, Other; Astronomy; Astrophysics; Atmospheric Chemistry and Climatology; Atmospheric Physics and Dynamics; Atmospheric Sciences and Meteorology, General; Atmospheric Sciences and Meteorology, Other; Atomic/Molecular Physics; Biochemistry; Biological and Biomedical Sciences, Other; Biological and Physical Sci.; others. **RELATED KNOWLEDGE/COURSES—Biology:** Knowledge of plant and animal organisms and their tissues, cells, functions, interdependencies, and interactions with each other and the environment. **Chemistry:** Knowledge of the chemical composition, structure, and properties of substances and of the chemical processes and transformations that they undergo. This includes uses of chemicals, their danger signs, production techniques, and disposal methods. **Administration and Management:** Knowledge of business and management principles involved in strategic planning, resource allocation, human resources modeling, leadership technique, production methods, and coordination of people and resources. **Law and Government:** Knowledge of laws, legal codes, court procedures, precedents, government regulations, executive orders, agency rules, and the democratic political process. **Engineering and Technology:** Knowledge of the practical application of engineering science and technology. This includes applying principles, techniques, procedures, and equipment to the design and production of various goods and services. **Customer and Personal Service:** Knowledge of principles and processes for providing customer and personal services. This includes customer needs assessment, meeting quality standards for services, and evaluation of customer satisfaction.

Network and Computer Systems Administrators

- Annual Earnings: $59,930
- Growth: 38.4%
- Annual Job Openings: 34,000
- Self-Employed: 0.6%
- Part-Time: No data available
- Education/Training Required: Bachelor's degree

The job openings listed here are shared with Computer Security Specialists.

Industries in Which Income Is Highest

Industry	Average Annual Wage	Number Employed
Securities, Commodity Contracts, and Other Financial Investments and Related Activities	$69,660	5,390
Telecommunications	$66,740	13,610
Chemical Manufacturing	$66,430	1,310
Computer and Electronic Product Manufacturing	$65,730	6,620
Transportation Equipment Manufacturing	$65,350	2,180

Metropolitan Areas Where Income Is Highest

Metropolitan Area	Average Annual Wage	Number Employed
San Jose–Sunnyvale–Santa Clara, CA	$85,960	3,910
San Francisco–Oakland–Fremont, CA	$75,970	5,880
New York–Northern New Jersey–Long Island, NY–NJ–PA	$74,630	20,100
Leominster–Fitchburg–Gardner, MA	$72,620	90
Danbury, CT	$72,070	120

Install, configure, and support an organization's local area network (LAN), wide area network (WAN), and Internet system or a segment of a network system. Maintain network hardware and software. Monitor network to ensure network availability to all system users and perform necessary maintenance to support network availability.

May supervise other network support and client server specialists and plan, coordinate, and implement network security measures. Diagnose hardware and software problems, and replace defective components. Perform data backups and disaster recovery operations. Maintain and administer computer networks and related computing environments, including computer hardware, systems software, applications software, and all configurations. Plan, coordinate, and implement network security measures in order to protect data, software, and hardware. Operate master consoles in order to monitor the performance of computer systems and networks, and to coordinate computer network access and use. Perform routine network startup and shutdown procedures, and maintain control records. Design, configure, and test computer hardware, networking software and operating system software. Recommend changes to improve systems and network configurations, and determine hardware or software requirements related to such changes. Confer with network users about how to solve existing system problems. Monitor network performance in order to determine whether adjustments need to be made, and to determine where changes will need to be made in the future. Train people in computer system use. Load computer tapes and disks, and install software and printer paper or forms. Gather data pertaining to customer needs, and use the information to identify, predict, interpret, and evaluate system and network requirements. Analyze equipment performance records in order to determine the need for repair or replacement. Maintain logs related to network functions, as well as maintenance and repair records. Research new technology, and implement it or recommend its implementation. Maintain an inventory of parts for emergency repairs. Coordinate with vendors and with company personnel in order to facilitate purchases. **SKILLS**—Troubleshooting; Installation; Programming; Repairing; Systems Evaluation; Systems Analysis; Technology Design; Service Orientation.

GOE—Interest Area: 11. Information Technology. **Work Group:** 11.01. Managerial Work in Information Technology. **PERSONALITY TYPE:** No data available.

EDUCATION/TRAINING PROGRAMS— Computer and Information Sciences and Support Services, Other; Computer and Information Sciences, General; Computer and Information Systems Security; Computer Systems Analysis/Analyst; Computer Systems Networking and Telecommunications; Information Science/Studies; System Administration/Administrator; System, Networking, and LAN/WAN Management/Manager. **RELATED KNOWLEDGE/COURSES—Computers and Electronics:** Knowledge of circuit boards, processors, chips, electronic equipment, and computer hardware and software, including applications and programming. **Telecommunications:** Knowledge of transmission, broadcasting, switching, control, and operation of telecommunications systems. **Customer and Personal Service:** Knowledge of principles and processes for providing customer and personal services. This includes customer needs assessment, meeting quality standards for services, and evaluation of customer satisfaction. **Education and Training:** Knowledge of principles and methods for curriculum and training design, teaching and instruction for individuals and groups, and the measurement of training effects. **Engineering and Technology:** Knowledge of the practical application of engineering science and technology. This includes applying principles, techniques, procedures, and equipment to the design and production of various goods and services. **Administration and Management:** Knowledge of business and management principles involved in strategic planning, resource allocation, human resources modeling, leadership technique, production methods, and coordination of people and resources.

Network Systems and Data Communications Analysts

- Annual Earnings: $61,750
- Growth: 54.6%
- Annual Job Openings: 43,000
- Self-Employed: 19.9%
- Part-Time: 9.7%
- Education/Training Required: Bachelor's degree

Industries in Which Income Is Highest

Industry	Average Annual Wage	Number Employed
Securities, Commodity Contracts, and Other Financial Investments and Related Activities	$74,450	3,840
Transportation Equipment Manufacturing	$71,360	1,410
Computer and Electronic Product Manufacturing	$70,780	3,850
Telecommunications	$66,720	16,750
Management of Companies and Enterprises	$65,740	13,330

Metropolitan Areas Where Income Is Highest

Metropolitan Area	Average Annual Wage	Number Employed
Rochester, MN	$84,170	140
Boulder, CO	$82,240	590
Poughkeepsie–Newburgh–Middletown, NY	$77,490	390
San Jose–Sunnyvale–Santa Clara, CA	$75,160	2,770
Bangor, ME	$74,980	90

Analyze, design, test, and evaluate network systems, such as local area networks (LAN), wide area networks (WAN), Internet, intranet, and other data communications systems. Perform network modeling, analysis, and planning. Research and recommend network and data communications hardware and software. Includes telecommunications specialists who deal with the interfacing of computer and communications equipment. Maintain needed files by adding and deleting files on the network server and backing up files to guarantee their safety in the event of problems with the network. Monitor system performance and provide security measures, troubleshooting and maintenance as needed. Assist users to diagnose and solve data communication problems. Set up user accounts, regulating and monitoring file access to ensure confidentiality and proper use. Design and implement network configurations, network architecture (including hardware and software technology, site locations, and integration of technologies), and systems. Maintain the peripherals, such as printers, that are connected to the network. Identify areas of operation that need upgraded equipment such as modems, fiber optic cables, and telephone wires. Train users in use of equipment. Develop and write procedures for installation, use, and troubleshooting of communications hardware and software. Adapt and modify existing software to meet specific needs. Work with other engineers, systems analysts, programmers, technicians, scientists and top-level managers in the design, testing and evaluation of systems. Test and evaluate hardware and software to determine efficiency, reliability, and compatibility with existing system, and make purchase recommendations. Read technical manuals and brochures to determine which equipment meets establishment requirements. Consult customers, visit workplaces or conduct surveys to determine present and future user needs. Visit vendors, attend conferences or training and study technical journals to keep up with changes in technology. **SKILLS**—Installation; Troubleshooting; Technology Design; Systems Analysis; Management of Material Resources; Programming; Systems Evaluation; Operations Analysis.

GOE—Interest Area: 11. Information Technology. **Work Group:** 11.02. Information Technology Specialties. **PERSONALITY TYPE:** Investigative. Investigative occupations frequently involve working with ideas and require an extensive amount of thinking. These occupations can involve searching for facts and figuring out problems mentally.

EDUCATION/TRAINING PROGRAMS—Computer and Information Sciences, General; Computer and Information Systems Security; Computer Systems Analysis/Analyst; Computer Systems Networking and Telecommunications; Information Technology. **RELATED KNOWLEDGE/COURSES**—**Computers and Electronics:** Knowledge of circuit boards, processors, chips, electronic equipment, and computer hardware and software, including applications and programming. **Customer and Personal Service:** Knowledge of principles and processes for providing customer and personal services. This includes customer needs assessment, meeting quality standards for services, and evaluation of customer satisfaction. **Telecommunications:** Knowledge of transmission, broadcasting, switching, control, and operation of telecommunications systems. **Education and Training:** Knowledge of principles and methods for curriculum and training design, teaching and instruction for individuals and groups, and the measurement of training effects. **Engineering and Technology:**

Knowledge of the practical application of engineering science and technology. This includes applying principles, techniques, procedures, and equipment to the design and production of various goods and services. **Design:** Knowledge of design techniques, tools, and principles involved in production of precision technical plans, blueprints, drawings, and models.

Nuclear Engineers

- Annual Earnings: $88,290
- Growth: 7.3%
- Annual Job Openings: 1,000
- Self-Employed: 0.0%
- Part-Time: 0.0%
- Education/Training Required: Bachelor's degree

Industries in Which Income Is Highest

Industry	Average Annual Wage	Number Employed
Professional, Scientific, and Technical Services	$89,000	5,130
Utilities	$87,880	4,660
Federal, State, and Local Government	$83,280	2,310

Metropolitan Areas Where Income Is Highest

Metropolitan Area	Average Annual Wage	Number Employed
Las Vegas–Paradise, NV	$115,100	100
Chicago–Naperville–Joliet, IL–IN–WI	$99,560	680
Augusta–Richmond County, GA–SC	$94,040	600
New York–Northern New Jersey–Long Island, NY–NJ–PA	$93,770	220
Boston–Cambridge–Quincy, MA–NH	$88,380	90

Conduct research on nuclear engineering problems or apply principles and theory of nuclear science to problems concerned with release, control, and utilization of nuclear energy and nuclear waste disposal. Examine accidents in order to obtain data that can be used to design preventive measures. Monitor nuclear facility operations in order to identify any design, construction, or operation practices that violate safety regulations and laws or that could jeopardize the safety of operations. Keep abreast of developments and changes in the nuclear field by reading technical journals and by independent study and research. Perform experiments that will provide information about acceptable methods of nuclear material usage, nuclear fuel reclamation, and waste disposal. Design and oversee construction and operation of nuclear reactors and power plants and nuclear fuels reprocessing and reclamation systems. Design and develop nuclear equipment such as reactor cores, radiation shielding, and associated instrumentation and control mechanisms. Initiate corrective actions and/or order plant shutdowns in emergency situations. Recommend preventive measures to be taken in the handling of nuclear technology, based on data obtained from operations monitoring or from evaluation of test results. Write operational instructions to be used in nuclear plant operation and nuclear fuel and waste handling and disposal. Conduct tests of nuclear fuel behavior and cycles and performance of nuclear machinery and equipment, in order to optimize performance of existing plants. Direct operating and maintenance activities of operational nuclear power plants in order to ensure efficiency and conformity to safety standards. Synthesize analyses of test results, and use the results to prepare technical reports of findings and recommendations. Prepare construction project proposals that include cost estimates, and discuss proposals with interested parties such as vendors, contractors, and nuclear facility review boards. Analyze available data and consult with other scientists in order to determine parameters of experimentation and suitability of analytical models. Design and direct nuclear research projects in order to discover facts, to test or modify theoretical models, or to develop new theoretical models or new uses for current models. **SKILLS**—Operation Monitoring; Technology Design; Systems Evaluation; Systems Analysis; Operations Analysis; Mathematics; Quality Control Analysis; Judgment and Decision Making.

GOE—Interest Area: 15. Scientific Research, Engineering, and Mathematics. **Work Group:** 15.07. Research and Design Engineering. **PERSONALITY TYPE:** Investigative. Investigative occupations frequently involve working with ideas and require an extensive amount of thinking. These occupations can involve searching for facts and figuring out problems mentally.

EDUCATION/TRAINING PROGRAM—Nuclear Engineering. **RELATED KNOWLEDGE/ COURSES—Engineering and Technology:** Knowledge of the practical application of engineering science and technology. This includes applying principles, techniques, procedures, and equipment to the design and production of various goods and services. **Physics:** Knowledge and prediction of physical principles and laws and their interrelationships and applications to understanding fluid, material, and atmospheric dynamics and mechanical, electrical, atomic, and subatomic structures and processes. **Design:** Knowledge of design techniques, tools, and principles involved in production of precision technical plans, blueprints, drawings, and models. **Chemistry:** Knowledge of the chemical composition, structure, and properties of substances and of the chemical processes and transformations that they undergo. This includes uses of chemicals, their danger signs, production techniques, and disposal methods. **Computers and Electronics:** Knowledge of circuit boards, processors, chips, electronic equipment, and computer hardware and software, including applications and programming. **Mechanical Devices:** Knowledge of machines and tools, including their designs, uses, repair, and maintenance.

Nuclear Equipment Operation Technicians

- ⊚ Annual Earnings: $61,120
- ⊚ Growth: 13.7%
- ⊚ Annual Job Openings: 1,000
- ⊚ Self-Employed: 0.0%
- ⊚ Part-Time: 0.0%
- ⊚ Education/Training Required: Associate degree

The job openings listed here are shared with Nuclear Monitoring Technicians.

Industries in Which Income Is Highest

Industry	Average Annual Wage	Number Employed
Utilities	$66,560	2,480
Educational Services	$61,740	190
Fabricated Metal Product Manufacturing	$58,640	680
Professional, Scientific, and Technical Services	$57,150	1,080
Hospitals	$56,830	200

Metropolitan Areas Where Income Is Highest

Metropolitan Area	Average Annual Wage	Number Employed
New York–Northern New Jersey–Long Island, NY–NJ–PA	$67,730	160
Boston–Cambridge–Quincy, MA–NH	$63,980	290
Idaho Falls, ID	$49,100	60

Operate equipment used for the release, control, and utilization of nuclear energy to assist scientists in laboratory and production activities. Follow policies and procedures for radiation workers in order to ensure personnel safety. Modify, devise, and maintain equipment used in operations. Set control panel switches, according to standard procedures, in order to route electric power from sources and direct particle beams through injector units. Submit computations to supervisors for review. Calculate equipment operating factors, such as radiation times, dosages, temperatures, gamma intensities, and pressures, using standard formulas and conversion tables. Perform testing, maintenance, repair, and upgrading of accelerator systems. Warn maintenance workers of radiation hazards, and direct workers to vacate hazardous areas. Monitor instruments, gauges, and recording devices in control rooms during operation of equipment, under direction of nuclear experimenters. Write summaries of activities and record experimental data, such as accelerator performance, systems status, particle beam specification and beam conditions obtained. **SKILLS—**Operation Monitoring; Operation and Control; Science; Instructing; Mathematics; Equipment Maintenance; Learning Strategies; Active Listening.

GOE—Interest Area: 15. Scientific Research, Engineering, and Mathematics. **Work Group:** 15.05. Physical Science Laboratory Technology. **PERSONALITY TYPE:** Realistic. Realistic occupations frequently involve work activities that include practical, hands-on problems and solutions. They often deal with plants, animals, and real-world materials like wood, tools, and machinery. Many of the occupations require working outside and do not involve a lot of paperwork or working closely with others.

EDUCATION/TRAINING PROGRAMS—Industrial Radiologic Technology/Technician; Nuclear and Industrial Radiologic Technologies/Technicians, Other; Nuclear Engineering Technology/Technician; Nuclear/ Nuclear Power Technology/Technician; Radiation Protection/Health Physics Technician. **RELATED KNOWLEDGE/COURSES—Physics:** Knowledge and prediction of physical principles and laws and their interrelationships and applications to understanding fluid, material, and atmospheric dynamics and mechanical, electrical, atomic, and subatomic structures and processes. **Chemistry:** Knowledge of the chemical composition, structure, and properties of substances and of the chemical processes and transformations that they undergo. This includes uses of chemicals, their danger signs, production techniques, and disposal methods. **Public Safety and Security:** Knowledge of relevant equipment, policies, procedures, and strategies to promote effective local, state, or national security operations for the protection of people, data, property, and institutions. **Engineering and Technology:** Knowledge of the practical application of engineering science and technology. This includes applying principles, techniques, procedures, and equipment to the design and production of various goods and services. **Mechanical Devices:** Knowledge of machines and tools, including their designs, uses, repair, and maintenance. **Computers and Electronics:** Knowledge of circuit boards, processors, chips, electronic equipment, and computer hardware and software, including applications and programming.

Nuclear Medicine Technologists

- Annual Earnings: $59,670
- Growth: 21.5%
- Annual Job Openings: 2,000
- Self-Employed: 0.5%
- Part-Time: 17.2%
- Education/Training Required: Associate degree

Industries in Which Income Is Highest

Industry	Average Annual Wage	Number Employed
Ambulatory Health Care Services	$62,020	4,600
Hospitals	$58,110	12,650

Metropolitan Areas Where Income Is Highest

Metropolitan Area	Average Annual Wage	Number Employed
Sacramento–Arden–Arcade–Roseville, CA	$80,030	70
San Francisco–Oakland–Fremont, CA	$75,440	120
San Diego–Carlsbad–San Marcos, CA	$73,160	100
Baltimore–Towson, MD	$71,630	240
Seattle–Tacoma–Bellevue, WA	$69,660	130

Prepare, administer, and measure radioactive isotopes in therapeutic, diagnostic, and tracer studies utilizing a variety of radioisotope equipment. Prepare stock solutions of radioactive materials and calculate doses to be administered by radiologists. Subject patients to radiation. Execute blood volume, red cell survival, and fat absorption studies following standard laboratory techniques. Calculate, measure and record radiation dosage or radiopharmaceuticals received, used and disposed, using computer and following physician's prescription. Detect and map radiopharmaceuticals in patients' bodies, using a camera to produce photographic or computer images. Explain test procedures and safety precautions to patients and provide them with assistance during test procedures. Administer radiopharmaceuticals or radiation to patients to detect or treat diseases, using radioisotope equipment, under direction of physician. Produce a computer-generated or film image for interpretation by a physician. Process cardiac function studies, using computer. Dispose of radioactive materials and store radiopharmaceuticals, following radiation safety procedures. Record and process results of procedures. Prepare stock radiopharmaceuticals, adhering to safety standards that minimize radiation exposure to workers and patients. Maintain and calibrate radioisotope and laboratory equipment. Gather information on patients' illnesses and medical history to guide the choice of diagnostic procedures for therapy. Measure glandular activity, blood volume, red cell survival, and radioactivity of patient, using scanners, Geiger counters, scintillometers, and other laboratory equipment. Train and supervise student or subordinate nuclear medicine technologists. Position radiation fields, radiation beams, and patient to allow for most effective treatment of patient's disease, using computer. Add radioactive substances to biological specimens, such as blood, urine and feces, to determine therapeutic drug or hormone levels. Develop treatment procedures for nuclear medicine treatment programs. **SKILLS—**Science; Operation Monitoring; Social Perceptiveness; Service Orientation; Operation and Control; Instructing; Active Learning; Persuasion.

GOE—Interest Area: 08. Health Science. **Work Group:** 08.06. Medical Technology. **PERSONALITY TYPE:** Investigative. Investigative occupations frequently involve working with ideas and require an extensive amount of thinking. These occupations can involve searching for facts and figuring out problems mentally.

EDUCATION/TRAINING PROGRAMS—Nuclear Medical Technology/Technologist; Radiation Protection/Health Physics Technician. **RELATED KNOWLEDGE/COURSES—Medicine and Dentistry:** Knowledge of the information and techniques needed to diagnose and treat human injuries, diseases, and deformities. This includes symptoms, treatment alternatives, drug properties and interactions, and preventive health-care measures. **Biology:** Knowledge of plant and animal organisms and their tissues, cells,

functions, interdependencies, and interactions with each other and the environment. **Customer and Personal Service:** Knowledge of principles and processes for providing customer and personal services. This includes customer needs assessment, meeting quality standards for services, and evaluation of customer satisfaction. **Chemistry:** Knowledge of the chemical composition, structure, and properties of substances and of the chemical processes and transformations that they undergo. This includes uses of chemicals, their danger signs, production techniques, and disposal methods. **Physics:** Knowledge and prediction of physical principles and laws and their interrelationships and applications to understanding fluid, material, and atmospheric dynamics and mechanical, electrical, atomic, and subatomic structures and processes. **Computers and Electronics:** Knowledge of circuit boards, processors, chips, electronic equipment, and computer hardware and software, including applications and programming.

Nuclear Monitoring Technicians

- Annual Earnings: $61,120
- Growth: 13.7%
- Annual Job Openings: 1,000
- Self-Employed: 0.0%
- Part-Time: 0.0%
- Education/Training Required: Associate degree

The job openings listed here are shared with Nuclear Equipment Operation Technicians.

Industries in Which Income Is Highest

Industry	Average Annual Wage	Number Employed
Utilities	$66,560	2,480
Educational Services	$61,740	190
Fabricated Metal Product Manufacturing	$58,640	680
Professional, Scientific, and Technical Services	$57,150	1,080
Hospitals	$56,830	200

Metropolitan Areas Where Income Is Highest

Metropolitan Area	Average Annual Wage	Number Employed
New York–Northern New Jersey–Long Island, NY–NJ–PA	$67,730	160
Boston–Cambridge–Quincy, MA–NH	$63,980	290
Idaho Falls, ID	$49,100	60

Collect and test samples to monitor results of nuclear experiments and contamination of humans, facilities, and environment. Calculate safe radiation exposure times for personnel, using plant contamination readings and prescribed safe levels of radiation. Provide initial response to abnormal events and to alarms from radiation monitoring equipment. Monitor personnel in order to determine the amounts and intensities of radiation exposure. Inform supervisors when individual exposures or area radiation levels approach maximum permissible limits. Instruct personnel in radiation safety procedures, and demonstrate use of protective clothing and equipment. Determine intensities and types of radiation in work areas, equipment, and materials, using radiation detectors and other instruments. Collect samples of air, water, gases, and solids in order to determine radioactivity levels of contamination. Set up equipment that automatically detects area radiation deviations, and test detection equipment in order to ensure its accuracy. Determine or recommend radioactive decontamination procedures, according to the size and nature of equipment and the degree of contamination. Decontaminate objects by cleaning with soap or solvents or by abrading with wire brushes, buffing wheels, or sandblasting machines. Place radioactive waste, such as sweepings and broken sample bottles, into containers for disposal. Calibrate and maintain chemical instrumentation sensing elements and sampling system equipment, using calibration instruments and hand tools. Place irradiated nuclear fuel materials in environmental chambers for testing, and observe reactions through cell windows. Enter data into computers in order to record characteristics of nuclear events and locating coordinates of particles. Operate manipulators from outside cells to move specimens into and out of shielded containers, to remove specimens from cells, or to place specimens on benches or equipment work stations. Prepare reports describing contamination tests, material and equipment decontaminated, and methods used in decontamination processes. Confer with scientists directing projects in order to determine significant events to monitor during tests. Immerse samples in chemical compounds in order to prepare them for testing. **SKILLS**—Science; Operation Monitoring; Coordination; Equipment Maintenance; Monitoring; Mathematics; Service Orientation; Technology Design.

GOE—Interest Area: 07. Government and Public Administration. **Work Group:** 07.03. Regulations Enforcement. **PERSONALITY TYPE:** Realistic. Realistic occupations frequently involve work activities that include practical, hands-on problems and solutions. They often deal with plants, animals, and real-world materials like wood, tools, and machinery. Many of the occupations require working outside and do not involve a lot of paperwork or working closely with others.

EDUCATION/TRAINING PROGRAMS—Industrial Radiologic Technology/Technician; Nuclear and Industrial Radiologic Technologies/Technicians, Other; Nuclear Engineering Technology/Technician; Nuclear/Nuclear Power Technology/Technician; Radiation Protection/Health Physics Technician. **RELATED KNOWLEDGE/COURSES—Physics:** Knowledge and prediction of physical principles and laws and their interrelationships and applications to understanding fluid, material, and atmospheric dynamics and mechanical, electrical, atomic, and subatomic structures and processes. **Chemistry:** Knowledge of the chemical composition, structure, and properties of substances and of the chemical processes and transformations that they undergo. This includes uses of chemicals, their danger signs, production techniques, and disposal methods. **Public Safety and Security:** Knowledge of relevant equipment, policies, procedures, and strategies to promote effective local, state, or national security operations for the protection of people, data, property, and institutions. **Engineering and Technology:** Knowledge of the practical application of engineering science and technology. This includes applying principles, techniques, procedures, and equipment to the design and production of various goods and services. **Design:** Knowledge of design techniques, tools, and principles involved in production of precision technical plans, blueprints, drawings, and models. **Customer and Personal Service:** Knowledge of principles and processes for providing customer and personal services. This includes customer needs assessment, meeting quality standards for services, and evaluation of customer satisfaction.

Nuclear Power Reactor Operators

- Annual Earnings: $66,230
- Growth: –0.5%
- Annual Job Openings: 1,000
- Self-Employed: 0.0%
- Part-Time: 0.8%
- Education/Training Required: Long-term on-the-job training

Industries in Which Income Is Highest

Industry	Average Annual Wage	Number Employed
Utilities	$66,750	3,290

Metropolitan Areas Where Income Is Highest

Metropolitan Area	Average Annual Wage	Number Employed

No data available.

Control nuclear reactors. Adjust controls to position rod and to regulate flux level, reactor period, coolant temperature, and rate of power flow, following standard procedures. Respond to system or unit abnormalities, diagnosing the cause, and recommending or taking corrective action. Monitor all systems for normal running conditions, performing activities such as checking gauges to assess output or assess the effects of generator loading on other equipment. Implement operational procedures such as those controlling start-up and shutdown activities. Note malfunctions of equipment, instruments, or controls, and report these conditions to supervisors. Monitor and operate boilers, turbines, wells, and auxiliary power plant equipment. Dispatch orders and instructions to personnel through radiotelephone or intercommunication systems to coordinate auxiliary equipment operation. Record operating data such as the results of surveillance tests. Participate in nuclear fuel element handling activities such as preparation, transfer, loading, and unloading. Conduct inspections and operations outside of control rooms as necessary. Direct reactor operators in emergency situations, in accordance with emergency operating procedures. Authorize maintenance activities on units and changes in equipment and system operational status. **SKILLS**—Operation Monitoring; Operation and Control; Science; Troubleshooting; Systems Analysis; Coordination; Active Listening; Equipment Maintenance.

GOE—Interest Area: 13. Manufacturing. **Work Group:** 13.16. Utility Operation and Energy Distribution. **PERSONALITY TYPE:** Realistic. Realistic occupations frequently involve work activities that include practical, hands-on problems and solutions. They often deal with plants, animals, and real-world materials like wood, tools, and machinery. Many of the occupations require working outside and do not involve a lot of paperwork or working closely with others.

EDUCATION/TRAINING PROGRAM—Nuclear/Nuclear Power Technology/Technician. **RELATED KNOWLEDGE/COURSES—Physics:** Knowledge and prediction of physical principles and laws and their interrelationships and applications to understanding fluid, material, and atmospheric dynamics and mechanical, electrical, atomic, and subatomic structures and processes. **Engineering and Technology:** Knowledge of the practical application of engineering science and technology. This includes applying principles, techniques, procedures, and equipment to the design and production of various goods and services. **Chemistry:** Knowledge of the chemical composition, structure, and properties of substances and of the chemical processes and transformations that they undergo. This includes uses of chemicals, their danger signs, production techniques, and disposal methods. **Public Safety and Security:** Knowledge of relevant equipment, policies, procedures, and strategies to promote effective local, state, or national security operations for the protection of people, data, property, and institutions. **Mechanical Devices:** Knowledge of machines and tools, including their designs, uses, repair, and maintenance. **Computers and Electronics:** Knowledge of circuit boards, processors, chips, electronic equipment, and computer hardware and software, including applications and programming.

Nursery and Greenhouse Managers

- Annual Earnings: $51,160
- Growth: 4.0%
- Annual Job Openings: 20,000
- Self-Employed: 0.0%
- Part-Time: 13.1%
- Education/Training Required: Work experience plus degree

The job openings listed here are shared with Agricultural Crop Farm Managers and Fish Hatchery Managers.

Industries in Which Income Is Highest

Industry	Average Annual Wage	Number Employed
Food Manufacturing	$57,140	90
Merchant Wholesalers, Nondurable Goods	$54,690	290
Administrative and Support Services	$54,540	160
Management of Companies and Enterprises	$52,780	70
Educational Services	$52,690	190

Metropolitan Areas Where Income Is Highest

Metropolitan Area	Average Annual Wage	Number Employed
New York–Northern New Jersey–Long Island, NY–NJ–PA	$76,240	50
Stockton, CA	$72,420	30
Riverside–San Bernardino–Ontario, CA	$67,640	40
Washington–Arlington–Alexandria, DC–VA–MD–WV	$64,020	30
Portland–Vancouver–Beaverton, OR–WA	$60,170	30

Plan, organize, direct, control, and coordinate activities of workers engaged in propagating, cultivating, and harvesting horticultural specialties, such as trees, shrubs, flowers, mushrooms, and other plants. Assign work schedules and duties to nursery or greenhouse staff, and supervise their work. Determine plant growing conditions, such as greenhouses, hydroponics, or natural settings, and set planting and care schedules. Determine types and quantities of horticultural plants to be grown, based on budgets, projected sales volumes, and/or executive directives. Explain and enforce safety regulations and policies. Hire employees, and train them in gardening techniques. Identify plants as well as problems such as diseases, weeds, and insect pests. Manage nurseries that grow horticultural plants for sale to trade or retail customers, for display or exhibition, or for research. Select and purchase seeds, plant nutrients, disease control chemicals, and garden and lawn care equipment. Tour work areas to observe work being done, to inspect crops, and to evaluate plant and soil conditions. Apply pesticides and fertilizers to plants. Confer with horticultural personnel in order to plan facility renovations or additions. Construct structures and accessories such as greenhouses and benches. Coordinate clerical, recordkeeping, inventory, requisitioning, and marketing activities. Cut and prune trees, shrubs, flowers, and plants. Graft plants. Inspect facilities and equipment for signs of disrepair, and perform necessary maintenance work. Negotiate contracts such as those for land leases or tree purchases. Position and regulate plant irrigation systems, and program environmental and irrigation control computers. Prepare soil for planting, and plant or transplant seeds, bulbs, and cuttings. Provide information to customers on the care of trees, shrubs, flowers, plants, and lawns. **SKILLS—** Management of Personnel Resources; Management of Financial Resources; Management of Material Resources; Negotiation; Systems Analysis; Systems Evaluation; Operations Analysis; Coordination.

GOE—Interest Area: 01. Agriculture and Natural Resources. **Work Group:** 01.01. Managerial Work in Agriculture and Natural Resources. **PERSONALITY TYPE:** Enterprising. Enterprising occupations frequently involve starting up and carrying out projects. These occupations can involve leading people and making many decisions. They sometimes require risk taking and often deal with business.

EDUCATION/TRAINING PROGRAMS— Agribusiness/Agricultural Business Operations; Agricultural Business and Management, General; Greenhouse Operations and Management; Horticultural Science; Ornamental Horticulture; Plant Nursery Operations and Management; Plant Protection and Integrated Pest Management. **RELATED KNOWLEDGE/COURSES—Biology:** Knowledge of plant and animal organisms and their tissues, cells, functions, interdependencies, and interactions with each other and the environment. **Food Production:** Knowledge of techniques and equipment for planting, growing, and harvesting food products (both plant and animal) for consumption, including storage/handling techniques. **Administration and Management:** Knowledge of business and management principles involved in strategic planning, resource allocation, human resources modeling, leadership technique, production methods, and coordination of people and resources. **Personnel and Human Resources:** Knowledge of principles and procedures for personnel recruitment, selection, training, compensation and benefits, labor relations and negotiation, and personnel information systems. **Chemistry:** Knowledge of the chemical composition, structure, and properties of substances and of the chemical processes and transformations that they undergo. This includes uses of chemicals, their danger signs, production techniques, and disposal methods. **Production and Processing:** Knowledge of raw materials, production processes, quality control, costs, and other techniques for maximizing the effective manufacture and distribution of goods.

Nursing Instructors and Teachers, Postsecondary

- ◎ Annual Earnings: $53,160
- ◎ Growth: 32.2%
- ◎ Annual Job Openings: 329,000
- ◎ Self-Employed: 0.4%
- ◎ Part-Time: 27.3%
- ◎ Education/Training Required: Master's degree

Our sources did not provide separate job openings data for this occupation. The job openings listed here are shared with 35 other postsecondary teaching occupations. For a complete list, see the beginning of this section.

Industries in Which Income Is Highest

Industry	Average Annual Wage	Number Employed
Hospitals	$62,990	3,360
Educational Services	$52,270	32,840

Metropolitan Areas Where Income Is Highest

Metropolitan Area	Average Annual Wage	Number Employed
San Diego–Carlsbad–San Marcos, CA	$77,290	210
Riverside–San Bernardino–Ontario, CA	$76,330	210
Trenton–Ewing, NJ	$73,820	60
New Haven, CT	$68,180	190
New York–Northern New Jersey–Long Island, NY–NJ–PA	$67,200	1,210

Demonstrate and teach patient care in classroom and clinical units to nursing students. Includes both teachers primarily engaged in teaching and those who do a combination of both teaching and research. Initiate, facilitate, and moderate classroom discussions. Prepare and deliver lectures to undergraduate and/or graduate students on topics such as pharmacology, mental health nursing, and community health care practices. Keep abreast of developments in their field by reading current literature, talking with colleagues, and participating in professional conferences. Prepare course materials such as syllabi, homework assignments, and handouts. Supervise students' laboratory and clinical work. Evaluate and grade students' class work, laboratory and clinic work, assignments, and papers. Collaborate with colleagues to address teaching and research issues. Plan, evaluate, and revise curricula, course content, and course materials and methods of instruction. Assess clinical education needs, and patient and client teaching needs, utilizing a variety of methods. Compile, administer, and grade examinations or assign this work to others. Advise students on academic and vocational curricula and on career issues. Maintain student attendance records, grades, and other required records. Maintain regularly scheduled office hours in order to advise and assist students. Supervise undergraduate and/or graduate teaching, internship, and research work. Conduct research in a particular field of knowledge and publish findings in professional journals, books, and/or electronic media. Participate in student recruitment, registration, and placement activities. Serve on academic or administrative committees that deal with institutional policies, departmental matters, and academic issues. Coordinate training programs with area universities, clinics, hospitals, health agencies, and/or vocational schools. Compile bibliographies of specialized materials for outside reading assignments. Select and obtain materials and supplies such as textbooks and laboratory equipment. Participate in campus and community events. Write grant proposals to procure external research funding. Act as advisers to student organizations. Demonstrate patient care in clinical units of hospitals. Perform administrative duties such as serving as department head. **SKILLS**—Instructing; Science; Social Perceptiveness; Learning Strategies; Writing; Service Orientation; Persuasion; Reading Comprehension.

GOE—Interest Area: 05. Education and Training. **Work Group:** 05.03. Postsecondary and Adult Teaching and Instructing. **PERSONALITY TYPE:** Social. Social occupations frequently involve working with, communicating with, and teaching people. These occupations often involve helping or providing service to others.

EDUCATION/TRAINING PROGRAMS—Adult Health Nurse/Nursing; Family Practice Nurse/Nurse Practitioner; Maternal/Child Health Nurse/Nursing; Nurse Anesthetist; Nurse Midwife/Nursing Midwifery; Nursing—Registered Nurse Training (RN, ASN, BSN, MSN); Nursing Clinical Specialist; Nursing Science (MS, PhD); Nursing, Other; Pediatric Nurse/Nursing; Perioperative/Operating and Surgical Nurse/Nur; Pre-Nursing Studies; Psychiatric/Mental Health Nurse/Nursing; Public Health/Community Nurse/Nursing. **RELATED KNOWLEDGE/COURSES—Therapy and Counseling:** Knowledge of principles, methods, and procedures for diagnosis, treatment, and rehabilitation of physical and mental dysfunctions and for career counseling and guidance. **Sociology and Anthropology:** Knowledge of group behavior and dynamics, societal trends and influences, human migrations, ethnicity, and cultures and their history and origins. **Education and Training:** Knowledge of principles and methods for curriculum and training design, teaching and instruction for individuals and groups, and the measurement of training effects. **Biology:** Knowledge of plant and animal organisms and their tissues, cells, functions, interdependencies, and interactions with each other and the environment. **Medicine and Dentistry:** Knowledge of the information and techniques needed to diagnose and treat human injuries, diseases, and deformities. This includes symptoms, treatment alternatives, drug properties and interactions, and preventive health-care measures. **Psychology:** Knowledge of human behavior and performance; individual differences in ability, personality, and interests; learning and motivation; psychological research methods; and the

assessment and treatment of behavioral and affective disorders.

Obstetricians and Gynecologists

- Annual Earnings: More than $146,500
- Growth: 24.0%
- Annual Job Openings: 41,000
- Self-Employed: 0.4%
- Part-Time: 9.6%
- Education/Training Required: First professional degree

The job openings listed here are shared with Anesthesiologists; Family and General Practitioners; Internists, General; Pediatricians, General; Psychiatrists; and Surgeons.

Industries in Which Income Is Highest

Industry	Average Annual Wage	Number Employed
Ambulatory Health Care Services	More than $146,500	19,070
Hospitals	More than $146,500	2,190

Metropolitan Areas Where Income Is Highest

Metropolitan Area	Average Annual Wage	Number Employed
Atlanta–Sandy Springs–Marietta, GA	More than $146,500	1,450
New York–Northern New Jersey–Long Island, NY–NJ–PA	More than $146,500	1,350
Dallas–Fort Worth–Arlington, TX	More than $146,500	1,090
Philadelphia–Camden–Wilmington, PA–NJ–DE–MD	More than $146,500	430
Boston–Cambridge–Quincy, MA–NH	More than $146,500	410

Diagnose, treat, and help prevent diseases of women, especially those affecting the reproductive system and the process of childbirth. Care for and treat women during prenatal, natal and post-natal periods. Explain procedures and discuss test results or prescribed treatments with patients. Treat diseases of female organs. Monitor patients' condition and progress and re-evaluate treatments as necessary. Perform cesarean sections or other surgical procedures as needed to preserve patients' health and deliver babies safely. Prescribe or administer therapy, medication, and other specialized medical care to treat or prevent illness, disease, or injury. Analyze records, reports, test results, or examination information to diagnose medical condition of patient. Collect, record, and maintain patient information, such as medical histories, reports, and examination results. Advise patients and community members concerning diet, activity, hygiene, and disease prevention. Refer patient to medical specialist or other practitioner when necessary. Consult with, or provide consulting services to, other physicians. Direct and coordinate activities of nurses, students, assistants, specialists, therapists, and other medical staff. Plan, implement, or administer health programs in hospitals, businesses, or communities for prevention and treatment of injuries or illnesses. Prepare government and organizational reports on birth, death, and disease statistics, workforce evaluations, or the medical status of individuals. **SKILLS**—Science; Judgment and Decision Making; Instructing; Social Perceptiveness; Active Learning; Reading Comprehension; Critical Thinking; Persuasion.

GOE—Interest Area: 08. Health Science. **Work Group:** 08.02. Medicine and Surgery. **PERSONALITY TYPE:** Investigative. Investigative occupations frequently involve working with ideas and require an extensive amount of thinking. These occupations can involve searching for facts and figuring out problems mentally.

EDUCATION/TRAINING PROGRAMS—Neonatal-Perinatal Medicine; Obstetrics and Gynecology. **RELATED KNOWLEDGE/COURSES**—**Medicine and Dentistry:** Knowledge of the information and techniques needed to diagnose and treat human injuries, diseases, and deformities. This includes symptoms, treatment alternatives, drug properties and interactions, and preventive health-care measures. **Therapy and Counseling:** Knowledge of principles, methods, and procedures for diagnosis, treatment, and rehabilitation of physical and mental dysfunctions and for career counseling and guidance. **Biology:** Knowledge of plant and animal organisms and their tissues, cells, functions, interdependencies, and interactions with each other and the environment. **Psychology:** Knowledge of human behavior and performance;

individual differences in ability, personality, and interests; learning and motivation; psychological research methods; and the assessment and treatment of behavioral and affective disorders. **Sociology and Anthropology:** Knowledge of group behavior and dynamics, societal trends and influences, human migrations, ethnicity, and cultures and their history and origins. **Chemistry:** Knowledge of the chemical composition, structure, and properties of substances and of the chemical processes and transformations that they undergo. This includes uses of chemicals, their danger signs, production techniques, and disposal methods.

Occupational Health and Safety Specialists

- Annual Earnings: $53,710
- Growth: 12.4%
- Annual Job Openings: 3,000
- Self-Employed: 5.0%
- Part-Time: 6.4%
- Education/Training Required: Master's degree

Industries in Which Income Is Highest

Industry	Average Annual Wage	Number Employed
Professional, Scientific, and Technical Services	$59,110	3,000
Transportation Equipment Manufacturing	$58,960	1,260
Chemical Manufacturing	$58,850	1,010
Hospitals	$55,790	2,560
Management of Companies and Enterprises	$53,580	1,150

Metropolitan Areas Where Income Is Highest

Metropolitan Area	Average Annual Wage	Number Employed
San Jose–Sunnyvale–Santa Clara, CA	$79,890	140
Davenport–Moline–Rock Island, IA–IL	$74,890	50
San Francisco–Oakland–Fremont, CA	$72,510	450
Kennewick–Richland–Pasco, WA	$69,510	170
Denver–Aurora, CO	$69,020	340

Review, evaluate, and analyze work environments and design programs and procedures to control, eliminate, and prevent disease or injury caused by chemical, physical, and biological agents or ergonomic factors. May conduct inspections and enforce adherence to laws and regulations governing the health and safety of individuals. May be employed in the public or private sector. Conduct audits at hazardous waste sites or industrial sites, and participate in hazardous waste site investigations. Conduct safety training and education programs, and demonstrate the use of safety equipment. Coordinate "right-to-know" programs regarding hazardous chemicals and other substances. Develop and maintain hygiene programs such as noise surveys, continuous atmosphere monitoring, ventilation surveys, and asbestos management plans. Develop and maintain medical monitoring programs for employees. Inspect and evaluate workplace environments, equipment, and practices, in order to ensure compliance with safety standards and government regulations. Inspect specified areas to ensure the presence of fire prevention equipment, safety equipment, and first-aid supplies. Investigate accidents to identify causes and to determine how such accidents might be prevented in the future. Investigate health-related complaints, and inspect facilities to ensure that they comply with public health legislation and regulations. Investigate the adequacy of ventilation, exhaust equipment, lighting, and other conditions that could affect employee health, comfort, or performance. Maintain and update emergency response plans and procedures. Maintain inventories of hazardous materials and hazardous wastes, using waste tracking systems to ensure that materials are handled properly. Collaborate with engineers and physicians to institute control and remedial measures for hazardous and potentially hazardous conditions or equipment. Collect samples of dust, gases, vapors, and other potentially toxic materials for analysis. Collect samples of hazardous materials, or arrange for sample collection. Order suspension of activities that pose threats to workers' health and safety. Perform laboratory analyses and physical inspections of samples in order to detect disease or to assess purity or cleanliness. Prepare hazardous, radioactive, and mixed waste samples for transportation and storage by treating, compacting, packaging, and labeling them. Provide new-employee health and safety orientations, and develop materials for these presentations. **SKILLS**—Science; Writing; Speaking; Mathematics; Systems Analysis; Management of Financial Resources; Operation Monitoring; Reading Comprehension.

GOE—Interest Area: 07. Government and Public Administration. **Work Group:** 07.03. Regulations Enforcement. **PERSONALITY TYPE:** Social. Social occupations frequently involve working with, communicating with, and teaching people. These occupations often involve helping or providing service to others.

EDUCATION/TRAINING PROGRAMS—Environmental Health; Industrial Safety Technology/Technician; Occupational Health and Industrial Hygiene; Occupational Safety and Health Technology/Technician; Quality Control and Safety Technologies/Technicians, Other. **RELATED KNOWLEDGE/COURSES—Medicine and Dentistry:** Knowledge of the information and techniques needed to diagnose and treat human injuries, diseases, and deformities. This includes symptoms, treatment alternatives, drug properties and interactions, and preventive health-care measures. **Public Safety and Security:** Knowledge of relevant equipment, policies, procedures, and strategies to promote effective local, state, or national security operations for the protection of people, data, property, and institutions. **Chemistry:** Knowledge of the chemical composition, structure, and properties of substances and of the chemical processes and transformations that they undergo. This includes uses of chemicals, their danger signs, production techniques, and disposal methods. **Physics:** Knowledge and prediction of physical principles and laws and their interrelationships and applications to understanding fluid, material, and atmospheric dynamics and mechanical, electrical, atomic, and subatomic structures and processes. **Biology:** Knowledge of plant and animal organisms and their tissues, cells, functions, interdependencies, and interactions with each other and the environment. **Law and Government:** Knowledge of laws, legal codes, court procedures, precedents, government regulations, executive orders, agency rules, and the democratic political process.

Occupational Therapists

◎ Annual Earnings: $56,860
◎ Growth: 33.6%
◎ Annual Job Openings: 7,000
◎ Self-Employed: 6.0%
◎ Part-Time: 29.4%
◎ Education/Training Required: Bachelor's degree

Industries in Which Income Is Highest

Industry	Average Annual Wage	Number Employed
Ambulatory Health Care Services	$59,440	26,940
Nursing and Residential Care Facilities	$58,380	10,180
Hospitals	$57,630	27,160
Federal, State, and Local Government	$56,720	3,120
Administrative and Support Services	$55,770	2,050

Metropolitan Areas Where Income Is Highest

Metropolitan Area	Average Annual Wage	Number Employed
San Francisco–Oakland–Fremont, CA	$76,940	1,090
Riverside–San Bernardino–Ontario, CA	$74,720	490
Oxnard–Thousand Oaks–Ventura, CA	$70,560	100
San Diego–Carlsbad–San Marcos, CA	$70,220	510
Rockford, IL	$70,130	90

Assess, plan, organize, and participate in rehabilitative programs that help restore vocational, homemaking, and daily living skills, as well as general independence, to disabled persons. Complete and maintain necessary records. Evaluate patients' progress and prepare reports that detail progress. Test and evaluate patients' physical and mental abilities and analyze medical data to determine realistic rehabilitation goals for patients. Select activities that will help individuals learn work and life-management skills within limits of their mental and physical capabilities. Plan, organize, and conduct occupational therapy programs in hospital, institutional, or community settings to help rehabilitate those impaired because of illness, injury or psychological or developmental problems. Recommend changes in patients' work or living environments, consistent with their needs and capabilities. Consult with rehabilitation team to select activity programs and coordinate occupational therapy with other therapeutic activities. Help clients improve decision making, abstract reasoning, memory, sequencing, coordination and perceptual skills, using computer programs. Develop and participate in health promotion programs, group activities, or discussions to promote client health, facilitate social adjustment, alleviate stress, and prevent physical or mental disability. Provide training and supervision in therapy techniques and objectives for students and nurses and other medical staff. Design and create, or requisition, special supplies and equipment, such as splints, braces and computer-aided adaptive equipment. Plan and implement programs and social activities to help patients learn work and school skills and adjust to handicaps. Lay out materials such as puzzles, scissors and eating utensils for use in therapy, and clean and repair these tools after therapy sessions. Advise on health risks in the workplace and on health-related transition to retirement. Conduct research in occupational therapy. **SKILLS**—Social Perceptiveness; Service Orientation; Science; Technology Design; Coordination; Instructing; Reading Comprehension; Persuasion.

GOE—Interest Area: 08. Health Science. **Work Group:** 08.07. Medical Therapy. **PERSONALITY TYPE:** Social. Social occupations frequently involve working with, communicating with, and teaching people. These occupations often involve helping or providing service to others.

EDUCATION/TRAINING PROGRAM—Occupational Therapy/Therapist. **RELATED KNOWLEDGE/COURSES—Therapy and Counseling:** Knowledge of principles, methods, and procedures for diagnosis, treatment, and rehabilitation of physical and mental dysfunctions and for career counseling and guidance. **Psychology:** Knowledge of human behavior and performance; individual differences in ability, personality, and interests; learning and motivation; psychological research methods; and the assessment and treatment of behavioral and affective disorders. **Customer and Personal Service:** Knowledge of principles and processes for providing customer and personal services. This includes customer needs assessment, meeting quality standards for services, and evaluation of customer satisfaction. **Medicine and Dentistry:** Knowledge of the information and techniques needed to diagnose and treat human injuries, diseases, and deformities. This includes symptoms, treatment alternatives, drug properties and interactions, and preventive health-care measures. **Education and Training:** Knowledge of principles and methods for curriculum and training design, teaching and instruction for individuals and groups, and the measurement of training effects. **Biology:** Knowledge of plant and animal organisms and their tissues, cells, functions, interdependencies, and interactions with each other and the environment.

Operations Research Analysts

- Annual Earnings: $62,180
- Growth: 8.4%
- Annual Job Openings: 7,000
- Self-Employed: 1.2%
- Part-Time: 5.5%
- Education/Training Required: Master's degree

Industries in Which Income Is Highest

Industry	Average Annual Wage	Number Employed
Computer and Electronic Product Manufacturing	$69,360	1,560
Merchant Wholesalers, Durable Goods	$69,130	1,390
Federal, State, and Local Government	$67,910	6,670
Postal Service	$66,960	1,490
Professional, Scientific, and Technical Services	$65,990	12,320

Metropolitan Areas Where Income Is Highest

Metropolitan Area	Average Annual Wage	Number Employed
Bakersfield, CA	$96,820	60
Las Cruces, NM	$84,580	80
Providence–Fall River–Warwick, RI–MA	$82,940	180
San Jose–Sunnyvale–Santa Clara, CA	$82,480	450
Huntsville, AL	$81,050	390

Formulate and apply mathematical modeling and other optimizing methods using a computer to develop and interpret information that assists **management with decision making, policy formulation, or other managerial functions. May develop related software, service, or products. Frequently concentrates on collecting and analyzing data and developing decision support software. May develop and supply optimal time, cost, or logistics networks for program evaluation, review, or implementation.** Formulate mathematical or simulation models of problems, relating constants and variables, restrictions, alternatives, conflicting objectives, and their numerical parameters. Collaborate with others in the organization to ensure successful implementation of chosen problem solutions. Analyze information obtained from management in order to conceptualize and define operational problems. Perform validation and testing of models to ensure adequacy; reformulate models as necessary. Collaborate with senior managers and decision-makers to identify and solve a variety of problems, and to clarify management objectives. Define data requirements; then gather and validate information, applying judgment and statistical tests. Study and analyze information about alternative courses of action in order to determine which plan will offer the best outcomes. Prepare management reports defining and evaluating problems and recommending solutions. Break systems into their component parts, assign numerical values to each component, and examine the mathematical relationships between them. Specify manipulative or computational methods to be applied to models. Observe the current system in operation, and gather and analyze information about each of the parts of component problems, using a variety of sources. Design, conduct, and evaluate experimental operational models in cases where models cannot be developed from existing data. Develop and apply time and cost networks in order to plan, control, and review large projects. **SKILLS—** Programming; Systems Analysis; Operations Analysis; Mathematics; Systems Evaluation; Science; Complex Problem Solving; Judgment and Decision Making.

GOE—Interest Area: 04. Business and Administration. **Work Group:** 04.05. Accounting, Auditing, and Analytical Support. **PERSONALITY TYPE:** Investigative. Investigative occupations frequently involve working with ideas and require an extensive amount of thinking. These occupations can involve searching for facts and figuring out problems mentally.

EDUCATION/TRAINING PROGRAMS— Management Science, General; Management Sciences and Quantitative Methods, Other; Operations

Research. **RELATED KNOWLEDGE/COURSES—Mathematics:** Knowledge of arithmetic, algebra, geometry, calculus, and statistics and their applications. **Engineering and Technology:** Knowledge of the practical application of engineering science and technology. This includes applying principles, techniques, procedures, and equipment to the design and production of various goods and services. **Computers and Electronics:** Knowledge of circuit boards, processors, chips, electronic equipment, and computer hardware and software, including applications and programming. **Production and Processing:** Knowledge of raw materials, production processes, quality control, costs, and other techniques for maximizing the effective manufacture and distribution of goods. **Administration and Management:** Knowledge of business and management principles involved in strategic planning, resource allocation, human resources modeling, leadership technique, production methods, and coordination of people and resources. **Economics and Accounting:** Knowledge of economic and accounting principles and practices, the financial markets, banking, and the analysis and reporting of financial data.

Optometrists

- Annual Earnings: $88,040
- Growth: 19.7%
- Annual Job Openings: 2,000
- Self-Employed: 27.4%
- Part-Time: 16.3%
- Education/Training Required: First professional degree

Industries in Which Income Is Highest

Industry	Average Annual Wage	Number Employed
Health and Personal Care Stores	$93,940	2,830
Ambulatory Health Care Services	$87,650	19,150

Metropolitan Areas Where Income Is Highest

Metropolitan Area	Average Annual Wage	Number Employed
Dayton, OH	More than $146,500	90
San Jose–Sunnyvale–Santa Clara, CA	More than $146,500	200
Greensboro–High Point, NC	$142,170	50
Anchorage, AK	$135,880	50
Tampa–St. Petersburg–Clearwater, FL	$134,870	110

Diagnose, manage, and treat conditions and diseases of the human eye and visual system. Examine eyes and visual system, diagnose problems or impairments, prescribe corrective lenses, and provide treatment. May prescribe therapeutic drugs to treat specific eye conditions. Examine eyes, using observation, instruments and pharmaceutical agents, to determine visual acuity and perception, focus and coordination and to diagnose diseases and other abnormalities such as glaucoma or color blindness. Analyze test results and develop a treatment plan. Prescribe, supply, fit and adjust eyeglasses, contact lenses and other vision aids. Prescribe medications to treat eye diseases if state laws permit. Educate and counsel patients on contact lens care, visual hygiene, lighting arrangements and safety factors. Consult with and refer patients to ophthalmologist or other health care practitioner if additional medical treatment is determined necessary. Remove foreign bodies from the eye. Provide patients undergoing eye surgeries, such as cataract and laser vision correction, with pre- and post-operative care. Prescribe therapeutic procedures to correct or conserve vision. Provide vision therapy and low vision rehabilitation. **SKILLS**—Science; Judgment and Decision Making; Management of Personnel Resources; Persuasion; Active Listening; Service Orientation; Reading Comprehension; Active Learning.

GOE—Interest Area: 08. Health Science. **Work Group:** 08.04. Health Specialties. **PERSONALITY TYPE:** Investigative. Investigative occupations frequently involve working with ideas and require an extensive amount of thinking. These occupations can involve searching for facts and figuring out problems mentally.

EDUCATION/TRAINING PROGRAM— Optometry (OD). **RELATED KNOWLEDGE/**

COURSES—Medicine and Dentistry: Knowledge of the information and techniques needed to diagnose and treat human injuries, diseases, and deformities. This includes symptoms, treatment alternatives, drug properties and interactions, and preventive health-care measures. Biology: Knowledge of plant and animal organisms and their tissues, cells, functions, interdependencies, and interactions with each other and the environment. Psychology: Knowledge of human behavior and performance; individual differences in ability, personality, and interests; learning and motivation; psychological research methods; and the assessment and treatment of behavioral and affective disorders. Personnel and Human Resources: Knowledge of principles and procedures for personnel recruitment, selection, training, compensation and benefits, labor relations and negotiation, and personnel information systems. Sales and Marketing: Knowledge of principles and methods for showing, promoting, and selling products or services. This includes marketing strategy and tactics, product demonstration, sales techniques, and sales control systems. Customer and Personal Service: Knowledge of principles and processes for providing customer and personal services. This includes customer needs assessment, meeting quality standards for services, and evaluation of customer satisfaction.

Oral and Maxillofacial Surgeons

- ◎ Annual Earnings: More than $146,500
- ◎ Growth: 16.2%
- ◎ Annual Job Openings: fewer than 500
- ◎ Self-Employed: 15.7%
- ◎ Part-Time: 22.6%
- ◎ Education/Training Required: First professional degree

Industries in Which Income Is Highest

Industry	Average Annual Wage	Number Employed
Ambulatory Health Care Services	More than $146,500	4,820
Nursing and Residential Care Facilities	$62,740	40
Hospitals	$54,290	220

Metropolitan Areas Where Income Is Highest

Metropolitan Area	Average Annual Wage	Number Employed
Fort Wayne, IN	More than $146,500	80
Boston–Cambridge–Quincy, MA–NH	More than $146,500	210
Philadelphia–Camden–Wilmington, PA–NJ–DE–MD	$52,350	40

Perform surgery on mouth, jaws, and related head and neck structure to execute difficult and multiple extractions of teeth, to remove tumors and other abnormal growths, to correct abnormal jaw relations by mandibular or maxillary revision, to prepare mouth for insertion of dental prosthesis, or to treat fractured jaws. Administer general and local anesthetics. Collaborate with other professionals such as restorative dentists and orthodontists in order to plan treatment. Perform surgery on the mouth and jaws in order to treat conditions such as cleft lip and palate and jaw growth problems. Perform surgery to prepare the mouth for dental implants, and to aid in the regeneration of deficient bone and gum tissues. Provide emergency treatment of facial injuries including facial lacerations, intra-oral lacerations, and fractured facial bones. Remove impacted, damaged, and non-restorable teeth. Remove tumors and other abnormal growths of the oral and facial regions, using surgical instruments. Restore form and function by moving skin, bone, nerves, and other tissues from other parts of the body in order to reconstruct the jaws and face. Evaluate the position of the wisdom teeth in order to determine whether problems exist currently or might occur in the future. Perform minor cosmetic procedures such as chin and cheek-bone enhancements, and minor facial rejuvenation procedures including the use of Botox and laser technology. Treat infections of the oral cavity, salivary glands, jaws, and neck. Treat problems affecting the oral mucosa such as mouth ulcers and infections. Treat snoring problems, using laser surgery. SKILLS— Science; Reading Comprehension; Judgment and Decision Making; Critical Thinking; Active Learning; Learning Strategies; Speaking; Service Orientation.

GOE—Interest Area: 08. Health Science. Work Group: 08.03. Dentistry. PERSONALITY TYPE: Investigative. Investigative occupations frequently involve working with ideas and require an extensive amount of thinking. These occupations can involve searching for facts and figuring out problems mentally.

EDUCATION/TRAINING PROGRAMS— Dental/Oral Surgery Specialty; Oral/Maxillofacial Surgery (Cert, MS, PhD). **RELATED KNOWLEDGE/COURSES—Medicine and Dentistry:** Knowledge of the information and techniques needed to diagnose and treat human injuries, diseases, and deformities. This includes symptoms, treatment alternatives, drug properties and interactions, and preventive health-care measures. **Biology:** Knowledge of plant and animal organisms and their tissues, cells, functions, interdependencies, and interactions with each other and the environment. **Chemistry:** Knowledge of the chemical composition, structure, and properties of substances and of the chemical processes and transformations that they undergo. This includes uses of chemicals, their danger signs, production techniques, and disposal methods. **Therapy and Counseling:** Knowledge of principles, methods, and procedures for diagnosis, treatment, and rehabilitation of physical and mental dysfunctions and for career counseling and guidance. **Psychology:** Knowledge of human behavior and performance; individual differences in ability, personality, and interests; learning and motivation; psychological research methods; and the assessment and treatment of behavioral and affective disorders. **English Language:** Knowledge of the structure and content of the English language, including the meaning and spelling of words, rules of composition, and grammar.

Orthodontists

- ◎ Annual Earnings: More than $146,500
- ◎ Growth: 12.8%
- ◎ Annual Job Openings: 1,000
- ◎ Self-Employed: 35.9%
- ◎ Part-Time: 22.6%
- ◎ Education/Training Required: First professional degree

Industries in Which Income Is Highest

Industry	Average Annual Wage	Number Employed
Ambulatory Health Care Services	More than $146,500	4,700
Hospitals	$63,010	70

Metropolitan Areas Where Income Is Highest

Metropolitan Area	Average Annual Wage	Number Employed
Cleveland–Elyria–Mentor, OH	More than $146,500	50
Kansas City, MO–KS	More than $146,500	30

Examine, diagnose, and treat dental malocclusions and oral cavity anomalies. Design and fabricate appliances to realign teeth and jaws to produce and maintain normal function and to improve appearance. Fit dental appliances in patients' mouths in order to alter the position and relationship of teeth and jaws, and to realign teeth. Study diagnostic records such as medical/dental histories, plaster models of the teeth, photos of a patient's face and teeth, and X-rays in order to develop patient treatment plans. Diagnose teeth and jaw or other dental-facial abnormalities. Examine patients in order to assess abnormalities of jaw development, tooth position, and other dental-facial structures. Prepare diagnostic and treatment records. Adjust dental appliances periodically in order to produce and maintain normal function. Provide patients with proposed treatment plans and cost estimates. Instruct dental officers and technical assistants in orthodontic procedures and techniques. Coordinate orthodontic services with other dental and medical services. Design and fabricate appliances, such as space maintainers, retainers, and labial and lingual arch wires. **SKILLS**—Management of Financial Resources; Management of Personnel Resources; Instructing; Service Orientation; Equipment Selection; Management of Material Resources; Time Management; Social Perceptiveness.

GOE—Interest Area: 08. Health Science. **Work Group:** 08.03. Dentistry. **PERSONALITY TYPE:** Investigative. Investigative occupations frequently involve working with ideas and require an extensive amount of thinking. These occupations can involve searching for facts and figuring out problems mentally.

EDUCATION/TRAINING PROGRAMS— Orthodontics Specialty; Orthodontics/Orthodontology (Cert, MS, PhD). **RELATED KNOWLEDGE/ COURSES—Medicine and Dentistry:** Knowledge of the information and techniques needed to diagnose and treat human injuries, diseases, and deformities. This includes symptoms, treatment alternatives, drug properties and interactions, and preventive health-care measures. **Biology:** Knowledge of plant and animal organisms and their tissues, cells, functions, interdependencies, and interactions with each other and the environment. **Sales and Marketing:** Knowledge of principles and methods for showing, promoting, and selling products or services. This includes marketing strategy and tactics, product demonstration, sales techniques, and sales control systems. **Customer and Personal Service:** Knowledge of principles and processes for providing customer and personal services. This includes customer needs assessment, meeting quality standards for services, and evaluation of customer satisfaction. **Personnel and Human Resources:** Knowledge of principles and procedures for personnel recruitment, selection, training, compensation and benefits, labor relations and negotiation, and personnel information systems. **Economics and Accounting:** Knowledge of economic and accounting principles and practices, the financial markets, banking, and the analysis and reporting of financial data.

Orthotists and Prosthetists

- Annual Earnings: $53,760
- Growth: 18.0%
- Annual Job Openings: fewer than 500
- Self-Employed: 14.4%
- Part-Time: 18.3%
- Education/Training Required: Bachelor's degree

Industries in Which Income Is Highest

Industry	Average Annual Wage	Number Employed
Rental and Leasing Services	$62,040	100
Miscellaneous Manufacturing	$60,800	1,030
Health and Personal Care Stores	$59,640	1,950
Federal, State, and Local Government	$54,530	310
Hospitals	$43,490	930

Metropolitan Areas Where Income Is Highest

Metropolitan Area	Average Annual Wage	Number Employed
Providence–Fall River–Warwick, RI–MA	$107,400	30
Houston–Sugar Land–Baytown, TX	$73,640	60
Philadelphia–Camden–Wilmington, PA–NJ–DE–MD	$56,400	70
Washington–Arlington–Alexandria, DC–VA–MD–WV	$54,740	30
Seattle–Tacoma–Bellevue, WA	$53,950	70

Assist patients with disabling conditions of limbs and spine or with partial or total absence of limb by fitting and preparing orthopedic braces or prostheses. Confer with physicians in order to formulate specifications and prescriptions for orthopedic and/or prosthetic devices. Construct and fabricate appliances or supervise others who are constructing the appliances. Design orthopedic and prosthetic devices, based on physicians' prescriptions, and examination and measurement of patients. Examine, interview, and measure patients in order to determine their appliance needs, and to identify factors that could affect appliance fit. Fit, test, and evaluate devices on patients, and make adjustments for proper fit, function, and comfort. Instruct patients in the use and care of orthoses and prostheses. Make and modify plaster casts of areas that will be fitted with prostheses or orthoses, for use in the device construction process. Repair, rebuild, and modify prosthetic and orthopedic appliances. Select materials and components to be used, based on device design. Maintain patients' records. Publish research findings, and present them at conferences and seminars. Research new ways to construct and use orthopedic and prosthetic devices. Show and explain orthopedic and prosthetic appliances to healthcare workers. Train and supervise orthopedic and prosthetic assistants and technicians, and other support staff. Update skills and knowledge by attending conferences and seminars. **SKILLS**—Technology Design; Speaking; Social Perceptiveness; Science; Management of Personnel Resources; Instructing; Active Listening; Quality Control Analysis.

GOE—Interest Area: 08. Health Science. **Work Group:** 08.06. Medical Technology. **PERSONALITY TYPE:** Social. Social occupations frequently involve working with, communicating with, and teaching people. These occupations often involve helping or providing service to others.

EDUCATION/TRAINING PROGRAMS— Assistive/Augmentative Technology and Rehabiliation Engineering; Orthotist/Prosthetist. **RELATED KNOWLEDGE/COURSES—Medicine and Dentistry:** Knowledge of the information and techniques needed to diagnose and treat human injuries, diseases, and deformities. This includes symptoms, treatment alternatives, drug properties and interactions, and preventive health-care measures. **Therapy and Counseling:** Knowledge of principles, methods, and procedures for diagnosis, treatment, and rehabilitation of physical and mental dysfunctions and for career counseling and guidance. **Building and Construction:** Knowledge of the materials, methods, and tools involved in the construction or repair of houses, buildings, or other structures such as highways and roads. **Design:** Knowledge of design techniques, tools, and principles involved in production of precision technical plans, blueprints, drawings, and models. **Engineering and Technology:** Knowledge of the practical application of engineering science and technology. This includes applying principles, techniques, procedures, and equipment to the design and production of various goods and services. **Biology:** Knowledge of plant and animal organisms and their tissues, cells, functions, interdependencies, and interactions with each other and the environment.

Park Naturalists

- ⊚ Annual Earnings: $53,350
- ⊚ Growth: 6.3%
- ⊚ Annual Job Openings: 2,000
- ⊚ Self-Employed: 9.0%
- ⊚ Part-Time: 7.3%
- ⊚ Education/Training Required: Bachelor's degree

The job openings listed here are shared with Range Managers and Soil Conservationists.

Industries in Which Income Is Highest

Industry	Average Annual Wage	Number Employed
Federal, State, and Local Government	$54,090	13,320

Metropolitan Areas Where Income Is Highest

Metropolitan Area	Average Annual Wage	Number Employed
Washington–Arlington–Alexandria, DC–VA–MD–WV	$83,690	460
Los Angeles–Long Beach–Santa Ana, CA	$74,340	90
Barnstable Town, MA	$71,250	80
San Diego–Carlsbad–San Marcos, CA	$71,120	60
Seattle–Tacoma–Bellevue, WA	$68,000	330

Plan, develop, and conduct programs to inform public of historical, natural, and scientific features of national, state, or local park. Provide visitor services by explaining regulations; answering visitor requests, needs and complaints; and providing information about the park and surrounding areas. Conduct field trips to point out scientific, historic, and natural features of parks, forests, historic sites or other attractions. Prepare and present illustrated lectures and interpretive talks about park features. Perform emergency duties to protect human life, government property, and natural features of park. Confer with park staff to determine subjects and schedules for park programs. Assist with operations of general facilities, such as visitor centers. Plan, organize and direct activities of seasonal staff members. Perform routine maintenance on park structures. Prepare brochures and write newspaper articles. Construct historical, scientific, and nature visitor-center displays. Research stories regarding the area's natural history or environment. Interview specialists in desired fields to obtain and develop data for park information programs. Compile and maintain official park photographic and information files. Take photographs and motion pictures for use in lectures and publications and to develop displays. Survey park to determine forest conditions and distribution and abundance of fauna and flora. **SKILLS—**Management of Personnel Resources; Management of Financial Resources; Service Orientation; Instructing; Persuasion; Writing; Learning Strategies; Management of Material Resources.

GOE—Interest Area: 01. Agriculture and Natural Resources. **Work Group:** 01.01. Managerial Work in Agriculture and Natural Resources. **PERSONALITY TYPE:** Social. Social occupations frequently involve working with, communicating with, and teaching people. These occupations often involve helping or providing service to others.

P

EDUCATION/TRAINING PROGRAMS—Forest Management/ Forest Resources Management; Forest Sciences; Forestry, General; Forestry, Other; Land Use Planning and Management/Development; Natural Resources and Conservation, Other; Natural Resources Management and Policy, Other; Natural Resources/ Conservation, General; Water, Wetlands, and Marine Resources Management; Wildlife and Wildlands Science and Management. **RELATED KNOWLEDGE/ COURSES—Biology:** Knowledge of plant and animal organisms and their tissues, cells, functions, interdependencies, and interactions with each other and the environment. **Customer and Personal Service:** Knowledge of principles and processes for providing customer and personal services. This includes customer needs assessment, meeting quality standards for services, and evaluation of customer satisfaction. **History and Archeology:** Knowledge of historical events and their causes, indicators, and effects on civilizations and cultures. **Geography:** Knowledge of principles and methods for describing the features of land, sea, and air masses, including their physical characteristics; locations; interrelationships; and distribution of plant, animal, and human life. **Education and Training:** Knowledge of principles and methods for curriculum and training design, teaching and instruction for individuals and groups, and the measurement of training effects. **Sociology and Anthropology:** Knowledge of group behavior and dynamics, societal trends and influences, human migrations, ethnicity, and cultures and their history and origins.

Pediatricians, General

- Annual Earnings: $136,600
- Growth: 24.0%
- Annual Job Openings: 41,000
- Self-Employed: 11.0%
- Part-Time: 9.6%
- Education/Training Required: First professional degree

The job openings listed here are shared with Anesthesiologists; Family and General Practitioners; Internists, General; Obstetricians and Gynecologists; Psychiatrists; and Surgeons.

Industries in Which Income Is Highest

Industry	Average Annual Wage	Number Employed
Ambulatory Health Care Services	$139,640	20,890
Hospitals	$131,710	4,020
Educational Services	$81,220	1,260

Metropolitan Areas Where Income Is Highest

Metropolitan Area	Average Annual Wage	Number Employed
Boston–Cambridge–Quincy, MA–NH	More than $146,500	790
St. Louis, MO–IL	More than $146,500	470
Baltimore–Towson, MD	More than $146,500	440
Cincinnati–Middletown, OH–KY–IN	More than $146,500	410
Salt Lake City, UT	More than $146,500	290

Diagnose, treat, and help prevent children's diseases and injuries. Examine patients or order, perform and interpret diagnostic tests to obtain information on medical condition and determine diagnosis. Examine children regularly to assess their growth and development. Prescribe or administer treatment, therapy, medication, vaccination, and other specialized medical care to treat or prevent illness, disease, or injury in infants and children. Collect, record, and maintain patient information, such as medical history, reports, and examination results. Advise patients, parents or guardians and community members concerning diet, activity, hygiene, and disease prevention. Treat children who have minor illnesses, acute and chronic health problems, and growth and development concerns. Explain procedures and discuss test results or prescribed treatments with patients and parents or guardians. Monitor patients' condition and progress and re-evaluate treatments as necessary. Plan and execute medical care programs to aid in the mental and physical growth and development of children and adolescents. Refer patient to medical specialist or other practitioner when necessary. Direct and coordinate activities of nurses, students, assistants, specialists, therapists, and other medical staff. Provide consulting services to other physicians. Plan, implement, or administer health programs or standards in hospital, business, or community for information, prevention, or treatment of injury or illness. Operate on patients to remove, repair, or improve functioning of diseased or injured body parts and systems. Conduct research to study anatomy and develop or test medications, treatments, or procedures to prevent, or control disease or injury. SKILLS— Social Perceptiveness; Science; Persuasion; Active Learning; Critical Thinking; Instructing; Negotiation; Management of Financial Resources.

GOE—Interest Area: 08. Health Science. Work Group: 08.02. Medicine and Surgery. PERSONALITY TYPE: Investigative. Investigative occupations frequently involve working with ideas and require an extensive amount of thinking. These occupations can involve searching for facts and figuring out problems mentally.

EDUCATION/TRAINING PROGRAMS—Child/Pediatric Neurology; Family Medicine; Neonatal-Perinatal Medicine; Pediatric Cardiology; Pediatric Endocrinology; Pediatric Hemato-Oncology; Pediatric Nephrology; Pediatric Orthopedics; Pediatric Surgery; Pediatrics. RELATED KNOWLEDGE/COURSES— Medicine and Dentistry: Knowledge of the information and techniques needed to diagnose and treat human injuries, diseases, and deformities. This includes symptoms, treatment alternatives, drug properties and interactions, and preventive health-care measures. Therapy and Counseling: Knowledge of principles, methods, and procedures for diagnosis, treatment, and rehabilitation of physical and mental dysfunctions and for career counseling and guidance. Biology: Knowledge of plant and animal organisms and their tissues, cells, functions, interdependencies, and interactions with each other and the environment. Psychology: Knowledge of human behavior and performance; individual differences in ability, personality, and interests; learning and motivation; psychological research methods; and the assessment and treatment of behavioral and affective disorders. Chemistry: Knowledge of the chemical composition, structure, and properties of substances and of the chemical processes and transformations that they undergo. This includes uses of chemicals, their danger signs, production techniques, and disposal methods. Sociology and Anthropology: Knowledge of group behavior and dynamics, societal trends and influences, human migrations, ethnicity, and cultures and their history and origins.

Personal Financial Advisors

- Annual Earnings: $63,500
- Growth: 25.9%
- Annual Job Openings: 17,000
- Self-Employed: 38.9%
- Part-Time: 8.4%
- Education/Training Required: Bachelor's degree

Industries in Which Income Is Highest

Industry	Average Annual Wage	Number Employed
Securities, Commodity Contracts, and Other Financial Investments and Related Activities	$71,070	63,790
Management of Companies and Enterprises	$62,220	1,850
Credit Intermediation and Related Activities	$57,070	22,320
Professional, Scientific, and Technical Services	$53,880	5,510
Insurance Carriers and Related Activities	$53,680	7,890

Metropolitan Areas Where Income Is Highest

Metropolitan Area	Average Annual Wage	Number Employed
Montgomery, AL	More than $146,500	130
Williamsport, PA	More than $146,500	50
Erie, PA	$135,850	50
Youngstown–Warren–Boardman, OH–PA	$128,750	60
Topeka, KS	$119,930	80

Advise clients on financial plans utilizing knowledge of tax and investment strategies, securities, insurance, pension plans, and real estate. Duties include assessing clients' assets, liabilities, cash flow, insurance coverage, tax status, and financial objectives to establish investment strategies. Participate in the selection of candidates for specific financial aid awards. Analyze financial information obtained from clients to determine strategies for meeting clients' financial objectives.

Answer clients' questions about the purposes and details of financial plans and strategies. Build and maintain client bases, keeping current client plans up-to-date and recruiting new clients on an ongoing basis. Contact clients periodically to determine if there have been changes in their financial status. Devise debt liquidation plans that include payoff priorities and timelines. Explain and document for clients the types of services that are to be provided, and the responsibilities to be taken by the personal financial advisor. Explain to individuals and groups the details of financial assistance available to college and university students, such as loans, grants, and scholarships. Guide clients in the gathering of information such as bank account records, income tax returns, life and disability insurance records, pension plan information, and wills. Implement financial planning recommendations, or refer clients to someone who can assist them with plan implementation. Interview clients to determine their current income, expenses, insurance coverage, tax status, financial objectives, risk tolerance, and other information needed to develop a financial plan. Monitor financial market trends to ensure that plans are effective, and to identify any necessary updates. Prepare and interpret for clients information such as investment performance reports, financial document summaries, and income projections. Recommend strategies clients can use to achieve their financial goals and objectives, including specific recommendations in such areas as cash management, insurance coverage, and investment planning. Research and investigate available investment opportunities to determine whether they fit into financial plans. Review clients' accounts and plans regularly to determine whether life changes, economic changes, or financial performance indicate a need for plan reassessment. Sell financial products such as stocks, bonds, mutual funds, and insurance if licensed to do so. **SKILLS**—Service Orientation; Management of Financial Resources; Speaking; Active Listening; Judgment and Decision Making; Mathematics; Critical Thinking; Writing.

GOE—Interest Area: 06. Finance and Insurance. **Work Group:** 06.05. Finance/Insurance Sales and Support. **PERSONALITY TYPE:** Social. Social occupations frequently involve working with, communicating with, and teaching people. These occupations often involve helping or providing service to others.

EDUCATION/TRAINING PROGRAMS Finance, General; Financial Planning and Services. **RELATED**

KNOWLEDGE/COURSES—Economics and Accounting: Knowledge of economic and accounting principles and practices, the financial markets, banking, and the analysis and reporting of financial data. **Mathematics:** Knowledge of arithmetic, algebra, geometry, calculus, and statistics and their applications. **Administration and Management:** Knowledge of business and management principles involved in strategic planning, resource allocation, human resources modeling, leadership technique, production methods, and coordination of people and resources. **Customer and Personal Service:** Knowledge of principles and processes for providing customer and personal services. This includes customer needs assessment, meeting quality standards for services, and evaluation of customer satisfaction.

Petroleum Engineers

- Annual Earnings: $93,000
- Growth: –0.1%
- Annual Job Openings: 1,000
- Self-Employed: 7.2%
- Part-Time: 5.1%
- Education/Training Required: Bachelor's degree

Industries in Which Income Is Highest

Industry	Average Annual Wage	Number Employed
Oil and Gas Extraction	$105,340	7,280
Professional, Scientific, and Technical Services	$88,960	2,000
Support Activities for Mining	$72,160	2,150

Metropolitan Areas Where Income Is Highest

Metropolitan Area	Average Annual Wage	Number Employed
Amarillo, TX	$110,260	70
Houston–Sugar Land–Baytown, TX	$108,270	5,050
Anchorage, AK	$106,550	150
Corpus Christi, TX	$100,940	80
Washington–Arlington–Alexandria, DC–VA–MD–WV	$97,570	60

Devise methods to improve oil and gas well production and determine the need for new or modified tool designs. Oversee drilling and offer technical advice to achieve economical and satisfactory progress. Assess costs and estimate the production capabilities and economic value of oil and gas wells, in order to evaluate the economic viability of potential drilling sites. Monitor production rates, and plan rework processes in order to improve production. Analyze data in order to recommend placement of wells and supplementary processes to enhance production. Specify and supervise well modification and stimulation programs, in order to maximize oil and gas recovery. Direct and monitor the completion and evaluation of wells, well testing, and well surveys. Assist engineering and other personnel to solve operating problems. Develop plans for oil and gas field drilling, and for product recovery and treatment. Maintain records of drilling and production operations. Confer with scientific, engineering, and technical personnel in order to resolve design, research, and testing problems. Write technical reports for engineering and management personnel. Evaluate findings in order to develop, design, or test equipment or processes. Assign work to staff in order to obtain maximum utilization of personnel. Interpret drilling and testing information for personnel. Design and implement environmental controls on oil and gas operations. Coordinate the installation, maintenance, and operation of mining and oil field equipment. Supervise the removal of drilling equipment, the removal of any waste, and the safe return of land to structural stability when wells or pockets are exhausted. Inspect oil and gas wells in order to determine that installations are completed. Simulate reservoir performance for different recovery techniques, using computer models. Take samples in order to assess the amount and quality of oil, the depth at which resources lie, and the equipment needed to properly extract them. Coordinate activities of workers engaged in research, planning, and development. Design or modify mining and oil field machinery and tools, applying engineering principles. **SKILLS—** Management of Financial Resources; Troubleshooting; Operations Analysis; Science; Mathematics; Judgment and Decision Making; Technology Design; Coordination.

GOE—Interest Area: 01. Agriculture and Natural Resources. **Work Group:** 01.02. Resource Science/Engineering for Plants, Animals, and the Environment. **PERSONALITY TYPE:** Realistic. Realistic occupations frequently involve work activities that include

practical, hands-on problems and solutions. They often deal with plants, animals, and real-world materials like wood, tools, and machinery. Many of the occupations require working outside and do not involve a lot of paperwork or working closely with others.

EDUCATION/TRAINING PROGRAM— Petroleum Engineering. **RELATED KNOWLEDGE/ COURSES—Engineering and Technology:** Knowledge of the practical application of engineering science and technology. This includes applying principles, techniques, procedures, and equipment to the design and production of various goods and services. **Physics:** Knowledge and prediction of physical principles and laws and their interrelationships and applications to understanding fluid, material, and atmospheric dynamics and mechanical, electrical, atomic, and subatomic structures and processes. **Geography:** Knowledge of principles and methods for describing the features of land, sea, and air masses, including their physical characteristics; locations; interrelationships; and distribution of plant, animal, and human life. **Chemistry:** Knowledge of the chemical composition, structure, and properties of substances and of the chemical processes and transformations that they undergo. This includes uses of chemicals, their danger signs, production techniques, and disposal methods. **Administration and Management:** Knowledge of business and management principles involved in strategic planning, resource allocation, human resources modeling, leadership technique, production methods, and coordination of people and resources. **Design:** Knowledge of design techniques, tools, and principles involved in production of precision technical plans, blueprints, drawings, and models.

Petroleum Pump System Operators

- Annual Earnings: $51,060
- Growth: –8.6%
- Annual Job Openings: 6,000
- Self-Employed: 0.1%
- Part-Time: 0.8%
- Education/Training Required: Long-term on-the-job training

The job openings listed here are shared with Gaugers; and Petroleum Refinery and Control Panel Operators.

Industries in Which Income Is Highest

Industry	Average Annual Wage	Number Employed
Oil and Gas Extraction	$52,700	8,680
Petroleum and Coal Products Manufacturing	$52,150	21,060
Pipeline Transportation	$50,740	4,530
Support Activities for Mining	$39,420	3,060

Metropolitan Areas Where Income Is Highest

Metropolitan Area	Average Annual Wage	Number Employed
Vallejo–Fairfield, CA	$81,650	90
Los Angeles–Long Beach–Santa Ana, CA	$58,990	1,800
Fairbanks, AK	$58,980	70
Billings, MT	$57,220	420
Denver–Aurora, CO	$55,610	280

Control or operate manifold and pumping systems to circulate liquids through a petroleum refinery. Starts battery of pumps, observes pressure meters and flowmeters, and turns valves to regulate pumping speeds according to schedules. Plans movement of products through lines to processing, storage, and shipping units, utilizing knowledge of interconnections and capacities system. Signals other workers by telephone or radio to operate pumps, open and close valves, and check temperatures. Records operating data, such as products and quantities pumped, stocks used, gauging results, and operating time. Reads operating schedules or instructions from dispatcher. Synchronizes activities with other pumphouses to ensure continuous flow of products and minimum of contamination between products. Turns handwheels to open line valves and direct flow of product. **SKILLS**—Operation and Control; Operation Monitoring; Repairing; Troubleshooting; Equipment Maintenance; Coordination; Systems Analysis.

GOE—Interest Area: 13. Manufacturing. **Work Group:** 13.16. Utility Operation and Energy Distribution. **PERSONALITY TYPE:** Realistic. Realistic occupations frequently involve work activities that include practical, hands-on problems and solutions. They often deal with plants, animals, and real-world materials like wood, tools, and machinery. Many of the occupations require working outside and do not involve a lot of paperwork or working closely with others.

EDUCATION/TRAINING PROGRAM—No data available. **RELATED KNOWLEDGE/COURSES**—**Mechanical Devices:** Knowledge of machines and tools, including their designs, uses, repair, and maintenance. **Chemistry:** Knowledge of the chemical composition, structure, and properties of substances and of the chemical processes and transformations that they undergo. This includes uses of chemicals, their danger signs, production techniques, and disposal methods. **Production and Processing:** Knowledge of raw materials, production processes, quality control, costs, and other techniques for maximizing the effective manufacture and distribution of goods. **Clerical Practices:** Knowledge of administrative and clerical procedures and systems such as word processing, managing files and records, stenography and transcription, designing forms, and other office procedures and terminology. **Engineering and Technology:** Knowledge of the practical application of engineering science and technology. This includes applying principles, techniques, procedures, and equipment to the design and production of various goods and services.

Petroleum Refinery and Control Panel Operators

- Annual Earnings: $51,060
- Growth: –8.6%
- Annual Job Openings: 6,000
- Self-Employed: 0.1%
- Part-Time: 0.8%
- Education/Training Required: Long-term on-the-job training

The job openings listed here are shared with Gaugers and Petroleum Pump System Operators.

Industries in Which Income Is Highest

Industry	Average Annual Wage	Number Employed
Oil and Gas Extraction	$52,700	8,680
Petroleum and Coal Products Manufacturing	$52,150	21,060
Pipeline Transportation	$50,740	4,530
Support Activities for Mining	$39,420	3,060

Metropolitan Areas Where Income Is Highest

Metropolitan Area	Average Annual Wage	Number Employed
Vallejo–Fairfield, CA	$81,650	90
Los Angeles–Long Beach–Santa Ana, CA	$58,990	1,800
Fairbanks, AK	$58,980	70
Billings, MT	$57,220	420
Denver–Aurora, CO	$55,610	280

Analyze specifications and control continuous operation of petroleum refining and processing units. Operate control panel to regulate temperature, pressure, rate of flow, and tank level in petroleum refining unit, according to process schedules. Reads and analyzes specifications, schedules, logs, and test results to determine changes to equipment controls required to produce specified product. Observes instruments, gauges, and meters to verify conformance to specified quality and quantity of product. Inspects equipment and listens for automated warning signals to determine location and nature of malfunction, such as leaks and breakage. Repairs, lubricates, and maintains equipment or reports malfunctioning equipment to supervisor to schedule needed repairs. Compiles and records operating data, instrument readings, documents, and results of laboratory analyses. Cleans interior of processing units by circulating chemicals and solvents within unit. Samples and tests liquids and gases for chemical characteristics and color of products, or sends products to laboratory for analysis. Operates auxiliary equipment and controls multiple processing units during distilling or treating operations. Monitors and adjusts unit controls to ensure safe and efficient operating conditions. Operates control panel to coordinate and regulate process variables and to direct product flow rate, according to prescribed schedules. **SKILLS—** Operation Monitoring; Operation and Control; Equipment Maintenance; Repairing; Science; Troubleshooting; Quality Control Analysis; Mathematics.

GOE—Interest Area: 13. Manufacturing. **Work Group:** 13.16. Utility Operation and Energy Distribution. **PERSONALITY TYPE:** Realistic. Realistic occupations frequently involve work activities that include practical, hands-on problems and solutions. They often deal with plants, animals, and real-world materials like wood, tools, and machinery. Many of the occupations require working outside and do not involve a lot of paperwork or working closely with others.

EDUCATION/TRAINING PROGRAM—No data available. **RELATED KNOWLEDGE/COURSES— Chemistry:** Knowledge of the chemical composition, structure, and properties of substances and of the chemical processes and transformations that they undergo. This includes uses of chemicals, their danger signs, production techniques, and disposal methods. **Mechanical Devices:** Knowledge of machines and tools, including their designs, uses, repair, and maintenance. **Physics:** Knowledge and prediction of physical principles and laws and their interrelationships and applications to understanding fluid, material, and atmospheric dynamics and mechanical, electrical, atomic, and subatomic structures and processes. **Production and Processing:** Knowledge of raw materials, production processes, quality control, costs, and other techniques for maximizing the effective manufacture and distribution of goods. **Engineering and Technology:** Knowledge of the practical application of engineering science and technology. This includes applying principles, techniques, procedures, and equipment to the design and production of various goods and services. **Public Safety and Security:** Knowledge of relevant equipment, policies, procedures, and strategies to promote effective local, state, or national security operations for the protection of people, data, property, and institutions.

Pharmacists

- ◎ Annual Earnings: $89,820
- ◎ Growth: 24.6%
- ◎ Annual Job Openings: 16,000
- ◎ Self-Employed: 1.7%
- ◎ Part-Time: 21.2%
- ◎ Education/Training Required: First professional degree

Industries in Which Income Is Highest

Industry	Average Annual Wage	Number Employed
General Merchandise Stores	$92,790	22,030
Health and Personal Care Stores	$90,880	103,230
Food and Beverage Stores	$90,820	18,770
Insurance Carriers and Related Activities	$90,090	1,140
Ambulatory Health Care Services	$89,600	6,390

Metropolitan Areas Where Income Is Highest

Metropolitan Area	Average Annual Wage	Number Employed
Chico, CA	$113,900	210
Merced, CA	$109,470	70
Salinas, CA	$109,090	170
Madera, CA	$108,850	90
Brownsville–Harlingen, TX	$108,530	170

Compound and dispense medications following prescriptions issued by physicians, dentists, or other authorized medical practitioners. Review prescriptions to assure accuracy, to ascertain the needed ingredients, and to evaluate their suitability. Provide information and advice regarding drug interactions, side effects, dosage and proper medication storage. Analyze prescribing trends to monitor patient compliance and to prevent excessive usage or harmful interactions. Order and purchase pharmaceutical supplies, medical supplies, and drugs, maintaining stock and storing and handling it properly. Maintain records, such as pharmacy files, patient profiles, charge system files, inventories, control records for radioactive nuclei, and registries of poisons, narcotics, and controlled drugs. Provide specialized services to help patients manage conditions such as diabetes, asthma, smoking cessation, or high blood pressure. Advise customers on the selection of medication brands, medical equipment and health-care supplies. Collaborate with other health care professionals to plan, monitor, review, and evaluate the quality and effectiveness of drugs and drug regimens, providing advice on drug applications and characteristics. Compound and dispense medications as prescribed by doctors and dentists, by calculating, weighing, measuring, and mixing ingredients, or oversee these activities. Offer health promotion and preven-

tion activities, for example, training people to use devices such as blood pressure or diabetes monitors. Refer patients to other health professionals and agencies when appropriate. Prepare sterile solutions and infusions for use in surgical procedures, emergency rooms, or patients' homes. Plan, implement, and maintain procedures for mixing, packaging, and labeling pharmaceuticals, according to policy and legal requirements, to ensure quality, security, and proper disposal. Assay radiopharmaceuticals, verify rates of disintegration, and calculate the volume required to produce the desired results, to ensure proper dosages. Manage pharmacy operations, hiring and supervising staff, performing administrative duties, and buying and selling non-pharmaceutical merchandise. Work in hospitals, clinics, or for HMOs, dispensing prescriptions, serving as a medical team consultants, or specializing in specific drug therapy areas such as oncology or nuclear pharmacotherapy. **SKILLS**—Instructing; Social Perceptiveness; Reading Comprehension; Active Listening; Science; Critical Thinking; Speaking; Persuasion.

GOE—Interest Area: 08. Health Science. **Work Group:** 08.02. Medicine and Surgery. **PERSONALITY TYPE:** Investigative. Investigative occupations frequently involve working with ideas and require an extensive amount of thinking. These occupations can involve searching for facts and figuring out problems mentally.

EDUCATION/TRAINING PROGRAMS—Clinical and Industrial Drug Development (MS, PhD); Clinical, Hospital, and Managed Care Pharmacy (MS, PhD); Industrial and Physical Pharmacy and Cosmetic Sciences (MS, PhD); Medicinal and Pharmaceutical Chemistry (MS, PhD); Natural Products Chemistry and Pharmacognosy (MS, PhD); Pharmaceutics and Drug Design (MS, PhD); Pharmacoeconomics/Pharmaceutical Economics (MS, PhD); Pharmacy (PharmD, BS/BPharm); Pharmacy Administration and Pharmacy Policy and Regulatory Affairs (MS, PhD); others. **RELATED KNOWLEDGE/COURSES**—**Medicine and Dentistry:** Knowledge of the information and techniques needed to diagnose and treat human injuries, diseases, and deformities. This includes symptoms, treatment alternatives, drug properties and interactions, and preventive health-care measures. **Chemistry:** Knowledge of the chemical composition, structure, and properties of substances and of the chemical processes and transformations that they undergo. This includes uses of chemicals, their danger signs, production techniques, and disposal methods. **Therapy**

and **Counseling:** Knowledge of principles, methods, and procedures for diagnosis, treatment, and rehabilitation of physical and mental dysfunctions and for career counseling and guidance. **Psychology:** Knowledge of human behavior and performance; individual differences in ability, personality, and interests; learning and motivation; psychological research methods; and the assessment and treatment of behavioral and affective disorders. **Customer and Personal Service:** Knowledge of principles and processes for providing customer and personal services. This includes customer needs assessment, meeting quality standards for services, and evaluation of customer satisfaction. **Biology:** Knowledge of plant and animal organisms and their tissues, cells, functions, interdependencies, and interactions with each other and the environment.

Philosophy and Religion Teachers, Postsecondary

- Annual Earnings: $53,210
- Growth: 32.2%
- Annual Job Openings: 329,000
- Self-Employed: 0.4%
- Part-Time: 27.3%
- Education/Training Required: Master's degree

Our sources did not provide separate job openings data for this occupation. The job openings listed here are shared with 35 other postsecondary teaching occupations. For a complete list, see the beginning of this section.

Industries in Which Income Is Highest

Industry	Average Annual Wage	Number Employed
Educational Services	$53,380	18,160

Metropolitan Areas Where Income Is Highest

Metropolitan Area	Average Annual Wage	Number Employed
Durham, NC	$94,560	100
Birmingham–Hoover, AL	$81,580	80
Springfield, MA–CT	$75,790	80
San Francisco–Oakland–Fremont, CA	$70,220	220
Providence–Fall River–Warwick, RI–MA	$70,090	110

Teach courses in philosophy, religion, and theology. Evaluate and grade students' class work, assignments, and papers. Initiate, facilitate, and moderate classroom discussions. Prepare and deliver lectures to undergraduate and/or graduate students on topics such as ethics, logic, and contemporary religious thought. Prepare course materials such as syllabi, homework assignments, and handouts. Compile, administer, and grade examinations or assign this work to others. Keep abreast of developments in their field by reading current literature, talking with colleagues, and participating in professional conferences. Maintain student attendance records, grades, and other required records. Plan, evaluate, and revise curricula, course content, and course materials and methods of instruction. Maintain regularly scheduled office hours in order to advise and assist students. Select and obtain materials and supplies such as textbooks. Advise students on academic and vocational curricula and on career issues. Conduct research in a particular field of knowledge and publish findings in professional journals, books, and/or electronic media. Perform administrative duties such as serving as department head. Serve on academic or administrative committees that deal with institutional policies, departmental matters, and academic issues. Collaborate with colleagues to address teaching and research issues. Participate in campus and community events. Compile bibliographies of specialized materials for outside reading assignments. Participate in student recruitment, registration, and placement activities. Supervise undergraduate and/or graduate teaching, internship, and research work. **SKILLS**—Instructing; Writing; Critical Thinking; Learning Strategies; Reading Comprehension; Social Perceptiveness; Speaking; Persuasion.

GOE—Interest Area: 05. Education and Training. Work Group: 05.03. Postsecondary and Adult Teaching and Instructing. PERSONALITY TYPE: No data available.

EDUCATION/TRAINING PROGRAMS—Bible/ Biblical Studies; Buddhist Studies; Christian Studies; Divinity/Ministry (BD, MDiv.); Ethics; Hindu Studies; Missions/Missionary Studies and Missiology; Pastoral Counseling and Specialized Ministries, Other; Pastoral Studies/Counseling; Philosophy; Philosophy and Religion, Other; Philosophy, Other; Pre-Theology/Pre-Ministerial Studies; Rabbinical Studies (M.H.L./Rav); Religion/Religious Studies; Religious Education; Religious/Sacred Music; Talmudic Studies; others. RELATED KNOWLEDGE/COURSES— **Philosophy and Theology:** Knowledge of different philosophical systems and religions. This includes their basic principles, values, ethics, ways of thinking, customs, and practices and their impact on human culture. **History and Archeology:** Knowledge of historical events and their causes, indicators, and effects on civilizations and cultures. **Education and Training:** Knowledge of principles and methods for curriculum and training design, teaching and instruction for individuals and groups, and the measurement of training effects. **English Language:** Knowledge of the structure and content of the English language, including the meaning and spelling of words, rules of composition, and grammar. **Sociology and Anthropology:** Knowledge of group behavior and dynamics, societal trends and influences, human migrations, ethnicity, and cultures and their history and origins. **Foreign Language:** Knowledge of the structure and content of a foreign (non-English) language, including the meaning and spelling of words, rules of composition and grammar, and pronunciation.

Physical Therapists

- Annual Earnings: $63,080
- Growth: 36.7%
- Annual Job Openings: 13,000
- Self-Employed: 4.5%
- Part-Time: 24.8%
- Education/Training Required: Master's degree

Industries in Which Income Is Highest

Industry	Average Annual Wage	Number Employed
Administrative and Support Services	$66,510	3,240
Nursing and Residential Care Facilities	$64,520	11,860
Ambulatory Health Care Services	$63,770	73,600
Hospitals	$62,660	50,410
Federal, State, and Local Government	$61,720	2,760

Metropolitan Areas Where Income Is Highest

Metropolitan Area	Average Annual Wage	Number Employed
Beaumont–Port Arthur, TX	$83,790	140
Modesto, CA	$82,400	250
Visalia–Porterville, CA	$80,470	200
Longview, TX	$78,970	110
Trenton–Ewing, NJ	$78,780	220

Assess, plan, organize, and participate in rehabilitative programs that improve mobility, relieve pain, increase strength, and decrease or prevent deformity of patients suffering from disease or injury. Plan, prepare and carry out individually designed programs of physical treatment to maintain, improve or restore physical functioning, alleviate pain and prevent physical dysfunction in patients. Perform and document an initial exam, evaluating the data to identify problems and determine a diagnosis prior to intervention. Evaluate effects of treatment at various stages and adjust treatments to achieve maximum benefit. Administer manual exercises, massage and/or traction to help relieve pain, increase the patient's strength, and decrease or prevent deformity and crippling. Instruct patient and family in treatment procedures to be continued at home. Confer with the patient, medical practitioners and appropriate others to plan, implement and assess the intervention program. Review physician's referral and patient's medical records to help determine diagnosis and physical therapy treatment required. Record prognosis, treatment, response, and progress in patient's chart or enter information into computer. Obtain patients' informed consent to proposed interventions. Discharge patient from physical therapy when goals or projected outcomes have been attained and provide for appropriate follow-up care or referrals. Test and measure patient's strength, motor development and function, sensory perception, functional capacity, and respiratory and circulatory efficiency and record data. Identify and document goals, anticipated progress and plans for reevaluation. Provide information to the patient about the proposed intervention, its material risks and expected benefits and any reasonable alternatives. Inform the patient when diagnosis reveals findings outside their scope and refer to an appropriate practitioner. Direct and supervise supportive personnel, assessing their competence, delegating specific tasks to them and establishing channels of communication. Administer treatment involving application of physical agents, using equipment, moist packs, ultraviolet and infrared lamps, and ultrasound machines. Teach physical therapy students as well as those in other health professions. Evaluate, fit, and adjust prosthetic and orthotic devices and recommend modification to orthotist. SKILLS—Science; Instructing; Social Perceptiveness; Reading Comprehension; Learning Strategies; Service Orientation; Time Management; Monitoring.

GOE—Interest Area: 08. Health Science. Work Group: 08.07. Medical Therapy. PERSONALITY TYPE: Social. Social occupations frequently involve working with, communicating with, and teaching people. These occupations often involve helping or providing service to others.

EDUCATION/TRAINING PROGRAMS— Kinesiotherapy/Kinesiotherapist; Physical Therapy/ Therapist. RELATED KNOWLEDGE/COURSES— Therapy and Counseling: Knowledge of principles, methods, and procedures for diagnosis, treatment, and rehabilitation of physical and mental dysfunctions and for career counseling and guidance. Psychology: Knowledge of human behavior and performance; individual differences in ability, personality, and interests; learning and motivation; psychological research methods; and the assessment and treatment of behavioral and affective disorders. Medicine and Dentistry: Knowledge of the information and techniques needed to diagnose and treat human injuries, diseases, and deformities. This includes symptoms, treatment alternatives, drug properties and interactions, and preventive health-care measures. Biology: Knowledge of plant and animal organisms and their tissues, cells, functions, interdependencies, and interactions with each other and the environment. Customer and Personal Service:

Knowledge of principles and processes for providing customer and personal services. This includes customer needs assessment, meeting quality standards for services, and evaluation of customer satisfaction. Education and Training: Knowledge of principles and methods for curriculum and training design, teaching and instruction for individuals and groups, and the measurement of training effects.

Physician Assistants

- Annual Earnings: $72,030
- Growth: 49.6%
- Annual Job Openings: 10,000
- Self-Employed: 1.3%
- Part-Time: 16.3%
- Education/Training Required: Bachelor's degree

Industries in Which Income Is Highest

Industry	Average Annual Wage	Number Employed
Administrative and Support Services	$79,600	1,110
Federal, State, and Local Government	$73,910	3,260
Hospitals	$73,110	14,330
Ambulatory Health Care Services	$71,360	41,970
Educational Services	$68,980	1,520

Metropolitan Areas Where Income Is Highest

Metropolitan Area	Average Annual Wage	Number Employed
Evansville, IN–KY	$98,400	70
Barnstable Town, MA	$95,870	130
Redding, CA	$92,190	50
San Jose–Sunnyvale–Santa Clara, CA	$88,230	150
Waterbury, CT	$87,740	50

Provide healthcare services typically performed by a physician, under the supervision of a physician. Conduct complete physicals, provide treatment, and counsel patients. May, in some cases, prescribe medication. Must graduate from an accredited educational program for physician assistants. Examine

P

patients to obtain information about their physical condition. Interpret diagnostic test results for deviations from normal. Make tentative diagnoses and decisions about management and treatment of patients. Obtain, compile and record patient medical data, including health history, progress notes and results of physical examination. Administer or order diagnostic tests, such as X-ray, electrocardiogram, and laboratory tests. Prescribe therapy or medication with physician approval. Perform therapeutic procedures, such as injections, immunizations, suturing and wound care, and infection management. Instruct and counsel patients about prescribed therapeutic regimens, normal growth and development, family planning, emotional problems of daily living, and health maintenance. Provide physicians with assistance during surgery or complicated medical procedures. Supervise and coordinate activities of technicians and technical assistants. Visit and observe patients on hospital rounds or house calls, updating charts, ordering therapy, and reporting back to physician. **SKILLS**—Science; Social Perceptiveness; Instructing; Critical Thinking; Reading Comprehension; Time Management; Active Listening; Active Learning.

GOE—Interest Area: 08. Health Science. **Work Group:** 08.02. Medicine and Surgery. **PERSONALITY TYPE:** Investigative. Investigative occupations frequently involve working with ideas and require an extensive amount of thinking. These occupations can involve searching for facts and figuring out problems mentally.

EDUCATION/TRAINING PROGRAM—Physician Assistant. **RELATED KNOWLEDGE/COURSES**— **Medicine and Dentistry:** Knowledge of the information and techniques needed to diagnose and treat human injuries, diseases, and deformities. This includes symptoms, treatment alternatives, drug properties and interactions, and preventive health-care measures. **Biology:** Knowledge of plant and animal organisms and their tissues, cells, functions, interdependencies, and interactions with each other and the environment. **Therapy and Counseling:** Knowledge of principles, methods, and procedures for diagnosis, treatment, and rehabilitation of physical and mental dysfunctions and for career counseling and guidance. **Psychology:** Knowledge of human behavior and performance; individual differences in ability, personality, and interests; learning and motivation; psychological research methods; and the assessment and treatment of behavioral and affective disorders. **Customer and Personal**

Service: Knowledge of principles and processes for providing customer and personal services. This includes customer needs assessment, meeting quality standards for services, and evaluation of customer satisfaction. **Chemistry:** Knowledge of the chemical composition, structure, and properties of substances and of the chemical processes and transformations that they undergo. This includes uses of chemicals, their danger signs, production techniques, and disposal methods.

Physicists

- Annual Earnings: $89,810
- Growth: 7.0%
- Annual Job Openings: 1,000
- Self-Employed: 0.0%
- Part-Time: 8.0%
- Education/Training Required: Doctoral degree

Industries in Which Income Is Highest

Industry	Average Annual Wage	Number Employed
Federal, State, and Local Government	$97,700	3,530
Professional, Scientific, and Technical Services	$91,650	6,500
Educational Services	$57,650	2,030

Metropolitan Areas Where Income Is Highest

Metropolitan Area	Average Annual Wage	Number Employed
Washington–Arlington–Alexandria, DC–VA–MD–WV	$107,660	1,570
Miami–Fort Lauderdale–Miami Beach, FL	$106,860	50
Los Angeles–Long Beach–Santa Ana, CA	$105,040	500
Huntsville, AL	$99,520	120
Dallas–Fort Worth–Arlington, TX	$99,320	90

Conduct research into the phases of physical phenomena, develop theories and laws on the basis of observation and experiments, and devise methods to apply laws and theories to industry and other fields. Analyze data from research conducted to detect and measure physical phenomena. Describe and express observations and conclusions in mathematical terms.

Design computer simulations to model physical data so that it can be better understood. Develop theories and laws on the basis of observation and experiments, and apply these theories and laws to problems in areas such as nuclear energy, optics, and aerospace technology. Observe the structure and properties of matter, and the transformation and propagation of energy, using equipment such as masers, lasers, and telescopes, in order to explore and identify the basic principles governing these phenomena. Perform complex calculations as part of the analysis and evaluation of data, using computers. Report experimental results by writing papers for scientific journals or by presenting information at scientific conferences. Collaborate with other scientists in the design, development, and testing of experimental, industrial, or medical equipment, instrumentation, and procedures. Conduct application evaluations and analyze results in order to determine commercial, industrial, scientific, medical, military, or other uses for electro-optical devices. Develop manufacturing, assembly, and fabrication processes of lasers, masers, infrared, and other light-emitting and light-sensitive devices. Provide support services for activities such as radiation therapy, diagnostic imaging, or seismology. Teach physics to students. Advise authorities of procedures to be followed in radiation incidents or hazards, and assist in civil defense planning. Conduct research pertaining to potential environmental impacts of atomic energy-related industrial development in order to determine licensing qualifications. Develop standards of permissible concentrations of radioisotopes in liquids and gases. Direct testing and monitoring of contamination of radioactive equipment, and recording of personnel and plant area radiation exposure data. SKILLS—Science; Mathematics; Writing; Technology Design; Active Learning; Reading Comprehension; Management of Personnel Resources; Operations Analysis.

GOE—Interest Area: 15. Scientific Research, Engineering, and Mathematics. Work Group: 15.02. Physical Sciences. PERSONALITY TYPE: Investigative. Investigative occupations frequently involve working with ideas and require an extensive amount of thinking. These occupations can involve searching for facts and figuring out problems mentally.

EDUCATION/TRAINING PROGRAMS— Acoustics; Astrophysics; Atomic/Molecular Physics;

Elementary Particle Physics; Health/Medical Physics; Nuclear Physics; Optics/Optical Sciences; Physics, General; Physics, Other; Plasma and High-Temperature Physics; Solid State and Low-Temperature Physics; Theoretical and Mathematical Physics. RELATED KNOWLEDGE/COURSES—Physics: Knowledge and prediction of physical principles and laws and their interrelationships and applications to understanding fluid, material, and atmospheric dynamics and mechanical, electrical, atomic, and subatomic structures and processes. Education and Training: Knowledge of principles and methods for curriculum and training design, teaching and instruction for individuals and groups, and the measurement of training effects. Mathematics: Knowledge of arithmetic, algebra, geometry, calculus, and statistics and their applications. Engineering and Technology: Knowledge of the practical application of engineering science and technology. This includes applying principles, techniques, procedures, and equipment to the design and production of various goods and services. Design: Knowledge of design techniques, tools, and principles involved in production of precision technical plans, blueprints, drawings, and models. Production and Processing: Knowledge of raw materials, production processes, quality control, costs, and other techniques for maximizing the effective manufacture and distribution of goods.

Physics Teachers, Postsecondary

- Annual Earnings: $65,880
- Growth: 32.2%
- Annual Job Openings: 329,000
- Self-Employed: 0.4%
- Part-Time: 27.3%
- Education/Training Required: Master's degree

Our sources did not provide separate job openings data for this occupation. The job openings listed here are shared with 35 other postsecondary teaching occupations. For a complete list, see the beginning of this section.

Industries in Which Income Is Highest

Industry	Average Annual Wage	Number Employed
Educational Services	$65,720	13,230

Metropolitan Areas Where Income Is Highest

Metropolitan Area	Average Annual Wage	Number Employed
Boston–Cambridge–Quincy, MA–NH	$84,720	500
Allentown–Bethlehem–Easton, PA–NJ	$81,420	60
Providence–Fall River–Warwick, RI–MA	$80,500	70
New York–Northern New Jersey–Long Island, NY–NJ–PA	$79,070	320
Columbus, OH	$77,200	110

Teach courses pertaining to the laws of matter and energy. Includes both teachers primarily engaged in teaching and those who do a combination of both teaching and research. Evaluate and grade students' class work, laboratory work, assignments, and papers. Prepare and deliver lectures to undergraduate and/or graduate students on topics such as quantum mechanics, particle physics, and optics. Compile, administer, and grade examinations or assign this work to others. Maintain student attendance records, grades, and other required records. Supervise students' laboratory work. Prepare course materials such as syllabi, homework assignments, and handouts. Maintain regularly scheduled office hours in order to advise and assist students. Supervise undergraduate and/or graduate teaching, internship, and research work. Keep abreast of developments in their field by reading current literature, talking with colleagues, and participating in professional conferences. Plan, evaluate, and revise curricula, course content, and course materials and methods of instruction. Initiate, facilitate, and moderate classroom discussions. Conduct research in a particular field of knowledge and publish findings in professional journals, books, and/or electronic media. Advise students on academic and vocational curricula and on career issues. Select and obtain materials and supplies such as textbooks and laboratory equipment. Collaborate with colleagues to address teaching and research issues.

Participate in student recruitment, registration, and placement activities. Serve on academic or administrative committees that deal with institutional policies, departmental matters, and academic issues. Write grant proposals to procure external research funding. Perform administrative duties such as serving as department head. **SKILLS**—Science; Instructing; Programming; Mathematics; Learning Strategies; Critical Thinking; Active Learning; Reading Comprehension.

GOE—Interest Area: 05. Education and Training. **Work Group:** 05.03. Postsecondary and Adult Teaching and Instructing. **PERSONALITY TYPE:** Investigative. Investigative occupations frequently involve working with ideas and require an extensive amount of thinking. These occupations can involve searching for facts and figuring out problems mentally.

EDUCATION/TRAINING PROGRAMS—Acoustics; Atomic/Molecular Physics; Elementary Particle Physics; Nuclear Physics; Optics/Optical Sciences; Physics, General; Physics, Other; Plasma and High-Temperature Physics; Solid State and Low-Temperature Physics; Theoretical and Mathematical Physics. **RELATED KNOWLEDGE/COURSES—Physics:** Knowledge and prediction of physical principles and laws and their interrelationships and applications to understanding fluid, material, and atmospheric dynamics and mechanical, electrical, atomic, and subatomic structures and processes. **Education and Training:** Knowledge of principles and methods for curriculum and training design, teaching and instruction for individuals and groups, and the measurement of training effects. **Mathematics:** Knowledge of arithmetic, algebra, geometry, calculus, and statistics and their applications. **Chemistry:** Knowledge of the chemical composition, structure, and properties of substances and of the chemical processes and transformations that they undergo. This includes uses of chemicals, their danger signs, production techniques, and disposal methods. **Computers and Electronics:** Knowledge of circuit boards, processors, chips, electronic equipment, and computer hardware and software, including applications and programming. **Engineering and Technology:** Knowledge of the practical application of engineering science and technology. This includes applying principles, techniques, procedures, and equipment to the design and production of various goods and services.

Pile-Driver Operators

- Annual Earnings: $48,900
- Growth: 11.9%
- Annual Job Openings: fewer than 500
- Self-Employed: 0.0%
- Part-Time: 16.7%
- Education/Training Required: Moderate-term on-the-job training

Industries in Which Income Is Highest

Industry	Average Annual Wage	Number Employed
Administrative and Support Services	$61,450	40
Specialty Trade Contractors	$57,970	920
Heavy and Civil Engineering Construction	$49,250	2,890
Construction of Buildings	$40,580	220

Metropolitan Areas Where Income Is Highest

Metropolitan Area	Average Annual Wage	Number Employed
Chicago–Naperville–Joliet, IL–IN–WI	$74,020	300
Los Angeles–Long Beach–Santa Ana, CA	$66,760	160
San Francisco–Oakland–Fremont, CA	$66,590	170
New York–Northern New Jersey–Long Island, NY–NJ–PA	$62,810	120
Seattle–Tacoma–Bellevue, WA	$62,140	190

Operate pile drivers mounted on skids, barges, crawler treads, or locomotive cranes to drive pilings for retaining walls, bulkheads, and foundations of structures, such as buildings, bridges, and piers. Clean, lubricate, and refill equipment. Conduct pre-operational checks on equipment to ensure proper functioning. Drive pilings to provide support for buildings or other structures, using heavy equipment with a pile driver head. Move hand and foot levers of hoisting equipment to position piling leads, hoist piling into leads, and position hammers over pilings. Move levers and turn valves to activate power hammers, or to raise and lower drophammers that drive piles to required depths. **SKILLS**—Operation and Control; Operation Monitoring.

GOE—Interest Area: 02. Architecture and Construction. **Work Group:** 02.04. Construction Crafts. **PERSONALITY TYPE:** Realistic. Realistic occupations frequently involve work activities that include practical, hands-on problems and solutions. They often deal with plants, animals, and real-world materials like wood, tools, and machinery. Many of the occupations require working outside and do not involve a lot of paperwork or working closely with others.

EDUCATION/TRAINING PROGRAM—Construction/Heavy Equipment/Earthmoving Equipment Operation. **RELATED KNOWLEDGE/COURSES**—**Building and Construction:** Knowledge of the materials, methods, and tools involved in the construction or repair of houses, buildings, or other structures such as highways and roads. **Engineering and Technology:** Knowledge of the practical application of engineering science and technology. This includes applying principles, techniques, procedures, and equipment to the design and production of various goods and services. **Mechanical Devices:** Knowledge of machines and tools, including their designs, uses, repair, and maintenance.

Pilots, Ship

- Annual Earnings: $50,940
- Growth: 4.8%
- Annual Job Openings: 2,000
- Self-Employed: 5.4%
- Part-Time: 8.3%
- Education/Training Required: Work experience in a related occupation

The job openings listed here are shared with Mates—Ship, Boat, and Barge; and Ship and Boat Captains.

Industries in Which Income Is Highest

Industry	Average Annual Wage	Number Employed
Support Activities for Transportation	$54,490	8,480
Water Transportation	$54,410	9,820
Federal, State, and Local Government	$53,760	1,600
Rental and Leasing Services	$52,030	1,360
Scenic and Sightseeing Transportation	$36,810	2,990

P

Metropolitan Areas Where Income Is Highest

Metropolitan Area	Average Annual Wage	Number Employed
Baton Rouge, LA	$67,280	470
Bremerton–Silverdale, WA	$66,460	70
New York–Northern New Jersey–Long Island, NY–NJ–PA	$62,450	1,970
Lake Charles, LA	$61,120	210
Seattle–Tacoma–Bellevue, WA	$60,990	850

Command ships to steer them into and out of harbors, estuaries, straits, and sounds, and on rivers, lakes, and bays. Must be licensed by U.S. Coast Guard with limitations indicating class and tonnage of vessels for which license is valid and route and waters that may be piloted. Serve as a vessel's docking master upon arrival at a port and when at a berth. Set ships' courses that avoid reefs, outlying shoals, and other hazards, utilizing navigational aids such as lighthouses and buoys. Steer ships into and out of berths, or signal tugboat captains to berth and unberth ships. Advise ships' masters on harbor rules and customs procedures. Learn to operate new technology systems and procedures, through the use of instruction, simulators, and models. Maintain and repair boats and equipment. Maintain ship logs. Oversee cargo storage on or below decks. Provide assistance in maritime rescue operations. Relieve crew members on tugs and launches. Report to appropriate authorities any violations of federal or state pilotage laws. Make nautical maps. Operate amphibious craft during troop landings. Consult maps, charts, weather reports, and navigation equipment to determine and direct ship movements. Direct courses and speeds of ships, based on specialized knowledge of local winds, weather, water depths, tides, currents, and hazards. Give directions to crew members who are steering ships. Operate ship-to-shore radios to exchange information needed for ship operations. Prevent ships under their navigational control from engaging in unsafe operations. Provide assistance to vessels approaching or leaving seacoasts, navigating harbors, and docking and undocking. **SKILLS**—Operation and Control; Systems Analysis; Operation Monitoring; Judgment and Decision Making; Systems Evaluation; Management of Personnel Resources; Monitoring; Science.

GOE—Interest Area: 16. Transportation, Distribution, and Logistics. **Work Group:** 16.05. Water Vehicle Operation. **PERSONALITY TYPE:** Realistic.

Realistic occupations frequently involve work activities that include practical, hands-on problems and solutions. They often deal with plants, animals, and real-world materials like wood, tools, and machinery. Many of the occupations require working outside and do not involve a lot of paperwork or working closely with others.

EDUCATION/TRAINING PROGRAMS—Commercial Fishing; Marine Science/Merchant Marine Officer; Marine Transportation Services, Other. **RELATED KNOWLEDGE/COURSES**—**Transportation:** Knowledge of principles and methods for moving people or goods by air, rail, sea, or road, including the relative costs and benefits. **Geography:** Knowledge of principles and methods for describing the features of land, sea, and air masses, including their physical characteristics; locations; interrelationships; and distribution of plant, animal, and human life. **Physics:** Knowledge and prediction of physical principles and laws and their interrelationships and applications to understanding fluid, material, and atmospheric dynamics and mechanical, electrical, atomic, and subatomic structures and processes. **Law and Government:** Knowledge of laws, legal codes, court procedures, precedents, government regulations, executive orders, agency rules, and the democratic political process. **Public Safety and Security:** Knowledge of relevant equipment, policies, procedures, and strategies to promote effective local, state, or national security operations for the protection of people, data, property, and institutions. **Engineering and Technology:** Knowledge of the practical application of engineering science and technology. This includes applying principles, techniques, procedures, and equipment to the design and production of various goods and services.

Plant Scientists

- Annual Earnings: $54,530
- Growth: 13.9%
- Annual Job Openings: 1,000
- Self-Employed: 35.9%
- Part-Time: 10.3%
- Education/Training Required: Bachelor's degree

The job openings listed here are shared with Soil Scientists.

Industries in Which Income Is Highest

Industry	Average Annual Wage	Number Employed
Federal, State, and Local Government	$61,680	3,450
Merchant Wholesalers, Nondurable Goods	$59,820	1,410
Professional, Scientific, and Technical Services	$49,710	2,710
Educational Services	$44,270	1,530

Metropolitan Areas Where Income Is Highest

Metropolitan Area	Average Annual Wage	Number Employed
New Haven, CT	$89,110	50
Denver–Aurora, CO	$88,830	90
Seattle–Tacoma–Bellevue, WA	$81,720	90
Washington–Arlington–Alexandria, DC–VA–MD–WV	$79,370	330
Fort Collins–Loveland, CO	$66,400	70

Conduct research in breeding, production, and yield of plants or crops, and control of pests. Conducts research to determine best methods of planting, spraying, cultivating, and harvesting horticultural products. Studies crop production to discover effects of various climatic and soil conditions on crops. Conducts experiments and investigations to determine methods of storing, processing, and transporting horticultural products. Aids in control and elimination of agricultural, structural and forest pests by developing new and improved pesticides. Identifies and classifies species of insects and allied forms, such as mites and spiders. Improves bee strains, utilizing selective breeding by artificial insemination. Conducts experiments regarding causes of bee diseases and factors affecting yields of nectar pollen on various plants visited by bees. Studies insect distribution and habitat and recommends methods to prevent importation and spread of injurious species. Develops methods for control of noxious weeds, crop diseases, and insect pests. Experiments to develop new or improved varieties of products having specific features, such as higher yield, resistance to disease, size, or maturity. **SKILLS**—Science; Writing; Critical Thinking; Active Learning; Quality Control Analysis; Complex Problem Solving; Operations Analysis; Reading Comprehension.

GOE—Interest Area: 01. Agriculture and Natural Resources. **Work Group:** 01.02. Resource Science/Engineering for Plants, Animals, and the Environment. **PERSONALITY TYPE:** Investigative. Investigative occupations frequently involve working with ideas and require an extensive amount of thinking. These occupations can involve searching for facts and figuring out problems mentally.

EDUCATION/TRAINING PROGRAMS—Agricultural and Horticultural Plant Breeding; Agriculture, General; Agronomy and Crop Science; Horticultural Science; Plant Protection and Integrated Pest Management; Plant Sciences, General; Plant Sciences, Other; Range Science and Management. **RELATED KNOWLEDGE/COURSES**—**Food Production:** Knowledge of techniques and equipment for planting, growing, and harvesting food products (both plant and animal) for consumption, including storage/handling techniques. **Biology:** Knowledge of plant and animal organisms and their tissues, cells, functions, interdependencies, and interactions with each other and the environment. **Chemistry:** Knowledge of the chemical composition, structure, and properties of substances and of the chemical processes and transformations that they undergo. This includes uses of chemicals, their danger signs, production techniques, and disposal methods. **English Language:** Knowledge of the structure and content of the English language, including the meaning and spelling of words, rules of composition, and grammar. **Communications and Media:** Knowledge of media production, communication, and dissemination techniques and methods. This includes alternative ways to inform and entertain via written, oral, and visual media. **Education and Training:** Knowledge of principles and methods for curriculum and training design, teaching and instruction for individuals and groups, and the measurement of training effects.

Podiatrists

- Annual Earnings: $100,550
- Growth: 16.2%
- Annual Job Openings: 1,000
- Self-Employed: 19.8%
- Part-Time: 22.4%
- Education/Training Required: First professional degree

P

Industries in Which Income Is Highest

Industry	Average Annual Wage	Number Employed
Ambulatory Health Care Services	$103,140	7,340
Federal, State, and Local Government	$92,640	560
Hospitals	$80,210	300

Metropolitan Areas Where Income Is Highest

Metropolitan Area	Average Annual Wage	Number Employed
Portland–Vancouver–Beaverton, OR–WA	More than $146,500	60
Denver–Aurora, CO	More than $146,500	50
Riverside–San Bernardino–Ontario, CA	More than $146,500	40
Virginia Beach–Norfolk–Newport News, VA–NC	More than $146,500	40
Charlotte–Gastonia–Concord, NC–SC	More than $146,500	30

Diagnose and treat diseases and deformities of the human foot. Treat bone, muscle, and joint disorders affecting the feet. Diagnose diseases and deformities of the foot using medical histories, physical examinations, x-rays, and laboratory test results. Prescribe medications, corrective devices, physical therapy, or surgery. Treat conditions such as corns, calluses, ingrown nails, tumors, shortened tendons, bunions, cysts, and abscesses by surgical methods. Advise patients about treatments and foot care techniques necessary for prevention of future problems. Refer patients to physicians when symptoms indicative of systemic disorders, such as arthritis or diabetes, are observed in feet and legs. Correct deformities by means of plaster casts and strapping. Make and fit prosthetic appliances. Perform administrative duties such as hiring employees, ordering supplies, and keeping records. Educate the public about the benefits of foot care through techniques such as speaking engagements, advertising, and other forums. Treat deformities using mechanical methods, such as whirlpool or paraffin baths, and electrical methods, such as short wave and low voltage currents. **SKILLS**—Science; Active Listening; Complex Problem Solving; Management of Financial Resources; Reading Comprehension; Instructing; Active Learning; Critical Thinking.

GOE—Interest Area: 08. Health Science. **Work Group:** 08.04. Health Specialties. **PERSONALITY TYPE:** Social. Social occupations frequently involve working with, communicating with, and teaching people. These occupations often involve helping or providing service to others.

EDUCATION/TRAINING PROGRAM—Podiatric Medicine/Podiatry (DPM). **RELATED KNOWLEDGE/COURSES**—**Medicine and Dentistry:** Knowledge of the information and techniques needed to diagnose and treat human injuries, diseases, and deformities. This includes symptoms, treatment alternatives, drug properties and interactions, and preventive health-care measures. **Biology:** Knowledge of plant and animal organisms and their tissues, cells, functions, interdependencies, and interactions with each other and the environment. **Therapy and Counseling:** Knowledge of principles, methods, and procedures for diagnosis, treatment, and rehabilitation of physical and mental dysfunctions and for career counseling and guidance. **Customer and Personal Service:** Knowledge of principles and processes for providing customer and personal services. This includes customer needs assessment, meeting quality standards for services, and evaluation of customer satisfaction. **Sales and Marketing:** Knowledge of principles and methods for showing, promoting, and selling products or services. This includes marketing strategy and tactics, product demonstration, sales techniques, and sales control systems. **Psychology:** Knowledge of human behavior and performance; individual differences in ability, personality, and interests; learning and motivation; psychological research methods; and the assessment and treatment of behavioral and affective disorders.

Poets and Lyricists

- Annual Earnings: $46,420
- Growth: 17.7%
- Annual Job Openings: 14,000
- Self-Employed: 67.7%
- Part-Time: 30.2%
- Education/Training Required: Bachelor's degree

The job openings listed here are shared with Caption Writers, Copy Writers, and Creative Writers.

Industries in Which Income Is Highest

Industry	Average Annual Wage	Number Employed
Motion Picture and Sound Recording Industries	$59,250	1,520
Federal, State, and Local Government	$58,640	1,710
Professional, Scientific, and Technical Services	$49,680	10,870
Religious, Grantmaking, Civic, Professional, and Similar Organizations	$49,100	4,330
Broadcasting (Except Internet)	$43,550	2,920

Metropolitan Areas Where Income Is Highest

Metropolitan Area	Average Annual Wage	Number Employed
Santa Barbara–Santa Maria, CA	$103,570	50
Austin–Round Rock, TX	$72,780	400
San Francisco–Oakland–Fremont, CA	$68,370	730
Los Angeles–Long Beach–Santa Ana, CA	$63,330	2,670
Raleigh–Cary, NC	$63,130	60

Write poetry or song lyrics for publication or performance. Writes words to fit musical compositions, including lyrics for operas, musical plays, and choral works. Chooses subject matter and suitable form to express personal feeling and experience or ideas or to narrate story or event. Adapts text to accommodate musical requirements of composer and singer. Writes narrative, dramatic, lyric, or other types of poetry for publication. **SKILLS**—Writing; Reading Comprehension.

GOE—Interest Area: 03. Arts and Communication. **Work Group:** 03.02. Writing and Editing. **PERSONALITY TYPE:** Artistic. Artistic occupations frequently involve working with forms, designs, and patterns. They often require self-expression, and the work can be done without following a clear set of rules.

EDUCATION/TRAINING PROGRAMS—Communications Studies/Speech Communication and Rhetoric; Creative Writing; English Composition. **RELATED KNOWLEDGE/COURSES—Fine Arts:** Knowledge of the theory and techniques required to compose, produce, and perform works of music, dance, visual arts, drama, and sculpture. **Communications**

and Media: Knowledge of media production, communication, and dissemination techniques and methods. This includes alternative ways to inform and entertain via written, oral, and visual media. **English Language:** Knowledge of the structure and content of the English language, including the meaning and spelling of words, rules of composition, and grammar.

Police Detectives

- Annual Earnings: $55,790
- Growth: 16.3%
- Annual Job Openings: 9,000
- Self-Employed: 0.0%
- Part-Time: 2.9%
- Education/Training Required: Work experience in a related occupation

The job openings listed here are shared with Child Support, Missing Persons, and Unemployment Insurance Fraud Investigators; Criminal Investigators and Special Agents; Immigration and Customs Inspectors; and Police Identification and Records Officers.

Industries in Which Income Is Highest

Industry	Average Annual Wage	Number Employed
Federal, State, and Local Government	$55,790	84,720

Metropolitan Areas Where Income Is Highest

Metropolitan Area	Average Annual Wage	Number Employed
Washington–Arlington–Alexandria, DC–VA–MD–WV	$79,180	4,270
Trenton–Ewing, NJ	$78,420	260
Chicago–Naperville–Joliet, IL–IN–WI	$76,080	3,170
Springfield, IL	$74,260	50
Oxnard–Thousand Oaks–Ventura, CA	$73,250	80

Conduct investigations to prevent crimes or solve criminal cases. Examine crime scenes to obtain clues and evidence, such as loose hairs, fibers, clothing, or weapons. Secure deceased body and obtain evidence from it, preventing bystanders from tampering with it prior to medical examiner's arrival. Obtain evidence from suspects. Provide testimony as a witness in court. Analyze completed police reports to determine what additional information and investigative work is needed. Prepare charges or responses to charges, or information for court cases, according to formalized procedures. Note, mark, and photograph location of objects found, such as footprints, tire tracks, bullets and bloodstains, and take measurements of the scene. Obtain facts or statements from complainants, witnesses, and accused persons and record interviews, using recording device. Obtain summary of incident from officer in charge at crime scene, taking care to avoid disturbing evidence. Examine records and governmental agency files to find identifying data about suspects. Prepare and serve search and arrest warrants. Block or rope off scene and check perimeter to ensure that entire scene is secured. Summon medical help for injured individuals and alert medical personnel to take statements from them. Provide information to lab personnel concerning the source of an item of evidence and tests to be performed. Monitor conditions of victims who are unconscious so that arrangements can be made to take statements if consciousness is regained. Secure persons at scene, keeping witnesses from conversing or leaving the scene before investigators arrive. Preserve, process, and analyze items of evidence obtained from crime scenes and suspects, placing them in proper containers and destroying evidence no longer needed. Record progress of investigation, maintain informational files on suspects, and submit reports to commanding officer or magistrate to authorize warrants. Take photographs from all angles of relevant parts of a crime scene, including entrance and exit routes and streets and intersections. Organize scene search, assigning specific tasks and areas of search to individual officers and obtaining adequate lighting as necessary. **SKILLS**—Persuasion; Negotiation; Social Perceptiveness; Coordination; Service Orientation; Active Listening; Speaking; Critical Thinking.

GOE—**Interest Area:** 12. Law and Public Safety. **Work Group:** 12.04. Law Enforcement and Public Safety. **PERSONALITY TYPE:** Enterprising. Enterprising occupations frequently involve starting up and carrying out projects. These occupations can involve leading people and making many decisions. They sometimes require risk taking and often deal with business.

EDUCATION/TRAINING PROGRAMS—Criminal Justice/Police Science; Criminalistics and Criminal Science. **RELATED KNOWLEDGE/COURSES**—**Public Safety and Security:** Knowledge of relevant equipment, policies, procedures, and strategies to promote effective local, state, or national security operations for the protection of people, data, property, and institutions. **Law and Government:** Knowledge of laws, legal codes, court procedures, precedents, government regulations, executive orders, agency rules, and the democratic political process. **Psychology:** Knowledge of human behavior and performance; individual differences in ability, personality, and interests; learning and motivation; psychological research methods; and the assessment and treatment of behavioral and affective disorders. **Therapy and Counseling:** Knowledge of principles, methods, and procedures for diagnosis, treatment, and rehabilitation of physical and mental dysfunctions and for career counseling and guidance. **Education and Training:** Knowledge of principles and methods for curriculum and training design, teaching and instruction for individuals and groups, and the measurement of training effects. **Philosophy and Theology:** Knowledge of different philosophical systems and religions. This includes their basic principles, values, ethics, ways of thinking, customs, and practices and their impact on human culture.

Police Identification and Records Officers

◎ Annual Earnings: $55,790
◎ Growth: 16.3%
◎ Annual Job Openings: 9,000
◎ Self-Employed: 0.0%
◎ Part-Time: 2.9%
◎ Education/Training Required: Work experience in a related occupation

The job openings listed here are shared with Child Support, Missing Persons, and Unemployment Insurance Fraud Investigators; Criminal Investigators and Special Agents; Immigration and Customs Inspectors; and Police Detectives.

Industries in Which Income Is Highest

Industry	Average Annual Wage	Number Employed
Federal, State, and Local Government	$55,790	84,720

Metropolitan Areas Where Income Is Highest

Metropolitan Area	Average Annual Wage	Number Employed
Washington–Arlington–Alexandria, DC–VA–MD–WV	$79,180	4,270
Trenton–Ewing, NJ	$78,420	260
Chicago–Naperville–Joliet, IL–IN–WI	$76,080	3,170
Springfield, IL	$74,260	50
Oxnard–Thousand Oaks–Ventura, CA	$73,250	80

Collect evidence at crime scene, classify and identify fingerprints, and photograph evidence for use in criminal and civil cases. Photograph crime or accident scenes for evidence records. Testify in court and present evidence. Dust selected areas of crime scene and lift latent fingerprints, adhering to proper preservation procedures. Look for trace evidence, such as fingerprints, hairs, fibers, or shoe impressions, using alternative light sources when necessary. Analyze and process evidence at crime scenes and in the laboratory, wearing protective equipment and using powders and chemicals. Package, store and retrieve evidence. Serve as technical advisor and coordinate with other law enforcement workers to exchange information on crime scene collection activities. Perform emergency work during off-hours. Submit evidence to supervisors. Process film and prints from crime or accident scenes. Identify, classify, and file fingerprints, using systems such as the Henry Classification system. **SKILLS**—Persuasion; Negotiation; Service Orientation; Judgment and Decision Making; Social Perceptiveness; Critical Thinking; Time Management; Speaking.

GOE—Interest Area: 12. Law and Public Safety. **Work Group:** 12.04. Law Enforcement and Public Safety. **PERSONALITY TYPE:** Conventional. Conventional occupations frequently involve following set procedures and routines. These occupations can include working with data and details more than with ideas. Usually there is a clear line of authority to follow.

EDUCATION/TRAINING PROGRAMS—Criminal Justice/Police Science; Criminalistics and Criminal Science. **RELATED KNOWLEDGE/COURSES—Law and Government:** Knowledge of laws, legal codes, court procedures, precedents, government regulations, executive orders, agency rules, and the democratic political process. **Customer and Personal Service:** Knowledge of principles and processes for providing customer and personal services. This includes customer needs assessment, meeting quality standards for services, and evaluation of customer satisfaction. **Public Safety and Security:** Knowledge of relevant equipment, policies, procedures, and strategies to promote effective local, state, or national security operations for the protection of people, data, property, and institutions. **Telecommunications:** Knowledge of transmission, broadcasting, switching, control, and operation of telecommunications systems. **Education and Training:** Knowledge of principles and methods for curriculum and training design, teaching and instruction for individuals and groups, and the measurement of training effects. **Psychology:** Knowledge of human behavior and performance; individual differences in ability, personality, and interests; learning and motivation; psychological research methods; and the assessment and treatment of behavioral and affective disorders.

Political Science Teachers, Postsecondary

- Annual Earnings: $59,850
- Growth: 32.2%
- Annual Job Openings: 329,000
- Self-Employed: 0.4%
- Part-Time: 27.3%
- Education/Training Required: Master's degree

Our sources did not provide separate job openings data for this occupation. The job openings listed here are shared with 35 other postsecondary teaching occupations. For a complete list, see the beginning of this section.

Industries in Which Income Is Highest

Industry	Average Annual Wage	Number Employed
Educational Services	$59,830	13,700

Metropolitan Areas Where Income Is Highest

Metropolitan Area	Average Annual Wage	Number Employed
Durham, NC	$86,490	230
Providence–Fall River–Warwick, RI–MA	$84,370	80
Springfield, MA–CT	$76,400	50
Riverside–San Bernardino–Ontario, CA	$74,780	70
Boston–Cambridge–Quincy, MA–NH	$74,640	380

Teach courses in political science, international affairs, and international relations. Initiate, facilitate, and moderate classroom discussions. Prepare and deliver lectures to undergraduate and/or graduate students on topics such as classical political thought, international relations, and democracy and citizenship. Evaluate and grade students' class work, assignments, and papers. Compile, administer, and grade examinations or assign this work to others. Prepare course materials such as syllabi, homework assignments, and handouts. Keep abreast of developments in their field by reading current literature, talking with colleagues, and participating in professional conferences. Plan, evaluate, and revise curricula, course content, and course materials and methods of instruction. Maintain student attendance records, grades, and other required records. Maintain regularly scheduled office hours in order to advise and assist students. Advise students on academic and vocational curricula and on career issues. Select and obtain materials and supplies such as textbooks. Conduct research in a particular field of knowledge and publish findings in professional journals, books, and/or electronic media. Supervise undergraduate and/or graduate teaching, internship, and research work. Collaborate with colleagues to address teaching and research issues. Serve on academic or administrative committees that deal with institutional policies, departmental matters, and academic issues. Participate in campus and community events. Participate in student recruitment, registration, and placement activities. Compile bibliographies of specialized materials for outside reading assignments. Act as advisers to student organizations. Perform administrative duties such as serving as department head. **SKILLS**—Instructing; Persuasion; Learning Strategies; Writing; Critical Thinking; Reading Comprehension; Active Learning; Speaking.

GOE—Interest Area: 05. Education and Training. **Work Group:** 05.03. Postsecondary and Adult Teaching and Instructing. **PERSONALITY TYPE:** Social. Social occupations frequently involve working with, communicating with, and teaching people. These occupations often involve helping or providing service to others.

EDUCATION/TRAINING PROGRAMS—American Government and Politics (United States); Political Science and Government, General; Political Science and Government, Other; Social Science Teacher Education. **RELATED KNOWLEDGE/COURSES—Philosophy and Theology:** Knowledge of different philosophical systems and religions. This includes their basic principles, values, ethics, ways of thinking, customs, and practices and their impact on human culture. **History and Archeology:** Knowledge of historical events and their causes, indicators, and effects on civilizations and cultures. **Sociology and Anthropology:** Knowledge of group behavior and dynamics, societal trends and influences, human migrations, ethnicity, and cultures and their history and origins. **Geography:** Knowledge of principles and methods for describing the features of land, sea, and air masses, including their physical characteristics; locations; interrelationships; and distribution of plant, animal, and human life. **Law and Government:** Knowledge of laws, legal codes, court procedures, precedents, government regulations, executive orders, agency rules, and the democratic political process. **Education and Training:** Knowledge of principles and methods for curriculum and training design, teaching and instruction for individuals and groups, and the measurement of training effects.

Political Scientists

- Annual Earnings: $84,100
- Growth: 7.3%
- Annual Job Openings: fewer than 500
- Self-Employed: 4.7%
- Part-Time: 15.6%
- Education/Training Required: Master's degree

Industries in Which Income Is Highest

Industry	Average Annual Wage	Number Employed
Federal, State, and Local Government	$94,920	3,210
Religious, Grantmaking, Civic, Professional, and Similar Organizations	$62,370	570
Professional, Scientific, and Technical Services	$51,460	1,110

Metropolitan Areas Where Income Is Highest

Metropolitan Area	Average Annual Wage	Number Employed
Washington–Arlington–Alexandria, DC–VA–MD–WV	$89,230	3,860
New York–Northern New Jersey–Long Island, NY–NJ–PA	$83,050	170
Seattle–Tacoma–Bellevue, WA	$55,660	70

Study the origin, development, and operation of political systems. Research a wide range of subjects, such as relations between the United States and foreign countries, the beliefs and institutions of foreign nations, or the politics of small towns or a major metropolis. May study topics, such as public opinion, political decision making, and ideology. May analyze the structure and operation of governments, as well as various political entities. May conduct public opinion surveys, analyze election results, or analyze public documents. Teach political science. Disseminate research results through academic publications, written reports, or public presentations. Identify issues for research and analysis. Develop and test theories, using information from interviews, newspapers, periodicals, case law, historical papers, polls, and/or statistical sources. Maintain current knowledge of government policy decisions. Collect, analyze, and interpret data such as election results and public opinion surveys; report on findings, recommendations, and conclusions. Interpret and analyze policies, public issues, legislation, and/or the operations of governments, businesses, and organizations. Evaluate programs and policies, and make related recommendations to institutions and organizations. Write drafts of legislative proposals, and prepare speeches, correspondence, and policy papers for governmental use. SKILLS—Writing; Critical Thinking; Reading Comprehension; Instructing; Active Learning; Speaking; Persuasion; Complex Problem Solving.

GOE—Interest Area: 15. Scientific Research, Engineering, and Mathematics. Work Group: 15.04. Social Sciences. PERSONALITY TYPE: Investigative. Investigative occupations frequently involve working with ideas and require an extensive amount of thinking. These occupations can involve searching for facts and figuring out problems mentally.

EDUCATION/TRAINING PROGRAMS— American Government and Politics (United States); Canadian Government and Politics; International/Global Studies; Political Science and Government, General; Political Science and Government, Other. RELATED KNOWLEDGE/COURSES—Law and Government: Knowledge of laws, legal codes, court procedures, precedents, government regulations, executive orders, agency rules, and the democratic political process. History and Archeology: Knowledge of historical events and their causes, indicators, and effects on civilizations and cultures. Philosophy and Theology: Knowledge of different philosophical systems and religions. This includes their basic principles, values, ethics, ways of thinking, customs, and practices and their impact on human culture. Sociology and Anthropology: Knowledge of group behavior and dynamics, societal trends and influences, human migrations, ethnicity, and cultures and their history and origins. English Language: Knowledge of the structure and content of the English language, including the meaning and spelling of words, rules of composition, and grammar. Foreign Language: Knowledge of the structure and content of a foreign (non-English) language, including the meaning and spelling of words, rules of composition and grammar, and pronunciation.

Postal Service Clerks

- Annual Earnings: $48,310
- Growth: 0.0%
- Annual Job Openings: 4,000
- Self-Employed: 0.0%
- Part-Time: 7.1%
- Education/Training Required: Short-term on-the-job training

Industries in Which Income Is Highest

Industry	Average Annual Wage	Number Employed
Postal Service	$48,310	78,710

Metropolitan Areas Where Income Is Highest

Metropolitan Area	Average Annual Wage	Number Employed
Des Moines–West Des Moines, IA	$50,350	110
Trenton–Ewing, NJ	$50,300	100
Manchester, NH	$50,250	50
Waterbury, CT	$50,200	70
Beaumont–Port Arthur, TX	$50,130	70

Perform any combination of tasks in a post office, such as receive letters and parcels; sell postage and revenue stamps, postal cards, and stamped envelopes; fill out and sell money orders; place mail in pigeon holes of mail rack or in bags according to State, address, or other scheme; and examine mail for correct postage. Transport mail from one work station to another. Weigh letters and parcels; compute mailing costs based on type, weight, and destination; and affix correct postage. Cash money orders. Post announcements or government information on public bulletin boards. Provide assistance to the public in complying with federal regulations of Postal Service and other federal agencies. Answer questions regarding mail regulations and procedures, postage rates, and post office boxes. Check mail in order to ensure correct postage and that packages and letters are in proper condition for mailing. Complete forms regarding changes of address, or theft or loss of mail, or for special services such as registered or priority mail. Feed mail into postage canceling devices or hand stamp mail to cancel postage. Keep money drawers in order, and record and balance daily transactions. Obtain signatures from recipients of registered or special delivery mail. Provide customers with assistance in filing claims for mail theft, or lost or damaged mail. Put undelivered parcels away, retrieve them when customers come to claim them, and complete any related documentation. Receive letters and parcels, and place mail into bags. Register, certify, and insure letters and parcels. Rent post office boxes to customers. Respond to complaints regarding mail theft, delivery problems, and lost or damaged mail, filling out forms and making appropriate referrals for investigation. Sell and collect payment for products such as stamps, prepaid mail envelopes, and money orders. Set postage meters, and calibrate them to ensure correct operation. Sort incoming and outgoing mail, according to type and destination, by hand or by operating electronic mail-sorting and scanning devices. SKILLS—None met the criteria.

GOE—Interest Area: 04. Business and Administration. Work Group: 04.07. Records and Materials Processing. PERSONALITY TYPE: Conventional. Conventional occupations frequently involve following set procedures and routines. These occupations can include working with data and details more than with ideas. Usually there is a clear line of authority to follow.

EDUCATION/TRAINING PROGRAM—General Office Occupations and Clerical Services. RELATED KNOWLEDGE/COURSES—Clerical Practices: Knowledge of administrative and clerical procedures and systems such as word processing, managing files and records, stenography and transcription, designing forms, and other office procedures and terminology. Customer and Personal Service: Knowledge of principles and processes for providing customer and personal services. This includes customer needs assessment, meeting quality standards for services, and evaluation of customer satisfaction.

Postal Service Mail Carriers

- ◎ Annual Earnings: $46,330
- ◎ Growth: 0.0%
- ◎ Annual Job Openings: 19,000
- ◎ Self-Employed: 0.0%
- ◎ Part-Time: 9.8%
- ◎ Education/Training Required: Short-term on-the-job training

Industries in Which Income Is Highest

Industry	Average Annual Wage	Number Employed
Postal Service	$46,330	347,180

Metropolitan Areas Where Income Is Highest

Metropolitan Area	Average Annual Wage	Number Employed
Fairbanks, AK	$49,730	50
Honolulu, HI	$49,110	850
New Haven, CT	$48,720	780
Casper, WY	$48,600	80
Dubuque, IA	$48,570	120

Sort mail for delivery. Deliver mail on established route by vehicle or on foot. Bundle mail in preparation for delivery or transportation to relay boxes. Deliver mail to residences and business establishments along specified routes by walking and/or driving, using a combination of satchels, carts, cars, and small trucks. Enter change of address orders into computers that process forwarding address stickers. Hold mail for customers who are away from delivery locations. Leave notices telling patrons where to collect mail that could not be delivered. Maintain accurate records of deliveries. Register, certify, and insure parcels and letters. Report any unusual circumstances concerning mail delivery, including the condition of street letter boxes. Sell stamps and money orders. Meet schedules for the collection and return of mail. Record address changes and redirect mail for those addresses. Return incorrectly addressed mail to senders. Return to the post office with mail collected from homes, businesses, and public mailboxes. Sign for cash-on-delivery and registered mail before leaving the post office. Sort mail for delivery, arranging it in delivery sequence. Travel to post offices to pick up the mail for routes and/or pick up mail from postal relay boxes. Turn in money and receipts collected along mail routes. Answer customers' questions about postal services and regulations. Complete forms that notify publishers of address changes. Obtain signed receipts for registered, certified, and insured mail; collect associated charges; and complete any necessary paperwork. Provide customers with change of address cards and other forms. **SKILLS**—None met the criteria.

GOE—**Interest Area:** 16. Transportation, Distribution, and Logistics. **Work Group:** 16.06. Other Services Requiring Driving. **PERSONALITY TYPE:** Conventional. Conventional occupations frequently involve following set procedures and routines. These occupations can include working with data and details more than with ideas. Usually there is a clear line of authority to follow.

EDUCATION/TRAINING PROGRAM—General Office Occupations and Clerical Services. **RELATED KNOWLEDGE/COURSES—Transportation:** Knowledge of principles and methods for moving people or goods by air, rail, sea, or road, including the relative costs and benefits. **Geography:** Knowledge of principles and methods for describing the features of land, sea, and air masses, including their physical characteristics; locations; interrelationships; and distribution of plant, animal, and human life.

Postmasters and Mail Superintendents

- ◎ Annual Earnings: $52,710
- ◎ Growth: 0.0%
- ◎ Annual Job Openings: 2,000
- ◎ Self-Employed: 0.0%
- ◎ Part-Time: 8.5%
- ◎ Education/Training Required: Work experience in a related occupation

Industries in Which Income Is Highest

Industry	Average Annual Wage	Number Employed
Postal Service	$52,710	26,120

Metropolitan Areas Where Income Is Highest

Metropolitan Area	Average Annual Wage	Number Employed
Los Angeles–Long Beach–Santa Ana, CA	$78,610	110
New York–Northern New Jersey–Long Island, NY–NJ–PA	$67,490	580
Detroit–Warren–Livonia, MI	$66,940	100
Milwaukee–Waukesha–West Allis, WI	$66,860	50
Chicago–Naperville–Joliet, IL–IN–WI	$65,310	230

Direct and coordinate operational, administrative, management, and supportive services of a U.S. post office; or coordinate activities of workers engaged in postal and related work in assigned post office. Organize and supervise activities such as the processing of incoming and outgoing mail. Direct and coordinate operational, management, and supportive services of one or a number of postal facilities. Resolve customer complaints. Hire and train employees, and evaluate their performance. Prepare employee work schedules. Prepare and submit detailed and summary reports of post office activities to designated supervisors. Negotiate labor disputes. Collect rents for post office boxes. Issue and cash money orders. Inform the public of available services, and of postal laws and regulations. Select and train postmasters and managers of associate postal units. **SKILLS**—Negotiation; Persuasion; Service Orientation; Management of Personnel Resources; Monitoring; Coordination; Management of Financial Resources; Social Perceptiveness.

GOE—Interest Area: 16. Transportation, Distribution, and Logistics. **Work Group:** 16.01. Managerial Work in Transportation. **PERSONALITY TYPE:** Enterprising. Enterprising occupations frequently involve starting up and carrying out projects. These occupations can involve leading people and making many decisions. They sometimes require risk taking and often deal with business.

EDUCATION/TRAINING PROGRAM—Public Administration. **RELATED KNOWLEDGE/COURSES—Production and Processing:** Knowledge of raw materials, production processes, quality control, costs, and other techniques for maximizing the effective manufacture and distribution of goods. **Personnel and Human Resources:** Knowledge of principles and procedures for personnel recruitment, selection, training, compensation and benefits, labor relations and negotiation, and personnel information systems. **Customer and Personal Service:** Knowledge of principles and processes for providing customer and personal services. This includes customer needs assessment, meeting quality standards for services, and evaluation of customer satisfaction. **Education and Training:** Knowledge of principles and methods for curriculum and training design, teaching and instruction for individuals and groups, and the measurement of training effects. **Public Safety and Security:** Knowledge of relevant equipment, policies, procedures, and strategies to promote effective local, state, or national security operations for the protection of people, data, property, and institutions. **Clerical Practices:** Knowledge of administrative and clerical procedures and systems such as word processing, managing files and records, stenography and transcription, designing forms, and other office procedures and terminology.

Power Distributors and Dispatchers

- Annual Earnings: $59,160
- Growth: 0.0%
- Annual Job Openings: 1,000
- Self-Employed: 0.0%
- Part-Time: 0.8%
- Education/Training Required: Long-term on-the-job training

Industries in Which Income Is Highest

Industry	Average Annual Wage	Number Employed
Management of Companies and Enterprises	$65,010	440
Federal, State, and Local Government	$60,440	1,790
Utilities	$58,610	4,830
Chemical Manufacturing	$53,490	30
Nonmetallic Mineral Product Manufacturing	$53,100	50

Metropolitan Areas Where Income Is Highest

Metropolitan Area	Average Annual Wage	Number Employed
Sacramento–Arden–Arcade–Roseville, CA	$82,340	50
Portland–Vancouver–Beaverton, OR–WA	$77,580	190
Salt Lake City, UT	$74,730	40
Wenatchee, WA	$70,640	50
Kennewick–Richland–Pasco, WA	$68,790	40

Coordinate, regulate, or distribute electricity or steam. Accept and implement energy schedules, including real-time transmission reservations and schedules. Calculate and determine load estimates or equipment requirements, in order to determine required control settings. Control, monitor, or operate equipment that regulates or distributes electricity or steam, using data obtained from instruments or computers. Coordinate with engineers, planners, field personnel, and other utility workers to provide information such as clearances, switching orders, and distribution process changes. Distribute and regulate the flow of power between entities such as generating stations, substations, distribution lines, and users, keeping track of the status of circuits and connections. Inspect equipment to ensure that specifications are met, and to detect any defects. Manipulate controls to adjust and activate power distribution equipment and machines. Monitor and record switchboard and control board readings to ensure that electrical or steam distribution equipment is operating properly. Record and compile operational data, such as chart and meter readings, power demands, and usage and operating times, using transmission system maps. Respond to emergencies, such as transformer or transmission line failures, and route current around affected areas. Tend auxiliary equipment used in the power distribution process. Track conditions that could affect power needs, such as changes in the weather, and adjust equipment to meet any anticipated changes. Direct personnel engaged in controlling and operating distribution equipment and machinery, for example, instructing control room operators to start boilers and generators. Prepare switching orders that will isolate work areas without causing power outages, referring to drawings of power systems. Repair, maintain, and clean equipment and machinery, using hand tools. **SKILLS**—Operation Monitoring; Repairing; Equipment Maintenance; Management of Personnel Resources; Operation and Control; Troubleshooting; Installation; Systems Evaluation.

GOE—Interest Area: 13. Manufacturing. **Work Group:** 13.16. Utility Operation and Energy Distribution. **PERSONALITY TYPE:** Realistic. Realistic occupations frequently involve work activities that include practical, hands-on problems and solutions. They often deal with plants, animals, and real-world materials like wood, tools, and machinery. Many of the occupations require working outside and do not involve a lot of paperwork or working closely with others.

EDUCATION/TRAINING PROGRAM—No data available. **RELATED KNOWLEDGE/COURSES**—**Mechanical Devices:** Knowledge of machines and tools, including their designs, uses, repair, and maintenance. **Physics:** Knowledge and prediction of physical principles and laws and their interrelationships and applications to understanding fluid, material, and atmospheric dynamics and mechanical, electrical, atomic, and subatomic structures and processes. **Engineering and Technology:** Knowledge of the practical application of engineering science and technology. This includes applying principles, techniques, procedures, and equipment to the design and production of various goods and services.

Power Generating Plant Operators, Except Auxiliary Equipment Operators

- Annual Earnings: $53,170
- Growth: –0.4%
- Annual Job Openings: 5,000
- Self-Employed: 0.0%
- Part-Time: 1.5%
- Education/Training Required: Long-term on-the-job training

The job openings listed here are shared with Auxiliary Equipment Operators, Power.

Industries in Which Income Is Highest

Industry	Average Annual Wage	Number Employed
Utilities	$55,330	23,660
Federal, State, and Local Government	$45,480	5,460

Metropolitan Areas Where Income Is Highest

Metropolitan Area	Average Annual Wage	Number Employed
Buffalo–Niagara Falls, NY	$66,950	150
Fresno, CA	$66,040	60
Albany–Schenectady–Troy, NY	$65,810	230
New York–Northern New Jersey–Long Island, NY–NJ–PA	$65,570	1,680
Riverside–San Bernardino–Ontario, CA	$65,310	470

Control or operate machinery, such as steam-driven turbogenerators, to generate electric power, often through the use of panelboards, control boards, or semi-automatic equipment. Operates or controls machinery that generates electric power, using control boards or semiautomatic equipment. Compiles and records operational data on specified forms. Maintains and repairs electrical power distribution machinery and equipment, using hand tools. Examines and tests electrical power distribution machinery and equipment, using testing devices. Monitors control and switchboard gauges to determine electrical power distribution meets specifications. Adjusts controls on equipment to generate specified electrical power. **SKILLS—** Operation Monitoring; Operation and Control; Equipment Maintenance; Troubleshooting; Repairing; Science; Quality Control Analysis; Installation.

GOE—Interest Area: 13. Manufacturing. **Work Group:** 13.16. Utility Operation and Energy Distribution. **PERSONALITY TYPE:** Realistic. Realistic occupations frequently involve work activities that include practical, hands-on problems and solutions. They often deal with plants, animals, and real-world materials like wood, tools, and machinery. Many of the occupations require working outside and do not involve a lot of paperwork or working closely with others.

EDUCATION/TRAINING PROGRAM—No data available. **RELATED KNOWLEDGE/COURSES— Mechanical Devices:** Knowledge of machines and tools, including their designs, uses, repair, and maintenance. **Engineering and Technology:** Knowledge of the practical application of engineering science and technology. This includes applying principles, techniques, procedures, and equipment to the design and production of various goods and services. **Physics:** Knowledge and prediction of physical principles and laws and their interrelationships and applications to understanding fluid, material, and atmospheric dynamics and mechanical, electrical, atomic, and subatomic structures and processes. **Computers and Electronics:** Knowledge of circuit boards, processors, chips, electronic equipment, and computer hardware and software, including applications and programming.

Pressure Vessel Inspectors

- Annual Earnings: $49,360
- Growth: 11.6%
- Annual Job Openings: 17,000
- Self-Employed: 0.0%
- Part-Time: 5.1%
- Education/Training Required: Long-term on-the-job training

The job openings listed here are shared with Coroners, Environmental Compliance Inspectors, Equal Opportunity Representatives and Officers, Government Property Inspectors and Investigators, and Licensing Examiners and Inspectors.

Industries in Which Income Is Highest

Industry	Average Annual Wage	Number Employed
Postal Service	$72,700	1,710
Utilities	$66,390	1,310
Securities, Commodity Contracts, and Other Financial Investments and Related Activities	$64,490	5,130
Computer and Electronic Product Manufacturing	$59,540	1,390
Telecommunications	$59,310	2,620

Metropolitan Areas Where Income Is Highest

Metropolitan Area	Average Annual Wage	Number Employed
Kankakee–Bradley, IL	$81,020	170
Brunswick, GA	$79,710	340
San Jose–Sunnyvale–Santa Clara, CA	$67,550	930
San Francisco–Oakland–Fremont, CA	$64,010	3,320
Santa Rosa–Petaluma, CA	$63,660	410

Inspect pressure vessel equipment for conformance with safety laws and standards regulating their design, fabrication, installation, repair, and operation. Inspects drawings, designs, and specifications for piping, boilers and other vessels. Performs standard tests to verify condition of equipment and calibration of meters and gauges, using test equipment and hand tools. Inspects gas mains to determine that rate of flow, pressure, location, construction, or installation conform to standards. Evaluates factors, such as materials used, safety devices, regulators, construction quality, riveting, welding, pitting, corrosion, cracking, and safety valve operation. Calculates allowable limits of pressure, strength, and stresses. Examines permits and inspection records to determine that inspection schedule and remedial actions conform to procedures and regulations. Keeps records and prepares reports of inspections and investigations for administrative or legal authorities. Investigates accidents to determine causes and to develop methods of preventing recurrences. Confers with engineers, manufacturers, contractors, owners, and operators concerning problems in construction, operation, and repair. Witnesses acceptance and installation tests. Recommends or orders actions to correct violations of legal requirements or to eliminate unsafe conditions. **SKILLS**—Quality Control Analysis; Operation Monitoring; Science; Mathematics; Operations Analysis; Systems Evaluation; Systems Analysis; Writing.

GOE—Interest Area: 07. Government and Public Administration. **Work Group:** 07.03. Regulations Enforcement. **PERSONALITY TYPE:** Realistic. Realistic occupations frequently involve work activities that include practical, hands-on problems and solutions. They often deal with plants, animals, and real-world materials like wood, tools, and machinery. Many of the occupations require working outside and do not involve a lot of paperwork or working closely with others.

EDUCATION/TRAINING PROGRAM—No data available. **RELATED KNOWLEDGE/COURSES**— **Physics:** Knowledge and prediction of physical principles and laws and their interrelationships and applications to understanding fluid, material, and atmospheric dynamics and mechanical, electrical, atomic, and subatomic structures and processes. **Mechanical Devices:** Knowledge of machines and tools, including their designs, uses, repair, and maintenance. **Public Safety and Security:** Knowledge of relevant equipment, policies, procedures, and strategies to promote effective local, state, or national security operations for the protection of people, data, property, and institutions. **Engineering and Technology:** Knowledge of the practical application of engineering science and technology. This includes applying principles, techniques, procedures, and equipment to the design and production of various goods and services. **Law and Government:** Knowledge of laws, legal codes, court procedures, precedents, government regulations, executive orders, agency rules, and the democratic political process. **Design:** Knowledge of design techniques, tools, and principles involved in production of precision technical plans, blueprints, drawings, and models.

Private Sector Executives

- ◎ Annual Earnings: $142,440
- ◎ Growth: 14.9%
- ◎ Annual Job Openings: 38,000
- ◎ Self-Employed: 16.2%
- ◎ Part-Time: 6.8%
- ◎ Education/Training Required: Work experience plus degree

The job openings listed here are shared with Chief Executives and Government Service Executives.

Industries in Which Income Is Highest

Industry	Average Annual Wage	Number Employed
Food Manufacturing	More than $146,500	2,810
Hospitals	More than $146,500	6,540
Machinery Manufacturing	More than $146,500	4,870
Motor Vehicle and Parts Dealers	More than $146,500	6,330
Telecommunications	More than $146,500	1,280

Metropolitan Areas Where Income Is Highest

Metropolitan Area	Average Annual Wage	Number Employed
Boston–Cambridge–Quincy, MA–NH	More than $146,500	17,530
New York–Northern New Jersey– Long Island, NY–NJ–PA	More than $146,500	15,260
Chicago–Naperville–Joliet, IL– IN–WI	More than $146,500	14,910
Los Angeles–Long Beach– Santa Ana, CA	More than $146,500	13,510
Atlanta–Sandy Springs– Marietta, GA	More than $146,500	11,950

Determine and formulate policies and business strategies and provide overall direction of private sector organizations. Plan, direct, and coordinate operational activities at the highest level of management with the help of subordinate managers. Directs and coordinates activities of business or department concerned with production, pricing, sales, and/or distribution of products. Directs and coordinates organization's financial and budget activities to fund operations, maximize investments, and increase efficiency. Directs, plans, and implements policies and objectives of organization or business in accordance with charter and board of directors. Directs activities of organization to plan procedures, establish responsibilities, and coordinate functions among departments and sites. Analyzes operations to evaluate performance of company and staff and to determine areas of cost reduction and program improvement. Confers with board members, organization officials, and staff members to establish policies and formulate plans. Reviews financial statements and sales and activity reports to ensure that organization's objectives are achieved. Assigns or delegates responsibilities to subordinates. Directs and coordinates activities of business involved with buying and selling investment products and financial services. Establishes internal control procedures. Presides over or serves on board of directors, management committees, or other governing boards. Directs inservice training of staff. Administers program for selection of sites, construction of buildings, and provision of equipment and supplies. Screens, selects, hires, transfers, and discharges employees. Promotes objectives of institution or business before associations, public, government agencies, or community groups. Negotiates or approves contracts with suppliers and distributors, and with maintenance, janitorial, and security providers. Prepares reports and budgets. Directs non-merchandising departments of business, such as advertising, purchasing, credit, and accounting. **SKILLS**—Management of Financial Resources; Systems Analysis; Systems Evaluation; Management of Personnel Resources; Judgment and Decision Making; Management of Material Resources; Coordination; Negotiation.

GOE—Interest Area: 04. Business and Administration. **Work Group:** 04.01. Managerial Work in General Business. **PERSONALITY TYPE:** Enterprising. Enterprising occupations frequently involve starting up and carrying out projects. These occupations can involve leading people and making many decisions. They sometimes require risk taking and often deal with business.

EDUCATION/TRAINING   PROGRAMS—Business Administration/Management; Entrepreneurship/Entrepreneurial Studies; InternationalBusiness/Trade/Commerce; Transportation/Transportation Management. **RELATED KNOWLEDGE/COURSES**—**Economics and Accounting:** Knowledge of economic and accounting principles and practices, the financial markets, banking, and the analysis and reporting of financial data. **Production and Processing:** Knowledge of raw materials, production processes, quality control, costs, and other techniques for maximizing the effective manufacture and distribution of goods. **Administration and Management:** Knowledge of business and management principles involved in strategic planning, resource allocation, human resources modeling, leadership technique, production methods, and coordination of people and resources. **Sales and Marketing:** Knowledge of principles and methods for showing, promoting, and selling products or services. This includes marketing strategy and tactics, product demonstration, sales techniques, and sales control systems. **Personnel and Human Resources:** Knowledge of principles and procedures for personnel recruitment, selection, training, compensation and benefits, labor relations and negotiation, and personnel information systems. **Building and Construction:** Knowledge of the materials, methods, and tools involved in the construction or repair of houses, buildings, or other structures such as highways and roads.

Producers

- Annual Earnings: $53,860
- Growth: 16.6%
- Annual Job Openings: 11,000
- Self-Employed: 30.4%
- Part-Time: 8.4%
- Education/Training Required: Work experience plus degree

The job openings listed here are shared with Directors—Stage, Motion Pictures, Television, and Radio, Program Directors, Talent Directors, and Technical Directors/Managers.

Industries in Which Income Is Highest

Industry	Average Annual Wage	Number Employed
Motion Picture and Sound Recording Industries	$70,820	16,180
Professional, Scientific, and Technical Services	$69,870	3,100
Federal, State, and Local Government	$55,810	1,690
Broadcasting (Except Internet)	$48,650	23,240
Educational Services	$44,150	2,950

Metropolitan Areas Where Income Is Highest

Metropolitan Area	Average Annual Wage	Number Employed
Bridgeport–Stamford–Norwalk, CT	$98,420	150
New York–Northern New Jersey–Long Island, NY–NJ–PA	$81,710	10,130
San Francisco–Oakland–Fremont, CA	$79,980	1,300
Los Angeles–Long Beach–Santa Ana, CA	$72,210	9,760
Buffalo–Niagara Falls, NY	$66,330	170

Plan and coordinate various aspects of radio, television, stage, or motion picture production, such as selecting script, coordinating writing, directing and editing, and arranging financing. Coordinate the activities of writers, directors, managers, and other personnel throughout the production process. Monitor post-production processes in order to ensure accurate completion of all details. Perform management activities such as budgeting, scheduling, planning, and marketing. Determine production size, content, and budget, establishing details such as production schedules and management policies. Compose and edit scripts, or provide screenwriters with story outlines from which scripts can be written. Conduct meetings with staff to discuss production progress and to ensure production objectives are attained. Resolve personnel problems that arise during the production process by acting as liaisons between dissenting parties when necessary. Produce shows for special occasions, such as holidays or testimonials. Edit and write news stories from information collected by reporters. Write and submit proposals to bid on contracts for projects. Hire directors, principal cast members, and key production staff members. Arrange financing for productions. Select plays, scripts, books, or ideas to be produced. Review film, recordings, or rehearsals to ensure conformance to production and broadcast standards. Perform administrative duties such as preparing operational reports, distributing rehearsal call sheets and script copies, and arranging for rehearsal quarters. Obtain and distribute costumes, props, music, and studio equipment needed to complete productions. Negotiate contracts with artistic personnel, often in accordance with collective bargaining agreements. Maintain knowledge of minimum wages and working conditions established by unions and/or associations of actors and technicians. Plan and coordinate the production of musical recordings, selecting music and directing performers. Negotiate with parties including independent producers, and the distributors and broadcasters who will be handling completed productions. Develop marketing plans for finished products, collaborating with sales associates to supervise product distribution. Determine and direct the content of radio programming. **SKILLS**—Negotiation; Coordination; Management of Personnel Resources; Monitoring; Management of Financial Resources; Writing; Social Perceptiveness; Persuasion.

GOE—Interest Area: 03. Arts and Communication. **Work Group:** 03.01. Managerial Work in Arts and Communication. **PERSONALITY TYPE:** Artistic. Artistic occupations frequently involve working with forms, designs, and patterns. They often require self-expression, and the work can be done without following a clear set of rules.

EDUCATION/TRAINING PROGRAMS— Cinematography and Film/Video Production; Directing and Theatrical Production; Drama and Dramatics/Theatre Arts, General; Dramatic/Theatre Arts and Stagecraft, Other; Film/Cinema Studies; Radio and Television; Theatre/Theatre Arts Management. **RELATED KNOWLEDGE/COURSES— Communications and Media:** Knowledge of media production, communication, and dissemination techniques and methods. This includes alternative ways to inform and entertain via written, oral, and visual media. **Fine Arts:** Knowledge of the theory and techniques required to compose, produce, and perform works of music, dance, visual arts, drama, and sculpture. **Clerical Practices:** Knowledge of administrative and clerical procedures and systems such as word processing, managing files and records, stenography and transcription, designing forms, and other office procedures and terminology. **Administration and Management:** Knowledge of business and management principles involved in strategic planning, resource allocation, human resources modeling, leadership technique, production methods, and coordination of people and resources. **Sales and Marketing:** Knowledge of principles and methods for showing, promoting, and selling products or services. This includes marketing strategy and tactics, product demonstration, sales techniques, and sales control systems. **Personnel and Human Resources:** Knowledge of principles and procedures for personnel recruitment, selection, training, compensation and benefits, labor relations and negotiation, and personnel information systems.

Product Safety Engineers

- Annual Earnings: $65,210
- Growth: 13.4%
- Annual Job Openings: 2,000
- Self-Employed: 0.5%
- Part-Time: 2.7%
- Education/Training Required: Bachelor's degree

The job openings listed here are shared with Fire-Prevention and Protection Engineers and Industrial Safety and Health Engineers.

Industries in Which Income Is Highest

Industry	Average Annual Wage	Number Employed
Transportation Equipment Manufacturing	$70,130	1,160
Professional, Scientific, and Technical Services	$69,370	2,750
Federal, State, and Local Government	$68,740	5,370
Chemical Manufacturing	$65,700	2,990
Construction of Buildings	$57,920	2,080

Metropolitan Areas Where Income Is Highest

Metropolitan Area	Average Annual Wage	Number Employed
San Jose–Sunnyvale–Santa Clara, CA	$84,920	390
Washington–Arlington–Alexandria, DC–VA–MD–WV	$84,880	960
Anchorage, AK	$84,300	70
Durham, NC	$83,530	100
Knoxville, TN	$78,820	130

Develop and conduct tests to evaluate product safety levels and recommend measures to reduce or eliminate hazards. Report accident investigation findings. Conduct research to evaluate safety levels for products. Evaluate potential health hazards or damage that could occur from product misuse. Investigate causes of accidents, injuries, or illnesses related to product usage in order to develop solutions to minimize or prevent recurrence. Participate in preparation of product usage and precautionary label instructions. Recommend procedures for detection, prevention, and elimination of physical, chemical, or other product hazards. **SKILLS**—Quality Control Analysis; Operations Analysis; Science; Mathematics; Technology Design; Writing; Active Learning; Troubleshooting.

GOE—Interest Area: 15. Scientific Research, Engineering, and Mathematics. **Work Group:** 15.08. Industrial and Safety Engineering. **PERSONALITY TYPE:** Investigative. Investigative occupations frequently involve working with ideas and require an extensive amount of thinking. These occupations can involve searching for facts and figuring out problems mentally.

EDUCATION/TRAINING PROGRAM—Environmental/Environmental Health Engineering. **RELATED KNOWLEDGE/COURSES**—**Chemistry:** Knowledge of the chemical composition, structure, and properties of substances and of the chemical processes and transformations that they undergo. This includes uses of chemicals, their danger signs, production techniques, and disposal methods. **Engineering and Technology:** Knowledge of the practical application of engineering science and technology. This includes applying principles, techniques, procedures, and equipment to the design and production of various goods and services. **Physics:** Knowledge and prediction of physical principles and laws and their interrelationships and applications to understanding fluid, material, and atmospheric dynamics and mechanical, electrical, atomic, and subatomic structures and processes. **Biology:** Knowledge of plant and animal organisms and their tissues, cells, functions, interdependencies, and interactions with each other and the environment. **Public Safety and Security:** Knowledge of relevant equipment, policies, procedures, and strategies to promote effective local, state, or national security operations for the protection of people, data, property, and institutions. **Production and Processing:** Knowledge of raw materials, production processes, quality control, costs, and other techniques for maximizing the effective manufacture and distribution of goods.

Program Directors

- Annual Earnings: $53,860
- Growth: 16.6%
- Annual Job Openings: 11,000
- Self-Employed: 30.4%
- Part-Time: 8.4%
- Education/Training Required: Work experience plus degree

The job openings listed here are shared with Directors—Stage, Motion Pictures, Television, and Radio, Producers, Talent Directors, Technical Directors/Managers.

Industries in Which Income Is Highest

Industry	Average Annual Wage	Number Employed
Motion Picture and Sound Recording Industries	$70,820	16,180
Professional, Scientific, and Technical Services	$69,870	3,100
Federal, State, and Local Government	$55,810	1,690
Broadcasting (Except Internet)	$48,650	23,240
Educational Services	$44,150	2,950

Metropolitan Areas Where Income Is Highest

Metropolitan Area	Average Annual Wage	Number Employed
Bridgeport–Stamford–Norwalk, CT	$98,420	150
New York–Northern New Jersey–Long Island, NY–NJ–PA	$81,710	10,130
San Francisco–Oakland–Fremont, CA	$79,980	1,300
Los Angeles–Long Beach–Santa Ana, CA	$72,210	9,760
Buffalo–Niagara Falls, NY	$66,330	170

Direct and coordinate activities of personnel engaged in preparation of radio or television station program schedules and programs, such as sports or news. Plan and schedule programming and event coverage based on broadcast length, time availability, and other factors such as community needs, ratings data, and viewer demographics. Monitor and review programming in order to ensure that schedules are met, guidelines are

P

adhered to, and performances are of adequate quality. Direct and coordinate activities of personnel engaged in broadcast news, sports, or programming. Check completed program logs for accuracy and conformance with FCC rules and regulations, and resolve program log inaccuracies. Establish work schedules and assign work to staff members. Coordinate activities between departments, such as news and programming. Perform personnel duties such as hiring staff and evaluating work performance. Evaluate new and existing programming for suitability and in order to assess the need for changes, using information such as audience surveys and feedback. Develop budgets for programming and broadcasting activities, and monitor expenditures to ensure that they remain within budgetary limits. Confer with directors and production staff to discuss issues such as production and casting problems, budgets, policies, and news coverage. Select, acquire, and maintain programs, music, films, and other needed materials, and obtain legal clearances for their use as necessary. Monitor network transmissions for advisories concerning daily program schedules, program content, special feeds, and/or program changes. Develop promotions for current programs and specials. Prepare copy and edit tape so that material is ready for broadcasting. Develop ideas for programs and features that a station could produce. Participate in the planning and execution of fundraising activities. Review information about programs and schedules in order to ensure accuracy and provide such information to local media outlets as necessary. Read news, read and/or record public service and promotional announcements, and otherwise participate as a member of an on-air shift as required. Operate and maintain on-air and production audio equipment. Direct setup of remote facilities and install or cancel programs at remote stations. **SKILLS**—Management of Financial Resources; Management of Personnel Resources; Coordination; Time Management; Operations Analysis; Monitoring; Social Perceptiveness; Writing.

GOE—Interest Area: 03. Arts and Communication. **Work Group:** 03.01. Managerial Work in Arts and Communication. **PERSONALITY TYPE:** Enterprising. Enterprising occupations frequently involve starting up and carrying out projects. These occupations can involve leading people and making many decisions. They sometimes require risk taking and often deal with business.

EDUCATION/TRAINING PROGRAMS—Cinematography and Film/Video Production; Directing and Theatrical Production; Drama and Dramatics/Theatre Arts, General; Dramatic/Theatre Arts and Stagecraft, Other; Film/Cinema Studies; Radio and Television; Theatre/Theatre Arts Management. **RELATED KNOWLEDGE/COURSES**—**Telecommunications:** Knowledge of transmission, broadcasting, switching, control, and operation of telecommunications systems. **Communications and Media:** Knowledge of media production, communication, and dissemination techniques and methods. This includes alternative ways to inform and entertain via written, oral, and visual media. **Customer and Personal Service:** Knowledge of principles and processes for providing customer and personal services. This includes customer needs assessment, meeting quality standards for services, and evaluation of customer satisfaction. **Computers and Electronics:** Knowledge of circuit boards, processors, chips, electronic equipment, and computer hardware and software, including applications and programming. **Personnel and Human Resources:** Knowledge of principles and procedures for personnel recruitment, selection, training, compensation and benefits, labor relations and negotiation, and personnel information systems. **Clerical Practices:** Knowledge of administrative and clerical procedures and systems such as word processing, managing files and records, stenography and transcription, designing forms, and other office procedures and terminology.

Prosthodontists

- Annual Earnings: More than $146,500
- Growth: 13.6%
- Annual Job Openings: fewer than 500
- Self-Employed: 38.2%
- Part-Time: 22.6%
- Education/Training Required: First professional degree

Industries in Which Income Is Highest

Industry	Average Annual Wage	Number Employed
Ambulatory Health Care Services	More than $146,500	390

Metropolitan Areas Where Income Is Highest

Metropolitan Area	Average Annual Wage	Number Employed
Washington–Arlington–Alexandria, DC–VA–MD–WV	More than $146,500	70

Construct oral prostheses to replace missing teeth and other oral structures to correct natural and acquired deformation of mouth and jaws, to restore and maintain oral function, such as chewing and speaking, and to improve appearance. Replace missing teeth and associated oral structures with permanent fixtures, such as crowns and bridges, or removable fixtures, such as dentures. Fit prostheses to patients, making any necessary adjustments and modifications. Design and fabricate dental prostheses, or supervise dental technicians and laboratory bench workers who construct the devices. Measure and take impressions of patients' jaws and teeth in order to determine the shape and size of dental prostheses, using face bows, dental articulators, recording devices, and other materials. Collaborate with general dentists, specialists, and other health professionals in order to develop solutions to dental and oral health concerns. Repair, reline, and/or rebase dentures. Restore function and aesthetics to traumatic injury victims, or to individuals with diseases or birth defects. Use bonding technology on the surface of the teeth in order to change tooth shape or to close gaps. Treat facial pain and jaw joint problems. Place veneers onto teeth in order to conceal defects. **SKILLS—** Management of Financial Resources; Social Perceptiveness; Science; Active Learning; Reading Comprehension; Instructing; Complex Problem Solving; Management of Personnel Resources.

GOE—Interest Area: 08. Health Science. **Work Group:** 08.03. Dentistry. **PERSONALITY TYPE:** Investigative. Investigative occupations frequently involve working with ideas and require an extensive amount of thinking. These occupations can involve searching for facts and figuring out problems mentally.

EDUCATION/TRAINING PROGRAMS— Prosthodontics Specialty; Prosthodontics/ Prosthodontology (Cert, MS, PhD). **RELATED KNOWLEDGE/COURSES—Medicine and Dentistry:** Knowledge of the information and techniques needed to diagnose and treat human injuries, diseases, and deformities. This includes symptoms, treatment alternatives, drug properties and interactions, and preventive health-care measures. **Biology:** Knowledge of plant and animal organisms and their tissues, cells, functions, interdependencies, and interactions with each other and the environment. **Psychology:** Knowledge of human behavior and performance; individual differences in ability, personality, and interests; learning and motivation; psychological research methods; and the assessment and treatment of behavioral and affective disorders. **Chemistry:** Knowledge of the chemical composition, structure, and properties of substances and of the chemical processes and transformations that they undergo. This includes uses of chemicals, their danger signs, production techniques, and disposal methods. **Sales and Marketing:** Knowledge of principles and methods for showing, promoting, and selling products or services. This includes marketing strategy and tactics, product demonstration, sales techniques, and sales control systems. **Customer and Personal Service:** Knowledge of principles and processes for providing customer and personal services. This includes customer needs assessment, meeting quality standards for services, and evaluation of customer satisfaction.

Psychiatrists

- Annual Earnings: More than $146,500
- Growth: 24.0%
- Annual Job Openings: 41,000
- Self-Employed: 11.0%
- Part-Time: 9.6%
- Education/Training Required: First professional degree

The job openings listed here are shared with Anesthesiologists; Family and General Practitioners; Internists, General; Obstetricians and Gynecologists; Pediatricians, General; and Surgeons.

Industries in Which Income Is Highest

Industry	Average Annual Wage	Number Employed
Ambulatory Health Care Services	More than $146,500	11,450
Federal, State, and Local Government	$140,340	2,830
Hospitals	$132,770	6,490

Metropolitan Areas Where Income Is Highest

Metropolitan Area	Average Annual Wage	Number Employed
Minneapolis–St. Paul–Bloomington, MN–WI	More than $146,500	220
Hartford–West Hartford–East Hartford, CT	More than $146,500	200
Detroit–Warren–Livonia, MI	More than $146,500	160
Bridgeport–Stamford–Norwalk, CT	More than $146,500	100
Phoenix–Mesa–Scottsdale, AZ	More than $146,500	100

Diagnose, treat, and help prevent disorders of the mind. Analyze and evaluate patient data and test or examination findings to diagnose nature and extent of mental disorder. Prescribe, direct, and administer psychotherapeutic treatments or medications to treat mental, emotional, or behavioral disorders. Collaborate with physicians, psychologists, social workers, psychiatric nurses, or other professionals to discuss treatment plans and progress. Gather and maintain patient information and records, including social and medical history obtained from patients, relatives, and other professionals. Counsel outpatients and other patients during office visits. Design individualized care plans, using a variety of treatments. Examine or conduct laboratory or diagnostic tests on patient to provide information on general physical condition and mental disorder. Advise and inform guardians, relatives, and significant others of patients' conditions and treatment. Review and evaluate treatment procedures and outcomes of other psychiatrists and medical professionals. Teach, conduct research, and publish findings to increase understanding of mental, emotional, and behavioral states and disorders. Prepare and submit case reports and summaries to government and mental health agencies. Serve on committees to promote and maintain community mental health services and delivery systems. **SKILLS**—Social Perceptiveness; Persuasion; Science; Active Learning; Active Listening; Systems Analysis; Negotiation; Complex Problem Solving.

GOE—Interest Area: 08. Health Science. **Work Group:** 08.02. Medicine and Surgery. **PERSONALITY TYPE:** Investigative. Investigative occupations frequently involve working with ideas and require an extensive amount of thinking. These occupations can involve searching for facts and figuring out problems mentally.

EDUCATION/TRAINING PROGRAMS—Child Psychiatry; Psychiatry; Psysical Medical and Rehabilitation/Psychiatry. **RELATED KNOWLEDGE/COURSES**—**Therapy and Counseling:** Knowledge of principles, methods, and procedures for diagnosis, treatment, and rehabilitation of physical and mental dysfunctions and for career counseling and guidance. **Medicine and Dentistry:** Knowledge of the information and techniques needed to diagnose and treat human injuries, diseases, and deformities. This includes symptoms, treatment alternatives, drug properties and interactions, and preventive health-care measures. **Psychology:** Knowledge of human behavior and performance; individual differences in ability, personality, and interests; learning and motivation; psychological research methods; and the assessment and treatment of behavioral and affective disorders. **Biology:** Knowledge of plant and animal organisms and their tissues, cells, functions, interdependencies, and interactions with each other and the environment. **Philosophy and Theology:** Knowledge of different philosophical systems and religions. This includes their basic principles, values, ethics, ways of thinking, customs, and practices and their impact on human culture. **Sociology and Anthropology:** Knowledge of group behavior and dynamics, societal trends and influences, human migrations, ethnicity, and cultures and their history and origins.

Psychology Teachers, Postsecondary

- Annual Earnings: $56,370
- Growth: 32.2%
- Annual Job Openings: 329,000
- Self-Employed: 0.4%
- Part-Time: 27.3%
- Education/Training Required: Master's degree

Our sources did not provide separate job openings data for this occupation. The job openings listed here are shared with 35 other postsecondary teaching occupations. For a complete list, see the beginning of this section.

Industries in Which Income Is Highest

Industry	Average Annual Wage	Number Employed
Educational Services	$56,390	30,170

Metropolitan Areas Where Income Is Highest

Metropolitan Area	Average Annual Wage	Number Employed
Columbia, SC	$78,930	110
Honolulu, HI	$75,070	130
Memphis, TN–MS–AR	$71,960	160
Riverside–San Bernardino–Ontario, CA	$70,580	170
San Diego–Carlsbad–San Marcos, CA	$69,450	270

Teach courses in psychology, such as child, clinical, and developmental psychology, and psychological counseling. Prepare and deliver lectures to under graduate and/or graduate students on topics such as abnormal psychology, cognitive processes, and work motivation. Evaluate and grade students' class work, laboratory work, assignments, and papers. Initiate, facilitate, and moderate classroom discussions. Compile, administer, and grade examinations or assign this work to others. Keep abreast of developments in their field by reading current literature, talking with colleagues, and participating in professional conferences. Prepare course materials such as syllabi, homework assignments, and handouts. Plan, evaluate, and revise curricula, course content, and course materials and methods of instruction. Maintain student attendance records, grades, and other required records. Supervise undergraduate and/or graduate teaching, internship, and research work. Maintain regularly scheduled office hours in order to advise and assist students. Conduct research in a particular field of knowledge and publish findings in professional journals, books, and/or electronic media. Advise students on academic and vocational curricula and on career issues. Select and obtain materials and supplies such as textbooks. Collaborate with colleagues to address teaching and research issues. Serve on academic or administrative committees that deal with institutional policies, departmental matters, and academic issues. Compile bibliographies of specialized materials for outside reading assignments. Participate in student recruitment, registration, and placement activities. Supervise students' laboratory work. Perform administrative duties such as serving as department head. Act as advisers to student organizations. Write grant proposals to procure external research funding. **SKILLS**—Instructing; Learning Strategies; Social Perceptiveness; Science; Active Learning; Critical Thinking; Persuasion; Writing.

GOE—Interest Area: 05. Education and Training. **Work Group:** 05.03. Postsecondary and Adult Teaching and Instructing. **PERSONALITY TYPE:** Social. Social occupations frequently involve working with, communicating with, and teaching people. These occupations often involve helping or providing service to others.

EDUCATION/TRAINING PROGRAMS—Clinical Psychology; Cognitive Psychology and Psycholinguistics; Community Psychology; Comparative Psychology; Counseling Psychology; Developmental and Child Psychology; Educational Psychology; Experimental Psychology; Industrial and Organizational Psychology; Marriage and Family Therapy/Counseling; Personality Psychology; Physiological Psychology/Psychobiology; Psychology Teacher Education; Psychology, General; Psychology, Other; Psychometrics and Quantitative Psychology; others. **RELATED KNOWLEDGE/COURSES**—**Psychology:** Knowledge of human behavior and performance; individual differences in ability, personality, and interests; learning and motivation; psychological research methods; and the assessment and treatment of behavioral and affective disorders. **Therapy and Counseling:** Knowledge of principles, methods, and procedures for diagnosis, treatment, and rehabilitation of physical and mental dysfunctions and for career counseling and guidance. **Education and Training:** Knowledge of principles and methods for curriculum and training design, teaching and instruction for individuals and groups, and the measurement of training effects. **Sociology and Anthropology:** Knowledge of group behavior and dynamics, societal trends and influences, human migrations, ethnicity, and cultures and their history and origins. **Philosophy and Theology:** Knowledge of different philosophical systems and religions. This includes their basic principles, values, ethics, ways of thinking, customs, and practices and their impact on human culture. **English Language:** Knowledge of the structure and content of the English language, including the meaning and spelling of words, rules of composition, and grammar.

P

Public Relations Managers

- Annual Earnings: $76,450
- Growth: 21.7%
- Annual Job Openings: 5,000
- Self-Employed: 1.6%
- Part-Time: 8.4%
- Education/Training Required: Work experience plus degree

Industries in Which Income Is Highest

Industry	Average Annual Wage	Number Employed
Professional, Scientific, and Technical Services	$97,110	6,340
Management of Companies and Enterprises	$91,340	3,460
Credit Intermediation and Related Activities	$87,170	1,570
Insurance Carriers and Related Activities	$82,950	1,250
Hospitals	$73,230	1,480

Metropolitan Areas Where Income Is Highest

Metropolitan Area	Average Annual Wage	Number Employed
San Jose–Sunnyvale–Santa Clara, CA	$112,020	410
New York–Northern New Jersey–Long Island, NY–NJ–PA	$107,610	5,180
Trenton–Ewing, NJ	$107,030	150
Bridgeport–Stamford–Norwalk, CT	$105,690	270
Washington–Arlington–Alexandria, DC–VA–MD–WV	$97,430	1,960

Plan and direct public relations programs designed to create and maintain a favorable public image for employer or client; or if engaged in fundraising, plan and direct activities to solicit and maintain funds for special projects and nonprofit organizations. Identify main client groups and audiences and determine the best way to communicate publicity information to them. Write interesting and effective press releases, prepare information for media kits and develop and maintain company internet or intranet web pages. Develop and maintain the company's corporate image and identity, which includes the use of logos and signage. Manage communications budgets. Manage special events such as sponsorship of races, parties introducing new products, or other activities the firm supports in order to gain public attention through the media without advertising directly. Draft speeches for company executives, and arrange interviews and other forms of contact for them. Assign, supervise and review the activities of public relations staff. Evaluate advertising and promotion programs for compatibility with public relations efforts. Establish and maintain effective working relationships with local and municipal government officials and media representatives. Confer with labor relations managers to develop internal communications that keep employees informed of company activities. Direct activities of external agencies, establishments and departments that develop and implement communication strategies and information programs. Formulate policies and procedures related to public information programs, working with public relations executives. Respond to requests for information about employers' activities or status. Establish goals for soliciting funds, develop policies for collection and safeguarding of contributions, and coordinate disbursement of funds. Facilitate consumer relations, or the relationship between parts of the company such as the managers and employees, or different branch offices. Maintain company archives. Manage in-house communication courses. Produce films and other video products, regulate their distribution, and operate film library. **SKILLS**—Management of Financial Resources; Social Perceptiveness; Service Orientation; Monitoring; Persuasion; Writing; Negotiation; Coordination.

GOE—Interest Area: 03. Arts and Communication. **Work Group:** 03.01. Managerial Work in Arts and Communication. **PERSONALITY TYPE:** No data available.

EDUCATION/TRAINING PROGRAM—Public Relations/Image Management. **RELATED KNOWLEDGE/COURSES—Sales and Marketing:** Knowledge of principles and methods for showing, promoting, and selling products or services. This includes marketing strategy and tactics, product demonstration, sales techniques, and sales control systems. **Economics and Accounting:** Knowledge of economic and accounting principles and practices, the financial markets, banking, and the analysis and reporting of financial data. **Education and Training:** Knowledge of principles and methods for curriculum and training design, teaching and instruction for individuals and groups, and the measurement of training effects. **Law and Government:** Knowledge of laws, legal codes, court procedures, precedents, government regulations, executive orders, agency rules, and the democratic political process. **Foreign Language:** Knowledge of the structure and content of a foreign (non-English) language, including the meaning and spelling of words, rules of composition and grammar, and pronunciation. **Customer and Personal Service:** Knowledge of principles and processes for providing customer and personal services. This includes customer needs assessment, meeting quality standards for services, and evaluation of customer satisfaction.

Public Transportation Inspectors

- Annual Earnings: $49,490
- Growth: 11.4%
- Annual Job Openings: 2,000
- Self-Employed: 1.9%
- Part-Time: 2.2%
- Education/Training Required: Work experience in a related occupation

The job openings listed here are shared with Aviation Inspectors, Freight Inspectors, Marine Cargo Inspectors, Motor Vehicle Inspectors, and Railroad Inspectors.

Industries in Which Income Is Highest

Industry	Average Annual Wage	Number Employed
Air Transportation	$67,590	1,460
Transportation Equipment Manufacturing	$55,200	1,100
Federal, State, and Local Government	$54,510	10,960
Rail Transportation	$45,840	2,680
Support Activities for Transportation	$37,870	4,350

Metropolitan Areas Where Income Is Highest

Metropolitan Area	Average Annual Wage	Number Employed
Washington–Arlington–Alexandria, DC–VA–MD–WV	$96,800	360
Oklahoma City, OK	$91,650	130
Milwaukee–Waukesha–West Allis, WI	$84,510	50
Miami–Fort Lauderdale–Miami Beach, FL	$84,490	680
Louisville–Jefferson County, KY–IN	$81,260	80

Monitor operation of public transportation systems to ensure good service and compliance with regulations. Investigate accidents, equipment failures, and complaints. Observes employees performing assigned duties to note their deportment, treatment of passengers, and adherence to company regulations and schedules. Observes and records time required to load and unload passengers or freight volume of traffic on vehicle and at stops. Investigates schedule delays, accidents, and complaints. Inspects company vehicles and other property for evidence of abuse, damage, and mechanical malfunction and directs repair. Determines need for changes in service, such as additional vehicles, route changes, and revised schedules to improve service and efficiency. Drives automobile along route to detect conditions hazardous to equipment and passengers and negotiates with local governments to eliminate hazards. Submits written reports to management with recommendations for improving service. Reports disruptions to service. Assists in dispatching equipment when necessary. Recommends promotions and disciplinary actions involving transportation personnel. SKILLS— Operations Analysis; Systems Evaluation; Writing; Management of Personnel Resources; Monitoring; Speaking; Systems Analysis.

GOE—**Interest Area:** 16. Transportation, Distribution, and Logistics. **Work Group:** 16.07. Transportation Support Work. **PERSONALITY TYPE:** Enterprising. Enterprising occupations frequently involve starting up and carrying out projects. These occupations can involve leading people and making many decisions. They sometimes require risk taking and often deal with business.

EDUCATION/TRAINING PROGRAM—No data available. **RELATED KNOWLEDGE/COURSES— Transportation:** Knowledge of principles and methods for moving people or goods by air, rail, sea, or road, including the relative costs and benefits. **Personnel and Human Resources:** Knowledge of principles and procedures for personnel recruitment, selection, training, compensation and benefits, labor relations and negotiation, and personnel information systems. **Public Safety and Security:** Knowledge of relevant equipment, policies, procedures, and strategies to promote effective local, state, or national security operations for the protection of people, data, property, and institutions. **Law and Government:** Knowledge of laws, legal codes, court procedures, precedents, government regulations, executive orders, agency rules, and the democratic political process. **Geography:** Knowledge of principles and methods for describing the features of land, sea, and air masses, including their physical characteristics; locations; interrelationships; and distribution of plant, animal, and human life. **Administration and Management:** Knowledge of business and management principles involved in strategic planning, resource allocation, human resources modeling, leadership technique, production methods, and coordination of people and resources.

Purchasing Agents and Buyers, Farm Products

- ◉ Annual Earnings: $46,680
- ◉ Growth: 7.0%
- ◉ Annual Job Openings: 2,000
- ◉ Self-Employed: 8.5%
- ◉ Part-Time: 10.1%
- ◉ Education/Training Required: Work experience in a related occupation

Industries in Which Income Is Highest

Industry	Average Annual Wage	Number Employed
Merchant Wholesalers, Nondurable Goods	$47,660	5,670
Food Manufacturing	$46,370	1,410
Food and Beverage Stores	$33,960	1,040

Metropolitan Areas Where Income Is Highest

Metropolitan Area	Average Annual Wage	Number Employed
Winston–Salem, NC	$69,610	70
Denver–Aurora, CO	$67,660	110
New York–Northern New Jersey–Long Island, NY–NJ–PA	$65,490	320
Visalia–Porterville, CA	$65,090	50
Dallas–Fort Worth–Arlington, TX	$63,510	130

Purchase farm products either for further processing or resale. Calculate applicable government grain quotas. Coordinate and direct activities of workers engaged in cutting, transporting, storing, or milling products and in maintaining records. Arrange for processing and/or resale of purchased products. Arrange for transportation and/or storage of purchased products. Examine and test crops and products to estimate their value, determine their grade, and locate any evidence of disease or insect damage. Maintain records of business transactions and product inventories, reporting data to companies or government agencies as necessary. Negotiate contracts with farmers for the production or purchase of farm products. Purchase for further processing or for resale farm products such as milk, grains, and Christmas trees. Review orders to determine product types and quantities required to meet demand. Advise farm groups and growers on land preparation and livestock care techniques that will maximize the quantity and quality of production. Estimate land production possibilities, surveying property and studying factors such as crop rotation history, soil fertility, and irrigation facilities. Sell supplies such as seed, feed, fertilizers, and insecticides, arranging for loans or financing as necessary. **SKILLS**—Negotiation; Management of Financial Resources; Writing; Mathematics; Persuasion; Management of Material Resources; Speaking; Coordination.

GOE—Interest Area: 01. Agriculture and Natural Resources. **Work Group:** 01.01. Managerial Work in Agriculture and Natural Resources. **PERSONALITY TYPE:** Enterprising. Enterprising occupations frequently involve starting up and carrying out projects. These occupations can involve leading people and making many decisions. They sometimes require risk taking and often deal with business.

EDUCATION/TRAINING PROGRAM—Agricultural/Farm Supplies Retailing and Wholesaling.

RELATED KNOWLEDGE/COURSES—Food Production: Knowledge of techniques and equipment for planting, growing, and harvesting food products (both plant and animal) for consumption, including storage/handling techniques. **Production and Processing:** Knowledge of raw materials, production processes, quality control, costs, and other techniques for maximizing the effective manufacture and distribution of goods. **Biology:** Knowledge of plant and animal organisms and their tissues, cells, functions, interdependencies, and interactions with each other and the environment. **Communications and Media:** Knowledge of media production, communication, and dissemination techniques and methods. This includes alternative ways to inform and entertain via written, oral, and visual media. **Economics and Accounting:** Knowledge of economic and accounting principles and practices, the financial markets, banking, and the analysis and reporting of financial data. **Sales and Marketing:** Knowledge of principles and methods for showing, promoting, and selling products or services. This includes marketing strategy and tactics, product demonstration, sales techniques, and sales control systems.

Purchasing Agents, Except Wholesale, Retail, and Farm Products

- Annual Earnings: $49,030
- Growth: 8.1%
- Annual Job Openings: 19,000
- Self-Employed: 3.5%
- Part-Time: 5.7%
- Education/Training Required: Work experience in a related occupation

Industries in Which Income Is Highest

Industry	Average Annual Wage	Number Employed
Telecommunications	$59,550	4,510
Publishing Industries (Except Internet)	$58,730	1,260
Federal, State, and Local Government	$57,140	40,570
Professional, Scientific, and Technical Services	$55,090	20,440
Utilities	$54,910	2,790

Metropolitan Areas Where Income Is Highest

Metropolitan Area	Average Annual Wage	Number Employed
Kennewick–Richland–Pasco, WA	$75,820	340
Washington–Arlington–Alexandria, DC–VA–MD–WV	$68,410	11,030
San Jose–Sunnyvale–Santa Clara, CA	$64,720	3,690
Huntsville, AL	$63,360	1,470
Dayton, OH	$62,170	1,400

Purchase machinery, equipment, tools, parts, supplies, or services necessary for the operation of an establishment. Purchase raw or semi-finished materials for manufacturing. Purchase the highest quality merchandise at the lowest possible price and in correct amounts. Prepare purchase orders, solicit bid proposals and review requisitions for goods and services. Research and evaluate suppliers based on price, quality, selection, service, support, availability, reliability, production and distribution capabilities, and the supplier's reputation and history. Analyze price proposals, financial reports, and other data and information to determine reasonable prices. Monitor and follow applicable laws and regulations. Negotiate, or renegotiate, and administer contracts with suppliers, vendors, and other representatives. Monitor shipments to ensure that goods come in on time, and in the event of problems trace shipments and follow up undelivered goods. Confer with staff, users, and vendors to discuss defective or unacceptable goods or services and determine corrective action. Evaluate and monitor contract performance to ensure compliance with contractual obligations and to determine need for changes. Maintain and review computerized or manual records of items purchased, costs, delivery, product performance, and inventories. Review catalogs, industry periodicals, directories, trade journals, and Internet sites, and consult with other department personnel to locate necessary goods and services. Study sales records and inventory levels of current stock to develop strategic purchasing programs that facilitate employee access to supplies. Interview vendors and visit suppliers' plants and distribution centers to examine and learn about products, services and prices. Arrange the payment of duty and freight charges. Hire, train and/or supervise purchasing clerks, buyers, and expediters. Write and review product specifications, maintaining a working technical knowledge of the goods or services to be purchased. Monitor changes affecting supply and demand, tracking market conditions, price trends, or futures markets. Formulate policies and procedures for bid proposals and procurement of goods and services. **SKILLS**—Management of Personnel Resources; Time Management; Persuasion; Management of Financial Resources; Negotiation; Speaking; Operations Analysis; Management of Material Resources.

GOE—Interest Area: 14. Retail and Wholesale Sales and Service. **Work Group:** 14.05. Purchasing. **PERSONALITY TYPE:** Enterprising. Enterprising occupations frequently involve starting up and carrying out projects. These occupations can involve leading people and making many decisions. They sometimes require risk taking and often deal with business.

EDUCATION/TRAINING PROGRAMS—Merchandising and Buying Operations; Sales, Distribution, and Marketing Operations, General; Sales, Distribution, and Marketing Operations, General. **RELATED KNOWLEDGE/COURSES—Clerical Practices:** Knowledge of administrative and clerical procedures and systems such as word processing, managing files and records, stenography and transcription, designing forms, and other office procedures and terminology. **Economics and Accounting:** Knowledge of economic and accounting principles and practices, the financial markets, banking, and the analysis and reporting of financial data. **Administration and Management:** Knowledge of business and management principles involved in strategic planning, resource allocation, human resources modeling, leadership technique, production methods, and coordination of people and resources. **Production and Processing:** Knowledge of raw materials, production processes, quality control, costs, and other techniques for maximizing the effective manufacture and distribution of goods. **Computers and Electronics:** Knowledge of circuit boards, processors, chips, electronic equipment, and computer hardware and software, including applications and programming. **Mathematics:** Knowledge of arithmetic, algebra, geometry, calculus, and statistics and their applications.

Purchasing Managers

- Annual Earnings: $76,270
- Growth: 7.0%
- Annual Job Openings: 8,000
- Self-Employed: 0.3%
- Part-Time: 1.5%
- Education/Training Required: Work experience plus degree

Industries in Which Income Is Highest

Industry	Average Annual Wage	Number Employed
Professional, Scientific, and Technical Services	$90,340	3,980
Management of Companies and Enterprises	$87,910	7,470
Computer and Electronic Product Manufacturing	$85,470	4,980
Federal, State, and Local Government	$81,720	6,330
Chemical Manufacturing	$81,510	1,800

Metropolitan Areas Where Income Is Highest

Metropolitan Area	Average Annual Wage	Number Employed
Trenton–Ewing, NJ	$111,530	130
Kennewick–Richland–Pasco, WA	$109,690	50
Bridgeport–Stamford–Norwalk, CT	$106,130	260
San Jose–Sunnyvale–Santa Clara, CA	$104,850	930
Washington–Arlington–Alexandria, DC–VA–MD–WV	$102,560	2,230

Plan, direct, or coordinate the activities of buyers, purchasing officers, and related workers involved in purchasing materials, products, and services. Maintain records of goods ordered and received. Locate vendors of materials, equipment or supplies, and interview them in order to determine product availability and terms of sales. Prepare and process requisitions and purchase orders for supplies and equipment. Control purchasing department budgets. Interview and hire staff, and oversee staff training. Review purchase order claims and contracts for conformance to company policy. Analyze market and delivery systems in order to assess present and future material availability. Develop and implement purchasing and contract management instructions, policies, and procedures. Participate in the development of specifications for equipment, products or substitute materials. Resolve vendor or contractor grievances, and claims against suppliers. Represent companies in negotiating contracts and formulating policies with suppliers. Review, evaluate, and approve specifications for issuing and awarding bids. Direct and coordinate activities of personnel engaged in buying, selling, and distributing materials, equipment, machinery, and supplies. Prepare bid awards requiring board approval. Prepare reports regarding market conditions and merchandise costs. Administer on-line purchasing systems. SKILLS—Management of Material Resources; Management of Financial Resources; Negotiation; Operations Analysis; Persuasion; Time Management; Active Learning; Coordination.

GOE—Interest Area: 14. Retail and Wholesale Sales and Service. Work Group: 14.01. Managerial Work in Retail/Wholesale Sales and Service. PERSONALITY TYPE: Enterprising. Enterprising occupations frequently involve starting up and carrying out projects. These occupations can involve leading people and making many decisions. They sometimes require risk taking and often deal with business.

EDUCATION/TRAINING PROGRAM—Purchasing, Procurement/Acquisitions and Contracts Management. RELATED KNOWLEDGE/ COURSES—Personnel and Human Resources: Knowledge of principles and procedures for personnel recruitment, selection, training, compensation and benefits, labor relations and negotiation, and personnel information systems. Economics and Accounting: Knowledge of economic and accounting principles and practices, the financial markets, banking, and the analysis and reporting of financial data. Administration and Management: Knowledge of business and management principles involved in strategic planning, resource allocation, human resources modeling, leadership technique, production methods, and coordination of people and resources. Production and Processing: Knowledge of raw materials, production processes, quality control, costs, and other techniques for maximizing the effective manufacture and distribution of goods. Education and Training: Knowledge of principles and methods for curriculum and training design, teaching and instruction for individuals and groups, and the measurement of training effects. Computers and Electronics: Knowledge of circuit boards, processors, chips, electronic equipment, and computer hardware and software, including applications and programming.

Radiation Therapists

- Annual Earnings: $62,340
- Growth: 26.3%
- Annual Job Openings: 1,000
- Self-Employed: 0.0%
- Part-Time: 6.0%
- Education/Training Required: Associate degree

Industries in Which Income Is Highest

Industry	Average Annual Wage	Number Employed
Ambulatory Health Care Services	$66,220	3,140
Hospitals	$60,700	10,310

Metropolitan Areas Where Income Is Highest

Metropolitan Area	Average Annual Wage	Number Employed
Seattle–Tacoma–Bellevue, WA	$78,180	160
Los Angeles–Long Beach–Santa Ana, CA	$76,760	240
Milwaukee–Waukesha–West Allis, WI	$76,720	100
New York–Northern New Jersey–Long Island, NY–NJ–PA	$76,030	640
Riverside–San Bernardino–Ontario, CA	$74,640	90

Provide radiation therapy to patients as prescribed by a radiologist according to established practices and standards. Duties may include reviewing prescription and diagnosis; acting as liaison with physician and supportive care personnel; preparing equipment, such as immobilization, treatment, and protection devices; and maintaining records, reports, and files. May assist in dosimetry procedures and tumor localization. Administer prescribed doses of radiation to specific body parts, using radiation therapy equipment according to established practices and standards. Position patients for treatment with accuracy according to prescription. Enter data into computer and set controls to operate and adjust equipment and regulate dosage. Follow principles of radiation protection for patient, self, and others. Maintain records, reports and files as required, including such information as radiation dosages, equipment settings and patients' reactions. Review prescription, diagnosis, patient chart, and identification. Conduct most treatment sessions independently, in accordance with the long-term treatment plan and under the general direction of the patient's physician. Check radiation therapy equipment to ensure proper operation. Observe and reassure patients during treatment and report unusual reactions to physician or turn equipment off if unexpected adverse reactions occur. Check for side effects such as skin irritation, nausea and hair loss to assess patients' reaction to treatment. Educate, prepare and reassure patients and their families by answering questions, providing physical assistance, and reinforcing physicians' advice regarding treatment reactions and post-treatment care. Calculate actual treatment dosages delivered during each session. Prepare and construct equipment, such as immobilization, treatment, and protection devices. Photograph treated area of patient and process film. Help physicians, radiation oncologists and clinical physicists to prepare physical and technical aspects of radiation treatment plans, using information about patient condition and anatomy. Train and supervise student or subordinate radiotherapy technologists. Act as liaison with physicist and supportive care personnel. Provide assistance to other health-care personnel during dosimetry procedures and tumor localization. Implement appropriate follow-up care plans. Store, sterilize, or prepare the special applicators containing the radioactive substance implanted by the physician. Assist in the preparation of sealed radioactive materials, such as cobalt, radium, cesium and isotopes, for use in radiation treatments. SKILLS—Operation Monitoring; Technology Design; Operation and Control; Time Management; Management of Personnel Resources; Instructing; Service Orientation; Social Perceptiveness.

GOE—Interest Area: 08. Health Science. Work Group: 08.07. Medical Therapy. PERSONALITY TYPE: Social. Social occupations frequently involve working with, communicating with, and teaching people. These occupations often involve helping or providing service to others.

EDUCATION/TRAINING PROGRAM—Medical Radiologic Technology/Science Radiation Therapist. RELATED KNOWLEDGE/COURSES—Medicine

and Dentistry: Knowledge of the information and techniques needed to diagnose and treat human injuries, diseases, and deformities. This includes symptoms, treatment alternatives, drug properties and interactions, and preventive health-care measures. Biology: Knowledge of plant and animal organisms and their tissues, cells, functions, interdependencies, and interactions with each other and the environment. Customer and Personal Service: Knowledge of principles and processes for providing customer and personal services. This includes customer needs assessment, meeting quality standards for services, and evaluation of customer satisfaction. Psychology: Knowledge of human behavior and performance; individual differences in ability, personality, and interests; learning and motivation; psychological research methods; and the assessment and treatment of behavioral and affective disorders. Therapy and Counseling: Knowledge of principles, methods, and procedures for diagnosis, treatment, and rehabilitation of physical and mental dysfunctions and for career counseling and guidance. Physics: Knowledge and prediction of physical principles and laws and their interrelationships and applications to understanding fluid, material, and atmospheric dynamics and mechanical, electrical, atomic, and subatomic structures and processes.

Railroad Conductors and Yardmasters

- Annual Earnings: $54,040
- Growth: 20.3%
- Annual Job Openings: 3,000
- Self-Employed: 0.0%
- Part-Time: 0.6%
- Education/Training Required: Work experience in a related occupation

Industries in Which Income Is Highest

Industry	Average Annual Wage	Number Employed
Rail Transportation	$53,910	35,560

Metropolitan Areas Where Income Is Highest

Metropolitan Area	Average Annual Wage	Number Employed

No data available.

Conductors coordinate activities of train crew on passenger or freight train. Coordinate activities of switch-engine crew within yard of railroad, industrial plant, or similar location. Yardmasters coordinate activities of workers engaged in railroad traffic operations, such as the makeup or breakup of trains, yard switching, and review train schedules and switching orders. Answer passengers' inquiries and announce information such as approaching train stops. Collect tickets, fares, or passes from passengers. Confer with engineers regarding train routes, timetables, and cargoes, and to discuss alternative routes when there are rail defects or obstructions. Confirm routes and destination information for freight cars. Direct and instruct workers engaged in yard activities, such as switching tracks, coupling and uncoupling cars, and routing inbound and outbound traffic. Direct engineers to move cars to fit planned train configurations, combining or separating cars to make up or break up trains. Instruct workers to regulate air-conditioning, lighting, and heating in passenger cars in order to ensure passengers' comfort. Keep records of the contents and destination of each train car, and make sure that cars are added or removed at proper points on routes. Observe lights on panelboards to monitor and chart locations of trains, and to estimate arrival times. Observe yard traffic to determine tracks available to accommodate inbound and outbound traffic. Review schedules, switching orders, way bills, and shipping records to obtain cargo loading and unloading information and to plan work. Signal engineers to begin train runs, stop trains, or change speed, using telecommunications equipment or hand signals. Supervise and coordinate crew activities to transport freight and passengers and to provide boarding, porter, maid, and meal services to passengers. Arrange for the removal of defective cars from trains at stations or stops. Document and prepare reports of accidents, unscheduled stops, or delays. Inspect each car periodically during runs. Inspect freight cars for compliance with sealing procedures, and record car numbers and seal numbers. Instruct workers to set warning signals in front and at rear of trains during emergency stops. Operate controls to activate track switches and traffic signals. Receive information regarding train or rail problems from dispatchers or from electronic monitoring devices. Receive instructions from dispatchers regarding trains' routes, timetables, and cargoes. SKILLS—Management of Personnel Resources; Coordination; Operation and Control; Operation Monitoring; Systems Evaluation; Systems Analysis; Troubleshooting; Instructing.

GOE—Interest Area: 16. Transportation, Distribution, and Logistics. Work Group: 16.01. Managerial Work in Transportation. PERSONALITY TYPE: Realistic. Realistic occupations frequently involve work activities that include practical, hands-on problems and solutions. They often deal with plants, animals, and real-world materials like wood, tools, and machinery. Many of the occupations require working outside and do not involve a lot of paperwork or working closely with others.

EDUCATION/TRAINING PROGRAM—Truck and Bus Driver/Commercial Vehicle Operation. RELATED KNOWLEDGE/COURSES— Transportation: Knowledge of principles and methods for moving people or goods by air, rail, sea, or road, including the relative costs and benefits. Administration and Management: Knowledge of business and management principles involved in strategic planning, resource allocation, human resources modeling, leadership technique, production methods, and coordination of people and resources. Mechanical Devices: Knowledge of machines and tools, including their designs, uses, repair, and maintenance. Public Safety and Security: Knowledge of relevant equipment, policies, procedures, and strategies to promote effective local, state, or national security operations for the protection of people, data, property, and institutions.

Railroad Inspectors

- Annual Earnings: $49,490
- Growth: 11.4%
- Annual Job Openings: 2,000
- Self-Employed: 1.9%
- Part-Time: 2.2%
- Education/Training Required: Work experience in a related occupation

The job openings listed here are shared with Aviation Inspectors, Freight Inspectors, Marine Cargo Inspectors, Motor Vehicle Inspectors, and Public Transportation Inspectors.

Industries in Which Income Is Highest

Industry	Average Annual Wage	Number Employed
Air Transportation	$67,590	1,460
Transportation Equipment Manufacturing	$55,200	1,100
Federal, State, and Local Government	$54,510	10,960
Rail Transportation	$45,840	2,680
Support Activities for Transportation	$37,870	4,350

Metropolitan Areas Where Income Is Highest

Metropolitan Area	Average Annual Wage	Number Employed
Washington–Arlington–Alexandria, DC–VA–MD–WV	$96,800	360
Oklahoma City, OK	$91,650	130
Milwaukee–Waukesha–West Allis, WI	$84,510	50
Miami–Fort Lauderdale–Miami Beach, FL	$84,490	680
Louisville–Jefferson County, KY–IN	$81,260	80

Inspect railroad equipment, roadbed, and track to ensure safe transport of people or cargo. Inspects signals and track wiring to determine continuity of electrical connections. Examines roadbed, switches, fishplates, rails, and ties to detect damage or wear. Examines locomotives and cars to detect damage or structural defects. Inspects and tests completed work. Operates switches to determine working conditions. Tests and synchronizes rail-flaw-detection machine, using circuit tester and hand tools, and reloads machine with paper and ink. Starts machine and signals worker to operate rail-detector car. Prepares reports on repairs made and equipment, railcars, or roadbed needing repairs. Tags rail cars needing immediate repair. Fills paint container on rail-detector car used to mark section of defective rail with paint. Directs crews to repair or replace defective equipment or to re-ballast roadbed. Places lanterns or flags in front and rear of train to signal that inspection is being performed. Seals leaks found during inspection that can be sealed with caulking compound. Replaces defective brake rod pins and tightens safety appliances. Notifies train dispatcher of railcar to be moved to shop for repair. Makes minor repairs. Packs brake bearings with grease. **SKILLS—** Repairing; Operation Monitoring; Troubleshooting; Equipment Maintenance; Quality Control Analysis; Management of Personnel Resources; Systems Analysis; Science.

GOE—Interest Area: 07. Government and Public Administration. **Work Group:** 07.03. Regulations Enforcement. **PERSONALITY TYPE:** Realistic. Realistic occupations frequently involve work activities that include practical, hands-on problems and solutions. They often deal with plants, animals, and real-world materials like wood, tools, and machinery. Many of the occupations require working outside and do not involve a lot of paperwork or working closely with others.

EDUCATION/TRAINING PROGRAM—No data available. **RELATED KNOWLEDGE/COURSES— Transportation:** Knowledge of principles and methods for moving people or goods by air, rail, sea, or road, including the relative costs and benefits. **Building and Construction:** Knowledge of the materials, methods, and tools involved in the construction or repair of houses, buildings, or other structures such as highways and roads. **Mechanical Devices:** Knowledge of machines and tools, including their designs, uses, repair, and maintenance. **Public Safety and Security:** Knowledge of relevant equipment, policies, procedures, and strategies to promote effective local, state, or national security operations for the protection of people, data, property, and institutions. **Engineering and Technology:** Knowledge of the practical application of engineering science and technology. This includes applying principles, techniques, procedures, and equipment to the design and production of various goods and services.

Railroad Yard Workers

- Annual Earnings: $49,700
- Growth: –38.5%
- Annual Job Openings: 1,000
- Self-Employed: 0.0%
- Part-Time: 1.3%
- Education/Training Required: Work experience in a related occupation

The job openings listed here are shared with Train Crew Members.

Industries in Which Income Is Highest

Industry	Average Annual Wage	Number Employed
Rail Transportation	$52,210	18,680
Support Activities for Transportation	$26,250	1,170

Metropolitan Areas Where Income Is Highest

Metropolitan Area	Average Annual Wage	Number Employed
Houston–Sugar Land–Baytown, TX	$24,870	240

Perform a variety of activities such as coupling railcars and operating railroad track switches in railroad yard to facilitate the movement of rail cars within the yard. Throws track switches to route cars to different sections of yard. Receives oral or written instructions indicating which cars are to be switched and track assignments. Raises lever to couple and uncouple cars for makeup and breakup of trains. Opens and closes chute gates to load and unload cars. Watches for and relays traffic signals to start and stop cars during shunting, using arm or lantern. Signals engineer to start and stop engine. Rides atop cars that have been shunted and turns handwheel to control speed or stop car at specified position. Attaches cable to cars being hoisted by cable or chain in mines, quarries or industrial plants. Connects airhose to car, using wrench. Opens and closes ventilation doors. SKILLS—Operation and Control.

GOE—Interest Area: 16. Transportation, Distribution, and Logistics. Work Group: 16.07. Transportation Support Work. PERSONALITY TYPE: Realistic. Realistic occupations frequently involve work activities that include practical, hands-on problems and solutions. They often deal with plants, animals, and real-world materials like wood, tools, and machinery. Many of the occupations require working outside and do not involve a lot of paperwork or working closely with others.

EDUCATION/TRAINING PROGRAM—Truck and Bus Driver/Commercial Vehicle Operation. RELATED KNOWLEDGE/COURSES—Trans-

portation: Knowledge of principles and methods for moving people or goods by air, rail, sea, or road, including the relative costs and benefits. Mechanical Devices: Knowledge of machines and tools, including their designs, uses, repair, and maintenance.

Range Managers

- Annual Earnings: $53,350
- Growth: 6.3%
- Annual Job Openings: 2,000
- Self-Employed: 9.0%
- Part-Time: 7.3%
- Education/Training Required: Bachelor's degree

The job openings listed here are shared with Park Naturalists and Soil Conservationists.

Industries in Which Income Is Highest

Industry	Average Annual Wage	Number Employed
Federal, State, and Local Government	$54,090	13,320

Metropolitan Areas Where Income Is Highest

Metropolitan Area	Average Annual Wage	Number Employed
Washington–Arlington–Alexandria, DC–VA–MD–WV	$83,690	460
Los Angeles–Long Beach–Santa Ana, CA	$74,340	90
Barnstable Town, MA	$71,250	80
San Diego–Carlsbad–San Marcos, CA	$71,120	60
Seattle–Tacoma–Bellevue, WA	$68,000	330

Research or study range land management practices to provide sustained production of forage, livestock, and wildlife. Regulate grazing, and help ranchers plan and organize grazing systems in order to manage, improve and protect rangelands and maximize their use. Measure and assess vegetation resources for biological assessment companies, environmental impact statements, and rangeland monitoring programs. Maintain soil stability and vegetation for non-grazing uses, such

R

as wildlife habitats and outdoor recreation. Mediate agreements among rangeland users and preservationists as to appropriate land use and management. Manage forage resources through fire, herbicide use, or revegetation to maintain a sustainable yield from the land. Study rangeland management practices and research range problems to provide sustained production of forage, livestock, and wildlife. Offer advice to rangeland users on water management, forage production methods, and control of brush. Plan and direct construction and maintenance of range improvements such as fencing, corrals, stock-watering reservoirs and soil-erosion control structures. Tailor conservation plans to landowners' goals, such as livestock support, wildlife, or recreation. Develop technical standards and specifications used to manage, protect and improve the natural resources of range lands and related grazing lands. Study grazing patterns to determine number and kind of livestock that can be most profitably grazed and to determine the best grazing seasons. Plan and implement revegetation of disturbed sites. Study forage plants and their growth requirements to determine varieties best suited to particular range. Develop methods for protecting range from fire and rodent damage and for controlling poisonous plants. Manage private livestock operations. **SKILLS**—Negotiation; Persuasion; Management of Financial Resources; Coordination; Science; Management of Personnel Resources; Complex Problem Solving; Judgment and Decision Making.

GOE—Interest Area: 01. Agriculture and Natural Resources. **Work Group:** 01.02. Resource Science/ Engineering for Plants, Animals, and the Environment. **PERSONALITY TYPE:** Investigative. Investigative occupations frequently involve working with ideas and require an extensive amount of thinking. These occupations can involve searching for facts and figuring out problems mentally.

EDUCATION/TRAINING PROGRAMS—Forest Management/ Forest Resources Management; Forest Sciences; Forestry, General; Forestry, Other; Land Use Planning and Management/Development; Natural Resources and Conservation, Other; Natural Resources Management and Policy, General; Natural Resources Management and Policy, Other; Natural Resources/Conservation, General; Water, Wetlands,

and Marine Resources Management; Wildlife and Wildlands Science and Management. **RELATED KNOWLEDGE/COURSES—Biology:** Knowledge of plant and animal organisms and their tissues, cells, functions, interdependencies, and interactions with each other and the environment. **Geography:** Knowledge of principles and methods for describing the features of land, sea, and air masses, including their physical characteristics; locations; interrelationships; and distribution of plant, animal, and human life. **Food Production:** Knowledge of techniques and equipment for planting, growing, and harvesting food products (both plant and animal) for consumption, including storage/handling techniques. **History and Archeology:** Knowledge of historical events and their causes, indicators, and effects on civilizations and cultures. **Law and Government:** Knowledge of laws, legal codes, court procedures, precedents, government regulations, executive orders, agency rules, and the democratic political process. **Customer and Personal Service:** Knowledge of principles and processes for providing customer and personal services. This includes customer needs assessment, meeting quality standards for services, and evaluation of customer satisfaction.

Real Estate Brokers

- ◎ Annual Earnings: $57,190
- ◎ Growth: 7.8%
- ◎ Annual Job Openings: 12,000
- ◎ Self-Employed: 59.9%
- ◎ Part-Time: 18.7%
- ◎ Education/Training Required: Work experience in a related occupation

Industries in Which Income Is Highest

Industry	Average Annual Wage	Number Employed
Real Estate	$57,250	35,940
Heavy and Civil Engineering Construction	$50,830	1,110

Metropolitan Areas Where Income Is Highest

Metropolitan Area	Average Annual Wage	Number Employed
San Francisco–Oakland–Fremont, CA	$138,880	780
Riverside–San Bernardino–Ontario, CA	$98,390	290
Davenport–Moline–Rock Island, IA–IL	$97,410	50
Minneapolis–St. Paul–Bloomington, MN–WI	$92,390	380
Portland–South Portland–Biddeford, ME	$89,080	160

Operate real estate office, or work for commercial real estate firm, overseeing real estate transactions. Other duties usually include selling real estate or renting properties and arranging loans. Sell, for a fee, real estate owned by others. Obtain agreements from property owners to place properties for sale with real estate firms. Monitor fulfillment of purchase contract terms to ensure that they are handled in a timely manner. Compare a property with similar properties that have recently sold, in order to determine its competitive market price. Act as an intermediary in negotiations between buyers and sellers over property prices and settlement details, and during the closing of sales. Generate lists of properties for sale, their locations and descriptions, and available financing options, using computers. Maintain knowledge of real estate law, local economies, fair housing laws, and types of available mortgages, financing options and government programs. Check work completed by loan officers, attorneys, and other professionals to ensure that it is performed properly. Arrange for financing of property purchases. Appraise property values, assessing income potential when relevant. Maintain awareness of current income tax regulations, local zoning, building and tax laws, and growth possibilities of the area where a property is located. Manage and operate real estate offices, handling associated business details. Supervise agents who handle real estate transactions. Rent properties or manage rental properties. Arrange for title searches of properties being sold. Give buyers virtual tours of properties in which they are interested, using computers. Review property details to ensure that environmental regulations are met. Develop, sell, or lease property used for industry or manufacturing. SKILLS— Management of Financial Resources; Negotiation; Persuasion; Service Orientation; Active Listening; Judgment and Decision Making; Mathematics; Complex Problem Solving.

GOE—Interest Area: 14. Retail and Wholesale Sales and Service. Work Group: 14.03. General Sales. PERSONALITY TYPE: No data available.

EDUCATION/TRAINING PROGRAM—Real Estate. RELATED KNOWLEDGE/COURSES— Sales and Marketing: Knowledge of principles and methods for showing, promoting, and selling products or services. This includes marketing strategy and tactics, product demonstration, sales techniques, and sales control systems. Customer and Personal Service: Knowledge of principles and processes for providing customer and personal services. This includes customer needs assessment, meeting quality standards for services, and evaluation of customer satisfaction. Law and Government: Knowledge of laws, legal codes, court procedures, precedents, government regulations, executive orders, agency rules, and the democratic political process. Personnel and Human Resources: Knowledge of principles and procedures for personnel recruitment, selection, training, compensation and benefits, labor relations and negotiation, and personnel information systems. Building and Construction: Knowledge of the materials, methods, and tools involved in the construction or repair of houses, buildings, or other structures such as highways and roads. Administration and Management: Knowledge of business and management principles involved in strategic planning, resource allocation, human resources modeling, leadership technique, production methods, and coordination of people and resources.

Recreation and Fitness Studies Teachers, Postsecondary

- Annual Earnings: $45,890
- Growth: 32.2%
- Annual Job Openings: 329,000
- Self-Employed: 0.4%
- Part-Time: 27.3%
- Education/Training Required: Master's degree

Our sources did not provide separate job openings data for this occupation. The job openings listed here are shared with 35 other postsecondary teaching occupations. For a complete list, see the beginning of this section.

Industries in Which Income Is Highest

Industry	Average Annual Wage	Number Employed
Educational Services	$47,520	14,920

Metropolitan Areas Where Income Is Highest

Metropolitan Area	Average Annual Wage	Number Employed
San Diego–Carlsbad–San Marcos, CA	$93,500	210
San Francisco–Oakland–Fremont, CA	$78,860	310
Los Angeles–Long Beach–Santa Ana, CA	$73,130	420
Sacramento–Arden–Arcade–Roseville, CA	$62,260	170
Birmingham–Hoover, AL	$59,390	50

Teach courses pertaining to recreation, leisure, and fitness studies, including exercise physiology and facilities management. Evaluate and grade students' class work, assignments, and papers. Maintain student attendance records, grades, and other required records. Prepare and deliver lectures to undergraduate and/or graduate students on topics such as anatomy, therapeutic recreation, and conditioning theory. Prepare course materials such as syllabi, homework assignments, and handouts. Compile, administer, and grade examinations or assign this work to others. Maintain regularly scheduled office hours in order to advise and assist students. Plan, evaluate, and revise curricula, course content, and course materials and methods of instruction. Initiate, facilitate, and moderate classroom discussions. Keep abreast of developments in their field by reading current literature, talking with colleagues, and participating in professional conferences. Advise students on academic and vocational curricula and on career issues. Participate in student recruitment, registration, and placement activities. Collaborate with colleagues to address teaching and research issues. Select and obtain materials and supplies such as textbooks. Participate in campus and community events. Serve on academic or administrative committees that deal with institutional policies, departmental matters, and academic issues. Compile bibliographies of specialized materials for outside reading assignments. Supervise undergraduate and/or graduate teaching, internship, and research work. Perform administrative duties such as serving as department heads. Prepare students to act as sports coaches. Conduct research in a particular field of knowledge and publish findings in professional journals, books, and/or electronic media. Act as advisers to student organizations. **SKILLS**—Instructing; Learning Strategies; Social Perceptiveness; Persuasion; Time Management; Service Orientation; Management of Financial Resources; Negotiation.

GOE—Interest Area: 05. Education and Training. **Work Group:** 05.03. Postsecondary and Adult Teaching and Instructing. **PERSONALITY TYPE:** No data available.

EDUCATION/TRAINING PROGRAMS—Health and Physical Education, General; Parks, Recreation and Leisure Studies; Sport and Fitness Administration/Management. **RELATED KNOWLEDGE/COURSES**—**Education and Training:** Knowledge of principles and methods for curriculum and training design, teaching and instruction for individuals and groups, and the measurement of training effects. **Psychology:** Knowledge of human behavior and performance; individual differences in ability, personality, and interests; learning and motivation; psychological research methods; and the assessment and treatment of behavioral and affective disorders. **Philosophy and Theology:** Knowledge of different philosophical systems and religions. This includes their basic principles, values, ethics, ways of thinking, customs, and practices and their impact on human culture. **Personnel and Human Resources:** Knowledge of principles and procedures for personnel recruitment, selection, training, compensation and benefits, labor relations and negotiation, and personnel information systems. **Therapy and Counseling:** Knowledge of principles, methods, and procedures for diagnosis, treatment, and rehabilitation of physical and mental dysfunctions and for career counseling and guidance. **Sociology and Anthropology:** Knowledge of group behavior and dynamics, societal trends and influences, human migrations, ethnicity, and cultures and their history and origins.

Registered Nurses

- Annual Earnings: $54,670
- Growth: 29.4%
- Annual Job Openings: 229,000
- Self-Employed: 0.7%
- Part-Time: 24.1%
- Education/Training Required: Associate degree

Industries in Which Income Is Highest

Industry	Average Annual Wage	Number Employed
Funds, Trusts, and Other Financial Vehicles	$58,810	1,050
Federal, State, and Local Government	$56,470	136,970
Hospitals	$55,740	1,424,860
Professional, Scientific, and Technical Services	$55,510	11,070
Insurance Carriers and Related Activities	$54,980	19,110

Metropolitan Areas Where Income Is Highest

Metropolitan Area	Average Annual Wage	Number Employed
San Jose–Sunnyvale–Santa Clara, CA	$89,070	13,350
Salinas, CA	$80,990	2,330
San Francisco–Oakland–Fremont, CA	$80,470	32,280
Modesto, CA	$71,580	3,340
Baltimore–Towson, MD	$69,990	28,220

Assess patient health problems and needs, develop and implement nursing care plans, and maintain medical records. Administer nursing care to ill, injured, convalescent, or disabled patients. May advise patients on health maintenance and disease prevention or provide case management. Licensing or registration required. Includes advance practice nurses such as: nurse practitioners, clinical nurse specialists, certified nurse midwives, and certified registered nurse anesthetists. Advanced practice nursing is practiced by RNs who have specialized formal, post-basic education and who function in highly autonomous and specialized roles. Maintain accurate, detailed reports and records. Monitor, record and report symptoms and changes in patients' conditions. Record patients' medical information and vital signs. Modify patient treatment plans as indicated by patients' responses and conditions. Consult and coordinate with health care team members to assess, plan, implement and evaluate patient care plans. Order, interpret, and evaluate diagnostic tests to identify and assess patient's condition. Monitor all aspects of patient care, including diet and physical activity. Direct and supervise less skilled nursing/health care personnel, or supervise a particular unit on one shift. Prepare patients for, and assist with, examinations and treatments. Observe nurses and visit patients to ensure that proper nursing care is provided. Assess the needs of individuals, families and/or communities, including assessment of individuals' home and/or work environments to identify potential health or safety problems. Instruct individuals, families and other groups on topics such as health education, disease prevention and childbirth, and develop health improvement programs. Prepare rooms, sterile instruments, equipment and supplies, and ensure that stock of supplies is maintained. Inform physician of patient's condition during anesthesia. Deliver infants and provide prenatal and postpartum care and treatment under obstetrician's supervision. Administer local, inhalation, intravenous, and other anesthetics. Provide health care, first aid, immunizations and assistance in convalescence and rehabilitation in locations such as schools, hospitals, and industry. Perform physical examinations, make tentative diagnoses, and treat patients en route to hospitals or at disaster site triage centers. Conduct specified laboratory tests. Hand items to surgeons during operations. Prescribe or recommend drugs, medical devices or other forms of treatment, such as physical therapy, inhalation therapy, or related therapeutic procedures. Direct and coordinate infection control programs, advising and consulting with specified personnel about necessary precautions. SKILLS—Social Perceptiveness; Service Orientation; Time Management; Instructing; Learning Strategies; Science; Coordination; Critical Thinking.

GOE—Interest Area: 08. Health Science. Work Group: 08.02. Medicine and Surgery. PERSONALITY TYPE: Social. Social occupations frequently involve working with, communicating with, and teaching people. These occupations often involve helping or providing service to others.

EDUCATION/TRAINING PROGRAMS—Adult Health Nurse/Nursing; Critical Care Nursing; Family Practice Nurse/Nurse Practitioner; Maternal/Child

Health Nurse/Nursing; Nurse Anesthetist; Nurse Midwife/Nursing Midwifery; Nursing—Registered Nurse Training (RN, ASN, BSN, MSN); Nursing Clinical Specialist; Nursing Science (MS, PhD); Nursing, Other; Occupational and Environmental Health Nursing; Pediatric Nurse/Nursing; Perioperative/Operating Room and Surgical Nurse/Nursing; Psychiatric/Mental Health Nurse/Nursing; others. **RELATED KNOWLEDGE/COURSES—Psychology:** Knowledge of human behavior and performance; individual differences in ability, personality, and interests; learning and motivation; psychological research methods; and the assessment and treatment of behavioral and affective disorders. **Medicine and Dentistry:** Knowledge of the information and techniques needed to diagnose and treat human injuries, diseases, and deformities. This includes symptoms, treatment alternatives, drug properties and interactions, and preventive health-care measures. **Therapy and Counseling:** Knowledge of principles, methods, and procedures for diagnosis, treatment, and rehabilitation of physical and mental dysfunctions and for career counseling and guidance. **Customer and Personal Service:** Knowledge of principles and processes for providing customer and personal services. This includes customer needs assessment, meeting quality standards for services, and evaluation of customer satisfaction. **Biology:** Knowledge of plant and animal organisms and their tissues, cells, functions, interdependencies, and interactions with each other and the environment. **Sociology and Anthropology:** Knowledge of group behavior and dynamics, societal trends and influences, human migrations, ethnicity, and cultures and their history and origins.

Sales Agents, Financial Services

- Annual Earnings: $67,130
- Growth: 11.5%
- Annual Job Openings: 37,000
- Self-Employed: 12.5%
- Part-Time: 8.3%
- Education/Training Required: Bachelor's degree

The job openings listed here are shared with Sales Agents, Securities and Commodities.

Industries in Which Income Is Highest

Industry	Average Annual Wage	Number Employed
Administrative and Support Services	$83,410	1,200
Securities, Commodity Contracts, and Other Financial Investments and Related Activities	$79,450	165,790
Professional, Scientific, and Technical Services	$76,530	2,070
Funds, Trusts, and Other Financial Vehicles	$68,940	2,030
Management of Companies and Enterprises	$66,430	5,130

Metropolitan Areas Where Income Is Highest

Metropolitan Area	Average Annual Wage	Number Employed
Barnstable Town, MA	More than $146,500	190
Rapid City, SD	$143,390	50
Bridgeport–Stamford–Norwalk, CT	$141,440	4,290
Sioux Falls, SD	$129,810	220
Ocala, FL	$125,970	90

Sell financial services, such as loan, tax, and securities counseling to customers of financial institutions and business establishments. Determine customers' financial services needs, and prepare proposals to sell services that address these needs. Contact prospective customers in order to present information and explain available services. Sell services and equipment, such as trusts, investments, and check processing services. Prepare forms or agreements to complete sales. Develop prospects from current commercial customers, referral leads, and sales and trade meetings. Review business trends in order to advise customers regarding expected fluctuations. Make presentations on financial services to groups in order to attract new clients. **SKILLS—** Persuasion; Service Orientation; Management of Financial Resources; Negotiation; Social Perceptiveness; Monitoring; Speaking; Time Management.

GOE—Interest Area: 06. Finance and Insurance. **Work Group:** 06.05. Finance/Insurance Sales and Support. **PERSONALITY TYPE:** Enterprising. Enterprising occupations frequently involve starting up and carrying out projects. These occupations can involve leading people and making many decisions. They sometimes require risk taking and often deal with business.

EDUCATION/TRAINING PROGRAMS— Business and Personal/Financial Services Marketing Operations; Financial Planning and Services; Investments and Securities. **RELATED KNOWLEDGE/ COURSES—Sales and Marketing:** Knowledge of principles and methods for showing, promoting, and selling products or services. This includes marketing strategy and tactics, product demonstration, sales techniques, and sales control systems. **Economics and Accounting:** Knowledge of economic and accounting principles and practices, the financial markets, banking, and the analysis and reporting of financial data. **Customer and Personal Service:** Knowledge of principles and processes for providing customer and personal services. This includes customer needs assessment, meeting quality standards for services, and evaluation of customer satisfaction. **Personnel and Human Resources:** Knowledge of principles and procedures for personnel recruitment, selection, training, compensation and benefits, labor relations and negotiation, and personnel information systems. **Law and Government:** Knowledge of laws, legal codes, court procedures, precedents, government regulations, executive orders, agency rules, and the democratic political process. **Computers and Electronics:** Knowledge of circuit boards, processors, chips, electronic equipment, and computer hardware and software, including applications and programming.

Sales Agents, Securities and Commodities

◎ Annual Earnings: $67,130

◎ Growth: 11.5%

◎ Annual Job Openings: 37,000

◎ Self-Employed: 12.5%

◎ Part-Time: 8.3%

◎ Education/Training Required: Bachelor's degree

The job openings listed here are shared with Sales Agents, Financial Services.

Industries in Which Income Is Highest

Industry	Average Annual Wage	Number Employed
Administrative and Support Services	$83,410	1,200
Securities, Commodity Contracts, and Other Financial Investments and Related Activities	$79,450	165,790
Professional, Scientific, and Technical Services	$76,530	2,070
Funds, Trusts, and Other Financial Vehicles	$68,940	2,030
Management of Companies and Enterprises	$66,430	5,130

Metropolitan Areas Where Income Is Highest

Metropolitan Area	Average Annual Wage	Number Employed
Barnstable Town, MA	More than $146,500	190
Rapid City, SD	$143,390	50
Bridgeport–Stamford–Norwalk, CT	$141,440	4,290
Sioux Falls, SD	$129,810	220
Ocala, FL	$125,970	90

Buy and sell securities in investment and trading firms and develop and implement financial plans for individuals, businesses, and organizations. Complete sales order tickets and submit for processing of client requested transactions. Interview clients to determine clients' assets, liabilities, cash flow, insurance coverage, tax status, and financial objectives. Record transactions accurately, and keep clients informed about transactions. Develop financial plans based on analysis of clients' financial status, and discuss financial options with clients. Review all securities transactions to ensure accuracy of information and that trades conform to regulations of governing agencies. Offer advice on the purchase or sale of particular securities. Relay buy or sell orders to securities exchanges or to firm trading departments. Identify potential clients, using advertising campaigns, mailing lists, and personal contacts. Review financial periodicals, stock and bond reports, business publications and other material in order to identify potential investments for clients and to keep abreast of trends affecting market conditions. Contact prospective customers to determine customer needs, present information, and explain available services. Prepare documents needed to implement plans selected by clients. Analyze market conditions in order to determine optimum times to execute securities transactions. Explain stock market terms and trading practices to clients. Inform and advise concerned parties regarding fluctuations and securities transactions affecting plans or accounts. Calculate costs for billings and commissions purposes. Supply the latest price quotes on any security, as well as information on the activities and financial positions of the corporations issuing these securities. Prepare financial reports to monitor client or corporate finances. Read corporate reports and calculate ratios to determine best prospects for profit on stock purchases and to monitor client accounts. **SKILLS**—Persuasion; Management of Financial Resources; Social Perceptiveness; Negotiation; Service Orientation; Time Management; Instructing; Active Learning.

GOE—Interest Area: 06. Finance and Insurance. **Work Group:** 06.05. Finance/Insurance Sales and Support. **PERSONALITY TYPE:** Enterprising. Enterprising occupations frequently involve starting up and carrying out projects. These occupations can involve leading people and making many decisions. They sometimes require risk taking and often deal with business.

EDUCATION/TRAINING PROGRAMS— Financial Planning and Services; Investments and Securities. **RELATED KNOWLEDGE/COURSES— Customer and Personal Service:** Knowledge of principles and processes for providing customer and personal services. This includes customer needs assessment, meeting quality standards for services, and evaluation of customer satisfaction. **Economics and Accounting:** Knowledge of economic and accounting principles and practices, the financial markets, banking, and the analysis and reporting of financial data. **Sales and Marketing:** Knowledge of principles and methods for showing, promoting, and selling products or services. This includes marketing strategy and tactics, product demonstration, sales techniques, and sales control systems. **Clerical Practices:** Knowledge of administrative and clerical procedures and systems such as word processing, managing files and records, stenography and transcription, designing forms, and other office procedures and terminology. **Law and Government:** Knowledge of laws, legal codes, court procedures, precedents, government regulations, executive orders, agency rules, and the democratic political process. **Administration**

and Management: Knowledge of business and management principles involved in strategic planning, resource allocation, human resources modeling, leadership technique, production methods, and coordination of people and resources.

Sales Engineers

- Annual Earnings: $74,200
- Growth: 14.0%
- Annual Job Openings: 8,000
- Self-Employed: 0.7%
- Part-Time: 2.4%
- Education/Training Required: Bachelor's degree

Industries in Which Income Is Highest

Industry	Average Annual Wage	Number Employed
Publishing Industries (Except Internet)	$103,340	1,470
Professional, Scientific, and Technical Services	$85,630	10,040
Electronics and Appliance Stores	$81,610	1,910
Wholesale Electronic Markets and Agents and Brokers	$78,920	6,480
Telecommunications	$77,110	4,790

Metropolitan Areas Where Income Is Highest

Metropolitan Area	Average Annual Wage	Number Employed
Hickory–Lenoir–Morgantown, NC	$113,890	50
Santa Cruz–Watsonville, CA	$111,340	90
Knoxville, TN	$107,240	190
Bridgeport–Stamford–Norwalk, CT	$98,800	410
Raleigh–Cary, NC	$98,660	420

Sell business goods or services, the selling of which requires a technical background equivalent to a baccalaureate degree in engineering. Arrange for demonstrations or trial installations of equipment. Attend company training seminars to become familiar with product lines. Collaborate with sales teams to understand customer requirements, to promote the sale of company products, and to provide sales support. Confer with customers and engineers to assess equipment needs, and to determine system requirements. Create sales or service contracts for products or services. Develop sales plans to introduce products in new markets. Develop, present, or respond to proposals for specific customer requirements, including request for proposal responses and industry-specific solutions. Identify resale opportunities, and support them to achieve sales plans. Keep informed on industry news and trends, products, services, competitors, relevant information about legacy, existing, and emerging technologies, and the latest product-line developments. Plan and modify product configurations to meet customer needs. Prepare and deliver technical presentations that explain products or services to customers and prospective customers. Recommend improved materials or machinery to customers, documenting how such changes will lower costs or increase production. Research and identify potential customers for products or services. Secure and renew orders and arrange delivery. Sell products requiring extensive technical expertise and support for installation and use, such as material handling equipment, numerical-control machinery, and computer systems. Visit prospective buyers at commercial, industrial, or other establishments to show samples or catalogs, and to inform them about product pricing, availability, and advantages. Attend trade shows and seminars to promote products or to learn about industry developments. Diagnose problems with installed equipment. Document account activities, generate reports, and keep records of business transactions with customers and suppliers. Maintain sales forecasting reports. Provide information needed for the development of custom-made machinery. Provide technical and non-technical support and services to clients or other staff members regarding the use, operation, and maintenance of equipment. **SKILLS**—Technology Design; Operations Analysis; Troubleshooting; Persuasion; Negotiation; Management of Material Resources; Speaking; Service Orientation.

GOE—Interest Area: 14. Retail and Wholesale Sales and Service. **Work Group:** 14.02. Technical Sales. **PERSONALITY TYPE:** Enterprising. Enterprising occupations frequently involve starting up and carrying out projects. These occupations can involve leading people and making many decisions. They sometimes require risk taking and often deal with business.

EDUCATION/TRAINING PROGRAM—Selling Skills and Sales Operations. **RELATED KNOWLEDGE/COURSES—Sales and Marketing:** Knowledge of principles and methods for showing, promoting, and selling products or services. This includes marketing strategy and tactics, product demonstration, sales techniques, and sales control systems. **Design:** Knowledge of design techniques, tools, and principles involved in production of precision technical plans, blueprints, drawings, and models. **Engineering and Technology:** Knowledge of the practical application of engineering science and technology. This includes applying principles, techniques, procedures, and equipment to the design and production of various goods and services. **Production and Processing:** Knowledge of raw materials, production processes, quality control, costs, and other techniques for maximizing the effective manufacture and distribution of goods. **Physics:** Knowledge and prediction of physical principles and laws and their interrelationships and applications to understanding fluid, material, and atmospheric dynamics and mechanical, electrical, atomic, and subatomic structures and processes. **Economics and Accounting:** Knowledge of economic and accounting principles and practices, the financial markets, banking, and the analysis and reporting of financial data.

Sales Managers

- Annual Earnings: $87,580
- Growth: 19.7%
- Annual Job Openings: 40,000
- Self-Employed: 3.5%
- Part-Time: 5.0%
- Education/Training Required: Work experience plus degree

Industries in Which Income Is Highest

Industry	Average Annual Wage	Number Employed
Securities, Commodity Contracts, and Other Financial Investments and Related Activities	$123,140	4,620
Internet Service Providers, Web Search Portals, and Data Processing Services	$115,910	2,880
Professional, Scientific, and Technical Services	$113,220	20,320
Computer and Electronic Product Manufacturing	$111,400	7,130
Broadcasting (Except Internet)	$108,100	3,870

Metropolitan Areas Where Income Is Highest

Metropolitan Area	Average Annual Wage	Number Employed
Bremerton–Silverdale, WA	More than $146,500	50
San Jose–Sunnyvale–Santa Clara, CA	$136,210	4,580
New York–Northern New Jersey–Long Island, NY–NJ–PA	$127,110	18,950
Sarasota–Bradenton–Venice, FL	$121,970	400
Bridgeport–Stamford–Norwalk, CT	$120,360	1,580

Direct the actual distribution or movement of a product or service to the customer. Coordinate sales distribution by establishing sales territories, quotas, and goals and establish training programs for sales representatives. Analyze sales statistics gathered by staff to determine sales potential and inventory requirements and monitor the preferences of customers. Resolve customer complaints regarding sales and service. Monitor customer preferences to determine focus of sales efforts. Direct and coordinate activities involving sales of manufactured products, services, commodities, real estate or other subjects of sale. Determine price schedules and discount rates. Review operational records and reports to project sales and determine profitability. Direct, coordinate, and review activities in sales and service accounting and recordkeeping, and in receiving and shipping operations. Confer or consult with department heads to plan advertising services and to secure information on equipment and customer specifications. Advise dealers and distributors on policies and operating procedures to ensure functional effectiveness of business. Prepare budgets and approve budg-

et expenditures. Represent company at trade association meetings to promote products. Plan and direct staffing, training, and performance evaluations to develop and control sales and service programs. Visit franchised dealers to stimulate interest in establishment or expansion of leasing programs. Confer with potential customers regarding equipment needs and advise customers on types of equipment to purchase. Oversee regional and local sales managers and their staffs. Direct clerical staff to keep records of export correspondence, bid requests, and credit collections, and to maintain current information on tariffs, licenses, and restrictions. Direct foreign sales and service outlets of an organization. **SKILLS**—Negotiation; Management of Personnel Resources; Persuasion; Service Orientation; Time Management; Monitoring; Instructing; Operations Analysis.

GOE—**Interest Area:** 14. Retail and Wholesale Sales and Service. **Work Group:** 14.01. Managerial Work in Retail/Wholesale Sales and Service. **PERSONALITY TYPE:** Enterprising. Enterprising occupations frequently involve starting up and carrying out projects. These occupations can involve leading people and making many decisions. They sometimes require risk taking and often deal with business.

EDUCATION/TRAINING PROGRAMS—Business Administration/Management; Business/Commerce, General; Consumer Merchandising/Retailing Management; Marketing, Other; Marketing/Marketing Management, General. **RELATED KNOWLEDGE/COURSES**—**Sales and Marketing:** Knowledge of principles and methods for showing, promoting, and selling products or services. This includes marketing strategy and tactics, product demonstration, sales techniques, and sales control systems. **Computers and Electronics:** Knowledge of circuit boards, processors, chips, electronic equipment, and computer hardware and software, including applications and programming. **Mathematics:** Knowledge of arithmetic, algebra, geometry, calculus, and statistics and their applications. **Customer and Personal Service:** Knowledge of principles and processes for providing customer and personal services. This includes customer needs assessment, meeting quality standards for services, and evaluation of customer satisfaction. **Administration and Management:** Knowledge of business and management principles involved in strategic planning, resource allocation, human resources modeling, leadership technique, production methods, and coordination of people and resources. **Law and Government:**

Knowledge of laws, legal codes, court procedures, precedents, government regulations, executive orders, agency rules, and the democratic political process.

Sales Representatives, Agricultural

◎ Annual Earnings: $60,760
◎ Growth: 14.4%
◎ Annual Job Openings: 47,000
◎ Self-Employed: 3.5%
◎ Part-Time: 7.5%
◎ Education/Training Required: Moderate-term on-the-job training

The job openings listed here are shared with Sales Representatives, Chemical and Pharmaceutical; Sales Representatives, Electrical/Electronic; Sales Representatives, Instruments; Sales Representatives, Mechanical Equipment and Supplies; and Sales Representatives, Medical.

Industries in Which Income Is Highest

Industry	Average Annual Wage	Number Employed
Internet Service Providers, Web Search Portals, and Data Processing Services	$70,730	4,050
Professional, Scientific, and Technical Services	$69,900	36,050
Publishing Industries (Except Internet)	$69,900	8,550
Computer and Electronic Product Manufacturing	$68,250	17,630
Wholesale Electronic Markets and Agents and Brokers	$67,520	41,440

Metropolitan Areas Where Income Is Highest

Metropolitan Area	Average Annual Wage	Number Employed
Peoria, IL	$86,400	370
Flint, MI	$84,800	210
Trenton–Ewing, NJ	$83,910	560
Pittsfield, MA	$81,970	60
San Jose–Sunnyvale–Santa Clara, CA	$81,880	5,850

Sell agricultural products and services, such as animal feeds, farm and garden equipment, and dairy, poultry, and veterinarian supplies. Solicits orders from customers in person or by phone. Demonstrates use of agricultural equipment or machines. Recommends changes in customer use of agricultural products to improve production. Prepares reports of business transactions. Informs customer of estimated delivery schedule, service contracts, warranty, or other information pertaining to purchased products. Displays or shows customer agricultural related products. Compiles lists of prospective customers for use as sales leads. Prepares sales contracts for orders obtained. Consults with customer regarding installation, set-up, or layout of agricultural equipment and machines. Quotes prices and credit terms. **SKILLS**—Persuasion; Negotiation; Speaking; Writing; Active Listening; Mathematics.

GOE—Interest Area: 14. Retail and Wholesale Sales and Service. **Work Group:** 14.02. Technical Sales. **PERSONALITY TYPE:** Enterprising. Enterprising occupations frequently involve starting up and carrying out projects. These occupations can involve leading people and making many decisions. They sometimes require risk taking and often deal with business.

EDUCATION/TRAINING PROGRAMS—Business, Management, Marketing, and Related Support Services; Selling Skills and Sales Operations. **RELATED KNOWLEDGE/COURSES—Sales and Marketing:** Knowledge of principles and methods for showing, promoting, and selling products or services. This includes marketing strategy and tactics, product demonstration, sales techniques, and sales control systems. **Economics and Accounting:** Knowledge of economic and accounting principles and practices, the financial markets, banking, and the analysis and reporting of financial data. **Mathematics:** Knowledge of arithmetic, algebra, geometry, calculus, and statistics and their applications.

Sales Representatives, Chemical and Pharmaceutical

◉ Annual Earnings: $60,760

◉ Growth: 14.4%

◉ Annual Job Openings: 47,000

◉ Self-Employed: 3.5%

◉ Part-Time: 7.5%

◉ Education/Training Required: Moderate-term on-the-job training

The job openings listed here are shared with Sales Representatives, Agricultural; Sales Representatives, Electrical/Electronic; Sales Representatives, Instruments; Sales Representatives, Mechanical Equipment and Supplies; and Sales Representatives, Medical.

Industries in Which Income Is Highest

Industry	Average Annual Wage	Number Employed
Internet Service Providers, Web Search Portals, and Data Processing Services	$70,730	4,050
Professional, Scientific, and Technical Services	$69,900	36,050
Publishing Industries (Except Internet)	$69,900	8,550
Computer and Electronic Product Manufacturing	$68,250	17,630
Wholesale Electronic Markets and Agents and Brokers	$67,520	41,440

Metropolitan Areas Where Income Is Highest

Metropolitan Area	Average Annual Wage	Number Employed
Peoria, IL	$86,400	370
Flint, MI	$84,800	210
Trenton–Ewing, NJ	$83,910	560
Pittsfield, MA	$81,970	60
San Jose–Sunnyvale–Santa Clara, CA	$81,880	5,850

Sell chemical or pharmaceutical products or services, such as acids, industrial chemicals, agricultural chemicals, medicines, drugs, and water treatment supplies. Promotes and sells pharmaceutical and chemical products to potential customers. Explains water treatment package benefits to customer and sells chemicals to treat and resolve water process problems. Estimates and advises customer of service costs to correct water-treatment process problems. Discusses characteristics and clinical studies pertaining to pharmaceutical products with physicians, dentists, hospitals, and retail/wholesale establishments. Distributes drug samples to customer and takes orders for pharmaceutical supply items from customer. Inspects, tests, and observes chemical changes in water system equipment, utilizing test kit, reference manual, and knowledge of chemical treatment. **SKILLS**—Science; Persuasion; Speaking; Social Perceptiveness.

GOE—Interest Area: 14. Retail and Wholesale Sales and Service. **Work Group:** 14.02. Technical Sales. **PERSONALITY TYPE:** Enterprising. Enterprising occupations frequently involve starting up and carrying out projects. These occupations can involve leading people and making many decisions. They sometimes require risk taking and often deal with business.

EDUCATION/TRAINING PROGRAMS—Business, Management, Marketing, and Related Support Services; Selling Skills and Sales Operations. **RELATED KNOWLEDGE/COURSES—Sales and Marketing:** Knowledge of principles and methods for showing, promoting, and selling products or services. This includes marketing strategy and tactics, product demonstration, sales techniques, and sales control systems. **Chemistry:** Knowledge of the chemical composition, structure, and properties of substances and of the chemical processes and transformations that they undergo. This includes uses of chemicals, their danger signs, production techniques, and disposal methods. **Mathematics:** Knowledge of arithmetic, algebra, geometry, calculus, and statistics and their applications.

Sales Representatives, Electrical/Electronic

- Annual Earnings: $60,760
- Growth: 14.4%
- Annual Job Openings: 47,000
- Self-Employed: 3.5%
- Part-Time: 7.5%
- Education/Training Required: Moderate-term on-the-job training

The job openings listed here are shared with Sales Representatives, Agricultural; Sales Representatives, Chemical and Pharmaceutical; Sales Representatives, Instruments; Sales Representatives, Mechanical Equipment and Supplies; and Sales Representatives, Medical.

Industries in Which Income Is Highest

Industry	Average Annual Wage	Number Employed
Internet Service Providers, Web Search Portals, and Data Processing Services	$70,730	4,050
Publishing Industries (Except Internet)	$69,900	8,550
Professional, Scientific, and Technical Services	$69,900	36,050
Computer and Electronic Product Manufacturing	$68,250	17,630
Wholesale Electronic Markets and Agents and Brokers	$67,520	41,440

Metropolitan Areas Where Income Is Highest

Metropolitan Area	Average Annual Wage	Number Employed
Peoria, IL	$86,400	370
Flint, MI	$84,800	210
Trenton–Ewing, NJ	$83,910	560
Pittsfield, MA	$81,970	60
San Jose–Sunnyvale–Santa Clara, CA	$81,880	5,850

Sell electrical, electronic, or related products or services, such as communication equipment, radiographic-inspection equipment and services, ultrasonic equipment, electronics parts, computers, and EDP systems. Analyzes communication needs of customer and consults with staff engineers regarding technical problems. Trains establishment personnel in equipment use, utilizing knowledge of electronics and product sold. Recommends equipment to meet customer requirements, considering salable features, such as flexibility, cost, capacity, and economy of operation. Negotiates terms of sale and services with customer. Sells electrical or electronic equipment, such as computers, data processing and radiographic equipment to businesses and industrial establishments. **SKILLS**—Persuasion; Negotiation; Operations Analysis; Instructing; Active Listening; Equipment Selection.

GOE—Interest Area: 14. Retail and Wholesale Sales and Service. **Work Group:** 14.02. Technical Sales. **PERSONALITY TYPE:** Enterprising. Enterprising occupations frequently involve starting up and carrying out projects. These occupations can involve leading people and making many decisions. They sometimes require risk taking and often deal with business.

EDUCATION/TRAINING PROGRAMS—Business, Management, Marketing, and Related Support Services; Selling Skills and Sales Operations. **RELATED KNOWLEDGE/COURSES—Sales and Marketing:** Knowledge of principles and methods for showing, promoting, and selling products or services. This includes marketing strategy and tactics, product demonstration, sales techniques, and sales control systems. **Computers and Electronics:** Knowledge of circuit boards, processors, chips, electronic equipment, and computer hardware and software, including applications and programming. **Economics and Accounting:** Knowledge of economic and accounting principles and practices, the financial markets, banking, and the analysis and reporting of financial data. **Education and Training:** Knowledge of principles and methods for curriculum and training design, teaching and instruction for individuals and groups, and the measurement of training effects. **Psychology:** Knowledge of human behavior and performance; individual differences in ability, personality, and interests; learning and motivation; psychological research methods; and the assessment and treatment of behavioral and affective disorders. **Mathematics:** Knowledge of arithmetic, algebra, geometry, calculus, and statistics and their applications.

Sales Representatives, Instruments

- Annual Earnings: $60,760
- Growth: 14.4%
- Annual Job Openings: 47,000
- Self-Employed: 3.5%
- Part-Time: 7.5%
- Education/Training Required: Moderate-term on-the-job training

The job openings listed here are shared with Sales Representatives, Agricultural; Sales Representatives, Chemical and Pharmaceutical; Sales Representatives, Electrical/Electronic; Sales Representatives, Mechanical Equipment and Supplies; and Sales Representatives, Medical.

Industries in Which Income Is Highest

Industry	Average Annual Wage	Number Employed
Internet Service Providers, Web Search Portals, and Data Processing Services	$70,730	4,050
Publishing Industries (Except Internet)	$69,900	8,550
Professional, Scientific, and Technical Services	$69,900	36,050
Computer and Electronic Product Manufacturing	$68,250	17,630
Wholesale Electronic Markets and Agents and Brokers	$67,520	41,440

Metropolitan Areas Where Income Is Highest

Metropolitan Area	Average Annual Wage	Number Employed
Peoria, IL	$86,400	370
Flint, MI	$84,800	210
Trenton–Ewing, NJ	$83,910	560
Pittsfield, MA	$81,970	60
San Jose–Sunnyvale–Santa Clara, CA	$81,880	5,850

Sell precision instruments, such as dynamometers and spring scales, and laboratory, navigation, and surveying instruments. Assists customer with product selection, utilizing knowledge of engineering specifications and catalog resources. Evaluates customer needs and emphasizes product features based on technical knowledge of product capabilities and limitations. Sells weighing and other precision instruments, such as spring scales, dynamometers, and laboratory, navigational, and surveying instruments to customer. **SKILLS**—Persuasion.

GOE—Interest Area: 14. Retail and Wholesale Sales and Service. **Work Group:** 14.02. Technical Sales. **PERSONALITY TYPE:** Enterprising. Enterprising occupations frequently involve starting up and carrying out projects. These occupations can involve leading people and making many decisions. They sometimes require risk taking and often deal with business.

EDUCATION/TRAINING PROGRAMS—Business, Management, Marketing, and Related Support Services; Selling Skills and Sales Operations. **RELATED KNOWLEDGE/COURSES—Sales and Marketing:** Knowledge of principles and methods for showing, promoting, and selling products or services. This includes marketing strategy and tactics, product demonstration, sales techniques, and sales control systems. **Engineering and Technology:** Knowledge of the practical application of engineering science and technology. This includes applying principles, techniques, procedures, and equipment to the design and production of various goods and services.

Sales Representatives, Mechanical Equipment and Supplies

- Annual Earnings: $60,760
- Growth: 14.4%
- Annual Job Openings: 47,000
- Self-Employed: 3.5%
- Part-Time: 7.5%
- Education/Training Required: Moderate-term on-the-job training

The job openings listed here are shared with Sales Representatives, Agricultural; Sales Representatives, Chemical and Pharmaceutical; Sales Representatives,

Electrical/Electronic; Sales Representatives, Instruments; and Sales Representatives, Medical.

Industries in Which Income Is Highest

Industry	Average Annual Wage	Number Employed
Internet Service Providers, Web Search Portals, and Data Processing Services	$70,730	4,050
Professional, Scientific, and Technical Services	$69,900	36,050
Publishing Industries (Except Internet)	$69,900	8,550
Computer and Electronic Product Manufacturing	$68,250	17,630
Wholesale Electronic Markets and Agents and Brokers	$67,520	41,440

Metropolitan Areas Where Income Is Highest

Metropolitan Area	Average Annual Wage	Number Employed
Peoria, IL	$86,400	370
Flint, MI	$84,800	210
Trenton–Ewing, NJ	$83,910	560
Pittsfield, MA	$81,970	60
San Jose–Sunnyvale–Santa Clara, CA	$81,880	5,850

Sell mechanical equipment, machinery, materials, and supplies, such as aircraft and railroad equipment and parts, construction machinery, material-handling equipment, industrial machinery, and welding equipment. Recommends and sells textile, industrial, construction, railroad, and oil field machinery, equipment, materials, and supplies, and services utilizing knowledge of machine operations. Computes installation or production costs, estimates savings, and prepares and submits bid specifications to customer for review and approval. Submits orders for product and follows-up on order to verify material list accuracy and delivery schedule meets project deadline. Appraises equipment and verifies customer credit rating to establish trade-in value and contract terms. Reviews existing machinery/equipment placement and diagrams proposal to illustrate efficient space utilization, using standard measuring devices and templates. Attends sales and trade meetings and reads related publications to obtain current market condition information, business trends, and industry developments. Inspects establishment premises to verify installation feasibility, and obtains building blueprints and elevator specifications to submit to engineering department for bid. Demonstrates and explains use of installed equipment and production processes. Arranges for installation and test-operation of machinery and recommends solutions to product-related problems. Contacts current and potential customers, visits establishments to evaluate needs, and promotes sale of products and services. **SKILLS—** Operations Analysis; Persuasion; Negotiation; Equipment Selection; Speaking; Active Listening; Instructing; Reading Comprehension.

GOE—Interest Area: 14. Retail and Wholesale Sales and Service. **Work Group:** 14.02. Technical Sales. **PERSONALITY TYPE:** Enterprising. Enterprising occupations frequently involve starting up and carrying out projects. These occupations can involve leading people and making many decisions. They sometimes require risk taking and often deal with business.

EDUCATION/TRAINING PROGRAMS— Business, Management, Marketing, and Related Support Services; Selling Skills and Sales Operations. **RELATED KNOWLEDGE/COURSES—Sales and Marketing:** Knowledge of principles and methods for showing, promoting, and selling products or services. This includes marketing strategy and tactics, product demonstration, sales techniques, and sales control systems. **Economics and Accounting:** Knowledge of economic and accounting principles and practices, the financial markets, banking, and the analysis and reporting of financial data. **Mathematics:** Knowledge of arithmetic, algebra, geometry, calculus, and statistics and their applications. **Design:** Knowledge of design techniques, tools, and principles involved in production of precision technical plans, blueprints, drawings, and models. **Mechanical Devices:** Knowledge of machines and tools, including their designs, uses, repair, and maintenance. **Engineering and Technology:** Knowledge of the practical application of engineering science and technology. This includes applying principles, techniques, procedures, and equipment to the design and production of various goods and services.

Sales Representatives, Medical

- Annual Earnings: $60,760
- Growth: 14.4%
- Annual Job Openings: 47,000
- Self-Employed: 3.5%
- Part-Time: 7.5%
- Education/Training Required: Moderate-term on-the-job training

The job openings listed here are shared with Sales Representatives, Agricultural; Sales Representatives, Chemical and Pharmaceutical: Sales Representatives, Electrical/Electronic; Sales Representatives, Instruments; and Sales Representatives, Mechanical Equipment and Supplies.

Industries in Which Income Is Highest

Industry	Average Annual Wage	Number Employed
Internet Service Providers, Web Search Portals, and Data Processing Services	$70,730	4,050
Professional, Scientific, and Technical Services	$69,900	36,050
Publishing Industries (Except Internet)	$69,900	8,550
Computer and Electronic Product Manufacturing	$68,250	17,630
Wholesale Electronic Markets and Agents and Brokers	$67,520	41,440

Metropolitan Areas Where Income Is Highest

Metropolitan Area	Average Annual Wage	Number Employed
Peoria, IL	$86,400	370
Flint, MI	$84,800	210
Trenton–Ewing, NJ	$83,910	560
Pittsfield, MA	$81,970	60
San Jose–Sunnyvale–Santa Clara, CA	$81,880	5,850

Sell medical equipment, products, and services. Does not include pharmaceutical sales representatives.

Advises customer regarding office layout, legal and insurance regulations, cost analysis, and collection methods. Designs and fabricates custom-made medical appliances. Selects surgical appliances from stock and fits and sells appliance to customer. Studies data describing new products to accurately recommend purchase of equipment and supplies. Promotes sale of medical and dental equipment, supplies, and services to doctors, dentists, hospitals, medical schools, and retail establishments. Writes specifications to order custom-made surgical appliances, using customer measurements and physician prescriptions. **SKILLS—** Technology Design; Operations Analysis; Persuasion; Negotiation; Writing; Active Listening; Speaking; Service Orientation.

GOE—Interest Area: 14. Retail and Wholesale Sales and Service. **Work Group:** 14.02. Technical Sales. **PERSONALITY TYPE:** Enterprising. Enterprising occupations frequently involve starting up and carrying out projects. These occupations can involve leading people and making many decisions. They sometimes require risk taking and often deal with business.

EDUCATION/TRAINING PROGRAMS— Business, Management, Marketing, and Related Support Services; Selling Skills and Sales Operations. **RELATED KNOWLEDGE/COURSES—Sales and Marketing:** Knowledge of principles and methods for showing, promoting, and selling products or services. This includes marketing strategy and tactics, product demonstration, sales techniques, and sales control systems. **Design:** Knowledge of design techniques, tools, and principles involved in production of precision technical plans, blueprints, drawings, and models. **Economics and Accounting:** Knowledge of economic and accounting principles and practices, the financial markets, banking, and the analysis and reporting of financial data. **Mathematics:** Knowledge of arithmetic, algebra, geometry, calculus, and statistics and their applications. **Engineering and Technology:** Knowledge of the practical application of engineering science and technology. This includes applying principles, techniques, procedures, and equipment to the design and production of various goods and services. **Law and Government:** Knowledge of laws, legal codes, court procedures, precedents, government regulations, executive orders, agency rules, and the democratic political process.

Sales Representatives, Wholesale and Manufacturing, Except Technical and Scientific Products

◎ Annual Earnings: $47,380
◎ Growth: 12.9%
◎ Annual Job Openings: 169,000
◎ Self-Employed: 3.5%
◎ Part-Time: 7.5%
◎ Education/Training Required: Moderate-term on-the-job training

Industries in Which Income Is Highest

Industry	Average Annual Wage	Number Employed
Paper Manufacturing	$61,790	10,490
Utilities	$58,510	1,890
Computer and Electronic Product Manufacturing	$57,210	10,590
Petroleum and Coal Products Manufacturing	$56,670	1,380
Chemical Manufacturing	$55,830	11,420

Metropolitan Areas Where Income Is Highest

Metropolitan Area	Average Annual Wage	Number Employed
Bridgeport–Stamford–Norwalk, CT	$74,200	5,390
Salinas, CA	$72,420	1,030
Danbury, CT	$69,080	950
Napa, CA	$68,220	830
San Jose–Sunnyvale–Santa Clara, CA	$62,910	7,210

Sell goods for wholesalers or manufacturers to businesses or groups of individuals. Work requires substantial knowledge of items sold. Answer customers' questions about products, prices, availability, product uses, and credit terms. Recommend products to customers, based on customers' needs and interests. Contact regular and prospective customers to demonstrate products, explain product features, and solicit orders. Estimate or quote prices, credit or contract terms, warranties, and delivery dates. Consult with clients after sales or contract signings in order to resolve problems and to provide ongoing support. Prepare drawings, estimates, and bids that meet specific customer needs. Provide customers with product samples and catalogs. Identify prospective customers by using business directories, following leads from existing clients, participating in organizations and clubs, and attending trade shows and conferences. Arrange and direct delivery and installation of products and equipment. Monitor market conditions, product innovations, and competitors' products, prices, and sales. Negotiate details of contracts and payments, and prepare sales contracts and order forms. Perform administrative duties, such as preparing sales budgets and reports, keeping sales records, and filing expense account reports. Obtain credit information about prospective customers. Forward orders to manufacturers. Check stock levels and reorder merchandise as necessary. Plan, assemble, and stock product displays in retail stores, or make recommendations to retailers regarding product displays, promotional programs, and advertising. Negotiate with retail merchants to improve product exposure such as shelf positioning and advertising. Train customers' employees to operate and maintain new equipment. Buy products from manufacturers or brokerage firms, and distribute them to wholesale and retail clients. SKILLS—Persuasion; Negotiation; Service Orientation; Time Management; Management of Financial Resources; Coordination; Active Learning; Speaking.

GOE—Interest Area: 14. Retail and Wholesale Sales and Service. Work Group: 14.03. General Sales. PERSONALITY TYPE: Enterprising. Enterprising occupations frequently involve starting up and carrying out projects. These occupations can involve leading people and making many decisions. They sometimes require risk taking and often deal with business.

EDUCATION/TRAINING PROGRAMS—Apparel and Accessories Marketing Operations; Business, Management, Marketing, and Related Support Services; Fashion Merchandising; General Merchandising, Sales, and Related Marketing Operations, Other; Sales, Distribution, and Marketing Operations, General; Sales, Distribution, and Marketing Operations, General; Sepecialized Merchandising, Sales, and Related Marketing Operations, Other; Special Products Marketing Operations. RELATED KNOWLEDGE/

COURSES—**Sales and Marketing:** Knowledge of principles and methods for showing, promoting, and selling products or services. This includes marketing strategy and tactics, product demonstration, sales techniques, and sales control systems. **Customer and Personal Service:** Knowledge of principles and processes for providing customer and personal services. This includes customer needs assessment, meeting quality standards for services, and evaluation of customer satisfaction. **Economics and Accounting:** Knowledge of economic and accounting principles and practices, the financial markets, banking, and the analysis and reporting of financial data. **Administration and Management:** Knowledge of business and management principles involved in strategic planning, resource allocation, human resources modeling, leadership technique, production methods, and coordination of people and resources. **Transportation:** Knowledge of principles and methods for moving people or goods by air, rail, sea, or road, including the relative costs and benefits. **Mathematics:** Knowledge of arithmetic, algebra, geometry, calculus, and statistics and their applications.

School Psychologists

- Annual Earnings: $57,170
- Growth: 19.1%
- Annual Job Openings: 10,000
- Self-Employed: 38.2%
- Part-Time: 23.3%
- Education/Training Required: Doctoral degree

The job openings listed here are shared with Clinical Psychologists and Counseling Psychologists.

Industries in Which Income Is Highest

Industry	Average Annual Wage	Number Employed
Hospitals	$61,740	8,950
Ambulatory Health Care Services	$60,260	21,730
Educational Services	$57,730	45,870
Federal, State, and Local Government	$57,260	9,190
Social Assistance	$45,800	8,020

Metropolitan Areas Where Income Is Highest

Metropolitan Area	Average Annual Wage	Number Employed
Napa, CA	$91,830	190
Salinas, CA	$83,160	170
Ogden–Clearfield, UT	$81,730	150
Trenton–Ewing, NJ	$81,710	270
Jonesboro, AR	$81,400	70

Investigate processes of learning and teaching and develop psychological principles and techniques applicable to educational problems. Compile and interpret students' test results, along with information from teachers and parents, in order to diagnose conditions, and to help assess eligibility for special services. Report any pertinent information to the proper authorities in cases of child endangerment, neglect, or abuse. Assess an individual child's needs, limitations, and potential, using observation, review of school records, and consultation with parents and school personnel. Select, administer, and score psychological tests. Provide consultation to parents, teachers, administrators, and others on topics such as learning styles and behavior modification techniques. Promote an understanding of child development and its relationship to learning and behavior. Collaborate with other educational professionals to develop teaching strategies and school programs. Counsel children and families to help solve conflicts and problems in learning and adjustment. Develop individualized educational plans in collaboration with teachers and other staff members. Maintain student records, including special education reports, confidential records, records of services provided, and behavioral data. Serve as a resource to help families and schools deal with crises, such as separation and loss. Attend workshops, seminars, and/or professional meetings in order to remain informed of new developments in school psychology. Design classes and programs to meet the needs of special students. Refer students and their families to appropriate community agencies for medical, vocational, or social services. Initiate and direct efforts to foster tolerance, understanding, and appreciation of diversity in school communities. Collect and analyze data to evaluate the effectiveness of academic programs and other services, such as behavioral management systems. Provide educational programs on topics such as classroom management, teaching strategies, or parenting skills. Conduct research to generate new knowledge that can be used to address learning and behavior issues. **SKILLS**—Social Perceptiveness; Negotiation; Learning Strategies; Persuasion; Service Orientation; Active Listening; Active Learning; Writing.

GOE—**Interest Area:** 15. Scientific Research, Engineering, and Mathematics. **Work Group:** 15.04. Social Sciences. **PERSONALITY TYPE:** Investigative. Investigative occupations frequently involve working with ideas and require an extensive amount of thinking. These occupations can involve searching for facts and figuring out problems mentally.

EDUCATION/TRAINING PROGRAMS—Clinical Psychology; Counseling Psychology; Developmental and Child Psychology; Psychoanalysis and Psychotherapy; Psychology, General; School Psychology. **RELATED KNOWLEDGE/COURSES**—**Therapy and Counseling:** Knowledge of principles, methods, and procedures for diagnosis, treatment, and rehabilitation of physical and mental dysfunctions and for career counseling and guidance. **Psychology:** Knowledge of human behavior and performance; individual differences in ability, personality, and interests; learning and motivation; psychological research methods; and the assessment and treatment of behavioral and affective disorders. **Sociology and Anthropology:** Knowledge of group behavior and dynamics, societal trends and influences, human migrations, ethnicity, and cultures and their history and origins. **Education and Training:** Knowledge of principles and methods for curriculum and training design, teaching and instruction for individuals and groups, and the measurement of training effects. **Philosophy and Theology:** Knowledge of different philosophical systems and religions. This includes their basic principles, values, ethics, ways of thinking, customs, and practices and their impact on human culture. **Customer and Personal Service:** Knowledge of principles and processes for providing customer and personal services. This includes customer needs assessment, meeting quality standards for services, and evaluation of customer satisfaction.

Ship and Boat Captains

- Annual Earnings: $50,940
- Growth: 4.8%
- Annual Job Openings: 2,000
- Self-Employed: 5.4%
- Part-Time: 8.3%
- Education/Training Required: Work experience in a related occupation

The job openings listed here are shared with Mates—Ship, Boat, and Barge; and Pilots, Ship.

Industries in Which Income Is Highest

Industry	Average Annual Wage	Number Employed
Support Activities for Transportation	$54,490	8,480
Water Transportation	$54,410	9,820
Federal, State, and Local Government	$53,760	1,600
Rental and Leasing Services	$52,030	1,360
Scenic and Sightseeing Transportation	$36,810	2,990

Metropolitan Areas Where Income Is Highest

Metropolitan Area	Average Annual Wage	Number Employed
Baton Rouge, LA	$67,280	470
Bremerton–Silverdale, WA	$66,460	70
New York–Northern New Jersey–Long Island, NY–NJ–PA	$62,450	1,970
Lake Charles, LA	$61,120	210
Seattle–Tacoma–Bellevue, WA	$60,990	850

Command vessels in oceans, bays, lakes, rivers, and coastal waters. Calculate sightings of land, using electronic sounding devices, and following contour lines on charts. Compute positions, set courses, and determine speeds, by using charts, area plotting sheets, compasses, sextants, and knowledge of local conditions. Direct and coordinate crew members or workers performing activities such as loading and unloading cargo, steering vessels, operating engines, and operating, maintaining, and repairing ship equipment. Inspect vessels to ensure efficient and safe operation of vessels and equipment, and conformance to regulations. Maintain records of daily activities, personnel reports, ship positions and movements, ports of call, weather and sea conditions, pollution control efforts, and/or cargo and passenger status. Monitor the loading and discharging of cargo or passengers. Signal crew members or deckhands to rig tow lines, open or close gates and ramps, and pull guard chains across entries. Steer and operate vessels, using radios, depth finders, radars, lights, buoys, and lighthouses. Arrange for ships to be fueled, restocked with supplies, and/or repaired. Assign watches and living quarters to crew members. Collect fares from customers, or signal ferryboat helpers to collect fares. Interview and hire crew members. Maintain boats and equipment on board, such as engines, winches, navigational systems, fire extinguishers, and life preservers. Measure depths of water, using depth-measuring equipment. Purchase supplies and equipment. Read gauges to verify sufficient levels of hydraulic fluid, air pressure, and oxygen. Resolve questions or problems with customs officials. Signal passing vessels, using whistles, flashing lights, flags, and radios. Tow and maneuver barges, or signal tugboats to tow barges to destinations. Contact buyers to sell cargo such as fish. Perform various marine duties such as checking for oil spills or other pollutants around ports and harbors, and patrolling beaches. Sort logs, form log booms, and salvage lost logs. **SKILLS**—Management of Personnel Resources; Operation Monitoring; Operation and Control; Management of Material Resources; Troubleshooting; Management of Financial Resources; Coordination; Judgment and Decision Making.

GOE—**Interest Area:** 16. Transportation, Distribution, and Logistics. **Work Group:** 16.05. Water Vehicle Operation. **PERSONALITY TYPE:** Enterprising. Enterprising occupations frequently involve starting up and carrying out projects. These occupations can involve leading people and making many decisions. They sometimes require risk taking and often deal with business.

EDUCATION/TRAINING PROGRAMS—Commercial Fishing; Marine Science/Merchant Marine Officer; Marine Transportation Services, Other. **RELATED KNOWLEDGE/COURSES**—**Transportation:** Knowledge of principles and methods for moving people or goods by air, rail, sea, or road, including the relative costs and benefits. **Geography:** Knowledge of principles and methods for describing the features of land, sea, and air masses, including their physical characteristics; locations; interrelationships;

and distribution of plant, animal, and human life. **Physics:** Knowledge and prediction of physical principles and laws and their interrelationships and applications to understanding fluid, material, and atmospheric dynamics and mechanical, electrical, atomic, and subatomic structures and processes. **Administration and Management:** Knowledge of business and management principles involved in strategic planning, resource allocation, human resources modeling, leadership technique, production methods, and coordination of people and resources. **Personnel and Human Resources:** Knowledge of principles and procedures for personnel recruitment, selection, training, compensation and benefits, labor relations and negotiation, and personnel information systems. **Mathematics:** Knowledge of arithmetic, algebra, geometry, calculus, and statistics and their applications.

Ship Engineers

- Annual Earnings: $52,780
- Growth: 12.7%
- Annual Job Openings: 1,000
- Self-Employed: 3.7%
- Part-Time: 16.7%
- Education/Training Required: Postsecondary vocational training

Industries in Which Income Is Highest

Industry	Average Annual Wage	Number Employed
Water Transportation	$54,860	7,300
Support Activities for Transportation	$54,790	2,660
Federal, State, and Local Government	$48,600	1,420

Metropolitan Areas Where Income Is Highest

Metropolitan Area	Average Annual Wage	Number Employed
Baton Rouge, LA	$66,000	170
Tampa–St. Petersburg–Clearwater, FL	$62,180	280
New York–Northern New Jersey–Long Island, NY–NJ–PA	$61,920	970
Seattle–Tacoma–Bellevue, WA	$55,620	540
Houma–Bayou Cane–Thibodaux, LA	$55,400	670

Supervise and coordinate activities of crew engaged in operating and maintaining engines, boilers, deck machinery, and electrical, sanitary, and refrigeration equipment aboard ship. Record orders for changes in ship speed and direction, and note gauge readings and test data, such as revolutions per minute and voltage output, in engineering logs and bellbooks. Fabricate engine replacement parts such as valves, stay rods, and bolts, using metalworking machinery. Install engine controls, propeller shafts, and propellers. Maintain and repair engines, electric motors, pumps, winches and other mechanical and electrical equipment, or assist other crew members with maintenance and repair duties. Maintain electrical power, heating, ventilation, refrigeration, water, and sewerage systems. Monitor and test operations of engines and other equipment so that malfunctions and their causes can be identified. Monitor engine, machinery, and equipment indicators when vessels are underway, and report abnormalities to appropriate shipboard staff. Perform general marine vessel maintenance and repair work such as repairing leaks, finishing interiors, refueling, and maintaining decks. Start engines to propel ships, and regulate engines and power transmissions to control speeds of ships, according to directions from captains or bridge computers. Supervise the activities of marine engine technicians engaged in the maintenance and repair of mechanical and electrical marine vessels, and inspect their work to ensure that it is performed properly. Act as a liaison between a ship's captain and shore personnel to ensure that schedules and budgets are maintained and that the ship is operated safely and efficiently. Clean engine parts, and keep engine rooms clean. Maintain complete records of engineering department activities, including machine operations. Monitor the availability, use, and condition of lifesaving equipment and pollution preventatives, in order to ensure that international regulations are followed. Operate and maintain off-loading liquid pumps and valves. Order and receive engine room's stores such as oil and spare parts; maintain inventories and record usage of supplies. Perform and participate in emergency drills as required. SKILLS—Operation Monitoring; Repairing; Operation and Control; Management of Personnel Resources; Equipment Maintenance; Coordination; Systems Evaluation; Troubleshooting.

GOE—Interest Area: 13. Manufacturing. Work Group: 13.16. Utility Operation and Energy Distribution. PERSONALITY TYPE: Realistic. Realistic occupations frequently involve work activities that include practical, hands-on problems and solutions. They often deal with plants, animals, and real-world materials like wood, tools, and machinery. Many of the occupations require working outside and do not involve a lot of paperwork or working closely with others.

EDUCATION/TRAINING PROGRAM—No data available. RELATED KNOWLEDGE/COURSES— Mechanical Devices: Knowledge of machines and tools, including their designs, uses, repair, and maintenance. Transportation: Knowledge of principles and methods for moving people or goods by air, rail, sea, or road, including the relative costs and benefits. Engineering and Technology: Knowledge of the practical application of engineering science and technology. This includes applying principles, techniques, procedures, and equipment to the design and production of various goods and services. Physics: Knowledge and prediction of physical principles and laws and their interrelationships and applications to understanding fluid, material, and atmospheric dynamics and mechanical, electrical, atomic, and subatomic structures and processes. Public Safety and Security: Knowledge of relevant equipment, policies, procedures, and strategies to promote effective local, state, or national security operations for the protection of people, data, property, and institutions. Administration and Management: Knowledge of business and management principles involved in strategic planning, resource allocation, human resources modeling, leadership technique, production methods, and coordination of people and resources.

Signal and Track Switch Repairers

- Annual Earnings: $49,200
- Growth: 2.3%
- Annual Job Openings: 1,000
- Self-Employed: 0.0%
- Part-Time: 0.0%
- Education/Training Required: Moderate-term on-the-job training

Industries in Which Income Is Highest

Industry	Average Annual Wage	Number Employed
Rail Transportation	$49,380	4,240
Support Activities for Transportation	$30,600	240

Metropolitan Areas Where Income Is Highest

Metropolitan Area	Average Annual Wage	Number Employed
Chicago–Naperville–Joliet, IL–IN–WI	$33,760	110

Install, inspect, test, maintain, or repair electric gate crossings, signals, signal equipment, track switches, section lines, or intercommunications systems within a railroad system. Inspect and test operation, mechanical parts, and circuitry of gate crossings, signals, and signal equipment such as interlocks and hotbox detectors. Inspect, maintain, and replace batteries as needed. Inspect electrical units of railroad grade crossing gates and repair loose bolts and defective electrical connections and parts. Inspect switch-controlling mechanisms on trolley wires and in track beds, using hand tools and test equipment. Install, inspect, maintain, and repair various railroad service equipment on the road or in the shop, including railroad signal systems. Lubricate moving parts on gate-crossing mechanisms and swinging signals. Replace defective wiring, broken lenses, or burned-out light bulbs. Test air lines and air cylinders on pneumatically operated gates. Tighten loose bolts, using wrenches, and test circuits and connections by opening and closing gates. Clean lenses of lamps with cloths and solvents. Drive motor vehicles to job sites. Maintain high tension lines, de-energizing lines for power companies when repairs are requested. Record and report information about mileage or track inspected, repairs performed, and equipment requiring replacement. **SKILLS**—Installation; Repairing; Equipment Maintenance; Troubleshooting; Operation Monitoring; Quality Control Analysis; Science; Systems Evaluation.

GOE—Interest Area: 13. Manufacturing. **Work Group:** 13.13. Machinery Repair. **PERSONALITY**

TYPE: Realistic. Realistic occupations frequently involve work activities that include practical, hands-on problems and solutions. They often deal with plants, animals, and real-world materials like wood, tools, and machinery. Many of the occupations require working outside and do not involve a lot of paperwork or working closely with others.

EDUCATION/TRAINING PROGRAM—Electrician. **RELATED KNOWLEDGE/COURSES**—**Transportation:** Knowledge of principles and methods for moving people or goods by air, rail, sea, or road, including the relative costs and benefits. **Mechanical Devices:** Knowledge of machines and tools, including their designs, uses, repair, and maintenance. **Telecommunications:** Knowledge of transmission, broadcasting, switching, control, and operation of telecommunications systems. **Engineering and Technology:** Knowledge of the practical application of engineering science and technology. This includes applying principles, techniques, procedures, and equipment to the design and production of various goods and services. **Physics:** Knowledge and prediction of physical principles and laws and their interrelationships and applications to understanding fluid, material, and atmospheric dynamics and mechanical, electrical, atomic, and subatomic structures and processes. **Public Safety and Security:** Knowledge of relevant equipment, policies, procedures, and strategies to promote effective local, state, or national security operations for the protection of people, data, property, and institutions.

Social and Community Service Managers

- Annual Earnings: $49,500
- Growth: 25.5%
- Annual Job Openings: 17,000
- Self-Employed: 2.2%
- Part-Time: 12.5%
- Education/Training Required: Bachelor's degree

Industries in Which Income Is Highest

Industry	Average Annual Wage	Number Employed
Federal, State, and Local Government	$56,780	24,290
Hospitals	$56,380	3,510
Management of Companies and Enterprises	$54,000	2,390
Educational Services	$52,570	2,350
Ambulatory Health Care Services	$50,080	3,580

Metropolitan Areas Where Income Is Highest

Metropolitan Area	Average Annual Wage	Number Employed
Seattle–Tacoma–Bellevue, WA	$82,550	520
Spokane, WA	$76,190	90
Olympia, WA	$73,500	50
Trenton–Ewing, NJ	$70,000	400
Tallahassee, FL	$69,840	150

Plan, organize, or coordinate the activities of a social service program or community outreach organization. Oversee the program or organization's budget and policies regarding participant involvement, program requirements, and benefits. Work may involve directing social workers, counselors, or probation officers. Establish and maintain relationships with other agencies and organizations in community in order to meet community needs and to ensure that services are not duplicated. Prepare and maintain records and reports, such as budgets, personnel records, or training manuals. Direct activities of professional and technical staff members and volunteers. Evaluate the work of staff and volunteers in order to ensure that programs are of appropriate quality and that resources are used effectively. Establish and oversee administrative procedures to meet objectives set by boards of directors or senior management. Participate in the determination of organizational policies regarding such issues as participant eligibility, program requirements, and program benefits. Research and analyze member or community needs in order to determine program directions and goals. Speak to community groups to explain and interpret agency purposes, programs, and policies. Recruit, interview, and hire or sign up volunteers and staff. Represent organizations in relations with governmental and media

institutions. Plan and administer budgets for programs, equipment and support services. Analyze proposed legislation, regulations, or rule changes in order to determine how agency services could be impacted. Act as consultants to agency staff and other community programs regarding the interpretation of program-related federal, state, and county regulations and policies. Implement and evaluate staff training programs. Direct fund-raising activities and the preparation of public relations materials. **SKILLS**—Social Perceptiveness; Management of Personnel Resources; Service Orientation; Negotiation; Persuasion; Instructing; Monitoring; Systems Evaluation.

GOE—**Interest Area:** 07. Government and Public Administration. **Work Group:** 07.01. Managerial Work in Government and Public Administration. **PERSONALITY TYPE:** Social. Social occupations frequently involve working with, communicating with, and teaching people. These occupations often involve helping or providing service to others.

EDUCATION/TRAINING PROGRAMS—Business Administration/Management; Business, Management, Marketing, and Related Support Services; Business/Commerce, General; Community Organization and Advocacy; Entrepreneurship/Entrepreneurial Studies; Human Services, General; Non-Profit/Public/Organizational Management; Public Administration. **RELATED KNOWLEDGE/COURSES**—**Sociology and Anthropology:** Knowledge of group behavior and dynamics, societal trends and influences, human migrations, ethnicity, and cultures and their history and origins. **Psychology:** Knowledge of human behavior and performance; individual differences in ability, personality, and interests; learning and motivation; psychological research methods; and the assessment and treatment of behavioral and affective disorders. **Therapy and Counseling:** Knowledge of principles, methods, and procedures for diagnosis, treatment, and rehabilitation of physical and mental dysfunctions and for career counseling and guidance. **Education and Training:** Knowledge of principles and methods for curriculum and training design, teaching and instruction for individuals and groups, and the measurement of training effects. **Customer and Personal Service:** Knowledge of principles and processes for providing customer and personal services. This includes customer needs assessment, meeting quality standards for services, and evaluation of customer satisfaction. **Clerical Practices:** Knowledge of administrative and clerical procedures and systems such as word processing, managing files and records, stenography and transcription, designing forms, and other office procedures and terminology.

Social Work Teachers, Postsecondary

- ◎ Annual Earnings: $52,660
- ◎ Growth: 32.2%
- ◎ Annual Job Openings: 329,000
- ◎ Self-Employed: 0.4%
- ◎ Part-Time: 27.3%
- ◎ Education/Training Required: Master's degree

Our sources did not provide separate job openings data for this occupation. The job openings listed here are shared with 35 other postsecondary teaching occupations. For a complete list, see the beginning of this section.

Industries in Which Income Is Highest

Industry	Average Annual Wage	Number Employed
Educational Services	$52,640	7,430

Metropolitan Areas Where Income Is Highest

Metropolitan Area	Average Annual Wage	Number Employed
St. Louis, MO–IL	$67,080	80
Springfield, MA–CT	$64,220	50
Philadelphia–Camden–Wilmington, PA–NJ–DE–MD	$63,150	280
Portland–Vancouver–Beaverton, OR–WA	$61,110	40
Milwaukee–Waukesha–West Allis, WI	$60,440	90

Teach courses in social work. Initiate, facilitate, and moderate classroom discussions. Evaluate and grade students' class work, assignments, and papers. Prepare and deliver lectures to undergraduate and/or graduate students on topics such as family behavior, child and adolescent mental health, and social intervention evaluation. Keep abreast of developments in their field by reading current literature, talking with colleagues, and participating in professional conferences. Conduct research in a particular field of knowledge and publish findings in professional journals, books, and/or electronic media. Supervise students' laboratory and field work. Prepare course materials such as syllabi, homework assignments, and handouts. Supervise undergraduate and/or graduate teaching, internship, and research work. Maintain regularly scheduled office hours in order to advise and assist students. Plan, evaluate, and revise curricula, course content, and course materials and methods of instruction. Collaborate with colleagues, and with community agencies, in order to address teaching and research issues. Compile, administer, and grade examinations or assign this work to others. Advise students on academic and vocational curricula and on career issues. Maintain student attendance records, grades, and other required records. Write grant proposals to procure external research funding. Serve on academic or administrative committees that deal with institutional policies, departmental matters, and academic issues. Perform administrative duties such as serving as department head. Compile bibliographies of specialized materials for outside reading assignments. Select and obtain materials and supplies such as textbooks and laboratory equipment. Participate in student recruitment, registration, and placement activities. Participate in campus and community events. Provide professional consulting services to government and/or industry. Act as advisers to student organizations. **SKILLS**—Social Perceptiveness; Instructing; Service Orientation; Learning Strategies; Critical Thinking; Negotiation; Complex Problem Solving; Writing.

GOE—Interest Area: 05. Education and Training. **Work Group:** 05.03. Postsecondary and Adult Teaching and Instructing. **PERSONALITY TYPE:** No data available.

EDUCATION/TRAINING PROGRAMS—Clinical/Medical Social Work; Social Work; Teacher Education and Professional Development, Specific Subject Areas, Other. **RELATED KNOWLEDGE/COURSES—Therapy and Counseling:** Knowledge of principles, methods, and procedures for diagnosis, treatment, and rehabilitation of physical and mental dysfunctions and for career counseling and guidance. **Sociology and Anthropology:** Knowledge of group behavior and dynamics, societal trends and influences, human migrations, ethnicity, and cultures and their history and origins. **Education and Training:** Knowledge of principles and methods for curriculum and training design, teaching and instruction for individuals and groups, and the measurement of training effects. **Psychology:** Knowledge of human behavior and performance; individual differences in ability, personality, and interests; learning and motivation; psychological research methods; and the assessment and treatment of behavioral and affective disorders. **Philosophy and Theology:** Knowledge of different philosophical systems and religions. This includes their basic principles, values, ethics, ways of thinking, customs, and practices and their impact on human culture. **English Language:** Knowledge of the structure and content of the English language, including the meaning and spelling of words, rules of composition, and grammar.

Sociologists

- Annual Earnings: $52,760
- Growth: 4.7%
- Annual Job Openings: fewer than 500
- Self-Employed: 11.7%
- Part-Time: 0.0%
- Education/Training Required: Master's degree

Industries in Which Income Is Highest

Industry	Average Annual Wage	Number Employed
Nursing and Residential Care Facilities	$67,460	70
Religious, Grantmaking, Civic, Professional, and Similar Organizations	$63,380	460
Professional, Scientific, and Technical Services	$60,630	1,510
Federal, State, and Local Government	$49,650	450
Educational Services	$43,960	970

Metropolitan Areas Where Income Is Highest

Metropolitan Area	Average Annual Wage	Number Employed
Atlanta–Sandy Springs–Marietta, GA	$96,850	70
Miami–Fort Lauderdale–Miami Beach, FL	$87,680	40
Washington–Arlington–Alexandria, DC–VA–MD–WV	$78,610	660
Sacramento–Arden–Arcade–Roseville, CA	$68,000	40
Philadelphia–Camden–Wilmington, PA–NJ–DE–MD	$59,850	60

Study human society and social behavior by examining the groups and social institutions that people form, as well as various social, religious, political, and business organizations. May study the behavior and interaction of groups, trace their origin and growth, and analyze the influence of group activities on individual members. Prepare publications and reports containing research findings. Analyze and interpret data in order to increase the understanding of human social behavior. Plan and conduct research to develop and test theories about societal issues such as crime, group relations, poverty, and aging. Collect data about the attitudes, values, and behaviors of people in groups, using observation, interviews, and review of documents. Develop, implement, and evaluate methods of data collection, such as questionnaires or interviews. Teach sociology. Direct work of statistical clerks, statisticians, and others who compile and evaluate research data. Consult with and advise individuals such as administrators, social workers, and legislators regarding social issues and policies, as well as the implications of research findings. Collaborate with research workers in other disciplines. Develop approaches to the solution of groups' problems, based on research findings in sociology and related disciplines. Observe group interactions and role affiliations to collect data, identify problems, evaluate progress, and determine the need for additional change. Develop problem intervention procedures, utilizing techniques such as interviews, consultations, role playing, and participant observation of group interactions. **SKILLS**—Science; Management of Financial Resources; Writing; Critical Thinking; Reading Comprehension; Active Learning; Complex Problem Solving; Management of Personnel Resources.

GOE—Interest Area: 15. Scientific Research, Engineering, and Mathematics. **Work Group:** 15.04. Social Sciences. **PERSONALITY TYPE:** Investigative. Investigative occupations frequently involve working with ideas and require an extensive amount of thinking. These occupations can involve searching for facts and figuring out problems mentally.

EDUCATION/TRAINING PROGRAMS—Criminology; Demography and Population Studies; Sociology; Urban Studies/Affairs. **RELATED KNOWLEDGE/COURSES—Sociology and Anthropology:** Knowledge of group behavior and dynamics, societal trends and influences, human migrations, ethnicity, and cultures and their history and origins. **Philosophy and Theology:** Knowledge of different philosophical systems and religions. This includes their basic principles, values, ethics, ways of thinking, customs, and practices and their impact on human culture. **History and Archeology:** Knowledge of historical events and their causes, indicators, and effects on civilizations and cultures. **Psychology:** Knowledge of human behavior and performance; individual differences in ability, personality, and interests; learning and motivation; psychological research methods; and the assessment and treatment of behavioral and affective disorders. **English Language:** Knowledge of the structure and content of the English language, including the meaning and spelling of words, rules of composition, and grammar. **Education and Training:** Knowledge of principles and methods for curriculum and training design, teaching and instruction for individuals and groups, and the measurement of training effects.

Sociology Teachers, Postsecondary

- Annual Earnings: $54,320
- Growth: 32.2%
- Annual Job Openings: 329,000
- Self-Employed: 0.4%
- Part-Time: 27.3%
- Education/Training Required: Master's degree

Our sources did not provide separate job openings data for this occupation. The job openings listed here are shared with 35 other postsecondary teaching occupations. For a complete list, see the beginning of this section.

Industries in Which Income Is Highest

Industry	Average Annual Wage	Number Employed
Educational Services	$54,320	14,980

Metropolitan Areas Where Income Is Highest

Metropolitan Area	Average Annual Wage	Number Employed
Riverside–San Bernardino–Ontario, CA	$86,400	80
Providence–Fall River–Warwick, RI–MA	$81,930	70
San Diego–Carlsbad–San Marcos, CA	$75,730	120
Rochester, NY	$74,080	90
Sacramento–Arden–Arcade–Roseville, CA	$73,050	80

Teach courses in sociology. Evaluate and grade students' class work, assignments, and papers. Prepare and deliver lectures to undergraduate and/or graduate students on topics such as race and ethnic relations, measurement and data collection, and workplace social relations. Initiate, facilitate, and moderate classroom discussions. Compile, administer, and grade examinations or assign this work to others. Prepare course materials such as syllabi, homework assignments, and handouts. Keep abreast of developments in their field by reading current literature, talking with colleagues, and participating in professional conferences. Maintain student attendance records, grades, and other required records. Maintain regularly scheduled office hours in order to advise and assist students. Plan, evaluate, and revise curricula, course content, and course materials and methods of instruction. Advise students on academic and vocational curricula and on career issues. Collaborate with colleagues to address teaching and research issues. Conduct research in a particular field of knowledge and publish findings in professional journals, books, and/or electronic media. Select and obtain materials and supplies such as textbooks and laboratory equipment. Supervise undergraduate and/or graduate teaching, internship, and research work. Serve on academic or administrative committees that deal with institutional policies, departmental matters, and academic issues. Participate in student recruitment, registration, and placement activities. Perform administrative duties such as serving as department head. Supervise students' laboratory and field work. Write grant proposals to procure external research funding. Act as advisers to student organizations. **SKILLS—** Instructing; Learning Strategies; Social Perceptiveness; Writing; Active Learning; Persuasion; Critical Thinking; Science.

GOE—Interest Area: 05. Education and Training. **Work Group:** 05.03. Postsecondary and Adult

Teaching and Instructing. **PERSONALITY TYPE:** Social. Social occupations frequently involve working with, communicating with, and teaching people. These occupations often involve helping or providing service to others.

EDUCATION/TRAINING PROGRAMS—Social Science Teacher Education; Sociology. **RELATED KNOWLEDGE/COURSES—Sociology and Anthropology:** Knowledge of group behavior and dynamics, societal trends and influences, human migrations, ethnicity, and cultures and their history and origins. **Education and Training:** Knowledge of principles and methods for curriculum and training design, teaching and instruction for individuals and groups, and the measurement of training effects. **Philosophy and Theology:** Knowledge of different philosophical systems and religions. This includes their basic principles, values, ethics, ways of thinking, customs, and practices and their impact on human culture. **History and Archeology:** Knowledge of historical events and their causes, indicators, and effects on civilizations and cultures. **English Language:** Knowledge of the structure and content of the English language, including the meaning and spelling of words, rules of composition, and grammar. **Psychology:** Knowledge of human behavior and performance; individual differences in ability, personality, and interests; learning and motivation; psychological research methods; and the assessment and treatment of behavioral and affective disorders.

Soil Conservationists

- Annual Earnings: $53,350
- Growth: 6.3%
- Annual Job Openings: 2,000
- Self-Employed: 9.0%
- Part-Time: 7.3%
- Education/Training Required: Bachelor's degree

The job openings listed here are shared with Park Naturalists and Range Managers.

Industries in Which Income Is Highest

Industry	Average Annual Wage	Number Employed
Federal, State, and Local Government	$54,090	13,320

Metropolitan Areas Where Income Is Highest

Metropolitan Area	Average Annual Wage	Number Employed
Washington–Arlington–Alexandria, DC–VA–MD–WV	$83,690	460
Los Angeles–Long Beach–Santa Ana, CA	$74,340	90
Barnstable Town, MA	$71,250	80
San Diego–Carlsbad–San Marcos, CA	$71,120	60
Seattle–Tacoma–Bellevue, WA	$68,000	330

Plan and develop coordinated practices for soil erosion control, soil and water conservation, and sound land use. Provide access to programs and training to assist in completion of government groundwater protection plans. Respond to complaints and questions on wetland jurisdiction, providing information and clarification. Review and approve amendments to comprehensive local water plans and conservation district plans. Review annual reports of counties, conservation districts, and watershed management organizations, certifying compliance with mandated reporting requirements. Review grant applications and make funding recommendations. Review proposed wetland restoration easements and provide technical recommendations. Revisit land users to view implemented land use practices and plans. Survey property to mark locations and measurements, using surveying instruments. Visit areas affected by erosion problems to seek sources and solutions. Apply principles of specialized fields of science, such as agronomy, soil science, forestry, or agriculture, to achieve conservation objectives. Develop and maintain working relationships with local government staff and board members. Advise land users such as farmers and ranchers on conservation plans, problems and alternative solutions, and provide technical and planning assistance. Analyze results of investigations to determine measures needed to maintain or restore proper soil management. Compute design specifications for implementation of conservation practices, using survey and field information technical guides, engineering manuals, and calculator. Develop, conduct and/or participate in surveys, studies and investigations of various land uses, gathering information for use in developing corrective action plans. Monitor projects during and after construction to ensure projects conform to design specifications. Plan soil management and conservation practices, such as crop rotation, reforestation, permanent vegetation, contour plowing, or terracing, to maintain soil and conserve water. Provide information, knowledge, expertise, and training to government agencies at all levels to solve water and soil management problems and to assure coordination of resource protection activities. **SKILLS**—Systems Analysis; Science; Systems Evaluation; Judgment and Decision Making; Mathematics; Complex Problem Solving; Monitoring; Active Learning.

GOE—**Interest Area:** 01. Agriculture and Natural Resources. **Work Group:** 01.02. Resource Science/Engineering for Plants, Animals, and the Environment. **PERSONALITY TYPE:** Investigative. Investigative occupations frequently involve working with ideas and require an extensive amount of thinking. These occupations can involve searching for facts and figuring out problems mentally.

EDUCATION/TRAINING PROGRAMS—Forest Management/ Forest Resources Management; Forest Sciences; Forestry, General; Forestry, Other; Land Use Planning and Management/Development; Natural Resources and Conservation, Other; Natural Resources Management and Policy, General; Natural Resources Management and Policy, Other; Natural Resources/Conservation, General; Water, Wetlands, and Marine Resources Management; Wildlife and Wildlands Science and Management. **RELATED KNOWLEDGE/COURSES**—**Biology:** Knowledge of plant and animal organisms and their tissues, cells, functions, interdependencies, and interactions with each other and the environment. **Food Production:** Knowledge of techniques and equipment for planting, growing, and harvesting food products (both plant and animal) for consumption, including storage/handling techniques. **Chemistry:** Knowledge of the chemical composition, structure, and properties of substances and of the chemical processes and transformations that they undergo. This includes uses of chemicals, their danger signs, production techniques, and disposal methods. **Engineering and Technology:** Knowledge of the practical

application of engineering science and technology. This includes applying principles, techniques, procedures, and equipment to the design and production of various goods and services. **Mathematics:** Knowledge of arithmetic, algebra, geometry, calculus, and statistics and their applications. **Physics:** Knowledge and prediction of physical principles and laws and their interrelationships and applications to understanding fluid, material, and atmospheric dynamics and mechanical, electrical, atomic, and subatomic structures and processes.

Soil Scientists

- Annual Earnings: $54,530
- Growth: 13.9%
- Annual Job Openings: 1,000
- Self-Employed: 35.9%
- Part-Time: 10.3%
- Education/Training Required: Bachelor's degree

The job openings listed here are shared with Plant Scientists.

Industries in Which Income Is Highest

Industry	Average Annual Wage	Number Employed
Federal, State, and Local Government	$61,680	3,450
Merchant Wholesalers, Nondurable Goods	$59,820	1,410
Professional, Scientific, and Technical Services	$49,710	2,710
Educational Services	$44,270	1,530

Metropolitan Areas Where Income Is Highest

Metropolitan Area	Average Annual Wage	Number Employed
New Haven, CT	$89,110	50
Denver–Aurora, CO	$88,830	90
Seattle–Tacoma–Bellevue, WA	$81,720	90
Washington–Arlington–Alexandria, DC–VA–MD–WV	$79,370	330
Fort Collins–Loveland, CO	$66,400	70

Research or study soil characteristics, map soil types, and investigate responses of soils to known management practices to determine use capabilities of soils and effects of alternative practices on soil productivity. Studies soil characteristics and classifies soils according to standard types. Provides advice on rural or urban land use. Performs chemical analysis on microorganism content of soil to determine microbial reactions and chemical mineralogical relationship to plant growth. Investigates responses of specific soil types to soil management practices, such as fertilization, crop rotation, and industrial waste control. Conducts experiments on farms or experimental stations to determine best soil types for different plants. **SKILLS**—Science; Operations Analysis; Writing; Reading Comprehension; Active Learning; Critical Thinking; Mathematics; Systems Evaluation.

GOE—Interest Area: 01. Agriculture and Natural Resources. **Work Group**: 01.02. Resource Science/ Engineering for Plants, Animals, and the Environment. **PERSONALITY TYPE**: Investigative. Investigative occupations frequently involve working with ideas and require an extensive amount of thinking. These occupations can involve searching for facts and figuring out problems mentally.

EDUCATION/TRAINING PROGRAMS—Soil Chemistry and Physics; Soil Microbiology; Soil Science and Agronomy, General. **RELATED KNOWLEDGE/ COURSES—Food Production**: Knowledge of techniques and equipment for planting, growing, and harvesting food products (both plant and animal) for consumption, including storage/handling techniques. **Biology**: Knowledge of plant and animal organisms and their tissues, cells, functions, interdependencies, and interactions with each other and the environment. **Chemistry**: Knowledge of the chemical composition, structure, and properties of substances and of the chemical processes and transformations that they undergo. This includes uses of chemicals, their danger signs, production techniques, and disposal methods. **Geography**: Knowledge of principles and methods for describing the features of land, sea, and air masses, including their physical characteristics; locations; interrelationships; and distribution of plant, animal, and human life. **Mathematics**: Knowledge of arithmetic, algebra, geometry, calculus, and statistics and their applications.

Special Education Teachers, Secondary School

- Annual Earnings: $46,820
- Growth: 17.9%
- Annual Job Openings: 11,000
- Self-Employed: 0.5%
- Part-Time: 10.5%
- Education/Training Required: Bachelor's degree

Industries in Which Income Is Highest

Industry	Average Annual Wage	Number Employed
Educational Services	$46,980	133,080
Federal, State, and Local Government	$44,880	1,710

Metropolitan Areas Where Income Is Highest

Metropolitan Area	Average Annual Wage	Number Employed
Stockton, CA	$70,550	210
Modesto, CA	$66,250	160
San Diego–Carlsbad–San Marcos, CA	$65,820	780
Waterbury, CT	$65,370	110
Holland–Grand Haven, MI	$65,330	130

Teach secondary school subjects to educationally and physically handicapped students. Includes teachers who specialize and work with audibly and visually handicapped students and those who teach basic academic and life processes skills to the mentally impaired. Maintain accurate and complete student records, and prepare reports on children and activities, as required by laws, district policies, and administrative regulations. Teach socially acceptable behavior, employing techniques such as behavior modification and positive reinforcement. Prepare materials and classrooms for class activities. Establish and enforce rules for behavior and policies and procedures to maintain order among students. Confer with parents, administrators, testing specialists, social workers, and professionals to develop individual educational plans designed to promote students' educational, physical, and social development. Instruct through lectures, discussions, and demonstrations in one or more subjects such as English, mathematics, or social studies. Employ special educational strategies and techniques during instruction to improve the development of sensory- and perceptual-motor skills, language, cognition, and memory. Plan and conduct activities for a balanced program of instruction, demonstration, and work time that provides students with opportunities to observe, question, and investigate. Teach personal development skills such as goal setting, independence, and self-advocacy. Prepare students for later grades by encouraging them to explore learning opportunities and to persevere with challenging tasks. Establish clear objectives for all lessons, units, and projects, and communicate those objectives to students. Develop and implement strategies to meet the needs of students with a variety of handicapping conditions. Modify the general education curriculum for special-needs students, based upon a variety of instructional techniques and technologies. Meet with other professionals to discuss individual students' needs and progress. Confer with parents or guardians, other teachers, counselors, and administrators in order to resolve students' behavioral and academic problems. Meet with parents and guardians to discuss their children's progress, and to determine their priorities for their children and their resource needs. Guide and counsel students with adjustment and/or academic problems, or special academic interests. **SKILLS**—Learning Strategies; Social Perceptiveness; Instructing; Negotiation; Persuasion; Service Orientation; Time Management; Coordination.

GOE—Interest Area: 05. Education and Training. Work Group: 05.02. Preschool, Elementary, and Secondary Teaching and Instructing. **PERSONALITY TYPE:** Social. Social occupations frequently involve working with, communicating with, and teaching people. These occupations often involve helping or providing service to others.

EDUCATION/TRAINING PROGRAM—Special Education, General. **RELATED KNOWLEDGE/COURSES**—**Therapy and Counseling:** Knowledge of principles, methods, and procedures for diagnosis, treatment, and rehabilitation of physical and mental

dysfunctions and for career counseling and guidance. **History and Archeology:** Knowledge of historical events and their causes, indicators, and effects on civilizations and cultures. **Geography:** Knowledge of principles and methods for describing the features of land, sea, and air masses, including their physical characteristics; locations; interrelationships; and distribution of plant, animal, and human life. **Psychology:** Knowledge of human behavior and performance; individual differences in ability, personality, and interests; learning and motivation; psychological research methods; and the assessment and treatment of behavioral and affective disorders. **Philosophy and Theology:** Knowledge of different philosophical systems and religions. This includes their basic principles, values, ethics, ways of thinking, customs, and practices and their impact on human culture. **Education and Training:** Knowledge of principles and methods for curriculum and training design, teaching and instruction for individuals and groups, and the measurement of training effects.

Speech-Language Pathologists

- ◉ Annual Earnings: $54,880
- ◉ Growth: 14.6%
- ◉ Annual Job Openings: 5,000
- ◉ Self-Employed: 6.0%
- ◉ Part-Time: 29.9%
- ◉ Education/Training Required: Master's degree

Industries in Which Income Is Highest

Industry	Average Annual Wage	Number Employed
Nursing and Residential Care Facilities	$65,800	4,930
Ambulatory Health Care Services	$60,070	18,450
Hospitals	$58,190	12,350
Federal, State, and Local Government	$57,880	3,040
Social Assistance	$54,540	3,540

Metropolitan Areas Where Income Is Highest

Metropolitan Area	Average Annual Wage	Number Employed
Las Vegas–Paradise, NV	$87,660	80
Grand Rapids–Wyoming, MI	$86,160	390
Lancaster, PA	$76,160	140
Santa Fe, NM	$74,250	130
Bridgeport–Stamford–Norwalk, CT	$72,540	270

Assess and treat persons with speech, language, voice, and fluency disorders. May select alternative communication systems and teach their use. May perform research related to speech and language problems. Monitor patients' progress and adjust treatments accordingly. Evaluate hearing and speech/language test results and medical or background information to diagnose and plan treatment for speech, language, fluency, voice, and swallowing disorders. Administer hearing or speech/language evaluations, tests, or examinations to patients to collect information on type and degree of impairments, using written and oral tests and special instruments. Record information on the initial evaluation, treatment, progress, and discharge of clients. Develop and implement treatment plans for problems such as stuttering, delayed language, swallowing disorders, and inappropriate pitch or harsh voice problems, based on own assessments and recommendations of physicians, psychologists, and social workers. Develop individual or group programs in schools to deal with speech or language problems. Instruct clients in techniques for more effective communication, including sign language, lip reading, and voice improvement. Teach clients to control or strengthen tongue, jaw, face muscles, and breathing mechanisms. Develop speech exercise programs to reduce disabilities. Consult with and advise educators or medical staff on speech or hearing topics such as communication strategies and speech and language stimulation. Instruct patients and family members in strategies to cope with or avoid communication-related misunderstandings. Design, develop, and employ alternative diagnostic or communication devices and strategies. Conduct lessons and direct educational or therapeutic games to assist teachers dealing with speech problems. Refer clients to additional medical or educational services if needed.

Participate in conferences or training, or publish research results, to share knowledge of new hearing or speech disorder treatment methods or technologies. Communicate with non-speaking students, using sign language or computer technology. Provide communication instruction to dialect speakers or students with limited English proficiency. Use computer applications to identify and assist with communication disabilities. **SKILLS**—Instructing; Learning Strategies; Social Perceptiveness; Service Orientation; Time Management; Speaking; Coordination; Active Learning.

GOE—Interest Area: 08. Health Science. **Work Group:** 08.07. Medical Therapy. **PERSONALITY TYPE:** Social. Social occupations frequently involve working with, communicating with, and teaching people. These occupations often involve helping or providing service to others.

EDUCATION/TRAINING PROGRAMS— Audiology/Audiologist and Speech-Language Pathology/Pathologist; Communication Disorders Sciences and Services, Other; Communication Disorders, General; Speech-Language Pathology/Pathologist. **RELATED KNOWLEDGE/COURSES—Therapy and Counseling:** Knowledge of principles, methods, and procedures for diagnosis, treatment, and rehabilitation of physical and mental dysfunctions and for career counseling and guidance. **Psychology:** Knowledge of human behavior and performance; individual differences in ability, personality, and interests; learning and motivation; psychological research methods; and the assessment and treatment of behavioral and affective disorders. **Education and Training:** Knowledge of principles and methods for curriculum and training design, teaching and instruction for individuals and groups, and the measurement of training effects. **Sociology and Anthropology:** Knowledge of group behavior and dynamics, societal trends and influences, human migrations, ethnicity, and cultures and their history and origins. **English Language:** Knowledge of the structure and content of the English language, including the meaning and spelling of words, rules of composition, and grammar. **Medicine and Dentistry:** Knowledge of the information and techniques needed to diagnose and treat human injuries, diseases, and deformities. This includes symptoms, treatment alternatives, drug properties and interactions, and preventive health-care measures.

Station Installers and Repairers, Telephone

- ☺ Annual Earnings: $50,620
- ☺ Growth: –4.9%
- ☺ Annual Job Openings: 21,000
- ☺ Self-Employed: 6.6%
- ☺ Part-Time: 4.8%
- ☺ Education/Training Required: Long-term on-the-job training

The job openings listed here are shared with Central Office and PBX Installers and Repairers; Communication Equipment Mechanics, Installers, and Repairers; Frame Wirers, Central Office; and Telecommunications Facility Examiners.

Industries in Which Income Is Highest

Industry	Average Annual Wage	Number Employed
Telecommunications	$52,170	136,200
Management of Companies and Enterprises	$51,670	2,520
Professional, Scientific, and Technical Services	$51,100	5,810
Wholesale Electronic Markets and Agents and Brokers	$48,990	1,400
Administrative and Support Services	$48,780	3,780

Metropolitan Areas Where Income Is Highest

Metropolitan Area	Average Annual Wage	Number Employed
Atlantic City, NJ	$68,240	50
Trenton–Ewing, NJ	$64,750	280
New York–Northern New Jersey–Long Island, NY–NJ–PA	$62,120	15,460
Rochester, NY	$61,530	620
State College, PA	$59,690	80

Install and repair telephone station equipment, such as telephones, coin collectors, telephone booths, and switching-key equipment. Installs communication equipment, such as intercommunication systems and related apparatus, using schematic diagrams, testing devices, and hand tools. Assembles telephone equipment, mounts brackets, and connects wire leads, using hand tools and following installation diagrams or work order. Analyzes equipment operation, using testing devices to locate and diagnose nature of malfunction and ascertain needed repairs. Operates and tests equipment to ensure elimination of malfunction. Climbs poles to install or repair outside service lines. Disassembles components and replaces, cleans, adjusts and repairs parts, wires, switches, relays, circuits, or signaling units, using hand tools. Repairs cables, lays out plans for new equipment, and estimates material required. **SKILLS**—Installation; Repairing; Troubleshooting; Equipment Maintenance; Quality Control Analysis; Operation Monitoring; Operations Analysis; Operation and Control.

GOE—Interest Area: 02. Architecture and Construction. **Work Group:** 02.05. Systems and Equipment Installation, Maintenance, and Repair. **PERSONALITY TYPE:** Realistic. Realistic occupations frequently involve work activities that include practical, hands-on problems and solutions. They often deal with plants, animals, and real-world materials like wood, tools, and machinery. Many of the occupations require working outside and do not involve a lot of paperwork or working closely with others.

EDUCATION/TRAINING PROGRAM—Communications Systems Installation and Repair Technology. **RELATED KNOWLEDGE/COURSES—Telecommunications:** Knowledge of transmission, broadcasting, switching, control, and operation of telecommunications systems. **Computers and Electronics:** Knowledge of circuit boards, processors, chips, electronic equipment, and computer hardware and software, including applications and programming. **Mechanical Devices:** Knowledge of machines and tools, including their designs, uses, repair, and maintenance. **Engineering and Technology:** Knowledge of the practical application of engineering science and technology. This includes applying principles, techniques, procedures, and equipment to the design and production of various goods and services. **Design:** Knowledge of design techniques, tools, and principles involved in production of precision technical plans, blueprints, drawings, and models.

Statisticians

- Annual Earnings: $62,450
- Growth: 4.6%
- Annual Job Openings: 2,000
- Self-Employed: 3.6%
- Part-Time: 10.7%
- Education/Training Required: Master's degree

Industries in Which Income Is Highest

Industry	Average Annual Wage	Number Employed
Federal, State, and Local Government	$68,140	5,640
Professional, Scientific, and Technical Services	$67,400	3,990
Insurance Carriers and Related Activities	$54,540	1,200
Educational Services	$51,140	1,760

Metropolitan Areas Where Income Is Highest

Metropolitan Area	Average Annual Wage	Number Employed
Washington–Arlington–Alexandria, DC–VA–MD–WV	$81,190	3,350
San Francisco–Oakland–Fremont, CA	$81,050	620
New Haven, CT	$80,910	90
San Jose–Sunnyvale–Santa Clara, CA	$77,330	210
Kansas City, MO–KS	$75,340	100

Engage in the development of mathematical theory or apply statistical theory and methods to collect, organize, interpret, and summarize numerical data to provide usable information. May specialize in fields, such as bio-statistics, agricultural statistics, business statistics, economic statistics, or other fields. Adapt statistical methods in order to solve specific problems in many fields, such as economics, biology and engineering. Analyze and interpret statistical data in order to identify significant differences in relationships among sources of information. Apply sampling techniques or utilize complete enumeration bases in order to determine and define groups to be surveyed. Design research projects that apply valid scientific techniques and utilize information obtained from baselines or historical data in order to structure uncompromised and efficient analyses. Develop and test experimental designs, sampling techniques, and analytical methods. Evaluate sources of information in order to determine any limitations in terms of reliability or usability. Evaluate the statistical methods and procedures used to obtain data in order to ensure validity, applicability, efficiency, and accuracy. Examine theories, such as those of probability and inference in order to discover mathematical bases for new or improved methods of obtaining and evaluating numerical data. Identify relationships and trends in data, as well as any factors that could affect the results of research. Plan data collection methods for specific projects, and determine the types and sizes of sample groups to be used. Process large amounts of data for statistical modeling and graphic analysis, using computers. Report results of statistical analyses, including information in the form of graphs, charts, and tables. Develop an understanding of fields to which statistical methods are to be applied in order to determine whether methods and results are appropriate. Prepare data for processing by organizing information, checking for any inaccuracies, and adjusting and weighting the raw data. Supervise and provide instructions for workers collecting and tabulating data. **SKILLS**—Mathematics; Science; Systems Evaluation; Critical Thinking; Active Learning; Complex Problem Solving; Systems Analysis; Judgment and Decision Making.

GOE—Interest Area: 15. Scientific Research, Engineering, and Mathematics. **Work Group:** 15.06. Mathematics and Data Analysis. **PERSONALITY TYPE:** Investigative. Investigative occupations frequently involve working with ideas and require an extensive amount of thinking. These occupations can involve searching for facts and figuring out problems mentally.

EDUCATION/TRAINING PROGRAMS—Applied Mathematics; Biostatistics; Business Statistics; Mathematical Statistics and Probability; Mathematics, General; Statistics, General; Statistics, Other. **RELATED KNOWLEDGE/COURSES**—**Mathematics:** Knowledge of arithmetic, algebra, geometry, calculus, and statistics and their applications. **Economics and Accounting:** Knowledge of economic and accounting principles and practices, the financial markets, banking, and the analysis and reporting of financial data. **Computers and Electronics:** Knowledge of circuit boards, processors, chips, electronic equipment, and computer hardware and software, including applications and programming. **English Language:** Knowledge of the structure and content of the English language, including the meaning and spelling of words, rules of composition, and grammar. **Administration and Management:**

Knowledge of business and management principles involved in strategic planning, resource allocation, human resources modeling, leadership technique, production methods, and coordination of people and resources. **Clerical Practices:** Knowledge of administrative and clerical procedures and systems such as word processing, managing files and records, stenography and transcription, designing forms, and other office procedures and terminology.

Storage and Distribution Managers

- Annual Earnings: $69,120
- Growth: 12.7%
- Annual Job Openings: 15,000
- Self-Employed: 2.8%
- Part-Time: 4.1%
- Education/Training Required: Work experience in a related occupation

The job openings listed here are shared with Transportation Managers.

Industries in Which Income Is Highest

Industry	Average Annual Wage	Number Employed
Computer and Electronic Product Manufacturing	$97,410	1,320
Rail Transportation	$85,160	1,540
Professional, Scientific, and Technical Services	$81,230	1,240
Utilities	$80,360	1,340
Air Transportation	$80,080	2,170

Metropolitan Areas Where Income Is Highest

Metropolitan Area	Average Annual Wage	Number Employed
Tallahassee, FL	$98,270	50
San Jose–Sunnyvale–Santa Clara, CA	$96,890	730
Bridgeport–Stamford–Norwalk, CT	$90,230	190
Durham, NC	$89,070	120
Cape Coral–Fort Myers, FL	$85,270	60

Plan, direct, and coordinate the storage and distribution operations within an organization or the activities of organizations that are engaged in storing and distributing materials and products. Supervise the activities of workers engaged in receiving, storing, testing, and shipping products or materials. Plan, develop, and implement warehouse safety and security programs and activities. Review invoices, work orders, consumption reports, and demand forecasts in order to estimate peak delivery periods and to issue work assignments. Schedule and monitor air or surface pickup, delivery, or distribution of products or materials. Interview, select, and train warehouse and supervisory personnel. Confer with department heads to coordinate warehouse activities, such as production, sales, records control, and purchasing. Respond to customers' or shippers' questions and complaints regarding storage and distribution services. Inspect physical conditions of warehouses, vehicle fleets and equipment, and order testing, maintenance, repair, or replacement as necessary. Develop and document standard and emergency operating procedures for receiving, handling, storing, shipping, or salvaging products or materials. Examine products or materials in order to estimate quantities or weight and type of container required for storage or transport. Negotiate with carriers, warehouse operators and insurance company representatives for services and preferential rates. Issue shipping instructions and provide routing information to ensure that delivery times and locations are coordinated. Examine invoices and shipping manifests for conformity to tariff and customs regulations. Prepare and manage departmental budgets. Prepare or direct preparation of correspondence, reports, and operations, maintenance, and safety manuals. Arrange for necessary shipping documentation, and contact customs officials in order to effect release of shipments. Advise sales and billing departments of transportation charges for customers' accounts. Evaluate freight costs and the inventory costs associated with transit times in order to ensure that costs are appropriate. Participate in setting transportation and service rates. Track and trace goods while they are en route to their destinations, expediting orders when necessary. **SKILLS**—Management of Personnel Resources; Operations Analysis; Monitoring; Persuasion; Management of Material Resources; Service Orientation; Systems Analysis; Social Perceptiveness.

GOE—Interest Area: 16. Transportation, Distribution, and Logistics. **Work Group:** 16.01. Managerial Work in Transportation. **PERSONALITY TYPE:** Enterprising. Enterprising occupations frequently involve starting up and carrying out projects. These occupations can involve leading people and making many decisions. They sometimes require risk taking and often deal with business.

EDUCATION/TRAINING PROGRAMS—Aeronautics/Aviation/Aerospace Science and Technology, General; Aviation/Airway Management and Operations; Business Administration/Management; Logistics and Materials Management; Public Administration; Transportation/Transportation Management. RELATED KNOWLEDGE/COURSES—**Customer and Personal Service:** Knowledge of principles and processes for providing customer and personal services. This includes customer needs assessment, meeting quality standards for services, and evaluation of customer satisfaction. **Sales and Marketing:** Knowledge of principles and methods for showing, promoting, and selling products or services. This includes marketing strategy and tactics, product demonstration, sales techniques, and sales control systems. **Administration and Management:** Knowledge of business and management principles involved in strategic planning, resource allocation, human resources modeling, leadership technique, production methods, and coordination of people and resources. **Personnel and Human Resources:** Knowledge of principles and procedures for personnel recruitment, selection, training, compensation and benefits, labor relations and negotiation, and personnel information systems. **Education and Training:** Knowledge of principles and methods for curriculum and training design, teaching and instruction for individuals and groups, and the measurement of training effects. **Production and Processing:** Knowledge of raw materials, production processes, quality control, costs, and other techniques for maximizing the effective manufacture and distribution of goods.

Subway and Streetcar Operators

- Annual Earnings: $47,500
- Growth: 13.7%
- Annual Job Openings: 1,000
- Self-Employed: 0.0%
- Part-Time: 0.0%
- Education/Training Required: Moderate-term on-the-job training

Industries in Which Income Is Highest

Industry	Average Annual Wage	Number Employed
No data available.		

Metropolitan Areas Where Income Is Highest

Metropolitan Area	Average Annual Wage	Number Employed
No data available.		

Operate subway or elevated suburban train with no separate locomotive, or electric-powered streetcar to transport passengers. May handle fares. Drive and control rail-guided public transportation, such as subways, elevated trains, and electric-powered streetcars, trams, or trolleys, in order to transport passengers. Make announcements to passengers, such as notifications of upcoming stops or schedule delays. Operate controls to open and close transit vehicle doors. Regulate vehicle speed and the time spent at each stop, in order to maintain schedules. Report delays, mechanical problems, and emergencies to supervisors or dispatchers, using radios. Monitor lights indicating obstructions or other trains ahead and watch for car and truck traffic at crossings to stay alert to potential hazards. Attend meetings on driver and passenger safety in order to learn ways in which job performance might be affected. Collect fares from passengers, and issue change and transfers. Complete reports, including shift summaries and incident or accident reports. Direct emergency evacuation procedures. Greet passengers, provide information, and answer questions concerning fares, schedules, transfers, and routings. Record transactions and coin receptor readings in order to verify the amount of money collected. SKILLS—Operation and Control; Operation Monitoring.

GOE—Interest Area: 16. Transportation, Distribution, and Logistics. **Work Group:** 16.04. Rail Vehicle Operation. **PERSONALITY TYPE:** Realistic. Realistic occupations frequently involve work activities that include practical, hands-on problems and solutions. They often deal with plants, animals, and real-world materials like wood, tools, and machinery. Many of the occupations require working outside and do not involve a lot of paperwork or working closely with others.

EDUCATION/TRAINING PROGRAM—Truck and Bus Driver/Commercial Vehicle Operation. RELATED KNOWLEDGE/COURSES— **Transportation:** Knowledge of principles and methods for moving people or goods by air, rail, sea, or road, including the relative costs and benefits. **Geography:** Knowledge of principles and methods for describing the features of land, sea, and air masses, including their physical characteristics; locations; interrelationships; and distribution of plant, animal, and human life. **Clerical Practices:** Knowledge of administrative and clerical procedures and systems such as word processing, managing files and records, stenography and transcription, designing forms, and other office procedures and terminology.

Surgeons

- ◎ Annual Earnings: More than $146,500
- ◎ Growth: 24.0%
- ◎ Annual Job Openings: 41,000
- ◎ Self-Employed: 11.0%
- ◎ Part-Time: 9.6%
- ◎ Education/Training Required: First professional degree

The job openings listed here are shared with Anesthesiologists; Family and General Practitioners; Internists, General; Obstetricians and Gynecologists; Pediatricians, General; and Psychiatrists.

Industries in Which Income Is Highest

Industry	Average Annual Wage	Number Employed
Hospitals	More than $146,500	4,790
Ambulatory Health Care Services	More than $146,500	46,430
Educational Services	$96,510	1,120

Metropolitan Areas Where Income Is Highest

Metropolitan Area	Average Annual Wage	Number Employed
New York–Northern New Jersey–Long Island, NY–NJ–PA	More than $146,500	4,050
Chicago–Naperville–Joliet, IL–IN–WI	More than $146,500	2,170
Minneapolis–St. Paul–Bloomington, MN–WI	More than $146,500	1,260
Los Angeles–Long Beach–Santa Ana, CA	More than $146,500	1,210
Philadelphia–Camden–Wilmington, PA–NJ–DE–MD	More than $146,500	1,050

Treat diseases, injuries, and deformities by invasive methods, such as manual manipulation or by using instruments and appliances. Analyze patient's medical history, medication allergies, physical condition, and examination results to verify operation's necessity and to determine best procedure. Operate on patients to correct deformities, repair injuries, prevent and treat diseases, or improve or restore patients' functions. Follow established surgical techniques during the operation. Prescribe preoperative and postoperative treatments and procedures, such as sedatives, diets, antibiotics, and preparation and treatment of the patient's operative area. Examine patient to provide information on medical condition and surgical risk. Diagnose bodily disorders and orthopedic conditions and provide treatments, such as medicines and surgeries, in clinics, hospital wards, and operating rooms. Direct and coordinate activities of nurses, assistants, specialists, residents and other medical staff. Provide consultation and surgical assistance to other physicians and surgeons. Refer patient to medical specialist or other practitioners when necessary. Examine instruments, equipment, and operating room to ensure sterility. Prepare case histories. Manage surgery services, including planning, scheduling and coordination, determination of procedures, and procurement of supplies and equipment. **SKILLS**—Science; Critical Thinking; Reading Comprehension; Instructing; Management of Financial Resources; Judgment and Decision Making; Complex Problem Solving; Active Learning.

GOE—Interest Area: 08. Health Science. **Work Group:** 08.02. Medicine and Surgery. **PERSONALITY TYPE:** Investigative. Investigative occupations frequently involve working with ideas and require an extensive amount of thinking. These occupations can involve searching for facts and figuring out problems mentally.

EDUCATION/TRAINING PROGRAMS—Adult Reconstructive Orthopedics (Orthopedic Surgery); Colon and Rectal Surgery; Critical Care Surgery; General Surgery; Hand Surgery; Neurological Surgery/Neurosurgery; Orthopedic Surgery of the Spine; Orthopedics/Orthopedic Surgery; Otolaryngology; Pediatric Orthopedics; Pediatric Surgery; Plastic Surgery; Sports Medicine; Thoracic Surgery; Urology; Vascular Surgery. **RELATED KNOWLEDGE/ COURSES—Medicine and Dentistry:** Knowledge of the information and techniques needed to diagnose and treat human injuries, diseases, and deformities. This includes symptoms, treatment alternatives, drug properties and interactions, and preventive health-care measures. **Biology:** Knowledge of plant and animal organisms and their tissues, cells, functions, interdependencies, and interactions with each other and the environment. **Therapy and Counseling:** Knowledge of principles, methods, and procedures for diagnosis, treatment, and rehabilitation of physical and mental dysfunctions and for career counseling and guidance. **Psychology:** Knowledge of human behavior and performance; individual differences in ability, personality, and interests; learning and motivation; psychological research methods; and the assessment and treatment of behavioral and affective disorders. **Customer and Personal Service:** Knowledge of principles and processes for providing customer and personal services. This includes customer needs assessment, meeting quality standards for services, and evaluation of customer satisfaction. **Chemistry:** Knowledge of the chemical composition, structure, and properties of substances and of the chemical processes and transformations that they undergo. This includes uses of chemicals, their danger signs, production techniques, and disposal methods.

Talent Directors

- Annual Earnings: $53,860
- Growth: 16.6%
- Annual Job Openings: 11,000
- Self-Employed: 30.4%
- Part-Time: 8.4%
- Education/Training Required: Long-term on-the-job training

The job openings listed here are shared with Directors—Stage, Motion Pictures, Television, and Radio, Producers, Program Directors, Technical Directors/Managers.

Industries in Which Income Is Highest

Industry	Average Annual Wage	Number Employed
Motion Picture and Sound Recording Industries	$70,820	16,180
Professional, Scientific, and Technical Services	$69,870	3,100
Federal, State, and Local Government	$55,810	1,690
Broadcasting (Except Internet)	$48,650	23,240
Educational Services	$44,150	2,950

Metropolitan Areas Where Income Is Highest

Metropolitan Area	Average Annual Wage	Number Employed
Bridgeport–Stamford–Norwalk, CT	$98,420	150
New York–Northern New Jersey–Long Island, NY–NJ–PA	$81,710	10,130
San Francisco–Oakland–Fremont, CA	$79,980	1,300
Los Angeles–Long Beach–Santa Ana, CA	$72,210	9,760
Buffalo–Niagara Falls, NY	$66,330	170

Audition and interview performers to select most appropriate talent for parts in stage, television, radio, or motion picture productions. Arrange for and/or design screen tests or auditions for prospective performers. Attend or view productions in order to maintain knowledge of available actors. Audition and interview performers in order to match their attributes to specific roles or to increase the pool of available acting talent. Contact agents and actors in order to provide notification of audition and performance opportunities and to set up audition times. Locate performers or extras for crowd and background scenes, and stand-ins or photo doubles for actors, by direct contact or through agents. Maintain talent files that include information such as performers' specialties, past performances, and availability. Negotiate contract agreements with performers, with agents, or between performers and agents or production companies. Prepare actors for auditions by providing scripts and information about roles and casting requirements. Read scripts and confer with producers in order to determine the types and numbers of performers required for a given production. Review performer information such as photos, resumes, voice tapes, videos, and union membership, in order to decide whom to audition for parts. Select performers for roles or submit lists of suitable performers to producers or directors for final selection. Hire and supervise workers who help locate people with specified attributes and talents. Serve as liaisons between directors, actors, and agents. SKILLS—Negotiation; Management of Personnel Resources; Speaking; Social Perceptiveness; Persuasion; Active Listening; Writing.

GOE—Interest Area: 03. Arts and Communication. Work Group: 03.07. Music. PERSONALITY TYPE: Artistic. Artistic occupations frequently involve working with forms, designs, and patterns. They often require self-expression, and the work can be done without following a clear set of rules.

EDUCATION/TRAINING   PROGRAMS— Cinematography and Film/Video Production; Directing and Theatrical Production; Drama and Dramatics/ Theatre Arts, General; Dramatic/Theatre Arts and Stagecraft, Other; Film/Cinema Studies; Radio and Television; Theatre/Theatre Arts Management. RELATED KNOWLEDGE/COURSES—Fine Arts: Knowledge of the theory and techniques required to compose, produce, and perform works of music, dance, visual arts, drama, and sculpture. Sales and Marketing: Knowledge of principles and methods for showing, promoting, and selling products or services. This includes marketing strategy and tactics, product demonstration, sales techniques, and sales control systems. Personnel and Human Resources: Knowledge of principles and procedures for personnel recruitment, selection, training, compensation and benefits, labor relations and negotiation, and personnel information systems. Administration and Management: Knowledge of business and management principles involved in strategic planning, resource allocation, human resources modeling, leadership technique, production methods, and coordination of people and resources. Communications and Media: Knowledge of media production, communication, and dissemination techniques and methods. This includes alternative ways to inform and entertain via written, oral, and visual media.

Technical Directors/Managers

- ◎ Annual Earnings: $53,860
- ◎ Growth: 16.6%
- ◎ Annual Job Openings: 11,000
- ◎ Self-Employed: 30.4%
- ◎ Part-Time: 8.4%
- ◎ Education/Training Required: Long-term on-the-job training

The job openings listed here are shared with Directors— Stage, Motion Pictures, Television, and Radio, Producers, Program Directors, and Talent Directors.

Industries in Which Income Is Highest

Industry	Average Annual Wage	Number Employed
Motion Picture and Sound Recording Industries	$70,820	16,180
Professional, Scientific, and Technical Services	$69,870	3,100
Federal, State, and Local Government	$55,810	1,690
Broadcasting (Except Internet)	$48,650	23,240
Educational Services	$44,150	2,950

Metropolitan Areas Where Income Is Highest

Metropolitan Area	Average Annual Wage	Number Employed
Bridgeport–Stamford–Norwalk, CT	$98,420	150
New York–Northern New Jersey–Long Island, NY–NJ–PA	$81,710	10,130
San Francisco–Oakland–Fremont, CA	$79,980	1,300
Los Angeles–Long Beach–Santa Ana, CA	$72,210	9,760
Buffalo–Niagara Falls, NY	$66,330	170

Coordinate activities of technical departments, such as taping, editing, engineering, and maintenance, to produce radio or television programs. Direct technical aspects of newscasts and other productions, checking and switching between video sources, and taking responsibility for the on-air product, including camera shots and graphics. Test equipment in order to ensure proper operation. Monitor broadcasts in order to ensure that programs conform to station or network policies and regulations. Observe pictures through monitors, and direct camera and video staff concerning shading and composition. Act as liaisons between engineering and production departments. Supervise and assign duties to workers engaged in technical control and production of radio and television programs. Schedule use of studio and editing facilities for producers and engineering and maintenance staff. Confer with operations directors in order to formulate and maintain fair and attainable technical policies for programs. Operate equipment to produce programs or broadcast live programs from remote locations. Train workers in use of equipment such as switchers, cameras, monitors, microphones, and lights. Switch between video sources in a studio or on multi-camera remotes, using equipment such as switchers, video slide projectors, and video effects generators. Set up and execute video transitions and special effects such as fades, dissolves, cuts, keys, and supers, using computers to manipulate pictures as necessary. Collaborate with promotions directors to produce on-air station promotions. Discuss filter options, lens choices, and the visual effects of objects being filmed with photography directors and video operators. Follow instructions from production managers and directors during productions, such as commands for camera cuts, effects, graphics, and takes. **SKILLS**—Operation Monitoring; Operation and Control; Time Management; Monitoring; Management of Personnel Resources; Coordination; Troubleshooting; Systems Analysis.

GOE—**Interest Area:** 03. Arts and Communication. **Work Group:** 03.01. Managerial Work in Arts and Communication. **PERSONALITY TYPE:** Realistic. Realistic occupations frequently involve work activities that include practical, hands-on problems and solutions. They often deal with plants, animals, and real-world materials like wood, tools, and machinery. Many of the occupations require working outside and do not involve a lot of paperwork or working closely with others.

EDUCATION/TRAINING PROGRAMS—Cinematography and Film/Video Production; Directing and Theatrical Production; Drama and Dramatics/Theatre Arts, General; Dramatic/Theatre Arts and Stagecraft, Other; Film/Cinema Studies; Radio and Television; Theatre/Theatre Arts Management. **RELATED KNOWLEDGE/COURSES**—Commu-

nications and Media: Knowledge of media production, communication, and dissemination techniques and methods. This includes alternative ways to inform and entertain via written, oral, and visual media. **Telecommunications:** Knowledge of transmission, broadcasting, switching, control, and operation of telecommunications systems. **Computers and Electronics:** Knowledge of circuit boards, processors, chips, electronic equipment, and computer hardware and software, including applications and programming. **Philosophy and Theology:** Knowledge of different philosophical systems and religions. This includes their basic principles, values, ethics, ways of thinking, customs, and practices and their impact on human culture. **Sales and Marketing:** Knowledge of principles and methods for showing, promoting, and selling products or services. This includes marketing strategy and tactics, product demonstration, sales techniques, and sales control systems. **Engineering and Technology:** Knowledge of the practical application of engineering science and technology. This includes applying principles, techniques, procedures, and equipment to the design and production of various goods and services.

Technical Writers

- Annual Earnings: $55,160
- Growth: 23.2%
- Annual Job Openings: 5,000
- Self-Employed: 7.3%
- Part-Time: 7.3%
- Education/Training Required: Bachelor's degree

Industries in Which Income Is Highest

Industry	Average Annual Wage	Number Employed
Federal, State, and Local Government	$61,120	1,380
Computer and Electronic Product Manufacturing	$59,670	4,410
Administrative and Support Services	$59,110	2,790
Professional, Scientific, and Technical Services	$55,300	17,780
Internet Service Providers, Web Search Portals, and Data Processing Services	$54,830	1,530

Metropolitan Areas Where Income Is Highest

Metropolitan Area	Average Annual Wage	Number Employed
San Jose–Sunnyvale–Santa Clara, CA	$82,820	1,530
San Francisco–Oakland–Fremont, CA	$73,590	1,270
Honolulu, HI	$70,040	80
Winston–Salem, NC	$69,970	60
Seattle–Tacoma–Bellevue, WA	$69,850	1,590

Write technical materials, such as equipment manuals, appendices, or operating and maintenance instructions. May assist in layout work. Organize material and complete writing assignment according to set standards regarding order, clarity, conciseness, style, and terminology. Maintain records and files of work and revisions. Edit, standardize, or make changes to material prepared by other writers or establishment personnel. Confer with customer representatives, vendors, plant executives, or publisher to establish technical specifications and to determine subject material to be developed for publication. Review published materials and recommend revisions or changes in scope, format, content, and methods of reproduction and binding. Select photographs, drawings, sketches, diagrams, and charts to illustrate material. Study drawings, specifications, mockups, and product samples to integrate and delineate technology, operating procedure, and production sequence and detail. Interview production and engineering personnel and read journals and other material to become familiar with product technologies and production methods. Observe production, developmental, and experimental activities to determine operating procedure and detail. Arrange for typing, duplication, and distribution of material. Assist in laying out material for publication. Analyze developments in specific field to determine need for revisions in previously published materials and development of new material. Review manufacturer's and trade catalogs, drawings and other data relative to operation, maintenance, and service of equipment. Draw sketches to illustrate specified materials or assembly sequence. **SKILLS**—Writing; Coordination; Active Listening; Active Learning; Reading Comprehension; Technology Design; Service Orientation; Speaking.

GOE—Interest Area: 03. Arts and Communication. **Work Group:** 03.02. Writing and Editing. **PERSONALITY TYPE:** Artistic. Artistic occupations frequently involve working with forms, designs, and patterns.

They often require self-expression, and the work can be done without following a clear set of rules.

EDUCATION/TRAINING PROGRAMS—Business/Corporate Communications; Communications Studies/Speech Communication and Rhetoric; Technical and Business Writing. **RELATED KNOWLEDGE/COURSES—Clerical Practices:** Knowledge of administrative and clerical procedures and systems such as word processing, managing files and records, stenography and transcription, designing forms, and other office procedures and terminology. **Communications and Media:** Knowledge of media production, communication, and dissemination techniques and methods. This includes alternative ways to inform and entertain via written, oral, and visual media. **English Language:** Knowledge of the structure and content of the English language, including the meaning and spelling of words, rules of composition, and grammar. **Education and Training:** Knowledge of principles and methods for curriculum and training design, teaching and instruction for individuals and groups, and the measurement of training effects. **Computers and Electronics:** Knowledge of circuit boards, processors, chips, electronic equipment, and computer hardware and software, including applications and programming. **Sales and Marketing:** Knowledge of principles and methods for showing, promoting, and selling products or services. This includes marketing strategy and tactics, product demonstration, sales techniques, and sales control systems.

Telecommunications Facility Examiners

- Annual Earnings: $50,620
- Growth: –4.9%
- Annual Job Openings: 21,000
- Self-Employed: 6.6%
- Part-Time: 4.8%
- Education/Training Required: Long-term on-the-job training

The job openings listed here are shared with Central Office and PBX Installers and Repairers; Communication Equipment Mechanics, Installers, and Repairers; Frame Wirers, Central Office; and Station Installers and Repairers, Telephone.

Industries in Which Income Is Highest

Industry	Average Annual Wage	Number Employed
Telecommunications	$52,170	136,200
Management of Companies and Enterprises	$51,670	2,520
Professional, Scientific, and Technical Services	$51,100	5,810
Wholesale Electronic Markets and Agents and Brokers	$48,990	1,400
Administrative and Support Services	$48,780	3,780

Metropolitan Areas Where Income Is Highest

Metropolitan Area	Average Annual Wage	Number Employed
Atlantic City, NJ	$68,240	50
Trenton–Ewing, NJ	$64,750	280
New York–Northern New Jersey–Long Island, NY–NJ–PA	$62,120	15,460
Rochester, NY	$61,530	620
State College, PA	$59,690	80

Examine telephone transmission facilities to determine equipment requirements for providing subscribers with new or additional telephone services. Examines telephone transmission facilities to determine requirements for new or additional telephone services. Visits subscribers' premises to arrange for new installations, such as telephone booths and telephone poles. Designates cables available for use. Climbs telephone poles or stands on truck-mounted boom to examine terminal boxes for available connections. SKILLS—Technology Design.

GOE—Interest Area: 02. Architecture and Construction. Work Group: 02.05. Systems and Equipment Installation, Maintenance, and Repair. PERSONALITY TYPE: Realistic. Realistic occupations frequently involve work activities that include practical, hands-on problems and solutions. They often deal with plants, animals, and real-world materials like wood, tools, and machinery. Many of the occupations require working outside and do not involve a lot of paperwork or working closely with others.

EDUCATION/TRAINING PROGRAM—Communications Systems Installation and Repair Technology. RELATED KNOWLEDGE/COURSES—Telecommunications: Knowledge of transmission, broadcasting, switching, control, and operation of telecommunications systems. Computers and Electronics: Knowledge of circuit boards, processors, chips, electronic equipment, and computer hardware and software, including applications and programming. Engineering and Technology: Knowledge of the practical application of engineering science and technology. This includes applying principles, techniques, procedures, and equipment to the design and production of various goods and services.

Train Crew Members

- Annual Earnings: $49,700
- Growth: –38.5%
- Annual Job Openings: 1,000
- Self-Employed: 0.0%
- Part-Time: 1.3%
- Education/Training Required: Work experience in a related occupation

The job openings listed here are shared with Railroad Yard Workers.

Industries in Which Income Is Highest

Industry	Average Annual Wage	Number Employed
Rail Transportation	$52,210	18,680
Support Activities for Transportation	$26,250	1,170

Metropolitan Areas Where Income Is Highest

Metropolitan Area	Average Annual Wage	Number Employed
Houston–Sugar Land–Baytown, TX	$24,870	240

Inspect couplings, airhoses, journal boxes, and handbrakes on trains to ensure that they function properly. Inspects couplings, airhoses, journal boxes, and handbrakes to ensure that they are securely fastened and function properly. Adjusts controls to regulate air-conditioning, heating, and lighting on train for comfort of passengers. Assists passengers to board and leave train. Answers questions from passengers concerning train rules, station, and timetable information. Collects tickets, fares, and passes from passengers. Pulls or pushes track switch to reroute cars. Observes signals from other crewmembers. Sets flares, flags, lanterns, or torpedoes in front and at rear of train during emergency stops to warn oncoming trains. Signals locomotive engineer to start or stop train when coupling or uncoupling cars. Makes minor repairs to couplings, airhoses, and journal boxes using hand tools. Places passengers' baggage in rack above seats on train. Reports to conductor any equipment requiring major repair. Climbs ladder to top of car to set brakes or to ride atop to control its speed when shunted. SKILLS—Repairing; Equipment Maintenance; Service Orientation; Operation and Control; Troubleshooting.

GOE—Interest Area: 16. Transportation, Distribution, and Logistics. Work Group: 16.07. Transportation Support Work. PERSONALITY TYPE: Realistic. Realistic occupations frequently involve work activities that include practical, hands-on problems and solutions. They often deal with plants, animals, and real-world materials like wood, tools, and machinery. Many of the occupations require working outside and do not involve a lot of paperwork or working closely with others.

EDUCATION/TRAINING PROGRAM—Truck and Bus Driver/Commercial Vehicle Operation. RELATED KNOWLEDGE/COURSES—Transportation: Knowledge of principles and methods for moving people or goods by air, rail, sea, or road, including the relative costs and benefits. Mechanical Devices: Knowledge of machines and tools, including their designs, uses, repair, and maintenance. Public Safety and Security: Knowledge of relevant equipment, policies, procedures, and strategies to promote effective local, state, or national security operations for the protection of people, data, property, and institutions. Customer and Personal Service: Knowledge of principles and processes for providing customer and personal services. This includes customer needs assessment, meeting quality standards for services, and evaluation of customer satisfaction.

Training and Development Managers

- Annual Earnings: $74,180
- Growth: 25.9%
- Annual Job Openings: 3,000
- Self-Employed: 1.3%
- Part-Time: 3.6%
- Education/Training Required: Work experience plus degree

Industries in Which Income Is Highest

Industry	Average Annual Wage	Number Employed
Professional, Scientific, and Technical Services	$86,340	2,500
Management of Companies and Enterprises	$82,090	4,180
Insurance Carriers and Related Activities	$77,550	1,710
Educational Services	$70,630	2,460
Hospitals	$69,020	2,140

Metropolitan Areas Where Income Is Highest

Metropolitan Area	Average Annual Wage	Number Employed
Oxnard–Thousand Oaks–Ventura, CA	$100,150	90
New York–Northern New Jersey–Long Island, NY–NJ–PA	$99,190	2,640
Boston–Cambridge–Quincy, MA–NH	$98,650	890
San Jose–Sunnyvale–Santa Clara, CA	$94,970	240
San Francisco–Oakland–Fremont, CA	$93,810	480

Plan, direct, or coordinate the training and development activities and staff of an organization. Conduct orientation sessions and arrange on-the-job training for new hires. Evaluate instructor performance and the effectiveness of training programs, providing recommendations for improvement. Develop testing and evaluation procedures. Conduct or arrange for ongoing technical training and personal development classes for staff members. Confer with management and conduct surveys to identify training needs based on projected production processes, changes, and other factors. Develop and organize training manuals, multimedia visual aids, and other educational materials. Plan, develop, and provide training and staff development programs, using knowledge of the effectiveness of methods such as classroom training, demonstrations, on-the-job training, meetings, conferences, and workshops. Analyze training needs to develop new training programs or modify and improve existing programs. Review and evaluate training and apprenticeship programs for compliance with government standards. Train instructors and supervisors in techniques and skills for training and dealing with employees. Coordinate established courses with technical and professional courses provided by community schools and designate training procedures. Prepare training budget for department or organization. **SKILLS**—Management of Personnel Resources; Management of Financial Resources; Learning Strategies; Negotiation; Service Orientation; Instructing; Social Perceptiveness; Persuasion.

GOE—**Interest Area**: 04. Business and Administration. **Work Group**: 04.01. Managerial Work in General Business. **PERSONALITY TYPE**: Enterprising. Enterprising occupations frequently involve starting up and carrying out projects. These occupations can involve leading people and making many decisions. They sometimes require risk taking and often deal with business.

EDUCATION/TRAINING PROGRAMS—Human Resources Development; Human Resources Management/Personnel Administration, General. **RELATED KNOWLEDGE/COURSES**—**Personnel and Human Resources**: Knowledge of principles and procedures for personnel recruitment, selection, training, compensation and benefits, labor relations and negotiation, and personnel information systems. **Clerical Practices**: Knowledge of administrative and clerical procedures and systems such as word processing, managing files and records, stenography and transcription, designing forms, and other office procedures and terminology. **Administration and Management**: Knowledge of business and management principles involved in strategic planning, resource allocation, human resources modeling, leadership technique, production methods, and coordination of people and resources. **Education and Training**: Knowledge of principles and methods for curriculum and training design, teaching and instruction for individuals and groups, and the measurement of training effects. **Psychology**: Knowledge of human behavior and performance; individual differences in ability, personality, and interests; learning and motivation; psychological research methods; and the assessment and treatment of behavioral and affective disorders. **Computers and Electronics**: Knowledge of circuit boards, processors, chips, electronic equipment, and computer hardware and software, including applications and programming.

Transit and Railroad Police

- Annual Earnings: $48,850
- Growth: 9.2%
- Annual Job Openings: fewer than 500
- Self-Employed: 0.0%
- Part-Time: 0.0%
- Education/Training Required: Long-term on-the-job training

Industries in Which Income Is Highest

Industry	Average Annual Wage	Number Employed
Rail Transportation	$52,800	1,050
Federal, State, and Local Government	$48,240	3,730
Food Manufacturing	$44,950	40

Metropolitan Areas Where Income Is Highest

Metropolitan Area	Average Annual Wage	Number Employed
Chicago–Naperville–Joliet, IL–IN–WI	$42,070	130
Los Angeles–Long Beach–Santa Ana, CA	$38,640	110

Protect and police railroad and transit property, employees, or passengers. Apprehend or remove trespassers or thieves from railroad property, or coordinate with law enforcement agencies in apprehensions and removals. Direct and coordinate the daily activities and training of security staff. Direct security activities at derailments, fires, floods, and strikes involving railroad property. Examine credentials of unauthorized persons attempting to enter secured areas. Investigate or direct investigations of freight theft, suspicious damage or loss of passengers' valuables, and other crimes on railroad property. Patrol railroad yards, cars, stations, and other facilities in order to protect company property and shipments, and to maintain order. Plan and implement special safety and preventive programs, such as fire and accident prevention. Prepare reports documenting investigation activities and results. Record and verify seal numbers from boxcars containing frequently pilfered items, such as cigarettes and liquor, in order to detect tampering. Seal empty boxcars by twisting nails in door hasps, using nail twisters. Interview neighbors, associates, and former employers of job applicants in order to verify personal references and to obtain work history data. **SKILLS**—Management of Personnel Resources; Speaking; Active Listening; Social Perceptiveness; Systems Analysis; Coordination; Writing; Critical Thinking; Complex Problem Solving.

GOE—**Interest Area:** 12. Law and Public Safety. **Work Group:** 12.04. Law Enforcement and Public Safety. **PERSONALITY TYPE:** Enterprising. Enterprising occupations frequently involve starting up and carrying out projects. These occupations can involve leading people and making many decisions. They sometimes require risk taking and often deal with business.

EDUCATION/TRAINING PROGRAMS—Protective Services, Other; Security and Loss Prevention Services. **RELATED KNOWLEDGE/COURSES**—**Public Safety and Security:** Knowledge of relevant equipment, policies, procedures, and strategies to promote effective local, state, or national security operations for the protection of people, data, property, and institutions. **Law and Government:** Knowledge of laws, legal codes, court procedures, precedents, government regulations, executive orders, agency rules, and the democratic political process. **Administration and Management:** Knowledge of business and management principles involved in strategic planning, resource allocation, human resources modeling, leadership technique, production methods, and coordination of people and resources.

Transportation Managers

- Annual Earnings: $69,120
- Growth: 12.7%
- Annual Job Openings: 15,000
- Self-Employed: 2.8%
- Part-Time: 4.1%
- Education/Training Required: Work experience in a related occupation

The job openings listed here are shared with Storage and Distribution Managers.

Industries in Which Income Is Highest

Industry	Average Annual Wage	Number Employed
Computer and Electronic Product Manufacturing	$97,410	1,320
Rail Transportation	$85,160	1,540
Professional, Scientific, and Technical Services	$81,230	1,240
Utilities	$80,360	1,340
Air Transportation	$80,080	2,170

Metropolitan Areas Where Income Is Highest

Metropolitan Area	Average Annual Wage	Number Employed
Tallahassee, FL	$98,270	50
San Jose–Sunnyvale–Santa Clara, CA	$96,890	730
Bridgeport–Stamford–Norwalk, CT	$90,230	190
Durham, NC	$89,070	120
Cape Coral–Fort Myers, FL	$85,270	60

Plan, direct, and coordinate the transportation operations within an organization or the activities of organizations that provide transportation services. Direct activities related to dispatching, routing, and tracking transportation vehicles, such as aircraft and railroad cars. Plan, organize and manage the work of subordinate staff to ensure that the work is accomplished in a manner consistent with organizational requirements. Direct investigations to verify and resolve customer or shipper complaints. Serve as contact persons for all workers within assigned territories. Implement schedule and policy changes. Collaborate with other managers and staff members in order to formulate and implement policies, procedures, goals, and objectives. Monitor operations to ensure that staff members comply with administrative policies and procedures, safety rules, union contracts, and government regulations. Promote safe work activities by conducting safety audits, attending company safety meetings, and meeting with individual staff members. Develop criteria, application instructions, procedural manuals, and contracts for federal and state public transportation programs. Monitor spending to ensure that expenses are consistent with approved budgets. Direct and coordinate, through subordinates, activities of operations department in order to obtain use of equipment, facilities, and human resources. Direct activities of staff performing repairs and maintenance to equipment, vehicles, and facilities. Conduct investigations in cooperation with government agencies to determine causes of transportation accidents and to improve safety procedures. Analyze expenditures and other financial information in order to develop plans, policies, and budgets for increasing profits and improving services. Negotiate and authorize contracts with equipment and materials suppliers, and monitor contract fulfillment. Supervise workers assigning tariff classifications and preparing billing. Set operations policies and standards, including determination of safety procedures for the handling of dangerous goods. Recommend or authorize capital expenditures for acquisition of new equipment or property in order to increase efficiency and services of operations department. Prepare management recommendations, such as proposed fee and tariff increases or schedule changes. SKILLS—Negotiation; Time Management; Coordination; Management of Financial Resources; Monitoring; Instructing; Critical Thinking; Management of Personnel Resources; Management of Material Resources.

GOE—Interest Area: 16. Transportation, Distribution, and Logistics. Work Group: 16.01. Managerial Work in Transportation. PERSONALITY TYPE: Enterprising. Enterprising occupations frequently involve starting up and carrying out projects. These occupations can involve leading people and making many decisions. They sometimes require risk taking and often deal with business.

EDUCATION/TRAINING PROGRAMS—Aeronautics/Aviation/Aerospace Science and Technology, General; Aviation/Airway Management and Operations; Business Administration/Management; Logistics and Materials Management; Public Administration; Transportation/Transportation Management. RELATED KNOWLEDGE/COURSES—Transportation: Knowledge of principles and methods for moving people or goods by air, rail, sea, or road, including the relative costs and benefits. Customer and Personal Service: Knowledge of principles and processes for providing customer and personal services. This includes customer needs assessment, meeting quality standards for services, and evaluation of customer satisfaction. Clerical Practices: Knowledge of administrative and

clerical procedures and systems such as word processing, managing files and records, stenography and transcription, designing forms, and other office procedures and terminology. Sales and Marketing: Knowledge of principles and methods for showing, promoting, and selling products or services. This includes marketing strategy and tactics, product demonstration, sales techniques, and sales control systems. Administration and Management: Knowledge of business and management principles involved in strategic planning, resource allocation, human resources modeling, leadership technique, production methods, and coordination of people and resources. Psychology: Knowledge of human behavior and performance; individual differences in ability, personality, and interests; learning and motivation; psychological research methods; and the assessment and treatment of behavioral and affective disorders.

Treasurers, Controllers, and Chief Financial Officers

- Annual Earnings: $86,280
- Growth: 14.8%
- Annual Job Openings: 63,000
- Self-Employed: 3.2%
- Part-Time: 4.3%
- Education/Training Required: Work experience plus degree

Industries in Which Income Is Highest

Industry	Average Annual Wage	Number Employed
Securities, Commodity Contracts, and Other Financial Investments and Related Activities	$132,390	31,320
Funds, Trusts, and Other Financial Vehicles	$107,590	1,860
Computer and Electronic Product Manufacturing	$100,940	9,420
Management of Companies and Enterprises	$99,280	37,340
Oil and Gas Extraction	$98,840	2,050

Metropolitan Areas Where Income Is Highest

Metropolitan Area	Average Annual Wage	Number Employed
Bridgeport–Stamford–Norwalk, CT	$125,300	3,070
New York–Northern New Jersey–Long Island, NY–NJ–PA	$125,200	53,490
San Jose–Sunnyvale–Santa Clara, CA	$119,540	6,360
Danbury, CT	$113,680	270
Burlington–South Burlington, VT	$107,760	240

Plan, direct, and coordinate the financial activities of an organization at the highest level of management. Includes financial reserve officers. Coordinate and direct the financial planning, budgeting, procurement, or investment activities of all or part of an organization. Develop internal control policies, guidelines, and procedures for activities such as budget administration, cash and credit management, and accounting. Prepare or direct preparation of financial statements, business activity reports, financial position forecasts, annual budgets, and/or reports required by regulatory agencies. Advise management on short-term and long-term financial objectives, policies, and actions. Analyze the financial details of past, present, and expected operations in order to identify development opportunities and areas where improvement is needed. Delegate authority for the receipt, disbursement, banking, protection, and custody of funds, securities, and financial instruments. Evaluate needs for procurement of funds and investment of surpluses, and make appropriate recommendations. Lead staff training and development in budgeting and financial management areas. Maintain current knowledge of organizational policies and procedures, federal and state policies and directives, and current accounting standards. Supervise employees performing financial reporting, accounting, billing, collections, payroll, and budgeting duties. Conduct or coordinate audits of company accounts and financial transactions to ensure compliance with state and federal requirements and statutes. Develop and maintain relationships with banking, insurance, and non-organizational accounting personnel in order to facilitate financial activities. Monitor and evaluate the performance of accounting and other financial staff; recommend and implement personnel actions such as promotions and dismissals. Monitor financial activities and details such as reserve levels to ensure that all legal and regulatory requirements are met. Perform tax planning work. Provide direction and assistance to other organizational units regarding accounting and budgeting policies and procedures, and efficient control and utilization of financial resources. Receive and record requests for disbursements; authorize disbursements in accordance with policies and procedures. **SKILLS**—Management of Financial Resources; Systems Analysis; Systems Evaluation; Judgment and Decision Making; Complex Problem Solving; Mathematics; Management of Personnel Resources; Operations Analysis.

GOE—Interest Area: 06. Finance and Insurance. **Work Group:** 06.01. Managerial Work in Finance and Insurance. **PERSONALITY TYPE:** Enterprising. Enterprising occupations frequently involve starting up and carrying out projects. These occupations can involve leading people and making many decisions. They sometimes require risk taking and often deal with business.

EDUCATION/TRAINING PROGRAMS—Accounting and Business/Management; Accounting and Finance; Credit Management; Finance and Financial Management Services, Other; Finance, General; International Finance; Public Finance. **RELATED KNOWLEDGE/COURSES—Economics and Accounting:** Knowledge of economic and accounting principles and practices, the financial markets, banking, and the analysis and reporting of financial data. **Administration and Management:** Knowledge of business and management principles involved in strategic planning, resource allocation, human resources modeling, leadership technique, production methods, and coordination of people and resources. **Law and Government:** Knowledge of laws, legal codes, court procedures, precedents, government regulations, executive orders, agency rules, and the democratic political process. **Mathematics:** Knowledge of arithmetic, algebra, geometry, calculus, and statistics and their applications. **English Language:** Knowledge of the structure and content of the English language, including the meaning and spelling of words, rules of composition, and grammar. **Sales and Marketing:** Knowledge of principles and methods for showing, promoting, and selling products or services. This includes marketing strategy and tactics, product demonstration, sales techniques, and sales control systems.

Urban and Regional Planners

- ● Annual Earnings: $55,170
- ● Growth: 15.2%
- ● Annual Job Openings: 3,000
- ● Self-Employed: 0.0%
- ● Part-Time: 10.2%
- ● Education/Training Required: Master's degree

Industries in Which Income Is Highest

Industry	Average Annual Wage	Number Employed
Professional, Scientific, and Technical Services	$61,070	5,180
Federal, State, and Local Government	$54,230	25,750

Metropolitan Areas Where Income Is Highest

Metropolitan Area	Average Annual Wage	Number Employed
Santa Rosa–Petaluma, CA	$82,380	80
San Francisco–Oakland–Fremont, CA	$76,880	1,030
San Jose–Sunnyvale–Santa Clara, CA	$74,150	330
Hartford–West Hartford–East Hartford, CT	$73,280	160
Las Vegas–Paradise, NV	$68,660	190

Develop comprehensive plans and programs for use of land and physical facilities of local jurisdictions, such as towns, cities, counties, and metropolitan areas. Design, promote and administer government plans and policies affecting land use, zoning, public utilities, community facilities, housing, and transportation. Hold public meetings and confer with government, social scientists, lawyers, developers, the public, and special interest groups to formulate and develop land use or community plans. Recommend approval, denial or conditional approval of proposals. Determine the effects of regulatory limitations on projects. Assess the feasibility of proposals and identify necessary changes. Create, prepare, or requisition graphic and narrative reports on land use data, including land area maps overlaid with geographic variables such as population density. Advise planning officials on project feasibility, cost-effectiveness, regulatory conformance, and possible alternatives. Conduct field investigations, surveys, impact studies or other research in order to compile and analyze data on economic, social, regulatory and physical factors affecting land use. Discuss with planning officials the purpose of land use projects such as transportation, conservation, residential, commercial, industrial, and community use. Keep informed about economic and legal issues involved in zoning codes, building codes, and environmental regulations. Mediate community disputes and assist in developing alternative plans and recommendations for programs or projects. Coordinate work with economic consultants and architects during the formulation of plans and the design of large pieces of infrastructure. Review and evaluate environmental impact reports pertaining to private and public planning projects and programs. Supervise and coordinate the work of urban planning technicians and technologists. Investigate property availability. SKILLS—Persuasion; Complex Problem Solving; Coordination; Service Orientation; Social Perceptiveness; Time Management; Writing; Speaking.

GOE—Interest Area: 07. Government and Public Administration. Work Group: 07.02. Public Planning. PERSONALITY TYPE: Investigative. Investigative occupations frequently involve working with ideas and require an extensive amount of thinking. These occupations can involve searching for facts and figuring out problems mentally.

EDUCATION/TRAINING PROGRAM— City/Urban, Community and Regional Planning. RELATED KNOWLEDGE/COURSES—Design: Knowledge of design techniques, tools, and principles involved in production of precision technical plans, blueprints, drawings, and models. Geography: Knowledge of principles and methods for describing the features of land, sea, and air masses, including their physical characteristics; locations; interrelationships; and distribution of plant, animal, and human life. Building and Construction: Knowledge of the materials, methods, and tools involved in the construction or repair of houses, buildings, or other structures such as highways and roads. Customer and Personal Service: Knowledge of principles and processes for providing customer and personal services. This includes customer needs assessment, meeting quality standards for services, and evaluation of customer satisfaction. Law and Government: Knowledge of laws, legal codes, court procedures, precedents, government regulations, executive orders, agency rules, and the democratic political process. **History and Archeology:** Knowledge of historical events and their causes, indicators, and effects on civilizations and cultures.

Veterinarians

- Annual Earnings: $68,910
- Growth: 17.4%
- Annual Job Openings: 8,000
- Self-Employed: 20.7%
- Part-Time: 11.2%
- Education/Training Required: First professional degree

Industries in Which Income Is Highest

Industry	Average Annual Wage	Number Employed
Federal, State, and Local Government	$73,850	1,840
Professional, Scientific, and Technical Services	$68,840	44,250

Metropolitan Areas Where Income Is Highest

Metropolitan Area	Average Annual Wage	Number Employed
San Antonio, TX	$118,340	200
Santa Cruz–Watsonville, CA	$112,710	70
Reno–Sparks, NV	$107,470	70
Anchorage, AK	$97,100	80
Barnstable Town, MA	$96,450	70

Diagnose and treat diseases and dysfunctions of animals. May engage in a particular function, such as research and development, consultation, administration, technical writing, sale or production of commercial products, or rendering of technical services to commercial firms or other organizations. Includes veterinarians who inspect livestock. Examine animals to detect and determine the nature of diseases or injuries. Treat sick or injured animals by prescribing medication, setting bones, dressing wounds, or performing surgery. Inoculate animals against various diseases such as rabies and distemper. Collect body tissue, feces, blood, urine, or other body fluids for examina-

tion and analysis. Operate diagnostic equipment such as radiographic and ultrasound equipment, and interpret the resulting images. Advise animal owners regarding sanitary measures, feeding, and general care necessary to promote health of animals. Educate the public about diseases that can be spread from animals to humans. Train and supervise workers who handle and care for animals. Provide care to a wide range of animals or specialize in a particular species, such as horses or exotic birds. Euthanize animals. Establish and conduct quarantine and testing procedures that prevent the spread of diseases to other animals or to humans, and that comply with applicable government regulations. Conduct postmortem studies and analyses to determine the causes of animals' deaths. Perform administrative duties such as scheduling appointments, accepting payments from clients, and maintaining business records. Direct the overall operations of animal hospitals, clinics, or mobile services to farms. Drive mobile clinic vans to farms so that health problems can be treated and/or prevented. Specialize in a particular type of treatment such as dentistry, pathology, nutrition, surgery, microbiology, or internal medicine. Inspect and test horses, sheep, poultry, and other animals to detect the presence of communicable diseases. Plan and execute animal nutrition and reproduction programs. Research diseases to which animals could be susceptible. Inspect animal housing facilities to determine their cleanliness and adequacy. Determine the effects of drug therapies, antibiotics, or new surgical techniques by testing them on animals. **SKILLS—** Science; Management of Financial Resources; Instructing; Reading Comprehension; Judgment and Decision Making; Management of Personnel Resources; Complex Problem Solving; Service Orientation.

GOE—Interest Area: 08. Health Science. **Work Group:** 08.05. Animal Care. **PERSONALITY TYPE:** Investigative. Investigative occupations frequently involve working with ideas and require an extensive amount of thinking. These occupations can involve searching for facts and figuring out problems mentally.

EDUCATION/TRAINING   PROGRAMS— Comparative and Laboratory Animal Medicine (Cert, MS, PhD); Laboratory Animal Medicine; Large Animal/Food Animal and Equine Surgery and Medicine (Cert, MS, PhD); Small/Companion Animal Surgery and Medicine (Cert, MS, PhD); Theriogenology; Veterinary Anatomy (Cert, MS, PhD); Veterinary Anesthesiology; Veterinary Biomedical and Clinical Sciences, Other (Cert, MS. PhD); Veterinary Dentistry; Veterinary Dermatology; Veterinary Emergency and Critical Care Medicine; others. **RELATED KNOWLEDGE/COURSES—Biology:** Knowledge of plant and animal organisms and their tissues, cells, functions, interdependencies, and interactions with each other and the environment. **Medicine and Dentistry:** Knowledge of the information and techniques needed to diagnose and treat human injuries, diseases, and deformities. This includes symptoms, treatment alternatives, drug properties and interactions, and preventive health-care measures. **Chemistry:** Knowledge of the chemical composition, structure, and properties of substances and of the chemical processes and transformations that they undergo. This includes uses of chemicals, their danger signs, production techniques, and disposal methods. **Customer and Personal Service:** Knowledge of principles and processes for providing customer and personal services. This includes customer needs assessment, meeting quality standards for services, and evaluation of customer satisfaction. **Therapy and Counseling:** Knowledge of principles, methods, and procedures for diagnosis, treatment, and rehabilitation of physical and mental dysfunctions and for career counseling and guidance. **Sales and Marketing:** Knowledge of principles and methods for showing, promoting, and selling products or services. This includes marketing strategy and tactics, product demonstration, sales techniques, and sales control systems.

Vocational Education Teachers, Postsecondary

- Annual Earnings: $41,750
- Growth: 32.2%
- Annual Job Openings: 329,000
- Self-Employed: 0.4%
- Part-Time: 27.3%
- Education/Training Required: Work experience in a related occupation

Our sources did not provide separate job openings data for this occupation. The job openings listed here are shared with 35 other postsecondary teaching occupations. For a complete list, see the beginning of this section.

Industries in Which Income Is Highest

Industry	Average Annual Wage	Number Employed
Federal, State, and Local Government	$44,100	3,740
Educational Services	$41,850	97,610
Social Assistance	$35,060	1,190

Metropolitan Areas Where Income Is Highest

Metropolitan Area	Average Annual Wage	Number Employed
Racine, WI	$66,150	60
Manchester, NH	$64,500	70
Fort Wayne, IN	$63,830	90
Ann Arbor, MI	$63,740	70
San Luis Obispo–Paso Robles, CA	$63,590	70

Teach or instruct vocational or occupational subjects at the postsecondary level (but at less than the baccalaureate) to students who have graduated or left high school. Includes correspondence school instructors; industrial, commercial and government training instructors; and adult education teachers and instructors who prepare persons to operate industrial machinery and equipment and transportation and communications equipment. Teaching may take place in public or private schools whose primary business is education or in a school associated with an organization whose primary business is other than education. Supervise and monitor students' use of tools and equipment. Observe and evaluate students' work to determine progress, provide feedback, and make suggestions for improvement. Present lectures and conduct discussions to increase students' knowledge and competence, using visual aids such as graphs, charts, videotapes, and slides. Administer oral, written, or performance tests in order to measure progress, and to evaluate training effectiveness. Prepare reports and maintain records such as student grades, attendance rolls, and training activity details. Supervise independent or group projects, field placements, laboratory work, or other training. Determine training needs of students or workers. Provide individualized instruction and tutorial and/or remedial instruction. Conduct on-the-job training, classes, or training sessions to teach and demonstrate principles, techniques, procedures, and/or methods of designated subjects. Develop curricula, and plan course content and methods of instruction. Prepare outlines of instructional programs and training schedules, and establish course goals. Integrate academic and vocational curricula so that students can obtain a variety of skills. Develop teaching aids such as instructional software, multimedia visual aids, or study materials. Select and assemble books, materials, supplies, and equipment for training, courses, or projects. Advise students on course selection, career decisions, and other academic and vocational concerns. Participate in conferences, seminars, and training sessions to keep abreast of developments in the field; and integrate relevant information into training programs. Serve on faculty and school committees concerned with budgeting, curriculum revision, and course and diploma requirements. Review enrollment applications, and correspond with applicants to obtain additional information. Arrange for lectures by experts in designated fields. **SKILLS**—Instructing; Learning Strategies; Social Perceptiveness; Service Orientation; Time Management; Persuasion; Speaking; Active Learning.

GOE—Interest Area: 05. Education and Training. **Work Group:** 05.03. Postsecondary and Adult Teaching and Instructing. **PERSONALITY TYPE:** Social. Social occupations frequently involve working with, communicating with, and teaching people. These occupations often involve helping or providing service to others.

EDUCATION/TRAINING PROGRAMS— Agricultural Teacher Education; Business Teacher Education; Health Occupations Teacher Education; Sales and Marketing Operations/Marketing and Distribution Teacher Education; Teacher Education and Professional Development, Specific Subject Areas, Other; Technical Teacher Education; Technology Teacher Education/Industrial Arts Teacher Education; Trade and Industrial Teacher Education. **RELATED KNOWLEDGE/COURSES—Education and Training:** Knowledge of principles and methods for curriculum and training design, teaching and instruction for individuals and groups, and the measurement of training effects. **Psychology:** Knowledge of human behavior and performance; individual differences in ability, personality, and interests; learning and motivation; psychological research methods; and the assessment and treatment of behavioral and affective disorders. **Computers and Electronics:** Knowledge of circuit boards,

processors, chips, electronic equipment, and computer hardware and software, including applications and programming. **Therapy and Counseling:** Knowledge of principles, methods, and procedures for diagnosis, treatment, and rehabilitation of physical and mental dysfunctions and for career counseling and guidance. **Sales and Marketing:** Knowledge of principles and methods for showing, promoting, and selling products or services. This includes marketing strategy and tactics, product demonstration, sales techniques, and sales control systems. **Customer and Personal Service:** Knowledge of principles and processes for providing customer and personal services. This includes customer needs assessment, meeting quality standards for services, and evaluation of customer satisfaction.

Vocational Education Teachers, Secondary School

- Annual Earnings: $47,090
- Growth: 9.1%
- Annual Job Openings: 10,000
- Self-Employed: 0.0%
- Part-Time: 9.5%
- Education/Training Required: Work experience plus degree

Industries in Which Income Is Highest

Industry	Average Annual Wage	Number Employed
Educational Services	$47,120	95,150

Metropolitan Areas Where Income Is Highest

Metropolitan Area	Average Annual Wage	Number Employed
New York–Northern New Jersey–Long Island, NY–NJ–PA	$69,220	3,290
Stockton, CA	$64,720	60
New Haven, CT	$63,200	280
Fresno, CA	$62,570	70
Rochester, NY	$62,560	660

Teach or instruct vocational or occupational subjects at the secondary school level. Prepare materials and classroom for class activities. Maintain accurate and complete student records as required by law, district policy, and administrative regulations. Instruct students individually and in groups, using various teaching methods such as lectures, discussions, and demonstrations. Establish and enforce rules for behavior and procedures for maintaining order among the students for whom they are responsible. Observe and evaluate students' performance, behavior, social development, and physical health. Instruct and monitor students the in use and care of equipment and materials, in order to prevent injury and damage. Plan and conduct activities for a balanced program of instruction, demonstration, and work time that provides students with opportunities to observe, question, and investigate. Prepare, administer, and grade tests and assignments in order to evaluate students' progress. Enforce all administration policies and rules governing students. Assign and grade class work and homework. Instruct students in the knowledge and skills required in a specific occupation or occupational field, using a systematic plan of lectures, discussions, audiovisual presentations, and laboratory, shop and field studies. Establish clear objectives for all lessons, units, and projects, and communicate those objectives to students. Use computers, audiovisual aids, and other equipment and materials to supplement presentations. Plan and supervise work-experience programs in businesses, industrial shops, and school laboratories. Prepare students for later grades by encouraging them to explore learning opportunities and to persevere with challenging tasks. Confer with parents or guardians, other teachers, counselors, and administrators in order to resolve students' behavioral and academic problems. Prepare objectives and outlines for courses of study, following curriculum guidelines or requirements of states and schools. Guide and counsel students with adjustment and/or academic problems, or special academic interests. Select, order, store, issue, and inventory classroom equipment, materials, and supplies. **SKILLS**—Instructing; Learning Strategies; Management of Financial Resources; Social Perceptiveness; Persuasion; Service Orientation; Management of Personnel Resources; Time Management.

GOE—Interest Area: 05. Education and Training. **Work Group:** 05.02. Preschool, Elementary, and Sec-

ondary Teaching and Instructing. **PERSONALITY TYPE:** Social. Social occupations frequently involve working with, communicating with, and teaching people. These occupations often involve helping or providing service to others.

EDUCATION/TRAINING PROGRAM—Technology Teacher Education/Industrial Arts Teacher Education. **RELATED KNOWLEDGE/COURSES**— **Education and Training:** Knowledge of principles and methods for curriculum and training design, teaching and instruction for individuals and groups, and the measurement of training effects. **Psychology:** Knowledge of human behavior and performance; individual differences in ability, personality, and interests; learning and motivation; psychological research methods; and the assessment and treatment of behavioral and affective disorders. **Therapy and Counseling:** Knowledge of principles, methods, and procedures for diagnosis, treatment, and rehabilitation of physical and mental dysfunctions and for career counseling and guidance. **Clerical Practices:** Knowledge of administrative and clerical procedures and systems such as word processing, managing files and records, stenography and transcription, designing forms, and other office procedures and terminology. **Computers and Electronics:** Knowledge of circuit boards, processors, chips, electronic equipment, and computer hardware and software, including applications and programming. **Sociology and Anthropology:** Knowledge of group behavior and dynamics, societal trends and influences, human migrations, ethnicity, and cultures and their history and origins.

Zoologists and Wildlife Biologists

- Annual Earnings: $52,050
- Growth: 13.0%
- Annual Job Openings: 1,000
- Self-Employed: 2.5%
- Part-Time: 8.6%
- Education/Training Required: Doctoral degree

Industries in Which Income Is Highest

Industry	Average Annual Wage	Number Employed
Professional, Scientific, and Technical Services	$56,870	4,060
Federal, State, and Local Government	$52,120	10,370

Metropolitan Areas Where Income Is Highest

Metropolitan Area	Average Annual Wage	Number Employed
Washington–Arlington–Alexandria, DC–VA–MD–WV	$82,260	640
Baltimore–Towson, MD	$75,430	80
Spokane, WA	$61,800	50
San Jose–Sunnyvale–Santa Clara, CA	$61,670	60
Albuquerque, NM	$61,360	50

Study the origins, behavior, diseases, genetics, and life processes of animals and wildlife. May specialize in wildlife research and management, including the collection and analysis of biological data to determine the environmental effects of present and potential use of land and water areas. Study animals in their natural habitats, assessing effects of environment and industry on animals, interpreting findings and recommending alternative operating conditions for industry. Inventory or estimate plant and wildlife populations. Analyze characteristics of animals to identify and classify them. Make recommendations on management systems and planning for wildlife populations and habitat, consulting with stakeholders and the public at large to explore options. Disseminate information by writing reports and scientific papers or journal articles, and by making presentations and giving talks for schools, clubs, interest groups and park interpretive programs. Study characteristics of animals such as origin, interrelationships, classification, life histories and diseases, development, genetics, and distribution. Perform administrative duties such as fundraising, public relations, budgeting, and supervision of zoo staff. Organize and conduct experimental studies with live animals in controlled or natural surroundings. Oversee the care and distribution of zoo animals, working with curators and zoo directors to determine the best way to contain animals, maintain their habitats and manage facilities. Coordinate preventive programs to control the outbreak of wildlife diseases. Prepare collections of preserved specimens or microscopic slides for species identification and study of development or disease. **SKILLS**—Science; Management of Financial Resources; Coordination; Persuasion; Writing; Management of Personnel Resources; Negotiation; Service Orientation.

GOE—Interest Area: 01. Agriculture and Natural Resources. **Work Group:** 01.02. Resource Science/Engineering for Plants, Animals, and the Environment. **PERSONALITY TYPE:** Investigative. Investigative occupations frequently involve working with ideas and require an extensive amount of thinking. These occupations can involve searching for facts and figuring out problems mentally.

EDUCATION/TRAINING PROGRAMS—Animal Behavior and Ethology; Animal Physiology; Cell/Cellular Biology and Anatomical Sciences, Other; Ecology; Entomology; Wildlife and Wildlands Science and Management; Wildlife Biology; Zoology/Animal Biology; Zoology/Animal Biology, Other. **RELATED KNOWLEDGE/COURSES**—**Biology:** Knowledge of plant and animal organisms and their tissues, cells, functions, interdependencies, and interactions with each other and the environment. **Geography:** Knowledge of principles and methods for describing the features of land, sea, and air masses, including their physical characteristics; locations; interrelationships; and distribution of plant, animal, and human life. **English Language:** Knowledge of the structure and content of the English language, including the meaning and spelling of words, rules of composition, and grammar. **Law and Government:** Knowledge of laws, legal codes, court procedures, precedents, government regulations, executive orders, agency rules, and the democratic political process. **Administration and Management:** Knowledge of business and management principles involved in strategic planning, resource allocation, human resources modeling, leadership technique, production methods, and coordination of people and resources. **Computers and Electronics:** Knowledge of circuit boards, processors, chips, electronic equipment, and computer hardware and software, including applications and programming.

Appendix: Skills Referenced in This Book

Definitions of the Skills

In each of the descriptions of the best-paying jobs found in Part II, we've included a listing of skills required for the job. This table contains specific definitions of each skill.

Definitions of Skills

Skill Name	Definition
Active Learning	Understanding the implications of new information for both current and future problem-solving and decision-making
Active Listening	Giving full attention to what other people are saying, taking time to understand the points being made, asking questions as appropriate, and not interrupting at inappropriate times
Complex Problem Solving	Identifying complex problems and reviewing related information to develop and evaluate options and implement solutions
Coordination	Adjusting actions in relation to others' actions
Critical Thinking	Using logic and reasoning to identify the strengths and weaknesses of alternative solutions, conclusions, or approaches to problems
Equipment Maintenance	Performing routine maintenance on equipment and determining when and what kind of maintenance is needed
Equipment Selection	Determining the kind of tools and equipment needed to do a job
Installation	Installing equipment, machines, wiring, or programs to meet specifications

(continued)

(continued)

Definitions of Skills

Skill Name	Definition
Instructing	Teaching others how to do something
Judgment and Decision Making	Considering the relative costs and benefits of potential actions to choose the most appropriate one
Learning Strategies	Selecting and using training/instructional methods and procedures appropriate for the situation when learning or teaching new things
Management of Financial Resources	Determining how money will be spent to get the work done and accounting for these expenditures
Management of Material Resources	Obtaining and seeing to the appropriate use of equipment, facilities, and materials needed to do certain work
Management of Personnel Resources	Motivating, developing, and directing people as they work, identifying the best people for the job
Mathematics	Using mathematics to solve problems
Monitoring	Monitoring or assessing your performance or that of other individuals or organizations to make improvements or take corrective action
Negotiation	Bringing others together and trying to reconcile differences
Operation and Control	Controlling operations of equipment or systems
Operation Monitoring	Watching gauges, dials, or other indicators to make sure a machine is working properly
Operations Analysis	Analyzing needs and product requirements to create a design
Persuasion	Persuading others to change their minds or behavior
Quality Control Analysis	Conducting tests and inspections of products, services, or processes to evaluate quality or performance
Reading Comprehension	Understanding written sentences and paragraphs in work-related documents
Repairing	Repairing machines or systems by using the needed tools
Science	Using scientific rules and methods to solve problems
Service Orientation	Actively looking for ways to help people
Social Perceptiveness	Being aware of others' reactions and understanding why they react as they do
Speaking	Talking to others to convey information effectively
Systems Analysis	Determining how a system should work and how changes in conditions, operations, and the environment will affect outcomes
Systems Evaluation	Identifying measures or indicators of system performance and the actions needed to improve or correct performance relative to the goals of the system

Definitions of Skills

Skill Name	Definition
Technology Design	Generating or adapting equipment and technology to serve user needs
Time Management	Managing one's own time and the time of others
Troubleshooting	Determining causes of operating errors and deciding what to do about it
Writing	Communicating effectively in writing as appropriate for the needs of the audience

The Skill-Income Connection

It's no secret that employers seek certain skills more than others. As part of the research for this book, we wondered whether high-paying occupations are associated with certain skills more than with others. So we employed a statistical procedure called *correlation* that shows how well one variable can predict another. In this case, we wanted to see how well the presence of a skill can predict income. We used skills ratings from the O*NET database and income figures from the Bureau of Labor Statistics.

Our analysis produced the following list of skills. Every skill on this list has at least a reasonably high correlation (better than 0.5) with income—which means that jobs that demand a high level of this skill tend to have a high level of income. The skills are ordered by the amount of correlation, which means that the skills nearest the top are the best predictors of high income. We also thought it would be handy for you to see which jobs in this book demand a high level of each skill, so for each skill we have listed the jobs that include the skill among its top three skills.

Keep in mind that most jobs demand a *combination* of skills, and one way to command higher pay is to have a special combination of skills that is scarce among other people with the same job title. For example, you may be the one chemist in your lab who is an excellent writer or the one sales representative in your company who has enough programming skill to advise the technology staff about how to improve sales-tracking software.

Skills Linked to High Occupational Earnings

Skill	Jobs That Demand a High Level of This Skill
Complex Problem Solving	Geographers; Mechanical Engineers; Podiatrists; Urban and Regional Planners
Judgment and Decision Making	Arbitrators, Mediators, and Conciliators; Directors—Stage, Motion Pictures, Television, and Radio; Financial Analysts; Immigration and Customs Inspectors; Industrial-Organizational Psychologists; Judges, Magistrate Judges, and Magistrates; Obstetricians and Gynecologists; Optometrists; Oral and Maxillofacial Surgeons
Reading Comprehension	Biophysicists; Coroners; Diagnostic Medical Sonographers; Epidemiologists; Oral and Maxillofacial Surgeons; Pharmacists; Poets and Lyricists; Political Scientists; Surgeons
Systems Evaluation	Accountants; Aerospace Engineers; Clinical Psychologists; Computer Hardware Engineers; Computer Security Specialists; Environmental Compliance Inspectors; First-Line Supervisors and Manager/Supervisors—Construction Trades Workers; First-Line Supervisors and Manager/Supervisors-Extractive Workers; Government Service Executives; Management Analysts; Marine Cargo Inspectors; Nuclear Engineers; Private Sector Executives; Public Transportation Inspectors; Soil Conservationists; Statisticians; Treasurers, Controllers, and Chief Financial Officers;
Critical Thinking	Anthropology and Archeology Teachers, Postsecondary; Arbitrators, Mediators, and Conciliators; Area, Ethnic, and Cultural Studies Teachers, Postsecondary; Child Support, Missing Persons, and Unemployment Insurance Fraud Investigators; Criminal Justice and Law Enforcement Teachers, Postsecondary; Law Teachers, Postsecondary; Lawyers; Philosophy and Religion Teachers, Postsecondary; Plant Scientists; Political Scientists; Sociologists; Surgeons
Active Learning	Actuaries; Atmospheric and Space Scientists; Cartographers and Photogrammetrists; Chemistry Teachers, Postsecondary; Dental Hygienists; Materials Scientists; Natural Sciences Managers
Monitoring	Business Teachers, Postsecondary; Financial Examiners; Licensing Examiners and Inspectors; Storage and Distribution Managers
Systems Analysis	Accountants; Aerospace Engineers; Computer Hardware Engineers; Computer Security Specialists; Computer Software Engineers, Systems Software; Electrical Engineers; Environmental Compliance Inspectors; Fashion Designers; Financial Managers, Branch or Department; Government

Skills Linked to High Occupational Earnings

Skill	Jobs That Demand a High Level of This Skill
	Property Inspectors and Investigators; Government Service Executives; Hydrologists; Operations Research Analysts; Pilots, Ship; Private Sector Executives; Soil Conservationists; Treasurers, Controllers, and Chief Financial Officers
Writing	Anthropology and Archeology Teachers, Postsecondary; Architecture Teachers, Postsecondary; Area, Ethnic, and Cultural Studies Teachers, Postsecondary; Auditors; Biochemists; Biophysicists; Caption Writers; Creative Writers; Criminal Justice and Law Enforcement Teachers, Postsecondary; Economics Teachers, Postsecondary; Education Teachers, Postsecondary; Environmental Science Teachers, Postsecondary; Equal Opportunity Representatives and Officers; Geography Teachers, Postsecondary; History Teachers, Postsecondary; Home Economics Teachers, Postsecondary; Immigration and Customs Inspectors; Insurance Underwriters; Library Science Teachers, Postsecondary; Licensing Examiners and Inspectors; Materials Scientists; Occupational Health and Safety Specialists; Philosophy and Religion Teachers, Postsecondary; Physicists; Plant Scientists; Poets and Lyricists; Political Scientists; Public Transportation Inspectors; Purchasing Agents and Buyers, Farm Products; Sociologists; Soil Scientists; Technical Writers
Science	Aerospace Engineering and Operations Technicians; Aerospace Engineers; Agricultural Engineers; Agricultural Sciences Teachers, Postsecondary; Airline Pilots, Copilots, and Flight Engineers; Anesthesiologists; Astronomers; Atmospheric and Space Scientists; Atmospheric, Earth, Marine, and Space Sciences Teachers, Postsecondary; Aviation Inspectors; Biochemists; Biological Science Teachers, Postsecondary; Biophysicists; Cartographers and Photogrammetrists; Chemical Engineers; Chemical Plant and System Operators; Chemistry Teachers, Postsecondary; Chemists; Civil Engineers; Commercial Pilots; Coroners; Dentists, General; Engineering Managers; Engineering Teachers, Postsecondary; Environmental Compliance Inspectors; Environmental Engineers; Environmental Science Teachers, Postsecondary; Environmental Scientists and Specialists, Including Health; Epidemiologists; Family and General Practitioners; Fish Hatchery Managers; Food Scientists and Technologists; Foresters; Forestry and Conservation Science Teachers, Postsecondary; Geographers; Geologists; Health Specialties Teachers,

(continued)

(continued)

Skills Linked to High Occupational Earnings

Skill	Jobs That Demand a High Level of This Skill
	Postsecondary; Hydrologists; Industrial Safety and Health Engineers; Industrial-Organizational Psychologists; Internists, General; Marine Architects; Marine Engineers; Materials Engineers; Materials Scientists; Mechanical Engineers; Medical Scientists, Except Epidemiologists; Microbiologists; Motor Vehicle Inspectors; Natural Sciences Managers; Nuclear Equipment Operation Technicians; Nuclear Medicine Technologists; Nuclear Monitoring Technicians; Nuclear Power Reactor Operators; Nursing Instructors and Teachers, Postsecondary; Obstetricians and Gynecologists; Occupational Health and Safety Specialists; Occupational Therapists; Optometrists; Oral and Maxillofacial Surgeons; Pediatricians, General; Physical Therapists; Physician Assistants; Physicists; Physics Teachers, Postsecondary; Plant Scientists; Podiatrists; Pressure Vessel Inspectors; Product Safety Engineers; Prosthodontists; Psychiatrists; Sales Representatives, Chemical and Pharmaceutical; Sociologists; Soil Conservationists; Soil Scientists; Statisticians; Surgeons; Veterinarians; Zoologists and Wildlife Biologists
Operations Analysis	Architects, Except Landscape and Naval; Budget Analysts; Commercial and Industrial Designers; Computer and Information Systems Managers; Computer Programmers; Database Administrators; Electronics Engineers, Except Computer; Engineering Managers; Fashion Designers; Film and Video Editors; Fire-Prevention and Protection Engineers; Landscape Architects; Management Analysts; Materials Engineers; Mechanical Engineers; Multi-Media Artists and Animators; Operations Research Analysts; Petroleum Engineers; Product Safety Engineers; Public Transportation Inspectors; Sales Engineers; Sales Representatives, Electrical/Electronic; Sales Representatives, Mechanical Equipment and Supplies; Sales Representatives, Medical; Soil Scientists; Storage and Distribution Managers
Management of Financial Resources	Accountants; Administrative Services Managers; Advertising of and Promotions Managers; Agents and Business Managers Artists, Performers, and Athletes; Agricultural Crop Farm Managers; Agricultural Sciences Teachers, Postsecondary; Architects, Except Landscape and Naval; Auditors; Budget Analysts; Chiropractors; Compensation and Benefits Managers; Computer and Information Systems Managers; Cost Estimators; Dentists, General; Education

Skills Linked to High Occupational Earnings

Skill	Jobs That Demand a High Level of This Skill
	Administrators, Elementary and Secondary School; Education Administrators, Postsecondary; Environmental Engineers; Fashion Designers; Financial Analysts; Financial Examiners; Financial Managers, Branch or Department; First-Line Supervisors/Managers of Non-Retail Sales Workers; First-Line Supervisors/Managers of Transportation and Material-Moving Machine and Vehicle Operators; Fish Hatchery Managers;Foresters; Forestry and Conservation Science Teachers, Postsecondary; Funeral Directors; Gaming Managers; General and Operations Managers; Geologists; Government Service Executives; Industrial Safety and Health Engineers; Instructional Coordinators; Landscape Architects; Librarians; Management Analysts; Marketing Managers; Medical Scientists, Except Epidemiologists; Nursery and Greenhouse Managers;Orthodontists; Park Naturalists; Personal Financial Advisors; Petroleum Engineers; Private Sector Executives; Program Directors; Prosthodontists; Public Relations Managers; Purchasing Agents and Buyers, Farm Products; Purchasing Managers; Range Managers; Real Estate Brokers; Sales Agents, Financial Services; Sales Agents, Securities and Commodities; Sociologists; Training and Development Managers; Treasurers, Controllers, and Chief Financial Officers; Veterinarians; Vocational Education Teachers, Secondary School; Zoologists and Wildlife Biologists
Mathematics	Actuaries; Astronomers; Budget Analysts; Economics Teachers, Postsecondary; Economists; Hydrologists; Marine Cargo Inspectors; Mathematical Science Teachers, Postsecondary; Physicists; Statisticians
Speaking	Child Support, Missing Persons, and Unemployment Insurance Fraud Investigators; Coroners; Credit Analysts; Equal Opportunity Representatives and Officers; Government Property Inspectors and Investigators; Graduate Teaching Assistants; Immigration and Customs Inspectors; Licensing Examiners and Inspectors; Occupational Health and Safety Specialists; Orthotists and Prosthetists; Personal Financial Advisors; Sales Representatives, Agricultural; Sales Representatives, Chemical and Pharmaceutical; Talent Directors; Transit and Railroad Police

Index

B

J–K

L

M

N

U